National Welfare Benefits Handbook

28th edition

Carolyn George
David Simmons
Paul Stagg
Geoff Tait

Child Poverty Action Group

Published by CPAG Ltd
1-5 Bath Street, London EC1V 9PY

CPAG Ltd 1998

A CIP record for this book is available from the British Library

ISBN 1 901698 04 1

Design by Devious Designs 0114 275 5634
Typeset by Page Bros, Norwich
Printed by Clays Ltd, Bungay, Suffolk

The authors

Carolyn George is a welfare rights worker with CPAG's Citizens' Rights Office and also works as a part-time lecturer at the University of Northumbria and as a freelance trainer.

David Simmons is a welfare rights worker with the National Association of Citizens' Advice Bureaux.

Paul Stagg is a barrister in a London chambers and specialises in social security law.

Geoff Tait is senior welfare rights officer for Wolverhampton Social Services.

Acknowledgements

We are especially grateful to Djuna Thurley, Lynn Webster, David Williams and Stewart Wright for their meticulous checking and helpful suggestions.

We would like to thank the many contributors who have come before and, in particular, those who have worked on the post-1988 versions of this *Handbook:* Martin Barnes, Sarah Campling, Rob Good, Andrew Grealey, Janet Gurney, John Hannam, Ian Hillier, Beth Lakhani, Jan Luba, Jim McKenny, Lee Ogilby-Webb, Anna Ravetz, Marcus Revell, Jim Read, Mark Rowland, Djuna Thurley, Gary Vaux, Penny Waterhouse, Lynn Webster, Penny Wood and Stewart Wright.

We would also like to acknowledge the generous help given by staff at the DSS, Benefits Agency, Further Education Funding Council, Independent Tribunal Service President's Office and the Department for Employment and Education; their co-operation has been invaluable.

Thanks are also due to Frances Ellery for editing and managing the production of the book; to Mary Shirley for her editorial work; to Paula McDiarmid for her proofreading; and to Katherine Dawson for her swift and conscientious indexing.

Finally we would like to say thank you to the staff of Page Bros and Clays Ltd for meeting a very tight schedule.

The law covered in this book was correct on 24 March 1998 and includes regulations laid up to this date.

Contents

PART THREE: BACK TO WORK BENEFITS, FAMILY CREDIT AND DISABILITY WORKING ALLOWANCE

PART FOUR: HOUSING BENEFIT AND COUNCIL TAX BENEFIT

Chapter 12: The basic rules

Chapter 13: The amount of benefit

Chapter 14: Special rules for students

Chapter 15: Claims, payments and reviews

Chapter 16: Council tax benefit

Abbreviations used in the text

AA	Attendance allowance
AMA	Adjudicating medical authority
AO	Adjudication officer
BAMS	Benefits Agency Medical Service
CCB	Community charge benefit
CCG	Community care grant
CSA	Child Support Agency
CTB	Council tax benefit
DAT	Disability appeal tribunal
DLA	Disability living allowance
DSS	Department of Social Security
DWA	Disability working allowance
EC	European Community
EEA	European Economic Area
EEC	European Economic Community
ECJ	European Court of Justice
EMO	Examining medical officer
EOC	Equal Opportunities Commission
ETU	Earnings top-up
FC	Family credit
GP	General practitioner
HB	Housing benefit
ICA	Invalid care allowance
IB	Incapacity benefit
IS	Income support
ITS	Industrial Tribunal Service
JSA	Jobseeker's allowance
MAT	Medical appeal tribunal
PAYE	Pay-as-you-earn
SDA	Severe disablement allowance
SERPS	State Earnings Related Pension Scheme
SF	Social fund
SFO	Social fund officer
SMP	Statutory maternity pay
SSAT	Social security appeal tribunal
SSP	Statutory sick pay

Means-tested benefit rates

Income support/income-based jobseeker's allowance applicable amounts £

Personal allowances

under 18* (usual rate)	30.30
under 18* (in certain circumstances)	39.85
aged 18-24	39.85
aged 25 or over	50.35

Lone parent

under 18* (usual rate)	30.30
under 18* (in certain circumstances)	39.85
aged 18 or over	50.35

Couple

both under 18*	60.10
both 18 or over	79.00

Dependent children

0 – September after 11th birthday	17.30
(from November 1998	19.80)
September after 11th birthday – September after 16th birthday	25.35
September after 16th birthday – day before 19th birthday	30.30

For eligibility of under-18s and calculating amounts, see pp60-61

Premiums

Family premium (see p361)	11.05
Family premium – lone parent rate (transitional)	15.75
Disabled child	21.45

Pensioner

single	20.10
couple	30.35

Enhanced pensioner

single	22.35
couple	33.55

Higher pensioner

single	27.20
couple	38.90

Disability   £
   single   21.45
   couple   30.60
Severe disability
   single   38.50
   couple (if one qualifies)   38.50
   couple (if both qualify)   77.00
Carers   13.65

Some claimants have their applicable amount calculated differently. This applies to claimants who are:
- only entitled to the urgent cases rate – see p49
- subject to a child support benefit penalty – see p114
- voluntarily unemployed – see p57
- on strike – see p61
- in residential care or nursing homes – see p87
- in hospital – see p97
- prisoners – see p101
- without accommodation – see p102.

Housing benefit applicable amounts
Personal allowances and premiums as for income support, except
   single person aged 16-24   39.85
   single parent under 18   39.85
   family premium – lone parent rate   22.05
   couple both under 18   60.10

Council tax benefit
Personal allowances and premiums as for income support, except
   family premium – lone parent rate   22.05

Family credit
Adult credit   48.80
Premium for working 30 hours or more   10.80
Child credit**
   under 11   12.35
   (from November 1998   14.85)
   aged 11-15   20.45
   aged 16-17   25.40
Applicable amount (ie, threshold level)   79.00

Disability working allowance   £

Adult credit

single	50.75
couple/lone parent	79.40
Premium for working 30 hours or more	10.80

Child credit   **

under 11	12.35
aged 11-15	20.45
aged 16-17	25.40

Applicable amount (ie, threshold level)

single	59.25
couple/lone parent	79.00

Social fund payments

Maternity expenses	100.00
Cold weather payment	9.50

Capital limits

Income support	8,000.00
Family credit	8,000.00

Residential accommodation (income support/housing benefit)

upper limit	16,000.00
disregarded	10,000.00
Housing benefit	16,000.00
Council tax benefit	16,000.00
Disability working allowance	16,000.00

**Rates for dependants change from the first Tuesday in September after their 11th and 16th birthdays.

Non-means-tested benefit rates

Earnings replacement benefits

	Claimant £pw	Adult dependant £pw	Child dependant £pw
Contribution-based jobseeker's allowance			
under 18	30.30		
under 25	39.85		
25 and over	50.35		
Short-term incapacity benefit			
lower rate	48.80	30.20	
lower rate (over pensionable age)	62.05	37.20	11.30*
higher rate	57.70	30.20	11.30*
higher rate (over pensionable age)	62.05	37.20	11.30*
Long-term incapacity benefit	64.70	38.70	11.30*
Invalidity allowance (transitional)			
higher rate	13.60		
middle rate	8.60		
lower rate	4.30		
Statutory sick pay	57.70		
Severe disablement allowance	39.10	23.20	11.30*
Age related addition –			
higher rate	13.90		
middle rate	8.60		
lower rate	4.30		
Statutory maternity pay (lower rate)	57.70		
Maternity allowance			
higher rate	57.70	30.20	
lower rate	50.10	30.20	
Invalid care allowance	38.70	23.15	11.30*

	Claimant £pw	Adult dependant £pw	Child dependant £pw
Widowed mother's allowance	64.70	11.30*	
Widow's pension (55 or over)	64.70		
(45-54)	from 19.41-60.17		

Retirement pension			
Category A	64.70	38.70	11.30*
Category B for a married woman	38.70		11.30*
Category B for a widow	64.70		11.30*
Category B for a widower	64.70		11.30*
Category C for a person not a married woman	38.70		11.30*
Category C for a married woman	23.15		11.30*
Category D	38.70		11.30*+

Benefits for the severely disabled

	£pw
Attendance allowance	
higher rate	51.30
lower rate	34.30

Disability living allowance

	£pw
Care component	
Higher	51.30
Middle	34.30
Lower	13.60
Mobility component	
Higher	35.85
Lower	13.60

Industrial injuries benefits

	£pw
Disablement benefit - variable, up to 100% (18 or over)	20.94-104.70

Industrial death benefit

	£pw
Widow	
higher permanent rate	64.70
lower permanent rate	19.41
Widower	64.70
Child	11.30*

Benefits for children   *£pw*

Child benefit
   –(for only/eldest child)   11.45
   –(for other child(ren)   9.30
   –for only/eldest child (lone parent rate)   17.10**
Guardian's allowance   11.30*
Child's special allowance   11.30*

* These are reduced by £1.40 if you receive child benefit for an only or eldest child.
⁺ Increase for child dependant only paid with Category D pension if there is an underlying entitlement to Category A, B or C pension.
** Some lone parents may only get the lower rate (£11.45). See CPAG's *Rights Guide to Non-Means-Tested Benefits* 1998/99 *for further details.*

Income tax allowances   *£pa*

Personal allowance   4,195
Married couple allowance   1,900
Additional personal allowance for caring for children   1,900
Blind person's allowance   1,330

National insurance contributions

gross weekly earnings
Below £64   Nil
£64-485   2% on the first £64 and
                                 10% on the rest, up to £485

This is the 'contract-in' rate for Class 1 contributions. For other NI rates, see CPAG's *Rights Guide to Non-Means-Tested Benefits*, Chapter 12.

Bands of taxable income (£)   *1998/99*

Lower rate – 20%   £0-£4,300
Basic rate – 23%   £4,301-£27,100
Upper rate – 40%   over £27,100

PART ONE

Introduction

CHAPTER ONE

An introduction to means tests

This *Handbook* covers only 'means-tested' benefits. This chapter explains:

1. Which benefits are means tested (below)
2. The administration of means-tested benefits (p4)
3. How means tests work (p5)

1. WHICH BENEFITS ARE MEANS TESTED

Non-means-tested benefits are those paid with only limited consideration of how much money you have (your 'means' of support), provided you satisfy certain basic conditions such as being available for work, disabled or widowed. Examples of non-means-tested benefits are *contribution-based* jobseeker's allowance and incapacity benefit (which replace earnings) and child benefit and disability living allowance (which are to meet specific needs).

To be entitled to some of the benefits which replace earnings you have to have paid sufficient national insurance contributions; for some non-means-tested benefits there is a requirement that you should have lived in Great Britain for a certain length of time. For information about non-means-tested benefits, see CPAG's *Rights Guide to Non-Means-Tested Benefits* (21st edn, 1998/99, £8.95, £3.00 for claimants) and the *Jobseeker's Allowance Handbook* (3rd edn, 1998/99, £8.95, £3.00 for claimants), both post-free from CPAG Ltd. However, the main benefit rates are included at the front of this book.

By contrast, to be entitled to **means-tested benefits** you do not have to pay any national insurance contributions. Instead, you must satisfy certain basic conditions and your income and capital must be sufficiently low for you to qualify. This involves detailed investigation of your means. The ways means tests work are outlined on pp5–6.

You may be entitled to a combination of non-means-tested and means-tested benefits. For example, you might receive incapacity benefit and child benefit topped up by income support. In addition, you might also qualify for help with your rent (housing benefit) and your council tax (council tax benefit).

The **means-tested benefits** covered in this *Handbook* are:

- income support (IS) (p8);
- family credit (FC) (p197);
- disability working allowance (DWA) (p212);
- earnings top-up (ETU) (p210);
- housing benefit (HB) (p228);
- council tax benefit (CTB))(p327);
- social fund payments (pp442 and 456);
- help with National Health Service charges (p500);
- free milk and vitamins (p511);
- free school meals and other education benefits (Appendix 1);
- housing renovation grants and other local authority grants and services (Appendix 1);
- discretionary payments for disabled people (Appendix 1).

This *Handbook* does not cover *income-based* jobseeker's allowance (JSA). A summary of the basic rules is given in Chapter 4, but for detailed information about income-based JSA, see the *Jobseeker's Allowance Handbook*, 3rd edn, 1998/99.

Some benefits are administered by the Benefits Agency (BA) on behalf of the Department of Social Security (DSS) and others are administered by local authorities or other organisations (see p4).

Working and entitlement to means-tested benefits

IS is restricted to those who are not working 'full time' (see p13). FC, ETU and DWA are restricted to those who are working full time.

- **Benefits only for people not in full-time work:**
  - income support
  - income-based jobseeker's allowance
  - social fund cold weather payments, community care grants and budgeting loans
  - free school meals
- **Benefits only for people in full-time work:**
  - family credit
  - disability working allowance
  - earnings top-up
- **Benefits for people both in and out of work:**
  - housing benefit
  - council tax benefit

- social fund maternity payments, funeral payments and crisis loans
- education benefits (other than free school meals)
- housing renovation grants

2. THE ADMINISTRATION OF MEANS-TESTED BENEFITS

The administration of the various benefits described in this *Handbook* varies enormously depending on who is responsible for them.

- The Benefits Agency administers IS, income-based JSA, FC, DWA and the social fund on behalf of the DSS. Initial claims for IS should be made and dealt with locally but most London claims are dealt with centrally by large centres in Glasgow, Belfast and Ashton-in-Makerfield. All FC and ETU claims are sent to offices in Blackpool, and DWA claims to an office in Preston.
- The Employment Service deals with claims for JSA.
- Local authorities (usually district councils outside London) administer HB, CTB and housing renovation grants.
- Local education authorities (county councils and metropolitan boroughs outside London) administer education benefits.
- The Health Benefits Division administers health benefits.
- Various other organisations deal with the other benefits covered in Appendix 1.

Standards of service

The Secretary of State sets annual performance targets for the Benefits Agency covering the time it takes to pay benefit, accuracy of decisions, customer satisfaction, recovery of overpayments and fraud detection. The Agency also sets internal targets after consultation with Ministers. These are included in a national *Business Plan* which is published annually. The Agency is also required to publish a national *Customer Charter*. Local offices should also produce a business plan and customer service statement, and benefit payment targets should be displayed in office waiting rooms. If you have a complaint about the way your benefit claim is handled, see p165.

3. HOW MEANS TESTS WORK

For most means-tested benefits there are complicated rules for assessing your needs and resources, and thus your entitlement. Some other benefits (known as 'passported' benefits – see p6) are payable once you have qualified for a different means-tested benefit. Some benefits are 'discretionary' even if you satisfy a means test (see p6).

The main means-tested benefits

- Income support
- Income-based jobseeker's allowance
- Family credit
- Disability working allowance
- Housing benefit
- Council tax benefit
- Health benefits (other than free milk and vitamins)
- Some housing renovation grants

It is not always necessary to consider all the benefits listed above separately because, if you qualify for IS or income-based JSA, you automatically satisfy the means test for the other benefits (excluding FC and DWA).

With the exception of FC and DWA, all the benefits have similar ways of taking account of your needs. These involve adding up personal allowances for each member of the family and then adding on extra amounts to take account of extra expenses you may have because of your circumstances (see Chapter 18).

All the benefits (including FC and DWA) also have similar ways of calculating resources to take into account both your income and your savings and other capital assets. If you have too much capital, you are not entitled to any benefit at all. If you have a lesser amount of capital, it may reduce the amount of benefit to which you are entitled because it is treated as producing an income (see Chapters 19 and 20).

Once your needs and your income have been calculated, your benefit entitlement can be worked out. In the case of IS, income-based JSA and health benefits, that is done simply by deducting your income from your needs. In the cases of HB and CTB, there are more complicated formulae which take into account the amount of your rent or council tax, as well as your other needs and your income. The higher your income, the less benefit you receive, but those with incomes substantially above IS or income-based JSA level may receive some help. The formulae are set out in Chapters 13 and 16.

FC and DWA are also calculated on the basis of a complicated formula. It takes into account your family's size but is not intended directly to represent your needs (see pp203 and 217).

Discretionary benefits

Where a benefit is discretionary, your means are obviously crucial in deciding whether or not to award the benefit. Earnings top-up, social fund crisis loans, budgeting loans and community care grants and are paid on a discretionary basis, although certain rules also have to be followed (see Chapters 10, 22, 23 and 24).

To get a budgeting loan or community care grant, you must be entitled to IS or income-based JSA. You do not need to be on benefit to get a crisis loan. Each local area has a limited budget for social fund payments, so your needs are assessed alongside those of other claimants.

Where local authorities have the power to make payments for things like school uniforms, they can do it on a purely discretionary basis. They often have local means tests similar to the IS means test.

Passported benefits

Some benefits do not have their own means tests. To be entitled you simply have to be entitled to another 'passporting' benefit. These are:

Passporting benefit	Passported benefit
IS, FC, DWA, income-based JSA	SF maternity expenses payments
IS, FC, DWA, HB, CTB, income-based JSA	SF funeral expenses payments
IS, FC, DWA, income-based JSA	Health benefits
IS, income-based JSA	SF cold weather payments
IS, income-based JSA	SF community care grants and budgeting loans
IS, income-based JSA	Free school meals
IS, income-based JSA	Housing renovation grants

In the case of all SF payments, it is a further condition of entitlement that your capital is not above a certain level (see pp468, 478 and 482). For free school meals there are no other tests. If you are entitled to IS or income-based JSA, your children are entitled to free school meals.

PART TWO

Income support

CHAPTER TWO

The basic rules of entitlement

This chapter covers:

1. Introduction to income support and basic rules (see below)
2. Who can claim income support? (p10)
3. Full-time work (p13)
4. Studying and claiming income support (p16)
5. Presence in and temporary absence from Great Britain (p23)

1. INTRODUCTION

Income support (IS) is a benefit for people with a low income. It is not paid to unemployed people who have to be available for and actively seeking work who may be able to claim jobseeker's allowance instead (see Chapter 4 and CPAG's *Jobseeker's Allowance Handbook*, 3rd edn, 1998/99 for further details). It is not paid to people in full-time work (see p13) who may be able to claim family credit (FC – see Chapter 10), earnings top-up (ETU - see Chapter 10) or disability working allowance (DWA – see Chapter 11) instead.

If you pay rent or council tax you may be entitled to housing benefit (see Chapter 12) and council tax benefit (see Chapter 16), as well as IS.

If you are entitled to IS you also qualify for:

- health service benefits such as free prescriptions (see Chapter 26); *and*
- education benefits such as free school meals (see Appendix 1).

You may also qualify for social fund payments (see Chapters 21-25).

If you or your partner start working full time (see p13) or increase your earnings and stop getting IS or jobseeker's allowance, you might be able to get a back-to-work benefit (see Chapter 9).

The principal conditions

You can claim IS if you satisfy the following rules:[1]

- You are at least 16. If you are at school or college, see p16-22.
- You fit into one of the groups of people who can claim IS (see p10).
- Your income is less than your applicable amount (see p25).
- Your savings and other capital are worth £8,000 or less. If you live in a residential or nursing care home, the capital limit is £16,000 (see p415). Some capital (in particular, your home) is ignored (see Chapter 20).
- Neither you nor your partner are in full-time paid work (see p13). You can claim if you are temporarily away from full-time work – eg, you are sick.
- You are not in full-time education (although there are exceptions to this rule – see p16). If you are studying part time, see p22.
- You are not getting either income-based or contribution-based jobseeker's allowance and your partner is not getting income-based jobseeker's allowance.
- You satisfy the 'habitual residence test' (see p72) and are present in Great Britain (although there are exceptions to this rule – see p23).

There are some groups of claimants to whom special rules apply. Those rules are covered in Chapter 5.

You do not have to have paid national insurance contributions to qualify for IS.

Who you can claim for

You can claim for your 'family'. See Chapter 17 for who counts as your family. If you do not fit into one of the groups of people who can claim IS, but your partner does (see p10) s/he could be the claimant (see p128). Whichever one of you claims IS, the other should seek advice about how to protect her/his national insurance record. See the *Rights Guide to Non-Means-Tested Benefits*, 21st edn, 1998/99 for more details about national insurance credits.

How to claim

You must claim IS in writing, on form A1 (SP1 for pensioners) which you can obtain free from your local Benefits Agency office. There are strict rules about the time limit for claiming and the information you must provide when you claim. For more detailed information about claims and how they are dealt with, see p128.

You may be able to get a crisis loan from the social fund to tide you over until your benefit is paid (see p479).

You have to make a separate claim to your local authority for housing benefit (see p282) and for council tax benefit (see p339).

2. WHO CAN CLAIM INCOME SUPPORT

IS is a benefit for people who do not work full time (see p13). You can claim IS if you satisfy the other rules for getting IS described on p8 and fit into one of the following groups:[2]

Age[3]

* You are aged 60 or more.
* On 6 October 1996, or at any time in the previous eight weeks:
  - you were aged 50–59; *and*
  - you had not been in full-time work (see p13) for 10 years; *and*
  - you had no prospect of getting full-time work; *and*
  - during the 10 years you were getting IS without having to sign on as available for and actively seeking work or would not have been required to sign on had you claimed IS.

  If you stop claiming IS for up to eight weeks you can still qualify under this rule when you claim again, so long as you do not work full time during the period.

Sick and disabled people[4]

* You are incapable of work because of illness or disability and you:
  - are receiving statutory sick pay; *or*
  - satisfy the 'own occupation' or 'all-work' test for incapacity benefit; *or*
  - are treated as incapable of work by an adjudication officer, for example because you suffer from a severe condition or have an infectious disease or are blind; *or*
  - are sick but are treated as capable of work because you are disqualified from receiving incapacity benefit due to misconduct or failure to accept treatment.

  (See *Rights Guide to Non-Means-Tested Benefits*, 21st edn, 1998/99.)
  If you have been claiming jobseeker's allowance (JSA) and are only likely to be sick for a short time, you do not necessarily have to claim IS. When you are sick for less than two weeks, you can sometimes continue to claim JSA even though you are incapable of work (see p56 and the *Jobseeker's Allowance Handbook*, 3rd edn, 1998/99 for further details).

* You are appealing a decision by the Benefits Agency not to treat you as incapable of work under:
  - the 'own occupation test' (if you continue to send in medical certificates during the period of your appeal); *or*

– the 'all-work' test (but you might be paid at a reduced rate - see below); *or*
– under the old incapacity rules that applied before 13 April 1995 (see *Rights Guide to Non-Means-Tested Benefits*, 21st edn; 1998/99 for details of the tests for incapacity).

You can get IS until your appeal has been decided. If you are appealing about the 'all-work' test and you do not come within any of the other groups of people who can claim IS, your IS is reduced by 20 per cent of the personal allowance for a single claimant of your age (unless on 12 April 1995 you had been off sick for 28 weeks, or on invalidity benefit or severe disablement allowance, and it is the first time the test has been applied to you).[5] If you are in this situation you would be better off signing on and claiming JSA, but it might be difficult for you to persuade the Employment Service to allow you to do so. If you do sign on as available for work, say you are doing so because the Benefits Agency has said you are capable of work. Signing on should not prejudice your appeal.[6] If your appeal is successful, any reduction in the amount of your benefit, for example because you lost the disability premium (see p362), must be repaid to you.

- You are mentally or physically disabled and because of this your earnings capacity or the number of hours you can work is reduced to 75 per cent or less of that for a person without your disability in the same job.
- You are registered blind (certified blind in Scotland). If you regain your sight you continue to be treated as blind for 28 weeks after you have been taken off the register.
- You work while living in a residential care or nursing home (see p15).

Carers and people with childcare responsibilities[7]

- You are a single parent claiming for a child under 16.
- You are a single person fostering a child under 16 through a local authority or voluntary organisation.
- You are looking after a child under 16 because their parent or the person who usually looks after them is temporarily away or ill.
- You are claiming for a child under 16 and your partner is temporarily out of the UK.
- You are pregnant and unable to work; or there are 11 weeks or less before the week your baby is due, or your baby was born not more than seven weeks ago.
- You are looking after your partner, or a child under 19 for whom you are claiming, who is temporarily ill.
- You are a carer *and*:

- receive invalid care allowance; *or*
- the person for whom you care either receives or has been awarded attendance allowance (AA) or the highest or middle rate care component of disability living allowance (DLA); *or*
- the person for whom you care has claimed AA or DLA. You are entitled to IS for up to 26 weeks from the date of the claim for AA/DLA or until the claim is decided, whichever comes first.

If you cease meeting these conditions or stop being a carer, you can continue to claim IS for a further eight weeks. After that, you will not get IS unless you fit into one of the other groups of people who can claim described in this chapter.

Pupils, students and people on training courses[8]

- You qualify for IS while in 'relevant education' (see p17).
- You are a disabled student and you satisfy one of the conditions on p21 – definition of 'disabled student'.
- You are a student who can claim IS (see p21).
- You are 16 to 24 and on a training course being provided by a Training and Enterprise Council (in Scotland, by a Local Enterprise Company). This covers people on work-based Training for Young People, which has replaced Youth Training. It may have different names in different areas.

   You are likely to qualify for IS if you:
   - are a 16-year-old on the lower rate training allowance;
   - have a dependent child;
   - qualify for a disability premium (see p362);
   - have to live away from home (see p48);
   - are aged 18 or over;
   - stopped getting severe disablement allowance when you started a training course but continue to be entitled to the disability premium.[9]

Some participants in training schemes have the legal status of employees (and are normally given contracts of employment). If you are an employee, you will not qualify for IS if you are in full-time work (see p13). You might qualify for family credit (FC), disability working allowance (DWA) or earnings top-up (ETU) instead (see pp197, 212 and 210).

Others[10]

- You have to go to court as a JP, juror, witness or party to the proceedings.

- You have been remanded in custody, or committed in custody but only until your trial or until you have been sentenced (see p101). See p27 to see if you qualify for help with your housing costs and p214 to see if you qualify for housing benefit.
- You are a refugee who is learning English in order to obtain employment. You must be on a course for more than 15 hours a week and, at the time the course started, you must have been in Britain for a year or less. You can get IS for up to nine months.
- You are a 'person from abroad' and are entitled to the urgent cases rate of IS (see p86).
- You are involved in a trade dispute or have been back to work for 15 days or less following a trade dispute (see p61).

3. FULL-TIME WORK

You cannot usually get IS if you or your partner are in full-time paid work.[11] If you are the one claiming IS, this means working 16 hours or more each week. For your partner it means 24 hours or more each week. If you both work less than this, you can get IS. See p14 for information about how your hours are calculated. If you or your partner normally work 16/24 hours or more but are off sick or on maternity leave you can claim.[12] If you work less than 16 hours and your partner works at least 16 hours but less than 24 hours each week, between you, you might choose to claim family credit (FC), disability working allowance (DWA) or earnings top-up (ETU) (see pp197, 212 and 210) instead of IS. However, you should seek advice before deciding which benefit to claim. For example, if you are paying a mortgage and can get IS to help you with your housing costs (see Chapter 3), you might be better-off on IS instead of FC, DWA or ETU.

What counts as paid work

Paid work includes work for which you expect payment. This means you expect to get payment for work you are doing now at some time in the future.[13] You must have a real likelihood of getting payment for your work, not just a hope or desire to make money. A self-employed writer who has never sold a manuscript may well be working with no real expectation of payment and thus not be treated as in full-time work even if s/he spends a lot of time writing.[14] However, if you have set up a business which is not yet making money but is likely to do so in the future (eg, an estate agency) you count as working in expectation of payment. Ultimately it depends on how viable your employment really is.[15]

How your hours are calculated

All the hours you are in paid work (see above) count towards the 16- or 24- hour total. Paid lunch hours also count.[16] Where your hours fluctuate, your weekly hours are worked out as follows:

- If you have a regular pattern of work, the average hours worked throughout each work 'cycle' is used – eg, if you regularly work three weeks on and one week off, your hours are the average over the four-week period.

  If you work for part of the year only, for example, in a school or other educational establishment and your work cycle is a year, your hours will be averaged in a different way. The school holidays or similar vacations when you do no work are ignored in calculating your average hours. So if you work less than 16 hours a week during term-time only, you are eligible for IS. However, if you work 16 hours or more each week you might be entitled to FC, ETU or DWA instead (see Chapters 10 and 11).[17] If you are a full-time 'term-time only' worker who is not paid during the school holidays, you might be able to claim IS during the holidays (see below).

- Where there is no pattern, the average over the five weeks before your claim is used, or a different period if this would be more accurate.[18]

- If you have just started work and no pattern is yet established or your working arrangements have changed and your previous work pattern no longer applies, the number of hours or average of hours you are expected to work each week is used.[19]

Appeal if you think the average was calculated unfairly, unless you are better off claiming FC/ETU/DWA instead (see Chapters 10 and 11).

Exceptions to the 16/24 hour rule

You are treated as in full-time work and are not entitled to IS, even if you work less than 16 hours in a week (in the case of your partner, 24 hours), if:[20]

- you are off work because of a holiday. If you do not get any holiday pay you could try for a crisis loan (see p479).

  Whether you count as being on holiday depends on the type of work you do. If you are what is known as a 'term-time only' worker, for example, a canteen assistant in a school or other educational establishment (as opposed to a teacher) and do not work in the school holidays, you can argue that you are not on holiday, nor are you in full-time work.[21] If your contract ends at the end of the school-term, you do not count as being on holiday and are entitled to IS in the usual way.[22] If your contract covers the school holidays, you might be able to argue you should get IS if you satisfy the other rules described on p8. You should seek advice before considering any changes to your contract of employment which might affect your employment rights;

• you are away from work without a good reason;
• you have ceased full-time work but have received pay in lieu of wages or in lieu of notice or holiday pay from your last job or an *ex gratia* payment in recognition of loss of employment (see p384);[23]
• you or your partner are involved in a trade dispute for seven days or less.[24]

You are not treated as in full-time work even if you work 16/24 hours or more each week if:[25]

• you are disabled and because of this:
  – your earnings are 75 per cent or less of what a person without your disability would reasonably expect to earn, working the same hours in that job, or in a comparable one;
  – your hours of work are 75 per cent or less than a person without your disability would reasonably be expected to do in that or a comparable job;
• you work at home as a childminder (see p391);
• you are getting a training allowance on a government scheme;
• you are working for a charity or voluntary organisation or you are a volunteer and are giving your services free (except for your expenses). However, where you receive any nominal payment, even if it is below your earnings disregard, you could be counted as in full-time work. The only way round this is for the organisation to pay you for a specific number of hours a week and for you to be a volunteer for the remainder of the time (but see p411 on notional income);
• you or your partner are involved in a trade dispute and it is more than seven days since the dispute started (see p61). This will also apply for the first 15 days following your return to work after having been involved in a trade dispute. You can claim if you satisfy the other rules for getting IS described in this chapter;
• you can claim IS because you are caring for someone (see p11 for further information). The Benefits Agency says that any hours of work you do are ignored, not just the hours you spend caring;[26]
• you are working while living in a residential care or nursing home, or a local authority home. This applies during temporary absences from the

home too. It only covers people who are being paid at the special rates for people in homes (see pp87-97);
- you work as a part-time firefighter, auxiliary coastguard, member of the territorial or reserve forces, or at running or launching a lifeboat;
- you are performing duties as a local authority councillor;
- you are a foster parent receiving an allowance for your caring responsibilities.

Self-employed people

The full-time work rule (see p13) applies to self-employed as well as employed earners. If you simply invest in a business and do not help to run it you are not treated as self-employed.[27]

A key problem for many self-employed people is that they work long hours for little financial reward, sometimes even making a loss. Nevertheless, the work is done in expectation of payment and counts as full-time work. If you are in this position and you are not entitled to FC, ETU or DWA (see Chapters 10 and 11), or it is not enough for your needs, you will want to claim IS or income-based JSA. You can only do this if you reduce your working hours to below 16 (in the case of your partner 24) or abandon self-employment altogether. If you want to claim income-based JSA, seek specialist advice before pursuing this course because there are very strict rules that you have to satisfy to get JSA (see the *Jobseeker's Allowance Handbook*, 3rd edn, 1998/99).

There may be a local scheme which pays you an allowance to help you set up your business. This allowance is not considered to be 'payment' in deciding if you are in full-time paid work. However, if you work in your business for 16 hours or more each week (in the case of your partner 24) and you reasonably expect to receive payment for the work (other than your allowance) you are treated as being in full-time work. If you work less than 16 hours a week (in the case of your partner 24), you should check that you still qualify for the allowance because this is usually paid to enable you to work full time.[28]

4. STUDYING AND CLAIMING INCOME SUPPORT

People in full-time education (see pp17 and 19) cannot usually qualify for IS, but there are some exceptions. You may be able to claim if you are studying part time (see p22). The rules of entitlement depend partly on your age and partly on your course as follows:

- You count as in 'relevant education' (see below) if you are under 19 and on a full-time non-advanced course. (See below to find out if you can claim IS.)
- You count as a student (see p19) if:
  - you are under 19 and on a full-time advanced course (see p21 to find out if you can claim IS);
  - you are 19 or over but under pensionable age (60 for women and 65 for men) and on a full-time advanced or non-advanced course. (See p21 to find out if you can claim IS.)

The rules about who can get IS are different for each of the groups above.

If you are not entitled to IS but you have a partner who is not studying, s/he could be the IS claimant instead.

Under 19 in 'relevant education'

If you are under 19 and on a full-time non-advanced course at school or college you count as being in what is known as **'relevant education'**. You usually cannot claim IS,[29] but there are exceptions (see below).

'Non-advanced course' means a course up to and including A-levels or higher level Scottish certificate of education. Your course is **full time** if it lasts 12 hours or more a week including instruction, tuition, supervised study, exams, practical work and projects provided for in the curriculum, but not including homework or other unsupervised study and meal breaks.[30] While you are in 'relevant education', your parents (or anyone acting as your parents) can get child benefit for you and claim for you if they get IS or one of the other means-tested benefits (see p353). See below to find out if you can claim IS in your own right.

Who can get IS while in 'relevant education'

You can get IS while in 'relevant education' (see above) if:[31]

- you have a child for whom you can claim (see p353);
- you are so severely disabled that you are unlikely to get a job in the next 12 months;
- you are an orphan, and have no one acting as your parent;
- you have left local authority care and cannot go home;
- you have to live away from your parents and any person acting in their place because:
  - you are estranged; *or*
  - you are in physical or moral danger; *or*
  - there is a serious risk to your physical or mental health.

The physical or moral danger does not have to be caused by your parents. Therefore a young person who is a refugee and cannot rejoin her/his parents can claim IS while at school.[32]

A 'person acting in place of your parents' includes a local authority or voluntary organisation if you are being cared for by them, or foster parents. In the last case this is only until you leave care.[33] It would not include a person who is your sponsor under the immigration laws.[34]

'Estrangement' implies emotional disharmony,[35] where you have no desire to have any prolonged contact with your parents or they feel similarly towards you. It is possible to be estranged even though your parents are providing some financial support or you still have some contact with them. If you are in care, it is also possible to be estranged from a local authority. If you are, then you could qualify for IS if you have to live away from local authority accommodation[36];

- you live apart from your parents and any person acting in their place and they are unable to support you *and*:
  - are in prison; *or*
  - are unable to come to Britain because they do not have leave to enter under UK immigration laws;[37] *or*
  - are chronically sick or are mentally or physically disabled. This covers people who could get a disability premium or higher pensioner premium or have an armed forces grant for car costs because of disability or are substantially and permanently disabled;
- you are a refugee and have started a course of 15 hours or more a week to learn English in order to obtain employment during your first year in Britain. This will apply for up to nine months.

Claiming IS when you leave 'relevant education'

Once you have left 'relevant education' (see p17) you might be able to claim IS if you satisfy the rules for getting IS described in this chapter. However, you might continue to be treated as in 'relevant education' after you have stopped studying. The day on which you cease to be treated as in 'relevant education' is called the **'terminal date'** (see p19) but your parents continue to get benefit for you until the end of that week. If you leave school before the legal school-leaving date, you are treated as having stayed on until that date.

From the Monday following your 'terminal date' (see p19), there are three possibilities:

- you might get IS if you fit into one of the groups of people who can claim (see p10);

- you might get jobseeker's allowance (if you are 16 or 17 you have to satisfy special rules, see CPAG's *Jobseeker's Allowance Handbook*, 3rd edn, 1998/99); *or*
- your parents might be able to go on claiming child benefit and IS or other means-tested benefits for you (see p353) during what is known as the child benefit extension period. The Monday after your 'terminal date' is the first day of the **child benefit extension period** (see the *Rights Guide to Non-Means-Tested Benefits*, 1998/99 edn, Chapter 10).

Terminal dates

Time of leaving school	Terminal date
Christmas	First Monday in January
Easter	First Monday after Easter Monday
June	First Monday in September

If you return to school or college solely to take exams, you still count as in 'relevant education'. So, for example, if you leave school at Easter and return to take exams in the following term, you will not be able to claim benefit in your own right until the first Monday in September,[38] unless you are a person who can claim while in full-time 'relevant education' (see p18).

You can claim earlier if you are 19 before the appropriate 'terminal date'[39] or if you are able to get IS while in full-time 'relevant education' (see p18) or come within one of the other qualifying groups (see p10–13) during the final vacation.

Students

If you are a student on a full-time course, you cannot usually claim IS for the duration of your course, including vacations.[40] See p21 for exceptions to this rule. See p22 if you give up or change your course and p22 if you are studying part time.

You count as a student if:[41]

- **You are under 19 and on a full-time course of advanced education.** 'Advanced education' means degree or postgraduate level qualifications, teaching courses, HND, diplomas of higher education, HND or HNC of the Business Technology Education Council or the Scottish Vocational Education Council and all other courses above advanced GNVQ or equivalent, OND, A-levels, highers or Scottish certificate of sixth year studies. See p20 for what counts as a full-time course.
- **You are 19 or over but under pensionable age** (currently 60 for women and 65 for men) **and on a full-time course of study.** If your

course is full time you are treated as a student regardless of the level of the course. See below for what counts as a full-time course.

Full-time courses[42]

In England and Wales your course counts as full time if:

- It is totally or partly funded by the Further Education Funding Council (FEFC) and involves more than 16 hours of **guided learning** each week.

    Courses funded by the FEFC are usually academic or vocational courses leading to a recognised qualification. The FEFC also funds basic literacy and numeracy courses, English as a second language programmes, courses which prepare you to move on to qualification-bearing courses, and courses developing independent living skills for people with learning difficulties. The FEFC does not fund leisure or general interest courses.

    'Guided learning' is not defined by the rules but the Benefits Agency says this means time which is spent in the presence of a teacher, lecturer or demonstrator as opposed to time which you spend doing homework or unsupervised private study at college.[43] Obviously, time which you spend in meal and other breaks cannot be 'guided learning', nor can time spent taking examinations. The number of guided learning hours you do each week will be set out in your learning agreement. This is signed by you and the college. The Benefits Agency will use this agreement to decide whether or not you are on a full-time course.

- It is not funded by the FEFC and is a **full-time course of study**. Whether a course counts as a full-time course depends on the college or university. Definitions are often based on local custom and practice within education authorities, or determined by the demands of course validating bodies, or by the fact that full-time courses can attract more resources. The college or university's definition is not absolutely final, but if you want to challenge it you will have to produce a good argument showing why it should not be accepted.[44] If your course is only for a few hours each week, you should argue that it is not full time. However, a course could be full time even though you only have to attend a few lectures a week.[45]

In Scotland your course counts as full time if:[46]

- It is totally or partly funded by the Secretary of State for Scotland (SOSS) at a college of further education, is not higher education *and*:
    - it involves more than 16 hours a week of classroom based or workshop based programmed learning under the guidance of a teacher; *or*

– it involves more than 21 hours study a week, 16 hours or less of which involve classroom based or workshop based programmed learning and the rest of which involve using structured learning packages with the help of a teacher.

The number of hours of 'learning' you do each week will be set out in a document. This is signed by you and the college. The Benefits Agency will use this document to decide whether or not you are on a full-time course.

• It is funded totally or partly by the SOSS and is a full-time course of higher education (see p20 for what counts as a full-time course of study).

• It is not funded by the SOSS and is a full-time course of study at a college of further education (see p20 for what counts as a full-time course of study).

Students who can claim IS

Even if you are a student, you can claim IS if you are:[47]

• a single parent or foster parent of a child under 16; *or*
• a student from abroad and entitled to an urgent cases payment because you are temporarily without funds (see p86); *or*
• a disabled student[48] and you satisfy one of the following conditions:
  – you qualify for the disability premium or severe disability premium (see pp362 and 367);
  – you have been incapable of work for 28 weeks (see p10). Two or more periods when you are incapable of work are joined to form a single period if they are separated by less than eight weeks;
  – you qualify for a disabled students' allowance because you are deaf. The rules changed on 1 September 1990. If you were a disabled student on IS around that time, see p15 of the 25th edition of the *National Welfare Benefits Handbook; or*
• a couple who are both full-time students, you fit into one of the groups of people who can claim IS (see p10) and you have a child, and it is the summer vacation; *or*
• a pensioner (aged 60 for women and 65 for men); *or*
• a refugee learning English (see p13); *or*
• a full-time student under the rules described on pp19–21 but were getting IS while studying part time under the rules that applied until 7 October 1996 (see *National Welfare Benefits Handbook* 1996/97 edn, pp12–16 for further details). You can continue to get IS if:
  – you were getting IS continuously from 31 July 1996 until 7 October 1996; *and*

- you were not claiming jobseeker's allowance in the week after 7 October 1996; *and*
- you are on the same course as you were on 31 July 1996; *and*
- you satisfy the rules for entitlement to IS (see p8) and fit within one of the groups of people who can claim (see p10).

You can get IS until your course ends or you abandon it. You can also get IS during a break in your claim of 12 weeks or less.

Giving up or changing your course

If you abandon your course or are dismissed from it you can claim IS from that date so long as you fit into one of the groups of people who can claim (see p10). This is also the case if you give up the course you are studying on, or your college requires you to change the type of course due to exam failure (eg, from 'A' level to GCSE) and you have a break before you restart studying. However, you still count as a student if you are pursuing your studies by, for example, spending an optional year abroad as part of a language course.[49] If you are not a student who can claim IS and you have to take time off due to sickness, you might be able to claim IS once you count as a 'disabled student' (see p21) – eg, where you have been sick for 28 weeks.[50]

If you are taking a year out to study for and resit exams, try to argue that you are not a student during this period because you are no longer on the full-time course you started.[51] The Government intends to amend the rules in the near future. Then this might no longer be possible.

If you are on a sandwich course you count as a student even if you have been unable to find a placement.[52]

Studying part time

You can get IS while studying part time if you fit into one of the groups of people who can claim (see p10). You count as studying part time if:[53]

- you are on a part-time course; *or*
- you are studying part time on a full-time course or you are currently studying part time on a course you previously attended full time. The Government intends to amend the rules in the near future. Then you might still count as a full-time student in these situations.

To see if your course counts as full time or part time see pp19–21.

Where you are attending a modular course, whether your course is part time will depend on such things as the number of modules you are taking, the number of hours you study each week and whether the course is one which you could attend part or full time.

5. PRESENCE IN AND TEMPORARY ABSENCE FROM GREAT BRITAIN

Normally you can only get IS while you are living in Great Britain (for more details, see the *Migration and Social Security Handbook*, 2nd edn, 1997). If you have recently come to this country from abroad either for the first time or because you have been living abroad, you must satisfy a 'habitual residence' test (see p72). If you do not satisfy the habitual residence test or you or your partner are a recently-arrived immigrant with restrictions on your stay, see p66.

Once you have established your right to IS, it is possible to claim during temporary absences abroad. Benefit can continue to be paid for up to either four or eight weeks. To qualify for IS while abroad you must:[54]

- have been entitled to IS before you left the country;
- not expect to be away for more than a year; *and*
- continue to satisfy the other rules for getting IS described in this chapter while you are away.

You can get IS for up to **four weeks** if you fall within one of the following groups:[55]

- you are going to Northern Ireland. (If you are going there long term, you should sign on at your local office in Northern Ireland and claim IS there);
- you and your partner are both abroad and your partner qualifies for a pensioner, enhanced pensioner, higher pensioner, disability or severe disability premium;
- you are incapable of work *and*:
  - you have been continuously incapable for the previous 28 weeks and you are terminally ill or receiving the highest rate of disability living allowance care component; *or*
  - you have been continuously incapable for 364 days.
  Two or more periods when you are incapable of work are joined together to form a single period if they are separated by less than eight weeks;
- you are incapable of work and going abroad specifically for treatment of the incapacity from an appropriately qualified person. Before you go you should check that the Benefits Agency accepts that this rule applies to you.
- You fit into one of the groups of people who can claim IS (see p10). However, you must *not* be:
  - in 'relevant education' (see p17);

    – involved in a trade dispute, or in the first 15 days after you have
      returned to work following the dispute;
    – receiving an urgent cases payment of IS as a 'person from abroad';
    – incapable of work for less than 28 weeks or appealing a decision of
      the Benefits Agency not to treat you as incapable of work (see p10).

You can get IS for up to **eight weeks** if you are taking a child abroad
specifically for medical, physiotherapy or similar treatment from an
appropriately qualified person. The child must count as part of your
family (see p353).

If you qualify for IS under the four- or eight-week rule, your benefit is
normally paid to you on your return, but if you are a member of a couple
you can ask for it to be paid to your partner during your absence instead.
If you are not entitled to IS while abroad or you have already used up
your four- or eight-week entitlement, your partner will have to make a
claim in her/his own right (see p128).

If it is your partner who goes abroad, your benefit is reduced after four
weeks (eight weeks if your partner is taking a child abroad for medical
treatment). You are then paid as if you were a single claimant or lone
parent, but your joint income and capital counts.[56]

While you are temporarily out of the country, you may be entitled to
housing benefit to cover your rent, and council tax benefit towards your
council tax (see p228 (HB) and p327 (CTB)). If your IS stops, you must
make a fresh claim for these benefits.

CHAPTER THREE

How your benefit is calculated

This chapter covers:

1. The basic calculation (below)
2. Housing costs (p27)
3. Rates of benefit paid to 16/17-year-olds (p47)
4. Transitional protection (p49)
5. Urgent cases payments (p49)

1. THE BASIC CALCULATION

Income support (IS) tops-up your income to a set level. The amount you get depends on your needs – the Benefits Agency calls these your 'applicable amount' (see below) – and on how much income and capital you have.[1] For the rules on income see Chapter 19, and on capital, Chapter 20.

There are three steps involved in working out your IS.

Step one: calculate your 'applicable amount'

Your applicable amount consists of:

- **personal allowances** (see Chapter 18) for you and each member of your family; *plus*
- **premiums** (see Chapter 18) for any special needs; *plus*
- **housing costs**, principally for mortgage interest payments, see p27.

Personal allowances and premiums are increased every April. If you do not qualify for IS currently, for example because your income is too high, you might qualify when the rates go up.

Your applicable amount might be reduced if you:

- are unwilling to apply for child support maintenance (see pp113-18); *or*
- are not signing on as available for and actively seeking work while appealing a decision of the Benefits Agency which says that you are

capable of work under the 'all-work' test (see p10). This does not apply if you fit into one of the other groups of people who can claim IS (see p10); *or*

• do not satisfy the ordinary rules for getting IS but are getting an urgent cases payment (see p49).

Step two: calculate your income

This is the amount you have coming in each week from other benefits, part-time earnings, maintenance etc (see Chapter 19). If you have capital over £3,000 (£10,000 if you live in a residential or nursing home) it also includes your 'tariff income' (see p405).

Step three: deduct your income from your applicable amount

Example
Mr and Ms Hughes aged 27 and 29 have a daughter aged 8. They have no housing costs to be covered by IS. Their applicable amount is:

£79.00	personal allowance
£17.30	personal allowance for child aged 8
£11.05	family premium
£107.35	total

Their income is £11.45 child benefit.

Their IS is £107.35 (applicable amount) minus £11.45 (income) = £95.90.

Different rules for deciding how your benefit is calculated apply to you if you are:

• in local authority residential accommodation (p95);
• in a residential care home or nursing home (p87);
• in hospital (p97);
• a prisoner (p101);
• a person without accommodation (p102);
• 16 or 17 years old (p47);
• a 'person from abroad' (p66);
• affected by a trade dispute (p61).

People who are members of, and fully maintained by, a religious order do not get any IS at all.

You may get more than your normal IS entitlement if you are receiving transitional protection (see p49).

2. HOUSING COSTS

If you own or are buying your home, IS can include a variety of payments for your housing costs. If you are a tenant you can get IS for some types of housing costs, but not for your rent (this is covered by housing benefit (HB) not IS – see Chapter 12). If you live in a residential care or nursing home your fees are treated differently (see p87).[2]

You can get help with your housing costs if:[3]

- the type of housing costs can be met by IS (see below);
- you, or someone in your family, are liable to pay the housing costs (see p28);
- the housing costs are for the home in which you normally live (see p29).

There are some situations in which you might not get help with housing costs. These are:

- for the first few weeks after you claim. You are expected to rely on mortgage protection payments or other income or savings initially (see p43);
- where you take out a loan while you are on IS or income-based JSA or during a period of 26 weeks between two claims (see p33).

There are restrictions on the amount you can be paid if:

- your housing costs are too high (see p41);
- you increase a loan while on IS or income-based JSA (see p33).

Which housing costs can be met[4]

Your IS can include the following housing costs:

- interest:
  - on mortgages and other house purchase loans;
  - under a hire purchase agreement taken out to buy your home.
  See p32 for further information;
- interest on loans used to pay for repairs and improvements or to meet a service charge for repairs and improvements (see p36);

- 'other housing costs':
  - rent or ground rent (feu duty in Scotland) if you have a lease of more than 21 years;
  - service charges (though some are excluded – see p38);
  - rentcharge payments;
  - payments under a co-ownership scheme;
  - rent if you are a Crown tenant (minus any water charges);
  - payments for a tent and its pitch if that is your home.

Are you liable to pay housing costs?[5]

You count as liable to pay housing costs (see p27 for the types that can be met) if:

- you, or your partner, are liable to pay them. You do not have to be legally liable.[6] However, you do not count as liable to pay housing costs if you pay these to someone who is a member of your household (see p346 for the meaning of household);
- you are treated as liable to pay them. You are treated as liable if:
  - you share the costs with other members of your household; *and*
  - at least one of those with whom you share is liable.

  In this case, you can be paid for your share,[7] as long as those you share with are not 'close relatives' of yourself or your partner and it is reasonable to treat you as sharing. ('Close relative' means a parent, parent-in-law, son, son-in-law, daughter, daughter-in-law, step-parent, stepson, stepdaughter, brother, sister or the partner of any of these. Sister or brother includes a half-sister or half-brother. An adopted child ceases to be related to her/his natural family on adoption and becomes the relative of her/his adoptive family.[8])
- someone else is liable to pay them but is not paying so you have to meet the cost yourself in order to continue to live in your home. You must show that it is reasonable for you to pay instead of her/him – eg, where you have given up your home to live with and care for someone and s/he has now gone into a nursing home, or where you have separated from your partner.

If, under the terms of your mortgage, you are not required to pay any interest currently, you cannot receive IS for housing costs. This applies to special mortgage schemes for pensioners where the mortgage is repaid from your estate when you die rather than by regular monthly payments.[9]

If you are on strike your partner is treated as liable for housing costs to enable her/him to make a claim.[10]

Are the housing costs for the home in which you normally live?

Housing costs are paid for the home in which you or a member of your family normally live (see Chapter 17 for who counts as your family). You cannot usually be paid for any other home,[11] but if you have to make payments on two properties, see p31 for exceptions to this rule. If you are liable to pay the mortgage on a property but have no immediate intention of living there you cannot get help with the cost.[12]

Your home is defined as the building, or part of the building, in which you live. This includes any garage, garden, outbuildings and other premises and land which it is not reasonable or practicable to sell separately.[13]

There are special rules if:

- you have just moved into your home (see below);
- you are away from home (see below);
- you are liable to pay housing costs on more than one home (see p31).

Moving house[14]

If you have just moved into your home but were liable to pay housing costs before moving in, your IS can include these costs for a period of up to four weeks before your move if your delay in moving was reasonable, you claimed IS before moving in, *and*:

- you were waiting for adaptations to be finished that meet needs you or a member of your family have because of a disability; *or*
- you became responsible for the housing costs while you were in hospital or residential care; *or*
- you were waiting for a social fund payment to help you set up home – eg, for help with removal costs or furniture and bedding. This only applies if you have a child of five or under, or you qualify for a pensioner, enhanced pensioner, higher pensioner, disability, severe disability or disabled child premium.

The IS for housing costs will not actually be paid until you move in. If the earlier IS claim you made before you moved was turned down you must claim again within four weeks of moving in to qualify.

Temporary absence from home

If you are temporarily away from home but are still entitled to IS, have not rented out your home and intend to return, your housing costs continue to be paid for a period. This can help you to keep your home, for example while you are in prison or hospital.

In most cases, you can get housing costs for **13 weeks** if you are unlikely to be away for longer than this.[15] However, you can get housing costs for **52 weeks** if you are unlikely to be away for longer than this (or in exceptional circumstances, unlikely to be away for substantially longer than this) and you are: [16]

- in hospital;
- receiving care (approved by a doctor) in the UK or abroad, as long as this is not in a residential care or nursing home;
- receiving medical treatment or convalescing in the UK or abroad (approved by a doctor) or your partner or a dependent child is, as long as this is not in a residential care or nursing home;
- attending a training course away from home in the UK or abroad. Your training course counts if it is provided by or on behalf of or by arrangement with or approved by a government department, the Secretary of State, Scottish Enterprise or Highlands and Islands Enterprise;
- in a bail hostel or in prison on remand;
- in a residential care or nursing home for short-term or respite care. However, if you are in the home for a trial period to see if you wish to move there permanently, you can only get your housing costs met for 13 weeks.[17] You must intend to return home if the accommodation is not suitable. If the home does not suit your needs you can have further trial periods in other homes, so long as you are not away from home for more than 52 weeks in total;
- providing care for someone living in the UK or abroad (approved by a doctor);
- caring for a child whose parent or guardian is receiving medical treatment or care (approved by a doctor) away from home;
- away from home through fear of violence (see below if you need to claim for two homes and for what counts as violence); *or*
- a student (see p19) who is neither able to get housing costs for two homes nor a single claimant or a lone parent who is liable to pay housing costs on one but not both of a term time and a home address (see p31).

There is no linking rule with these provisions, which means that a new period can start if you return home even for a short stay – eg, a day or a weekend.[18]

If you have to live in temporary accommodation while essential repairs are done to your normal home and you only have to pay for housing costs for one of the homes, your IS covers those costs.[19] This is not subject to the normal limits on temporary absence from home (see p29).[20] If you have to pay housing costs for both homes, you may be able to claim IS for both for up to four weeks (see below). After that you are only paid for one home. This could be your normal home if you are unlikely to be away for more than 13 or 52 weeks (see p29) or your temporary home if you will be away for longer.

Housing costs for more than one home

In most cases you can only be paid housing costs for one home. However, if you have to pay housing costs for two homes you can get IS for both:[21]

- for up to four weeks if you have moved into a new home and cannot avoid having to pay for the other one as well;
- indefinitely if you left your home because of either domestic violence or fear of other violence in that home. Remember that your garden and garage, for example, count as your home (see p29). So long as you left home because of the violence and are still away from home because of it, it does not matter if you were away from home for some other reason during this period – for example, because you were in prison.[22]

  'Violence' means violence against you and not caused by you[23] and includes violence in your old home or from a former member of your family. Fear of a racial attack should be covered provided the attack would take place *in* the old home (see p29 for what counts as your home). You will have to show that it is reasonable for you to get payment for two homes. Thus, if you do not intend to return home or someone else is paying the mortgage, you might not get IS for both homes;
- indefinitely if you are one of a couple and you or your partner are a student (see p19) or on a training course (see p30) and living away from your home (see below).

If you have to live in temporary accommodation while essential repairs are done to your normal home see p30.

If you have to live away from your normal home because you are a student (see p19) **or on a training course** (see p30) IS can cover the housing costs as follows:

- if you are one of a couple and have to live apart, you can get IS for both of your homes if it is reasonable for both to be met;[24]
- if you are a single person or lone parent and are having to pay housing costs for *either* your normal home or your term-time accommodation you can get IS for the home for which you pay but not both.[25]

If neither of the above apply you may only get IS for your normal home for up to 52 weeks (see p29).[26]

If you are getting IS for your term-time accommodation and you stop living there during a vacation, you cannot get housing costs unless you are away because you are in hospital.[27]

Mortgages and loans

An amount for mortgage payments is included in your IS applicable amount (see p25) under the rules described below. We use the term 'mortgage' to refer to mortgages, hire purchase agreements or loans.

It is important to remember that:

- not all loans qualify for help;
- your IS for housing costs only covers interest on your loan(s) and the amount you are paid is calculated in a special way (see p35);
- you might not get your full housing costs met initially (see p43);
- deductions can be made if other people live in your home (see p39);
- restrictions might be made – eg, if your housing costs are too high (see p41) or if you took out or increased your loan while on IS or income-based JSA (see p33). For circumstances in which you are allowed to take out or increase your loan, see p33;
- payment is made direct to the lender (see p150).

Loans that qualify

You are only paid where your loan qualifies. If your mortgage was taken out to pay for repairs or improvements, see p36. If you have other housing costs, see p37. Your loan qualifies if it was:[28]

- **taken out to buy the home in which you live**. Loans taken out to buy an existing property as well as those to pay for materials and labour to build your own home are covered.[29] If all or part of your loan was taken out to pay for something other than your home (eg, to buy a car or set up a business) you cannot get help with the cost even if the loan is secured on your home (but see p46);
- **taken out to buy an additional interest in the home in which you live** for example:
  - by buying out your ex-partner's share in your home after you separated. However, where your ex-partner has registered a right to occupy your home (what is known as a 'Class F land charge') you cannot get help with a loan to pay her/him to remove it;[30]
  - by purchasing the freehold on a leasehold property;[31]

- by buying your partner's share back from a trustee in bankruptcy if s/he is bankrupt;[32]
- by buying out sitting tenants;[33]
- **taken out to repay a loan which itself would have qualified** (see above). However, if the second loan is also for things that do not qualify for help (eg, to pay debts or to pay for a holiday) you only get help with the amount of the original loan.

Example
Mr Clay took out a new mortgage of £60,000. £45,000 was to pay off the mortgage he took out to buy his home and £15,000 was to pay off business debts. He will get help with the loan for £45,000.

Remember that even if all of your loan qualifies, you might not get help if you took it out or increased it while on IS or income-based JSA (see below). Where your home is used for both business and domestic purposes and neither part can be sold off separately, you can only get help with the interest payable on the loan for the part where you live.[34]

Taking out or increasing loans while on IS or income-based JSA[35]

Even if your loan qualifies (see p32) you cannot get IS to help you pay the cost if you took it out or increased it:[36]

- when you were on IS or income-based JSA; *or*
- when you were living as a member of the family with someone who was on IS or income-based JSA (see Chapter 17 for who counts as your family); *or*
- during a period of 26 weeks between two IS or income-based JSA claims as described above.

For these purposes, you and your partner are treated as being on IS or income-based JSA when you are on a New Deal programme or scheme (see p58), but only if as a result you:

- count as in full-time work (see p13); *or*
- have too much income (see p26).[37]

You can get IS for your housing costs even if you took out your loan during one of the periods listed above if: [38]

- your loan was taken out before 2 May 1994;
- your loan was taken out between 2 May 1994 and 2 October 1995 and you got IS for it under the rules that applied between those dates;

- your loan was taken out after 2 May 1994 but you have since stopped getting IS and income-based JSA for more than 26 weeks;
- you have taken out, or increased, your loan to buy a home which is better suited than your former home to the needs of a disabled person.[39] The person has to qualify as disabled at the time the loan is taken out.[40] S/he does not have to be a member of your family nor to have previously lived with you. A 'disabled person' is anybody for whom you or someone living with you is getting a disabled child, disability, enhanced pensioner or higher pensioner premium as well as other people living in your home who would get one of these premiums if they were on IS. It also includes a person who is sick, but, under the incapacity rules, is either disqualified from receiving benefit or is treated as capable of work (see p10 and the *Rights Guide to Non-Means-Tested Benefits*, 21st edn, 1998/99);
- you have a boy and a girl aged 10 or over and you increased your loan to move to a home where they could have separate bedrooms.[41] You can argue that this should apply if one of the children is 10 or over and the other will be 10 in the reasonably near future.[42]

You can get IS for your housing costs even if you took out your loan during one of the periods listed on p33 (although the amount you get might be restricted) if:

- you re-mortgaged your home to pay off your original house purchase loan,[43] *or* you sold your previous home, paid off a loan which you took out to buy a home or pay for repairs or improvements, and have now taken out a new loan for a new property, even if this is some time later.[44]

The original loan must have qualified (see p32) and be one for which you can get IS even if it was taken out during any of the periods described on p33. Unless the loan was to buy a home for a disabled person (see above) or to provide separate bedrooms for a boy and girl aged 10 or over (see above) you cannot get help with any increase in your housing costs. Thus, if your original mortgage was £30,000 and you took out a new loan for £35,000 to buy a new home, you can only get IS housing costs on £30,000 of the second loan.

It seems that the rule *is* intended to apply if, following divorce or separation, you buy out your former partner's share of your home – you will not get the mortgage interest paid in relation to that share. Similarly, if you take out a loan or increase an existing loan to buy a home after separation, the rule will in principle apply. However, where couples on IS or income-based JSA separate, it can be argued that each should be entitled to housing costs up to the amount of the loan they were liable to pay when they were together.[45] So, for example, if you

were liable to pay a mortgage of £50,000 when you were together, you can argue that you should each be entitled to housing costs on a mortgage of up to £50,000 when you separate;
* you buy your home and immediately beforehand you were in rented accommodation and getting HB. Your housing costs are restricted to the amount of HB you previously received plus any 'other housing costs'(see p37) you were already getting.[46] You get any subsequent increases in the standard rate of interest (see below) or the 'other housing costs' and do not lose these if the interest rate or costs go down again;[47]
* you were only getting 'other housing costs' (see p37) paid with your IS (eg, as a Crown Tenant) and you then buy a home.[48] To begin with you will only get the amount you had been getting for those other costs. You get any subsequent increases in the standard rate of interest or the 'other housing costs' and do not lose these if the interest rate or costs go down again.

How are my mortgage payments calculated?

Your IS does not cover the whole of your mortgage payments. You can get help with interest on the loan(s) but not with capital repayments or the cost of associated insurance premiums.[49] Thus claimants with an endowment mortgage will not get the insurance element paid.

There is therefore a short-fall between the IS you get for your housing costs and what you have to pay your lender. Your lender may be prepared to accept interest-only payments for a while and it is important to discuss this with them so that you do not fall into arrears and risk losing your home. If you have to make capital repayments you may be able to increase your income by taking in lodgers (see p404 for how this affects your IS). Payments made direct to the lender by relatives, friends or a charity towards the capital repayments can also be ignored (see 403).

Your weekly IS housing costs are worked out using a special formula.[50] The amount of your loan which qualifies (see p32) is taken into account less any restrictions that have been made (see pp33 and 41). IS housing costs are worked out net of tax relief (known as MIRAS) provided this is deducted at source by your lender.

A **standard rate of interest** is used, not what you actually have to pay.[51] The standard rate of interest is set by the DSS and is currently 7.97 per cent. If your repayments are higher because your lender charges a higher rate of interest you have to meet the shortfall yourself. However, if you are paying less than 5 per cent interest (eg, under a special low-start mortgage scheme) your payments are calculated using the interest rate you pay. If the interest rate on your mortgage goes above 5 per cent, the standard rate will be used.

Your housing costs for repairs and improvements (see below) are calculated in the same way as for mortgages.

Example

Mr and Mrs Khan have a repayment mortgage. The outstanding loan of £30,000 qualifies (see p32). Tax relief is deducted at source. They pay interest at the rate of 8.5%.

£30,000 x 90% (loan net of tax relief at 10%) x 7.97% (standard interest rate) = £2,151.90

Their weekly IS housing costs are £2,159.90 ÷ 52 = £41.38.

There can be a limit on how much interest will be paid. If your loan is for more than £100,000 you might only be paid interest on this figure (see p41). If your housing costs are lower than this but still thought to be too high they might be restricted (see p42).

Note: The rules for calculating your weekly housing costs changed on 2 October 1995. If you have been claiming IS or income-based JSA since before that date, see p46 to see if you are entitled to transitional protection.

Loans for repairs and improvements[52]

It is important to remember that:

- not all loans for repairs and improvements qualify for help;
- you might not get your full costs met initially (see p43);
- deductions can be made if other people live in your home (see p39);
- your IS only covers interest on your loan(s) and there is a special way the amount you can be paid is calculated (see p35).

IS will not meet the cost of repairs and improvements to the home or the cost of service charges for these (but see p38). However, if you take out a loan to pay for the repairs and improvements or the service charge (or to pay off an earlier loan taken out for this purpose) you may get help with the interest. See below for what repairs or improvements qualify. You must use the loan for the repairs and improvements or service charge within six months (longer if this is reasonable). A bank overdraft you arrange to pay for the repairs or improvements counts as a loan.[53]

Repairs and improvements that qualify

You can only get help with loans for repairs or improvements to maintain your current home,[54] or any part of the building in which it is contained, in a habitable condition. Loans towards the cost of necessary survey work should also be included.[55] You can get interest on a loan for any of the following:

- provision of a bath, shower, toilet, wash basin and the necessary plumbing and hot water;
- repairs to your heating system;
- damp-proof measures;
- provision of ventilation and natural lighting;
- provision of drainage facilities;
- facilities for preparing and cooking food (but not for storing it[56]);
- home insulation;
- provision of electric lighting and sockets;
- storage facilities for fuel or refuse;
- repairs of unsafe structural defects;
- adaptations for a disabled person (see p34 for who counts);
- providing separate bedrooms for children of different sexes aged 10 or over who are part of your family (see p346 for who counts as your family). You can argue that this should apply if one of the children is 10 or over and the other will be 10 in the reasonably near future.[57]

If your loan is also for other repairs and improvements, you will only be paid housing costs for the proportion which relates to any of the items listed above.

The rules for help with loans for repairs and improvements changed on 2 October 1995. If you took out your loan before that date, you might be able to get help under the old, more favourable rules (see p46).

If your loan is for the right sort of repairs or improvements, the amount payable is calculated as for mortgages – you do not get full help when you first claim (see p43) and the standard interest rate is used (see p35). The restriction on taking out loans while on IS or income-based JSA does not apply to those taken out for repairs and improvements.

Help with 'other housing costs'

You are paid the normal weekly charge for all other housing costs covered by IS.[58] See p28 for what is covered. Where you pay your 'other housing costs' annually or irregularly, the weekly amount will be worked out by dividing what is payable for the year by 52. You might not get your full costs met initially (see p43).

If your other housing costs have been waived because you have paid for repairs or redecoration which are not your responsibility, you can still get IS for them for up to eight weeks.[59]

Service charges

A 'service' is something which is agreed and arranged on your behalf and for which you are required to pay. Thus, if you own a flat and the lessor arranges the exterior painting of the building for which you have to pay a share of the cost, your IS includes this as a service charge. Some service charges are specifically excluded (see the list of ineligible service charges listed on p246). Some service charges only count if they relate to the provision of 'adequate accommodation' (see p245).[60]

House insurance paid under the terms of your lease can be a service charge, but insurance required by a building society as a condition of your mortgage is not.[61] Service charges to cover minor repairs and maintenance are covered but service charges for repairs and improvements listed on p37 are not – you must take out a loan to pay for these, and the interest on the loan can be covered by IS housing costs (see p36).

Services provided by an outside authority which you arrange yourself are not covered. Thus charges for water and sewerage paid to a water board are not met.[62]

Charges for the following items cannot be met:[63]

- fuel, where this is included in your housing costs. If there is no specific charge for fuel, set deductions are made as follows:

heating	£9.25	lighting	£0.80
hot water	£1.15	cooking	£1.15

- repairs and improvements listed on p37. You are expected to take out a loan to pay for these and can claim the interest (see p36);
- ineligible services listed on p246.

If you normally pay service charges annually you will have to ask if you can make weekly payments.

Calculating your total housing costs

Once you have worked out which housing costs can be met by IS you need to:

- calculate the weekly amount of:
  - mortgage interest (see p32);
  - interest on loans for repairs and improvements (see p36);
  - other housing costs (see p37);

- add these amounts together;
- deduct any restrictions being made because your housing costs are too high (see p41);
- deduct any amounts for non-dependants living in your home (see below).

Remember that a reduced amount is paid for the early weeks of your claim (see p43).

Deductions for other people living in your home[64]

If other people normally live with you in your home who are not part of your family for benefit purposes (see p346) – they are called 'non-dependants' – a set deduction is usually made from your housing costs. Thus, if an adult son or daughter, or an elderly relative shares your home, you may need to ask her/him for a contribution towards your outgoings.

A person can only be treated as living with you if s/he shares rooms with you. This includes the kitchen (unless it is only used by someone else to prepare food for her/him[65]), but not a bathroom, toilet or common access areas.[66] A person who is separately liable to pay rent to a landlord is not counted as living with you.

When no deduction is made
No deduction is made from your housing costs if the person living with you is not treated as a 'non-dependant' (though any rent or lodging charges they pay to you affects the amount of your IS, see p404). A person does not count as a non-dependant if s/he:[67]

- is liable to pay you, or your partner, in order to live in your home – eg, a sub-tenant, licensee or boarder. This also applies to other members of her/his household. The payment must be on a commercial basis. A low charge does not necessarily mean that the arrangement is not commercial, nor do you have to make a profit. An arrangement between friends can be commercial.[68] Close relatives (see p28) count as non-dependants even if they pay for their accommodation;
- is someone other than a close relative (see p28) to whom you, or your partner, are liable to make payments on a commercial basis (ie, as a sub-tenant, licensee or boarder) in order to live in her/his property. Other members of her/his household do not count as non-dependants either;
- jointly occupies your home and is a co-owner or joint tenant with you or your partner. Your joint occupier's partner is not a non-dependant. Close relatives (see p28) who jointly occupy your home are treated as non-dependants unless they had joint liability prior to 11 April 1988 or it existed on or before the date you first lived in the property (or your

partner did if s/he is the joint owner/tenant). However, no non-dependant deduction is made for them even though they are non-dependants;

- is employed by a charitable or voluntary organisation as a resident carer for you, or your partner, and you pay for that service (even if the charge is nominal). If the carer's partner also lives in your home s/he does not count as a non-dependant.

Even if you do have a non-dependant in your home no deduction is made if:[69]

- a deduction is already being made from your HB;
- you, or your partner, are blind or treated as blind (see p11);
- you, or your partner, get attendance allowance (or equivalent benefits paid because of injury at work or a war injury) or the care component of disability living allowance.

In addition no deduction is made for a non-dependant who is:

- staying with you but who normally lives elsewhere;
- 16 or 17 years old, or getting a Youth Training allowance;
- a full-time student (see p19). This also applies during the summer vacation as long as s/he is not working full time;
- 18–24 years old and getting IS or income-based JSA;
- not living with you at present because s/he has been in hospital for more than six weeks, or is in prison;
- a co-owner or joint tenant with you, or your partner, even if s/he is a close relative (see p28).

The amount of deductions

If you have a non-dependant living with you who is 18 or over, a fixed amount is usually deducted from your housing costs, whatever s/he pays you. If your non-dependant is working full time (see p13), the amount depends on her/his weekly gross income as follows:

Gross weekly income	*Non-dependant deduction*
£250 or more	£45
£200–249.99	£41
£152–199.00	£36
£116–151.99	£22
£78–115.99	£16
Less than £78	£7

In all other cases, a £7 deduction is made, but see above for situations when no deduction is made.

Gross income includes wages before tax and national insurance are deducted plus any other income the non-dependant has (but not attendance allowance, disability living allowance or payments from the Macfarlane Trusts, the Eileen Trust, the Fund or the Independent Living Funds – see p514).[70]

A deduction is made for each non-dependant in your home, but if there is more than one and they include a couple only one deduction is made for the couple. In this case their joint income counts and the highest possible deduction is made.

If you are a joint owner with someone other than your partner, any deductions are shared proportionally between you and the other owner(s).

Restrictions if your housing costs are too high

Your housing costs can be restricted if:

- your loans exceed an upper limit (see below); *or*
- your housing costs are thought to be too high (see p42).

If you are left with insufficient money to pay your housing costs you may be in danger of losing your home, particularly if you are on IS for a long time. You should inform your lender and discuss with them how to resolve the situation. You should also seek independent debt advice.

Ultimately, you may have to sell your home and buy somewhere cheaper but you could try and make up any shortfall by taking in a lodger (see p404) or finding a part-time job and benefiting from an earnings disregard (see pp386-88). Another way around the problem is to move out and put your house up for sale. The capital value of your house can be disregarded for a period while you take reasonable steps to sell it (see p421).[71] If you also rent it out while trying to sell, the income from any tenants can be disregarded up to the value of any mortgage outgoings which you have on the property.[72]

The upper limit

If your loans amount to more than £100,000 in total, your housing costs might not be met in full.[73] This includes all mortgages taken out to buy your home and also any loans for repairs and improvements. The restriction is applied proportionately to each loan. If a loan was taken out to adapt your home for a disabled person (see p34 for who counts), it is ignored when working out if your loans exceed the upper limit. If you are getting housing costs on more than one home (see p31) you can be paid up to the limit for each.[74]

Upper limits for loans have only existed since 2 August 1993 and have changed twice since that date. The limit has been £100,000 since 10 April 1995. However:

- your limit is £125,000 if you have been entitled to IS or income-based JSA since 11 April 1994;
- your limit is £150,000 if you have been entitled to IS or income-based JSA since 2 August 1993;
- there is no limit if you have been entitled to IS or income-based JSA from before 2 August 1993.

If you are uncertain about which limit applies to you, you should seek advice. If you are considering increasing your mortgage or loan, see p33.

Excessive housing costs

Even if you have borrowed less than the upper limit (see above), your housing costs can be restricted if:[75]

- your home (excluding any part which you let) is too big for you and your family. When deciding if your home is too big, a comparison is made with other accommodation which would be suitable given the size of your household. Any non-dependants (see p39) or foster children in your home count as part of your family for this purpose. The needs of everyone in your family must be considered. For example, if a member of your family needs extra space because of a disability, or you have a child or elderly relative in care who regularly comes to stay with you, your need for a large home may be justified;
- the area in which you live is more expensive than other areas where there is accommodation suitable for your needs. An area is 'something more confined, restricted and compact than a locality or district...It might consist of...a number of roads, refer to a neighbourhood and even to a large block of flats.'[76] The area should not be chosen on too wide a basis – ie, you should not be expected to move to a completely different part of the country;
- the outgoings on your home which are met by IS housing costs (see pp32, 36 and 37) are higher than on other properties in the area which are suitable for your needs.

The capital value of your home cannot be taken into account.[77]

No restriction should be made even if suitable accommodation is available if it is not reasonable for you to look for cheaper accommodation. Account should be taken of:[78]

- the general level of housing costs in the area and whether a suitable alternative is available. This means that property must be generally available, not necessarily available to you personally;[79]

- your family circumstances – eg, your employment prospects, the age and state of health of your family members and whether the move would have a detrimental effect on a child's education if s/he would have to change schools.

These are not the only situations which count.[80] A move may not be reasonable where:

- the size of your family would make it difficult to find accommodation;
- you need to be near relatives or friends to provide (or receive) care or support;
- you have moved a number of times recently;
- it would be difficult to sell your property[81] or you have negative equity or selling would cause you financial hardship;[82]
- you have lived in your home for many years and it is now too large because you are separated or divorced, or your children have left home, or your partner has died;
- prior to your claim you were advised by the Benefits Agency that full mortgage interest would be paid;[83]
- you could not get another mortgage on a property.[84]

Even if it is reasonable for you to move, your housing costs should not be restricted for 26 weeks if you, or a member of your family, were able to meet these costs when they were first taken on. Your housing costs are not restricted for a further 26 weeks if you are trying to find cheaper accommodation. If full payment is made initially but later, following a review, your housing costs are restricted, the 26-week periods begin from the date of the review.[85] Periods of 12 weeks or less when you were not getting IS or income-based JSA are included when calculating these periods. If you have only recently become one of a couple or separated from your partner and you make a new claim within 12 weeks, periods when your partner was in receipt of IS count towards the 26-week period. You should be notified of any intention to restrict your benefit.[86]

If it is appropriate to restrict your housing costs, the amount paid is limited to what you would have to pay for a suitable alternative property. This is a subjective test – if the equity in your property was sufficient to buy a new home outright your IS housing costs could be nil.[87]

Reduced payment during the first weeks of your claim

Even if you are entitled to IS to cover your housing costs, these are not usually paid until you have been claiming IS for a number of weeks – what is known as a 'waiting period'.[88] This applies to mortgages and loans (see p32), loans for repairs and improvements (see p36) and 'other housing costs' (see p37). To help you get help with your housing costs sooner, you are treated as being on IS for certain weeks prior to your claim even though you were not actually receiving it (see p45).

You can be paid straight away if:[89]

• you have already been entitled to IS or income-based JSA for the relevant number of weeks when you take out your loan or agreement to pay 'other housing costs' (but see p33 for the rules restricting housing costs if you take out or increase a loan while on IS or income-based JSA);
• you or your partner are 60 or over;
• you are claiming for payments as a Crown tenant, under a co-ownership scheme or for a tent.

All other claimants get a reduced amount of help initially. How long your waiting period is depends on when you took out your mortgage or loan or agreed to pay 'other housing costs' and how long you have been on (or treated as on) IS or income-based JSA (see below). You are expected to use mortgage protection policy payments, savings or disregarded income to meet any shortfall. If you do not have enough to pay the shortfall you should approach your lender to discuss how you can protect your home.

If you took your loan out or agreed to pay 'other housing costs' before 2 October 1995 (the Benefits Agency calls these 'existing housing costs') you get:[90]

• nothing for the first eight weeks of your claim;
• 50 per cent of your housing costs for the next 18 weeks;
• full housing costs after 26 weeks on IS.

This 26-week waiting period can also apply if you take out a loan after 2 October 1995, provided it replaces a loan taken out before that date and is with the same lender, for the same property and for the same amount (or lower) as the earlier loan.

If you took your loan out or agreed to pay 'other housing costs' after 1 October 1995 (the Benefits Agency calls these 'new housing costs') you get:[91]

• nothing for the first 39 weeks of your claim;
• full housing costs after 39 weeks on IS.

However, if the loan replaces another loan taken out before 2 October 1995, see above.

Certain claimants are exempt from this 39-week waiting period. Instead the 26-week waiting period described above applies. This is the case if you:[92]

• are a lone parent and have claimed IS because your partner has left you or died, unless you become one of a couple again;

- are claiming IS because you are a carer (see p11);
- are in prison awaiting trial or sentence;
- have been refused payments under a mortgage protection policy due to a pre-existing medical condition or because you are HIV positive.

If you have two loans or agreements to pay 'other housing costs' and one was taken out before and one after 1 October 1995, the relevant waiting periods apply to each.[93]

To help you get full housing costs earlier, you are treated as being on IS for certain weeks prior to your claim even though you were not actually receiving it. You are treated as in receipt of IS:[94]

- for any period when you were getting or were treated as entitled to income-based JSA;[95]
- during a period of 12 weeks or less between two periods when:
  - you were getting IS or income-based JSA; *or*
  - you were treated as entitled to IS or income-based JSA.
  This period is extended to 26 weeks if you were getting full housing costs but stopped getting IS because you received child support maintenance, and this has now reduced as a result of child support rule changes in April 1995 or because an interim maintenance assessment has been replaced or terminated (see the *Child Support Handbook*, 1998/99 edn for details);
- during any period for which you are awarded IS or income-based JSA after a review or an appeal;
- during any period when you were getting contribution-based JSA immediately before starting on a New Deal programme or scheme (see p58);
- during the time when your partner was claiming IS or income-based JSA on her/his own, provided you make a claim for IS within 12 weeks of becoming a couple;
- during the time when your ex-partner was claiming IS or income-based JSA for you both, provided you claim IS within 12 weeks of separating;
- during the time when your partner was claiming IS or income-based JSA for you both, if you take over the claiming role;
- during the time when you or your partner were on a New Deal programme or scheme (see p58) so long as your partner was claiming IS or income-based JSA for you immediately before this and you claim IS immediately after;
- during the time when someone who was not your partner was claiming IS or income-based JSA for you and another dependent child or young person. You must claim within 12 weeks of this and you must be a member of another family (see p346 for who counts as your family) and be claiming for that other child;

- during periods when you stop getting IS or income-based JSA because you or your partner are:
  - doing an employment training rehabilitation course;
  - on a New Deal programme or scheme (see p58) and as a result count as in full-time work (see p13) or have too much income (see p26);
- for up to 39 weeks where you were not entitled to IS because your income or capital was too high *and*:[96]
  - you have been getting contribution-based JSA, statutory sick pay or incapacity benefit (or credits for unemployment or incapacity); *or*
  - you are a lone parent or a carer (see p11) and you or someone claiming on your behalf has previously been refused IS. This does not apply if you or your partner are working full-time (see p13), or you are a student who cannot claim IS (see p19) or are temporarily absent from Great Britain and not entitled to IS (see p23).

  Where you were not entitled to IS because your income was too high, you are treated as entitled for any period where you were getting payments under a mortgage protection policy. This could be longer than 39 weeks.

If you reclaim IS within 26 weeks of a previous claim during which you were getting housing costs and you have been receiving payments under an employment insurance policy which has since run out, periods when you were getting those payments are ignored in calculating the 26/39-week waiting periods. This means that you can requalify for housing costs sooner.

Transitional protection if you have been claiming since before 2 October 1995

The rules on payment of housing costs changed on 2 October 1995. Some people will qualify for a lower amount of housing costs than they did before that date. However, there are two types of transitional protection which ensure that you should be no worse off than you were under the old rules.

- You can continue to get certain types of housing costs for which, since 2 October 1995, IS can no longer be paid. These are:[97]
  - accumulated arrears of interest;
  - interest on a secured loan which was not for house purchase, taken out when you were one of a couple, where your partner had left and could not or would not pay the cost or had died;
  - interest on a loan for repairs and improvements under the pre-2 October 1995 rules.

  You can continue to get these if they were included in your housing costs before 2 October 1995, for as long as you remain on IS (or are treated as being on IS – see p45) and fulfil the qualifying conditions. See the *National Welfare Benefits Handbook*, 1995/96 edn, pp30-32 for more details on how these costs were assessed.

* If you were on IS both on and after 1 October 1995 and the amount of housing costs to which you are now entitled is less because of the new rules, you can get an extra payment to make up the loss.[98]

  This payment is called an 'add-back' and is equal to the difference between your IS housing costs in the week including 1 October 1995 and your entitlement in the next week. Where you have more than one loan, the 'add-back' for each is calculated separately.

  The 'add-back' reduces if your new entitlement to housing costs increases. You lose the 'add-back' when your new entitlement equals what you used to get under the old rules. You also lose it if you stop getting (or being treated as getting – see p45) IS for more than 12 weeks or if you cease to qualify for housing costs. If you lose the 'add-back' but your partner makes a claim for you within 12 weeks, s/he can continue to get the 'add-back' to which you were entitled.

  If you are on a fixed-rate mortgage, where your interest rate stays the same throughout, the way the 'add-back' rule is applied means you lose out if the standard rate of interest used to calculate your housing costs goes down. Although difficult, you could try to argue that the rule is unlawful because it has operated retrospectively and Parliament cannot have intended that you lose out in this way.[99]

3. RATES OF BENEFIT PAID TO 16/17-YEAR-OLDS

Special rates of IS are paid if you are 16 or 17 years old. Your applicable amount (see p25) depends partly on your age and that of your partner, if you have one.

Single people and lone parents

There are two levels of payment:[100]
  – lower rate   £30.30
  – higher rate   £39.85

You are paid at the higher rate if:[101]

* you qualify for the disability premium (see p362); *or*
* you are an orphan with no one acting as your parent (which includes foster parents, a local authority or a voluntary organisation if you are in care or are being looked after by them); *or*

- you are living away from parents and any person acting as your parent, and immediately before you were 16 you were in custody, or being looked after by a local authority who placed you with someone other than a close relative (see p28); *or*
- you are living away from parents and any person acting as your parent, and instead are living elsewhere:
  - as part of a programme of resettlement or rehabilitation under the supervision of the probation service or a local authority; *or*
  - to avoid physical or sexual abuse; *or*
  - because you need special accommodation due to mental or physical illness or handicap; *or*
- you are living in accommodation away from your parents and any person acting as your parent, they are unable to support you financially and they are:
  - in custody; *or*
  - unable to enter Great Britain because of the immigration laws; *or*
  - 'chronically sick or mentally or physically disabled' (see p18); *or*
- you have to live away from parents and any person acting as your parent, because:
  - you are estranged from them (see p18); *or*
  - you are in physical or moral danger; *or*
  - there is a serious risk to your physical or mental health.

Couples[102]

The amount paid to couples depends on your ages and whether one or both of you would be eligible for IS as a single person.

- One partner aged 18 or over and the other under   £79.00
  18 *and*
  - entitled to IS (or would be if not a member
    of a couple); *or*
  - entitled to income-based JSA; *or*
  - entitled to discretionary JSA on grounds of severe
    hardship
  (see CPAG's *Jobseeker's Allowance Handbook* 3rd edn, 1998/99 for further information about JSA).
- Both under 18 *and*   £60.10
  - both entitled to IS (or would be if not a member
    of a couple; *or*
  - one is responsible for a child; *or*
  - the partner of the person claiming is entitled to
    income-based JSA; *or*

- the partner of the person claiming is entitled to
discretionary JSA on grounds of severe hardship
(see p48).
- The claimant is aged 25 or over and the other under   £50.35
18 *and*
  - not entitled to IS (even if s/he were not a member of a
couple); *and*
  - not entitled to income-based JSA; *and*
  - not entitled to discretionary JSA on grounds of
severe hardship (see p48).
- The claimant is 18–24 and the other under 18 *and*   £39.85
  - not entitled to IS (even if s/he was not a member of a
couple); *and*
  - not entitled to income-based JSA; *and*
  - not entitled to discretionary JSA on grounds of
severe hardship (see p48).
- Both under 18 and one is entitled to IS   £39.85
at the higher rate for under-18s.
- Both under 18 and one is entitled to IS   £30.30
at the lower rate for under-18s.

4. TRANSITIONAL PROTECTION

Some claimants are paid more than their basic IS entitlement because
they receive an amount of transitional protection. This protection
ensured people were not worse-off when IS replaced supplementary
benefit in April 1988. It covers people who were claiming supplementary
benefit immediately before 11 April 1988 who have been on IS or
income-based JSA ever since. For more details see the 19th edition of the
National Welfare Benefits Handbook. If you do not have this we can supply a
photocopy of the relevant parts. Write to CPAG, 1-5 Bath Street,
London EC1V 9PY.

5. URGENT CASES PAYMENTS

Who can claim

If you do not satisfy the normal rules for IS, you may be able to get an
urgent cases payment if you come within one of the following groups:[103]

- you are a 'person from abroad' and meet certain conditions (see p86);

- you are treated as possessing income which was due to be paid to you but which has not been paid (see p412). If you were due to receive a social security benefit but it has not yet been paid you will not be treated as possessing it. The income you are treated as possessing must not be readily available to you and there must be a likelihood that if you do not get a payment, you or your family will suffer hardship.[104]

Even if your partner is entitled to ordinary IS you can claim urgent cases payments instead if the amount you receive would be higher.

It is important to note that an urgent cases payment is a payment of IS and thus you are automatically eligible for other benefits (see p6).

If you do not come within these rules but have no money, you may be able to get a crisis loan from the social fund (see p479).

How much you can get

Applicable amounts

Urgent cases payments of IS are paid at a reduced rate. Your applicable amount is:

- a personal allowance for you (and your partner) (see p25). It is paid at 90 per cent of the personal allowance that would have been paid had you qualified for IS in the normal way; *plus*
- full personal allowances for your children; *plus*
- premiums (see p25) and housing costs (see p27) or residential allowance (see pp89, 93 and 95), if any, and any 'protected sum' paid because you were a boarder prior to 10 April 1989.[105]

If you are living in a residential or nursing home and have 'preserved rights' (see p88), you receive 90 per cent of the personal allowance for you (and your partner) plus full personal allowances for any children plus the amount normally allowed for your accommodation. You get 98 per cent of the amount paid if you are in a local authority home.[106]

If your benefit is reduced by 20 per cent because you are appealing a decision of the Benefits Agency which says that you are capable of work under the 'all-work' test and are not signing on for work in the meantime (see p11) that reduction is applied before the 10 per cent urgent cases reduction.[107]

Income and capital

Almost all of your income and capital is taken into account before an urgent cases payment is made.

Income

Most of your income counts, but the following is ignored:[108]

- assumed income from capital between £3,000 and £8,000 (£10,000 and £16,000 if you live in a residential or nursing home – see p405);
- income you are treated as having if you are applying for an urgent cases payment for that reason;
- backdated payments of IS made to you once the Home Office accepts you are a refugee (see p79);
- concessionary urgent cases payments of IS or income-based JSA;
- any housing benefit (HB) and/or council tax benefit (CTB);
- any payment made to compensate you for the loss of entitlement to HB;
- social fund payments;
- any payment from any of the Macfarlane Trusts, the Eileen Trust, the Fund, or the Independent Living Funds;
- payments made by haemophilia sufferers to their partner or children, out of money originally provided by one of the Macfarlane Trusts. If the sufferer has no partner or children, payments made to a parent, step-parent or guardian are also disregarded, but only for two years. These payments are also disregarded if the sufferer dies and the money is paid out of the estate;
- payments arising from the Macfarlane Trusts which are paid by a person to a haemophiliac partner, or to their child(ren).

Certain income is treated as capital if you get IS under the normal rules (see p420). However, if you apply for an urgent cases payment the following is treated as income:[109]

- any lump sum paid to you not more than once a year for your work, as a part-time firefighter, part-time member of a lifeboat crew, auxiliary coastguard or member of the Territorial Army;
- any refund of income tax;
- holiday pay which is not payable until more than four weeks after your job ended;
- any irregular charitable or voluntary payment.

Capital[110]

Your capital is calculated in the usual way (see Chapter 20) but certain types cannot be disregarded. Any capital taken into account affects your urgent cases payment, not just that over the capital limit (see p415). The following cannot be disregarded:

- money from the sale of your home which you intend to use to buy another;

- the liquid assets of a business (eg, cash in hand);
- arrears of the following: mobility supplement, disability living or disability working allowance, attendance allowance, earnings top-up, family credit or any concessionary payments made to compensate for non-payment of any of these benefits;
- arrears of IS or income-based JSA but not:
  – arrears of urgent cases payments;
  – concessionary urgent cases payments;
- backdated payments of IS, HB or CTB made to you once the Home Office accepts you are a refugee (see p79);
- money which had been deposited with a housing association and which is now to be used to buy a home;
- up to £200 of a training bonus received after being on Training for Work;
- a refund of tax on a mortgage or loan taken out to buy, or to do repairs and/or improvements to your home.

CHAPTER FOUR

Jobseeker's allowance

This chapter covers:

1. Introduction to jobseeker's allowance (below)
2. Income-based jobseeker's allowance (p54)
3. The labour market conditions (p55)
4. Sanctions and hardship payments (p57)
5. The New Deal (p58)
6. Should you claim jobseeker's allowance or income support? (p58)

1. INTRODUCTION TO JOBSEEKER'S ALLOWANCE

Jobseeker's allowance (JSA) is paid instead of income support (IS) to those who have to look for work in order to qualify for benefit. Claims for JSA are made at local JobCentres.

This chapter gives only a summary of the main jobseeker's allowance rules. For full details, see CPAG's *Jobseeker's Allowance Handbook*, 3rd edn, 1998/99.

JSA has two elements:

- *Contribution-based* JSA can be paid for the first 26 weeks of your 'jobseeking period' (see below) if you satisfy contribution conditions. It can be paid on its own, but if you satisfy a means-test, you can be paid income-based JSA as well.
- *Income-based* JSA can be paid during your 'jobseeking period' (see below) if you satisfy the means test (see p55). It can be paid on its own or in addition to *contribution-based* JSA.

Your 'jobseeking period' is the period during which you meet the conditions of entitlement for JSA or in which you receive a hardship payment.[1]

You cannot get JSA for the first three days of your 'jobseeking period' unless you have been entitled to IS, incapacity benefit or invalid care allowance within the 12 weeks before you became entitled to JSA *or* you are aged 16 or 17 and are getting JSA under the 'severe hardship' rules (see the *Jobseeker's Allowance Handbook,* 3rd edn, 1998/99).[2]

Passported benefits

If you get income-based JSA, you may have a right to receive the following payments from the social fund:

- a cold weather payment (see p451)
- a funeral expenses payment (see p444)
- a maternity expenses payment (see p442)

You can also be considered for community care grants (see p467), budgeting loans (see p477) and crisis loans (see p479).

If you get income-based JSA, you automatically qualify for a number of other benefits and types of help such as free prescriptions and free school meals (see p6). The rules about these are the same as for IS (see Chapter 26 and Appendix 1).

2. INCOME-BASED JOBSEEKER'S ALLOWANCE

If you have not paid or been credited with enough national insurance contributions to get *contribution-based* JSA, you might still qualify for *income-based* JSA if your income and savings are low enough to pass the means test. If you do qualify for contribution-based JSA, you could claim income-based JSA as well if, for example:

- you have a family and want to claim benefit for them as well as yourself;
- you need help with your housing costs (the rules are generally the same as for IS, see the *Jobseeker's Allowance Handbook,* 3rd edn, 1998/99).

You can claim income-based JSA if you satisfy the following rules:[3]

- neither you nor your partner are in full-time paid work (see p13 for what counts as full-time work);
- you satisfy the 'labour market conditions' (see p55);
- you are at least 16 but under pensionable age (60 for women and 65 for men). 16- and 17-year-olds have to satisfy special rules;
- you are not in full-time education.

The means test

The way income-based JSA is calculated is broadly the same as for IS (see Chapters 3, 18, 19 and 20). The capital limit is £8,000 – £16,000 if you live in residential care or similar accommodation (see p415).

If you are 'sanctioned' (see p57), for example because you have left a job without a good reason, you only get JSA if you qualify for a hardship payment. If you do, you are paid JSA at a reduced rate. Your JSA can also be paid at a reduced rate if you are a lone parent and refuse – without a good reason – to co-operate with the Child Support Agency in seeking maintenance for your children (see p113 for the IS rules, which are the same).

3. THE LABOUR MARKET CONDITIONS

To get JSA, you must prove that you are genuinely looking for work. To qualify you must:

- be capable of work; *and*
- be available for work; *and*
- be actively seeking work; *and*
- have a current jobseeker's agreement with the Employment Service.

'Available for work'

You are treated as available for work if you are willing and able to take up any job immediately. There are exceptions to this rule. For example:

- if you have caring responsibilities or are doing voluntary work you do not have to be available for work immediately;[4]
- you are allowed to place restrictions on the sort of job you are prepared to take, for example, the pay you will accept (for the first six months of your claim only), the type of work you will do or where you are willing to work, so long as you can show that you still have a reasonable chance of getting a job.[5] In deciding whether you still have a reasonable chance, the Employment Service must consider such things as, for example, your skills and experience and the length of time you have been unemployed;[6]
- you can be allowed to concentrate your search for work on vacancies in your normal occupation for up to 13 weeks at the beginning of your claim (your 'permitted period');[7]
- although you generally must be prepared to accept any offer of employment which would involve at least 40 hours a week, you can

restrict your availability to less than this in certain circumstances, for example, if this is reasonable in the light of your physical or mental condition.

You can be **treated as available for work** in certain circumstances, for example, during short spells of sickness (a maximum of two periods of two weeks in 12 months you are unemployed) or for the week following your discharge from prison.[8]

Even if you are available for work, you will nevertheless be **treated as unavailable** if:[9]

* you are a full-time student;
* you are on temporary release from prison;
* you are receiving maternity allowance or statutory maternity pay (for further details of these benefits see the *Rights Guide to Non-Means-Tested Benefits*, 21st edn, 1998/99).

'Actively seeking work'

You must be actively trying to find work in each week you are unemployed. You must take such 'steps' as you can reasonably be expected to take, to have the best prospects of getting employment. Steps include applying for jobs by letter or telephone, getting information about possible jobs from employers, registered employment agencies, and advertisements in newspapers and preparing a CV.[10]

When deciding whether you have taken reasonable steps to find work the adjudication officer must take account of, for example, your skills, qualifications, any health and physical or mental limitations, the attempts you have made to find work in previous weeks, whether you are doing voluntary work, whether you are homeless, and attempts you have made to find accommodation.[11]

You can be **treated as actively seeking work** in certain weeks including:[12]

* the first and last weeks for which you claim;
* two weeks in any period of 12 months while you are away from home – eg, on holiday, in the UK. You must give the Employment Service advance notice;
* during short spells of sickness (see p10).

The jobseeker's agreement

You must enter into a jobseeker's agreement to get JSA. It must be signed both by you and an Employment Service Officer (EO).[13] The EO will not sign it unless s/he believes you qualify as available for and actively seeking work (see pp55 and 56). The agreement must contain certain information, including:[14]

- the hours you are available for work each week;
- any restriction you are allowed to place on the work you are prepared to do;
- the type of job you are looking for;
- the steps you will take to actively seek work; *and*
- a statement of your rights if you and the EO cannot agree about what should be in the agreement.

4. SANCTIONS AND HARDSHIP PAYMENTS

There are a number of situations when you might be 'sanctioned' and JSA might not be paid to you even if you would otherwise be entitled.[15] No JSA will be paid for the length of your sanction period unless you qualify for a hardship payment (see below). The length of your sanction period could be a fixed period of two or four weeks (for example, if you refuse to carry out a reasonable jobseeker's direction or lose your place on a compulsory training scheme through misconduct) or for a period from one to 26 weeks – for example, if you lose your job through misconduct or give up your job voluntarily without just cause.

If you are sanctioned but your partner qualifies for IS or JSA, s/he could claim instead of you. Her/his claim is not affected by your sanction so s/he can be paid IS or JSA in full.

Hardship payments

If you are sanctioned, you will not be paid *contribution-based* JSA at all during your sanction period (see above). However, if you are entitled to *income-based* JSA, you might be able to get a hardship payment. To qualify for a hardship payment, you must prove that you, your partner or a member of your family (see p346 for who counts as your family) will suffer hardship if no payment is made.[16] Many people cannot get a hardship payment for the first two weeks of their sanction period. However, you can get a hardship payment straight away if, for example:

- you or your partner is pregnant and will suffer hardship if no payment is made; *or*
- you or your partner have children who will suffer hardship; *or*
- you qualify for a disability premium with your income-based JSA.

If you get a hardship payment, premiums and housing costs are paid in full, but your income-based JSA is reduced by an amount equal to 40 per cent of the personal allowance for a single claimant of your age.[17] The reduction is the same even if you are one of a couple. A smaller reduction of 20 per cent is made where you, your partner or child is pregnant or seriously ill.

5. THE NEW DEAL

As part of its 'welfare to work' policy, the Government has set up programmes and schemes to assist people back to work. These are:

- the New Deal for 18 to 24-year-olds. You will be offered a place if you have been claiming JSA for six months or more;
- the New Deal for people of 25 or over who are long-term unemployed (currently for more than two years).

If you refuse to participate in the New Deal or leave a programme or scheme without just cause, you might be 'sanctioned' (see p57). You might not be paid any JSA during your sanction period (see p57).

There is also a New Deal for lone parents and a New Deal for disabled people. However, you cannot be 'sanctioned' (see p57) if you refuse to participate or leave these schemes or programmes.

See the *Jobseeker's Allowance Handbook,* 3rd edn, 1998/99 for further details of the New Deal.

6. SHOULD YOU CLAIM JOBSEEKER'S ALLOWANCE OR INCOME SUPPORT?

Although you cannot claim JSA and income support (IS) at the same time,[18] you might be able to choose which benefit to claim. For example, you might want to claim IS instead of JSA if:

- you automatically qualify as incapable of work without having to satisfy the 'all-work' test, for example because you are registered blind, terminally ill or have a severe learning disability (see *Rights Guide to Non-Means-Tested Benefits,* 21st edn, 1998/99);
- you are caring for a disabled person and qualify for invalid care allowance;
- you are 60 or over; *or*
- you are a lone parent of a child under 16.

If you are in this position, you should claim IS instead of JSA, together with any other benefit you may be entitled to such as incapacity benefit, severe disablement allowance or invalid care allowance. The rates of benefit are the same, but you will not have to sign on every fortnight or look for work or risk being sanctioned (see p57). However, you should ensure that you are getting national insurance contribution credits or home responsibilities protection. See the *Rights Guide to Non-Means-Tested Benefits*, 21st edn, 1998/99 for more information.

There are other situations when you can claim either JSA or IS. However, you might want to claim JSA to protect your national insurance record. You should seek advice before deciding which benefit to claim if:

- you are 16 or 17 years old and claiming benefit while you are in 'relevant education' (see p17);
- you are looking after a member of your family who is temporarily ill.

If you have a partner and you are claiming *contribution-based* JSA, you could claim *income-based* JSA to top up your income but your partner might be able to claim IS for you instead (see p10). If you are in this situation, you should check to see how you would be better off financially. For example, your partner should claim IS if s/he qualifies for the IS disability premium (see p362) because s/he is entitled to statutory sick pay or has been incapable of work for 196 days (if terminally ill) or 364 days (see p363). You cannot get the disability premium for her/him if you claim income-based JSA.

If you work part time (see p13) **and your partner works at least 16 hours but no more than 24 hours each week, between you, you might choose to claim family credit (FC), disability working allowance (DWA) or earnings top-up (ETU)** (see pp197, 212 and 210) **instead of** JSA or IS. However, you should seek advice before deciding whether to claim. For example, if you are paying a mortgage and can get income-based JSA or IS to help you with your housing costs, you might be better off on income-based JSA or IS instead of FC, DWA or ETU.

CHAPTER FIVE

Special rules for special groups

This chapter covers:
1. 16/17-year-olds (below)
2. People involved in a trade dispute (p61)
3. People from abroad (p66)
4. Residential and nursing care (p87)
5. People in hospital (p97)
6. Prisoners (p101)
7. People without accommodation (p102)

I. 16/17-YEAR-OLDS

If you are aged 16 or 17, you are entitled to income support (IS) in your own right if you satisfy the normal rules of entitlement.[1] You should not have your claim refused or be turned away by the Benefits Agency simply because of your age.

You should note the following points, however:

- You are only entitled to income support (IS) if you fall into one of the categories of claimants eligible for IS listed on p10.[2]
- If you are in 'relevant education', you are only entitled to IS in specified circumstances (see p17).[3] If you are in or have recently left non-advanced education and are living with someone who is 'responsible' for you, you can be included in their IS claim (see p354).
- Your IS personal allowance depends on your (and your partner's) age and circumstances. See p47 for details.
- If you are not entitled to IS, you may be entitled to income-based jobseeker's allowance (JSA), if you satisfy the special rules which apply to 16/17-year-olds. See CPAG's *Jobseeker's Allowance Handbook* 1998/99 for details. You must normally be registered with the Careers Service and be available for and actively seeking work and training. In addition, you are only entitled to JSA in specified circumstances and sometimes for a limited period. You cannot get JSA if you are in 'relevant' education (see p54).

- If you are not entitled to IS or JSA, you can claim discretionary payments of JSA, if you will otherwise suffer severe hardship. See CPAG's *Jobseeker's Allowance Handbook 1998/99* for details.
- In certain circumstances, you may satisfy the rules for both IS and income-based JSA. In particular, if you are eligible for IS but not claiming it, you will also be eligible for income-based JSA (unless you are in relevant education).[4] You cannot claim both IS and income-based JSA.[5] It will usually be better to claim IS to avoid the requirement to be available for and actively seeking work and training and the attendant risk of benefit sanctions (see *Jobseeker's Allowance Handbook* for details). If you claim IS rather than JSA, however, you will not receive national insurance credits (see CPAG's *Rights Guide to Non-Means-Tested Benefits 1998/99* for information about credits).

2. PEOPLE INVOLVED IN A TRADE DISPUTE

You are not entitled to JSA for any week in which you are involved in a trade dispute.[6] You can claim IS, but the amount payable is reduced under special rules if you or your partner are involved in a trade dispute.[7] If your partner is claiming IS or JSA for you, a reduced rate of benefit is also payable.[8]

Involvement in a trade dispute

A trade dispute is any dispute relating to an employment matter whether between employers and employees or between different groups of employees.[9] You are treated as involved in a trade dispute if:

- you are not working because of a stoppage of work due to a trade dispute at your place of work; *or*
- you otherwise withdraw your labour in furtherance of any trade dispute.[10]

Your 'place of work' means the place or premises where you work. It does not include a separate department carrying out a separate branch of work which is commonly undertaken as a separate business elsewhere.[11] It may, however, be difficult to show that separate branches of work are carried on as separate businesses, and that the separate branches are not integrated.[12]

You are not treated as involved in a trade dispute during a period of 'incapacity for work' (four or more days of incapacity) or during a maternity period (six weeks before your baby is due until the end of the seventh week after the birth).[13]

You are not treated as involved in a trade dispute at your place of work if:

- you can prove you are 'not directly interested' in the dispute – ie, you will not be affected by its outcome (this could apply if your terms and conditions will not be affected whatever the outcome, or you leave your job and will not gain anything when the dispute is resolved);[14] *or*
- during a stoppage, you are made redundant, or you become genuinely employed elsewhere, or you genuinely resume work with your employer but then leave for a reason other than the trade dispute.[15]

You are assumed to be involved in a trade dispute pending a decision by an adjudication officer as to whether you are actually so involved.[16]

You are treated as engaged in full-time work for the first seven days you or your partner stop work because of a trade dispute in the circumstances described above.[17] This means neither you, nor your partner, can claim IS during this period.[18] If there is a series of stoppages caused by the same trade dispute, the rule only applies for the first seven days of the first stoppage.[19] If you were getting IS immediately before the stoppage, the rule should not apply at all.[20]

Calculation of IS

Applicable amounts

If you are treated as involved in a trade dispute, your IS applicable amount (see Chapter 18) is calculated as follows:[21]

For a single person involved in a trade dispute:	Nil
For a couple without children where both are involved in a trade dispute:	Nil
For a couple without children where only one partner is involved in a trade dispute:	Half the personal allowance for a couple *plus* half the couple rate of any premium payable for the person not involved in the dispute, *plus* housing costs, if applicable.
For a lone parent who is involved in a trade dispute:	The normal personal allowances for the children, *plus* the family premium (lone parent rate if still applicable), *plus* the disabled child premium, if applicable, *plus* housing costs, if applicable.

For a couple with children where only one is involved in a trade dispute:
Half the personal allowance for a couple, *plus* half the couple rate of any premium payable for the person not involved in the dispute, *plus* the normal personal allowances for the children and the family premium, *plus* the disabled child premium, if applicable *plus* housing costs, if applicable.

For a couple with children where both are involved in a trade dispute:
The normal personal allowances for children, *plus* the family premium, *plus* the disabled child premium, if applicable *plus* housing costs, if applicable.

Housing costs are payable unless all members of the family are involved in a trade dispute. Those members not involved in the dispute are treated as responsible for the costs.[22]

Actual and 'assumed' strike pay

If you, or your partner, are involved in a trade dispute, special rules apply relating to actual and 'assumed' strike pay.

First, any payments you actually receive from a trade union in excess of £27 a week count as income and are deducted from your IS applicable amount. Payments of up to £27 a week are ignored. If you and your partner are both involved in a trade dispute, only £27 in total is ignored.[23]

Secondly, whether or not you actually receive any payments, £27 is deducted from your IS as 'assumed strike pay'. If you and your partner are both involved in a trade dispute, £27 is still deducted.[24] This deduction may extinguish your entitlement to any IS.

Example
Childless couple, one on strike, whose only income is £30 a week strike pay.

Applicable amount:	£39.50	(half normal amount)
less income:	£ 3.00	(strike pay in excess of £27)
	£36.50	
less	£27.00	(assumed strike pay)
= IS payable	£ 9.50	

If their strike pay was £40, their income of £13 (strike pay in excess of £27) and their assumed strike pay of £27, would extinguish their entitlement to any IS.

Other income and capital

Other income and capital is treated in the way described in Chapters 19 and 20 except that the following are taken into account in full as income:

- any tax refund due because of the stoppage of work;[25]
- any payment made under sections 17 or 24 of the Children Act 1989 (in Scotland, sections 12, 24 or 26 Social Work (Scotland) Act 1968);[26]
- all charitable or voluntary payments (whether regular or irregular, with no £20 disregard for regular payments) except any payment from the Macfarlane Trusts, the Eileen Trust or the Fund, or either of the Independent Living Funds;[27]
- payments of income in kind except any payment from the Macfarlane Trusts, the Eileen Trust or the Fund, or either of the Independent Living Funds;[28]
- holiday pay which is not payable until more than four weeks after your employment ends or is interrupted[29] (this counts as earnings and therefore attracts an earnings disregard – see p386);
- any advance of earnings or a loan made by your employer.[30] Where these payments are earnings, they attract an earnings disregard.

Any payments received or due because the person involved in the trade dispute is currently unemployed are also treated as income and counted in full.[31]

Benefit loans on return to work

If you return to work with the same employer, whether or not the trade dispute has ended, you can receive IS for the first 15 days back at work, in the form of a loan.[32] You are not treated as in full-time work for this period.[33] If you are a member of a couple you are not entitled to IS if your partner is in full-time work.[34] Your applicable amount is calculated according to the normal rules. Your income (including any earnings you receive from your employer) is calculated in the same way as if you were still involved in the dispute (see above) except that any income tax refunds are ignored, and there is no deduction from your benefit for assumed strike pay.

Any IS that you are awarded is paid in advance.[35] You may not get IS if you are entitled to less than £5.[36]

Repayment of the loan

Any IS paid during your first 15 days back at work can be recovered by deductions from your earnings.[37] If this is not practical (eg, because you are currently unemployed) it can be recovered directly from you.[38]

The amount deducted from your earnings is worked out by comparing your 'protected earnings' with your 'available earnings'.

Your **'protected earnings'** are an amount equal to:

- your applicable amount excluding housing costs; *plus*
- £27; *less*
- child benefit paid at ordinary or lone parent rate.[39]

Your **'available earnings'** are the whole of your earnings, including sick pay, after all 'lawful' deductions have been made.[40] These include tax and national insurance contributions, trade union subscriptions and any amount being deducted under a court order or, for instance, a child support deduction order. Any bonus or commission if paid on a different day is treated as paid on your next normal pay day.[41]

If your available earnings are less than £1 above your protected earnings level, there will be no deduction. If they are £1 or more above, your employer will deduct half of the difference between your protected and available earnings. If you are paid monthly, your protected earnings are multiplied by five. If your monthly available earnings are less than £5 above this level, no deduction is made. Otherwise, half the excess is deducted. If your earnings are paid daily, the amount of your protected earnings and the £1 figure is divided by five to determine the amount (if any) of the deduction. The calculation can be adjusted as appropriate where your wages are paid at other intervals.[42] If you are paid more than one amount of earnings on a pay day, your protected earnings and the £1 figure are multiplied to reflect this.[43]

A deduction notice is sent to your employer by the Benefits Agency setting out your protected earnings level and the amount of IS to be recovered.[44] If you have not actually received the IS and you can satisfy your employer that you have not, no deduction should be made.[45] Your employer *can* begin making the deductions from the first pay day after receiving the notice and *must* start doing so one month after getting it.[46] A deduction notice ceases to have effect if:

- it is cancelled or replaced; *or*
- you stop working for that employer; *or*
- your IS loan has been repaid; *or*
- 26 weeks have passed since the date of the notice.[47]

If you stop work, another deduction notice can be sent if you get another job and part of your IS loan is still outstanding.[48]

You must tell the Benefits Agency within ten days if you leave a job or start another while part of your IS loan remains unpaid.[49] If you fail to do so you can be prosecuted.[50] It is a criminal offence for your employer to fail to keep records of deductions and supply the Benefits Agency with these.[51] If your employer fails to make a deduction which should have been made from your pay, the Benefits Agency can recover the amount from your employer instead.[52]

Other benefits during a trade dispute

- You can get a social fund payment for **maternity** and **funeral expenses** (see Chapter 21) and travel expenses to visit a close relative or a member of the same household who is ill[53] (see p476).
- A crisis loan can only be awarded in cases of **disaster** (see p482) or for items needed for **cooking or space heating**.[54] Budgeting loans are not available to strikers.[55]
- Strikers and their families may be entitled to **free prescriptions, free dental treatment and free glasses** (see Chapter 26).

3. PEOPLE FROM ABROAD

This section gives a brief outline of the rights of claimants who are classed as 'persons from abroad' for IS purposes.

It covers:

- Introduction (p67)
- 'Persons from abroad' (p67)
- People entitled to normal rate IS (p69)
- Couples and families (p70)
- The habitual residence test (p72)
- European Economic Area nationals (p75)
- Refugees (p78)
- People with 'exceptional leave' (p79)
- Asylum-seekers (p80)
- Sponsorship undertakings (p85)
- Urgent cases payments (p86)

The interrelationship between immigration and social security law is extremely complex. For more information, you should consult CPAG's *Migration and Social Security Handbook* and JCWI's *Immigration and Nationality Law Handbook* (listed in Appendix 5).

Introduction

Your right to IS depends on:

- your immigration status; *and*
- whether you satisfy, or are exempt from, the 'habitual residence' test (see p72).

Certain categories of claimants are classed as 'persons from abroad' under the IS regulations because of their immigration status (see below). *All* claimants, including British citizens, who fail to satisfy or gain exemption from the 'habitual residence' test are also classed as 'persons from abroad'. If you are a 'person from abroad' you are not entitled to normal rate IS. In most cases your applicable amount will be nil. In some cases, however, you are entitled to urgent cases payments of IS, which are paid at a reduced rate (see p86).

The IS claim forms ask whether you, or anyone you are claiming for, have come to live in the UK in the last five years. If the answer is 'yes', you are likely to be interviewed to determine whether any one of you is a 'person from abroad'. The forms also ask whether you have come to the UK under a sponsorship undertaking (see p85).

Your immigration status may not always be clear. There are close links between the Benefits Agency and the Home Office. Making a claim for IS could alert the immigration authorities to the fact that you are here unlawfully, or that you have broken your conditions of entry by claiming 'public funds' (see p68).

It is vitally important, therefore, to get specialist advice before claiming IS if you are unsure about your position. You can get advice from your local law centre, citizens advice bureau or other advice agency which deals with immigration problems. You can also get specialist advice from the Joint Council for the Welfare of Immigrants (JCWI), 115 Old Street, London EC1V 9JR (tel: 0171 251 8706) or the Immigration Advisory Service (various offices - tel: 0171 357 6917). If you are a refugee or asylum-seeker, you can contact the Refugee Council, 3 Bondway, London SW8 1SJ (tel: 0171 582 6922/1162).

The rules relating to 'persons from abroad' also apply to income-based JSA. You will not be eligible for income-based JSA (including urgent cases payments), however, if there are any immigration restrictions on your right to work.

'Persons from abroad'

If you are classed as a 'person from abroad' under the IS regulations, you are not entitled to normal rate IS. Your IS applicable amount will be nil, unless you are entitled to urgent cases payments (see p86).[56] If your partner is not a 'person from abroad', s/he can claim IS but will not receive any benefit for you (see p70).

You are classed as a 'person from abroad' under the IS regulations if you fall into any of the following categories.[57] The first category can apply to *any* person including a British citizen. The remaining categories apply to people who are subject to immigration control and refer to various types of immigration status.

- You are not 'habitually resident' or treated as 'habitually resident' in the UK, Republic of Ireland, Channel Islands or the Isle of Man. The 'habitual residence' test is discussed on p72.
- You have 'limited leave' to enter or remain in the UK subject to the condition or requirement that you do not have recourse to 'public funds'. The meaning and scope of this is discussed below.
- You have been allowed temporary admission to the UK (this applies to people liable to be detained).
- Your immigration status has not been determined by the Secretary of State – ie, whether you require leave rather than whether you should be granted leave.
- You have been in the UK for less than five years, subject to a sponsorship *undertaking* (see p85). **Note:** You are entitled to normal rate IS if you become a British citizen, and to urgent cases payments of IS if your sponsor dies (see p86).
- You are an asylum-seeker. **Note:** Some asylum-seekers are entitled to urgent cases payments of IS (see p80).
- You are a European Economic Area (EEA) national, 'required to leave the UK' by the Secretary of State – ie, you are subject to a deportation or removal order - see p78.
- The immigration authorities have decided that you are an illegal entrant with no permission to stay.
- You are an 'overstayer' – ie, your limited leave has expired and you have not applied for permission to stay prior to that expiry.
- You are subject to a deportation order

If you come within the last three categories you should always seek independent advice before approaching the Benefits Agency.

Limited leave and public funds

- 'Limited leave' means permission to enter, or remain in, the UK for a specified period of time.
- 'Public funds' is defined in the immigration rules as IS, income-based JSA, housing benefit (HB), council tax benefit (CTB), family credit

(FC), disability working allowance (DWA), disability living allowance, attendance allowance, invalid care allowance, severe disablement allowance, child benefit and housing provided by local authorities.

- Having recourse to public funds in breach of your leave conditions could render you liable to deportation, refusal of further leave and prosecution. Claiming IS urgent cases payments, however, is usually safe (see p86). If you are a member of a couple and one of you is claiming a public funds benefit, see p70 (Implications of claiming public funds).
- Most people admitted to the UK as visitors, students, business and self-employed people, people with a work permit, artists, writers, au pairs, people of independent means, fiancé(e)s, spouses and dependent relatives (unless given indefinite leave) are given limited leave with a public funds prohibition.
- Nationals of the EEA States (see p75) do not require leave to enter or remain in the UK, and are specifically excluded from the 'limited leave' category of 'persons from abroad'.[58] In restricted circumstances, EEA nationals can be classed as 'persons from abroad' if they are 'required to leave the UK' (see p78).
- Cypriot nationals with limited leave are not classed as 'persons from abroad'. Nor are Maltese or Turkish nationals, unless they have applied for a variation of their conditions of leave.[59] Turkish nationals who have worked in the European Union (EU) may have special rights and should seek specialist advice (see p67).

People entitled to normal rate IS

If you are not a 'person from abroad' (see p67) you are entitled to IS at the normal rate.[60] In practical terms, this means you are entitled to normal rate IS if you satisfy (or are exempt from) the 'habitual residence' test (see p72) and you fall into any of the following categories:

- You are a British citizen.
- You have the right of abode in the UK or a certificate of patriality.
- You have 'indefinite leave' to enter or remain in the UK (ie, 'settled' status), unless you have been in the UK for less than five years, subject to a sponsorship undertaking (see p85).
- You have been granted refugee status (see p78).
- You have been given exceptional leave to enter or remain in the UK (see p79).
- You are a national of Eire, the Channel Islands, or the Isle of Man.
- You are a national of Cyprus, Malta or Turkey (unless in the case of Malta or Turkey, you have applied for your leave conditions to be varied).

- You are an EEA national (but see p75).
- You are in GB and you left Montserrat after 1 November 1995 because of a volcanic eruption there.

Couples and families

Entitlement to IS

The following rules apply where one or more members of your family are 'persons from abroad' (see p67):

- If you claim IS as a 'person from abroad', you are not entitled to any benefit for yourself or for any members of your family, unless you qualify for an urgent cases payment (see p86).[61]
- If your partner is not a 'person from abroad' but you are, s/he can claim IS under the normal rules but will not receive any benefit for you or any other family member who is a 'person from abroad'.[62] Full housing costs are payable.[63] You are still treated as a couple for IS purposes (see p351), so your joint resources are taken into account.
- Couples where both partners are not 'persons from abroad' and lone parents who are not 'persons from abroad', can claim IS for children who are.[64] But claimants who are 'persons from abroad' cannot claim benefit for children even if the children are *not* 'persons from abroad'.[65]
- Foreign fiancé(e)s and spouses who are admitted for settlement on the condition that they can maintain and accommodate themselves, count as 'persons from abroad' and are not entitled to IS until they are granted indefinite leave to remain in the UK.[66]

Implications of claiming public funds

A claim for urgent cases payments of IS should not have any effect on your immigration status (see p86).

If you are a 'person from abroad' and your partner is not, s/he can claim IS under the normal rules. Although s/he will not receive any benefit in respect of you (see above), you could still be treated as having 'recourse to public funds' (albeit indirectly) if s/he is maintaining you. This could result in you being refused leave to remain in the UK or even being deported.

This issue, however, is yet to be fully resolved (see CPAG's *Migration and Social Security Handbook* for more details). There have been conflicting decisions by the courts and immigration appellate authorities. Home Office policy has so far been that there is only recourse to public funds where *additional* benefit is payable in respect of the person from abroad.

In the case of IS, income-based JSA, FC, DWA, attendance allowance, disability living allowance and HB/CTB (where maximum benefit is payable because the claimant receives IS or income-based JSA), no additional benefit is payable because of the presence of a partner who is a 'person from abroad'. You should still get advice (see p67) before a claim is made for these benefits in case Home Office policy changes. You should also seek advice before claiming a public funds benefit where an additional amount is payable because of the presence of a family member from abroad. This could apply to HB/CTB, severe disablement allowance, invalid care allowance and child benefit, FC and DWA (where there is a child subject to the 'no public funds' restriction).

You should also always seek advice before claiming a public funds benefit if your fiancé(e) or spouse is applying for entry clearance to join you in the UK, or for indefinite leave to remain in the UK after being here with limited leave. This is because leave to enter or remain may be refused if you are unable to maintain yourselves without recourse to public funds (see CPAG's *Migration and Social Security Handbook* for more details).

Partner or child abroad

If you or your partner go abroad temporarily, you may be entitled to continue to claim IS as a couple for four or eight weeks (see p352). After four or eight weeks, if you qualify for benefit you will be paid as a single person or lone parent.[67]

If your partner is abroad permanently, you no longer count as a couple for IS purposes, and you can claim IS as a single person or lone parent. If your partner is abroad temporarily, however, you may still be treated as a couple for IS purposes (see p351), which means your partner's income and capital will be taken into account and if s/he is in full-time work, you will not be entitled to benefit.[68] This can apply even if you have not lived together in the UK, because the rules relate to absence from each other, not absence from home. If your partner is waiting for entry clearance to come to the UK, you can argue that because this is a lengthy process and refusal rates are high, your separation is likely to exceed 52 weeks substantially, so you should not be treated as a couple (see p351). [69]

Alternatively, you can argue that you should not be treated as a couple because your intention to live together depends on entry clearance being granted.[70]

If your child is abroad temporarily, you can continue to get IS for her/him for four or eight weeks (see p355).

The habitual residence test

You are not entitled to IS, income-based JSA, HB or CTB unless you are habitually resident or are treated as habitually resident in the UK, Republic of Ireland, the Channel Islands or the Isle of Man. You are classed as a 'person from abroad' (see p67).[71]

The habitual residence test is applied to all claimants (but not partners or dependants), including British citizens. The following people, however, are automatically treated as habitually resident in the UK and are therefore exempt from the test: [72]

- EEA nationals who are classed as 'workers', or have the right to reside in the UK under specified EC legislation. See p75 for details.
- Refugees or people who have been granted 'exceptional leave to enter or remain' in the UK (see pp78 and 79).
- People in GB who left Montserrat after 1 November 1995 because of a volcanic eruption there.

If you are entitled to urgent cases payments as a 'person from abroad' (see p86), you do not have to satisfy the habitual residence test.

If you were entitled to IS on 31 July 1994, you do not have to satisfy the habitual residence test unless you make a new claim after that date.[73] Completing a new claim form on a change of circumstances where IS is already in payment should not count as a new claim. Swapping claimants, however, does (see p128).

The meaning of 'habitually resident'

The term 'habitually resident' is not defined in the benefit regulations. Although there has been a certain amount of case law, 'habitual residence' remains a problematic and imprecise concept. The 'habitual residence test' is therefore open to highly subjective, restrictive and inconsistent decision-making by adjudication officers (AOs) and social security appeal tribunals (SSATs). Particular groups tend to be targeted, including EU nationals and people (especially from ethnic minority communities) who spend lengthy periods overseas.

The concept of 'habitual residence' occurs in EU law relating to migrant workers[74] but the DSS appears to have accepted that this interpretation is not applicable to means-tested benefits.[75]

Two social security commissioner decisions which considered the meaning of 'habitual residence' in the context of IS (and are now the basis for DSS guidance), have established the following principles:[76]

- The term 'habitual residence' must be given its ordinary and natural meaning. There is no definitive definition or list of factors which determines a person's habitual residence. Each case must be considered on its merits, taking into account all the relevant circumstances and facts.

- You must have a 'settled intention' to reside in a country – ie, to make your home there for a temporary or permanent period. Events subsequent to your arrival can help confirm that your intentions were settled from the outset.

- You must be actually resident for an 'appreciable period of time' before you become 'habitually resident'. What counts as an appreciable period of time depends on the facts of each case. There is no minimum period but habitual residence cannot be acquired immediately. One of the commissioners' decisions suggested, by way of example, that a UK citizen could establish habitual residence after three to six months.[77] The other commissioner's decision, however, said such examples should not be relied upon as normal or minimum 'appreciable periods'.[78] In spite of this, AOs and SSATs often treat three months as an unofficial minimum period. There is no legal basis for this. Family case law has found an 'appreciable period' to be as little as a month[79] and each case must be decided on its own circumstances. Previous visits to the UK to prepare for settled status can form part of the 'appreciable period'. (See note below for the latest legal developments.)

- If you go abroad for a temporary period, you may retain your home and your habitual residence in the UK, so that you will be habitually resident from the first day of your return. You can also be habitually resident in more than one country at the same time.

- The 'viability' of your residence may be one relevant factor but whereas one commissioner held that living arrangements dependent on public funds, including IS, were not viable,[80] the other firmly stated that there was no condition that only residence without recourse to public funds counted towards the required 'appreciable period'.[81]

Note: One of the commissioners' decisions referred to above was appealed to the Court of Appeal on the 'appreciable period' issue. The Court upheld by a majority the requirement of an appreciable period of time before residence could become habitual.[82] This decision is being appealed to the House of Lords. See *Welfare Rights Bulletin* for further developments.

Tactics

- Only the claimant is subject to the habitual residence test. If you cannot satisfy the test, your partner could be the claimant if s/he would satisfy the test (eg, s/he has been in the UK longer than you) or would be exempt (eg, as an EEA national - see p75).

- Since the habitual residence test operates as an exclusion from IS and income-based JSA, the onus of proof lies with the Benefits Agency to establish that you are *not* habitually resident.[83] It is vital, nevertheless, that you produce as much evidence as possible to show that you *are* habitually resident, taking into account the above points on the meaning of the term. You should prepare your case thoroughly before attending a Benefits Agency interview or a SSAT.
- If you fail the test, you may be able to satisfy it at a later date, particularly if there is a change in your circumstances, or simply through the passage of time. Repeated claims for benefit can highlight your determination to remain in the UK, as well as the unfairness of the test. Some local offices are refusing to accept repeat claims if there is an appeal pending. This is wrong – the local office should accept the claim and make a decision.
- If you are refused IS or income-based JSA because of the habitual residence test, you can request a review, or appeal to a SSAT. You can ask for an expedited hearing of your appeal if you are suffering hardship (see p168). Always ask for an oral hearing, so that you can explain your circumstances in person. The tribunal must apply the test from the date of claim to the date of your appeal hearing.[84]
- If you have no money to live on because you have failed the habitual residence test, you could:
  - apply to the Benefits Agency for an 'extra-statutory payment' (the most effective way of doing this is to ask your MP to put your case in writing to the Secretary of State for Social Security);
  - apply to your local social services department for financial assistance if you have children. (If you do not have children then you can ask your local authority to pay you under the National Assistance Act if you face destitution – see Asylum-seekers, p84.);
  - apply for a social fund crisis loan. Although you have to be able to repay a loan, if you are likely to be counted as habitually resident in the near future you will then qualify for benefit and will be in a position to repay the loan.
- The legality of the habitual residence test has been challenged, so far unsuccessfully,[85] but there may be further challenges. See future editions of CPAG's *Welfare Rights Bulletin* for latest developments. One challenge, on the application of the test to a person who has worked in another EEA State, is pending a decision by the European Court of Justice.[86]
- The Government is currently reviewing the operation of the habitual residence test. See CPAG's *Welfare Rights Bulletin* for latest developments.

European Economic Area nationals

If you are a national of the EEA (see below for countries covered), you and your dependants have rights under European Community (EC) and UK law to enter and reside in the UK.[87] You also have the right to claim IS or income-based JSA on the same basis as British citizens.[88]

You are not entitled to IS or income-based JSA unless you satisfy or are treated as satisfying the 'habitual residence' test (see p72). Certain categories of EEA nationals are automatically treated as habitually resident in the UK (see below).

EC law is particularly complex and can only be covered briefly here. See CPAG's *Migration and Social Security Handbook* for more details. If you are unsure about your rights, always seek specialist advice (see Appendix 4 for sources of further information and advice).

Who is an EEA national?

You are an EEA national if you are a national of one of the following countries:

- the Member States of the EU - ie, Austria, Belgium, Denmark, Finland, France, Germany, Greece, Italy, Luxembourg, Netherlands, Portugal, Republic of Ireland, Spain, Sweden, UK; *plus*
- Iceland, Liechtenstein and Norway.

Those treated as 'habitually resident'

In order to qualify for IS or income-based JSA, you must normally satisfy the 'habitual residence' test (see p72). You are, however, automatically treated as habitually resident in the UK and therefore exempt from the test if you are:[89]

- a 'worker' for the purposes of EEC Regulations 1612/68 or 1251/70 (see below); *or*
- a person with the right to reside in the UK under EC Directives 68/360 or 73/148 (see p77).

If you are a British citizen, you can only be a 'worker' or person with the right to reside in the UK under the above provisions, if you are returning after working or exercising an EC right in another EEA country.[90]

'Workers'

The term 'worker' is not defined in EC legislation. Its meaning and scope remain somewhat unclear and have been the subject of complex and sometimes contradictory case law. What is clear, however, is that many people who are not actually working are still classed as 'workers'.[91]

Workers under Regulation 1612/68

Regulation 1612/68 covers freedom of movement and equality of treatment for 'workers'. You should be treated as a worker for the purposes of the Regulation if you fall into any of the following categories:

- You are working in the UK, whether full- or part-time. Any 'genuine' and 'effective work' should count, so long as it is not so irregular and limited that it is a purely marginal and ancillary activity.[92]
- You have worked in the UK (at any time and even for a short period) but have become involuntarily unemployed or temporarily incapable of work.[93]
- You have worked in the UK, have become involuntarily unemployed and must take on occupational retraining to compete in the job market.[94]
- You have voluntarily given up work in the UK to take up vocational training linked to your previous job.[95] If you have voluntarily given up work for other reasons, your position is not entirely clear. DSS guidance suggests you are not a worker[96] but you may be able to argue otherwise, if you remain in the labour market and are trying to find alternative work or are seeking reinstatement.[97]
- You have been temporarily laid off and are seeking to return to work with the same employer in the UK.[98]

Note: Work-seekers

If you are looking for work but have not worked in the UK before, EC and domestic case law has so far held that you are not a 'worker' for the purposes of Regulation 1612/68.[99] This applies even if you have worked in another EEA State[100] (although you may be able to argue that this *does* make you a 'worker for the purposes of Regulation 1612/68' even though you will not have acquired the full range of EC workers' rights in the UK until you have worked here).

Workers under Regulation 1251/70

Regulation 1251/70 allows certain incapacitated or retired workers to remain in the State where they have worked.

You are a worker for the purposes of the Regulation if you fall into one of the following categories:

- You have given up work in the UK because of permanent incapacity and either:
  – you had resided continuously in the UK for at least two years when you gave up work; *or*

- your incapacity resulted from an industrial injury or disease which entitles you to a disability or incapacity benefit; *or*
- your spouse is (or was before marrying you) British.[101]
• You retired on or after pensionable age and either:
- you had resided continuously in the UK for at least three years and were employed in the UK for at least 12 months immediately before retiring; *or*
- your spouse is (or was before marrying you) British.[102]

Notes:[103]

• Absences from the UK of up to 3 months a year (or longer for military service) are ignored when calculating your period of residence.
• Periods of unemployment recorded by the JobCentre and absences from work because of illness or accident are ignored when calculating your period of employment.
• Periods of employment as a 'frontier worker' in another EEA State can count if you returned to your home in the UK at least once a week.

Right to reside in the UK

EC Directives 68/360 and 73/148 deal with residence rights and the issuing of residence permits.

You have the right to reside in the UK under the Directives if you fall into one of the following categories:

• You are a 'worker' for the purposes of EC Regulation 1612/68 (see p76).[104] Case law has so far held that if you are a work-seeker, who has not worked in the UK, your right of residence does not derive from Directive 68/360, which means you cannot secure exemption from the habitual residence test on that basis.[105]
• You are self-employed or provide a service on a commercial basis in the UK.[106] If you are *seeking* self-employment or to provide a service, your rights are not entirely clear. DSS guidance and UK case law suggests you do not have the right to reside[107] but UK immigration law suggests you do.[108] Seek specialist advice if this applies to you (see p67).
• You are receiving commercial services in the UK.[109] These could include tourism, private education or health care and business or professional services.[110]
• You are a member of the family of any of the above. This covers spouses, children under 21, and other dependent relatives.[111]

Your right to reside in the UK is confirmed by the issue of a residence permit but the lack of a permit does not negate that right.[112] Permits are normally issued for five years on confirmation of employment.

'Requirement to leave' the UK

In certain circumstances, EEA nationals can be 'required to leave the UK' if they are no longer exercising EC rights as a worker, work-seeker or self-sufficient person.[113] This could apply to you if:

- you have been seeking employment for more than six months and there is no evidence that you have genuine chances of finding work;[114] *or*
- you have claimed benefit when your right to reside in the UK is subject to the condition that you are self-supporting (this applies to students, pensioners and others not covered by EC Directives 68/360 and 73/148 - see p77).[115]

In practice, the Home Office is very unlikely to remove you in these circumstances and cannot do so until any appeal against such removal has been decided.

In rare circumstances, you can also be deported or removed (subject to appeal) on the grounds of public policy, security or health – eg, you have committed a serious offence.

If you are 'required to leave the UK', you are treated as a 'person from abroad' under the IS, income-based JSA, HB and CTB regulations and are no longer entitled to any of these benefits.[116] The House of Lords has ruled that you are only 'required to leave the UK' if a deportation or removal order has been made against you, after any appeals against such an order have run their course.[117]

It has been Home Office practice to send letters to EEA nationals after they have been claiming IS or income-based JSA for six months, informing them that they are no longer lawfully resident in the UK under EC law (see above) and should make arrangements to leave. Following the House of Lords ruling, such letters do *not* amount to a 'requirement to leave' and benefit *cannot* be stopped on the basis of their issue.

Refugees

The UK is a signatory to the 1951 United Nations Convention on the Status of Refugees which gives refugees certain rights of asylum in a foreign country, including the right to public relief and assistance. A refugee is defined under the convention as someone who is unable or unwilling to return to his own country because of a '... well founded fear of persecution for reasons of race, religion, nationality, membership of a particular social group or political opinion ...'

If the Home Office accepts that you are a refugee, you and your family are entitled to remain in the UK and claim IS or income-based JSA under the normal rules from the date you are recorded as a refugee by the Secretary of State.[118] You do not have to satisfy the 'habitual residence' test (see p72).[119]

You, or your partner, can also claim backdated urgent cases payments of IS for any period following the first refusal of your asylum claim (if you claimed asylum 'on arrival in the UK' – see p81), or the date of your asylum claim (if you claimed asylum other than 'on arrival in the UK'). You cannot, however, get IS for any period prior to 5 February 1996 and you must submit your claim for IS within 28 days of being notified that you have been accepted as a refugee. The normal restrictions on backdating IS do not apply.[120] Any IS already paid to you or your partner for the backdated period is offset against the amount you get. You cannot get backdated payments for any week in which you were receiving contribution-based JSA.[121] If your partner has been recognised as a refugee and was not getting contribution-based JSA, s/he could claim instead. Only IS, and not income-based JSA, can be backdated when you are granted refugee status. If you are only entitled to income-based JSA on becoming a refugee, you must submit a separate claim for backdated IS within the 28-day time limit to receive your arrears of urgent cases payments. The arrears are disregarded as capital for 52 weeks from the date of receipt.[122]

You may be able to get backdated IS at the normal rate (rather than the 90 per cent urgent cases rate) if you have worked in the UK or EEA (see p75) by arguing that you are entitled to equal treatment with British citizens under EC law.[123] Seek advice if this applies to you (see p67).

People with 'exceptional leave'

In some circumstances, the Home Office will not accept that you are a refugee but will grant you 'exceptional leave' to enter or remain in the UK on humanitarian grounds or because of the political situation in your country (your family will not normally be allowed to join you until you have been in the UK for four years). Some people are also granted exceptional leave for other reasons. Exceptional leave may initially be given for a year but this does not count as 'limited leave'. A person applying for an extension of their exceptional leave, continues to be treated as a person with exceptional leave, provided their application was made before their original leave had expired.

If you are granted 'exceptional leave' to enter or remain in the UK, you are entitled to claim IS or income-based JSA under the normal rules. You do not have to satisfy the 'habitual residence' test (see p72).[124] There is normally no prohibition on claiming 'public funds' if you are granted exceptional leave to remain, but if you have any doubts about this, you should get advice (see p67). The Benefits Agency sometimes wrongly refuses benefit to people with exceptional leave because it mistakenly thinks they have 'limited leave' (see p68). Seek advice if this happens to you (see p67).

Asylum-seekers

Immigration issues

You are treated as an 'asylum-seeker' while you are waiting for a Home Office decision on an application for refugee status (see p78). If you applied for asylum when you arrived in the UK, you will normally have been given 'temporary admission' while your case is considered (although you can be detained or removed in certain circumstances). You may also have applied for asylum while you were in the UK with limited leave or as an illegal entrant or overstayer. If your application for asylum is refused, you have the right of appeal. It can take a long time before your application is finally decided, although the Government has now introduced quicker procedures and curtailed appeal rights for many asylum-seekers.

You can apply to the Home Office for permission to work after six months as an asylum-seeker (including while you are appealing). Claiming IS or other public funds benefits (see p68) should not affect your application for asylum, but in most cases, you are excluded from entitlement by the benefit rules (see below).

Restrictions on benefit entitlement

The Government introduced sweeping restrictions to the rights of asylum-seekers to claim benefits from 5 February 1996.[125] Previously, asylum-seekers were entitled to claim urgent cases payments of IS and other benefits until their applications for asylum were finally decided. Under the new rules, most asylum-seekers were excluded from all entitlement to IS and most other non-contributory benefits.

The rules were widely criticised as unjust and contrary to international conventions. A legal challenge was successfully mounted and some of the new rules were declared invalid by the Court of Appeal in June 1996.[126] One of the Judges commented that '... the Regulations necessarily contemplate for some a life so destitute that to my mind no civilised nation can tolerate it'. Despite this, the Government re-introduced the rules by Act of Parliament and thus in a valid form, with effect from 24 July 1996.[127]

Entitlement to IS

If you are an asylum-seeker, you are not entitled to normal rate IS because you are classed as a 'person from abroad' (see p68).[128] You are entitled to urgent cases payments of IS (see p86) if you fall into one of the following categories:

(a) You applied for asylum 'on arrival' in the UK[129]

* The term 'on arrival' is not defined in the regulations. A social security commissioner has decided that it means 'while clearing immigration control at the port of entry'. He does recognise, however, that there may be cases when a person cannot clear immigration control immediately while at the port of entry – eg, because there is no interpreter available.[130] Other cases might include where you are too ill to make an application immediately or you arrive secretly at an entry point with no immigration officer. In such cases, your application should be treated as made 'on arrival' if you make it as soon as practicable after arrival.[131]
* Your application for asylum does not have to be made in any particular form. It could be verbal or written, in any language, and doesn't necessarily have to include the words 'asylum' or 'refugee'. The application must be made to the 'Secretary of State'. In practice, this should mean any immigration officer. The claim must be recorded as having been made (again not in any particular form).
* You must have arrived in the UK from a country outside the 'Common Travel Area' of Eire, the Channel Islands or the Isle of Man.
* You must not be re-entering the UK on your arrival. It is not entirely clear what 're-entry' means. Presumably the rule is designed to prevent people going abroad for a short period, in order to apply for asylum on re-entry. Arguably, however, it should only apply to re-entry during the period covered by your previous grant of leave to enter the UK.
* Decisions about whether you applied for asylum on arrival in accordance with the above rules are made by AOs and not the Home Office. You have the right to appeal any question to a SSAT (see p167).
* You can claim urgent cases payments of IS until your entitlement ends in accordance with the rules on p49.[132]

(b) You apply for asylum following an 'upheaval declaration' by the Secretary of State[133]

* The declaration is a written announcement from the Home Office that because a country is subject to such a fundamental change of circumstances, a person would not be ordered to return there by the Secretary of State.

- You must be a national of the country concerned. Stateless people are not covered.
- You must submit your application for asylum within three months of the date of the declaration and your application must be recorded by the Secretary of State (see p81). If you have an asylum application or appeal awaiting determination when the declaration is made, you will only be covered if you make a fresh application for asylum within the three-month time limit. You should always seek advice before you do this, however, because a fresh application could prejudice your case for asylum.
- At the time of writing, only two countries have been subject to declarations – Zaire (May 1997) and Sierra Leone (July 1997).
- You can claim urgent cases payments of IS until your entitlement ends in accordance with the rules on p83.[134] You do not have to make your claim within the three-month time limit for asylum applications, referred to above.

(c)   You were entitled to IS as an asylum-seeker before 5 February 1996[135]

- All asylum-seekers were eligible for urgent cases payments of IS before 5 February 1996. If you were entitled to IS as an asylum-seeker before that date, you can continue to claim it until your entitlement ends in accordance with the rules on p83.[136]
- Although the regulations do not state that you must have been entitled to IS 'immediately before' 5 February 1996, the Court of Appeal and a social security commissioner have ruled that you must have been entitled to IS on 4 February 1996.[137] There may be further challenges on the scope of transitional protection, however. See CPAG's *Welfare Rights Bulletin* for developments.
- Although the rules imposing restrictions on an asylum-seeker's rights to claim benefit were only validly in force from 24 July 1996 (see p80), transitional protection was only given to asylum-seekers entitled to IS before 5 February 1996. The Court of Appeal rejected a challenge that the relevant date for transitional protection should have been 24 July 1996.[138] Asylum-seekers first claiming IS between 5 February and 24 July 1996 were therefore entitled to benefit under the old rules but lost their entitlement from 24 July unless they satisfied the new rules.
- Transitional protection is also extended to anyone who was a member of your family (see p346) on 5 February 1996, allowing them to claim IS urgent cases payments if, for example, they leave your household, leave education or you 'swap' claimants (see p128).[139] They can claim until their entitlement ends in accordance with the rules on p83.

Notes:

- If you have worked in the UK or EEA (see p75), you may be able to argue that you are a refugee entitled to normal rate IS under EC law (see p79). Seek specialist advice if this applies to you.
- You are only excluded from normal rate IS if you apply for asylum when you are already classed as a 'person from abroad' because you fall into one of the categories listed on p68. Get advice if you think you may not fall into any of those categories. If you are a national of Cyprus, Malta or Turkey and apply for asylum while you have leave to be in the UK, you should be eligible for normal rate IS or income-based JSA but you will have to satisfy the habitual residence test (see p72).[140]
- The above rules apply to income-based JSA as well as IS. You are not entitled to urgent cases payments of income-based JSA, however, unless you hold a work permit or have been given permission to work by the Home Office (see p80).[141] It is normally better to claim IS, rather than income-based JSA, to avoid the labour market conditions and sanctions (see p54). If you are entitled to contribution-based JSA, you cannot claim IS (although your partner may be able to).[142]

When your entitlement ends

- You are only normally entitled to urgent cases payments of IS as an asylum-seeker until the Home Office makes and records an initial decision on your asylum application.[143] This applies to all three categories of eligible asylum-seekers set out on pp81-82. There is no requirement that you must be notified of the asylum decision before your IS can be stopped, although according to Home Office practice, you should be notified at the same time as the Benefits Agency.[144] The asylum decision, however, must be clearly recorded and dated to be valid.[145]
- You are not entitled to IS while you are appealing against an asylum decision, unless that decision was made before 5 February 1996 and an appeal was pending on that date or was submitted within the time limits laid down in the immigration rules.[146] The appeal could be to an adjudicator, immigration appeal tribunal or court. You are entitled to IS until the appeal is determined. It is unclear whether you remain entitled while you appeal against an appeal decision. Seek advice in this situation (see p67).

Documentation

There are often problems in providing acceptable evidence of identification and status when you claim IS as an asylum-seeker if you have come to the UK without the usual travel and identity documents, or with false documentation.

- If you apply for asylum 'on arrival in the UK' (see p81), you should be issued with a 'standard acknowledgement letter' (SAL1). You should also be given a form IS96 confirming you have been granted 'temporary admission' to the UK. These documents should be accepted by the Benefits Agency as proof of your identity and status.
- If you apply for asylum after entry to the UK, you will be given a GEN32 form calling you for interview. You should subsequently be given a standard acknowledgement letter (SAL2) which should be accepted by the Benefits Agency as proof of your identity and status.
- If you do not have a SAL, the Benefits Agency can contact the Home Office by telephone for confirmation of your status. The Benefits Agency should be willing to interview you to establish identity and should take account of relevant correspondence concerning your application for asylum produced by a lawyer or advice agency. If you cannot produce evidence of your identity, you may have to produce an affidavit sworn before a solicitor.
- A SAL issued before 12 October 1995 was not numbered so as to indicate whether it was issued at the port of entry or after entry.

Other sources of help

If you are not entitled to IS, you could try to access the following alternative sources of help:

- If you have children, you should approach your local authority social services department for help under the Children Act 1989. The local authority has a duty under the Act to safeguard the welfare of children and can provide services such as accommodation, food, heat and emergency cash payments.[147]
- The Court of Appeal has ruled that destitute asylum-seekers are entitled to assistance from local authorities under s21 of the National Assistance Act 1948, which covers accommodation, board and other services.[148] There have been a number of other legal challenges to clarify the nature of the assistance which should be provided but the situation remains somewhat unclear. It appears local authorities cannot make cash payments or provide only food but you do not have to be homeless to qualify for help.[149]
- You are entitled to apply for a crisis loan from the social fund to alleviate the consequences of a disaster (see p482). The *Social Fund Guide* advises social fund officers to give particular attention to the clothing needs of asylum-seekers.[150] The problem is that you must be able to show that you are likely to be able to repay the loan (see p485).

- You can qualify for health service benefits on the grounds of low income (see p500).
- You could ask your MP to request an extra-statutory payment from the Secretary of State for Social Security. The more MPs are aware of the hardship caused by the rules, the more likely it is that the law will be changed.
- For advice on charitable sources of help, contact the Refugee Council (see Appendix 4). A network of emergency provision has been established to alleviate the effects of the rules.

Sponsorship undertakings

Most people subject to immigration control are admitted to the UK on the condition that they can maintain and accommodate themselves. A relative or friend in the UK can act as a sponsor to help satisfy this condition.

In some cases, sponsors are required to give a written undertaking under the terms of the Immigration Act 1971 (on a special Home Office form – RON 112), that they will provide maintenance and accommodation. Such undertakings are only usually required for dependent elderly relatives or children, and *not* for spouses. Other sorts of voluntary or informal sponsorship which are commonly used to support applications to enter the UK are *not* undertakings (this distinction is often misunderstood by the Benefits Agency).

If you have been resident in the UK subject to a mandatory sponsorship undertaking for less than five years, you are not entitled to normal rate IS unless you become a British citizen.[151] After five years, you are entitled to IS under the normal rules. The five years runs either from your date of entry into the UK, or the date the undertaking was given, whichever was later.[152] You are entitled to urgent cases payments of IS during the five-year period if your sponsor dies.[153]

If you were entitled to IS before 5 February 1996 as a person subject to a mandatory sponsorship undertaking, the above rules do not apply to you and you remain entitled to IS.[154] The High Court and a social security commissioner have ruled that you must have been entitled to IS on 4 February 1996 (see p82).

If you have a right to remain in the UK under EC law (see p75), you should not be denied IS because of a sponsorship undertaking.

If you are paid benefit as a sponsored immigrant and your sponsor signed an undertaking, the Benefits Agency can recover the amount of benefit paid to you from your sponsor.[155] It has been government policy not to enforce this power if your sponsor cannot afford to pay. If the undertaking was given before 23 May 1980, the Benefits Agency does *not* have the power to recover any money from the sponsor.[156]

Urgent cases payments

If you are not entitled to normal rate IS because you are classed as a 'person from abroad' (see p67), you are entitled to urgent cases payments of IS if any of the following circumstances apply to you:

- You have 'limited leave' to remain in the UK on the condition that you do not have recourse to 'public funds' (see p68), but you are temporarily without money. You are entitled to urgent cases payments of IS for a maximum of 42 days if:
  - you have supported yourself without recourse to public funds during your limited leave; *and*
  - you are temporarily without funds because remittances from abroad have been disrupted; *and*
  - there is a reasonable expectation that your supply of funds will be resumed.[157]
- You are an asylum-seeker and you satisfy the rules set out on pp81-82.[158]
- You have been in the UK subject to a sponsorship undertaking for less than five years and your sponsor has died (see p85).[159]

Notes:

- Urgent cases payments of IS are less than normal rate IS. Your personal allowance is 10 per cent less and there are modified rules relating to income and capital. Asylum-seekers are not eligible to claim non-contributory benefits including disability living allowance and attendance allowance. They will, therefore, not be able to qualify for the disability-related premiums except where an adult establishes incapacity for work for a period of a year. See p49 for full details of urgent cases payments and CPAG's *Rights Guide to Non-Means-Tested Benefits* 1998/99 edn.
- There has been a problem in the past where arrears of urgent cases payments (eg, caused by Benefits Agency delays in processing your claim) are treated as capital when they are eventually paid, resulting in IS being stopped. The Government has removed this problem from 1 April 1998 by amending the regulations so that arrears of IS, income-based JSA and Social Fund payments are disregarded when calculating urgent cases payments (see p51 for details).[160]
- You do not have to satisfy the 'habitual residence' test to receive urgent cases payments.
- Urgent cases payments are payments of IS and therefore act as a 'passport' to other benefits – eg, social fund and health benefits.
- Urgent cases payments count as 'public funds' under the immigration rules (see p68). Asylum-seekers, however, are not normally prohibited

from claiming public funds. A claim from people with limited leave for a short period or from a sponsored immigrant whose sponsor has died is unlikely to affect their immigration status. If in doubt, seek advice (see p67).

- As an asylum-seeker you should be allowed to work after six months. If you are looking for work you can opt to claim income-based JSA at the urgent cases rate but it will generally be simpler to continue to claim IS urgent cases.

4. RESIDENTIAL AND NURSING CARE

This section covers:

- IS for people with 'preserved rights' (p88)
- IS for people without 'preserved rights' in independent homes (p93)
- IS for people in local authority homes (p95)
- Local authority funding and charges for residential and nursing care (p96)

Residential or nursing care in this section means:

- local authority care homes (see p95 for definition); *and*
- independent (ie, private or voluntary sector) residential care or nursing homes (see p94 for definition).

If you go into residential or nursing care, you are entitled to IS if you satisfy the normal rules, but your 'applicable amount' is usually calculated differently. There are also more generous capital rules, including an upper limit of £16,000 (see p416 for details).

The Government's community care reforms introduced a new funding structure for residential care from 1 April 1993.[161] Under the previous system, people entering independent residential care or nursing homes were entitled to claim special higher rates of IS to help pay their fees. Most people who have remained in independent homes since 31 March 1993 have 'preserved rights' to continue to claim these special rates of IS (see p88).

If you enter independent care for the first time after 31 March 1993 you do not have 'preserved rights'. You can still claim IS, but only at the normal rates plus a 'residential allowance' (see p93). If you need more public funding to pay for a place in an independent home you must apply to your local authority social services department (see p96).

If you are in a local authority home, you do not have 'preserved rights'. Your IS applicable amount is worked out differently to that for people in independent care (see p95).

If you are in a local authority home or a local authority is funding your place in an independent home, any IS you are entitled to will be clawed back in weekly charges, together with most other income you have. See p96 for details.

People with preserved rights

Who has preserved rights?[162]

You have preserved rights to claim special higher rates of IS if you were living in most types of independent residential care or nursing homes (see definition on p94) on 31 March 1993 and:

- you were getting IS at the special higher rates; *or*
- you were not getting IS because you were able to afford to pay for the home yourself; *or*
- you were living with a partner, to whom either of the above applied;
- one of the above would have applied but for the fact that you were absent from the home for:
  - up to 4 weeks if you were a temporary resident;
  - up to 13 weeks if you were a permanent resident;
  - up to 52 weeks if you were in hospital.

You are covered if the home you were living in was a residential care or nursing home, as defined on p94. Complex rules apply if you were living in a home with less than four residents or provided by a close relative or the Abbeyfield Society.[163] You should seek specialist advice if this applies to you.

Losing preserved rights[164]

You will lose your preserved rights if you are absent from an independent home for:

- more than four weeks if you are a temporary resident;
- more than 13 weeks if you are a permanent resident;
- more than 52 weeks if you are in hospital.

Note: You do not lose your preserved rights if you move from one independent home to another, as long as any gap does not exceed the above periods.

Calculation of IS

If you have preserved rights, your IS applicable amount consists of an amount for personal expenses and an accommodation allowance to cover all or part of the charge made by the home. You are not entitled to any premiums. If you are a member of a couple see p352. Attendance allowance and disability living allowance are taken into account as income when calculating your IS.[165]

Personal expenses[166]
These are as follows:

Single claimant	£14.45
Couple	£28.00
Dependent child aged 18+	£14.45
16-17	£10.05
11-15	£-8.65
0-10	£-5.95

Accommodation allowance

The amount you receive will cover the weekly charge for your accommodation including meals and services where these are provided, but only up to a maximum level (see below).[167]

If you have to pay for some meals separately, your accommodation allowance will include for each person, either an amount to cover the actual cost of the meals if they can be purchased in the home, *or*, if they cannot, the following standard amounts:[168]

- £1.10 for breakfast
- £1.55 for lunch
- £1.55 for dinner

The above amounts are reduced if meals are provided free or at a lower cost.

If you pay additional charges for heating, attendance needs, extra baths, laundry or a special diet you follow for medical reasons, these will be included in the accommodation allowance, so long as they are provided by the home and not by an outside agency.[169]

If you receive housing benefit towards part of your accommodation charge this will be deducted from that charge and reduce your IS accordingly.[170]

Maximum accommodation allowances[171]

Your accommodation charge (including any charges for additional services and meals) will usually only be met up to a maximum level. This maximum varies depending on the type of home you are in and the type of care you receive.[172] You may find that the amount payable does not fully cover your home fees.

If you are in a residential care home the maximum varies according to the type of care the home is registered to provide, or if the home is not registered, according to the type of care you receive.[173] The type of care depends on the health conditions and/or age of the residents – see the table on p91 for details. If more than one category could apply to you, the amount you get is decided as follows:[174]

* Where the home is registered to provide the type of care you get, you will receive the amount that is allowed for that type of care.
* If the care you receive is different from the type the home is registered to provide, you will receive the allowance for the lower or lowest of the categories of care which the home is registered to provide.
* In any other case you will receive the amount most consistent with the care you receive.

If you are in a nursing home the maximum varies according to the type of care you actually receive. The type of care depends on your health conditions and/or age – see the table on p91 for details. If more than one category could apply to you, you receive the amount most consistent with the care you receive.[175] You could, for example, get the 'terminal illness' rate if that is the level of care you receive even though you are not, in fact, terminally ill.[176]

Some homes may be registered both as a residential care and a nursing home. In these cases your maximum accommodation allowance will be decided according to whether you are receiving residential or nursing care.

The tables below list the maximum amounts payable in residential care and nursing homes. The following definitions apply to the categories of health conditions noted in the tables:

'**Mental disorder**' is defined as 'mental illness, arrested or incomplete development of mind, psychopathic disorder, and any other disorder or disability of mind'.[177]

'**Mental handicap**' is defined as 'a state of arrested or incomplete development of mind which includes impairment of intelligence and social functioning'.[178] 'Senility' is not mental handicap but can amount to a mental disorder.[179]

'**Disablement**' is defined as meaning that you are 'blind, deaf or dumb or substantially and permanently handicapped by illness, injury or congenital deformity or any other disability prescribed by the Secretary of State'.[180]

'**Very dependent elderly**' means you are over pension age and *either*:

* registered or certified as blind; *or*

- entitled to attendance allowance or disability living allowance care component at the highest rate (even if it is not payable because you have not met the qualifying period); *or*
- getting war or industrial injury constant attendance allowance.[181]

Residential care homes

Health condition/age	*Maximum payable*
Old age	£213
Past or present mental disorder but excluding mental handicap	£225
Past or present drug or alcohol dependence	£225
Mental handicap	£257
Physical disablement if under pension age, or, if over pension age, claimant had become disabled before reaching 60 (65 if a man)	£292
Physical disablement (over pension age and not disabled before reaching 60 (woman) or (65 man))	£213
Very dependent elderly (see p90)	£247
Any other condition	£213

The above amounts are increased by £44 a week for homes in the Greater London area (see p93 for definition).

Nursing homes

Health condition/age	*Maximum payable*
Past or present mental disorder but excluding mental handicap	£319
Mental handicap	£325
Past or present drug or alcohol dependence	£319
Physical disablement, if under pension age, or if over pension age, claimant had become disabled before reaching 60 (65 if a man)	£359
Over pension age and had become physically disabled after reaching 60 (65 if a man)	£318
Terminal illness	£318
Any other condition (including elderly)	£318

The above amounts are increased by £49 a week for homes in the Greater London area (see p93 for definition).

Getting more than the maximum

You can get more than the maximum if one of the following applies:

- You have lived in the same accommodation for over 12 months and could afford it without IS when you moved in. You will get your full accommodation charge for up to 13 weeks after you claim IS if you are trying to move but need time to find suitable alternative accommodation.[182] Income which is normally disregarded for IS may be taken into account during the 13 weeks.[183] The 13-week concession does not apply if you are being accommodated by the local authority because you are homeless or under the authority's duty to promote the welfare of children.
- You have been living in a residential care or nursing home since 28 April 1985 and your accommodation allowance under the present rules is lower than what you received then plus £10. (For further details on this see the 22nd edition of the *Handbook*, p78.)[184]

Money from other sources

If your IS does not meet your accommodation fees, you will have to try to obtain the balance from other sources. Money from charities or relatives which is used to pay fees is ignored for IS purposes.[185] Your local authority can only provide 'topping-up' finance in restricted circumstances. They are only responsible for providing funding if:[186]

- you lose your preserved rights (see p88); *or*
- you were under pension age on 31 March 1993; *or*
- you are over pension age, have been evicted from a residential care home and need to move to another residential care home (not a nursing home), which is owned or managed by a different person.

When the special rates are not payable

You will not receive the special rates of IS if:[187]

- your accommodation and any meals are provided wholly or partially by a 'close relative' (see p28) or other than on a commercial basis; *or*
- you are away on holiday for up to 13 weeks.

Temporary absences

If you go into hospital, see p97.

If you have to pay a retaining fee to keep your home while you are temporarily absent from it, up to 80 per cent of your accommodation allowance is payable to cover it (in addition to any other IS you are entitled to) for up to four weeks, or 52 weeks if you have been in hospital for more than six weeks or you are in a local authority home.[188] Commissioners disagree about your entitlement to a retaining fee if you are temporarily away from your usual care home and are temporarily living in another independent residential care home.[189]

People without preserved rights in independent homes

If you do not have 'preserved rights', you are not entitled to the special higher rates of IS. This applies to everybody first entering an independent care or nursing home after 31 March 1993.

You are still entitled to claim IS if you satisfy the normal rules. Your applicable amount is calculated in the normal way – ie, personal allowances plus premiums (see p357). You are also, in most cases, entitled to a 'residential allowance' to help pay your home fees (see below). If you are a member of a couple, see p352. If you go into hospital, see p100.

If you go into an independent home for a temporary period (either for respite care or a trial period) and you have housing costs in your own home, see p30. If you go into an independent home permanently you cannot be paid housing costs on your former home or claim housing benefit to cover your residential care fees.[190]

Residential allowance[191]

You are entitled to a residential allowance if:

- you live in an independent residential care or nursing home (see p94 for definition); *and*
- you require and receive personal care because of old age, disablement, past or present alcohol or drugs dependence, past or present mental disorder or a terminal illness; *and*
- you are aged 16 or over and do not have 'preserved rights' (see p88); *and*
- your accommodation and any meals are provided on a commercial basis and no part of your weekly charge is met by housing benefit.

The residential allowance is £57.50 a week; or £64 a week if the home is in Greater London, which covers all the London Boroughs, plus parts of Essex (Chigwell and Waltham Cross), Hertfordshire (Elstree, Ridge, Shenley, South Mimms and South Broxbourne) and Surrey (Spelthorne and part of Elmbridge).[192]

The residential allowance stops after three weeks' absence from your home, or six weeks if you are in hospital.[193] See p97 for when you count as being in hospital. Separate periods in hospital are linked if they are less than 28 days apart.

Definition of independent care and nursing homes

An independent residential care home is a home which is: [194]

- registered or deemed to be registered under the Registered Homes Act 1984 or the Social Work (Scotland) Act 1968 (all homes providing board and personal care are required to be registered); *or*
- run by a body established by Royal Charter or Act of Parliament (other than a local authority) and provides board and personal care.

An independent nursing home is a home which is: [195]

- registered as a nursing home under the Registered Homes Act 1984 or the Nursing Homes Registration (Scotland) Act 1938 or the Mental Health (Scotland) Act 1984; *or*
- run by a body established by Royal Charter or special Act of Parliament.

A hospice does not count as a nursing home.[196]

Effects of local authority funding

If you cannot afford or can no longer afford to pay for a place in an independent home, you can apply to your local authority for funding (see p96). You will have to use most of your income, including your IS, to pay local authority charges.

If you are funded by the local authority you may find that your IS goes down after four weeks. This is because your attendance allowance (AA) or disability living allowance (DLA) (care component) will stop and you will therefore lose entitlement to the severe disability premium (and sometimes the higher pensioner premium) – see p367.[197] In some circumstances, you may be better off not receiving funding from your local authority, so that you can retain entitlement to AA/DLA and the severe disability premium. This could apply, for example, where you would have to refund charges to the local authority when your property is sold (see p97). The issue of the payability of AA/DLA to people in residential care is a complex one. For more details, see CPAG's *Rights Guide to Non-Means-Tested Benefits*.

If you are receiving local authority funding, charitable or voluntary payments used to top up the funding to pay for a more expensive home are disregarded as income for IS purposes.[198] If you are not receiving local authority funding, charitable or voluntary payments towards the home fees are disregarded up to a maximum of the difference between your applicable amount (less the amounts listed as personal expenses on p89) and the home fees.[199]

People in local authority homes

If you are permanently in a local authority home, your IS applicable amount is worked out in a special way. You do not have 'preserved rights' (see p88) and you are not entitled to a 'residential allowance' (see p93). You will get less IS than if you were in an independent home. You will also always lose your AA/DLA care component after four weeks. You will have to use your IS to pay local authority charges (see p96).

Definition of a local authority home

For IS purposes, you live in a local authority home if:[200]

- the home is owned or managed by a local authority; *and*
- the accommodation is provided under sections 21 and 24 of Part III of the National Assistance Act 1948 or sections 13B and 59 of the Social Work (Scotland) Act 1968 or section 7 of the Mental Health (Scotland) Act 1984; *and*
- board is provided (but if you buy and pay for food when you want – eg, in a café or canteen on the premises, this does not count as board – this will apply to many local authority hostels, the residents of which can claim ordinary rate IS and housing benefit); *and*
- you are not a person who is under 18 and in the care of a local authority in Scotland.

If you are living in a home which transferred from the local authority to the independent sector after 11 August 1991 while you were there, you will still be treated as living in a local authority home for IS purposes.[201]

IS entitlement

If you or your partner are in a local authority home, your IS applicable amount is worked out as follows:[202]

- **If you are a single person** your applicable amount is a set figure of £64.70 a week (no premiums are payable). If you are temporarily in the home, you can continue to get housing costs on your normal home (see p30).
- **If you are a lone parent** your applicable amount is a set figure of £64.70 a week. If you are temporarily in the home, you can continue to get IS for your children (see Chapter 17), the family premium plus IS housing costs (see p27).

- **If you are one of a couple:**
  - If you or your partner are temporarily in the home you are still treated as a couple for IS. Your applicable amount will be £64.70 for the partner in the home plus the normal allowance (including premiums) for a single person for the other partner.
  - If you or your partner have permanently moved into a home, you are no longer treated as a couple for IS. The partner in the home will have an applicable amount of £64.70 a week. The other partner must claim IS separately as a single person or parent.
  - If you are both in a home, you will each have an applicable amount of £64.70. If you are temporary residents, you can continue to get IS housing costs for your normal home (see p30).
- If your child is living with you in a home you can claim the normal child allowance for her/him.
- If you go into hospital, see p97.

Local authority funding and charges for residential care

Funding

If you cannot afford to pay for a place in a home and you do not have 'preserved rights' (see p88), you can apply for funding from your local authority social services department. This may happen if you are going into a home for the first time, or you are already in a home and your capital falls below £16,000 (see p416). If social services assess you as needing residential or nursing care, they must provide and fund a suitable placement for you.[203] This could either be in a local authority home or an independent home, in which case the local authority must contract to pay the full fees to the provider. There are no legal maximum rates of funding but the local authority is not obliged to pay more than is necessary to provide a placement which is suitable for your needs.

Charges

If you are in a local authority home or being funded by a local authority in an independent home, you will have to pay a weekly accommodation charge to the authority.[204] The charge is means-tested and the charging rules are laid down in national regulations.[205] They are based on the IS regulations but there are important differences. Guidance on the regulations is set out in the *Charging for Residential Accommodation Guide* issued by the Department of Health.

The main features of the charging rules are:

- **If you have more than £16,000 capital**, you must pay a charge equal to the full cost of your placement. Property is treated as for IS (see p421), but:
  - property up for sale is not disregarded;
  - property occupied by anyone can be disregarded;
  - the share of a jointly owned property may be valued differently.

Notional capital rules are similar to the IS rules (see p428). If you cannot afford to pay your charge because your capital is tied up in a property, the local authority can place a legal charge on the property and collect the debt when it is sold.[206]

- **If you have less than £16,000 capital**, your charge will be:
  - your total weekly income (including IS and tariff income from capital over £10,000 (see p405) but excluding most income disregarded under the IS rules); *less*
  - a personal allowance of at least £14.45 a week – ie, you must be left with at least this amount after paying your charge.

You cannot be charged more than the full fees for the home.

- Unlike the IS rules, only *your* income and capital counts – *not* your partner's. Joint savings are divided in half.
- The local authority can impose a standard reasonable charge for temporary placements of up to eight weeks.[207] If you have housing costs on your normal home, see p30.

5. PEOPLE IN HOSPITAL

If you, your partner or child goes into hospital, your IS is usually reduced after a specified period. Other benefits (eg, incapacity benefit, retirement pension) may also be reduced, which means you may still be entitled to some IS or you might even qualify for IS for the first time. The loss of attendance allowance (AA) or disability living allowance (DLA) after four weeks in hospital will result in the loss of the severe disability premium. See CPAG's *Rights Guide to Non-Means-Tested Benefits* for details of the effects of a stay in hospital on non-means-tested benefits.

The reductions apply if you are receiving free in-patient treatment in a hospital or similar institution under NHS legislation.[208] They do not apply if you are a fee-paying patient under NHS legislation.[209] People in nursing homes funded by health authorities or health boards may also be caught by the rules.[210]

Housing costs

IS housing costs (see p30) are payable for your normal home for up to 52 weeks while you are in hospital, providing you are unlikely to be away for substantially longer than 52 weeks.[211] Someone else may be able to get IS housing costs no longer paid to you (see p28).

Single people in hospital

After four weeks any AA or DLA you receive stops and you therefore lose your severe disability premium[212] (carers lose their carer's premium eight weeks after their invalid care allowance stops[213]).

After six weeks your IS applicable amount is reduced to £16.20[214] plus any housing costs.

After 52 weeks your applicable amount is reduced to £12.95.[215] You can be paid less than this if:[216]

- you are unable to look after your own affairs (eg, mentally ill or senile) and another person has been appointed to act on your behalf; *and*
- the IS is paid to the hospital at the request of the appointee, or to the hospital as the appointee; *and*
- a doctor who is treating you certifies that you cannot make use of all or part of your benefit, and that it cannot be used on your behalf.

This rule could leave you without any income at all, though your relatives and the hospital staff should be consulted about how much you should receive. Your appointee could refuse to allow the Benefits Agency to pay the hospital direct. S/he could receive payments on your behalf instead to make sure you get the money.

Lone parents in hospital

After four weeks any AA/DLA you receive stops and you therefore lose your severe disability premium[217] (carers lose their carer's premium eight weeks after their invalid care allowance stops[218]).

After six weeks your IS applicable amount is reduced to £16.20 *plus* your children's personal allowances, *plus* the family and disabled child premiums,[219] *plus* housing costs.

After 52 weeks you will lose your housing costs. You will also be treated as a single person (see p351) once you are likely to be in hospital for substantially longer than 52 weeks.[220] If your child is also in hospital, see below.

Couples

After four weeks if one of you is in hospital, s/he will lose her/his AA/DLA. If both of you are in hospital, you will both lose your AA/DLA. In either case, you can continue to get the severe disability premium, but only at the single person rate.[221] Carers lose their carer's premium eight weeks after their invalid care allowance stops.[222]

After six weeks if one of you is in hospital, your IS applicable amount is reduced by £12.95. This also applies if both of you are in hospital but only one of you has been there for over six weeks. If both of you are in hospital for over six weeks your applicable amount is £32.40 personal allowance for you both, *plus* personal allowances for your children and family and disabled child premiums (if applicable), *plus* housing costs.[223]

After 52 weeks if one or both of you are in hospital, you will count as single people once one of you is likely to be in hospital for substantially longer than 52 weeks.[224]

If only one of you is in hospital, that person's applicable amount will be £12.95 and the other person must claim separately as a single claimant or lone parent. If both of you are in hospital and have no children, you will each have an applicable amount of £12.95.[225] If both of you are in hospital and you have children, one of you is treated as responsible for the children and has an applicable amount of £16.20 *plus* the children's personal allowances, disabled child premiums (if applicable) and the family premium.[226] The other partner has an applicable amount of £12.95.[227]

If a child is also in hospital, see below.

Children in hospital

If your child goes into hospital, your IS stays the same for 12 weeks. After that the personal allowance you receive for the child reduces to £12.95.[228] Any premiums you receive in relation to the child remain in payment. Even if your child loses the care component of DLA because s/he has been in hospital for over 12 weeks, you still get a disabled child premium, as long as s/he continues to be treated as a member of your family (see p353).[229]

The rule about adjustment to IS for a child in hospital applies equally where parent(s) and child are in hospital.[230]

People in residential care or nursing homes

Up to six weeks in hospital

- If you have 'preserved rights' (see p88) and you go into hospital for six weeks or less you will still get your personal allowance and your accommodation allowance as long as you still have to pay the charge for the home – or a reduced allowance if the charge is reduced.[231] If you are single, do not have to pay the charge, and are unlikely to return to the home, you will get IS as a hospital patient (see p97). If you do not have to pay the charge but are likely to return to the home, you will get your personal allowance as a home resident (see p89), *plus* meals allowance, if any.[232]
- If you do not have preserved rights, you will continue to receive your usual IS, including the residential allowance, for the first six weeks in hospital.[233] If you are a single claimant who is permanently resident in a local authority home, however, you are only entitled to an applicable amount of £14.45.[234]

After six weeks in hospital

- If you have preserved rights (see p88) your personal allowance is £16.20 (£32.40 if your partner is also in hospital). You can also get IS housing costs or an amount to cover a retaining fee for the home (see p92 for how this is calculated). If a member of your family remains in the home you are entitled to your normal accommodation allowance (less your meals allowance) taking into account any reduction in the charge. Children in hospital for a longer period than 12 weeks have a personal allowance of £12.95.[235]
- If you do not have preserved rights your IS is reduced in accordance with the rules explained on pp97-99. If you are a single claimant who is permanently in a local authority home, your applicable amount remains £14.45.[236]

Patients detained under the Mental Health Act

Single people detained under the Mental Health Act 1983 (in Scotland, Mental Health (Scotland) Act 1984), who were in prison immediately before their detention have an applicable amount of £12.95.[237]

Going in and out of hospital

- The date your IS applicable amount reduces depends on whether your IS is paid in advance or arrears.[238] If you are paid in arrears, the reduction takes place from the first day of the benefit week in which you have been in hospital for six weeks (not counting the day of admission). If your IS is paid in advance, the reduction takes effect from the first day of the benefit week which coincides with, or follows, the date when you have been in hospital for six weeks. In the first case you could *lose* up to six days' full benefit; in the second you could *gain* up to six days' full benefit.

- Separate stays in hospital less than 28 days apart are added together in calculating the length of time you have been in hospital.[239]
- If you or a member of your family stop being a patient for any period of less than a week you should be paid your full IS for the days you are at home.[240]
- Your entitlement on the days you enter and leave hospital is not entirely clear and there have been conflicting commissioners' decisions on the issue.[241] DSS guidance probably reflects the current legal situation by stating that for IS purposes, the day you enter hospital does not count as a day in hospital but the day you leave does.[242] Note that the law relating to AA/DLA is different and for the purposes of these benefits, days of admission and discharge count as days in hospital.[243] If you go home for part of the day while you are an in-patient, you still count as an in-patient on that day.[244]

6. PRISONERS

If you are a prisoner (see below), you are not entitled to any IS, apart from housing costs (see p27), which are only payable while you are detained in custody, awaiting trial or sentence.[245] You will also not be entitled to jobseeker's allowance (JSA) (see CPAG's *Jobseeker's Allowance Handbook 1998/99*). Your partner can claim IS/JSA as a single person or lone parent while you are a prisoner.[246] If your dependent child becomes a prisoner, you cannot get IS for her/him.[247] If you have no other children you will no longer qualify for IS as a lone parent (you can claim income-based JSA instead), or for the family premium.

You count as a prisoner if you are detained in custody awaiting trial or sentence, are serving a custodial sentence or are on temporary release.[248] You do *not* count as a prisoner if you are released on licence or parole or you are remanded in a bail or probation hostel.[249] If you and your partner are temporarily separated because one of you is in a bail or probation hostel, you may still count as a couple for IS purposes and your applicable amount is subject to special rules (see p352).[250]

Other sources of help

- Housing benefit and council tax benefit are payable for up to 52 weeks if you are remanded in custody or a bail hostel pending trial or sentence; or up to 13 weeks if you are serving a custodial sentence (see p231-32).
- Somebody caring for you while you are on temporary release can claim a community care grant for living expenses (see p468). The Prison Department can make a payment for your home leave if your family is not getting IS, but cannot afford to support you. It can also pay for board and lodging during a period of temporary release if you are homeless.
- Help with the cost of visiting a close relative in prison comes from the Home Office. For this purpose, 'close relative' means husband, wife (including an established unmarried partner), brother, sister, parent and child. Adopted and fostered children and adoptive and foster parents are included. If you are too ill, or too young, to travel alone, the fares of an escort can also be paid. It is normal policy to cover the travel costs (including an overnight stay and meals allowance where necessary), of up to 26 visits in a 12-month period if you are receiving IS or family credit. If your income is low but above IS level, the Home Office may pay part of the cost. Your income is assessed in the same way as for health benefits (see p502). You apply for help with the cost of visits on form F2022 obtainable from your local Benefits Agency office, or from the Assisted Prison Visits Unit, PO Box 2152, Birmingham B15 1SD, tel: 0121 626 2797. There is no right of appeal against a refusal by the Home Office of fares or a warrant for a visit but you could take up the matter with your MP.
- When you are released from prison, you may receive a discharge grant, which is treated as capital for IS purposes.[251] If you need help with the cost of basic essentials (eg, clothing, furniture, rent in advance), you may be able to get a social fund payment (see p456).

7. PEOPLE WITHOUT ACCOMMODATION

If you are a person 'without accommodation', you are entitled to the normal IS personal allowances, for yourself and your partner (see p358) but you are not entitled to any allowances for dependent children, nor any premiums for yourself, your partner or your children.[252]

The term 'accommodation' is not defined in the legislation and should be interpreted widely and flexibly. The *Adjudication Officers' Guide* describes it as, 'An effective shelter from the elements which is capable of being heated; and in which occupants can sit, lie, cook and eat; and which is reasonably suited for continuous occupation. The site of the accommodation may alter from day to day, but it is still accommodation if the structure is habitable'.[253] This would cover tents, caravans and other vehicles.

If you are known in an area, you should get your IS by giro, payment card or order book in the normal way, but if you are 'likely to move on or mis-spend your money' you may be required to collect your benefit on a daily or part-week basis.[254] If you become homeless and have no money, you may initially need a crisis loan (see p479).

If you set up home as part of a resettlement programme after you have been homeless, you may be entitled to a community care grant (see p468).

The Benefits Agency may decide you have an unsettled way of life and refer you to a voluntary project centre as an alternative. This should only be done with your consent and if a place is available. IS should not be refused or delayed if you are unwilling to take the 'advice' being offered, or are not interested in being resettled.[255]

It may be argued that if you are forced to live on the streets that this is a threat to your health and that the local authority has a duty to provide accommodation for you under the National Assistance Act.[256]

CHAPTER SIX

Maintenance payments

This chapter is divided as follows:

1. Lone parents (below)
2. Who is 'liable to maintain' you and your children (p106)
3. Getting maintenance (p108)
4. The child support scheme (p110)
5. How maintenance affects your income support (p120)

This chapter tells you about who is 'liable to maintain' you and your children (see p106). It also deals with the effect any maintenance payments have on income support (IS) (see p120). Some of the provisions affect sponsors who have signed undertakings to maintain people from abroad; the implications for them are dealt with on p85.

If you are claiming income-based jobseeker's allowance (JSA), see the *Jobseeker's Allowance Handbook*, 3rd edn, 1998/99.

The rules about maintenance for children under the Child Support Act 1991 are included where they affect your right to benefit or the amount to which you are entitled (see p110). For further information about the child support scheme, see CPAG's *Child Support Handbook*.

Payments of maintenance for yourself could be on a voluntary basis or under a court order. Detailed advice about maintenance orders is beyond the scope of this *Handbook*. You should see a solicitor for advice about this. If you are receiving IS you can apply for legal aid for court proceedings. In addition, you can get free advice from a solicitor under what is known as the Green Form scheme.

If you have been getting child maintenance (see p190) and you or your partner start working full time (see p13) or increase your earnings and stop getting IS, you might be able to get a child maintenance bonus (see p189).

I. LONE PARENTS

If you are a lone parent claiming for a child under 16, you fit into one of the groups of people who can claim IS (see p10). You can claim if you satisfy the other rules of entitlement described in Chapter 2.

If you claim IS within three months of the birth of a child, claim a maternity expenses payment from the social fund (see p443).

You are entitled to maintenance payments for your child(ren) whether or not you were married and possibly for yourself if you were married. You are required to apply for child support maintenance if you claim IS, income-based jobseeker's allowance (JSA), family credit (FC) or disability working allowance (DWA), unless you are exempt (see p111). The money you get affects your benefit (see p120).

As part of its 'welfare to work' policy, the Government is offering a New Deal for lone parents. Under the New Deal, lone parents are assisted back to work and given help with jobsearch, training and childcare. The scheme is not compulsory. If you are interested you should contact your local JobCentre.

Child benefit

As a lone parent or someone looking after a child on your own, you can claim child benefit. It is not necessary to be a parent of the child. You can claim it at a higher rate for your oldest child (£17.10 a week). However, by claiming the higher rate you might be taken off IS. If you are not on IS you will not get free school meals (see p513) or access to the social fund (see Chapters 21, 22 and 23). If you are currently claiming child benefit you do not have to claim the higher rate (but see below). For full details, see CPAG's *Rights Guide to Non-Means-Tested Benefits*.

If you stop claiming IS, for example because you start working full-time (see p13), you could be better off financially if you claim the higher rate of child benefit. You should seek advice because the Government intends to abolish this rate of child benefit in June 1998 (see below).

Note: The Government intends to abolish the higher (lone parent) rate of child benefit in June 1998 (see Appendix 2). However, it says that it intends to allow lone parents who are on IS continously from 5 April 1998 to claim it when they go into full-time work (see p13). If you are in this situation, you should seek advice. The Government also says that lone parents already getting the lone parent rate when it is abolished will continue to get it. From April 1999, the Government intends to increase the amount of benefit paid to both lone parents and parents in couples. See Appendix 2 for further details. For information about future developments, see CPAG's *Welfare Rights Bulletin*.

Young mothers

If you are under 16, you cannot claim IS but can claim child benefit and also health benefits (see p500). If your parents (or someone else) are entitled to include you in their family (see p353), they can also include your baby in their family for the purpose of a claim for IS or other means-tested benefits. They can claim a maternity payment for you from the social fund (see p442) if they are entitled to IS, income-based JSA, FC or DWA.

If you are 16 or over, you can claim IS if you fit into one of the groups of people who can claim (see p10) and satisfy the other rules of entitlement described in Chapter 2. If you are still in school or college – what is known as 'relevant education' – see p17.

You can get maintenance for your child from the father, and will be required to apply for it if you are claiming IS/income-based JSA/FC/DWA in your own right unless you are exempt (see p111).

Claiming after a relationship breakdown

If your marriage or other relationship breaks down you can claim benefit in your own right as a single person or lone parent. If you and your ex-partner remain living under the same roof but live separate lives, you can make separate claims for IS (and other means-tested benefits). You should not be treated as a married or cohabiting couple, provided that you keep separate households (see p347). You may be entitled to maintenance for yourself from your ex-spouse and this affects the amount of benefit to which you are entitled (see p121). You must apply for maintenance for your children if you are on IS/income-based JSA/FC/DWA unless you are exempt (see p111) and this also affects the amount of your benefit (see p120).

2. WHO IS 'LIABLE TO MAINTAIN' YOU AND YOUR CHILDREN

While you are on IS, certain people are 'liable to maintain' you and your children.[1] If someone is 'liable to maintain' you or your children, s/he must pay maintenance. The Secretary of State can take proceedings against anyone who has a liability to maintain you or your children while you are on IS (see p107). If that person fails to maintain you or your children, s/he can be prosecuted (see p107).

Your right to claim benefit is not affected by the fact that the DSS can get money back from someone who is liable to maintain you. You should therefore not be refused IS while maintenance is being pursued.

However, maintenance that is recovered might affect your benefit (see pp120 and 121).

- **You** must be maintained by your spouse, if you are married or separated.[2]

  If you have to live apart from your spouse because you need care or treatment (eg, in hospital, or in a residential or nursing home) you may be assessed and paid as separate individuals for benefit purposes (see p351). However, your spouse is still 'liable to maintain' you and may be asked to make a financial contribution towards your care.

- **Your children** must be maintained by both their parents.[3] A parent who does not live with the person who is looking after her/his child(ren) is expected to pay child support maintenance on a regular basis to that person.[4] If you are the parent looking after the child(ren) and claiming IS/income-based JSA/FC/DWA you are required to apply for this maintenance unless you are exempt (see p111). However, you can opt not to apply for maintenance and have your benefit paid at a reduced rate (but see p114 before you decide to do this).

  A parent is not 'liable to maintain' children over 16 who are independent or any children over the age of 19.

- If you are a **'person from abroad'**, you must be maintained by a sponsor who has given an undertaking to support you (see p85). This includes your ex-spouse after you are divorced.

Maintenance Orders

The Secretary of State can take proceedings against anyone who is 'liable to maintain' (see above) if they fail to do so. This enables the DSS to pursue maintenance on your behalf while you are on benefit. The magistrates' court can make an order telling the person who is liable what s/he has to pay.[5] Since 5 April 1993, the courts have not had the power to make new orders for maintenance for children, other than consent orders.[6] Instead, you can apply for child support maintenance (see p110).

The fact that there was an agreement that you would not ask for maintenance is not a bar to an order being made,[7] although all the circumstances must be taken into account.[8] The court is entitled to refuse to make an order for maintenance if you have been guilty of adultery, cruelty or desertion.[9]

Prosecution

As a last resort a person who is 'liable to maintain' (see above) can be prosecuted if IS is paid as a result of her/his persistently refusing or neglecting to maintain you or your children. You can even be prosecuted for failing to maintain yourself (this is uncommon). Although the power remains in respect of children, it is very unlikely to be used given that child maintenance is now being dealt with by the Child Support Agency (see below). In either case, the maximum penalty is three months' imprisonment or a fine of £2,500 or both.[10] If you are charged with such an offence, see a solicitor. Legal aid may be available to help meet the cost.

3. GETTING MAINTENANCE

If you are having problems with your maintenance (eg, you have difficulties getting it or the amount is too low) the Secretary of State can take action on your behalf. If there is already an order in favour of, or for the benefit of, you or your children, the Secretary of State may do anything which you could do to enforce or vary the order.[11] Furthermore, if the Secretary of State notifies the relevant court officer that s/he wishes to be informed of any application to vary or enforce the order or to have any arrears remitted, by either a benefit claimant or a 'liable relative' (see p121) s/he will be given that information and is entitled to take part in the proceedings.[12] Nevertheless, any maintenance which then has to be paid is paid to you (unless diverted – see below).

Where the Child Support Agency has taken over cases with previous court orders for maintenance for children (see below), this is no longer necessary.

Collection by the Benefits Agency

If maintenance is payable through a magistrates' court (including orders made in the county court or High Court but registered in the magistrates' court) it can be paid direct to the Benefits Agency.[13] In return, the Benefits Agency gives you an order book for the amount of IS you would receive if no maintenance was being paid. The Benefits Agency does not usually accept this sort of arrangement unless payments have actually been missed, but may if you have a good reason for wanting it done and you explain why.

Maintenance for children

Maintenance for children is dealt with by the **Child Support Agency (CSA)** and is called child support maintenance (see p110). If you are getting maintenance for a child under a voluntary agreement or court order, this can continue until the CSA takes on your case. If you want to apply for child support maintenance and have not been approached by the CSA, you can request a maintenance application form.

If you make a new or repeat claim for IS/income-based JSA/FC/DWA, you must apply for child support maintenance unless you are exempt (see p111). The CSA may collect other types of maintenance at the same time as child support maintenance.[14]

Collection by the CSA

Child support maintenance (see p110) can be paid to the CSA rather than direct to you as the carer, if the Secretary of State agrees.[15] If you want this to happen, ask the CSA. You can request this on the maintenance application form or at a later date. This is useful where maintenance payments are likely to be irregular or unreliable, or where you do not want to be located by the other party. If the CSA is collecting the payments for you, enforcement action should begin automatically when a payment is missed. Where payment should be made direct to you, it is up to you to contact the CSA and the Benefits Agency when a maintenance payment does not arrive.

If you are on IS and your child(ren)'s absent parent is making payments to the CSA, your child support maintenance is paid in the same order book/girocheque as your IS. The CSA retains the payments made by the absent parent. If the Agency does not receive your child support maintenance payment, you can still cash the full amount of IS.

Amount of maintenance

The CSA's formula for calculating **child support maintenance** (see p110) is rigid. However, departures from the formula are allowed in certain circumstances, for example, where you or an absent parent have a disabled child or where an absent parent's travel costs to see your children are expensive or if a parent's life style is more extravagant than the income s/he has declared allows. See the *Child Support Handbook* for an explanation of the formula and details of the departure rules.

There is more flexibility about how much **maintenance your spouse is required to pay for you.** S/he can negotiate with the Benefits Agency to pay an amount s/he can afford given her/his outgoings. As a starting point for negotiations, the Benefits Agency compares your spouse's net income with the total of:[16]

• the IS personal allowances and premiums s/he would qualify for if entitled to IS;

- household expenses including rent, mortgage and council tax (excluding arrears);
- 15 per cent of her/his net wage (to cover expenses for work); *and*
- the balance of any other expenses exceeding the 15 per cent margin that are considered essential.

If your spouse has a new partner, two calculations are performed – one as if s/he was single and the other using joint incomes. The lower figure is used as the basis for negotiation.

If the Benefits Agency feels that your spouse is not paying enough it has the right to take her/him to court (see p107).

4. THE CHILD SUPPORT SCHEME

A child must be maintained by both parents (see p107). If you are a child's absent parent (see p118) and are on IS or JSA, a deduction is made from your benefit as a contribution towards your child's maintenance (see p118). If you are a lone parent or are looking after children on your own, and make a new or repeat claim for IS/income-based JSA/FC/DWA, you must apply to the Child Support Agency (CSA) for a maintenance assessment unless you are exempt (see p111). Any maintenance you receive counts as income when calculating your benefit. Your benefit claim should not be held up by the CSA, but failure to apply for child support maintenance could affect the amount of benefit you receive (see p113).

The CSA assessment overrides any previous maintenance agreement you have for your children, including a court order.

Pursuing maintenance

On your IS claim form, you are asked if any child for whom you are claiming has another parent who does not normally live with you. If so, you are asked whether you are willing, if required, to authorise the CSA to pursue child support maintenance on your behalf. If you think you or your child(ren) would be at risk of harm or undue distress were you required to authorise the CSA (see p112), there is a space on the form for you to say so. You are given time (currently 14 days) to decide what you want to do.

Unless you have indicated there is a risk of harm or undue distress on your claim form (see above), if you are not getting child support maintenance currently, you are usually visited by an officer of the Benefits Agency. If you said on your form that you are willing to authorise the CSA to pursue maintenance, s/he helps you complete a maintenance application form. Otherwise, s/he explains your options (see above). You are given more time to decide what you want to do if you need this. See the *Child Support Handbook* for full details of the child support scheme.

The requirement to co-operate

If you are claiming IS, income-based JSA, FC or DWA the Secretary of State may require you to apply for child support maintenance from your child's other parent where you are living apart and you have care of your child for at least part of the week[17] (see the *Child Support Handbook* for details of shared care situations). This is what is known as the 'requirement to co-operate' with the CSA. You will be required to:

* authorise the CSA to pursue child support maintenance for your children (see below); *and*
* provide information and evidence to the CSA (see p112).

You are generally required to apply for child support maintenance. However:

* the Secretary of State has the discretion not to require you to co-operate and must consider the welfare of any children involved;[18]
* you can be exempt from the requirement to co-operate where you or your child would be put at risk of suffering **harm or undue distress** if you gave your authorisation for child support maintenance to be pursued (see p112).

If you are required to co-operate with the CSA and refuse to do so, your benefit may be paid at a reduced rate (see pp113 and 114).

The requirement to co-operate applies not only to lone parents, but also to couples where one of the children in the family has a parent who is living elsewhere. It even applies if you are not receiving an IS personal allowance for the child (see p359).[19] The requirement does not apply where a child lives with neither parent. In this case, an application for child support maintenance from the person looking after the child is voluntary.

Providing authorisation

Unless you have given the CSA details of a risk of harm or undue distress (see p112), if you claim IS/income-based JSA/FC/DWA you are asked to complete a child support maintenance application form. If you sign the form, you are giving your authorisation to the CSA to pursue child support maintenance. Without your signature, the CSA cannot take any action to pursue maintenance. **Do not sign the maintenance application form unless you are sure that you want to apply for child support maintenance**. You can opt not to authorise the CSA to pursue maintenance but your benefit may be paid at a reduced rate (see pp113 and 114).

If you are looking after children who have different parents, see the *Child Support Handbook*.

Withdrawing authorisation

If you sign the maintenance application form and later find that you or your children are at risk of harm or undue distress (see below) as a result of the maintenance assessment, you can ask the CSA to stop pursuing maintenance.[20]

The CSA will go through the same procedure as if you had refused to co-operate at the beginning. If the child support officer decides you are no longer required to co-operate (see p113), the CSA must stop pursuing the maintenance. Otherwise, the CSA continues to act on the original authorisation and pursues the maintenance. You do not have the option of having your benefit paid at a reduced rate (see p114) at this stage. You may want to contact your MP for support.

Providing information

Unless you or your children would be at risk of harm or undue distress (see below), as well as providing authorisation (see p111) you must provide information and evidence to enable the CSA to trace your children's absent parent and to assess and collect child support maintenance.[21] See the *Child Support Handbook* for details of the information the CSA can expect you to provide.

Harm or undue distress

You do not have to provide authorisation or information (see above and p111) if doing so would put you or your child at risk of harm or undue distress.

When you claim IS you are asked on the claim form if you or your child(ren) would be put at risk of suffering harm or undue distress if you were required to pursue maintenance. If you think this applies to you, you should say so and give details of your situation. This will be followed up by the CSA. See the *Child Support Handbook* for further details.

If you believe that you or any of the children living with you would be at risk of harm or distress if you applied for child support maintenance, you should explain this to the CSA. There is no legal definition of 'harm or undue distress'. It certainly covers situations where there is a possibility of violence or where there has been rape, sexual abuse, threats or other harassment.[22] There does not need to have been a history of actual violence – fear of violence is enough. A child support officer decides if a fear of violence is reasonably held.

There will be many other situations in which you might find it distressing to pursue maintenance. Examples are where:

- you have not had any contact with the other parent for many years;
- you had a clean-break divorce;
- the other parent is threatening to contest who the child lives with;
- you chose to have the child against the father's wishes;
- you believe that seeking child support maintenance would threaten the arrangement between the children and their other parent.

Each case is decided on its merits. Your word should be accepted without any supporting evidence unless you contradict yourself or the child support officer thinks the information is improbable,[23] for example, where you have named a celebrity as the father of your child.

It will take the CSA many weeks to decide whether you have to provide authorisation or information (see pp111 and 112). It is important not to sign a maintenance application form in the meantime. See below for the procedure the CSA must follow if you refuse to co-operate.

Refusal to co-operate with the CSA

If you refuse to authorise the CSA to seek maintenance for your child(ren) (see p111) or to provide information to help them do so (see p112), your benefit (IS, income-based JSA, FC or DWA) may be paid at a reduced rate (see p114).[24] However, your benefit claim must still be processed by the Benefits Agency. You do not need to withdraw your benefit claim to avoid child support maintenance being pursued. If you do not want to apply for child support maintenance, do not sign the maintenance application form (see p112).

You do not have to provide authorisation or information if you or your child(ren) would be at risk of harm or undue distress (see p112). You should be notified in writing whether or not you are required to do so.

The procedure

If you are required to provide authorisation and information (see pp111 and 112), you will be warned in writing that your benefit could be paid at a reduced rate (see p114) unless you do so.[25] You must respond within two weeks, giving your reasons why you think you or your children would suffer harm or undue distress (see p112) if you were required to co-operate. You can submit supporting letters – eg, from friends and relatives, your doctor, child's school, or other helpful organisations – if you wish. It is important to do this to avoid having your benefit paid at a reduced rate (see below).

If you do submit further information, the Secretary of State should let you know if it is accepted that there is a risk of harm or undue distress (see p112) if you are required to co-operate. If there is not, your case will be referred to the area manager of the CSA. S/he will write to you asking you either to provide the authorisation or information requested, or to explain why you have not done this. You are given 14 days in which to respond.[26] Even at this stage, you should not sign the maintenance application form if you believe you should not be required to co-operate (see p111). You do not have a right of appeal until the end of the procedure. See the *Child Support Handbook* for more details about the procedure.

To ensure that your benefit is not paid at a reduced rate (see below) it is important that you explain the harm or undue distress (see p112) which could arise if you authorise the CSA to pursue child support maintenance. Make it clear that this is why you do not wish to co-operate. You do not have to reply in writing – a telephone call is acceptable.[27] Nor do you have to provide evidence to prove that you would be under threat. Your word should be accepted,[28] though it is always useful to point to specific examples of problems which have occurred in the past or reasons why you believe they might occur in the future, to help illustrate what effect your co-operation might have. If there are reasonable grounds for believing that you or your child would suffer harm or undue distress were authorisation to be given, no further action is taken and you are advised of this.[29]

The rules about the procedure the CSA must follow if you refuse to co-operate changed on 7 October 1996. If you failed to co-operate before that date, the old rules still apply.[30] See the *Child Support Handbook* 1996/97 edn, pp101–12.

Payment of benefit at a reduced rate

Your IS/income-based JSA/FC/DWA can be paid at a reduced rate if:

- you refuse to provide authorisation or information to enable the CSA to pursue child support maintenance for your children (see pp111 and 112); *and*
- the child support officer does not accept that there is any risk of harm or undue distress to you or your children (see p112).

If this is the case, the child support officer makes what is known as a 'reduced benefit direction'.[31] When deciding whether to issue a reduced benefit direction, the child support officer must consider whether the welfare of any child involved would be adversely affected, for example, because of her/his age or state of health or that of her/his parent's.[32] See p116 for more information about the amount by which your benefit can be reduced.

A reduced benefit direction cannot be issued where:[33]

- IS or income-based JSA is paid to you or your partner which includes a disabled child premium, a disability premium or a higher pensioner premium (this applies even if it is your partner who has the disability);
- the disabled child premium or the disability premium is included in your exempt income for child support maintenance purposes (see the *Child Support Handbook* for details) if you are in receipt of FC/DWA (this does not recognise your partner's disability).

Right of appeal

You have a right of appeal to an independent child support appeal tribunal against a reduced benefit direction.[34] You must appeal within 28 days of the decision being sent to you, although a late appeal will be accepted if you have special reasons.[35] The special reasons do not have to relate to your own personal circumstances or actions. They could include things like the amount of money involved or how strong your case is. The reduced benefit direction will be imposed in the meantime, unless you decide to co-operate by providing the authorisation or information (see pp111 and 112) after it is issued.

The reduced rate of benefit

The adjudication officer at the Benefits Agency must follow a reduced benefit direction (see above) issued by a child support officer. Your benefit should be paid in full until a direction is issued but it will then be adjusted. A current award of FC/DWA can be changed immediately if a reduced benefit direction is issued, cancelled or suspended (see p209) and not at the end of your current award as is usually the case.

Benefit can be paid at a reduced rate even if it does not include an amount for the child(ren) for whom maintenance is being claimed.[36] However, no reduction is made if you are in hospital, a residential care or nursing home, or a local authority residential home.[37]

If your FC or DWA is being paid at a reduced rate and you then go on to IS or income-based JSA, this is paid at a reduced rate.[38]

Only one reduced benefit direction (see above) can be in operation at a time even if you refuse to co-operate in seeking maintenance for children from different relationships.[39] However, if another child is born or joins your household you can be asked to give authorisation and information (see pp111 and 112) in relation to that additional child. A second reduced benefit direction could be issued if you again fail to co-operate. The second direction replaces the original one which ceases even if it would otherwise have run for several more months.[40]

The amount by which benefit is reduced and how long this lasts

If a reduced benefit direction is issued (see p115), unless it ends early (see p117), your benefit is reduced by £20.14 a week for three years.[41] If the reduction would take your benefit to below 10 pence (IS or income-based JSA) or 50 pence (FC or DWA), a lower reduction is made so that you are left with this minimum amount of benefit.[42] When benefit rates are increased in April the amount of the reduction also increases. For IS, this happens straightaway but with FC or DWA it is adjusted when your claim is next renewed.[43]

The three year period begins on the first day of the second benefit week after the adjudication officer has reviewed and revised your claim.[44] At the end of the three-year period, if you still refuse to co-operate, another reduced benefit direction can be issued.

The rules about the amount of the reduction and how long it lasts changed on 7 October 1996. If your reduced benefit direction began before that date, the old rules still apply.[45] You cannot get more than one reduced benefit direction for the same children. See the *Child Support Handbook* 1996/97 edn, pp112-14.

Second reduced benefit directions

If a second reduced benefit direction is made against you because you refuse to co-operate in relation to an additional child (see above), the original direction lapses and the reduction under the new direction lasts for a fresh three years.[46]

Example
Paula has been paid benefit at a reduced rate for seven months because she refused to sign a maintenance application form for her first child. She has now refused to authorise the CSA to pursue maintenance for her new baby. The first reduced benefit direction ends early. However, she is penalised for a further three years under a new reduced benefit direction.

If the second reduced benefit direction terminates because it is reviewed (see p118) or because you decide to provide the required authorisation or information (see pp111 and 112), the original direction can be brought back into operation for the balance of the three-year period. This can only be done if you are still refusing to co-operate in relation to the original child support maintenance application.[47]

Example

After a second reduced benefit direction (RBD) has been in operation for one year, Paula has decided to co-operate with the CSA in seeking child support maintenance for her baby. However, she still does not want to seek maintenance for her first child. The original RDB had been in place for seven months. It is re-instated for one year and five months.

3 years – 1 year (second RBD) – 7 months (original RBD) = 1 year and 5 months.

The rules about what happens when a second reduced benefit direction ends early changed on 7 October 1996. If your earlier reduced benefit direction was made before 7 October 1996, the old rules still apply, even if the second direction was made after that date.[48] See the *Child Support Handbook* 1996/97 edn, p114.

When a reduced benefit direction ends early

A reduced benefit direction can end early. It:

- is **cancelled** if it was made in error, or not ended earlier due to an error (in this case the money will be repaid).[49] This can include situations where the child support officer did not at first accept your explanation why you or your children were at risk of harm or undue distress (see p112) but now does;
- **terminates** if you decide to provide the authorisation (see p111) or information (see p112) requested by the CSA.[50] It can also be terminated on review (see p118);
- is **suspended or withdrawn** where:
  – you stop getting IS/income-based JSA/FC/DWA.[51] However, if you claim one of these benefits again within 52 weeks, the reduced benefit direction is reinstated for the remainder of the three year period. You must be given 14 days notice of this. If you make your new claim more than 52 weeks after you last received IS/income-based JSA/FC/DWA the direction is no longer valid. However, the requirement to co-operate (see p111) still applies and you will be asked to complete a maintenance application form. A new direction

could be made, though it should only run for the balance of the three years which was not used up on the previous claim;
- your child(ren) cease(s) to be eligible for maintenance because they are over 16 and have left non-advanced education, or are 19 or over. If they become eligible again (eg, because they return to full-time education) the reduced benefit direction can be reinstated;[52]
- you stop living with and caring for the child(ren). The reduced benefit direction can be reinstated if you resume your role as carer;[53]
- you are paid IS at a special rate because you are in hospital, a residential care or nursing home or a local authority residential home (see Chapter 5). Initially the reduced benefit direction is suspended, but if you stay there for more than 52 weeks it ceases completely;[54]
- your child(ren) (if in Scotland) or their absent parent successfully apply to the CSA for a maintenance assessment.[55]

Both you and the Benefits Agency adjudication officer should be notified if a reduced benefit direction ceases, and given an explanation.[56]

The rules about what happens when a reduced benefit direction ends early changed on 7 October 1996. If your earlier reduced benefit direction was made before 7 October 1996, the old rules still apply, even if the second direction was made after that date.[57] See the *Child Support Handbook* 1996/97 edn, p114.

Reviewing a reduced benefit direction

A reduced benefit direction (see p115) must be **reviewed** if you, or someone on your behalf, provides additional reasons explaining why: [58]

- you failed to co-operate with the CSA (see p111);
- you are no longer obliged to co-operate (see p111).

It should also be reviewed if the child(ren)'s welfare is likely to be put in jeopardy by the continuing existence of a direction.

The review is done by a child support officer (but not the one who issued the direction). S/he may decide to terminate the direction from the date that the reasons were supplied. You should be given a full written decision and informed of your right of appeal if the direction is not terminated.

Child support maintenance paid by absent parents on IS or income-based JSA

If you are an absent parent you are liable to maintain your children (see p106). If you are on IS or income-based JSA, deductions of £5.10 a week can be made from your benefit as a contribution towards their maintenance.[59] This does not apply if you:[60]

* are aged under 18;
* qualify for a family premium or have day-to-day care of any child (see the *Child Support Handbook* for details of 'day-to-day care');
* receive incapacity benefit, maternity allowance, statutory sick pay or maternity pay, severe disablement allowance, attendance allowance, disability living or working allowances, invalid care allowance, industrial injuries disablement benefit, a war pension or a payment from either of the Independent Living Funds. If this benefit is not paid solely because of overlapping benefit rules, or an inadequate contribution record, you are still exempt from deductions.

If you are an absent parent on IS or income-based JSA and have children from two or more different relationships, only one deduction can be made and the £5.10 is apportioned between the people who care for the child(ren).[61]

If you think that a decision to make deductions from your IS or income-based JSA is wrong, you can apply in writing to the CSA for a review. You should try to show that the decision was:

* given in ignorance of relevant facts; *or*
* based on a mistake about the facts; *or*
* wrong in law.

A different child support officer will review the decision. If you still do not agree with the decision you can appeal to a child support appeal tribunal but must do this within 28 days.[62] If your circumstances change you can also apply for a review.

If you are not exempt from the deductions, the CSA sends a notification to the Benefits Agency. This request for deductions to be made is binding on the adjudication officer of the Benefits Agency, unless other deductions are being made from IS which are of a higher priority (see p155). Deductions for child support maintenance cannot be made from any benefit other than IS or jobseeker's allowance, unless incapacity benefit, severe disablement allowance or retirement pension are paid in the same girocheque or order book as IS. If you are an absent parent who is not exempt from the deductions but disagree that the Benefits Agency can make them because other higher priority deductions are being made from your benefit, you have a right of appeal to a social security appeal tribunal (see Chapter 8).

5. HOW MAINTENANCE AFFECTS YOUR INCOME SUPPORT

The following types of maintenance are taken into account in working out the amount of IS to which you are entitled:

- child support maintenance payments (see below);
- other maintenance payments made by 'liable relatives' (see p121).

See Chapter 3 for further information about how your IS is calculated.

Child support maintenance

All payments of child support maintenance are treated as income and are taken into account in full on a weekly basis.[63] Where payments are made monthly, multiply by 12 and divide by 52 to obtain a weekly amount. Where regular payments are made at intervals other than each week or month, the payments are spread over the period, including any part week. It is the actual payments made, and not the amount due under the Child Support Agency (CSA) assessment, which are taken into account in this way.[64]

The Benefits Agency should not calculate IS on the assumption that child support maintenance payments are being made where this has not been happening. So a parent who would be floated off IS if payments were made can continue to receive IS if the child support maintenance is not received. If there is a delay in obtaining increased or reinstated IS you should seek advice.

Child support maintenance can be paid direct to the CSA rather than to you. See p109 for further details.

Arrears at the beginning of the child support assessment

Arrears of child support maintenance have always accrued by the time an assessment is made. Usually these arrears will be paid to, and retained by, the CSA if you are on IS. However, if the payment is made to you, the IS which has been overpaid to you can be recovered by the Benefits Agency.[65]

Arrears due during a claim

The CSA is responsible for collecting arrears of child support maintenance if you are on IS. If you were paid IS because the maintenance was not paid when it was due, the CSA retains an amount equal to the IS you were paid.[66]

Arrears paid for a period before the claim

Only child support maintenance both due for and received in the weeks of the claim can be taken into account by the Benefits Agency. A payment of child support maintenance due before but paid after you claim IS is treated as paid in the week in which it was due.[67]

Other maintenance payments made by 'liable relatives'

If someone who is a 'liable relative' (see below) makes maintenance payments to you which are not child support maintenance (see p110) these are dealt with in a special way.[68] For the rules about child support maintenance, see p120.

How such a payment affects your benefit depends on whether it:

- counts as a 'liable relative payment' – either:
  - a regular payment – known as a 'periodical payment' (see p122); *or*
  - a lump sum – in one go or by instalments – treated as income (see p125) or capital (see p124); *or*
- does not count as a 'liable relative payment' (see p126).

You and your solicitor should look at these rules carefully *before* negotiating payments from your former partner.

Liable relative payments

Most payments by 'liable relatives' (see below) count as liable relative payments. They are usually treated as income and are taken into account fully to reduce your IS (see pp122 and 125). If you are receiving IS, it is usually not a good idea to have a lump sum instead of periodical payments (see p122). This is because a lump sum is usually treated as income (see p125) at a sufficiently high level to disqualify you from benefit altogether even if the amount is well below the usual capital limit (see p415).

For information about lump sums which can be treated as capital, see p124. For information about payments which do not count as liable relative payments, see p126. Some of these do not affect your benefit (see p126).

If you are on FC/DWA, see p398.

Unless it is a payment that does not count (see p126) payments from the following people (known as **'liable relatives'**) count as liable relative payments:[69]

- a husband or wife. This includes one from whom you are separated or divorced;

- a parent of a child or young person under 19 for whom you are claiming (this could include a step-parent);
- a parent of a young person under 19 who is claiming IS in her/his own right (this could include a step-parent);
- a person who has been living with and maintaining a child or young person under 19 or maintaining a young person under 19 who is claiming IS in her/his own right and can therefore reasonably be treated as her/his father;
- if you are a 'person from abroad', a sponsor who has given an undertaking to support you financially (see p85).

There are special rules about how payments to you or to someone else on your behalf by one of the people above are taken into account (see below and pp124 and 125).

However, it is important to note that not all of them are legally 'liable to maintain' you (see p106). The Secretary of State can only pursue those who are liable to maintain you (see p107).

Periodical payments

Periodical payments are any of the following payments made by 'liable relatives' (see p121):[70]

- any payment made, or due to be made, regularly, whether voluntarily or under a court order or other formal agreement;
- any other small payment no higher than your weekly IS;
- any payment made instead of one or more regular payments due under an agreement (whether formal or voluntary), either as payment in advance or arrears. This does not include any arrears due before the beginning of your entitlement to IS (see p124).

Periodical payments which are received on time are each spread over a period equal to the interval between them – ie, monthly payments are spread over a month. Payments are converted to a weekly amount – ie, they are multiplied by 12 and divided by 52 to produce a weekly income figure.[71]

Arrears of periodical payments due during your claim

When a payment arrives during a claim and it includes a lump sum for arrears (or in advance), the payment is spread over a period calculated by dividing it by the weekly amount of maintenance you should have received.[72]

Example

Tia should receive maintenance of £80 a month. It is not paid for three months and she then receives £200.

£80 a month is treated as producing a weekly income of:

$$\frac{£80 \times 12}{52} = £18.46$$

The £200 is taken into account for:

$$\frac{200}{18.46} = 10.83 \text{weeks}$$

Tia is assumed to have an income of £18.46 for the next 10 weeks and six days. The maintenance payments due are still two weeks and one day in arrears (£40).

If a payment is specifically identified as being arrears of maintenance for a particular period, the Benefits Agency can:

- take it into account for a forward period from the week you report you have received it; *or*
- attribute it to the past period which it was intended to cover, unless it is 'more practicable' to choose a later week.[73] In this case the Secretary of State can recover the full amount of extra benefit paid to you while maintenance was not being received.[74] (This can still be done when you receive a payment after your claim ends which is for arrears of maintenance that should have been paid while you were still claiming.)

It is important to work out how you would be better-off financially. You should then argue for the payment to be spread over whichever period is more advantageous to you. This will depend on the amount of IS you would otherwise receive, the amount of the payment and whether any other periodical payments (see p122) are being made. You should appeal if your argument is not accepted.

Examples

Connie should have been receiving maintenance at the rate of £25 a week. Her husband misses eight weeks and she has to claim IS at the rate of £15 a week to top up her part-time earnings. When she reduces her hours her entitlement to IS increases to £30 a week. Then her husband pays her eight weeks arrears of maintenance (£200).

The Benefits Agency might try to take the maintenance into account for eight weeks at the rate of £25 a week from the date it is paid to Connie. If it does this, she loses £200 (£25 × 8 weeks).

Connie argues that the maintenance should be attributed to the eight-week period it was intended to cover. The Benefits Agency can then recover the IS she was paid for that period. She says that she will pay the Benefits Agency what she owes out of the arrears of maintenance. This is a very good case for arguing that it is not 'more practicable' to spread the payment forwards rather than over the past period. She loses £120 (£15 × 8 weeks).

Gwen is in the exact same position as Connie. However, when her husband paid her arrears of maintenance of £200, he also started making regular maintenance payments. She is better off having the payment of arrears spread forwards from the date of payment. The new maintenance payments of £25 a week reduce her IS to £5 a week (£30 − 25). If the Benefits Agency takes the arrears into account for eight weeks from the date it is paid to Gwen, she only loses £40 (£5 × 8 weeks).

Arrears of periodical payments due before your claim

If arrears of maintenance are paid for a period before the date of your claim they do not count as periodical payments (see p122).[75] The Benefits Agency deals with such payments as lump sums treated as income (see p125). This means that they spread them over a future period (see p125). You should try to argue that this is wrong and that such payments should be treated as capital. The benefit rules do not exclude arrears from the definition of periodical payments just to have them brought back into the calculation in this way. Any other interpretation is unfair and gives the Secretary of State an unwarranted windfall at your expense.[76] It is also contrary to the rule for arrears of child support maintenance (see p121).

Lump sum payments treated as capital

If a 'liable relative' (see p121) is already paying you periodical payments (see p122) equal to:

- your IS if the payments include payments for you; *or*
- your child's applicable amount and any family premium if the payments are only for a child, *then*

a lump sum payment from her/him counts as capital. [77]

If the periodical payments stop or fall below the level shown above, what is left of the lump sum is taken into account as income (see p125).[78] Lump sum payments that count as capital do not affect your IS unless they take your capital over £3,000 (£10,000 if you live in a residential care or nursing home). See Chapter 20 for more information about the capital rules.

Lump sum payments treated as income

Unless they do not count as liable relative payments (see p121) or are lump sums treated as capital (see p124), lump sums are treated as income.[79] They are spread over a period so as to disqualify you from IS for as long as possible.

The lump sum is treated as producing a weekly income (see below). You are then disqualified from getting IS for a period beginning on the first day of the benefit week in which the payment is received and lasting for a number of weeks calculated by dividing the amount of the payment by the weekly income. The period can start in a later week if that is more practical.[80]

If you are **not receiving periodical payments** (see p122), the lump sum is treated as producing a weekly income equal to:[81]

* if the lump sum is for you or for you and any children, your IS plus £2;
* if the lump sum is just for a child or children, the personal allowance for you and each child for whom you get maintenance, any disabled child premium or family premium, and any carer's premium if it is paid because you are caring for a disabled child for whom you receive maintenance. However, if your IS entitlement plus £2 would be less than this amount (eg, because you had other income), the lower amount is used. This means that the lump sum disqualifies you from IS for a longer period.

If you are **also receiving periodical payments** (see p122), the lump sum is treated as producing a weekly income equal to the difference between the periodical payment and:[82]

* the amount of IS plus £2 which would be paid if you did not get the periodical payment when it is paid for you alone or for you and your children;
* the child's personal allowance plus family premium if the periodical payment is just for a child.

If the periodical payments are varied or stop, the calculation is done again taking the balance of the lump sum into account.[83]

Example
Fiona receives a lump sum of £2,000 from her husband. Her IS is £48. Under the rules, the lump sum is treated as producing a weekly income of £50. She does not receive IS for 40 weeks (£2,000 divided by £50 = 40 weeks).

If you receive a lump sum which is treated as income, and are disqualified from receiving IS under the rules described above, you should ask the Benefits Agency to recalculate the period of your disqualification whenever:

• your circumstances change so that your entitlement to IS would be higher; *or*
• benefit rates increase.

Arrears of periodical payments due before your claim are often treated as described above so as to disqualify you from benefit. However, you should try to argue that that is wrong (see p124).

Payments that do not count as liable relative payments

Certain types of payment from 'liable relatives' (see p121) do not count as liable relative payments.[84] They are therefore dealt with under the normal income and capital rules (see Chapters 19 and 20) and you are usually better off. You should ensure that your solicitor takes account of this in negotiating payments with your former partner. For example:

• some payments can be disregarded as income or capital (see pp408 and 421 for more information about disregarded income and capital);
• some payments made to someone else for the benefit of you or a member of your family, or paid to you or a member of the family to pay to someone else (see p127), do not count as your income or capital (see pp411 and 428 for more information about notional income and notional capital which does not affect your IS).

If you receive a payment which does not count as a liable relative payment (see below), it is usually better if it can be treated as capital. If it is treated as capital it does not affect your benefit if it does not take your capital over £3,000 (£10,000 if you live in a residential care or nursing home). If the payment is more than the capital limit (£8,000 – £16,000 if you live in a residential or nursing home – see p415), you will not receive any benefit whether it is capital or a lump sum treated as income (see p125), but you might be able to reclaim sooner if it is capital.

The following types of payment from 'liable relatives' (see p121) do not count as liable relative payments:[85]

• any payment arising from a 'disposition of property' (see p127) in consequence of your separation, divorce or the nullity of your marriage;
• any gifts not exceeding £250 in any period of 52 weeks (and not so regular as to amount to periodical payments – see p122);

- payments made after the liable relative has died;
- any payment in kind;
- any payment made to someone else for the benefit of you or a member of your family (such as mortgage capital payments), or paid to you or a member of your family to pay to someone else, which it is unreasonable to take into account – you can appeal to a tribunal which may take a different view from the adjudication officer about what is reasonable;
- any boarding school fees (but see p374);
- any payment to, or for, a child or young person who does not count as a member of your household;
- money from a liable relative which has already been taken into account under a previous claim, or which has already been recovered out of overpaid IS;
- any payment which you have used before the adjudication officer makes her/his decision provided that you did not use it for the purpose of gaining entitlement to IS. It should not be taken into account if you have used it to clear debts such as your solicitor's bill.

'Disposition of property'

Any payment arising from a 'disposition of property' does not count as a liable relative payment (see p126). It is therefore vital to distinguish between payments arising from a disposition of property and those that are not. 'Property' is not confined to houses and land, but includes any asset such as the contents of your former home or a building society account. There is a 'disposition' when those contents are divided up or your former partner buys out your interest.[86] Therefore, any lump sum which is paid in settlement of a claim to a share in any property does not count as a liable relative payment. It is only those lump sums which are paid instead of income which are liable to be treated as income.[87] It is important to take this into account in any negotiations with your former partner. You should make sure your solicitor knows about this rule.

It is best that court orders are drawn up to make it clear that any lump sum is in settlement of a claim to an interest in property. However, this is not essential and the Benefits Agency should accept a letter from your solicitor explaining why a lump sum was asked for and agreed.

Note that the proceeds of sale of your former home may be disregarded altogether for a period of time (see p422). Other capital, such as the home itself and its contents, may also be disregarded (see p421). There is therefore an advantage, while you are on benefit, to ask for a greater share of the home and accept less in the way of capital or income which would be taken into account to reduce your benefit.

CHAPTER SEVEN

Claims, reviews and getting paid

This chapter is about how income support is administered. It covers:
1. Claims (below)
2. Decisions and reviews (p137)
3. Payments of benefit (p144)
4. Overpayments and fraud (p156)
5. Complaints about administration (p165)

1. CLAIMS

To be entitled to income support (IS), you must make a claim.[1] Claims are usually dealt with by your local branch office and this is where your claim should go. See p129 for information about the claim form and the information you must provide. You can obtain leaflets and information there and ask a benefit adviser to give advice and help with claims. S/he has access to your computerised records.

London claimants have their claims dealt with by social security centres set up to deal with work which does not require face-to-face contact with the public. There are three centres, in Glasgow, Belfast and Ashton-in-Makerfield. Although the benefit centres decide your claim, you should still use your branch office to make initial claims or if you have any queries about your claim.

Who should claim?

If you are a single person, a lone parent or one of a lesbian or gay couple, you claim on your own behalf. If you are a heterosexual couple you must choose which one of you will claim for you both (see p347). However, if you are a member of a couple claiming backdated IS after one of you is awarded refugee status (see p79), the claim must be made by the refugee.[2] Where you have a choice about who can claim and you cannot agree, the Secretary of State decides.[3]

You can change which partner claims, provided the partner previously claiming is agreeable.[4] But if you get transitional protection because you used to get supplementary benefit, you lose this if you swap. It can be worth swapping who claims, for example, if:

- it would entitle you to a disability premium (see p362);
- one of you is about to go abroad or otherwise lose entitlement – eg, become a student;
- one of you fits into one of the groups of people who can claim IS but not the other (see p10). However, you should both seek advice about how to protect your national insurance record;
- one of you is working less than 16 hours a week and the other is working between 16 and 24 hours a week (see p13 for what counts as working full time). In this case, between you might be able to choose to claim family credit, disability working allowance or earnings top-up or IS (see p59). However, you should seek advice about how you would be better-off financially.

You might be able to choose whether to claim IS or income-based jobseeker's allowance. See p58 for further information.

Appointees

The Secretary of State can authorise an 'appointee' to act on your behalf if you cannot claim for yourself – eg, you are mentally ill or suffering from senile dementia.[5] If this happens, the appointee takes on all your responsibilities as a claimant. Normally this would only apply from the date the appointment is agreed, but if someone acts on your behalf before becoming your official appointee her/his actions can be validated in retrospect by her/his appointment.[6] Someone can become an appointee by applying in writing to the Benefits Agency. S/he must be over 18.

If you are an appointee for a claimant who dies, you must re-apply for appointee status in order to settle any outstanding benefit matters.[7] An executor under a will can also pursue an outstanding claim or appeal on behalf of a deceased claimant even if the decision was made before the formal grant of probate.[8]

How to claim

A claim for IS must be in writing and on the appropriate form,[9] which is free of charge.[10] Get form SP1 (for pensioners) or A1 (other claimants) from your local Benefits Agency office, or by filling in the tear-off slip in leaflet IS1 available from your local post office. The form tells you the address to which it must be sent.

Remember:

- you must fill in the claim form completely and provide any information or evidence required by the Benefits Agency (see p131). You might not count as having made a claim until you do;
- you must usually claim on the first day you want your benefit to start. See p133 for more information about your date of claim and p134 for when your claim can be backdated.

The Benefits Agency will send you an IS claim form if you just telephone your local office, write a letter, have someone contact it on your behalf, or send in the wrong form. You should complete the form and return it to your local office within one month of your initial contact with it. If you do not, you might lose benefit (see p133).

If you want to withdraw or amend your claim, notify the Benefits Agency office before it makes its decision.[11]

The NINO requirement

When you claim IS you may be asked to provide proof of your identity (see p132). In addition you must satisfy what is known as the 'NINO requirement':[12]

- by providing a national insurance number and information or evidence to show that it is yours; *or*
- if you do not know your national insurance number, by providing evidence or information to enable the Benefits Agency to trace it; *or*
- if you do not have a national insurance number, by applying for one to the Contributions Agency and providing enough information and evidence to allow one to be allocated to you.

From 5 October 1998, if you are claiming IS as a couple (see p347), your partner also has to satisfy the NINO requirement unless you claimed for her/him (or are treated as having done so) before that date.[13]

Completing the claim form

It is your responsibility to complete your claim form fully and to produce information and evidence to verify your claim.[14] This is known as the 'onus of proof rule'. See p131 for the information you can be asked to provide.

If you do not fill in the form properly or provide all the information and evidence required, the Benefits Agency will notify you that your claim is defective and contact you to put things right. It might telephone or write to you or even visit you to get the information or evidence. But it might simply return your claim form. You should provide the information or evidence or complete the form and return it to your local office within one month of your initial contact with it (or that of someone contacting the Benefits Agency on your behalf). If you do not, you might lose benefit (see p133).

You are exempt from the 'onus of proof' rule if:[15]

- you could not complete the form or get the information or evidence required because of a physical, mental, learning or communication difficulty. You must show that it is not 'reasonably practicable' for someone to help you complete the form or get the proof on your behalf; *or*
- the information or evidence required does not exist; *or*
- you could not get the information or evidence required without serious risk of physical or mental harm. You must show that it is not 'reasonably practicable' to get it in another way; *or*
- you could only get the information or evidence required from a third party and it is not 'reasonably practicable' to get it from her/him; *or*
- the Secretary of State thinks sufficient proof has been provided to show that you are not entitled to IS – eg, because your capital is too high, so it would be inappropriate to require further proof.

If you are unable to complete your claim form or provide required information or evidence for one of the reasons listed above, you should give your local office notice of this as soon as possible, ideally on the claim form provided. The Benefits Agency says this must be done within one month of when you first contacted it. Explain your circumstances fully. You can provide supporting letters, for example, from a social worker or a solicitor. If the Benefits Agency accepts you are exempt from the 'onus of proof rule', it can help you to fill in the form or give you longer to complete it or collect evidence or information on your behalf.

Information to support your claim

Besides proof of your identity and a national insurance number (see pp132 and 130), you can be asked to supply any 'certificates, documents, information or evidence' considered relevant to your claim or to an issue arising from your claim.[16] It is very important that you provide any information or evidence required. Until you do, you might not count as having made a claim and you could lose benefit (see p133).

Currently you are asked for:

- payslips;
- proof of income – eg, pensions, war widow's pension or other money coming in;
- proof of savings over £2,500;

- proof of any payments from a credit insurance policy;
- details of payments you receive on ceasing work – eg, redundancy payments, lump sum payments or holiday pay;
- proof of the service charges and ground rent you pay;
- if you are claiming because you are incapable of work, an SC1 form;
- if you or your partner are 60 or over, details of any personal pension scheme or retirement annuity contract which you have taken out. Your pension fundholder may also be asked to give details of your pension rights.[17]

If you have a mortgage, you are given form MI12 with your IS claim form. Give this to your lender, who will provide details about your mortgage and return the form to the Benefits Agency. Your lender is also required to notify the Benefits Agency of any changes to the amount you owe or the interest payable during your claim. If you have this information you must also advise the Benefits Agency just in case your lender fails to do so. Make sure the Benefits Agency takes this information into account so you are not overpaid IS (see p157).

If you are asked to provide information which you do not have, ask what other evidence would be accepted. Press the Benefits Agency to be clear about what is required and why, and complain if you feel that any requests for information are unreasonable (see p165).

If it is not possible to assess your housing costs accurately or your entitlement to severe disability premium the adjudication officer can exclude these from your IS until they can be calculated.[18]

Proof of identity

The Benefits Agency might ask you to produce documents or evidence that help to prove your identity. This could be a passport, a national identity card issued by an EU member state, or a letter issued by the Home Office acknowledging your application for asylum (known as a SAL). However, there are many things that can help you to prove who you are. Examples include your birth certificate, full driving licence or even paid fuel or telephone bills. Remember:

- you should not be refused benefit simply because you do not have any documents, especially where it is unreasonable for you to have or obtain them;
- it is important to tell the Benefits Agency about any other people who can confirm what you have told it – eg, your solicitor or other representative, or a support group or official organisation.

In some cases the Benefits Agency may refuse to accept evidence that you are who you say you are. Many travellers and Irish claimants find that the evidence they provide is simply not accepted as genuine – eg, there is suspicion about the validity of birth certificates. Asylum-seekers and Black people may also face hostility and mistrust when claiming. Where, for example, you have had to use forged papers to flee from persecution, the Benefits Agency might assume you are making a fraudulent claim. Press it to be clear about what is required and why, and complain if you feel any requests for information are unreasonable (see p165). You may also wish to approach your local race equality council if you feel that you have suffered racial discrimination.

Your date of claim

You are usually not entitled to IS for any day before your 'date of claim'.[19] However, in some cases you can claim before you qualify (see below) and sometimes your date of claim can be backdated (see p134). If you want this to be done you should make this clear on your claim form. Your **date of claim** is usually the earliest of:[20]

- the date you first contact a benefit office (eg, you ask to claim IS by telephone or letter) or someone does this on your behalf so long as a fully completed form and all the information and evidence required (see p130) are provided within one month; *or*
- the date your fully completed claim form and all the information and evidence required (see p130) are received in the benefit office.

Something counts as being received in the benefit office even if it is a day on which the office is closed.[21] If you send something by post it should be accepted as having been delivered unless it is proved not to have been. However, you will have to persuade the adjudication officer that you did post it.[22]

You can claim up to three months before you qualify,[23] thus giving the Benefits Agency time to ensure you receive benefit as soon as you are entitled. This can be useful if you know you are going to qualify – eg, you are due to come out of hospital or a care home. In this case, your date of claim is the date you qualify.[24]

You might not be entitled to IS currently, but would be once you or a member of your family become entitled to another benefit. You should make your claim for IS at the same time as the claim for the other benefit. If you are awarded IS, you might be entitled to a higher rate once the outcome of the claim for the other benefit is known (see p143). If you are not awarded IS initially you should see p143 and seek advice.

If you claim family credit (FC) or disability working allowance (DWA) when you should have claimed IS, the day you claimed FC or DWA counts as your date of claim for IS. However, you must:[25]

- have been refused FC or DWA because neither you nor your partner are in full-time work (see p13); *and*
- claim IS within 14 days of the decision refusing your claim.

You can ask for your claim to start on a later date, for example, where you have just finished work and have earnings that will be taken into account for a certain period of time (see p384).

If you are claiming backdated IS because you have been awarded refugee status, see p78.

Backdating claims

If you want to get IS for a period before your date of claim (see p133), your claim can be backdated:

- for up to one month if the Secretary of State decides there are good administrative reasons (see p135);
- for up to three months if you can show that it was not reasonable to expect you to claim before you did and your delay was for one of the specified reasons on p135.

If you want your claim to be backdated you must ask for this to happen or the Benefits Agency will not consider it.[26]

If you are claiming backdated IS after you are awarded refugee status these rules do not apply (see p78).[27]

If you claimed FC or DWA when you should have claimed IS, see above.

Note 1: The rules about backdating of claims changed on 7 April 1997. If you claimed backdated IS before that date, the old, more favourable, rules apply (see pp126-27 of the *National Welfare Benefits Handbook*, 1996/97 edn).

Note 2: The Government intends to limit backdating of IS to one month when the new Social Security Bill (see Appendix 2) becomes law. This is likely to be June 1998. The DSS says the situations in which your claim can be backdated are likely to be similar to those described on p135.

One month backdating – for good administrative reasons

The Secretary of State can backdate your claim for up to one month, but only if one of the following applies:[28]

- your claim is late because the office where you are supposed to claim was closed and there were no other arrangements for claims to be made;
- you could not get to the Benefit Office due to difficulties with the type of transport you normally use and there was no reasonable alternative;
- there were adverse postal conditions – eg, bad weather or a postal strike;
- you stopped getting another benefit but were not informed before your entitlement ceased so you could not claim IS in time;
- you claimed IS in your own right within one month of separating from your partner;
- a close relative of yours died in the month before your claim. Close relative in these circumstances means your partner, parent, son, daughter, brother or sister.

Three months backdating – for other specified reasons

Your claim can be backdated for up to three months if you can show that it was not reasonable to expect you to claim earlier than you did for one of the following specified reasons:[29]

- you have learning, language or literacy difficulties *or* are deaf or blind *or* were sick or disabled *or* were caring for someone who is sick or disabled *or* were dealing with a domestic emergency which affected you *and* it was not 'reasonably practicable' for you to get help to make your claim from anyone else;
- you were given information by an officer of the Department of Social Security or the Department for Education and Employment and as a result thought you were not entitled to benefit;
- you were given advice in writing by a CAB or other advice worker, a solicitor or other professional adviser (eg, an accountant), a doctor or a local authority and as a result thought you were not entitled to benefit;
- you or your partner were given written information about your income or capital by your employer or former employer or a bank or building society and as a result you thought you were not entitled to benefit;
- you could not get to the office because of bad weather.

You might be paid less than three months' arrears if you claim because of a new interpretation of the law.[30]

The rules on backdating are very strict. If you are claiming IS late, it is important to explain why. Provide evidence or information that backs this up, for example, a copy of the letter from your adviser or information from your employer which misled you (see p135). If you have been misled, misinformed or insufficiently informed by an officer of the DSS, explain how and when this happened and where possible, give the name and a description of the officer concerned. Where relevant, you should explain why there is no one else who could help you make your claim.

If you are prevented from receiving benefit because your claim was more than three months late due to an error on the part of the Benefits Agency, you should try to persuade the Benefits Agency to meet its moral obligation and make an *ex gratia* payment or extra-statutory payment to you, as compensation (see p148). To do this, simply write to your Benefits Agency office and ask. The intervention of an MP or the Ombudsman (see p166) may help in these circumstances.

If a person has been formally appointed by a court or the Secretary of State to act on your behalf, it is the appointee not you who must show that it was not reasonable to expect her/him to claim sooner than s/he did for one of the reasons listed above.[31] If someone is informally acting on your behalf, you must show this. You must also show that it was reasonable for you to delegate responsibility for your claim and that you took care to supervise the person helping you.[32]

Note: The rules about backdating of claims changed on 7 April 1997. If you claimed backdated IS before that date, you might be able to get up to 12 months' arrears (see pp126–27 of the *National Welfare Benefits Handbook*, 1996/97 edn).

Changes of circumstance after you claim

You may be on benefit for quite a long time, during which your circumstances may change. You must inform the benefit office, in writing, of any change which might affect the amount of, or your right to, benefit.[33] Keep a copy of the letter you send reporting such changes. The Benefits Agency can accept notification by some other method (ie, by telephone), but this is not always acted on so it is best to do it in writing.

If you fail to report a change and, as a result, you receive too much benefit, the Benefits Agency might take steps to recover the overpayment (see p157) or even treat this as fraud (see p164).

2. DECISIONS AND REVIEWS

It is important to know who makes the decision on any particular question in your claim because that determines how you challenge it if you disagree.

Most decisions are made by an **adjudication officer** at the Benefits Agency office where you claimed IS.[34]

An adjudication officer at the Child Benefit Centre may advise:

• whether you are in 'relevant education' (see p17).

While an adjudication officer elsewhere is being consulted on your case, it will be assumed s/he has decided against you and IS will be refused in the meantime.[35]

If you think an adjudication officer's decision is wrong you can:

• seek a review of the decision (see p140);
• appeal against the decision (see Chapter 8).

Decisions made by the **Secretary of State** are:

• whether to accept a claim made other than on the approved form;
• whether a claim for one benefit can be treated instead of, or in addition to, a claim for another benefit;[36]
• whether to demand recovery of an overpayment, and the amount of weekly deductions (subject to the maximum, see p162);
• whether to suspend benefit pending determination of a question on review or appeal;
• whether to take action against people who are liable to maintain claimants (see p106);
• whether to appoint a person as an appointee;
• who should be the claimant when a couple are unable to decide;
• whether to issue or replace giros and order books and how IS should be paid;
• whether to pay an interim payment;
• whether a school or college is a 'recognised educational establishment';
• circumstances in which a claim is to be treated as withdrawn.

If you think a Secretary of State's decision is wrong you can:

• ask her/him to use her/his discretion to review the decision;
• seek advice about whether you can apply for Judicial Review (see p185).

You should be notified in writing of the decision on your claim unless the decision is to pay you in cash, or your benefit is being stopped and it is reasonable not to give you a written decision.[37] Sometimes a decision is unclear or difficult to understand or you may simply want to know the reasons for it. To get these, write to the appropriate office within three months of that decision,[38] or seek independent advice. If you disagree with the decision, you can seek a review (see p140). You can also appeal but must do this within three months (see p168). If you appeal against an adjudication officer's decision (see Chapter 8) the papers you receive will give the full background to the decision.

You should automatically receive a letter showing how your benefit has been worked out.[39] You can ask for a more detailed breakdown. Check the details on this form.

Note: A new Social Security Bill is due to become law in June 1998. Provisions which will radically alter the system for decision making, reviews and appeals will be brought in from April 1999. See Appendix 2 for more information.

Contacting benefit offices

Writing to your office is nearly always the best way to have your case dealt with. It ensures there is a permanent record of what you said and enables you to cover all the points you want to make clearly. Always put your name, address, the date and your national insurance number at the top of your letter. If possible, make a copy of it. You should also keep all letters and forms sent to you. Such a record may help you or your adviser to work out later whether any decision can be challenged.

The Benefits Agency says it will reply to all letters within 10 working days (seven days if it is a letter of complaint). If you are sent a partial reply you should be told how long it will be before your letter can be fully answered. The person writing to you should give their name and telephone number.

If there is a delay in getting a reply, you can telephone to find out why, but it may be better to write a short reminder and only telephone if you still receive no response.

On occasion, **telephoning your benefit office** may be necessary. If you are a London claimant, try your branch office first. If you have to ring the centre in Belfast, Glasgow or Ashton-in-Makerfield, you are only charged the local rate. If you telephone your office:

- ask for the income support section;
- be ready to give your surname and national insurance number;
- try to get the name, title and telephone extension number of the person you speak to as this may be useful in the future;

- make a brief note of what is said, together with the date. If the information is important, follow up the telephone call with a letter confirming what the Benefits Agency said so that any misunderstanding can be cleared up. Offices are usually reluctant to write merely to confirm a telephone conversation.

Visiting your office enables you to have a detailed conversation with an officer. Check the opening times first. An appointment can usually be arranged by telephone. You should expect the receptionist to see you within 10 minutes. However, at busy times you should not have to wait more than 30 minutes. Be prepared to wait longer if you need to see someone else. The receptionist should tell you how long it is likely to take. If you want a private interview, this should be provided. Staff you see will wear name badges so you can make a note of their names. Remember:

- to take any documents with you which may be relevant otherwise you may be asked to make a second visit to provide the additional information;
- to follow up any important meeting with a letter confirming the points you or the Benefits Agency have made or ask the office to confirm in writing any advice to you;
- that you can take a friend or relative with you, not only for moral support, but also as a witness to what is said.

If you cannot get to the office (eg, because of your age, health or a disability) an officer may be able to make a **home visit** if your case cannot be dealt with by telephone. Ask for a visit if you need one. If you are refused and are not satisfied with the explanation, ask to speak to a supervisor or the customer care manager.

If you are a London claimant, you can go to your local branch office to discuss your claim. The staff will contact the social security centre in Belfast, Glasgow or Ashton-in-Makerfield if necessary.

Delays

It is very unlikely that you will get an immediate decision on your claim because the facts need to be checked and your benefit calculated. However, an adjudication officer should decide a claim for IS within 14 days 'so far as is practicable'.[40]

If you have been waiting more than 14 days for a decision, contact the benefit office. First, check that your claim has been received. If it has not, let the office have a copy of your claim or fill out a new form and refer them to the claim form you sent in earlier.

If your claim has been received but not dealt with, ask for an explanation. If you are not satisfied with the explanation for the delay, make a complaint (see p165). The Benefits Agency has target times for dealing with claims and these are displayed in local offices. The target time for IS claims is five working days.

In addition to taking the steps already described, you should ask the office to make interim payments to you while you wait for the decision (see p145). You may also be able to obtain a crisis loan (see p479).

Reviews

An adjudication officer can review a decision of an adjudication officer, social security appeal tribunal (SSAT), or social security commissioner if there are grounds for review (see p141).[41] This can be done even if the original decision was made a long time ago.

You can ask for a review or the adjudication officer may decide that one is necessary. The person who wants the review is the one who has to show there are grounds (see p141).[42] It is best to ask for a review in writing giving the reasons why you think one should take place. Claims for benefit or questions you ask about your entitlement can be treated as requests for a review.[43]

Following a review, the original decision may be changed either to increase *or* decrease the amount of your IS *or* remove entitlement to benefit altogether. You should seek advice before you seek a review if you are concerned about what could happen in your case. If a review decision does not give you all that you wanted, you can try to appeal against the original decision[44] (but if the original decision was made more than three months ago see p168).

Awards of IS are made for an indefinite period. If you cease to satisfy the conditions of entitlement, the decision awarding you benefit must be reviewed if one of the grounds for review applies (see p141).[45] This is the case even where the amount of benefit to which you are entitled is simply reduced or increased – eg, where you are claiming IS because you are sick but you then recover and have to claim on the basis that you are a lone parent.

Note: A new Social Security Bill is due to become law in June 1998. Provisions which will radically alter the system for decision making, reviews and appeals will be brought in from April 1999. See Appendix 2 for more information.

The grounds for review

A decision may only be reviewed if:[46]

- **There was a mistake about the facts of your case or it was made in ignorance of relevant facts.** If a decision is reviewed on this ground, the review decision takes effect from the beginning of the period covered by the original decision.
- The original decision was made by an adjudication officer (not a tribunal or commissioner) and was **legally wrong.** This is what is known as an 'error of law' (see p181).
- **Your circumstances have changed since the original decision** or it is anticipated that they will do so and this means the decision is no longer correct. A decision can only be reviewed on this basis if you are currently entitled to benefit and your situation changes. If you were correctly refused IS in the past and your circumstances are now different, you must make a fresh claim.[47] An amendment to the law counts as a change of circumstances, but a decision of a court or commissioner that the law has been wrongly interpreted does not.[48] A new medical opinion is not a change of circumstances,[49] but a medical opinion following an examination might give evidence of such a change.[50] Some situations never count as a change of circumstance – the repayment of a student loan, and your absence from a nursing or residential care home for less than a week.[51]

  If a decision is reviewed on this ground, the review decision takes effect from the first day of the week in which the change occurs if you are paid in arrears, or the week following the change if you are paid in advance (unless the change occurs on the first day of your benefit week in which case it is that day).[52]
- The original decision on your claim was based on a **Secretary of State's decision** which has itself now been changed.

If a decision is reviewed in your favour, you receive arrears (but see p142 for how far back your arrears can be paid). If it is not you may have been overpaid and the adjudication officer decides whether or not to recover the overpayment (see p157). There is no limit on how far back an overpayment can be recovered.

After an adjudication officer carries out a review s/he makes a new decision. S/he can decide:

- there are no grounds for a review (see above); *or*
- there are grounds for review (see above), but the original decision was correct; *or*
- there are grounds for review (see above) and the original decision should be changed.

If you do not agree with the new decision, you can appeal against it (see p167). This can be useful if you did not appeal against the original decision in time and cannot make a late appeal (see p169). Where the adjudication officer says there are no grounds for a review, you must show why there are, as well as give your reasons for disputing the original decision.

In an appeal the tribunal must identify which decision is to be reviewed, establish whether there are grounds for review and from what date, and then, if you are entitled to benefit, check if the limitations on backdating restrict the arrears which can be paid (see below).[53]

Although in an appeal the tribunal is usually considering whether the adjudication officer had grounds to review a decision, it is possible for them to review a decision themselves if new facts, of which the adjudication officer was unaware but which give grounds for review, come to light during the hearing.[54] It is not necessary for them to adjourn the hearing and refer the matter back to the adjudication officer, though they may choose to do this instead.

A review can be a quicker and simpler way to challenge a decision with which you disagree than an appeal. It can also be a way of getting round the three-month time limit for appeals (see p168). But see p144 if you are seeking a review because you think a test case applies to you.

Payment of arrears of benefit on review

If the adjudication officer agrees to change a decision in your favour, you can usually get arrears of benefit going back one month before the date you requested a review, or if you did not request a review, from the date the review took place.[55] It is important to make it clear that you want payment for the past period. You can sometimes get more than one month's arrears (see below).

If you were underpaid benefit because of a clear error by the DSS/ Benefits Agency you could apply for compensation as well as getting arrears owed to you (see p148).

Note: The rules about payment of arrears of benefit changed on 7 April 1997. If you requested a review before that date, the old, more favourable, rules apply (see pp131-33 of the *National Welfare Benefits Handbook*, 1996/97 edn).

More than one month's backdating

You can get more than one month's backdating if:

• the ground for review was that the decision was legally wrong (see p141) because the adjudication officer overlooked or misinterpreted part of an Act, Order, regulation, or decision of a commissioner or court when deciding your claim; [56]

- the ground for review was ignorance of, or mistake about, the facts (see p141) and you can show that the decision is being changed because:[57]

- there is specific evidence which the adjudication officer (or SSAT) who originally decided the claim had, but which they failed to take into account even though it was relevant. This applies even if the evidence does not conclusively prove your entitlement. So long as it raised a strong possibility that you were entitled, it should have been taken into account;[58]

- there is documentary or other written evidence of your entitlement which the DSS, DHSS or Department of Employment had, but failed to give to the adjudication officer (SSAT or commissioner), at the time of the earlier decision;

- new evidence has come to light which did not exist earlier and could not have been obtained. This will only apply if you provide this evidence as soon as possible after it is available to you;

- you want your IS to be reviewed because you or a member of your family have become entitled to another benefit or to an increase in its rate, and arrears of that benefit are payable for more than one month.[59] See p346 for who counts as your family. This provision helps you if you did not get certain premiums paid with your IS because of delays in assessing another benefit – eg, where a DLA claim took 18 months to be decided and you have missed out on the severe disability premium for this period. You can only ask for a review if you have claimed IS. It is therefore important to claim IS while you are waiting to hear about your claim for another benefit. If you wait to claim IS until you hear, you can only get arrears if you satisfy the backdating rules on p134.

  Currently you can only get arrears of IS back to the date you or a member of your family are awarded another benefit, or an increase in its rate, if you were on IS while you were waiting to hear about the other benefit. If you claimed IS but were refused, you cannot get the decision refusing you IS revised even though you can now show that you were actually entitled.[60] In this situation, you must make a fresh claim for IS and should do this as soon as possible. CPAG understands the DSS did not intend the rule to operate in this unfair way. You should seek advice. You might also ask for an extra-statutory payment to cover the period before your fresh IS claim;

- your IS is being reviewed to include help with mortgage interest (see p32) or interest on a loan for repairs and improvements (see p36), but only if the review could not take place sooner because your lender did not supply the Benefits Agency with your mortgage details. In this case, you can get up to eight weeks arrears.[61]

If you are trying to get arrears going back several years, it may be difficult to identify the grounds for review, particularly where the Benefits Agency has destroyed old papers relating to your claim. The onus is on you to show that your claim should be reviewed and you cannot simply rely on the Benefits Agency's lack of evidence.[62]

The 'anti-test case' rule

You may get less than one month's backdating if your entitlement is reviewed following a new interpretation of the law by a social security commissioner or court. In this case you get arrears back to the date of the decision by the commissioner or court.[63] This is what is known as the 'anti-test case' rule. This rule only applies if you ask for a review on the grounds that the decision in your case was found to be legally wrong by the decision of the commissioner or court in the test case (and not for some other reason – see p141). In addition, you must have asked for the review after the test case decision.[64] You can avoid the anti-test case rule by applying for a late appeal rather than a review (but see p169). You can do this even if a review has taken place but has not given you all the arrears you are claiming.[65] See the *Rights Guide to Non-Means-Tested Benefits* for more information.

Note: The Government intends to amend the 'anti-test case' rule so it will apply whether you ask for a review before *or* after the test case decision. This is likely to take effect in June 1998. See Appendix 2 for more information about the new Social Security Bill.

3. PAYMENTS OF BENEFIT

The Secretary of State decides how benefit is paid to you.[66] You are paid by giro, benefit order book, or directly into a bank or building society account.[67] It may be possible to be paid cash in certain circumstances.[68] The Government intends to introduce benefit payment cards in the future.

Once you have been awarded benefit you must cash the payment within a year of it being due.[69] This period can be extended if you can show good cause for the delay.[70] However, an order book is only valid for three months and a giro for one month. If you do not cash them within this period you will have to try to get a replacement.

If you are entitled to less than 10 pence a week you are not paid IS at all, unless you are receiving another social security benefit which can be paid with IS. If you are entitled to less than £1 a week the Secretary of State can decide to pay you quarterly in arrears.[71] If your IS includes a fraction of a penny it is rounded up to a full penny if it is more than a half penny. Otherwise the fraction is ignored.[72]

You are paid in advance if you are:[73]

* receiving retirement pension; *or*
* over pension age (60 for a woman, 65 for a man) and not receiving incapacity benefit or severe disablement allowance nor involved in a trade dispute (unless you were receiving IS immediately before the dispute began); *or*
* receiving widows' benefits (but only if you are not providing or required to provide medical evidence of incapacity for work); *or*
* returning to work after a trade dispute.

If you are paid in advance, your entitlement begins on the first pay day of any other social security benefit to which you are entitled (or would be entitled if you had sufficient contributions) following the date of your claim for IS. For example, retirement pension is paid on a Monday. If you claim IS on a Wednesday you are entitled to IS in advance from the following Monday. But if you claim on a Monday you get it from that day.

You are paid in arrears if you are not in one of the above groups.[74] Your entitlement to IS starts from the date of your claim (see p133).[75]

Once your entitlement has been worked out, the Secretary of State decides how often and on which day of the week you are paid[76] unless you are entitled to incapacity benefit, severe disablement allowance, retirement pension or widows' benefits. If you are entitled to one of these (or would be if you satisfied the contribution conditions), you are paid IS on the same day of the week as that other benefit and at the same intervals.[77] If you are incapable of work and not getting incapacity benefit you are paid fortnightly in arrears.

Interim payments

If payment of your IS is delayed you may be in urgent need of money. If this is the case, you can ask for what are known as 'interim payments'.

An interim payment can be made where it seems that you are or may be entitled to IS and where:[78]

* you have claimed IS but not in the correct way (eg, you have filled in the wrong form, or filled in the right form incorrectly or incompletely – see p130) and you cannot put in a correct claim immediately (eg, because the Benefits Agency office is closed); *or*

- you have claimed IS correctly, but it is not possible for the claim or for a review or appeal which relates to it to be dealt with immediately; *or*
- you have been awarded benefit, but it is not possible to pay you immediately other than by means of an interim payment.

However, if your claim is being appealed, an interim payment can only be made if the Secretary of State thinks you are entitled to some benefit. This rule might be invalid in a case involving EC law.[79] If you think this applies to you, you should seek advice.

The decision whether or not to award an interim payment is the Secretary of State's and therefore you cannot appeal to a tribunal if you are refused, though it may be possible to apply for judicial review (see p185). If you are refused an interim payment, contact your MP and see Chapter 24 for whether you can get a crisis loan. You could also try using the emergency service (see p148).

An interim payment can be deducted from any later payment of IS and if it is more than your actual entitlement, the overpayment can be recovered.[80] You should be notified of this in advance, unless the interim payment is made because you have not received child support maintenance. In this case, any overpayment is recovered from the arrears of maintenance rather than your benefit.

Suspension and withholding of payments

The Secretary of State can order payment of your IS to be *suspended* if:

- **a question has arisen about your entitlement to benefit.**[81] In this case, all or part of the benefit due to you is suspended pending a review or appeal of the decision about your entitlement. For example, if you are being paid IS but it is thought that you are in full-time work, your benefit may be suspended while information is gathered about the true situation;
- **it looks as though your IS award should be revised;**[82]
- **you are awarded benefit by a tribunal, commissioner or court but the Benefits Agency wants to appeal against that decision.**[83] If this happens, your award can only be suspended for three months after the adjudication officer receives the decision while the Benefits Agency considers an appeal to the Social Security Commissioner or courts. If it decides to appeal, it must notify you in writing within the three months. You will then not be paid until your case is resolved;
- **you are due to be paid arrears of a benefit but you may also have been overpaid.**[84] Your arrears may be withheld in whole or in part while the possible overpayment is investigated.

The Benefits Agency used to suspend your benefit if it was appealing (or considering an appeal) to the courts about someone else's claim, and the issue in the appeal affected your claim. However, this rule was found to be unlawful.[85] However, the Government intends to reinstate the rule when the new Social Security Bill (see Appendix 2) becomes law. This is likely to be June 1998. In the meantime, if your benefit has been suspended in this way you should ask the Benefits Agency to start paying your benefit immediately and to give you what has been withheld so far. You should be given what was withheld even if the appeal about someone else's claim has already been decided. Even if the decision was negative, you should be paid up to the date of that decision. If the Benefits Agency refuses to pay, you should seek advice. Where a tribunal, a commissioner or a court has awarded you benefit, the Benefits Agency can only suspend your benefit if it appeals your case (see p146).[86]

The decision to suspend benefit is made by the Secretary of State and you cannot appeal against it to a tribunal. Your only remedy is judicial review (see p185). You must negotiate to get your benefit reinstated and/or request an interim payment. You should try to persuade the Secretary of State that it is unreasonable to suspend payment of your benefit, particularly if hardship is caused.

Your benefit can be *withheld* if:[87]

- **you fail to provide information in support of your claim** within 28 days of being asked;
- **you do not send in sick notes;**
- there are **doubts about where you are living**.

If you later fulfil these requirements you can be paid any benefit that has been withheld, but you must normally apply within 12 months.[88]

Lost and missing payments

If you lose a giro or order book after you have received it, report the loss immediately to the benefit office by telephone or personal visit and confirm the loss in writing, requesting a replacement at the same time. If your giro is lost or stolen before you have had a chance to cash it, the Secretary of State has a duty to replace it. This applies even if the giro is later cashed by someone else,[89] though you will need to satisfy the Benefits Agency that it was not you who cashed it. You should also report the matter to the police, and note the investigating officer's name and number.

If the benefit office refuses to issue a replacement, or takes too long considering your request, you can take legal action to get the benefit due to you. You cannot appeal to a tribunal if a payment goes missing, but you can sue the Secretary of State in the county court.[90] This can take time, so you may wish to claim a crisis loan to tide you over (see p479).

Before taking legal action you should write to the local Benefits Agency office requesting it to replace the giro within a reasonable time – eg, seven days. Explain that court action will be taken if it does not respond. Keep a copy of the letter.

If the Benefits Agency does not replace your giro or order book, you need to begin proceedings in the local county court. The forms to do this are available from the county court. Complete these and return them to the court. You have to pay a court fee, calculated as a percentage of your unpaid giro. The fee is refundable if you win. The Benefits Agency is allowed time to respond to your summons, but you will almost certainly find that the local Benefits Agency office will replace your giro without the need to proceed to a court hearing. Your court fee is repaid separately by the Benefits Agency Solicitors (see Appendix 3 for address), and you should not withdraw the summons until you have received both a replacement giro and your court fee. If the Benefits Agency refuses to pay benefit for a future period covered by a lost order book, you can take court action in the High Court (see p185).

Emergencies

If you have lost all your money or there has been a similar crisis, it is possible to get help at any time.

Any local police station should have a contact number for Benefits Agency staff on call outside normal office hours. In London there is a special Benefits Agency office open in the evenings and at weekends for emergencies. It is Keyworth House, Keyworth Street, London SE1 (tel: 0171 401 9692).

There will also be a duty social worker who can be contacted via your local social services department or council, or via the police.

Compensation payments

You should expect prompt, courteous and efficient service from Benefits Agency staff dealing with your claim. If you are dissatisfied with the way your claim has been administered you can seek compensation. The Benefits Agency uses a circular, *Financial Redress for Maladministration*, to help it decide when and how much compensation should be paid. The circular is available from the Stationery Office (see Appendix 5).

Benefits Agency errors

Sometimes the Benefits Agency makes mistakes about the amount of your benefit. Also, you might be given incorrect advice or information by the Benefits Agency which means you do not claim in time. Where possible it corrects the mistake by carrying out a review and awarding you the correct benefit (see p140) or by backdating your claim (see p134).

If the procedures for review or backdating do not apply or do not properly compensate you for the effects of the mistake that has occurred, you may claim compensation (known as an *ex gratia* payment). You should ask for a payment equal to the money you have lost, but you could also ask for additional amounts to cover interest on arrears, extra expenses you had to pay out, and to compensate you for any hardship or distress suffered because of the mistake. Payments are discretionary, so you should stress the Benefits Agency error and the fact that you have suffered as a consequence of official negligence, in order to ensure payment. If your loss was as a clear result of incorrect advice or negligence on the part of the Benefits Agency, you may be able to bring a court action for damages. You will need the help of an advice agency or solicitor to do this.

Delays by the Benefits Agency

Benefits Agency offices have target times for dealing with claims, but they are not always able to meet these. If there is a long delay (eg, in assessing your entitlement or paying you benefit) you are entitled to compensation if:[91]

- a significant reason for the delay was Benefits Agency error; *and*
- the amount of benefit involved was more than £100; *and*
- the delay in payment was more than two months (IS), six months (family credit), one month (disability working allowance), five months (social fund funeral payments) or three months (other types of social fund payments; *and;*
- any compensation would be £10 or more.

You are not automatically awarded compensation although the Benefits Agency should automatically consider whether it should be paid where you are owed arrears of benefit. However, you should still write to your local Benefits Agency office and ask. If you do not get a sympathetic response you could ask your MP to write on your behalf, or to take up your case with the Social Security Minister.

Payments to other people

Payment is usually made direct to you but there are some circumstances in which payments can be made to other people or organisations on your behalf.

- If you are unable to manage your own money, your benefit is paid to a person appointed to act on your behalf (see p129).[92]
- If it is in the interests of you, your partner or your children, the Secretary of State can pay your benefit to someone else.[93] For example, if your partner is refusing to support you, all or part of her/his benefit can be paid to you. If you are neglecting your children even though benefit is being paid for them, it might be paid to another person to help look after them.

Mortgage direct payments

When you first claim IS you may not receive help with your housing costs (see p43) and you must meet these costs from other income – eg, a mortgage protection policy. Once you qualify for help with housing costs the amount for mortgage interest is usually paid direct to your lender for each complete week that you are on benefit.[94] The only exceptions to this are where your lender is not covered by, or has opted out of, the mortgage payments scheme.[95] The Benefits Agency should tell you if this is the case and you must pay your own mortgage.

Your housing costs (see p27) are deducted from your total IS entitlement and you get the balance.[96] You have to make up any difference between what the Benefits Agency pays to your lender and the amount you owe them. This could include such things as mortgage capital, non-dependant deductions or a restriction due to excessive housing costs. If you get incapacity benefit, severe disablement allowance or retirement pension paid on the same giro/order book as your IS, deductions can be made from these benefits too. If you do not have enough benefit to meet the full cost, all but 10 pence of your benefit is paid over and you must pay the rest yourself.[97]

Payments are made four-weekly in arrears[98] even if your payments are due on a calendar month basis, so you may appear to be in arrears even though your full mortgage is being met. You might need to explain this to your lender. If the Benefits Agency deducts your housing costs from your IS but fails to pay these to your lender in time and as a result you have to pay interest on arrears that build up or you lose your home, you should seek advice. You might be able to claim compensation.[99]

If you have more than one type of housing cost, deductions for non-dependants (see p39) and certain restrictions for excessive housing costs are apportioned using a formula (see p155).[100]

If you are in mortgage arrears, no amount towards the arrears can be deducted from your benefit if your lender is covered by the mortgage payments scheme (see p150). If you are in this situation, you should seek financial advice. If you are in arrears of other housing costs, see p152.

If an overpayment of mortgage interest is paid to your lender see p157.

Other direct deductions

Amounts can also be deducted from your IS to pay for other housing costs, fuel, water charges, the recovery of social fund loans (see p486), council tax arrears, community charge arrears, child support maintenance (see p118), fines and overpayments (see p162).[101]

Deductions are made at the Benefits Agency office before you receive your regular benefit payment. If you want to have deductions made to help you clear any arrears or debts, ask at the Benefits Agency office dealing with your IS claim. If you disagree with a decision about deductions, you can appeal (see p167).

When can direct deductions be made?[102]

Rent arrears[103]
If you are in arrears with your rent (including any inclusive water, fuel and service charges) while on benefit, an amount can be deducted from your IS and paid direct to your landlord.

'Rent arrears' do not include the amount of any non-dependant deductions (see p270), but can cover any water charges or service charges payable with your rent and not met by housing benefit. Fuel charges included in your rent cannot be covered by direct deductions if they change more than twice a year.

To qualify for direct deductions your rent arrears must amount to at least four times your full weekly rent. If you have not paid your full rent for more than eight weeks, direct deductions can be made automatically if your landlord asks the Benefits Agency to make them.[104] If your arrears relate to a shorter period, deductions can only be made if it is in the 'overriding interests' of your family to do so.[105] In either case the adjudication officer must be satisfied that you are in rent arrears. Even if you are, you can ask her/him not to make direct deductions – eg, where you are claiming compensation from your landlord because of the state of repair of your home.[106] Once your arrears are paid off, direct payments can continue for any fuel and water charges inclusive in your rent.[107]

Housing costs[108]

The IS for your mortgage interest is usually paid direct to your lender (see p150). If this applies to you (or would if your lender had not opted out of the scheme) then the deductions under this provision only cover payments for other types of housing costs (see p27).[109]

If your current IS includes money for such housing costs and you are in debt for these costs (excluding payments for ground rent/feu duty unless paid with your service charges or for a tent[110]), deductions can be made from your benefit both to clear the debt and to meet current payments. Deductions are made if it would be 'in the interests' of you or your family to do so.

You can only qualify for direct deductions if you owe more than half of the annual total of the relevant housing cost. This condition can be waived if it is in the 'overriding interests' of you or your family that deductions start as soon as possible – eg, repossession of your home is imminent.[111]

In the case of mortgage payments, the adjudication officer must be satisfied there are arrears.[112] You must have paid less than eight weeks' worth of full payments in the last 12 weeks. The amount of mortgage interest taken into account is the amount after deductions for non-dependants (see p39).

Residential accommodation charges[113]

If you receive IS, the amount you are paid may cover charges for your accommodation if you live in a residential care or nursing home, or local authority residential accommodation (see p87).

These charges can be met by direct deductions from your benefit if you have failed to budget for the charges from your benefit and it is in your interest that deductions should be made. Even if these conditions do not apply direct payments can be made if you are in a home run by a voluntary organisation for alcoholics or drug addicts.

Water charges[114]

If you get into debt with charges for water and sewerage, direct deductions might be made – 'debt' includes any disconnection, reconnection and legal charges. If you pay your landlord for water with your rent, deductions are made under the arrangements for rent arrears (see p151).[115]

Deductions can be made if you failed to budget and it is in the interests of your family to make deductions.[116] If you get into debt with water charges you should consider making an agreement for direct deductions because the water authority can cut off your water supply if you do not meet your debts and current charges. If you are in debt to two water companies you can only have a deduction for arrears made to one of them at a time. Your debts for water charges should be cleared before your debts for sewerage costs, but the amount paid for current consumption can include both water and sewerage charges.[117]

Fuel debts[118]
If you are in debt, an amount can be deducted from your benefit each week and paid over to the fuel board in instalments – usually once a quarter. This is known as 'fuel direct'. In return, the fuel board agrees not to disconnect you. Deductions can be made where:[119]

- the amount you owe is £50.35 or more (including reconnection or disconnection charges if you have been disconnected); *and*
- you continue to need the fuel supply; *and*
- it is in your interest to have deductions made.

An amount is deducted for the fuel you use each week (your 'current consumption') as well as for the arrears you owe. The amount deducted for current consumption is whatever is necessary to meet your current weekly fuel costs. This is adjusted if the cost increases or decreases. Deductions for current consumption can be continued after the debt has been cleared.[120]

Council tax and community charge arrears[121]
Deductions for council tax or community charge arrears can be made from IS if the local authority gets a liability order from a magistrates' court (in Scotland, a summary warrant or decree from a sheriff's court) and applies to the Benefits Agency for recovery to be made in this way. For community charge purposes, if they want to recover arrears from both partners in a couple the order must be against both of them. Deductions can be made for arrears and any unpaid costs or penalties imposed. Deductions cannot be made for council tax arrears while community charge deductions are being made.

Hostel payments[122]
If you (or your partner) live in a hostel *and* you have claimed housing benefit (HB) to meet your accommodation costs *and* your payments to the hostel cover fuel, meals, water charges, laundry and/or cleaning of your room, part of your benefit can be paid direct to the hostel for these items. You do not have to be in arrears for this to apply. These costs are all items which cannot be covered by HB (see p243) and which you must meet from your IS. Fuel costs are not paid direct if the charge varies according to actual consumption, unless the charge is altered less than three times a year.

Fines, costs and compensation orders[123]

Magistrates' courts (any court in Scotland) can apply to the Benefits Agency for a fine, costs or compensation order to be deducted from your IS. Only one court application can be dealt with at a time – if a second application is made it is not dealt with until the first debt is paid.

Deductions can only be made if you are 18 or over, on IS, and you have defaulted on payments. Payments continue until the debt is paid off, or your IS ceases or is too low to cover the repayments.

Maintenance for children

Deductions can be made from an absent parent's IS as a contribution towards the maintenance of her/his child(ren) – see p118.[124]

How much can be deducted?

Deductions are made to pay off the debt, or current weekly costs or both.[125] Deductions are made from your IS and from any incapacity benefit, retirement pension or severe disablement allowance paid with it in the same giro or order book.[126] You must be left with at least 10 pence. Council tax and community charge arrears can be deducted from IS only.[127]

Type of arrears	Deduction for arrears	Deduction for ongoing cost
Mortgage direct payments*	Nil	Current weekly cost
Housing costs*	£2.55 each housing debt (maximum of £7.65 payable)	Current weekly cost
Rent arrears	£2.55	Nil (met by HB)
Fuel	£2.55 each fuel debt (maximum of £5.10 payable)	Estimated amount of current consumption
Water charges	£2.55	Estimated costs (adjusted every 26 weeks)
Council tax	£2.55	Nil (met by council tax benefit)
Community charge	£2.55 (single person) £3.95 (couple)	Not applicable
Fines	Nil	£2.55
Child maintenance	Nil	£5.10

| Residential accommodation charges | Nil | The accommodation allowance (for those in local authority homes). All but £14.45 of your IS (for those in private or voluntary homes). |
| Hostel charges | Nil | Weekly amount assessed by local authority. |

* If you have more than one type of housing cost and these are not met in full because of a restriction on the amount which can be covered (see p41), or a non-dependant deduction (see p39) the direct payment to meet current weekly costs is reduced as follows:[128] Multiply the amount of the restriction and/or deduction by the amount of the item of housing costs to be paid direct and then divide by the amount of total housing costs. This ensures that such reductions are shared proportionately between different items of housing costs.

More than one debt

Deductions for arrears can be made for more than one debt. See above for what can be deducted. However:

- the maximum deduction that can be made for arrears (excluding community charge arrears) and a contribution towards child maintenance (if you have to make one) is £7.65 a week.[129] If you have more debts and charges than this, see below;
- if deductions of £5.10 are being made for items of a higher priority than child maintenance (see p155), half of the child maintenance deduction will be made – ie, £2.55;
- in the case of fuel, rent arrears, water charges and housing costs arrears (see p151), if the combined cost of deductions for arrears and current consumption is more than 25 per cent of your total applicable amount (see p25) the deductions cannot be made without your consent.[130]

Priority between debts

If you have more debts or charges than can be met within the limits for direct deductions (see above), they are paid in the following order of priority:[131]

1st other IS housing costs
2nd rent arrears (and related charges)
3rd fuel charges

4th   water charges
5th   council tax and community charge arrears
6th   unpaid fines, costs and compensation orders
7th   payments for maintenance of children

If you owe both gas and electricity, the Benefits Agency chooses which one to pay first, depending on your circumstances. If you have been overpaid benefit or given a social fund loan, you may have to repay these too by having deductions from your IS.[132] You should argue that these deductions should take a lower priority. If you have arrears for both council tax and community charge, only one application can be dealt with at a time and the earliest debt should be dealt with first.[133]

4. OVERPAYMENTS AND FRAUD

There are a number of ways that you might be paid too much IS by the Benefits Agency, some of these through no fault of your own. The rules for each type of overpayment spell out if and when you have to repay it.

- If you have been paid too much IS because other income was paid late, see below for information about duplication of payments.
- If too much mortgage interest has been paid direct to your lender, see p157;
- For all other overpayments, see p157.

Duplication of payments

Sometimes you receive too much IS because money which is owing to you does not arrive on time. For example, if you claim child benefit but it is not paid for several weeks, your IS continues at the full rate while you are not actually receiving child benefit. However, if child benefit had been promptly paid, your IS would have been paid at a lower rate.

When you get your arrears, you must repay the IS which you would not have received if the other income had been paid on time.[134] This is to prevent a 'duplication of payment'. The rule applies to any income which affects the amount of your IS. This includes other social security benefits and arrears of child support maintenance paid to you for the period from your application to the date it is assessed by the Child Support Agency (see p120). It also applies to benefits paid by other EU member states.[135] You always have to pay the money back, even though it was not your fault that the income was paid late. See p162 to see how it can be recovered.

Mortgage interest paid direct to a lender

Any overpayment of mortgage interest which is paid direct to your lender (see p150) must be sent back to the Benefits Agency by that lender if it arose because:[136]

- you ceased to be entitled to IS, but only if the Benefits Agency asks for repayment within four weeks of you going off benefit; *or*
- you were entitled to less IS because there was a reduction in:
  - the amount of your outstanding loan; *or*
  - the standard interest rate (see p35); *or*
  - your actual mortgage interest rate;

  but the Benefits Agency did not reduce your mortgage direct payments.

In the latter case your mortgage account should simply be corrected, but where you come off IS and interest is recovered, you will be in arrears unless you have started to make payments yourself.

In practice, the Benefits Agency often stops sending your lender your ongoing housing costs until they have recovered the overpayment, rather than ask a lender to return what was overpaid. However, the Benefits Agency should not do this if you are put into arrears as a result.[137] If you are put into arrears, you should seek advice.

You can appeal to a tribunal (see p167) if, for example, you think the rules do not apply to you or if the Benefits Agency has not reviewed your IS properly (see p140) or if you dispute the amount being recovered.[138] If you are not to blame for the overpayment or would suffer hardship, you can also ask the Secretary of State to use her/his discretion not to ask your lender to repay the overpayment.

The Benefits Agency can also recover overpaid mortgage interest under the rules for other overpayments[139] described below – eg, where it fails to ask your lender to repay within four weeks of you going off IS. If it tries to do this, you should make sure that those rules actually apply.

All other overpayments

Overpayments (other than duplication of payments – see p156 – or mortgage interest paid direct to the lender – see above), only have to be repaid if:[140]

- you have misrepresented or failed to disclose a material fact (see pp159-61); *and*
- as a result, too much benefit has been paid (see p161).

It does not matter if you innocently misrepresented your situation or you failed to tell the local office certain facts because you did not understand how the benefit scheme works. You might still have to repay.

If you do not agree that you owe the Benefits Agency money you can appeal (see p167). You can also appeal if you disagree that an overpayment can be recovered, or with the amount to be recovered. Do not pay back any of the money until your appeal has been decided, as the Benefits Agency may keep any money you voluntarily repay, even if you later win your case![141]

If the Benefits Agency thinks an overpayment was made due to fraud, as well as recovering the overpayment it can prosecute you or offer you the option of paying a penalty as an alternative to going to court. You should seek advice before agreeing to pay. See p317 for further information.

Correct benefit entitlement

If you have been (or are being) overpaid, an adjudication officer must review your entitlement to benefit (see p140) and decide the correct amount you should have been (or should be) paid. Until your entitlement has been reviewed, you cannot be asked to repay an overpayment. You can argue that the decision that you have been overpaid is invalid and you should not have to repay.[142] However, it is likely that your entitlement will then be reviewed correctly and benefit may then be recoverable (see p140). Pending this review, some or all of your current benefit can be suspended (see p146).

Prior to 24 July 1996, an overpayment could generally only be recovered if the adjudication officer made a decision to recover it at the same time as s/he reviewed your entitlement to benefit (see above).[143] However, at that time, most decisions about recovering overpayments were made after benefit entitlement had been reviewed. In this circumstance, an overpayment could only be recovered if an appeal was made against the review decision and the adjudication officer asked the tribunal to decide whether the overpayment was recoverable. If you think the rules have not been applied correctly in your case, you should seek advice.

Can an overpayment be recovered?

Whether an overpayment can be recovered depends on the answer to the following three questions. For all three, the burden of proving the case lies with the adjudication officer.

Did you fail to disclose or misrepresent a material fact?

The first thing to check is whether you have been accused of failing to disclose (see below) or of misrepresenting (see p160) a 'material fact'. A material fact is one which makes a difference to how much benefit you should be paid.[144]

You have a duty to report your circumstances correctly and to notify the Benefits Agency when they have changed (see p136). Failure to disclose occurs where you do not give the Benefits Agency relevant information – eg, you forget to tell it that your or your partner's hours or pay have increased. Misrepresentation occurs where you have given the Benefits Agency information which is inaccurate – eg, you gave an incorrect answer to a specific question on the claim form.

Failure to disclose

- You cannot be said to have failed to disclose a fact you did not know about (because of, for example, your mental incapacity).
- It must be reasonable to have expected you to notify the office of the particular facts. It is irrelevant that you did not personally realise the need to tell the Benefits Agency these facts – the test is whether a reasonable person would have realised that disclosure was required.[145]
- You cannot assume that changes in your social security benefits, paid by one section of the Benefits Agency, are known to the other sections. You should give the IS section any information which might affect your IS.[146]
- It is not necessary for you to show that you told the office in writing about your situation. It will do just as well if you give the information over the telephone, or in an office interview, either verbally or by presenting the relevant documents.[147]
- If you filled in a form while giving information, a tribunal should look at what you said on the form, but also consider whether you gave the necessary information in another way.[148] If you fail to fill in a form correctly, but give the relevant information in the wrong place, you have disclosed the facts.[149]
- If you have made a statement in person or over the telephone but the Benefits Agency says there is no record of this, you only have a case to answer once the adjudication officer has shown, 'on the balance of probabilities', that there would be a record of the conversation at the local office if it had taken place. In order to do this, the adjudication officer must give a tribunal information on:[150]
  - the instructions which should have applied for recording and attaching information to a claimant's file;

- whether there were the appropriate administrative arrangements to
enable these instructions to be carried out;
- to what extent *in practice* these instructions are, or are not, carried out.
Where there is no record of what happened, other than your own
statement, the Benefits Agency will not be able to prove that there has
been a recoverable overpayment.[151]
- You need not report a change direct to the Benefits Agency if you give
the information in another way which might reasonably be expected to
reach the relevant local office – eg, you tell the pensions section and
ask it to inform the IS section too. However, if you realise or should
have realised that the information has not reached the IS section, you
are under an obligation to take further steps to inform it.[152] A short
time may elapse before you can reasonably be expected to realise that
the original information has not been acted on.[153]

Misrepresentation

- This can be completely innocent[154] – eg, where you meant to declare
your partner's earnings but forgot to put these on the claim form.
- You would not be guilty of misrepresentation if you add the phrase
'not to my knowledge' to your statement.[155]
- It must relate to your current claim. If you have declared a fact on a
previous claim but inadvertently give incorrect information on a later
claim, you have misrepresented. The Benefits Agency is not required
to check back for you.[156] However, if what you say on your claim form
is obviously incorrect and the adjudication officer does not check this
out, the overpayment will be due to DSS error not your
misrepresentation and you do not have to pay it back. For example,
if you say you pay ground rent and are a freeholder, the adjudication
officer should recognise that this must be incorrect and check before
paying you benefit.[157]
- If you are incapable of managing your affairs but nevertheless sign a
claim form which is incorrectly completed, you cannot later argue that
you were not capable of making a true representation of your
circumstances to avoid recovery.[158]

Most overpayments arise due to a failure to disclose facts (see p159) and
it is easier to challenge such a decision than to show that you did not
misrepresent anything. Because of this the Benefits Agency relies on
general statements which you have signed to argue that a failure to
disclose facts can later become a misrepresentation.

This can occur in two situations:[159]

- **when you sign the claim form for IS**. The form ends with a statement:
'I declare that the information I have given is correct and complete'. If

you gave correct answers but left out relevant information because you were unaware of it, the information is incomplete and you have failed to disclose. You can argue that signing the declaration does not convert this into a misrepresentation as the declaration means 'complete insofar as I have knowledge of the material facts';[160]

- **when you cash a giro or an order book.** Each time you do this you are signing a declaration that you have reported any facts which could affect the amount of your IS. If you knew a fact but failed to declare it (eg, where you start getting incapacity benefit but did not tell the Benefits Agency your circumstances had changed) you are misrepresenting your circumstances each time you sign the declaration, and the overpayment is recoverable due to *both* your original 'failure to disclose' *and* the later misrepresentation.

However:

- if you did not declare a fact because you were unaware of it, signing the declaration does not amount to a misrepresentation because all you are declaring is that you have correctly disclosed those facts *which were known to you;*[161]
- if you were told by the Benefits Agency that certain facts are irrelevant to your claim, then signing the declaration cannot be a misrepresentation if you fail to disclose those facts.[162]

Did an overpayment result?

Even if you admit that there is information you failed to give the Benefits Agency or that you did misrepresent your circumstances, you can still argue that this was not the cause of the overpayment. If something else caused the overpayment, it should not be recovered. If the Benefits Agency has been given the correct information to decide your claim by someone else, but fails to act on it, you could argue that any overpayment did not arise because of your failure.[163]

How much is repayable?

It is always worth checking how the overpayment has been calculated as you may be asked to repay too much by mistake. Do not be afraid to ask the Benefits Agency for more information if you need it.

The amount of the overpayment is the difference between what you were paid and what you should have been paid.[164] The Benefits Agency works out what you should have been paid using the information that you originally gave it, plus any facts which you misrepresented or did not disclose.[165] The adjudication officer must consider whether you have also been underpaid benefit for a past period.

- If your **claim contained enough information** to alert the adjudication officer to your potential need, but s/he did not investigate this fully, you can argue that the underpayment should be offset against the overpayment. It does not matter if the overpayment was for a different period, so long as there was sufficient information to alert the adjudication officer to your need for extra benefit.[166]
- If **additional facts are needed** to prove you were underpaid, you cannot offset the underpayment against the overpayment.[167] However, you can ask the Benefits Agency to review your claim (see p140). It could then withhold any arrears owed to you (see p142) to reduce the overpayment.[168]

If you were not entitled to IS at all (eg, if you were working full time – see p13), you should claim any other benefits to which you may have been entitled – eg, family credit (FC), disability working allowance (DWA) or earnings top-up (see Chapters 10 and 11) – and ask for these to be backdated (see p134).

If you were overpaid because you had too much capital, the overpayment is calculated taking account of the fact that, had you received no benefit, you would have had to use your capital to meet everyday expenses. For each 13-week period, the Benefits Agency assumes that your capital is reduced by the amount of overpaid benefit.[169] This is known as the 'diminishing capital rule'. It can help to reduce the period of the overpayment.

Recovery of overpayments

If an overpayment of IS must be repaid, it can be done through deductions from any national insurance benefit, FC, DWA, income-based JSA or IS, but no deduction can be made from guardian's allowance, child benefit, HB, or council tax benefit (CTB).[170]

If the overpayment occurred because of a duplication of payment (see p156), the Benefits Agency normally deducts any overpaid IS from the arrears owing to you.[171] However, if it omits to do so you must still repay even if you have spent the money.

Other overpayments can also be recovered from arrears you are owed, except arrears where benefit has previously been suspended.[172]

When it comes to your current weekly benefit, the following are the maximum amounts which can be deducted:[173]

- £10 if you have admitted fraud or been found guilty of fraud; *or*
- £7.65 in any other case.

The deduction can be increased by half of any:[174]

- earnings subject to the £5, £10 or £15 disregard (see p386); *or*
- charitable income subject to a disregard (see p403); *or*
- benefit subject to a disregard (see p397).

Remember, the above are maximum amounts. The Benefits Agency might be persuaded to deduct less, especially if you have other direct deductions made from your benefit.

As long as a couple are married or living together as husband and wife (see p347), the amount of overpaid benefit can be recovered from either partner's IS or FC.[175] If you are an appointee who misrepresents circumstances, or fails to disclose something, you can argue that it is the claimant who has to repay any overpayment, not you as you are simply acting on her/his behalf.[176]

The money can be recovered from a claimant's estate if s/he dies.[177]

The Secretary of State's discretion

It is important to note that a tribunal cannot 'write off' part of the overpayment even if there are mitigating circumstances. It can only decide if it is recoverable and, if so, how much is repayable. In a case where you acted in all innocence and hardship is likely to be caused, the best tactic is to apply to the Secretary of State who has the discretion to decide whether or not to recover the overpayment. You can do this by writing to the local office, but it is sometimes more effective to write direct to the Secretary of State at the House of Commons. Although s/he does not deal with your case personally, it can ensure that local staff take your case seriously if they are asked to investigate by the Secretary of State. In either case you may wish to involve your MP. If you have been underpaid in the past but cannot now get arrears, ask the Secretary of State to reduce the amount to be recovered by this sum if s/he will not write it off altogether.

Recovery using common law

In the drive to recoup money lost through overpayments the Benefits Agency is increasingly trying to use other means to get money back. If an overpayment made to you is not recoverable under the social security rules described above, the Benefits Agency might try to recover it under what is known as the 'common law'. In such cases you do not have a right of appeal. There is some doubt about whether recovery in this way is lawful given that there is a clear legal code for social security which defines when payments are and are not recoverable. Nevertheless, court action is commonly threatened and has sometimes been pursued. If this happens to you, contact a local advice agency as soon as possible for help in challenging the decision.

Fraud

There is a lot of concern currently among government ministers and DSS officials about fraudulent benefit claims. As a result, a lot of resources are being put into fraud investigations. Stricter rules were introduced in 1997. In addition, if the Secretary of State thinks you are guilty of fraud, you can now be given the option of paying a penalty instead of being taken to court. You should seek urgent advice before agreeing to pay a penalty. See p317 for further information.

The definition of fraud and the way in which it is investigated is broadly the same for all means-tested benefits. A fuller explanation of this and what to do if you are under investigation can be found on p313. The footnotes to that section contain IS references where these differ.

Fraud involves a deliberate and dishonest intention to obtain benefit to which you are not entitled. Thus, if you deliberately fail to let the Benefits Agency know that you have extra money coming in which reduces your right to benefit, you are guilty of fraud. Other cases are less clear cut: for example, you may be suspected of living with someone as husband and wife and fail to declare this. However, this may not be because of any fraudulent intent, but rather because you are not sure how the relationship will develop and whether it will last in the longer term. You may not even have realised that you had to claim as a couple rather than as separate individuals in such situations (see p347). Nevertheless, your claim could come under scrutiny by a fraud officer and any irregularities will be checked out.

Your benefit can be suspended while your claim is being investigated (see p146). However, you cannot have your benefit withdrawn solely because of fraud; only if the investigation reveals that you are no longer entitled. If your benefit is suspended, you should push for a decision to be made as speedily as possible, or for your benefit to be reinstated while the investigation is completed if this is likely to take some time.

If your benefit is stopped, you can do three things:

- **make a fresh claim for benefit**. Benefit should be paid regardless of what the situation was in the past if your circumstances are now different – eg, you were working full time, but have now stopped;
- **appeal to a tribunal** (see p167) against any alleged overpayment. If you dispute that you have claimed fraudulently, you should argue that there has been no overpayment. If you accept that you have been overpaid, you can still check the calculation of the overpayment – adjudication

officers often forget the normal rules about earnings disregards, etc, when calculating the figure. It is best to appeal before any criminal proceedings have been decided;
- **apply for a social fund payment** (see p479, Crisis loans) **or an interim payment** (see p145).

Being under suspicion of fraud is very distressing and it can be difficult to re-establish your entitlement once your claim is under investigation. Fraud officers often take your papers away from the section which normally deals with your claim and it can sometimes be difficult to find out what is happening or to persuade other Benefits Agency staff to reinstate payments. Remember that a fraud officer cannot make a decision on your entitlement. S/he can only provide the adjudication officer with evidence that you are no longer entitled. If a fraud officer tries to make you give up your order book or persuade you not to claim, you should insist on a proper decision from an adjudication officer. Never withdraw your claim unless you know you are not entitled to benefit.

Some claimants have found the attitude and behaviour of fraud officers to be intimidating. While such officers are clearly required to check any irregularities on your claim, they should not threaten you or force you to do or say anything with which you do not agree. If you feel you are under undue pressure, you should ask for the interview to be terminated and complain about the manner of the investigation.

Although a fraud investigator cannot make a decision on your claim, s/he can decide whether or not to prosecute you or to offer you the option of paying a penalty instead of being taken to court. See pp313 and 317 for further details. Remember that you can be required to repay any overpayment as well as being prosecuted or paying a penalty.

5. COMPLAINTS ABOUT ADMINISTRATION

The procedures for appeal and review allow you to challenge decisions about your entitlement to benefit (including the refusal of benefit). If you want to make a complaint simply about the way in which your benefit claim was handled there are other procedures you can follow. The things you might want to complain about could include:

- delay in dealing with your claim;
- poor administration in the benefit office (eg, they keep losing your papers, or you can never get through on the telephone);
- poor or negligent advice from Benefits Agency staff;

- the behaviour of members of staff. Most Benefits Agency staff do a good job and try to be helpful, but you should certainly complain about staff rudeness or sexist or racist remarks.

You should ask your local office for any written information on the standards and level of service which you can expect. The Benefits Agency produces a leaflet, *Tell us about it*, which explains your rights and contains a form which you can use to explain your complaint. It is available from local Benefits Agency offices and on the internet (see Appendix 5 for address). You might also wish to seek compensation (see p148).

Complaining to the Benefits Agency

The Benefits Agency suggests that as a first step you should speak to the person who dealt with you. If they cannot help or you would prefer to speak to someone else, contact the supervisor or assistant manager. If you are still dissatisfied, you can contact the customer services manager of your branch office. S/he will investigate your complaint and should respond within seven days. If this does not solve the problem you should write to the manager of your district office with details of the complaint. Keep a copy of your letter. If you are still unhappy, you can ask the Benefits Agency for independent consideration of your complaint. You may also wish to write a letter for the personal attention of the Chief Executive of the Benefits Agency (for address, see Appendix 3).

Complaining to your MP

If you are not satisfied with the reply from the officers to whom you have written, the next step is to take up the matter with your MP.

Most MPs have 'surgeries' in their areas where they meet constituents to discuss problems. You can get the details from your local library or citizens advice bureau. You can either go to the surgery or write to your MP with details of your complaint.

Your MP will probably want to write to the benefit authorities for an explanation of what has happened. If you or s/he are not satisfied with the reply, the next stage is to complain to the Ombudsman, via your MP.

The Parliamentary Commissioner for Administration (commonly called the 'Parliamentary Ombudsman' – see Appendix 3) investigates complaints made by MPs against government departments. The Ombudsman's office will send you a leaflet providing further information. Many of the complaints are about benefits. If s/he investigates your case, your MP will be sent a full report. If the Ombudsman finds you were badly treated, s/he will recommend an apology and possibly compensation.

CHAPTER EIGHT

Appeals

This chapter covers:
1. Appealing to social security appeal tribunals (below)
2. How to prepare an appeal (p178)
3. Appealing to the Social Security Commissioner (p181)
4. Appealing to the courts (p184)

I. APPEALING TO SOCIAL SECURITY APPEAL TRIBUNALS

You can appeal to an independent social security appeal tribunal (SSAT) against any decision taken by an adjudication officer. Decisions made by the Secretary of State cannot be appealed (see p137). However, you can still try to persuade the Secretary of State to change her/his decision as your only legal remedy is to apply to the High Court for judicial review (see p185).

Sometimes, an adjudication officer will refuse to make a decision on your claim. If an adjudication officer does this, it effectively prevents you having the right to appeal. An adjudication officer must make a decision on every valid claim.[1] You can then appeal and it is up to the tribunal to decide whether the decision is correct.

Note: A new Social Security Bill is due to become law in spring 1998. Radical changes to the system and procedure for appeals will be introduced from April 1999. In addition, the time limit for appealing is likely to be reduced to one month. See Appendix 2 for more information.

How to appeal

It is important to remember that:

- there is a strict time limit for appealing – normally only three months (see p168);
- there is information you must provide (see p169);

- you must appeal in writing and normally on the appropriate form. If you do not use the appropriate form, the chair of a tribunal can accept your appeal so long as it is in writing and includes all the information required (see p169).[2] There is no guarantee the chair will do this, so use the form wherever possible. The appeal form is contained in leaflet NI246, *How to appeal,* which is available at Benefits Agency offices;
- the completed appeal form (see above) should be sent or delivered to the Benefits Agency office that made the decision with which you disagree. It must pass forms or appeal letters to the Independent Tribunal Service (ITS) (see p174);
- the ITS decides if your appeal is valid, not the Benefits Agency.[3]

If you want the tribunal to deal with your appeal quickly, make this plain on your appeal form, explaining why. You could also telephone the clerk to the tribunal at the ITS to check that your appeal has been received and to ask her/him to deal with the matter quickly.

Before challenging a decision, it is useful to know why it was given. You have a right to a written statement of reasons for a decision if you apply for it within three months of being given the decision in writing.[4] Ask for this as soon as possible so you can appeal within the strict time limit for appealing (see below). On receiving the statement of reasons, if there are grounds for a review, you may decide it is worth asking for a review of the decision rather than appealing straightaway (see p140). In any case, if you appeal an adjudication officer will look at the decision again (see p170).

The time limit for appealing

Your appeal, including all the information described on p169, must arrive within the three months beginning with the date the written decision was sent to you. [5] This time limit is very strict, but see p169 for information about appealing late. It is very important that you provide all the information required (see p169) within the time limit. Your appeal is not treated as made until you do.[6] If you do not include all the information on your appeal form, the chair or clerk to the tribunal can make what is known as a 'direction' requiring you to provide the information you left out within a certain period of time.[7] The chair or clerk to a tribunal can give you extra time beyond the three-month time limit to provide the information required,[8] but there is no guarantee that s/he will do so. In any case, s/he can only give you a maximum of 14 more days.

If you do not provide the information within the time limit, you have to ask the chair of a tribunal to accept a late appeal (see p169). However, it is extremely difficult to get a chair to do this so it is better that you provide all the information in time. If you have sent your appeal form but the chair or clerk only asks for extra information after the time limit has expired, the DSS have said it is their intention that your appeal should be allowed under the late appeal rules (see below).

Information you must provide when you appeal

When you appeal you must provide the following information:[9]

- the name of the benefit you are appealing about – eg, income support or family credit;
- the date the Benefits Agency sent you the decision with which you disagree. You can find this date on the letter notifying you of the decision;
- a summary of your arguments for saying the decision was wrong. You should not simply say you think the decision was wrong, but explain why.

Examples

'The Benefits Agency says I have been overpaid income support because I failed to disclose that my wife had started working part time, but I wrote to them as soon as she started work and told them what her take-home pay would be.'

'The decision is that I should not get income support for my son because he left school in June. This decision is wrong because my son decided to stay on at school and do his 'A' levels.'

It might also be helpful to include information and evidence which supports your appeal because an adjudication officer looks at the decision again and might review it (see p170).

Late appeals

You need the chair of an appeal tribunal's permission to appeal if you miss the three months' time limit (see p168) and this is extremely difficult to get. It is often simpler to ask for a review of the adjudication officer's decision instead of making a late appeal, so long as there are grounds for review and this would give you everything to which you are entitled (see p140). However, you can often only get one month's arrears of benefit if you seek a review (see p142).

The chair of an appeal tribunal can only accept a late appeal if:[10]

- your appeal is likely to succeed; *and*
- it is in the 'interests of justice' (see p170).

Even if you meet the two conditions above, a late appeal cannot be accepted if it is more than six years since the decision you want to appeal against was made.[11] It is considered to be in the 'interests of justice' to allow a late appeal if:[12]

- there are special reasons which are 'wholly exceptional' and relate to the history and facts of your case; *and*
- the special reasons are sufficiently strong to give you a reasonable excuse for your delay in appealing; *and*
- the special reasons have existed since your deadline for appealing expired (see p168).

In addition to the information you must provide on your appeal form (see p169) you must explain the special reasons why your appeal is late (see above).[13] The longer you have delayed in appealing, the more compelling the special reasons have to be.

When deciding if there are special reasons, the chair cannot take account of the fact that:[14]

- a court or a commissioner has interpreted the law in a different way than previously understood and applied;
- you (or your adviser) misunderstood or were unaware of the relevant law, including the time limits for appealing.

You must be notified of the chair's decision as soon as is practicable, and must be sent written reasons for it if you ask for these in writing within three months.[15]

You cannot appeal against the refusal of the chair to accept a late appeal,[16] but you can ask the chair to look at her/his decision again, or you may be able to apply to the High Court for judicial review if the decision is clearly unreasonable (see p185).

What happens after you appeal

An adjudication officer will look at the decision you are appealing about again and might change the decision, for example, on the basis of any facts, information or evidence that you provided with your appeal form. However, if you do not get everything you think you are entitled to, your appeal must still go ahead.[17]

After your appeal is received at the local office, you should receive an acknowledgement (form AT38) from the clerk of the Independent Tribunal Service, together with a questionnaire (form AR4) asking you whether you want an oral hearing (see p171) and, if so, when you and your representative (if you have one) are available to attend. You must return the questionnaire within 14 days (the chair or clerk to a tribunal could give you more or fewer days than this).[18] You are also sent a leaflet containing information about appeals and how to find someone to represent you at the hearing if this would be helpful.

Oral or paper hearings

If you want an **oral hearing**, you must tell the clerk to the tribunal.[19] You are more likely to succeed if you attend an oral hearing, particularly where there is an argument about the facts of your case. The clerk also asks the adjudication officer if s/he wants an oral hearing. Even if neither you nor the adjudication officer want an oral hearing, the chair of the tribunal might decide that one should take place.[20] This could happen if the chair feels an oral hearing is necessary to help the tribunal make its decision.

If neither of you opt for an oral hearing and the chair does not think one is necessary, the tribunal will make its decision by looking at what you said on your appeal form, any evidence or other information you provided to support your appeal, and the adjudication officer's submission (see p172). This is what is known as a **'paper hearing'**.

You should consider carefully whether to opt for an oral or a paper hearing. You may feel that you would rather not attend an oral hearing, for example, because you are worried about speaking for yourself or would have difficulties getting there. But if you attend an oral hearing, you can explain your side of the story to the tribunal. You may want to seek advice before you decide what to do. Consider whether you need representation (see Appendix 4). If you take someone with you to an oral hearing your chances of winning are much higher. You can take a friend, relative, adviser or representative with you[21] – you can have more than one person if the chair of the tribunal agrees.[22]

If you opt for a paper hearing, think about what other information and evidence you can get to support your appeal, and send it to the tribunal. You must send this to the clerk to the tribunal within 10 days of being sent the adjudication officer's submission about your appeal (see below). See pp178-80 for information about sorting out the facts and checking the law and the case law that applies in your case.

A chair can decide your appeal should be heard straightaway if s/he thinks you have no chance of winning – eg, where you have claimed income support but you are 15 years old or where you have claimed family credit but have no children.[23] You must be offered an oral hearing and be given proper notice (see p173).

You might find that your appeal is not dealt with if there is a test case pending which deals with the same issues. You can insist that your appeal is dealt with but it might then be adjourned (but see p175).

The Adjudication Officer's submission

The Benefits Agency prepares a detailed explanation of the reasons for its decision (known as the adjudication officer's submission) and this is sent to you on form AT2. This should be sent to you as soon as it is received by the Independent Tribunal Service, usually six to eight weeks after you appeal. If you opted for an oral hearing you are normally also told when and where the hearing will be. Your oral hearing should take place within one month of receiving the adjudication officer's submission. See p173 for information about how much notice you must be given.

If you opted for a paper hearing (see p171), but now that you have seen the adjudication officer's submission you want an oral hearing after all, you may be able to change your mind. You must tell the clerk to the tribunal before the tribunal makes its decision.

Providing other information

The chair or clerk to the tribunal might issue 'directions' requiring you or the adjudication officer to provide further information or documents.[24] A chair can require you or the adjudication officer to provide information or documents that are needed to help the tribunal make its decision. You can also ask the chair to require an adjudication officer to provide these.

The chair or the clerk can require you to:

- provide information, where your appeal form is incomplete (see p169);
- reply to the letter asking you about when you are available for a hearing (see p170).

If you are required to provide any information or documents, it is important that you do so. If you do not, the chair can:[25]

- strike out your appeal (see p173);
- decide to hear your appeal straightaway, but only if:
  - you have not explained why you have not provided what has been required; *and*
  - the tribunal has sufficient information to make its decision.

This might happen, for example, where your appeal was adjourned for you to get evidence, but you have not done so after a considerable period of time. You must still be asked whether you want an oral hearing (see p170) and if you do, must be given proper notice (see p173).

When can a chair strike out your appeal?

A chair can strike out your appeal for 'want of prosecution' if you do not appear to be pursuing it. This might happen where you fail to provide information or documents that have been required by a chair or clerk (see p172) or to tell the clerk when you can attend a hearing (see p172).[26] This cancels your appeal and it does not go ahead.

You must be notified if this is being considered and given a reasonable amount of time to explain why you think your appeal should not be struck out. You do not have to be given notice where your address is not known or cannot be found out easily. If the chair is satisfied with your explanation and decides not to strike out your appeal, s/he might decide to hear your case straightaway (see above), or to give instructions to speed your appeal along.

If a chair strikes out your appeal, you have three months to ask for it to be reinstated.[27] It will be reinstated if you did not receive notice that your appeal might be struck out (see above) unless no notice was sent to you because your address was not known or could not have been found out easily.

Withdrawing an appeal[28]

If you change your mind about appealing, you can withdraw your appeal. You must apply in writing to the clerk to the tribunal. S/he must allow you to withdraw your appeal unless the adjudication officer has already notified the clerk that s/he is opposed to this. However, once the appeal tribunal hearing has begun, you can only withdraw your appeal with the consent of the chair and provided the tribunal has not yet made a decision. Once an appeal has been withdrawn it cannot be reinstated, but if you decide that you want to go ahead after all, you could try to make a late appeal against the adjudication officer's original decision (but see p169).[29]

The oral hearing

You have a right to at least seven days' notice of the oral hearing unless you agree to less notice than this. If you have not been given the correct notice, the tribunal can only go ahead if you agree.[30] If you give up your right to notice the tribunal can go ahead with the hearing even if you are not there.[31]

If the hearing date is inconvenient or you want more time to prepare your case, you can ask for it to be **postponed**. You must apply in writing to the clerk to the tribunal, saying why you want your case to be postponed. You should do this as soon as you decide that you want a postponement.[32] The Independent Tribunal Service is very keen to avoid postponements, so you should ring before the hearing is due to take place to check if this has been agreed. If you do not attend and have not asked for a postponement, the tribunal can hear the case without you, and you are less likely to succeed.[33] However, they should not go ahead if you have advised them that you cannot attend and have asked for another hearing date, especially if you have a good reason for not attending.[34] If the tribunal makes a decision in your absence with which you disagree, you can try to appeal to a Social Security Commissioner (see p181) or ask for the decision to be set aside (but see p177).

A social security appeal tribunal is heard in public unless you request a private hearing, or the chair thinks it should be in private. In practice, it is extremely rare for members of the public to turn up. However, the rule does mean that you could sit in on the case before your own.[35]

The tribunal members

A tribunal is independent of the Benefits Agency. The standards of tribunals are the responsibility of the President of the Independent Tribunal Service (ITS). The ITS is divided into regions, with a chair for each region who recruits and trains tribunal members. The President issues circulars to guide tribunals on how they should conduct themselves. If you have a complaint about a tribunal member, or the way a hearing is conducted, write to your regional chair or the President (see Appendix 3 for addresses).

A tribunal usually consists of three people. There is a **chair**, who is a lawyer, and two **'wing members'**, who sit on either side of the chair. They are supposed to be people who have knowledge or experience of conditions in your area, and who are representative of people living or working there. Wherever possible, at least one member of the tribunal should be the same sex as you.[36]

Tribunals can sit with only one wing member, but only if you agree. In this case, the chair has the casting vote.[37]

The chair has to record the tribunal's decision, and a statement of its findings on the relevant facts of the case and the reasons for its decision (see p176). S/he makes a note of what is said by you, your representative, the adjudication officer and any witnesses.

Other people present at the oral hearing

The **clerk to the tribunal** is there in an administrative capacity – eg, to pay expenses. You, your representative, an interpreter if needed and any witnesses may be able to get travel expenses paid. You can also claim for meals, loss of earnings and childcare costs.[38] The clerk takes no part in making the decision on your appeal and should not express any views on the case.

The **presenting officer** represents the adjudication officer. S/he explains the reasons for the decision you are appealing about, but is not there to defend the Benefits Agency's decision at all costs. S/he may provide information which helps your case.[39]

If your appeal concerns whether you are incapable of work (see p10) a **medical assessor** is present at the hearing. S/he is.a doctor who is there in an advisory capacity. S/he advises the tribunal on medical issues but takes no part in making the decision on your appeal.

Procedure at the oral hearing

When the tribunal is ready to hear your case, you are taken in with the presenting officer.

There are no strict rules of procedure. The chair should start by introducing the members of the tribunal and everyone else who is present. The presenting officer then summarises the adjudication officer's written submission and you are asked to explain your reasons for disagreeing with it. Alternatively, you may be asked to explain your position first. You can call any witnesses and can ask questions of the presenting officer, and the tribunal members ask questions of you both.

The tribunal considers all the facts, evidence, law (see p179) and caselaw (see p180) and makes a decision. It must look at what has happened since the date of the decision with which you disagree and take any changes of circumstance into account.[40] However, this is due to change. From summer 1998, when the new Social Security Bill becomes law, the tribunal will only be able to look at your circumstances as they were on the date of the decision with which you disagree. See p516 for further details.

Your case may be adjourned unfinished to be heard on another day because, for instance, more evidence is required. Failure to adjourn to allow you to get relevant evidence is an error of law (see p181) and you can appeal to the commissioner to get the decision overturned (see p181).[41] A tribunal might adjourn your case if there is a test case pending which deals with the same issues as your appeal.[42] If this happens, you should ask them to hear your appeal based on the law as it currently stands, if this is in your interests, rather than waiting for the result of the test case.

If your case is adjourned the new tribunal must rehear your case from the beginning unless it has the same three members as before or you agree to it being heard by two members of the previous tribunal without the third.[43]

You can appeal against a decision to adjourn your appeal though it will often be quicker to press for a fresh hearing.[44]

The tribunal decision

Usually you are told of the tribunal's decision at the hearing and you are given a decision notice confirming it. The decision notice includes a summary of the tribunal's reasons for its decision. If it is not given at the hearing or you opted for a paper hearing, the decision notice is sent to you later by the clerk. You must also be informed of:[45]

• your right to request a 'full decision' (see below);
• the conditions for appealing to the commissioner (see p181).

The 'full decision'

A chair might decide to give you a 'full decision' at the hearing or to send one to you later on.[46] If not, you have a right to request one. The chair **must** provide one if you ask for it within 21 days of being sent or given the decision notice (see above). If you ask after the 21 day time-limit has expired, the chair might agree to provide one but there is no guarantee of this.

If you lose your appeal and want to appeal to the commissioner (see p181) you **must** have a 'full decision'. You should ask for one as soon as possible after the decision is made. If the chair fails to provide a 'full decision', whether or not you ask for it in time (see above), you should seek advice.

A full decision must include the tribunal's reasons for its decision and the relevant findings of fact. This must be a legible record of the evidence.[47] If the decision is not unanimous, the full decision must give the reasons why a tribunal member disagreed with the decision.[48]

Winning your appeal

If you have won, the Benefits Agency ought to carry out the tribunal's decision straightaway. They can do this on the basis of the decision notice (see above). However, they have three months in which to appeal against the tribunal's decision to a social security commissioner (see p181). If considering an appeal, you will not be paid while they decide what to do. If they decide to appeal, you will not be paid until the commissioner hears the case.[49] See p146 for details of what the Benefits Agency must do before it can suspend your benefit. If you are left without any money, you might be able to apply for an interim payment (see p145), or get a crisis loan (see p479).

What if you disagree with the tribunal's decision?

A tribunal's decision is final. However:

- it can be reviewed in the normal way – eg, where your circumstances have changed since the decision was made or new facts have come to light (see p140). However, where the tribunal made a mistake about the law you must appeal (see below);
- you or the adjudication officer can appeal to the Social Security Commissioners (see p181);
- A decision can be 'set aside', which means the decision is cancelled and your appeal is heard again. A tribunal can only do this if it thinks it is *just* and:[50]
  - you, your representative or the presenting officer did not receive the appeal papers or other relevant documents, or did not receive them in sufficient time before the hearing; *or*
  - you, your representative or the presenting officer were not present at the hearing. However, if you or the presenting officer chose not to attend it may not be just to set the decision aside. If you did not ask for an oral hearing (see p171) the decision cannot be set aside for this reason unless it would clearly be in the 'interests of justice' (see below); *or*
  - 'the interests of justice so require'. This applies where there has been a 'procedural irregularity'.[51] A failure to produce sufficient evidence at the hearing is not a 'procedural irregularity'.

An adjudication officer may also ask for a decision to be set aside.

You must apply for the decision to be set aside within three months of the decision being sent to you. A late application is only accepted if there are special reasons. The special reasons do not have to relate to your own personal circumstances or actions. They could include the amount of money involved or how strong your case is. Applications are normally decided without a hearing, so make sure you give a full explanation of your reasons when you apply.[52] You cannot appeal against a refusal to set aside, but you may be able to apply for judicial review (see p185).

If a decision is wrongly set aside, any subsequent rehearing by a tribunal is invalid. The second tribunal could thus refuse to rehear the case if there was no power to set aside the previous decision.[53]

- If the written decision contains an accidental error this can be corrected by the tribunal.[54]

2. HOW TO PREPARE AN APPEAL

Your appeal may concern a dispute about the facts or the law, or both. Always try, if possible, to link the facts of your case and your arguments to the rules laid down in the benefit regulations.

Sorting out the facts

The tribunal has to decide your appeal on the evidence given by you and the Benefits Agency. A tribunal hearing is a complete rehearing of your case, so fresh facts and arguments can be put by either side.[55] Remember to:

- check through the appeal papers carefully to work out where there are disagreements between you and the Benefits Agency. This will help you decide what evidence you need to win your case;
- gather helpful evidence (see below). If you want to give any evidence or information to the tribunal, you should send it to the clerk to the tribunal at least five days before your oral hearing. Otherwise, the tribunal might decide to adjourn your case (see p175);
- ask any witnesses who support your case to attend the appeal. Both you and the Benefits Agency can ask witnesses to come and give information. Chairs do have the power to refuse to hear witnesses who are not relevant, but they should always be fair to claimants and generally allow witnesses to speak, even if it looks as if they may have nothing useful to say.[56]

Evidence

Evidence consists of what you (and any witnesses) actually say at the hearing and any documents which you produce to support your case. Written evidence would include letters of support, medical reports, wage slips, bank statements, birth certificates and anything else which helps to prove the facts. If, for example, the Benefits Agency says that you failed to disclose an increase in your earnings and you have been overpaid, you could explain to the tribunal how and when you told them, but you may also be able to produce a copy of the letter which you sent informing them of the change.

Proving your case with additional evidence is useful but not essential. A tribunal cannot dismiss your verbal evidence without a proper explanation of why it has done so.[57]

The presenting officer puts the adjudication officer's case at the tribunal but is very rarely the person who actually made the decision in your case. The presenting officer's submissions are not evidence,[58] nor are comments made by another adjudication officer if s/he did not decide your claim.[59]

The presenting officer can report what other people have said. This is called hearsay evidence. Tribunals can accept hearsay evidence but they should carefully weigh up its value as proof, given that the person who originally made the statement is not present at the hearing. Most evidence relied on by adjudication officers is written and you can point out that you have not had the opportunity of questioning the witnesses. You are not entitled to insist on the presence of any particular witness,[60] but you should argue that the tribunal should not place any weight on the written evidence of, say, an interviewing officer if you are disputing the interview.

Checking the law

Adjudication officers must look at the law, the case law and the guidance (see below) before making a decision. The adjudication officer often gets the law wrong so it is worth checking the benefit rules to see if they have been correctly applied in your case. This *Handbook* explains what the law says and the footnotes give you the legal references if you want to look them up for yourself. The adjudication officer quotes certain parts of the law which support her/his decision and you should check these. It is quite common for the adjudication officer to quote a large number of commissioners' decisions (see p180), but these are not always of direct relevance to your appeal so check them carefully. Also, check to see if you can find others which help your case.

The law consists of Acts of Parliament and regulations. You can ask to see the law concerning income support, disability working allowance and family credit at the local Benefits Agency office. It should be available for public inspection at all reasonable hours and without payment.[61]

Benefit laws are collected together in a large looseleaf book called the *Law Relating to Social Security*. It is in several volumes and is known as the 'Blue Book'. It is kept up-to-date with regular supplements. You can look at a copy of the 'Blue Book' at your nearest major library as well as at the Benefits Agency.

Most of the law you need is contained in CPAG's *Income Related Benefits: The Legislation* (see Appendix 5). As well as giving the law it gives explanations of what each bit means and tells you about relevant case law (see p180). Tribunal members have this textbook.

Benefit laws are complicated and the staff who administer benefits are issued with **guidance** manuals and circulars. However, adjudication officers and tribunals are only bound by what the law says, not by the guidance. The *Adjudication Officers' Guide* covers benefits administered by the Benefits Agency. It is written by the Chief Adjudication Officer, who is responsible for advising local adjudication officers about the law.[62]

Case law is made by the Social Security Commissioners who are part of the appeal system and by the Courts.[63] Rulings they make about the meaning of benefit law are binding and must be applied in similar cases by adjudication officers and tribunals. Sometimes commissioners' decisions conflict. If so, the tribunal must follow a reported decision in preference to an unreported one (see below), and a tribunal of commissioners' decision to that of a single commissioner.[64] Starred unreported decisions are generally given more weight than unstarred ones. If there is a decision on the same point by the High Court on judicial review, the Court of Appeal or the House of Lords, it must be followed in preference to a commissioner's decision.

The most important commissioners' decisions are published by The Stationery Office and are called 'reported decisions'. They are prefixed by the letter 'R'. Income support decisions are reported as R(IS), disability working allowance as R(DWA) and family credit as R(FC). Sometimes you will be referred to supplementary benefit decisions which are R(SB), and to decisions on other benefits. Only the most important decisions are reported.

Example
R(IS) 1/90 was the first commissioner's decision on IS to be reported in 1990.

Unreported decisions are prefixed by the letter 'C', and the year is written out in full – eg, CIS/13/1989. Some unreported decisions are 'starred' by the commissioner if, for example, they deal with an important issue or with an aspect of benefit law for the first time. Unreported decisions are available from the Office of the Social Security Commissioners (see Appendix 3 for address). From April 1998, the price is likely to be £3 each. Some are available on the internet at http://hywels.demon.co.uk/commis/decns.htm

This *Handbook* gives references to commissioners' decisions and you can keep up-to-date with the latest commissioners' decisions by reading CPAG's bi-monthly *Welfare Rights Bulletin*. The main library in your area may have copies of reported commissioners' decisions or you can ask to see them at any Benefits Agency office.

If you want to refer to an unreported commissioner's decision, it is best to circulate it to the SSAT and Benefits Agency in advance. If this is not possible, take copies for them to the hearing.

3. APPEALING TO THE SOCIAL SECURITY COMMISSIONER

Both you and the Benefits Agency have a further right of appeal to a social security commissioner, but only if the tribunal has made an error of law.[65]

The tribunal made an error of law if:[66]

- the tribunal got the law wrong – eg, it misunderstood the particular benefit regulation concerned;
- there is no evidence to support its decision;
- the facts it found are such that, had it acted reasonably, and interpreted the law correctly, it could not have made the decision it did. This argument would be used where the facts are inconsistent with the decision – eg, a tribunal finds that a man and a woman live in separate households, but decides they are living together as husband and wife;
- there is a breach of the rules of natural justice. This is where the procedure followed by the tribunal leads to unfairness (eg, you are not allowed to call witnesses to support you or the tribunal refuses a postponement, even though you cannot attend for a good reason and have told it so), and the result is that you lost without having a chance to put your case properly;[67]
- it does not give proper findings of fact or provide adequate reasons for its decision (see p176). The tribunal must not simply say what its decision was. It must put down sufficient reasons so that you can see why, on the evidence, it reached the conclusion it did. It can rely on the adjudication officer's summary of the facts, but only if these are not in dispute and s/he has covered all relevant issues.[68] If you and the adjudication officer disagree about the facts the tribunal must explain which version it prefers and why.

How to appeal

You must first obtain permission to appeal to the commissioner – what is known as 'leave'.[69] This means that you have to show that there has possibly been an error of law (see above) and that you have the beginnings of a case.

If you wish to appeal, you must have the tribunal's 'full decision' (see p176). You should first apply for leave to appeal to the chair of the tribunal.[70] You must do this by writing to the clerk of the tribunal at the regional office within three months of being sent the 'full decision' of the tribunal.[71] You must include a copy of the 'full decision' (see p176) with your application for leave to appeal.

If the chair refuses you leave to appeal, you may make a fresh application direct to a commissioner. You must do this within 42 days, beginning on the day after the date on the notification that you were refused leave to appeal by the tribunal chair.[72] You must include a copy of the 'full decision' (see p176) with your application for leave to appeal.

If you miss the time limit, you may still apply for leave to appeal but any application must be made direct to a commissioner who will give you leave only if there are special reasons for the delay.[73] The special reasons do not have to relate to your own personal circumstances or actions. They could include things like the amount of money involved or how strong your case is. Delays by the post office (but not other courier firms) in delivering your appeal can be disregarded, so long as your application was prepaid and properly addressed.

Once you have been given leave to appeal, you must send what is known as a notice of appeal within six weeks.[74] You are sent a form on which to do this. The time may, again, be extended for special reasons (see above). You may have been told that your notice of application for leave has been treated as a notice of appeal, in which case you do not have to send in another.[75]

The adjudication officer might agree with you that the tribunal made an error of law (see p181). After the new Social Security Bill becomes law (which is likely to be in June 1998 – see p516), if this happens your appeal will not go ahead. Instead, the commissioner must send your case back to be heard by a different tribunal.

The written procedure

Adjudication officers at the Central Adjudication Services (see Appendix 3 for address) deal with the Benefits Agency's side of the case. A bundle of documents is prepared by that office and sent to the commissioners' office where it is added to any submissions from you. The commissioners' office then sends copies of the bundle, including the adjudication officer's submission, to you.

You are given 30 days in which to reply to the submission of the adjudication officer, although the commissioner may extend the time limit. There is a right of reply, if required, within 30 days.[76] If you have nothing to add and do not want to reply at any stage, tell the commissioners' office. A commissioner has the power to strike out an appeal that appears to have been abandoned, although you can apply for it to be reinstated.[77]

When the commissioner has all the written submissions, s/he decides whether or not there should be an oral hearing of the appeal. If you ask for an oral hearing, the commissioner will hold one unless s/he feels that the case can be dealt with properly without one.[78] Occasionally, the commissioner decides to hold an oral hearing even if you have not asked for one.

If there is no oral hearing, the commissioner reaches a decision on the basis of written submissions and other documents.

Because of the length of time you usually have to wait before your case is dealt with, you should make a fresh claim for benefit if, for example, your circumstances change.

The hearing

If there is an oral hearing, it will be at the commissioners' offices in London, Edinburgh or Belfast, or at the law courts in Cardiff, Leeds or Liverpool. You are told the date in good time and your fares are paid in advance if you want to attend. At least half a day is set aside for each case. Usually, one commissioner hears your case. However, if there is a 'question of law of special difficulty', the hearing may be before a tribunal of three commissioners,[79] but the procedure is the same.

The hearing is more formal than those before social security appeal tribunals but the commissioner will let you say everything you want to. Commissioners usually intervene a lot and ask questions so you need to be prepared to argue your case without your script. A full set of commissioners' decisions (see p180) and the 'Blue Books' (see p179) are available for your use. The adjudication officer is usually represented by a lawyer, so you should consider trying to obtain representation as well. The commissioner may exclude members of the public if intimate personal or financial circumstances, or matters of public security are involved.[80] This is not usually necessary because it is rare for anyone not involved in the case to attend.

The decision

The decision is always given in writing[81] – often at some length – and it may be a few weeks before it is sent to you.

After a successful appeal, the case is often sent back to a differently constituted social security appeal tribunal with directions as to how the tribunal should go about reconsidering the issues.[82] However, if the commissioner feels that the record of the decision of the original tribunal contains all the material facts, or s/he feels that it is 'expedient' to make findings on any extra factual issues necessary to the decisions, the commissioner makes the final decision.[83] It is unusual for a commissioner not to send a case back to a tribunal if there is a dispute about facts not determined by the original tribunal, unless all the evidence points in one direction.[84]

A commissioner may correct or set aside her/his decision in the same way as a tribunal (see p177).[85]

In certain circumstances, an adjudication officer may review a commissioner's decision (see p140).

4. APPEALING TO THE COURTS

You may appeal against a decision of a commissioner to the Court of Appeal (in Scotland, the Court of Session) but only if the commissioner has made an error of law (see p181) and you must first obtain permission to appeal – what is known as 'leave'.[86] If you want to appeal you should seek help from a solicitor, but first check that you qualify for legal aid to cover the costs.

The application for leave to appeal must first be made to a commissioner, in writing, within three months of the date when you were sent the commissioner's decision. The commissioner may extend the time limit if s/he thinks fit.[87] If you do not apply to the commissioner within the time limit and the commissioner refuses to extend it, the Court of Appeal (or Court of Session) cannot hear your appeal and you can only proceed by applying to the High Court (in Scotland, the Court of Session) for judicial review of the refusal to extend the time allowed for the appeal (see p185).[88]

Applications to a commissioner for leave to appeal are almost always considered without an oral hearing. If the commissioner refuses, you can apply direct to the court for leave.[89] Your notice of application should be lodged with the Civil Appeals Office within six weeks of being sent notification of the commissioner's refusal.[90] The court may extend the time but you must explain the reasons for your delay and file an affidavit in support of an application for an extension of time.[91] Generally, the Court of Appeal considers your application without an oral hearing. If leave is refused, you may renew your application in open court within seven days. Similarly, if leave is granted, the Chief Adjudication Officer or the Secretary of State has seven days in which to ask for an oral hearing.[92]

If leave to appeal is granted by a commissioner or the Court of Appeal you must serve a notice of appeal on the relevant parties. There are strict time limits for doing this.[93] The solicitor to the Benefits Agency will accept service on behalf of the Chief Adjudication Officer (see Appendix 3 for address).

You cannot appeal to the Court of Appeal against a commissioner's refusal to grant you leave to appeal against a tribunal's decision, but you can apply to the High Court for judicial review of such a refusal (see below).[94]

The procedures in Scotland are similar.

The Chief Adjudication Officer or the Secretary of State has the same rights of appeal as you.

Applying for judicial review

Occasionally it is possible to challenge the Benefits Agency by going to court for a judicial review. You will need the services of a solicitor, law centre or legal advice centre.

You can apply for judicial review of a decision made by:

* the Secretary of State;
* a tribunal chair refusing to grant you leave to appeal; *or*
* a social security commissioner refusing to grant you leave to appeal.

However, this procedure cannot usually be used if you have an independent right of appeal, such as against the decision of an adjudication officer or a social security appeal tribunal.

Meeting the cost of going to court

Legal aid is available for cases in the Court of Appeal, the High Court and the Court of Session and you should certainly seek legal advice and representation (see Appendix 4). In the past, the legal aid authorities have taken the view that an application to a commissioner for leave to appeal to the Court of Appeal cannot be covered by legal aid. However, it is arguable that such an application is a step 'preliminary to' proceedings in the Court of Appeal and is thus work for which legal aid is available.[95]

PART THREE

Back to work benefits, family credit and disability working allowance

CHAPTER NINE

Back to work benefits

This chapter covers:
1. Back to work bonus (below)
2. Child maintenance bonus (p189)
3. Extended payments of housing benefit and council tax benefit (p196)

If you or your partner start working full time or increase your earnings and, as a result, stop claiming income support (IS) or income-based jobseeker's allowance (JSA), you might be able to claim a back to work bonus (see below) or a child maintenance bonus (see p189). You might also be able to claim an extended payment of housing benefit and council tax benefit at the rate you were getting on IS or income-based JSA (see p196). In addition, you might be able to claim benefit to top up your pay. If you have children, this is family credit or if you do not, earnings top-up (see Chapter 10). If you have a disability this is disability working allowance (see Chapter 11).

I. BACK TO WORK BONUS

Back to work bonus is a tax free lump sum of up to £1,000 which you can accumulate by working part time while you are receiving jobseeker's allowance (JSA) or income support (IS). It is paid when you return to full-time work (16 or more hours a week) or when your earnings increase so that you are no longer entitled to JSA or IS.

Receiving JSA or IS can qualify you for a bonus. They are the only 'qualifying benefits'. Both *contribution-based* JSA and *income-based* JSA count.

How do you qualify for a bonus?

The detailed rules about back to work bonus are beyond the scope of this *Handbook*. For further details see CPAG's *Jobseeker's Allowance Handbook*, 3rd edn, 1998/99.

The following is a *summary* of the main qualifying conditions.

To qualify for a back to work bonus:[1]

- You must have been entitled to JSA or IS for at least 91 days. This is called the **waiting period.** The 91-day period does not have to be continuous. Separate periods adding up to 91 days will count if the breaks in between are 12 weeks or less. Days when you are entitled to JSA or IS but during which you are not actually paid can count.
- After the waiting period, you must remain entitled to JSA or IS have earnings from employment which are taken into account by the Benefits Agency to reduce your JSA or IS. Earnings that are disregarded (see p386) do not count for the back to work bonus.
- You or your partner must satisfy the **work condition.** The work condition for back to work bonus purposes is that you or your partner are no longer entitled to JSA or IS because:
  - you work for 16 hours or more a week; *or*
  - your partner (if you are entitled to income-based JSA or IS) works for 24 hours or more a week; *or*
  - your earnings (or the combined earnings of you and your partner) increase to a level at which you are no longer entitled to JSA or IS. The waged option of the New Deal (see p58) counts as work.
- You must usually claim the bonus within 12 weeks of JSA or IS stopping or within 12 weeks of the end of a period of training which followed a period when you were entitled to JSA or IS.

There are special rules for:

- couples who get together or separate while claiming JSA or IS;
- partners of people who die while claiming JSA or IS;
- people who reach age 60 (if coming off IS) or pensionable age – 60 for women and 65 for men (if coming off JSA).

You can qualify for the bonus if your earnings are from self-employment.

A back to work bonus is treated as capital but disregarded for 52 weeks for family credit, disability working allowance, housing benefit and council tax benefit purposes.

2. CHILD MAINTENANCE BONUS

If you have been getting or are meant to be paid child maintenance (see p190) while on IS or income-based JSA, you can be paid a child maintenance bonus of up to £1,000 if you or your partner return to work or increase your hours or your pay and, as a result, your entitlement to those benefits ceases. See p192 to find out how much you can get.

Child maintenance includes:[2]

- child support maintenance (see p110);
- maintenance paid to you for your child(ren) by voluntary agreement or under a court order;
- maintenance being deducted from the benefit of an absent parent (see p118) who is liable to maintain your child(ren) see p106).

You can get a child maintenance bonus if:[3]

- You or your partner's entitlement to IS or income-based JSA ceases because one of you satisfies the 'work condition', ie:
  - takes up a new job or the waged option of the New Deal (see p58) or returns to work (but not if you return to work for the same employer at the same place of work following a trade dispute[4]); *or*
  - increases your weekly hours of work; *or*
  - has an increase in earnings.
- If your IS or income-based JSA ceases for another reason, you satisfy the work condition:
  - within the 14 days after your bonus period ends (see p191); *or*
  - within 12 weeks of the earliest of the dates an absent parent dies or stops being habitually resident in the UK or is found not to be your child(ren)'s parent; *or*
  - where you get maintenance for one child and s/he dies, within 12 months of her/his date of death.
- You or your partner start or resume work or increase your pay or hours (see above) prior to the day before:
  - your 60th birthday if you are coming off IS; *or*
  - you reach pensionable age (currently 60 for women and 65 for men) if you are coming off income-based JSA.
  Special rules apply if you do not satisfy the work condition before those ages (see p194).
- You have been getting child maintenance (see above) during a period when you or your partner were on IS or income-based JSA (your 'bonus period' – see p191).
- You claim within the time limit (see p193).

A child maintenance bonus is treated as capital,[5] but disregarded for 52 weeks for family credit, disability working allowance, housing benefit and council tax benefit purposes (see p426).

The bonus period

You accumulate a child maintenance bonus during your bonus period – ie, any period from 7 April 1997 when:[6]

- you or your partner were entitled or treated as entitled to IS or income-based JSA whether or not it was paid (unless you were getting an urgent cases payment because you were treated as having income which had not been paid – see p50); *and*
- you are getting or are meant to be paid child maintenance (see p190) for a child who lives with you but whose other parent does not. Your child still counts as living with you if s/he is away temporarily but not for more than 12 weeks. You count as getting child maintenance if it is being collected by the Child Support Agency or Benefits Agency on your behalf (see pp109 and 108), even if they retain the payments *or* it is being taken into account as income in working out how much IS or income-based JSA you can get (see p120).

When you or your partner stop claiming IS or income-based JSA due to work (see p190) the Benefits Agency looks at how much child maintenance (see p190) you were paid during your bonus period to calculate how much child maintenance bonus you can get (see p192).

If your bonus period ends but you cannot claim a child maintenance bonus (eg, because you do not satisfy the work condition), you do not necessarily lose out. The bonus period that ended can link to a second bonus period.

Two bonus periods link to count as one if they are separated by not more than 12 weeks *or* one of the following periods:[7]

- while you are getting maternity allowance; *or*
- of not more than two years throughout which you were getting incapacity benefit, severe disablement allowance or invalid care allowance.

Example
Beth stopped getting IS but could not claim a child maintenance bonus as she was not working (see p190). Three weeks later she started getting IS again. When she takes up full-time work the Benefits Agency should look at the child maintenance she was paid during both bonus periods when they calculate her child maintenance bonus.

Although bonus periods can link, it is best to claim your child maintenance bonus as soon as you satisfy the work condition (see p190) – eg, if you are uncertain how long a temporary job will last. See p193 for information about how and when you must claim.

A person's bonus period ends if s/he dies. See p195 for further information about what happens when a person with the care of a child dies.

How much child maintenance bonus can you get?

To calculate your child maintenance bonus, the Benefits Agency looks at how much child maintenance (see p190) you were paid or were meant to be paid during your 'bonus period' (see p191). Your child maintenance bonus is the lower of the following amounts:[8]

- £5, for every week where you were meant to be paid at least £5 child maintenance (see p190) *plus* for each week you were meant to be paid less than £5, the amount due; *or*
- the actual amount of child maintenance (see p190) you were paid. If it is not clear how much maintenance is being paid for your child(ren) because you are also getting it for yourself, £5 is taken into account as child maintenance (or all of what you are paid if this is less than £5).[9] Any child maintenance you get above what has been taken into account as income in working out your IS (see p120) or income-based JSA or what has been collected on your behalf by the Benefits Agency or Child Support Agency (see pp108 and 109) is not included; *or*
- £1,000.

Examples
Avni's ex-husband Sanjay agreed to pay £20 child maintenance a week. He did so during her bonus period of 250 weeks. Her bonus is the lower of:

$£5 \times 250 = £1,250$ *or*
$£20 \times 250 = £5,000$ *or*
£1,000

Avni will get a child maintenance bonus of £1,000.

Sarah's ex-husband Phil was meant to pay £20 child maintenance a week during her bonus period of 100 weeks. During that time Phil actually paid her £4 a week. Her bonus is the lower of:

$£5 \times 100$ weeks $= £500$ *or*
$£4 \times 100$ weeks $= £400$ *or*
£1,000

Sarah will get a child maintenance bonus of £400.

Lynn's former partner Robert was meant to pay £12 child maintenance a week during her bonus period of 50 weeks. He actually paid £6 a week. She will get the lower of:

£5 × 50 = £250 *or*

£6 × 50 = £300 *or*

£1,000

Lynn will get a child maintenance bonus of £250.

If your child maintenance bonus would be less than £5, you are not paid at all.[10]

While you are on IS or income-based JSA, the Secretary of State can send estimates of how much child maintenance bonus you might be paid were you to take up work.[11] If the DSS knows you are getting child maintenance (see p190) you should get a statement every six months. However, you can ask for a statement at any time – eg, if you are considering taking a job and want to know how much child maintenance bonus you have accumulated.

Claims

A claim for child maintenance bonus must be in writing and on the appropriate form.[12] You should return the form to the office where you or your partner claimed IS or income-based JSA.

If you are one of a couple, you should claim the child maintenance bonus if you are the one caring for a child for whom child maintenance (see p190) is paid.[13] If both you and your partner care for different children for whom child maintenance is paid, you can both qualify for a child maintenance bonus. In this case, each of you must claim. If you separate, you count as entitled to IS or income-based JSA on days when your former partner was claiming for you to help you qualify.[14]

You can claim in the week before the week in which you or your partner's entitlement to IS or income-based JSA ceases. This is useful, for example, where you know you or your partner are returning to work. Otherwise, you must claim within the time limits as follows:[15]

- no later than 28 days after you or your partner stop getting IS or income-based JSA; *or*
- where you are claiming because you stopped getting IS/income-based JSA in the 12 weeks before you reached age 60/pensionable age (see p194), no later than 28 days after you reach that age.

Different rules apply if you are an appointee claiming the child maintenance bonus of someone who has died (see p195).

Your claim is usually treated as made on the date it is received by the benefit office.[16] Your claim can be backdated but only if you can show that throughout the period between the date by which you should have claimed, and the date you actually claimed, you had 'good cause' for failing to claim.[17] However, your claim can never be backdated more than six months. See p285 for what counts as 'good cause' for a late claim.

If you do not complete the form properly or provide sufficient information and evidence to support your claim, you will be asked to do so, usually within one month.[18] You can be given longer than this if the Secretary of State thinks it is reasonable. It is important that you reply in time. If you do not complete the form properly, you might not get a child maintenance bonus unless you can show that you have 'good cause' for claiming late (see above).

You can ask for your claim to be amended or withdrawn.[19] You must do this in writing before a decision is made about your claim.

Special rules if you reach age 60 or retire

You can get a child maintenance bonus without having to make a claim even if you do not satisfy the work condition (see p190) if you:[20]

- turn 60 and on the day before you or your partner were entitled to IS; *or*
- reach pensionable age (60 for women and 65 for men) and on the day before you or your partner were entitled to income-based JSA; *or*
- stop getting income-based JSA after your 60th birthday but before you reach pensionable age and you become entitled to IS within 12 weeks or during any of the periods that link bonus periods listed on p191.

You can get a child maintenance bonus even if you do not satisfy the work condition, but you have to make a claim (see p193) if:[21]

- you or your partner's entitlement to IS ceases in the 12 weeks before your 60th birthday or to income-based JSA ceases in the 12 weeks before you reach pensionable age.

Your bonus period ends when you are paid a child maintenance bonus. You cannot get another one.[22]

Death of the person with care of the child

If someone who has been getting child maintenance dies, the child maintenance bonus s/he has already accumulated can be paid to an appointee (see below) or can help the person who takes over the care of her/his child(ren) get a higher child maintenance bonus (see below).

Payment to an appointee

If a person satisfies all of the conditions of entitlement to a child maintenance bonus described on p190 but does not claim and s/he dies within 28 days of her/his entitlement to IS or income-based JSA ceasing, the Secretary of State can appoint someone to claim a child maintenance bonus in her/his place.[23] You must apply to be an appointee within six months of the date of death and claim the child maintenance bonus, in writing, within six months of the date you are appointed. The Secretary of State can accept an application for appointment or a claim up to 12 months after the date of death in exceptional circumstances. However, if the time limit for one is extended, the other is shortened by the same amount of time. Any time between the date you apply to be an appointee and the date you are appointed is ignored.

Payment to a new carer

If you take over the care of someone's child(ren) when s/he dies, you might be able to claim any child maintenance bonus accumulated at the date of her/his death or within 12 weeks of that date. Unless you have already accumulated bonus for the same weeks, her/his bonus period (see p191) must be treated as part yours if:[24]

- on the date the person died, s/he or her/his partner was entitled to IS or income-based JSA or had been within the 12 weeks before the death;
- you are her/his close relative (see p28);
- you or your partner were entitled to IS or income-based JSA on the date of her/his death or within 12 weeks of when s/he was last entitled to those benefits.

3. EXTENDED PAYMENTS OF HOUSING BENEFIT AND COUNCIL TAX BENEFIT

If you or your partner start working full time or increase your earnings, you might be able to get four weeks housing benefit (HB) and council tax benefit (CTB) at the same rate you were getting when you were claiming IS or income-based JSA. This is what is known as an extended payment of HB and CTB. There are very strict time limits for claiming extended payments. See p266 for further details.

CHAPTER TEN

Family credit

This chapter covers all the rules about family credit and gives an outline of the new benefit, earnings top-up. It contains:

1. INTRODUCTION

Family credit (FC) is a tax-free benefit for low-paid workers with children. It tops up your wages if you are in full-time work (see p199). If you have a disability, you should consider claiming disability working allowance (DWA) instead as this may give you more money than FC (see p212). Part-time workers should claim income support (IS) instead of FC. If you pay rent and/or council tax you may get housing benefit (HB) (see p228) and/or council tax benefit (CTB) (see p327) as well, but your FC counts as income for these benefits.

If you receive FC you will not have to pay for certain health service benefits such as prescriptions (see Chapter 26), or certain discretionary education benefits (but you will not get free school meals), or certain help from social services provided for children or young people in need (see Appendix 1). You may also qualify for social fund payments for maternity or funeral expenses and crisis loans (see Chapters 21 and 24), and you can qualify for a discretionary grant from the local authority towards the cost of certain home improvements or for insulating your home (see Appendix 1).

Family credit is a weekly payment which normally continues at the same rate for 26 weeks, regardless of any changes in your circumstances (see p209).

You qualify for FC if:

- your income is low enough (see Chapter 19);
- your savings and capital are not worth over £8,000 (see Chapter 20);
- you are in GB (see below);
- you, or your partner (if you have one), normally work full time (ie, for 16 hours or more a week) (see p119);
- you have at least one dependent child (see p202);
- you have made a proper claim (see p205);
- neither you nor your partner are getting DWA instead (see p202).

You can claim for your 'family' (see Chapter 17).

You must claim in writing on the form in leaflet FC1 which you can get from your local post office or Benefits Agency office. For more details about claims, see p205.

2. THE BASIC RULES

Residence in Great Britain

The residence rules are explained in more detail in CPAG's *Migration and Social Security Handbook* (see Appendix 5).

To be entitled to FC you must be in Great Britain (GB).[1] This means England, Scotland and Wales. You can be treated as being in GB if:[2]

- you are present and ordinarily resident in GB; *and*
- your right to reside in GB is not subject to any limitation or condition (but see p199); *and*
- your partner (if any) is ordinarily resident in the United Kingdom (UK) (but see below); *and*
- at least part of your earnings (or your partner's earnings) are derived from full-time work in the UK; *and*
- your earnings (or those of your partner) do not come wholly from paid work done outside the UK.

You are ordinarily resident here if you normally live in GB (or, if relevant, the UK).[3] This means that the residence here has been adopted voluntarily and for settled purposes, although not necessarily with the intention of remaining indefinitely or for more than a limited period.[4] The United Kingdom includes Northern Ireland as well as GB. If you and your partner used to live together abroad but you now live in this country and s/he lives abroad, s/he is counted as your 'partner' for social security purposes if you intend to resume living together.[5] The fact that s/he is not ordinarily resident in the UK would therefore disentitle you.

The position is the same if your partner was living with you in this country but is now living abroad – if you intend to resume living together s/he is still regarded as your 'partner'. Again, the fact that s/he is not ordinarily resident in the UK would therefore disentitle you.[6]

You cannot be treated as being in GB during any period you or your partner are entitled to FC or DWA in Northern Ireland.[7]

There is no requirement that a child for whom you are responsible and who is a member of your household (see p346) should be present in GB.[8]

Even if you are resident in GB you will not be entitled to FC if your right to be here is subject to any limitation or condition[9] – eg, if you have been granted leave to remain in GB for six months as a visitor. This rule will not apply to you if:[10]

- you are a refugee;
- you are a person who has been granted exceptional leave to remain in the UK;
- you, or a member of your family, is a national of a state which is a signatory to the Agreement on the European Economic Area (the 'Oporto Agreement') – this includes all EU nationals;
- you are lawfully working in GB and you, or a member of your family, is a national of a state which the European Community has an agreement with concerning equal treatment of workers;
- you were getting FC before 5 February 1996 (it will apply if subsequently there is a relevant change of circumstances – see p209). A social security commissioner has, however, now held[11] that this exception no longer applies when you make a renewal claim (see p207) for FC – ie, after the award which was current on 5 February 1996 expired.

For more details, see the *Migration and Social Security Handbook*.

Full-time work

To be entitled to FC, you, or your partner (if any), must be 'engaged and normally engaged in remunerative work'.[12] Work includes self-employment and can also include people who work from home (eg, childminders, writers or some carers) if they are paid[13] or expect to be paid. If you have been getting a Business Start-Up Allowance, the work you do will not count as 'remunerative work' unless you are receiving (or have a realistic expectation of receiving) payment from other sources.[14] You may still be treated as in 'remunerative work' where you are employed but receive no earnings but are only paid in kind – eg, free accommodation[15] or free produce for farmworkers[16]. Note that payments in kind are generally not treated as 'earnings' (see p380) but as other income which may be disregarded (see p409).

Unless you are claiming FC on account of any other work you do, you will *not* be treated as in work if you are:

- on a scheme for which a training allowance is paid;[17] *or*
- on a course of education as a student;[18] *or*
- a volunteer or working for a charitable or voluntary organisation and only your expenses are paid;[19] *or*
- a carer paid by the health or local authority, or a voluntary organisation, for looking after someone who is not normally a member of your household.[20]

You are entitled if you:[21]

- work for not less than 16 hours, or, if your hours fluctuate, 16 hours on average, a week; *and*
- are employed at the date of claim; *and*
- are paid, or expect to be paid. Any expectation of payment must be realistic – a mere hope or desire that you will be paid is not enough to make your work count as 'remunerative' work.[22]

In addition[23] you must:

- actually work for 16 hours or more in either the week in which you claim or one of the two preceding weeks; *or*
- be expected by your employers (or yourself if you are self-employed) to work for 16 hours or more in the week after the week you claim (this applies if you have just started work); *or*
- if you are on holiday from work but are expected to (or, if you are self-employed, you expect to) work 16 hours or more in the week after you return. You are not treated as on holiday if you are off sick or on maternity leave.[24]

The work must be your normal work and you must be likely to continue in that job for at least five weeks after your claim.[25] What is 'normal' depends on your individual circumstances[26] – eg, the likely future pattern of work, the past pattern and all other relevant circumstances.[27] If you have only just started work, but are likely to continue working, this should be sufficient to enable you to qualify.[28]

If you do not do at least 16 hours' work in one of the three relevant weeks, your claim will be disallowed (unless you are starting or resuming work after a holiday and thus covered because you are expected to work more than 16 hours). This applies even if the reason you have not been working the necessary hours is because of sickness,[29] maternity leave, suspension, short-time working, lay-off or because you are only on call.[30]

However, you should be treated as working if you are on duty and required to be available during a part of the day and/or night – eg, if you are a warden in sheltered housing.

In calculating your hours, include all the hours you actually work for which you are paid. If you routinely need to work over your contractual hours, these extra hours can also count even if you are not paid for them.[31] Lunch-breaks (and for DWA, paid time off to attend a hospital or clinic in relation to your disability) should be included in the total if they are paid.[32] Your total hours can be made up from more than one job but, where you are claiming as a couple, you may not add your partner's hours to your own.[33] If you are self-employed, you can count not only the hours spent on services for which you are paid, but also other time which is essential to your business – eg, preparation time.[34]

If you are employed and you have not got a normal pattern of working hours (because you have just started a new job, or just changed your hours, or just returned to work after a break of more than four weeks – 13 for DWA), you qualify if it is expected that you will work 16 or more hours on average each week.[35] If you are self-employed and have not yet worked for five weeks (or your hours have gone up to 16 or more over the past five weeks), take the average hours that you expect to work.[36]

Otherwise hours are calculated by looking at your normal cycle of work and assessing your weekly hours. If you always work the same number of hours a week this is straightforward. If your work pattern is different (eg, you work one week on and one week off) your hours are averaged out. Periods when you do not normally work (eg, the 'week off') are included when working out the average but other absences (eg, for sickness) are not.[37]

If you have no recognisable cycle of work, the average over the five-week period immediately before the week in which you claim is used, or over another period if this would more accurately reflect your average working hours.[38]

If you have a recognisable cycle of work of one year, including school or similar holidays during which you do not work, in calculating your average number of hours you should ignore those holidays and also any other periods when you do not have to work.[39]

If you are unsure about whether you are working for 16 hours or more at the time of your claim, you should make a further claim in a week when you are more certain that you are working for 16 hours or more. This is because it may take the Benefits Agency a long time to send you a decision on the first claim and, if the first claim is refused because you were working for less than 16 hours a week, any second claim will only run from the date it is made unless you meet one of the qualifying reasons for having the claim backdated (see p134).

Family credit or income support?

Sometimes it is difficult to show that you normally work at least 16 hours a week and the distinction between FC and IS is not absolute. For example, you may fail to qualify for IS because you are found to be in full-time work, yet still fail to qualify for FC because the work is held not to be the work you normally do. You may also be refused both FC and IS because adjudication officers at the local Benefits Agency office and the Family Credit Unit interpret the rules, on the same facts, differently. If this happens, appeal against both decisions and ask for them to be heard together so a tribunal can decide which benefit is appropriate. In the meantime you could apply for interim payments. Note, however, that you will only be eligible for an interim payment when you are appealing if it is clear that you are entitled to some benefit, and even then you may get turned down (see p145).

You will fall within *both* schemes if you have a partner and s/he works for 16 hours or more a week but less than 24 hours a week.[40] Alternatively, if you are a childminder working from home for 16 hours or more a week, you are not treated as in full-time work for the purposes of IS (see p15), and so may be entitled to claim either IS or FC/DWA. In either case you may choose which benefit to claim. If you have to pay housing costs (see p27), in most cases it will be better to claim IS. You may even claim both IS and FC at the same time. Although FC counts as income for IS purposes (see p395), it may still be worthwhile claiming FC if your circumstances are likely to improve in the foreseeable future as you may still keep your FC award for up to 26 weeks (see p209). Seek advice if this applies to you.

Responsibility for a child

To get FC, you or your partner must be responsible for at least one child who is a member of your household.[41] You do not have to be their parent. (For when you are responsible for a child, see p353.)

Overlap with disability working allowance

You cannot get FC if you or your partner have been awarded DWA. This does not apply if:

- your DWA is due to expire within six weeks of the date you claim FC; *and*
- you fulfil all the other conditions of entitlement to FC; *and*
- you are claiming FC for the period immediately after your DWA ends.[42]

In all other cases, you have to wait until your DWA award comes to an end before claiming FC (see p207).

Check whether you are better off claiming FC or DWA (see p216).

3. THE AMOUNT OF BENEFIT

Your FC is calculated by taking account of the number and ages of your children, the income and capital you and your family possess and the amount of hours you and/or your partner work.

To work out FC, first of all calculate the **maximum FC** for your family (see below). Then compare your income (see Chapter 19) with a set figure of £79 (called the applicable amount).[43] If your income is the same as or below the applicable amount you receive maximum FC. If your income exceeds the applicable amount, your maximum FC is reduced by 70 per cent of the difference.[44]

Maximum family credit

The maximum family credit is made up of an adult credit and a credit for each child.[45] The current rates are:[46]

Credit for adult (lone parent or couple)	£48.80
Credit for adult working 30 hours or more a week	£10.80
Credit for child aged	
0–10	£12.35*
11–15	£20.45
16–18	£25.40
Additional partners in a polygamous marriage	£25.40

* This will be increased to £14.85 from November 1998.

Example of maximum FC
For a couple (working less than 30 hours) with three children aged 5, 7 and 13 the maximum is:

£48.80	for the couple
£24.70	for the two children under 11
£20.45	for the eldest child
£93.95	is the total maximum FC for this family

You do not receive a credit for any child who:[47]

- has more than £3,000 capital (savings etc) of their own (see p416); *or*
- has a higher weekly income (other than disregarded income or that from maintenance) than the appropriate credit for a child of that age; *or*

- has been in hospital or residential accommodation because of illness or disability for 52 weeks before the date of claim (see p355).

A child is not treated as being aged 11 or 16 until the first Tuesday in September following her/his 11th or 16th birthday.[48]

Your maximum FC will include an extra £10.80 a week if you and/or your partner work for 30 hours or more a week.[49] The way your hours are calculated is the same as for those working 16 hours or more[50] (see p201).

The family credit calculation

You now compare your income (see Chapter 19) with the applicable amount.

Example

Shahida has a partner and two children aged 3 and 5. Her partner works 30 hours a week and the total family income taken into account for the purposes of FC is £107.60. The maximum FC in her case is £84.30 (£48.80 for the couple, £12.35 for each child and £10.80 because her partner works 30 hours a week).

Her income exceeds the applicable amount by £28.60 (£107.60 less £79); 70 per cent of the excess is £20.02.

Maximum FC   £84.30
less   £20.02 (70% of excess)
equals   £64.28 weekly FC
Shahida will therefore receive £64.28 each week in FC.

If her income had been £79 or less she would have received the maximum FC.

Any fractions produced at the end of the FC calculation are rounded up to a penny if they are a half-penny or more, and are ignored if less than a half-penny.[51]

The minimum amount of FC that will be paid is 50 pence a week.[52]

Your FC can be reduced if you fail to apply for child support maintenance (see p114).

Note: Some childcare costs can be deducted when working out your income (see p392).

4. SPECIAL RULES FOR SPECIAL GROUPS

People from abroad

Most people from abroad can no longer claim FC because of the residence conditions (see p198).

People involved in a trade dispute

If you are involved in a trade dispute, you can still claim FC but your normal weekly earnings are taken as those prior to the dispute[53] and so do not reflect your actual income during the dispute. Also, you, or your partner, would have to have worked in one of the three weeks around the date of your claim (see p200), or else you would need to argue that, in spite of the dispute, your employer is still expecting you to work in the following week. If you are already getting FC when you become involved in a trade dispute you continue to receive it at the same rate for the rest of the 26 weeks of your award.[54]

Since there are no other special rules under FC for the assessment of your income and capital if you or your partner are involved in a trade dispute, the normal rules apply.

5. CLAIMS AND GETTING PAID

Claims

There is an FC Helpline which can give advice about FC. The number is 01253 500050 and it is open 7.30 am – 6.30 pm Monday to Friday.

Your claim should be on form FC1. For couples, the claim must be made by the female partner unless the Secretary of State decides that it is reasonable to accept a claim from the male partner.[55] The claim is usually considered to have been made on the day it reaches the Family Credit Unit (see Appendix 3 for address).[56] However, if you get the claim form by contacting your local Benefits Agency office, the Family Credit Unit or JobCentre, your claim will count as having been made on the day your request for the claim form was received in the office, as long as you get the claim form back to the Family Credit Unit within one month of requesting it.[57]

You must provide your national insurance number. From 5 October 1998, you also have to provide your partner's national insurance number unless your claim is made or treated as made before that date. If you do not know your national insurance number, you must provide evidence or information to enable the Benefits Agency to trace it. This is known as the 'NINO requirement'. If you do not have a national insurance number, the NINO requirement is satisfied if you apply for one, so long as information and evidence is provided to enable one to be allocated.

The NINO requirement does not apply:

- to children or young people for whom you are claiming benefit;
- if your claim was made or treated as made before 9 February 1998.

If you do not use the right form or if you fill it in incorrectly, the date of your first attempt to claim will still count provided you correct it within one month of being asked to do so. This time limit can be extended.[58] If you are just starting work after being unemployed you can ask a claimant adviser at the JobCentre to give you the form. Alternatively you can get it from your local Benefits Agency. Both will help you fill it in and, in either case, your claim is likely to be dealt with more speedily as the JobCentre/ Benefits Agency should mark the FC1 to ensure that you get a quick decision. If you prefer, you can get the form from a post office or your local advice centre (see Appendix 4).

If you claim income support (IS) or jobseeker's allowance (JSA) when you should have claimed FC, your claim for FC can be treated as made on the day you claimed IS or JSA. This will apply if you have been refused IS or JSA because you, or your partner (if any), are in full-time work (see p13), and you claim FC within 14 days of the decision refusing your claim for IS/JSA.[59] You can ask for the FC claim to start on a later date – eg, if your wages are about to go down.

A claim for FC can be backdated for a maximum of three months but only in exceptional circumstances. The rules on backdating are the same as for IS (see pp134-36), except that in relation to backdating for up to one month for *good administrative reasons* (see p137):

- the fact that you claimed FC within one month of your entitlement to IS or JSA stopping is an *additional* qualifying reason;[60] *and*
- the fact that the claim was made within one month of separating from your partner is *not* a qualifying reason.[61]

Note: Backdating will be restricted to only one month when the new Social Security Bill is introduced, probably in June 1998 (see Appendix 2).

If you have made a claim but then your circumstances change (eg, your income suddenly drops), you can amend or withdraw your claim. But you must act quickly. Your letter must arrive before the adjudication officer has decided your claim.[62]

Renewal claims

If you are renewing your claim[63] after a period on FC you should be reminded that it is about to run out and invited to re-apply. You can put in your renewal claim up to 28 days before the current award expires or within 14 days of it running out. Your renewal claim then follows on immediately from your previous award. If you are changing from disability working allowance (DWA) to FC you can make your claim up to 42 days before your DWA award expires or 14 days afterwards and FC is then paid from the date the DWA ends.

When to claim

It is worth thinking carefully about when you should claim, bearing in mind:

* Awards of FC run from a Tuesday so you should try to get your claim to the Benefits Agency on a Tuesday or on the Monday before. If your claim arrives on a Wednesday, your entitlement will not start until the following Tuesday and you lose benefit for that week.[64]
* Make sure your claim is made during a week in which you are eligible to claim (see p200).
* If you are thinking about making a claim in late February or March it might be to your advantage to consider delaying the claim until April. This is because the amounts for FC are uprated in April. You will need to work out whether it is worth losing three or four weeks' FC in order to receive the higher rate for the next 26 weeks. However, if you claim no more than 28 days before benefits are increased and you do not qualify for FC at the old rates but would under the new ones, you can be treated as entitled and paid from the date the increases take effect.[65] In all other cases, even if you are not entitled on the date your claim is made, provided you would be entitled for the period beginning within three days of that date, your claim will be treated as if it had been made from the later date.[66]
* A claim for DWA can be treated as a claim for FC.[67] If you are refused DWA, you could ask for this to happen and thus have FC paid from the date of your DWA claim. If you are entitled to both you must choose which one to claim *before* a decision is made. Once you have been awarded FC you cannot change to DWA until 26 weeks have elapsed and *vice versa*.
* Consider whether your family circumstances are about to change in a way which might affect your FC. For example, if you are about to take a drop in income or have another child, it might be worth delaying your claim.

208 *Back to work benefits, FC and DWA* 10: *Family credit*

- As renewal claims will be determined as if they were made on the first day after your previous award expires, they will not normally take into account any changes of circumstances occurring within the 14-day renewal period (see p207). If any such changes would be likely to result in an increase in your new award (eg, your partner's unemployment benefit is about to end), you should consider foregoing your entitlement for this 14 days and either submit a fresh claim after the 14 days have passed, or else state in your renewal claim that you wish it to be treated as a fresh claim instead. The adjudication officer has a duty to treat your new application in the way you indicate.[68]

Send off your claim form even if you cannot complete all the details. You can send missing details or documents on later. Keep a copy of your claim in case queries arise.

How your claim is dealt with

When your claim is received by the Family Credit Unit, the information you have provided is checked and verification can be obtained from your employer about your wages or salary.[69] You should ask your employer to reply promptly. If you have claimed through a claimant adviser or local Benefits Agency, your wages are checked by telephone which speeds up your claim. On a renewal claim, if you are still working for the same employer, the Benefits Agency may accept your wage slips as evidence of your earnings and not contact your employer again.

Then your claim is referred to an adjudication officer for decision. The law requires that all claims should be dealt with within 14 days 'so far as practicable'.[70] However, since April 1996 the intention has been to process most new claims within five days.[71] You are given the decision concerning your claim in writing. The letter from the Family Credit Unit should give the reasons for the decision and tell you about your right to appeal.[72]

Delays and complaints

If you suffer delays, or wish to complain about how your claim has been dealt with, see pp148 and 165. The advice given there applies equally to FC.

Family credit – getting paid

You are paid by order book or into an account (including your partner's account), whichever you have requested. If your weekly FC is £4 or less, you will usually be paid in a lump sum covering the whole 26-week period,[73] but if it is less than 50 pence a week, FC will not be paid at all.[74]

Payments will start from the first Tuesday of the week after your claim is treated as made. Payments by order book are made weekly in arrears.[75] If you have asked to be paid by direct credit transfer,[76] these payments should be credited to your account every seven days in arrears.

If your order book is lost or stolen or your FC is suspended, the rules are the same as for IS (see p147). There are similar rules for when your FC can be suspended (see p146).

Change of circumstances

If your circumstances change during the 26 weeks, this does not usually affect the amount you are paid.[77] However:

- if a child or young person leaves your household while FC is being paid and IS, DWA or FC is awarded to them or for them in a different household, your FC stops from the first day of any overlap[78] and you will need to make a fresh claim if you have another child and are still entitled to FC;
- if a child for whom you are responsible (see p353) ceases full-time education (see p16), and if there are no other children for whom you are responsible and who are in full-time education, your award of FC will be reviewed and you will stop getting benefit. Your FC will stop on the date the child turns 16 or the date s/he ceases full-time education, whichever is the later.[79] Note that there is now a single school-leaving date which is the last Friday in June in the school year when the child reaches 16 (for 1998 this date is 26 June);
- if a claimant dies during the 26-week period, FC stops if s/he was single. If s/he was one of a couple (see p347), the partner is paid the rest of the award provided that s/he was the partner when FC was claimed;[80]
- if you are later notified that FC or DWA has been awarded to you for a period beginning before your existing award, and the new award overlaps with any period of your existing award, your existing award will be terminated from the date you are notified of this, so that the new award can take its place (this may happen as a result of the time taken to complete a review of or an appeal against an earlier claim or because a later claim is backdated);[81]
- if you fail to comply with the requirement to apply for child support maintenance and a reduced benefit direction is issued (see p114), the amount of your FC is adjusted during your current award. This also applies where the reduced benefit direction ceases, is cancelled or suspended, or reinstated after a suspension.

Where your earnings are estimated and it transpires that the estimate was wrong, this does not amount to a change of circumstances and your benefit cannot be reviewed.[82] However, if you appeal against the amount of FC your award might be revised to take account of your actual earnings.

Overpayments and fraud

The rules on overpayments and fraud are the same as for IS (see p156). The IS rules limiting the maximum amount that can be recovered from your weekly benefit[83] do not apply to FC, but you should argue for realistic repayments.

6. CHALLENGING A FAMILY CREDIT DECISION

You can apply for a review of an FC decision, or appeal against it, see p140 and Chapter 8. The advice given there in relation to IS applies equally to FC, except that reviews on the grounds of a change of circumstances are very limited in relation to FC (see p209).

When an FC decision is reviewed, payment of arrears is not restricted *unless* the review was because of ignorance of, or a mistake about, the facts, and you were aware of (or should have been aware of) these facts but you failed to tell the Benefits Agency. In this case you can only get up to one month's arrears.[84]

7. EARNINGS TOP-UP

From October 1996, a new benefit, earnings top-up (ETU), has been introduced on a pilot basis in eight areas. Earnings top-up is similar to FC, but it is available to people in low-paid work who do *not* have dependent children.

In four of the areas, ETU is paid at a **lower rate** (Scheme A), and in the other four at a **higher rate** (Scheme B).

The Scheme A areas are:
- Newcastle-upon-Tyne;
- Castleford and Pontefract, Wakefield and Dewsbury, and Barnsley;
- Southend; *and*
- Bangor and Caernarfon, Conway and Colwyn, Denbigh, Dolgellau and Barmouth, Holyhead, Shotton, Flint and Rhyl, and Wrexham.

The Scheme B areas are:
- Sunderland;
- Doncaster;
- Bournemouth; *and*
- Perth and Crieff, Dumbarton, and Stirling.

The pilot scheme is intended to run for three years until 1999. The details are contained in the scheme rules, not regulations.

The calculation for ETU is very similar to that for FC. The maximum amount you will receive if you work less than 30 hours a week is as follows:

	Single under 25	*Single 25+*	*Couple*
Scheme A (lower)	£23.90	£29.45	£48.80
Scheme B (higher)	£23.90	£29.45	£58.90

CHAPTER ELEVEN

Disability working allowance

This chapter deals with the rules about disability working allowance. It covers:

1. Introduction (below)
2. The basic rules (p213)
3. The amount of benefit (p217)
4. Special rules for special groups (p218)
5. Claims and getting paid (p218)
6. Challenging a DWA decision (p223)
7. Giving up work because of sickness or disability (p224)

1. INTRODUCTION

Disability working allowance (DWA) is a tax-free benefit for low-paid workers with a disability. It tops up your wages if you are in full-time work (see p213). Part-time workers can claim income support (IS) instead. If you are in low-paid work but do not have a disability you could claim family credit (FC) if you have children (see Chapter 10). If you pay rent and/or council tax you may get housing benefit (HB) (see p228) and/or council tax benefit (CTB) (see p327) as well, but your DWA counts as income for these benefits.

Receipt of DWA helps you to qualify for a disability premium with IS/HB/CTB.[1] In addition, if you receive DWA you do not have to pay for health service benefits such as prescriptions (see Chapter 26), or certain discretionary education benefits (but you will not get free school meals), or certain help from social services provided for children or young people in need (see Appendix 1). You may also qualify for social fund payments for maternity or funeral expenses and crisis loans (see Chapters 21 and 24), and you can qualify for a discretionary grant from the local authority towards the cost of certain home improvements or for insulating your home (see Appendix 1).

Disability working allowance is a weekly payment which normally continues at the same rate for 26 weeks regardless of changes in your circumstances (see p222). If your earnings are too low to pay national insurance you will get a credit for each week on DWA.[2]

Who can claim

You qualify for DWA if:

- you are 16 or over;
- your income is low enough (see Chapter 19);
- your savings and capital are not worth more than £16,000 (see Chapter 20);
- you are in Great Britain (see below);
- you normally work full time – ie, for 16 hours or more a week (see below);
- you have a physical or mental disability which puts you at a disadvantage in getting a job (see p214);
- you are, or have recently been, getting a sickness or disability benefit (see p215);
- you have made a proper claim (see p218);
- neither you nor your partner (if any) are getting FC instead (see p216).

Who you claim for

You claim for your 'family' (see Chapter 17). For more details about claims, see p218.

If you become sick while on DWA

There are special rules to protect your entitlement to the incapacity benefits which you were claiming before you took up work (see p224).

2. THE BASIC RULES

Residence in Great Britain[3]

The rules are the same as for FC[4] (see p198).

Full-time work

The rules are the same as for FC (see p199).

The disability and disadvantage test

To qualify for DWA you must have a physical or mental disability which puts you at a disadvantage in getting a job.[5] If you are claiming for the first time, or after a period of two years when you were not getting DWA, you simply have to sign a declaration that this applies to you. This will be accepted *unless* the information given on your claim form is contradictory, *or* the adjudication officer has other evidence which indicates that you do not fulfil that condition.[6] For all other claims, you fulfil this condition if one of the following applies:[7]

- you are paid one of the following benefits (or a Northern Ireland equivalent) – but see below:
  - the higher or middle rate care component or the higher rate mobility component of the disability living allowance;
  - attendance allowance;
  - industrial disablement benefit or a war pension, where you are at least 80 per cent disabled;
  - mobility supplement;
- you have an invalid 'trike' or similar vehicle (but see below);
- you were paid severe disablement allowance (or a Northern Ireland equivalent) for at least one day in the eight weeks prior to your 'initial claim'. Initial claim means your first successful claim for DWA, or a new claim where you have not been getting DWA during the last two years;
- you cannot keep your balance without continually holding on to something when standing;
- you cannot walk 100 metres on level ground without stopping or suffering severe pain. You are expected to use a walking aid (eg, crutches, a stick, a frame or an artificial limb) if you normally do so;
- you cannot use either of your hands behind your back (as you would when putting on a jacket or tucking your shirt in);
- you cannot extend either of your hands forwards in order to shake hands with someone without difficulty;
- you cannot put either of your hands up to your head without difficulty (as when putting on a hat);
- you cannot, with one hand, pick up a coin of 2.5cm diameter because of a lack of manual dexterity;
- you cannot pick up a full one-litre jug and pour from it into a cup without difficulty;
- you cannot turn either of your hands sideways through 180 degrees;
- you are registered blind or partially sighted;

- you cannot read 16-point print from more than 20cm distance, even when wearing your normal glasses, if any;
- you cannot hear a telephone ring when in the same room, even with your hearing aid, if any;
- you cannot hear someone talking in a loud voice when the room is quiet and they are only two metres away from you, even with your hearing aid, if any;
- people who know you well have difficulty understanding what you say;
- you have difficulty understanding a person you know well when s/he speaks to you;
- you lose consciousness during a fit or go into a coma at least once a year during waking hours;
- you are mentally ill for which you are receiving regular medical treatment;
- you are often confused or forgetful due to mental disability;
- you cannot do simple addition and subtraction;
- you hit people, or damage property or cannot socialise because of your mental disability;
- you cannot manage an eight-hour working day or a five-day week because of your medical condition or because you suffer from intermittent or continuous severe pain;
- following illness or accident you are undergoing rehabilitation. You can only use this condition to qualify on an initial claim (see p214).

If you fulfil the disability test for DWA because you are paid one of the specified benefits, or have an invalid trike, you will nevertheless be refused DWA if there is evidence that none of the above disability conditions are fulfilled.[8]

Receipt of a sickness or disability benefit

To qualify for DWA you must also be, or have been, receiving a sickness or disability benefit.[9] You are entitled if, *when you claim*, you are receiving:

- disability living allowance;
- attendance allowance;
- an increase of your industrial disablement benefit or war pension for attendance needs;
- a corresponding benefit from Northern Ireland.

Alternatively, you qualify if, *for at least one day in the eight weeks prior to your claim*, you were getting:

- the higher rate of short-term incapacity benefit or long-term incapacity benefit (or invalidity benefit[10]) or severe disablement allowance;

- IS, income-based jobseeker's allowance (JSA), HB or CTB, if your applicable amount included the disability or higher pensioner (on the ground of disability) premium either for yourself or your partner (see pp362 and 365);
- a corresponding benefit from Northern Ireland.

You also meet this condition if you have an invalid trike or similar vehicle when you claim.

Similarly, you will also qualify if, for at least one day in the eight weeks prior to your claim you were on a 'training for work' course, and within the eight weeks before your first day of training you were getting either the higher rate of short-term or long-term incapacity benefit (or invalidity benefit), or severe disablement allowance (or a corresponding benefit from Northern Ireland). A 'training for work' course means one under the Employment and Training Act 1973 or, in Scotland, the Enterprise and New Towns (Scotland) Act 1990, or one you attend for at least 16 hours a week and the main purpose of which is to teach occupational or vocational skills.[11]

If you are renewing your DWA claim within eight weeks of a previous award running out, you are deemed to be receiving the appropriate award of incapacity benefit (or invalidity benefit), severe disablement allowance or a disability or higher pensioner premium paid with IS, HB or CTB (or a Northern Ireland equivalent) where your previous award was made on this basis.[12]

Entitlement to family credit

You are not entitled to DWA if, when you claim, you (or your partner) are entitled to FC.[13] However, this does not apply if:[14]

- your FC claim runs out within 28 days of your DWA claim;
- you are otherwise entitled to DWA;
- your DWA claim is for the period immediately after your FC runs out.

Check whether you are better off claiming FC or DWA. Disability working allowance is usually paid at a higher rate and entitles you to a disability premium for HB/CTB (see p362).

3. THE AMOUNT OF BENEFIT

To work out DWA, first of all calculate your maximum DWA (see below). Then compare your income (see Chapter 19) with your applicable amount which is a set figure of:

    £59.25 (single claimants)

or   £79.00 (couples or lone parents)

If your income is the same as or less than your applicable amount you receive maximum DWA. If it is more, you get the maximum DWA minus 70 per cent of the difference between your income and the applicable amount.[15]

Maximum DWA

This is made up of allowances for each member of your family (see p346). These are as follows:[16]

single claimant	£50.75
couple/lone parent	£79.40
credit for adult working 30 hours or more a week	£10.80
child aged:	
0-10	£12.35*
11-15	£20.45
16-18	£25.40
disabled child allowance (if applicable)	£21.45
additional partners in a polygamous marriage	£25.40

* This will be increased to £14.85 from November 1998.

The conditions of entitlement to the disabled child allowance are similar to those for the IS/HB/CTB disabled child premium (see p362), but there is no capital condition.[17]

Note that the age allowance for a child (as distinct from the disabled child allowance) is not payable for a child who has:

- capital of over £3,000 (see p416); *or*
- weekly income (excluding maintenance or disregarded income) which is greater than their allowance; *or*
- been in hospital or local authority residential accommodation for the 52 weeks prior to your claim because of physical or mental illness/disability.

A child is not treated as being aged 11 or 16 until the first Tuesday in September following her/his 11th or 16th birthday.[18]

As for FC, your maximum DWA will be increased by an extra £10.80 a week if you and/or your partner work for 30 hours or more a week.[19] The way your hours are calculated is the same as for FC[20] (see p201).

Calculating DWA

Work out your income (see Chapter 19), and compare this to your applicable amount.

Example

Winston is 19 and single. He works 35 hours a week. His income for DWA is £75. He has no savings.

His maximum DWA is £61.55 (single person's allowance of £50.75 and £10.80 because of the number of hours he works).

His income exceeds the applicable amount of £59.25 by £15.75. Thus his maximum DWA is reduced by £11.03 (70 per cent of £15.75) and he is paid £50.52 a week (£61.55 less £11.03).

If his income had been at or below £59.25 he would have received the maximum DWA.

Any fractions produced at the end of the DWA calculation are rounded up to a penny if they are half a penny or more, and are ignored if less than half a penny.[21]

The minimum amount of DWA that will be paid is 50 pence a week.[22]

Your DWA can be reduced if you fail to apply for child support maintenance (see p114).

Note: As with FC (see p392), childcare costs can sometimes be deducted from your income.

4. SPECIAL RULES FOR SPECIAL GROUPS

The rules for people from abroad are the same as for FC (see p205). The rules for people involved in a trade dispute are similar to those for FC (see p205). Earnings for set periods immediately prior to the trade dispute (or periods of short-term working) are normally used to calculate your normal weekly earnings.[23]

5. CLAIMS AND GETTING PAID

Claims

You claim DWA using the claim pack[24] which you can get from the Benefits Agency, a post office or JobCentre.

If you prefer, you can ring the Benefits Enquiry Line free of charge on 0800 882200. Benefits Agency staff will discuss your claim and complete the appropriate forms for you. These are sent to you to sign and post.

You must provide your national insurance number. From 5 October 1998, you also have to provide your partner's national insurance number unless your claim is made or treated as made before that date. If you do not know your national insurance number, you must provide evidence or information to enable the Benefits Agency to trace it. This is known as the 'NINO requirement'. If you do not have a national insurance number, the NINO requirement is satisfied if you apply for one, so long as information and evidence is provided to enable one to be allocated.

The NINO requirement does not apply:

• to children or young people for whom you are claiming benefit;
• if your claim was made or treated as made before 9 February 1998.

Do not delay sending in the DWA1 just because you do not yet have your payslips or a completed form EEF 200 from your employer (this form confirms your hours/earnings if you have not yet worked for nine weeks) – these can be sent later.

If you are one of a couple the disabled partner should claim. If both of you are disabled you can choose who should be the claimant, but if you cannot agree the Secretary of State decides for you.[25]

If you do not use the proper form or fill it in incorrectly and then return the corrected form within one month of being asked to do so, the date of your first claim counts. This period can be extended if you have a good reason but it is best to act promptly.[26] If you want to amend or withdraw your claim, write to the Benefits Agency immediately. Your letter must arrive before the adjudication officer has decided your claim.[27]

If you claim FC, this can be treated as a claim for DWA if you would be better off.[28] However, you must let both the FC and DWA Units know that you want them to do this *before* your FC claim is assessed.

Your claim is normally treated as made on the date it is received at the DWA Unit.[29]

However, if you got the claim pack by contacting your local Benefits Agency office, the DWA Unit or JobCentre, your claim will count as having been made on the day your request for the claim pack was received in the office, as long as you get the claim pack back to the DWA Unit within one month of requesting it.[30] Also, if you start work on a Monday or Tuesday and claim DWA in the same week your claim is treated as made on the Tuesday of that week.[31]

If you claim IS or income-based JSA when you should have claimed DWA, your claim for DWA can be treated as made on the day you claimed IS or income-based JSA. This will apply if you have been refused IS or JSA because you, or your partner (if any), are in full-time work (see p13), and you claim DWA within 14 days of the decision refusing your claim for IS/income-based JSA.[32] You can ask for the DWA claim to start on a later date – eg, if your wages are about to go down.

Your claim for DWA will also be treated as having been made on an earlier date if:[33]

• you had made an earlier claim for DWA which had been refused because at the time of the claim you were not, or had not been, receiving one of the relevant sickness or disability benefits (see p215); *and*

• at the time of the earlier claim for DWA you had made a claim for one of the relevant sickness or disability benefits but the claim had not been decided; *and*

• after being refused DWA, the claim for one of the relevant sickness or disability benefits is decided in your favour; *and*

• you make a further claim for DWA within three months of the decision awarding you one of the relevant sickness or disability benefits.

In these circumstances, the further claim for DWA will be treated as having been made on either the date of your earlier claim for DWA or the date from which you are awarded the relevant sickness or disability benefit, whichever is the later.[34]

Note: This rule will not apply to you if you qualify for DWA through having been on a 'training for work' course[35] (see p216). It will also not apply if the second claim for DWA is made within three months of you being turned down on the first claim for DWA.[36] In this circumstance, the second claim is treated as a review request,[37] though your claim date is still treated as that of your later claim.[38]

A claim can be backdated for up to three months but only in exceptional circumstances. The rules on backdating are the same as for IS (see pp134-36), except that, in relation to backdating (for up to one month) for *good administrative reasons* (see p135):

• the fact that you claimed DWA within one month of your entitlement to IS, JSA, incapacity benefit or severe disablement allowance stopping is an *additional* qualifying reason;[39] *and*

• the fact that the claim was made within one month of separating from your partner is *not* a qualifying reason.[40]

Note: Backdating will be restricted to only one month when the new Social Security Bill is introduced, probably in June 1998 (see Appendix 2).

Renewal claims

If you are currently getting DWA, you should be sent a claim form eight weeks before your payments end. You can reclaim from six weeks before your award runs out and up to two weeks afterwards. It is usually best to claim as early as possible to ensure that your payments are not interrupted. On your renewal claim you have to fill in a fresh DWA1 and you will also be sent form DWA2 which asks you questions about the extent of your disability and how it affects you.

If you are currently getting FC, you can claim DWA up to four weeks before your FC expires or two weeks afterwards.[41]

When to claim

For practical advice on when to claim DWA, see p207 as the rules for FC are the same.

How your claim is dealt with

When your claim is received, the information in it is checked to see if further details are needed. If so, you are asked to provide extra information or documents. You are obliged to provide this if requested and should do so *within a month*.[42] If there is a good reason this time limit can be extended, but if you reply quickly your DWA will be paid sooner. The Benefits Agency can also approach your employer for confirmation of your earnings and s/he must reply.[43]

Your claim is then passed to an adjudication officer for decision, and this should be made within 14 days if possible.[44]

If this is your first claim for DWA or you are reclaiming after two years of not getting DWA, it is usually accepted that your disability puts you at a disadvantage in getting a job if you say it does on form DWA1.[45] You do not have to fill in form DWA2 to prove this unless there is other evidence to suggest that you do not qualify, in which case the adjudication officer will ask you to do so. In all other cases, the adjudication officer considers your answers to the disability questions to decide if you qualify. The DWA2 form asks you to give the names of two health professionals who know about your disability and the adjudication officer may contact them to confirm your answers to the questions. S/he can also ask for advice from DSS doctors about your condition and how it is likely to affect you but s/he must make the decision.[46]

If necessary you can be asked to go for a medical, though this is unlikely.[47] You should be sent a written decision and informed that you can appeal if you disagree with it.[48]

Delays and complaints

If you suffer delays, or wish to complain about how your claim has been dealt with, see pp148 and 165. The advice given there applies equally to DWA.

Payment of benefit

Disability working allowance is normally paid on a Tuesday. If you claim on a different day of the week you are paid from the following Tuesday[49] (but see p219 if you have just started a job). If you are currently getting DWA or FC and you reclaim within the time limits (see p221) you are paid from the day after your last award runs out.[50] If you claim up to 28 days before the annual benefit increases (which happen each April) and you are not entitled at the old benefit rates, you can be paid from the date the new ones come in.[51]

If you are awarded DWA it is paid for 26 weeks.[52] You are paid by an order book or, if you wish and the Secretary of State agrees, into an account (including your partner's account),[53] whichever you have requested. Benefit is paid a week in arrears (by order book) or four-weekly in arrears (into a bank). If your weekly DWA is £4 or less, you will usually be paid in a lump sum covering the whole 26-week period, but if it is less than 50 pence it will not be paid at all.[54]

Payment is usually made to the claimant but it can be paid to a partner instead.[55] You could apply to the Benefits Agency for this to happen if it is more convenient, but it is the Secretary of State's decision so there is no right of appeal if this is refused. If there is a delay in assessing your DWA, you can claim an interim payment (see p145).

If your order book is lost or stolen or your DWA is suspended, the rules are the same as for IS (see p147). There are similar rules about when your DWA can be suspended (see p146).

Change of circumstances

If your circumstances change during the 26 weeks, this does not usually affect the amount you are paid.[56] However:

- if your DWA includes an amount for a child or young person (see p353), but s/he ceases to be a member of your household and someone else is claiming for her/him as a dependant in their DWA/FC/IS, your DWA stops from the first day of any overlap[57] and you will need to make a fresh claim if you are still entitled to DWA;
- if the claimant dies, DWA will stop unless there is a surviving partner and s/he is included in the claim, when DWA will continue to be paid for the remainder of the 26 weeks;[58]

- if you fail to comply with the requirement to apply for child support maintenance and a reduced benefit direction is issued (see p114), the amount of your DWA is adjusted during your current award. This also applies where the reduced benefit direction ceases, is cancelled or suspended, or reinstated after a suspension;
- if you are later notified that DWA or FC has been awarded to you for a period beginning before your existing award, and the new award overlaps with any period of your existing award, your existing award will be terminated from the date you are notified of this, so that the new award can take its place (this may happen as a result of the time it takes to complete a review of or appeal against an earlier claim or because a later claim is backdated).[59]

Note: Unlike FC (see p209), DWA awards are not affected when a child finishes full-time education.

Overpayments and fraud

The rules on overpayments and fraud are the same as for IS[60] (see p156) except that the maximum rate of recovery does not apply to DWA. Nevertheless, you should argue for realistic repayments.

6. CHALLENGING A DWA DECISION

You can apply for a review of a DWA decision, or appeal against it, see p140 and Chapter 8. The advice there in relation to IS applies equally to DWA, except for the following differences:

- Your appeal may be heard by a disability appeal tribunal if any question about your disability arises, rather than a social security appeal tribunal. One of the members of the disability appeal tribunal has to be a doctor.
- Reviews on the grounds of a change of circumstances are very limited in relation to DWA (see p222).
- You cannot appeal against an initial decision. First you have to write and ask for a review. If the request for review is made within three months of receiving the decision, but the review is unsuccessful, you can then appeal against that decision.

If your review request is outside the three-month time limit the decision can only be reviewed if:[61]

- there was a mistake about or ignorance of a fact which is relevant to your claim;

- you have claimed in advance and been awarded DWA, but then do not fulfil the conditions on the date it is due to be paid. The review is to stop payment being made;
- the adjudication officer got the law wrong;
- there has been one of the changes of circumstances set out on p222.

If you were refused DWA, and made a further claim (rather than an application for a review) within three months of the decision, and are then awarded DWA, you are paid only from the date you made the further claim.[62]

If you were awarded DWA and apply for a review within three months about the amount of the award, the general rule that reviews take effect from the beginning of an award should operate. However, only up to one month's arrears of DWA can be paid if:

- you apply for a review within three months or because there was a mistake about, or ignorance of, relevant facts; *and*
- the review arises because you provide some information which you knew (or should have known) but did not previously give to the Benefits Agency; *and*
- the review leads to a new award of DWA or an increase in the amount you are getting.

The month runs from the date you first provided the information.[63] Note the way this rule is phrased; it applies to a new award of DWA, as well as an increased award.

The rules for getting more than one month's arrears are the same as for IS (see p142).

7. GIVING UP WORK BECAUSE OF SICKNESS OR DISABILITY

If you have to stop working and you are sick, there are special rules to ensure that you can go back on to the benefit which you were claiming for your incapacity before you took a job and claimed DWA. The rules differ depending on whether you are temporarily off sick or stop work altogether.

Temporary sickness

You should claim statutory sick pay from your employer (unless you were getting sickness/invalidity/incapacity benefit or severe disablement allowance within the last eight weeks, in which case you go back on to that benefit). You continue to get your DWA and you may also be entitled to claim IS, HB and CTB if your income is low enough (see Chapters 2, 12 and 16 respectively).

Giving up work

If you give up work or training for work through ill-health and have been claiming invalidity/incapacity benefit or severe disablement allowance within the last two years, you can go straight back on to that benefit from your first day of sickness.[64] This is because days on DWA count as days of incapacity for work (and also as days when you were disabled for severe disablement allowance purposes) and your two periods of sickness are linked together. As well as any basic incapacity benefit/severe disablement allowance you get increases for your partner or child (if any) under the rules which applied on your last claim.[65] You must show that you are now incapable of work. If you have been working for some time, your incapacity may be questioned by the adjudication officer. Make it clear that you have had to give up work due to ill-health or disability when you reclaim.

Periods when you have been on DWA do not in themselves help you to get the disability premium, higher pensioner premium or the severe disability premium with IS/HB/CTB. You must requalify for these in the normal way (see pp362, 365 and 367).

If your job ends after the two-year period but you are nevertheless incapable of work, claim incapacity benefit when you stop working. With the introduction of incapacity benefit on 13 April 1995, the Government brought in special rules to give some protection to people who had been on DWA. The rules are very complicated, but the stated intention is to enable incapacity benefit, for a period, to be paid at a protected rate in certain circumstances when you have been getting DWA and then give up work because of sickness.[66]

If you give up work for reasons other than sickness or disability you should claim jobseeker's allowance instead. If you qualify you can also claim IS/HB/CTB (see Chapters 2, 12 and 16 respectively).

For details about claiming incapacity and severe disablement allowance, see the *Rights Guide to Non-Means-Tested Benefits,* 21st edn, 1998/99. For detailed information about JSA, see the *Jobseeker's Allowance Handbook,* 3rd edn, 1998/99.

PART FOUR

Housing benefit and council tax benefit

CHAPTER TWELVE

The basic rules

This chapter covers:
1. Introduction (below)
2. 'Eligible rent' (p242)
3 Rent restrictions (p247)

I. INTRODUCTION

Housing benefit (HB) is paid to people who have a low income and who pay rent. It is paid whether or not the claimant is available for or in full-time work and may be paid as well as other social security benefits, or just by itself. HB is paid by local authorities, although it is a national scheme and the rules are mainly determined by DSS regulations.

Who can claim?

You can claim HB for your family (see Chapter 17) if the following conditions are satisfied:[1]

* your income is low enough. How low it has to be depends on your circumstances (see p263);
* your savings and other capital are not worth more than £16,000 (see Chapter 20);
* you or your partner are treated as liable to pay rent for accommodation (see p229);
* you normally occupy that accommodation as your home (see p231), or are only temporarily absent from it (see p232);
* you are not excluded under the rules explained on p234.

The amount of HB you receive depends on a number of factors. The full calculation is explained on p263. Also note that:

* HB is non-taxable and is not dependent on you having paid national insurance contributions;
* unlike income support (IS), there is no lower age limit for claiming HB.

Liability to pay rent

When are you treated as liable?

To get HB, you must normally be either the person who is liable to pay the rent,[2] or the partner of the person who is liable.[3] You can also be treated as liable to pay rent in the following situations:

• Where your former partner is liable to make the payments on your home but is not doing so and you have to pay rent in order to remain living there.[4] It does not matter whether or not the landlord is prepared to transfer the tenancy to you or wants to evict you. Some local authorities may refuse to accept your HB claim in this situation because they allow their own interests as landlords to override their duties under the HB scheme. This is wrong. You should point out that the eligibility rules for HB and for transferring council tenancies are quite separate.

• Where you have taken over paying the rent but are not the former partner of the liable person. In such a case, the council has the discretion to treat you as liable if it considers that it is reasonable to do so.[5] If it refuses to exercise this discretion in your favour, request a review (see pp319-21).

• Where your landlord allows you a rent-free period as compensation for undertaking repairs or re-decoration which s/he would otherwise have had to carry out.[6] This only applies where you have actually carried out the work and then only for a maximum of eight benefit weeks in respect of any one rent-free period. If you expect the work to last for more than eight weeks, you should arrange with your landlord to schedule the work in periods of eight weeks or less separated by at least one complete benefit week where you resume paying rent.

• Where you are the partner of a full-time student who is treated as not liable to pay rent (see p277).[7]

Even if you fall into one of these categories, you can still be treated as not being liable to pay rent in certain circumstances (see p234).

Joint liability – couples

If you are a married or unmarried couple (see p347) and are jointly liable for the rent, only one of you can claim HB (see p282).[8]

The definition of 'unmarried couple' does not apply to lesbian or gay couples. You are regarded as two single people.

Joint liability – single people sharing accommodation

A group of single people living together and paying rent together to their landlord is treated differently according to whether they are all liable under the agreement, some of them are liable or only one is liable.

If all or some of you have joint liability for the rent, you can all make separate claims for HB on your share (except in any case where the local authority thinks the joint tenancy has been created to take advantage of the HB scheme – see p235). The local authority apportions the eligible rent between you by considering:

- the number of jointly liable persons in the property; *and*
- the proportion of the rent actually paid by each liable person; *and*
- any other relevant factors – such as the number of rooms occupied by each jointly liable person and whether any formal or informal agreement exists between you regarding the use and occupation of the home.[9]

Where the rent includes any ineligible service charges etc, these will be apportioned between you on the same basis as the rent.[10] Note that the HB rules are different from those applying to the apportionment of joint council tax liability for council tax benefit (CTB) purposes (see p330).

If only one of you is responsible for the rent, s/he is treated as the tenant and the other(s) as a non-dependant(s) (see p268).

What does 'liable' mean?

In order for you to be 'liable' to pay rent, your agreement must be legally enforceable.[11] It is not enough if you only have a moral obligation, such as a promise to pay something whenever you can afford to do so.

However, your agreement can be enforceable even if it is not in writing. Some authorities have refused to accept that you have a legal liability unless you produce a written agreement, a rent book or some other evidence in writing of the agreement. You should argue that this is wrong and seek a review (see p319).[12] It is always better to have your agreement with your landlord in writing, but if you have made a firm promise to pay money to your landlord in return for your occupation of the property, that should be treated as sufficient to allow you to claim HB.

What is rent?

'Rent' includes many payments that are not normally treated as being rent, such as payments as a licensee and payments for bed and breakfast and hostel accommodation (see p243 for a full list). However, the payment must be in return for your occupation of the home. This usually means that the payments must be made to the person who has the right to let you occupy it or somebody acting on their behalf. Payments to someone else may not qualify for HB.[13] If you think you may be in this situation, seek advice.

You are still treated as liable to pay rent if you pay it before the period which the rent refers to, even where you pay it before claiming HB.[14]

Occupying accommodation as your home

Housing benefit can normally only be paid for accommodation which you normally occupy as your home.[15] See below for circumstances in which you can be treated as occupying a home even when you are not.

Where you or your family have more than one home, HB is only payable if the accommodation for which you claim is regarded as your main home, except in the limited circumstances set out below in which you can claim for two homes.

Cases where you are treated as occupying a home

Even if you are not occupying the accommodation for which you are claiming HB, or it is not your main home, you can be treated as occupying it in the following circumstances:

- Where you have two homes, and you make payments for only one of them (including mortgage payments), you are always treated as occupying the home for which you pay if: *either*
  - you are a single claimant (including lone parents), and you are either a student who is not excluded from HB entitlement (see p277) or on a training course (see p232 for the meaning of this), and you live in one home during periods of study or training and another home for vacations;[16] *or*
  - you have had to move into temporary accommodation due to essential repairs being carried out on your main home.[17] 'Essential repairs' means basic works rather than luxuries, but they need not be crucial to make the house habitable;[18]
- you are in a vulnerable category and you have been delayed from moving in to a new home (see p233);
- you have left your home due to a fear of violence (see p233) and you could not reasonably avoid having to pay rent for that home.[19] If, as will usually be the case, you leave without giving notice, then you should argue that you had to leave in a hurry and it is not reasonable to expect you to live with violence during the period of notice to your landlord. You can only be treated as occupying your home for a

maximum of four weeks, but see below and p233 if you intend to return to your home;

- you have moved into residential accommodation on a trial basis to see if it suits you with the intention of returning if it is not right for you, and you have not rented your home out to someone in the meantime. You can be treated as occupying your home for up to 13 weeks for each stay in residential accommodation up to a maximum of 52 weeks from different periods in residential accommodation;[20]
- where you are temporarily absent from your home for up to 13 weeks if you are unlikely to be away for longer than this (but see the next category), provided that you have not rented the property out;[21]
- where you are temporarily absent from your home for up to 52 weeks if you are unlikely to be away for longer (or in exceptional circumstances, unlikely to be away for substantially longer), and you have not rented the property out, and you are in one of the following categories:[22]
  - you are a remand prisoner held in custody pending trial or sentencing (including where you are in a bail hostel);
  - you are a hospital in-patient;
  - you or a dependant are undergoing medical treatment or medically approved convalescence in the UK or abroad;
  - you are providing, or receiving, 'medically approved' (ie, certified by a medical practitioner) care in the UK or abroad;
  - you are caring for a child whose parent or guardian is away from home receiving medically approved care or medical treatment;
  - you are undertaking a training course in the UK or abroad which is provided by, or on behalf of, or approved by a government department, the Secretary of State, Scottish Enterprise or Highlands and Islands Enterprise;
  - you are a student who is not excluded from HB (see p277) and you neither fall into the first category on p231 nor are entitled to HB on two homes (see p233);
  - you are in residential accommodation and you are not there on a trial basis (see above);
  - you are in fear of violence (see p233), and are not liable for rent at your temporary address (if you are liable, see p233).

For the purposes of the last two categories above, a new period of absence starts if you return home for even a short stay. DSS guidance states that a stay of at least 24 hours may be enough.[23] This does not apply, however, if you are a prisoner on temporary leave.[24]

Fear of violence

To show that you are in fear of violence, you need not have suffered actual violence provided there are grounds for you to fear violence, but you must be in fear of violence in your home or from a former family member outside the home. DSS guidance suggests that the former category includes violence by neighbours and racial attacks on your home.[25]

Vulnerable people who move

If you are not liable for rent on your old home, you can claim HB on your new home for a period of up to four weeks before moving in, although you will not be paid until after the move.[26] To qualify for this retrospective HB you must have:

- moved into your new home; *and*
- been liable to make payments on your new home before moving in; *and*
- claimed HB before moving in and either, it was not decided until after you moved in, or it was refused (because you had not yet moved in) and you made a second claim within four weeks of moving in.

Furthermore, the delay in moving into your new home must have been reasonable and *either*

- a member of your family is aged five or under, or your applicable amount includes one of the pensioner or disability premiums, and your move was delayed while the Benefits Agency decided on a claim for a social fund payment for a need connected with the move – eg, removal expenses or a household item or furniture; *or*
- the delay was necessary in order to adapt your new home to the disability needs of either you or a family member (see below if you are obliged to pay rent on your old home as well); *or*
- you became liable to make payments on your new home while you were a hospital patient or in residential accommodation.

Getting HB for two homes

You can usually only get HB on one home. However, you can get HB paid on two homes (but not more than two) where:

- you have left your home due to fear of violence (see above) but you intend to return to your former home, and it is reasonable for you to receive HB for both homes.[27] You can get HB on both homes for up to 52 weeks;

- where you or your partner is a student who is not excluded from HB (see p277) or a trainee on a government course, and it is necessary for you to live apart, and it is reasonable for you to receive HB for both homes;[28]
- where your family is large and the local authority has housed your family in more than one home;[29]
- where you have moved into a new home and you could not reasonably avoid having to pay rent on your old home.[30] DSS guidance suggests that authorities must consider the reasons why a person had to move quickly, and that people forced to move quickly to take advantage of better accommodation may not be able to avoid leaving without given a notice period.[31] You can only receive HB on both homes for a maximum of four weeks;
- you are a person in a vulnerable category (see p233) who has a move delayed because you are adapting your new home for the disability needs of a member of your family.[32] Again, you can get HB on both homes for up to four weeks prior to the date you move.

Who cannot claim

You cannot get HB if: *either*

- you fall into one of the groups of people who are treated as not liable for rent; *or*
- the payments you make are not eligible rent for HB purposes (see p236).

People treated as not liable for rent

You are not entitled to HB if you fall into one of the groups of people who, even though they have to pay rent, are treated as though they are not liable to do so:

- you are a full-time student[33] and you do not come within the categories of those who can get HB (see Chapter 14);
- you are a 'person from abroad' (see p236);[34]
- you are a member of, and are fully maintained by, a religious order;[35]
- you are living in a residential care or nursing home[36] (but see p242);
- you pay rent to someone you live with and that person is a close relative of you or your partner.[37] You are regarded as living with your landlord if you share some accommodation with her/him other than a bathroom, toilet or a hall or passageway.[38] It does not matter if you use the accommodation at different times or if you pay to use it.[39] A 'close relative' is a parent, son, daughter, in-laws or step-relatives of those three kinds, or a brother, sister or spouse.[40] It also includes half-

brothers and sisters.[41] Relations with in-laws or step-relatives are severed by divorce or death;[42]

- you pay rent to someone you live with (see p34) and the agreement is not a on commercial basis. In deciding whether or not your agreement is 'commercial', the authority must look at the whole agreement, not just the rent you pay.[43] The rent need not necessarily be a market rent.[44] Similarly, just because you are a relative of, or have a close friendship with, the person you pay rent to does not mean that your agreement is non-commercial;[45] neither does the fact that you or your landlord regard the agreement as non-commercial.[46] DSS guidance suggests that a foster child who continues to live with her/his foster parents on reaching the age of 18 should usually be treated as renting on a commercial basis.[47]
- your liability to pay rent has been created to take advantage of the HB scheme (see below).[48] This does not apply if you had already been liable to make payments to your landlord for eight weeks before the agreement that is alleged to take advantage of the HB scheme;
- you became jointly liable to pay rent within eight weeks of having been a non-dependant of one of the other joint occupiers, unless you can satisfy the local authority that the change in arrangements was not made to take advantage of the HB scheme.[49]

Agreements taking advantage of the HB scheme

In order for your agreement to come within this category, it must be shown that it amounts to an abuse of the HB scheme, and that the main reason for you entering the agreement was to obtain HB.[50] *All* the circumstances should be taken into account. One factor will rarely be conclusive in determining whether such an abuse has taken place.

Your agreement does not 'take advantage' of the HB scheme just because you hope to be able to claim HB to help you with your rent. In such a case, your main purpose is to get accommodation for yourself, not to obtain HB.[51] In particular, you should not be seen as taking advantage of the HB scheme just because you seek to find out the 'eligible rent' (see p256) from the rent officer before moving in.

It is not necessary that you and your landlord should have plotted to take advantage of the HB scheme.[52] So tenants of a landlord who deliberately charges high rents to try and get them paid by HB may fall foul of this provision, even if they had no such intention themselves.[53] The fact that a rent is above the market average does not mean that the liability takes advantage of the HB scheme, [54] unless perhaps the rent is extremely high. If your landlord is going to evict you if you cannot get HB, that suggests that the agreement does not take advantage of the HB scheme.[55]

If the authority refuses you HB on the basis that you are taking advantage of the scheme, you should always request a review (see p319). Set out in your letter the reasons why you entered into the agreement.

Payments which are not eligible rent

You cannot get HB if the payments you make for your accommodation do not count as 'eligible rent' (see p242). This applies where:

- you are provided with residential accommodation by a local authority and it is either registered under the Registered Homes Act 1984 or owned or managed by the local authority and the charge includes meals.[56] Even if meals are not provided you cannot get HB for your accommodation costs if you were in the home on 31 March 1993 and excluded from HB at that time;[57]
- you own your accommodation or have a lease of more than 21 years – unless you are a 'shared owner' (ie, buying part of your house or flat and renting the rest), in which case you can get HB on the part you rent.[58] You are treated as the owner of the property if you have the right to sell it – even though you may not be able to do this without the consent of other joint owners;[59]
- you are getting income support (IS) and housing costs are included in your IS applicable amount (see p25).[60] If you are now getting your housing costs met through IS but were previously getting HB for the same accommodation, your HB continues for your first four weeks on IS. This is deducted from your IS so you do not get any extra benefit; it is merely an administrative arrangement to help with the transfer of housing costs from HB to IS;[61]
- you are a Crown tenant. There is a separate scheme for some Crown tenants, check with the Crown Agent;[62]
- you make payments under a co-ownership scheme under which you will receive a payment related to the value of the accommodation when you leave;[63]
- you make payments under a hire purchase (for, say, the purchase of a mobile home), credit sale or a conditional sale agreement except to the extent that it is in respect of land.[64]

Persons from abroad

'Persons from abroad' is a legal term rather than a literal description of the claimant. If you are classed as a person from abroad, you are not entitled to HB. The term applies to some foreign nationals but also to British nationals who fail the habitual residence test (see p238).

Local authorities have been advised to add questions to their claim forms asking about your nationality and whether you have come to this country in the last five years. Some local authorities substitute two years for five years (see p238). Detailed guidance has been issued to them to decide if you are a person from abroad, but there will sometimes be liaison between them and the Immigration and Nationality Department to check your immigration status. You should be advised if they are intending to do this. There will also be liaison between the local authority and the Benefits Agency if you are claiming IS as well, and information which you give to one department could be passed to the other.[65]

You may be interviewed to check out whether you are entitled to claim and you will certainly be asked to produce proof of your identity and immigration status. You do not have to produce your passport, but you will need some other way of verifying your status. If you do not have this, the local authority should interview you and make a decision on the balance of probabilities.

If you are a couple and your partner is not classed as a person from abroad, s/he can claim for you both and you are paid the full amount for a couple. However, in some cases your immigration status could be jeopardised by your partner's claim for HB, as it counts as 'public funds' under the Immigration Rules (see p68). If you are here subject to the condition that you should not have recourse to public funds, you should seek independent immigration advice before your partner claims HB. See p68 for more information – it may not be wise for your partner to claim.

If you are a married or unmarried couple and both of you are persons from abroad, you will not be entitled to HB.

If you are unsure about how a claim for HB might affect your right to remain in the UK, you should get independent advice about this before making a claim. If you subsequently discover that you can claim with no problems, you should ask for your benefit to be backdated on the grounds that you have 'good cause for a late claim' (see p285).

You are classed as a **person from abroad** if you do not satisfy either:

- the immigration status test (see below); *or*
- the habitual residence test (see p238).

The immigration status test

You are **not classed as a person from abroad** under the immigration status test if:

- you are an **asylum-seeker** and satisfy certain conditions (see p239);
- you are a **sponsored immigrant** and satisfy certain conditions;

- you are in receipt of **IS/income-based jobseeker's allowance (JSA)**;
- you are in GB and left **Montserrat** after 1 November 1995 because of the effects of a volcanic eruption.[66]

You are classed as a person from abroad because of your immigration status if you do not fall into one of the above groups *and*;

- you have limited leave to enter or remain in the UK subject to the requirement that you have no recourse to public funds[67] but this does not apply if:[68]
  - either you are a national of the European Economic Area (EEA) (see p75 for a list of countries), Malta, Turkey or Cyprus; *or*
  - your funds from abroad have been temporarily disrupted and there is a reasonable expectation that they will resume (provided you have not been without funds for more than 42 days in one period of limited leave);
- you were given limited leave to enter or remain in the UK and have overstayed the period of your leave;[69]
- you are subject to a deportation order unless your removal has been deferred in writing by the Secretary of State;[70]
- you are an illegal entrant unless you have the Secretary of State's written consent to stay;[71]
- you are an EEA national who has been required to leave by the Secretary of State (see p78);[72]
- you are an asylum-seeker in certain circumstances (see p239);
- you are a sponsored immigrant in certain circumstances (see p239).

The habitual residence test

You are also classed as a person from abroad if you are **not habitually resident** in the UK.[73] The DSS recommended that the test be applied to any claimant who has been resident here for under five years.[74] Some local authorities have decided to follow the advice of the Social Security Advisory Committee and apply the test only to those claimants resident for less than two years.[75]

Are you treated as habitually resident?

You do not have to satisfy the habitual residence test if you fall within one of the exempt groups. You are treated as habitually resident if you are:[76]

- an **asylum-seeker** and satisfy certain conditions;
- a **sponsored immigrant** and satisfy certain conditions;
- in receipt of **IS/income-based JSA**;

- you are in GB and left **Montserrat** after 1 November 1995 because of a volcanic eruption there;
- you are an EEA worker or from an EEA state or have a right to reside in the UK;
- you are a refugee;
- you have exceptional leave to remain (see p79) or, from April 1998, you have been given exceptional leave to enter by an immigration officer;[77]
- your funds from abroad have been temporarily disrupted and there is a reasonable expectation that they will resume (provided you have not been without funds for more than 42 days in one period of limited leave);
- you are subject to a deportation order but your deportation has been deferred in writing by the Secretary of State;
- you are an illegal entrant who has the Secretary of State's written consent to stay.

Passing the habitual residence test

If you are not within one of the exempt groups, you will have to show that you are habitually resident in the UK. The phrase means the same as for IS and so the same principles should apply (see p72). Case law relating to IS should be persuasive for HB purposes. Remember that if you get IS or JSA, the local authority has to treat you as habitually resident (see p238). It may not proceed to carry out the test itself.

People with sponsorship undertakings

If you were given leave to enter the UK subject to a sponsorship undertaking, you are entitled to HB if:[78] *either*

- you have been resident in the UK for at least five years; *or*
- the person who gave the undertaking has died; *or*
- you were entitled to or were receiving HB before 5 February 1996.[79]

For more about sponsorship undertakings and benefit see p85.

Asylum-seekers

If you are an asylum-seeker, you are entitled to HB if either:

- you applied for asylum on arrival in the UK (for the meaning of this see pp80-85); *or*
- you applied for asylum within the three months following a declaration by the Secretary of State that your country is subject to such a fundamental change of circumstances that you would not normally be ordered to return there;[80] *or*

- you were entitled to HB as an asylum-seeker immediately before 5 February 1996.[81] This means that you must have been in receipt of HB on 4 February – a period of entitlement prior to that is insufficient.[82] However, provided you were receiving HB on 4 February, the fact that you have had a break in your claim subsequently or have made a renewal claim ought not to prevent you getting HB.[83] If you were getting HB on 4 February 1996, you remain entitled until you receive a decision on your application. You are not entitled pending an appeal unless the decision was made before 5 February 1996.[84]

For more about asylum-seekers, see p80.

Backdating HB and CTB when you get refugee status

If you are notified that you have been granted refugee status, you do not count as a person from abroad and can therefore claim HB/council tax benefit (CTB) from that date. If, while you were seeking asylum, you were not entitled to HB/CTB because you were classed as a person from abroad, you may be entitled to a retrospective award of HB/CTB for that past period.

Claims

You must make a claim for retrospective HB/CTB within 28 days of the date you are notified by the Secretary of State that you have been recorded as a refugee.[85] You must claim within the time limit as a late claim cannot be backdated.[86] If you have lived in more than one local authority area, you should make your claim to the local authority in whose area you last lived before being granted refugee status.[87]

Date of claim

Your HB/CTB claim will be treated as made on: *either*[88]

- *if you applied for asylum on arrival* in the UK, the date your application was first refused or 5 February 1996, whichever is later; *or*
- *if you applied for asylum other than on arrival* in the UK (see p81), the date of your asylum application or 5 February 1996, whichever is later.

HB/CTB can be paid for whole or part of the period from the date the claim is treated as made until the date you were notified of your refugee status.[89] Any HB/CTB which has already been paid to you or any partner of yours over this period is deducted from your award.[90]

Example
Meral applied for asylum on arrival in the UK in December 1995. She was paid HB until March 1996, when her asylum application was refused. In October 1996, she started living as a couple with Barry who has since been claiming HB for both of them. In April 1997, she is granted refugee status. She claims HB immediately.

Meral is entitled to retrospective HB from the March 1996 (when her asylum application was refused) until April 1997 when she was granted refugee status. However, the award is reduced by the amount of HB paid to her partner for both of them from October 1996 onwards.

How your claim is assessed

You must provide any evidence and information you have or could reasonably get which the local authority may reasonably require to determine your entitlement.[91] The authority can ask for information from your landlord, from the person you paid rent to, from any person who paid the rent on your behalf or from another local authority.[92]

You must notify the local authority of any changes of circumstances which might be relevant to your HB/CTB entitlement over the period for which you are claiming.[93] Where you are unable to provide the necessary evidence, the local authority must determine your claim on the basis of the information you have been able to provide.[94]

Your HB claim will be assessed using the rules for rent and rent restrictions as they stood on 1 January 1996.[95] In particular, this means that the rent officer's assessment of the appropriate rent for your home is not conclusive (see p258).

Payment of benefit

Once the local authority decides you are entitled to retrospective HB/CTB they must make payment within 14 days.[96] Any outstanding council tax liability for the period covered by the award is paid off before any remaining CTB is paid to you. If your rent has not been paid, part or all of your HB award can be paid direct to the landlord. If your landlord was a local authority, any eligible rent owing to them is deducted from your award and only the balance paid to you.[97] Otherwise, HB can be paid to your landlord where the local authority considers it reasonable to do so.[98] The landlord must show that you have not paid your rent for part or all of the period of your award and the local authority must give you an opportunity to give reasons why payment should not be made to the landlord.

Residential care or nursing homes

Payments for residential care and nursing homes are usually not covered by HB.[99]

If you are provided with accommodation by a local authority see p236. If you live in a private or voluntary home you can claim if:

- you were entitled, or became entitled, to HB before 30 October 1990.[100] This protection lasts for life;
- you lived there prior to 1 April 1993 and were either in full-time work, or making payments on a commercial basis in a home run by a close relative, or living in a home for less than four people. This protection applies until you leave the home (apart from temporary absences) or if you cease to qualify for HB;[101]
- you live in a Royal Charter or Act of Parliament residential home – eg, Salvation Army establishments. You can claim either IS or HB to cover your accommodation costs. This does not apply if you are in a nursing home;
- you live in a small home which is not required to be registered under the Registered Homes Act 1984 – eg, some adult placement or supported lodging schemes.

If you are entitled to HB while in a residential care or nursing home, the tariff income and capital rules differ from the normal ones – see p236.

2. 'ELIGIBLE RENT'

Your 'eligible rent' is the amount of your rent which is taken into account for the purpose of calculating your housing benefit (HB). It may be less than the actual amount that you pay because it might not include all payments.

Your eligible rent is your contractual rent, minus:

- any ineligible charges (see p243); *and minus*
- any amount above the level to which your rent is restricted under the rent restriction rules (see p247).

Students may find their eligible rent further reduced by the student rent deduction (see p279).

If you are jointly liable you can claim HB on your 'share' (see p230).

What counts as 'eligible rent'

The following charges are eligible rent for HB purposes:[102]

- rent you pay in respect of a tenancy;
- payments you make in respect of a licence or other permission to occupy premises;
- mesne profits (in Scotland, violent profits) which include payments made if you remain in occupation when a tenancy has been ended;
- other payments for use and occupation of premises;
- payments of eligible service charges (see p245) required as a condition of occupation;
- rent, including mooring charges for a houseboat;
- site rent for a caravan or mobile home (but not a tent, although that might be met through IS – see p27);
- rent paid on a garage or land (unless used for business purposes). Either you must be making a reasonable effort to end your liability for it, or you must have been unable to rent your home without it;[103]
- contributions made by a resident of a charity's almshouse;
- payments made under a rental purchase agreement under which the purchase price is paid in more than one instalment and you will not finally own your home until all, or an agreed part of, the purchase price has been paid;
- in Scotland, payments in respect of croft land.

Parts of your rent which are not eligible

You may find that your HB is less than your contractual rent because ineligible charges are deducted. Ineligible charges include:

- most fuel charges (see p244);
- some service charges (see p245);
- charges for meals (see p247);
- water rates;[104]
- payments for any part of your accommodation which is used exclusively for business purposes;[105]
- rent supplements charged to clear your rent arrears;[106]
- any amount above the level to which your rent is restricted under the rent restriction rules (see p247).[107]

Fuel charges

As a rule of thumb, if the charge is specified this amount is deducted from your rent. If the charge is not specified, a fixed amount is deducted.

- If your fuel charge is specified on your rent book or is readily identifiable from your agreement with your landlord – the full amount of the charge is deducted in arriving at your eligible rent.[108] Where your fuel charge is specified but the local authority considers it to be unrealistically low in relation to the fuel provided, the charge is treated as unspecified and a flat-rate deduction made instead (see below).

  This is also the case where your total fuel charge is specified but contains an unknown amount for communal areas. If you are a council tenant, the regulations assume your fuel charges are always specified or readily identifiable since the local authority is also your landlord.[109]

- If your fuel charge is not readily identifiable – a flat-rate deduction is made for fuel.[110] The flat-rate fuel deductions are:

(a) Where you and your family occupy more than one room:
   - for heating (other than hot water)   £9.25
   - for hot water   £1.15
   - for lighting   £0.80
   - for cooking   £1.15

(b) Where you and your family occupy one room only:
   - for heating alone, or heating combined with either hot water or lighting or both   £5.60
   - for cooking   £1.15

These amounts are added together where fuel is supplied for more than one purpose. If you are a joint tenant, all the deductions are apportioned according to your share of the rent.[111]

Where flat-rate fuel deductions have been made in calculating your HB, the local authority must notify you about this and explain that if you can produce evidence from which the actual or approximate amount of your fuel charge can be estimated, the flat-rate deductions may be varied accordingly.[112] However, there is no point in providing such evidence unless it is likely to show that your charge is less than the flat-rate deductions – eg, where you live in a small bedsit.

Guidance suggests that the lower deduction for one room only should apply where you occupy one room exclusively – even if you share other rooms (such as a bathroom or kitchen, or communal lounge in a hotel).[113] You should also argue for the lower level of deductions to be made where you are forced to live in one room because the other room(s) in your accommodation are, in practice, unfit to live in – eg, because of severe mould/dampness etc).

Fuel for communal areas

If you pay a service charge for the use of fuel in communal areas, and that charge is separately identified from any other charge for fuel used within your accommodation, it may be included as part of your eligible rent.[114] Communal areas include access areas like halls and passageways, but not rooms in common use except those in sheltered accommodation – eg, a shared TV lounge or dining-room etc.[115] If you pay a charge for the provision of a heating system (eg, regular boiler maintenance etc), this is also eligible where the amount is separately identified from any other fuel charge you pay.[116]

Service charges

Most service charges are covered by HB, but only if payment is a condition of occupying the accommodation rather than an optional extra.[117] Some service charges are specifically excluded (see p246).

The following services are eligible for HB:

- services for the provision of adequate accommodation including general management costs, gardens, children's play areas, lifts, entry phones, communal telephone costs, portering and rubbish removal. TV and radio relay is covered, but only relay for ordinary UK channels and not satellite dishes or decoders. Cable TV is also excluded unless it is the only practicable way of providing you with ordinary domestic channels;[118]
- laundry facilities (eg, a laundry room in an apartment block), but not charges for the provision of personal laundry;[119]
- furniture and household equipment, but not if there is an agreement that the furniture will eventually become yours;[120]
- cleaning of communal areas;[121]
- cleaning within your own accommodation, but only if no one living in the household is able to do it;[122]
- emergency alarm systems in accommodation designed or adapted for elderly, sick or disabled people, or which is otherwise suitable for them taking into account factors such as size, heating system or other facilities. In all other cases, emergency alarms are ineligible;[123]
- counselling and support services, but only to the extent that they are:
  - necessary for the provision of adequate accommodation.[124] This concerns only keeping the accommodation fit for use and does not cover counselling designed to ensure that you do not break the terms of your tenancy[125] (but see p246); *or*

- provided by someone (whether a landlord or her/his employee) who spends the majority of time during which s/he provides services, providing services which are not within the list of ineligible charges below;[126] *or*
- payable where you are in 'supported accommodation' and payment of the charges is a condition of your occupancy.[127] 'Supported accommodation' is accommodation that is provided by the Resettlement Agency; or a home provided by a local authority, a housing association, a charity or similar voluntary body where care, support or supervision is given to the occupants; or similar accommodation where your landlord does not come within any of those categories but you are exempt from the local rent reference rules (see p252). Accommodation is not supported accommodation unless it was used for the same purpose on 18 August 1997 or was closed for refurbishment, cleaning or pest control on that date.[128] At the time of writing, this exception will only apply until 31 October 1998.[129]

If the local authority regards any of the above charges as excessive it will estimate a reasonable amount given the cost of comparable services.[130]
The following services are not eligible for HB:[131]

- food including prepared meals (see p247);
- sports facilities;
- TV rental and licence fees (but see p245);
- transport;
- personal laundry service;
- medical expenses;
- nursing and personal care;
- counselling and other support services (but see p245);
- any other charge not connected with the provision of adequate accommodation (see p245 for the meaning of this) and not specifically included in the list of eligible charges above.

Any ineligible service charge must be deducted in full from your rent. Where the ineligible charge is specified, this amount is deducted. Authorities have the power to substitute their own estimate where they consider the amount is unreasonably low.[132] Where the amount is not specified in your rent agreement, the local authority estimates how much is fairly attributable to the service, given the cost of comparable services.[133] Where a HB claim is referred to the rent officer, s/he will provide a valuation for certain services (see p251).

Charges for meals

Where your housing costs include an amount for meals, the local authority makes set deductions.[134] These always apply, regardless of the actual cost of your meals.[135]

Where at least three meals a day are provided:
- for the claimant and each additional member of the family aged 16 (see below) or over £17.95
- for each additional member of the family aged under 16 £ 9.05

Where breakfast only is provided:
- for the claimant and each additional member of the family, regardless of age £ 2.15

In all other cases (part-board):
- for the claimant and each additional member of the family aged 16 or over £11.95
- for each additional member of the family aged under 16 £ 6.00

For these purposes, a person is treated as having attained the age of 16 on the first Monday in September following her/his 16th birthday.

The standard deductions are made for everyone who has meals paid for by you – including meals for someone who is not part of your 'family' such as a non-dependant.[136]

3. RENT RESTRICTIONS

The amount of your eligible rent may be restricted if the local authority decides that either your rent is too high or accommodation too large. If you have a deregulated private tenancy, new rules for deciding whether your rent should be restricted came into force on 2 January 1996 (the 'local reference rent' rules). The rules in force before January 1996 continue to apply to certain claimants who are exempt from the local reference rent rules. Where the local reference rent rules do apply and you are a single claimant aged under 25 you may find your rent restricted to the level of the 'single room rent' by the rules which came into force on 7 October 1996.

If the local reference rent rules apply, your eligible rent is restricted to the level of the 'maximum rent' (see p253). If the pre-January 1996 rules apply, your eligible rent may be restricted to an amount the local authority considers appropriate (see p258).

Summary of local authority rent restriction procedure

The procedure for restricting rent can be summarised as follows:

Step 1: The local authority refers your claim to the rent officer unless you have an excluded tenancy (see below).

Step 2: The rent officer makes determinations as to the level of rent and size of your accommodation (see p249).

Step 3: The local authority decides whether you are exempt from the local reference rent rules (see p252).

Step 4: If you are not exempt, the local reference rent rules apply. The local authority calculates your maximum rent on the basis of the rent officer determinations. If your rent is restricted the local authority may use its discretion to pay extra (see p255). The local authority checks to see whether there should be a delay before any restriction is imposed (see p254).

Step 5: If you are exempt from the local reference rent rules, the local authority decides whether to restrict your rent using the rules in force pre-January 1996 (see p258). The local authority checks to see whether there should be a delay before any restriction is imposed (see p254).

Excluded tenancies (Step 1 – see above)

Following a claim for HB, the local authority must make a reference to the rent officer unless your tenancy is an 'excluded tenancy'.[137] Excluded tenancies are:[138]

- a regulated tenancy (that is a tenancy entered into before 15 January 1989 or, in Scotland, 2 January 1989);
- a Home Office bail hostel or probation hostel;
- a housing action trust tenancy;
- a former local authority or new town letting which has been transferred to a new owner, unless there has been a rent increase since the transfer, and the local authority considers your accommodation is unreasonably large or expensive;
- a registered housing association letting, unless the local authority considers your accommodation to be unreasonably large or expensive.

If your tenancy is excluded, the local authority can uses its general power to decrease your eligible rent (see p250) to an amount it considers 'appropriate'. It should have evidence and objective justification to do so and must exercise its discretion properly. You can ask for a review (see p319).

Rent officer determinations (Step 2 – see p248)

If your tenancy is not excluded (see p248), the local authority refers it to the rent officer.[139] The rent officer may make a number of determinations about your rent making comparison with other private sector rents in the locality. These determinations are valid for 12 months. However, a tenancy can be referred back to the rent officer within this period – eg, if there is a change in the terms of the tenancy, the composition of the household, the condition of the property or if a child reaches the age of 10 or 16.[140] This means that a determination made for a previous tenant may be valid for your claim. If you are not given details of the rent officer's determinations, consider asking for a written statement of reasons (see p289).

The rent officer may make determinations relevant to your specific property (the significantly high rent, size-related rent and exceptionally high rent) as well as determinations which indicate the average rents for specific types of accommodation in the locality (the local reference rent and single room rents).

Significantly high rent determination

If your rent is significantly higher than that paid for similar tenancies and dwellings, the rent officer determines an amount your landlord might reasonably have got for your tenancy.[141]

Size-related rent determination

If your accommodation is larger than you are allowed under the size criteria, the rent officer determines an amount your landlord might reasonably have got for a similar tenancy of an appropriate size.[142]

The size criteria

One bedroom, or room suitable for living in, is allowed for each of the following occupiers (each occupier coming only into the first category for which they are eligible):[143]

- a married or unmarried couple;
- a person who is not a child (ie, aged 16 or over);
- two children of the same sex;
- two children under 10;
- a child.

In addition, you are allowed the following number of rooms suitable for living in:

Number of occupiers	Number of rooms
less than 4	1
4-6	2
7 or more	3

A person counts as an 'occupier' if the local authority includes them on the form they use to refer your tenancy to the rent officer.[144] You may be able to argue that, for example, a child who comes to stay regularly, although not a member of your family, is an occupier and should be included on the form so that their needs can be taken into account.

If any of the rooms in your home are not suitable for living in (eg, because of their size, condition or lack of ventilation) you should argue that they should be ignored.

Exceptionally high rent determination

If your rent or the lowest of the determinations made so far is exceptionally high, the rent officer determines the highest amount which your landlord might reasonably have got for an assured tenancy of an appropriate size.[145]

Single room rent

The single room rent is the midpoint of 'reasonable market rents' for accommodation in which the tenant has exclusive use of one room only and other than that only shares a kitchen, shares a toilet and makes no payment for board or attendance.[146]

The single room rent only applies if you are a 'young individual'. A young individual is a single person under the age of 25. However, the single room rent does not apply if:

• you are a housing association tenant;[147]
• you are under the age of 22 and were formerly in the care of the local authority;[148]
• you have a severe disability premium as part of your applicable amount (see p367);[149] *or*
• you have a non-dependant (see p268) living with you.[150]

Local reference rent

The local reference rent is the midpoint of 'reasonable market rents' for assured tenancies of an appropriate size (under the size criteria).[151] It is only provided if your rent or the lowest of the rent officer determinations (excluding the single room rent) exceeds it.

Example 1

Tina lives in a one-bedroom flat. It has a separate living room. Her rent is £60 a week. The rent officer decides that, although the accommodation is an appropriate size, the rent is too high for the tenancy and so notifies the local authority of the following:

Significantly high rent determination   £55

Local reference rent   £50

Example 2

Paul and Sarah share a two-bedroom flat which has a living room and a dining room. They pay £75 rent a week. The rent officer decides that the accommodation is too big and the rent too high for the property, so notifies the local authority of the following:

Significantly high rent determination   £65

Size-related rent determination   £60

Local reference rent   £50

Example 3

Carl has a two-bedroom flat with two living rooms. He pays £90 a week rent. The rent officer decides that, not only is the flat too big but the rent is too high. S/he also thinks that the rent is exceptionally high. The local authority is notified of the following:

Significantly high rent determination   £80

Size-related rent determination   £70

Exceptionally high rent determination   £75

Local reference rent   £50

Service charges in rent officer determinations

Except where you live in a hostel, rent officer determinations are required to determine whether your rent includes any ineligible service charges (see p245).[152] The significantly high, size-related and local reference rent figures include charges for fuel, meals and water if these are included in your contractual rent.[153] If the determinations include other ineligible charges, the rent officer will provide a valuation of these services.[154] The local reference rent (see p250) excludes ineligible charges apart from fuel, meals and water.[155] The single room rent does not include any payments for charges.[156]

Notification

The rent officer notifies the local authority of her/his determinations within five working days or 25 if s/he intends to visit.[157]

Exemption from the local reference rent rules (Step 3 – see p248)

The local authority must decide whether you are exempt from the local reference rent rules. You are exempt if you are either an exempt claimant or live in exempt accommodation.[158]

You are an **exempt claimant** if:

- you have been continuously entitled to and in receipt of HB since 1 January 1996. Breaks in your claim of up to four weeks are ignored;[159] *and*
- you continue to occupy the same property as your home (except where you are forced to move because fire, flood or natural catastrophe makes it uninhabitable).

If you are thinking of making any changes to your claim, you should check that you will not lose your exemption by doing so. This would happen, for example, if you moved (including moving rooms within the same house) or if your partner took over the claim (but see below).

An exemption can be **transferred** to a new claimant in some limited circumstances. You are an exempt claimant if:

- you claim HB because an exempt claimant dies and you are a member of the former claimant's family, or any relative occupying the same accommodation without a separate right to do so. You must continue to occupy the same property and make your claim within four weeks of the death. If you can get your claim backdated (see p285) to within the four weeks, you may be able to argue that the exemption should be transferred to you;
- you claim HB because your partner (who was exempt) has been detained in custody and is not entitled to HB under the temporary absence rules. You must continue to occupy the same property and must make your claim within four weeks of the imprisonment;
- you claim HB because your former partner (who was exempt) has left the dwelling and you are no longer living together as husband and wife. You must continue to occupy the same property and claim within four weeks of the date it left.

You live in **exempt accommodation** if:

- you live in hostel accommodation for people without a fixed way of life which is funded by the Resettlement Agency;[160]
- you live in accommodation provided by a housing association, non-metropolitan county council, registered charity or voluntary organisation where care, support or supervision is provided either by your

landlord or, on her/his behalf, by someone else.[161] These terms are not defined in law and are open to review. It may be possible to argue that your accommodation is provided by one of the relevant organisations even if they are not actually your landlord.

If you are exempt, the local authority has to decide whether to restrict your rent using the pre-January 1996 rules (see p258).

The local authority determines the maximum rent (Step 4 – see p248)

If you are not exempt, the local reference rent rules apply and the local authority calculates your 'maximum rent' on the basis of the rent officer's determinations.

Definitions[162]
- The *reckonable rent* is your contractual rent minus ineligible charges apart from fuel, meals and water.
- The *relevant rent* is the lowest of the significantly high, size- related and exceptionally high rent determinations minus ineligible charges apart from fuel, meals and water.
- The *appropriate rent* is the lowest of the reckonable and relevant rents. (This is a local authority term, not one found in regulations.)
- The *maximum rent* is the figure to which your eligible rent is restricted after the calculation has been done.

The calculation

To calculate your maximum rent, the local authority identifies your appropriate rent (see above). It then compares the appropriate rent with the local reference rent (see p250).

If your appropriate rent is less than the local reference rent, the maximum rent is the appropriate rent.
If the appropriate rent is higher than the local reference rent, the maximum rent is the local reference rent. If you have transitional protection (see p254) you then add half the difference between the local reference rent and appropriate rent (subject to a maximum of twice the local reference rent).[163]
Any amount for fuel, meals and water is deducted after the above calculations are made[164]

Your HB will be restricted to the level of the maximum rent although the local authority can use its discretion to pay extra HB (see p255). There may also be a delay before the restriction is imposed (see p254).

Transitional protection

You are still entitled to add on half the difference between the local reference rent and the appropriate rent in the calculation above if you come within one of the following categories:

- You were entitled to and in receipt of HB on 5 October 1997.[165] However, this protection only lasts until the **earlier** of the following dates:
  - the date on which your benefit period (see p291) on that claim ends, though you may make a further claim for HB (see below); *or*
  - the date that you move away from the accommodation you occupied on 5 October 1997.
- Where you make a further claim for HB (see p287) and have been in receipt of HB continuously since 5 October 1997 under an assessment which included the addition.[166]

Remember that you may be able to get your claim backdated to 5 October 1997 in order to qualify for transitional protection (see p285).

Renegotiating your rent

Once the maximum rent figure has been calculated, your HB will continue to be paid at this level for the rest of the benefit period unless you negotiate a level below that of the maximum rent, in which case you get HB up to the level to which you have renegotiated.[167] (The same applies if you renegotiate your rent following a pre-tenancy determination.[168])

If the landlord increases your rent, you can ask for a discretionary payment to cover the increase (see p255).

Delay in applying rent restrictions

If a member of your family or a relative dies, and s/he occupied the same home without a separate right to do so, either no restriction applies for 12 months from the date of death or any maximum rent which applied at the time of death continues to do so for the 12 months.[169]

If you, or a family member or relative (as above), could meet the payments when you took the tenancy on, no restriction can be made for 13 weeks provided you did not receive HB in the preceding 52 weeks.[170]

Discretion to increase entitlement

If you are entitled to some HB but the local authority has restricted your entitlement, you should ask it to exercise its discretion to increase your HB.[171] You must be entitled to some HB on the basis of the maximum rent figure.

You will also have to show that unless your HB is increased, you or a member of your family will suffer 'exceptional hardship'. This is not defined but should be given its ordinary everyday meaning. If in doubt, apply. The amount of the discretionary payment cannot take your HB entitlement to a level higher than that to which you would be entitled had no rent restriction taken place.

Local authorities have been issued with guidance providing a list of factors that they may want to consider when deciding whether there is exceptional hardship.[172] The guidance is neither exhaustive nor binding – every claim should be considered on its merits.

The factors the local authority may take into account include:

- Is there a risk of eviction if the shortfall in the rent is not met? The local authority may consider other outgoings you have which may make it harder for you to meet the shortfall.
- Do you have any assets or disregarded income which might be used to meet the shortfall? If you do have savings or disregarded income, it does not automatically follow that it is reasonable for them to be used to meet any shortfall. It may be, for example, that you have other priority expenses or debts, or that your savings are small and would soon be exhausted.
- Is it possible for you to negotiate with the landlord for a reduction in your rent? The local authority should not assume that it is reasonable or possible for you to negotiate with your landlord. However, a statement from your landlord that your rent cannot be reduced may improve your chances of getting a payment.
- Is there anywhere else that you could move to which would cost less? If so, the authority should not refuse a discretionary increase outright. It ought to consider the effect of such a move on you and your family – eg, on your attempts to find work.
- Do you, or a member of your family, suffer from any health problems? If so, this may affect your ability to find cheaper alternative accommodation. The shortfall in HB may lead to a deterioration in your health or the health of a member of your family.
- Would the shortfall have particular effects on individuals within your family? It may interfere with the education of your children or your ability to care for an elderly relative if you have to meet the shortfall from your own resources.

- Can you get financial help from any non-dependants (see p268) in the home?
- Will the local authority have to rehouse you if you are made homeless?

It may be helpful to see any local guidance before making an application or, if unsuccessful, applying for review. Local authorities only have a limited amount of money to spend on discretionary payments, so you should include as much information and evidence to support your request as possible. Some local authorities use standard forms for applications for discretionary payments.

The increased amount of HB is paid for the length of the benefit period, although the local authority can review your entitlement if your circumstances change (see p296). The authority may also give you a shorter benefit period if it thinks it appropriate – eg, if it thinks that your need is short term.

It is possible for you to be awarded a discretionary payment as outlined above in addition to an exceptional circumstances payment (see p272).[173] It is probably best to ask for both types of payment in the same letter.

Discretion to decrease entitlement

If the local reference rent rules have been applied but the local authority does not think it reasonable for the full amount of the maximum rent to be met by HB, it has a discretion to decrease your weekly entitlement further.[174] It may only reduce your HB to a reasonable level. Since the whole point of having rent officer determinations is to determine reasonable rent levels, this power should be exercised rarely. If the authority does utilise this power, ask for a review (see p319).

Pre-tenancy determinations

If you are thinking of renting accommodation privately you can apply to the local authority for a pre-tenancy determination (PTD).[175] This will tell you what rent figure will be used to calculate your HB. You can apply if you are already receiving HB and your tenancy is due for renewal. You can also apply if you are already renting accommodation privately and think you are going to have to claim HB in the near future – eg, because of a drop in your income.

If you wish to apply for a PTD you obtain a form from your local authority. You will need to complete it and ask your prospective landlord to sign it. You then return it to the local authority, which must forward it to the rent officer within three days of receipt.[176] The rent officer will then send you, the prospective landlord and the local authority the rent figures which s/he has decided within five working days unless s/he needs more details from the local authority.[177]

If you rent the property these will be the figures used to calculate your HB. A PTD is valid for a year unless there is a change in the tenancy agreement or in the claimant's family position. If you apply for a PTD, you may find that there is already one in force if someone else in the same circumstances as you applied for a PTD in the previous 12 months. Her/his PTD is binding on you.

You cannot appeal against a PTD unless you accept the tenancy and claim HB, in which case you can request a review and ask that the rent officer considers the determination again.

If you subsequently negotiate a lower rent with your landlord, see p254.

Review

You have the right, under the standard HB review procedures (see p319), to challenge a restriction on your eligible rent. However, because of the way that maximum rent is calculated, the scope for review is limited. Your review request could relate to: *either*

- the rent officer determinations; *or*
- a local authority decision to refuse to use its discretion to increase the amount of benefit payable so that the full amount of your eligible rent is met.

If your request relates to the **rent officer** figures, the local authority must pass any representations you make or evidence you supply to the rent officer within seven days. While it is not easy to challenge rent officers because they have access to a large database with information of rents in the area, it may be possible in some circumstances. If, for example, the rent officer has said your rent is significantly high, you may be able to get her/him to reconsider by providing evidence of similar tenancies where tenants who are not on HB are paying the same rent as you. The rent officer must get the advice of one or two other rent officers and notify the local authority of their decision within 20 working days.

The rent officer can reduce your maximum rent if you request a review so you need carefully to consider your position before doing so. You could end up with less HB as a result. However, the reduced amount will only apply from the date of the new decision and you will not have been overpaid.[178] An increase in your entitlement will apply from the date of the original decision and you should be paid any arrears.

If your review request relates to a decision on discretionary payments, put forward any arguments that will help to satisfy the authority that you will suffer exceptional hardship if extra payments are not made. Even if they are satisfied of this, they will not be able to make the payments if the budget would be exceeded. If you are asking for a further review (see p321), the review board can only review determinations the local authority has made, so make sure you have already asked for discretionary payments to be considered at an earlier stage.

The pre-January 1996 rules (Step 5 – see p248)

If you are exempt from the local reference rent rules (see p252), the local authority uses the pre-January 1996 rules in deciding whether to restrict your eligible rent.

If the local authority decides to impose a rent restriction in your case, you should insist on a full explanation. If you believe that the local authority has failed to apply all the proper tests or has been influenced by irrelevant facts, you should ask for a review (see p319).

The various steps which local authorities must take are as follows:

- The local authority considers whether your rent or accommodation is unreasonable (see below).
- If your rent or accommodation is unreasonable, the local authority must consider whether you are in a protected group.
- If you are in a protected group, the local authority cannot restrict your rent unless there is suitable alternative accommodation available to you and it is reasonable to expect you to move.
- If your rent or accommodation is unreasonable and either you are not in a protected group, or you are, but there is cheaper suitable alternative accommodation for you to move to, the local authority can restrict to an appropriate level (see p261).
- The local authority considers whether there should be a delay before the restriction applies.

Is your rent or accommodation unreasonable?

The local authority can only consider your rent or accommodation unreasonable if either of the following apply:[179]

- your accommodation is larger than is reasonably needed for you and anyone who also occupies the accommodation (including non-dependants and sub-tenants) – taking account of suitable alternative accommodation occupied by other households of the same size; *or*
- your rent is unreasonably high compared with that for suitable alternative accommodation elsewhere.

Is your home too large?

The important question is the size of home that you need, rather than the size of home that you want.[180] The needs of everyone living in your accommodation, whether or not they are part of your family, must be considered. For example, you might need additional space because someone has a disability, or they live elsewhere but regularly come to visit you. If you are elderly and have lived in a house for a long time, you should argue that because you are used to living there and are settled, you need to stay in your existing accommodation.

Is it too expensive?

Rent includes, among other things, any service charges or licence fees you have to pay.[181]

When deciding whether your rent is too high, the local authority may ask a rent officer to assess a reasonable rent for your property, but the figures are not binding on the authority. Although it may have regard to them, its decision should be made on the criterion of whether your rent is unreasonably high, which is different from the rent officer's criteria.[182]

It is not enough for the local authority to argue that your rent is merely higher than that for suitable alternative accommodation. It must be 'unreasonably' higher.[183] In making this comparison, the local authority must consider the full spectrum of rents which could be paid for such accommodation and not just the cheapest.[184] If your rent is within the bracket[185] or just above it[186] the authority will find it difficult to justify a finding that your rent is unreasonably high.

What is suitable alternative accommodation?

The Court of Appeal has said that comparisons should only be made with suitable alternative accommodation which forms part of an 'active housing market'. This means that the accommodation must currently be available for rent, although not necessarily to the claimant.[187] Typically, authorities will produce a list of comparable properties at review board hearings to justify their assertions that there is suitable alternative accommodation. Local authorities should not 'make comparisons with other parts of the country where accommodation costs differ widely from those which apply locally',[188] but it may compare your property to one in a less expensive area within a city.[189]

It is not sufficient for the local authority to show that cheaper or smaller alternative accommodation exists. It must also be 'suitable' for the age and health of all the people that the authority must take into account, having regard to the nature of the accommodation and the facilities available.[190] The people that the authority must consider are:[191]

- you;
- members of your family;
- if you are in a polygamous marriage, any of your partners or children for which you or they are responsible; *and*
- any relative of yours who lives in the same home, whether or not you are in the same household as them (see p346). This only applies where the relative does not have her/his own agreement with your landlord.[192]

The authority must compare your home with properties that have reasonably equivalent facilities. It is not enough, for example, just to compare flats with the same number of bedrooms. Some effort must be made to establish what other facilities are available.[193]

If you currently have security of tenure, then the local authority must compare your home with other properties offering the same security of tenure.[194] So if you have an assured tenancy, the authority may not rely on accommodation which will only be let on an assured shorthold tenancy,[195] or with council or housing association properties.[196] If you have a long-term assured shorthold tenancy for a number of years, you should also argue that property on let on assured shorthold tenancies for six months is not suitable, because the landlord can require you to leave much earlier.[197] If you are not sure what type of tenure you have, seek advice.

The local authority is not required to exclude properties that you cannot take because the landlord wants a deposit which you cannot afford.[198]

Are you in a protected group?

If the local authority has decided that your rent is unreasonable, it must then consider whether you are in a protected group.[199] You are in a protected group if any of the people that the local authority must consider (see above) fulfils any of the following criteria:

- s/he is aged 60 or over; *or*
- s/he satisfies any of the tests of being incapable of work for social security purposes (see p10); *or*
- s/he has a child or young person living with her/him for whom s/he is responsible (see p353).

If you are in a protected group, the local authority must go on to consider whether cheaper suitable alternative accommodation is available and whether it is reasonable to expect you to move.[200]

Is there cheaper suitable alternative accommodation?

The local authority is required to prove that suitable alternative accommodation does not merely exist, but is actually available to you. However, if a local authority considers that suitable alternative accommodation is available, it does not need to refer to specific properties, but must have sufficient evidence to demonstrate the existence of an 'active housing market' in accommodation of a suitable type, rent and location for you.[201]

In considering whether accommodation is 'available', the authority must have regard to personal factors such as whether you can afford to pay a deposit.[202] You should insist on being told exactly what accommodation is being referred to, why it is considered 'suitable' for you and those who live with you, and on what evidence it is considered to actually be available to you. Even if the authority produces a list of properties which are available to you, you can seek to show that they are not available to you due to your personal circumstances.[203]

Is it reasonable to expect you to move?

The regulations compel local authorities to consider the adverse effects of a move on the following factors:[204]

- your ability to retain your job; *and*
- the education of any child or young person living with you. In considering this, the authority must justify any decision that it is reasonable to make the child travel to school or move school.[205]

A judge has decided that the authority need not consider any other factors, such as your health.[206] It is arguable that this is wrong, since the regulations only say that the authority must 'take into account' the two factors above.[207] If you are in this position, seek advice.

The rent restriction

The authority *must* reduce your rent if it finds that:

- your accommodation is too large or too expensive; *and*
- if you are in a protected group, that:
  - suitable alternative accommodation is available to you at a lower cost; *and*
  - it is reasonable to expect you to move.

Although it cannot decide not to reduce your rent, the authority has a discretion as to how much it reduces it by. It must take into account your individual circumstances and the cost of suitable alternative accommodation elsewhere. Although the local authority should not be unduly influenced by the amount of subsidy payable, it could take this into account when deciding on a reasonable level of eligible rent. The reduction cannot reduce the eligible rent below that payable for suitable alternative accommodation.[208]

Should there be a delay before a restriction is applied?

No restriction can be made within 12 months of the death of a member of your family or a relative who occupied the same accommodation without a separate right to do so.[209] If you, a family member or relative (as above) could meet the payments when you took on the tenancy, no restriction applies for 13 weeks providing you were not in receipt of HB in the preceding 52 weeks.[210]

Rent increases

If your rent is assessed under the local reference rent rules – see p255. If the pre-January rules apply, and your rent is increased, the local authority has the power not to increase your HB by the full amount if it decides that:

- the increase is unreasonably high compared with the increases in suitable alternative accommodation; *or*
- the increase is unreasonable because a previous increase has occurred within the preceding 12 months.[211]

Where the local authority considers a rent increase to have been unreasonable, it may either refuse to meet all of that increase or only so much of it as it considers appropriate. If your rent has been increased for the second time in under 12 months but is still below the market level for suitable alternative accommodation, or the increase reflects improvements made to your accommodation, you should press for the full amount to be allowed.[212] If the local authority refuses, you should ask for a review (see p319).

CHAPTER THIRTEEN

The amount of benefit

This chapter covers:

1. THE BASIC CALCULATION

How your benefit is worked out

This depends on:

- your 'applicable amount' (see Chapter 18);
- your 'eligible rent' (see p242);
- whether any deductions are to be made for non-dependants (see p263);
- your income (see Chapter 19).

The most housing benefit (HB) you can get is called your 'maximum housing benefit'. This is your 'eligible rent' less any deductions for non-dependants.[1] In some exceptional cases you can get extra HB (see p272).

Because entitlement to income support (IS) or income-based jobseeker's allowance (JSA) acts as an automatic passport to maximum HB (once you have made a claim for HB), the local authority does not need to work out applicable amounts, income or capital.[2] However, if you are not on IS or income-based JSA, you do need to work them out (see p264).

No HB is payable if the amount would be less than 50 pence a week.[3] A local authority may round any figure used in working out your entitlement to the nearest penny (a half-penny is rounded upwards). The steps on p264 will help you to calculate HB.

If you are on IS/income-based JSA
- Work out your **maximum HB.** This is your eligible rent minus any non-dependant deductions.
- If you are on IS/income-based JSA, you are entitled to maximum HB.

If you are not on IS/income-based JSA
- Check that your capital is not too high (see Chapter 20).
- Work out your **maximum HB.** This is your eligible rent minus any non-dependant deductions.
- Work out your applicable amount (see Chapter 18).
- Work out your income (see Chapter 19 but also p279 if you are a student).
- **If your income is less than or equal to your applicable amount,** you are entitled to maximum HB.
- **If your income is greater than your applicable amount,** work out the difference. The amount of HB you are entitled to is maximum HB minus 65 per cent of the difference between your income and applicable amount.

Example 1

Mr and Mrs Feinstein and their adult son live together in a flat. Mrs Feinstein is the sole tenant and pays rent of £65 a week, which includes all their fuel. Mr Feinstein receives income-based JSA for himself and his wife while they are looking for work. Their son earns £110 a week gross. Mr Feinstein claims HB.

His eligible rent is £52.65 a week (ie, £65 – £12.35 deducted because of the fuel charges – see p244).

His son counts as a non-dependant and the appropriate deduction for him is £16 a week (see p270).

Therefore, his maximum HB is £36.65 a week (£52.65 – £16). Because he receives income-based JSA, his HB is £36.65 a week. The amount is lower than his actual rent because his fuel charge is not covered by HB and because his son is expected to make a contribution to the rent.

Example 2
Mrs Feinstein then finds a job for which she is paid £120 a week after deductions of tax and national insurance contributions. There is no occupational pension scheme. Her husband ceases to be entitled to income-based JSA because she now works full time and he makes a new claim for HB.
Mr Feinstein's maximum HB is still £36.65 a week.
His applicable amount is £79.00 (the standard rate for a couple – see p359).
His income is £110 a week (because £10 of his wife's earnings is disregarded – see p386).
The difference between his income and his applicable amount is therefore £31.00 a week.
65 per cent of £31.00 a week is £20.15 a week.
Mr Feinstein's HB is therefore £36.65 – £20.15 = £16.50 a week.

If you come off IS/income-based JSA because of starting work or increasing your income from work, you may be entitled to an extended payment of the same amount of HB you were getting while on IS/income-based JSA for a further four weeks (see p266).

Calculating a weekly amount of HB

Entitlement to HB is always paid for a specific benefit week, a period of seven consecutive days beginning with a Monday and ending on a Sunday.[4] If you pay rent at different intervals (eg, monthly) the amount has to be converted to a weekly figure before HB can be calculated.[5]

If the rent period is not a whole number of weeks, you divide the figure by the number of days in the period. This 'daily rent' is then multiplied by seven to give the equivalent weekly figure to be used in the calculation.[6]

Rent-free periods

If you have a regular rent-free period (eg, you pay rent on a 48-week rent year) you get no HB during your rent-free period. Your applicable amount, weekly income, non-dependant deductions, the set deductions for meals and fuel charges and the minimum amount payable (but not your eligible rent) are adjusted.[7] The rules for doing this are:

• Where your rent is paid weekly or in a whole multiple of weeks, you should multiply the figures to be converted by 52 (or 53 as appropriate) to give the annual amounts. Then divide by the number of weeks in the year in which you actually pay rent. So, for a 48-week rent year, all the figures would need to be multiplied by 52 and the result divided by 48.[8]

- Where your rent is paid on some other basis, you should multiply all the figures to be converted by 365 (or 366 as appropriate) and divide the result by the number of days in the rent year for which rent is actually payable. So, if you pay rent every calendar month except December (31 days), all the figures would need to be multiplied by 365 and the result divided by 334 (365 − 31).[9]

This rule does not apply if your landlord has temporarily waived the rent in return for you doing repairs (see p229).

2. EXTENDED PAYMENTS OF HOUSING BENEFIT/COUNCIL TAX BENEFIT

If you are on **income support** (IS)/income-based jobseeker's allowance (JSA) and your entitlement ends because you start work or increase your hours of or income from work, you may be entitled to an extended payment of housing benefit (HB)/council tax benefit (CTB). This means that for four weeks you continue to receive the same amount of HB/CTB as you did in your last week of entitlement to IS/income-based JSA.

You are entitled to an extended payment of HB/CTB if:[10]

- you were entitled to and in receipt of IS/income-based JSA and your entitlement ended because you or your partner started work (including self-employed work) or increased your earnings from or hours of work; *and*
- before your IS/income-based JSA entitlement ceased:
  − you were available for and actively seeking work; *or*
  − you were a lone parent; *or*
  − you were a carer and your applicable amount included the carer premium; *or*
  − you were on a government training scheme and getting a training allowance; *and*
- you had been continuously entitled to and in receipt of either IS or JSA or both for 26 weeks for any combination of the above reasons; *and*
- you expect the work (or increase) to last for five weeks or more; *and*
- your liability for rent will continue for at least four weeks; *and*
- if you were getting IS, you are under 60. (It does not matter if your partner is over 60, even if it is s/he who is starting work.); *and*
- you make a claim within eight days of the day your entitlement to IS/income-based JSA ceased (see p267).

Claims for extended payments

You can claim extended payments from the Benefits Agency, Employment Service or local authority. You must claim on the approved form, properly completed, within eight days of the day your entitlement to IS/income-based JSA ceased.[11] A claim for an extended payment cannot be backdated. If you fail to claim in time because of incorrect advice from a member of staff from the Benefits Agency or Employment Service, you should complain and request compensation. Your HB claim is given priority if, as well as claiming an extended payment within eight days, you claim standard in-work HB within 15 days of IS/income-based JSA ceasing.[12]

The amount of the extended payment

If you continue to live in the same property, the weekly amount of your extended payment is the actual HB payable in your last full week of your IS/income-based JSA claim.[13] (Ignore rent-free weeks.) If extra HB was in payment for exceptional hardship (see p255) or circumstances (see p272), it continues to be paid for the extended payment period. If you move house (except when you move into local authority accommodation), you continue to get the weekly amount of HB payable on your old home.[14] No account is taken of changes in circumstances over the extended payment period – eg, non-dependants, rent increases, increases in income, rent-free weeks.

The only change of circumstances which affects the amount of your extended payment is where you move to local authority accommodation. In this case, the amount of the extended payment is the eligible rent at your new address minus any non-dependant deductions which applied at the old address.

Even if you get an extended payment, you may still qualify for HB on two homes (see p233).[15]

In-work claims for benefit

An extended payment is a payment of HB/CTB, so if you make a claim for standard in-work HB/CTB within four weeks of the end of the extended payment period, your HB/CTB entitlement will be continuous.[16] This will mean, for example, that if you are exempt from the local reference rent rules, you should continue to be exempt unless you move home (see p252). In some cases, your entitlement to standard, in-work HB/CTB might be more than the amount on top of your extended payment. This could happen where, for example, your rent increases or a non-dependant with a high income moves out. In this case HB/CTB can be paid up to the level of your standard, in-work HB/CTB entitlement.[17]

3. DEDUCTIONS FOR NON-DEPENDANTS

What is a non-dependant?

A non-dependant is a person who 'normally resides' with you,[18] with certain exceptions (see p269). Most non-dependants are assumed to contribute towards your rent, whether they do so or not, and a deduction is made from your housing benefit (HB) to reflect this. You should consider asking them to reimburse you at least the amount of the deduction.

A person does not normally live with you if s/he has not been there long enough to regard the home as her/his normal home[19] or if s/he spends a lot of her/his time elsewhere. If you think the local authority has wrongly assumed that a person is normally living with you, ask for a review (see p319). DSS guidance says that a number of factors have to be taken into account to decide whether a person is normally living with you:[20]

- the relationship between you;
- how much time the person spends at your address;
- where the person has her/his post sent;
- where the person keeps most of her/his clothes and personal belongings;
- whether the person's stay in or absence from your address is temporary or permanent;
- whether the person has another place that could be regarded as home or whether s/he just travels around.

In addition, a non-dependant is only regarded as living with you if s/he is not separately liable for her/his own housing costs (eg, if you have separate tenancy agreements with your landlord) and s/he shares some accommodation with you.[21]

A person does not live with you, and so cannot be a non-dependant, if you share only a bathroom, lavatory, or a communal area such as a hall, passageway or a room in common use in sheltered accommodation.[22] For example, where part of your home has been converted to include a self-contained 'granny-flat', the person occupying it would not be a non-dependant even though s/he may share your bathroom and toilet.[23] However, if any other areas of the house are shared, such as the kitchen, the other person is treated as living with you. This is the case even if you only use it at different times and you maintain different households (see p346 for the meaning of 'household').[24]

People who are not non-dependants

The following people cannot count as non-dependants even if they normally live with you:[25]

- a member of your family (see p346);
- if you are in a polygamous marriage, a partner of yours and any child or young person in your household (see p353) for which you or a partner is responsible;
- a child or young person living with you who is not a member of your household (see p346);
- someone who is employed by a charitable or voluntary organisation as a resident carer for you or your partner and you pay for the service. This can also apply if a public body pays on your behalf;
- any person, or a member of their household, to whom you or your partner are liable to pay rent on a commercial basis.
- someone who jointly occupies your home and is either a co-owner or jointly liable with you or your partner to make payments in respect of occupying it. You do not 'jointly occupy' the home with someone unless you made a joint agreement with your landlord to occupy the home. The fact that s/he lives in the same home as you does not make you joint occupiers;[26]
- someone who is liable to pay rent on a commercial basis (see p235) to you or your partner.

If the person comes within the last three categories above, s/he can still be treated as a non-dependant if s/he falls within any of the *last four* categories of people who are treated as if they were not liable for rent (see pp234-35).[27]

Deductions from your eligible rent

When no deduction is made

- No non-dependant deductions are made if either you or your partner are registered blind or have regained your eyesight within the last 28 weeks, or receive attendance allowance, constant attendance allowance, or the care component of the disability living allowance.[28]
- No deduction is made in respect of any non-dependant who is:[29]
  - currently staying in your household but whose normal home is elsewhere;
  - receiving a youth training allowance;
  - a full-time student during her/his period of study, unless it is the summer vacation and s/he is in full-time work;

- in hospital for more than six weeks;
- in prison;
- under 18 years old;[30]
- aged under 25 and receiving IS/income-based JSA.[31]

The amount of deductions

You should try to provide information to show which deduction applies. If you cannot, ask the local authority to consider your circumstances – eg, are you doing a job which is normally very low-paid.

Unless you or your non-dependant(s) are exempt, a deduction is made from your eligible rent for every non-dependant living in your household except in the case of a non-dependant couple (see below). These are:[32]

Circumstances of the non-dependant	*Deduction*
Aged 18 or over and in full-time work with a weekly gross income of:	
– £250 or more	£45.00
– £200–£249.99	£41.00
– £152–£199.99	£36.00
– £116–£151.99	£22.00
– £78–£115.99	£16.00
All others (for whom a deduction is made)	£ 7.00

Full-time work is paid employment of 16 hours or more each week.[33] In averaging the number of hours worked, any recognised holidays or leave are ignored. The local authority also ignores any absences from work which, in its opinion, are without good cause.[34] Where the number of hours worked fluctuates, the average is taken.[35] However, where a person is on IS/income-based JSA for more than three days in any benefit week, they are not treated as being in full-time work for that week.[36]

Generally, non-dependants on training schemes are not regarded as being in full-time work. If they are aged 18/24 and were on IS/income-based JSA prior to the training scheme, no deduction should be made.[37]

A non-dependant who is on sick or maternity leave is not in full-time work, even if the employer is making up the non-dependant's full wages.[38]

The earnings amounts are gross figures – ie, in the case of wages the amount before any deductions. They relate to the total income of the non-dependant (apart from attendance allowance, constant attendance allowance, disability living allowance and payments from any of the Macfarlane Trusts, the Eileen Trust, the Fund and the Independent Living Funds[39]), and not just income from employment.

The earnings bands only apply to non-dependants in full-time work. A non-dependant who works less than 16 hours will not attract the higher levels of deduction even if her/his weekly gross income exceeds £78.

The DSS guidance stresses that local authorities are not expected to investigate the income of non-dependants in every case.[40]

Non-dependant couples

Only one deduction is made for a married or unmarried couple (or the members of a polygamous marriage) who are non-dependants. Where the individual circumstances of each partner are different, the highest deduction is made.[41] For the purpose of deciding which earnings band applies (see p270), their joint income counts, even if only one of them is in full-time work.[42]

Non-dependants of joint occupiers

Where joint occupiers share a non-dependant, the deduction is divided between them. This should be done taking into account the proportion of housing costs paid by each one. But no apportionment should be made between the members of a couple.[43] Where the person is a non-dependant of only one of the joint occupiers, the full deduction will be made from that person's benefit only.

Income and capital of a non-dependant

Normally, the income and capital of any non-dependant is completely ignored when assessing your HB entitlement, except for deciding which non-dependant deduction applies. However, if:

- you are not on IS/income-based JSA; *and*
- the income and capital of the non-dependant are both greater than yours; *and*
- the local authority is satisfied you have made an arrangement with the non-dependant to take advantage of the HB scheme (see p235);

your benefit entitlement is assessed on the basis of the non-dependant's income and capital rather than your own.[44] Any income and capital normally treated as belonging to you is completely ignored, but the rest of the calculation proceeds as normal.[45]

If this applies to you, seek a review of the decision (see p319).

4. EXTRA BENEFIT IN EXCEPTIONAL CIRCUMSTANCES

If the local authority considers your circumstances to be 'exceptional', it can pay you extra housing benefit (HB) over and above your normal entitlement.[46] This is in addition to the discretion the local authority has to increase HB where exceptional hardship would be caused by the local reference rent restriction rules (see p255). The meaning of the term 'exceptional circumstances' is not defined, and you should argue for it to be used wherever hardship would otherwise arise. Your circumstances do not have to be unique to count as exceptional.[47]

It is your individual circumstances that count and this power should not be used to pay extra benefit on the basis of predefined conditions. In any case where additional HB is paid, it can either be paid on a weekly basis for as long as the exceptional circumstances warrant it, or can be made as a 'one-off award'.

You will not be considered for any additional HB unless you specifically ask for it. Many local authorities use special forms for requests for extra HB. Make sure you give clear reasons why you need the additional help. If you are refused, you should ask for a review.

The overall limit is your eligible rent (see p242).[48] The local authority cannot use this power unless you are entitled to receive HB during the period of payment of the extra benefit. The power can only be used to pay HB in addition to, and not as a substitute for, normal entitlement.[49]

The local authority also has the power to pay extra HB/CTB to people getting either a war disablement pension or a war widow's pension including similar pensions paid by non-UK governments, by disregarding all of them as income, rather than just disregarding £10.[50] If the authority uses this power it must apply the income disregard to all people in receipt of these benefits.

5. PEOPLE IN HOSPITAL

If you remain entitled to income support (IS)/income-based jobseeker's allowance (JSA) while in hospital you will receive maximum housing benefit (HB), provided you continue to satisfy the temporary absence rules (see p232). If you or your partner go into hospital and you cease to be entitled to IS/income-based JSA your HB is affected as follows:

- up to six weeks – there is no change to your HB;
- after six weeks – benefit is reduced for adults in hospital.

If you are likely to be in hospital for more than 52 weeks you will not be entitled to HB under the temporary absence rules. If someone remains living in your home, they will need to make the claim for HB.

There are no reductions to your benefit if a dependent child goes into hospital.

After six weeks in hospital

- Single claimant – your applicable amount is reduced to £16.20.[51]
- Lone parent – your applicable amount is reduced to £16.20 personal allowance plus any children's personal allowances, plus any family premium (including the lone parent rate where applicable) and disabled child premiums.[52]
- Couple with one adult in hospital – your applicable amount is reduced by £12.95.[53]
- Couple with both adults in hospital – your applicable amount is reduced to £32.40 personal allowance for you both, plus any children's personal allowances, plus any family and disabled child premiums.[54]
- Partners of polygamous marriages where not all partners have been in hospital for six weeks. Your applicable amount is reduced by £12.95 for each adult in hospital for over six weeks.[55]
- Partners of polygamous marriages where all adults are in hospital. Your applicable amount reduces to £16.20 for each partner, plus any allowances for children, plus any family or disabled child premiums.[56]

The six weeks are calculated by adding together any separate stays in hospital less than 28 days apart.[57] The reduction takes effect from the beginning of the benefit week (see p290) after you have been in hospital for six weeks.

6. TRANSITIONAL PAYMENTS

In April 1988, HB was changed. Some people who were worse off under the new scheme were made payments to compensate for their losses.

For information on how payments were originally calculated, see the 19th edition of the *Handbook*, p209.

CHAPTER FOURTEEN

Special rules for students

This chapter covers:

1. General rules (below)
2. Students who are eligible (p277)
3. Students who are ineligible (p277)
4. Students from overseas (p279)
5. Calculating students' benefit (p279)
6. Payments (p281)

Most full-time students cannot claim housing benefit (HB) during their course, including all the vacation periods falling within it. Students who remain eligible for HB are subject to additional rules. There are special rules for the treatment of students' income (see p279). For students and council tax benefit, see Chapter 16.

1. GENERAL RULES

Note: The Government intends to change the definitions of 'student' and related terms in the Regulations from May 1998. From 1 June 1998, participants on certain other training courses will count as students. See CPAG's *Welfare Rights Bulletin* for more details.

Who counts as a student?

A student is someone attending a course of study at an educational establishment.[1] This covers any full-time, part-time or sandwich course, either advanced or non-advanced, whether or not you get a grant for attending it. The term educational establishment is not defined in law, but DSS guidance suggests it should include private as well as state-funded institutions. You are treated as a student until either the last day of the course or until you abandon it or are dismissed from it. 'Last day of the course' means the date on which the last day of the final academic year is officially scheduled to fall and not the date you actually leave if you do so just before then.[2]

If you have to take time off, change your course or give up studying, see p22.

Full-time students

You are a 'full-time student' if you are on a full-time course (including a sandwich course).[3] The rules for deciding whether your course is full or part time depend on whether it is funded by the Further Education Funding Council (FEFC).

If your course is not funded by the FEFC, the local authority is expected to decide whether your course is full time by looking at the nature of the course you are attending and, if in doubt, by consulting the educational establishment involved. Local authorities are advised that student grants are normally only payable for full-time courses. If you get a grant, and especially if the level of your grant seems appropriate to a full-time course, the local authority will probably decide to treat you as a full-time student.[4]

Some types of course, such as modular courses, give you a choice as to how much study you undertake. One judge has said that because you are not *required* to study full-time on such a course, it cannot be classified as a full-time course, and so you are not a full-time student regardless of the number of hours you study.[5] Even if this is not right, if you change from full-time to part-time study during the course, the course becomes part time.[6] If you disagree with a decision made by the local authority, you should request a review (see p319).

If your course is funded by the FEFC, then whether it is classed as full or part time depends on the number of guided learning hours it involves. (In Scotland the reference is to classroom or workshop based programmed learning under the guidance of teaching staff.) Guided learning hours include lectures, tutorials and supervised study but exclude unsupervised study, homework and meal breaks. Your college can provide a document showing the number of such hours your course involves.[7] Your course is full time if it involves:

- more than 16 guided learning hours; *or*
- in Scotland, more than 16 hours classroom or workshop based programmed learning under the guidance of teaching staff; *or*
- in Scotland, more than 21 hours a week, made up of 16 hours classroom or workshop based learning and additional hours using structured learning packages.

Transitional protection

If you were entitled to HB on 31 July 1996 while on an FEFC-funded course, you may be able to continue to get HB even if your course would now be defined as full time. Provided you satisfy the other conditions of entitlement, you can continue to get HB if:[8]

* you continue to attend the same course; *and*
* you have been continuously entitled to HB since 31 July 1996 (periods of up to 12 weeks during which you are not entitled after 7 October 1996 are ignored).

The period of study

If you are eligible for HB, the amount of your entitlement depends on whether that week falls either inside or outside a period of study. Your 'period of study' for HB purposes depends on the length and type of the course:[9]

* Where your course is for one year or less, the period of study is the period from the first to the last day of the course.
* Where your course is for more than one year and a grant is payable on the basis of you studying throughout the year, the period of study is the period from the first day of the course until the day before the next year of the course. In the final year the period of study ends with the last day of your final academic term. Many post-graduate courses come under this heading.
* In any other case where your course is for more than one year, the period of study is from the first day of each academic year until the day before the start of the recognised summer vacation. In the final year the period of study ends with the last day of your final academic term.

In deciding whether or not your grant has been assessed on the basis of you studying throughout the whole year (as in the second category above), the local authority should ignore supplements to your grant (eg, dependants' allowances) which are paid for the full year, regardless of the length of the course.

Your period of study includes periods of practical experience outside the educational establishment for students on sandwich courses.[10]

Your HB entitlement is calculated differently during the period of study than outside it. For example, the student rent deduction only applies during the period of study (see p279 – and also p399 for treatment of grant income). You may find, therefore, that your HB entitlement is higher during the summer vacation and that you need to make a new claim or check that your entitlement is reviewed at that time.

2. STUDENTS WHO ARE ELIGIBLE

Part-time students can claim housing benefit (HB). Full-time students are not normally entitled to HB, but there are a number of exceptions. You can claim if:[11]

- you are on income support (IS)/income-based jobseeker's allowance (JSA);
- you are under 19 and not following a course of higher education. Higher education includes degree courses, teachers' training, HND, HNC, post-graduate courses and professional examination courses;
- you and your partner are both full-time students and have a dependent child or young person;
- you are a lone parent;
- you are a lone foster parent where the child has been formally placed with you by a local authority or voluntary agency;
- you meet the conditions for the disability premium, or would do if you were not disqualified from incapacity benefit (see p10); *or*
- you have been incapable of work for 28 weeks (see p10). Two or more periods when you are incapable are joined to form a single period if they are separated by less than eight weeks; *or*
- you meet the conditions for the severe disability premium; *or*
- you satisfy the conditions for a grant supplement in the form of a disabled student's allowance award because of deafness; *or*
- you are a pensioner who satisfies the conditions for one of the pensioner premiums.

There are also certain exceptions for disabled students getting IS around 1 September 1990 – see the 27th edition of the *Handbook*, p261.

Partners who are not themselves ineligible as students can claim HB.[12] The claim will be assessed in the normal way, except that the rules about being away from term-time accommodation (see p278) and the student deduction from eligible rent (see p279) apply to the partner's claim.[13]

3. STUDENTS WHO ARE INELIGIBLE

Full-time students

Full-time students are not entitled to housing benefit (HB), except for the exceptions noted above.

Being away from your term-time accommodation

If you are a full-time student who is eligible for HB (see p277) and your main reason for occupying your home is to enable you to attend your course, you cannot get HB on that home for any full week of absence falling outside the period of study.[14]

This rule does not apply if:

- you are away from home because you are in hospital;[15]
- the main reason for occupying your home is not to enable you to attend your course but for some other purpose – eg, to provide a home for your children or for yourself if you do not have a normal home elsewhere;[16] *or*
- you are a non-student partner.

In these cases, any absences are dealt with under the temporary absence rules (see p232).

Accommodation rented from an educational establishment

If you rent your accommodation from your educational establishment you are not eligible to claim HB during your period of study (see p276).[17]

This only applies where you pay rent to the same educational establishment as the one you attend for your studies. It does not apply where your educational establishment itself rents the accommodation from a third party, unless this is on a long lease or where the third party is an education authority providing the accommodation as part of its functions.[18]

However, the local authority can still apply this rule if it decides that your educational establishment has arranged for your accommodation to be provided by a person or body other than itself in order to take advantage of the HB scheme.[19]

If you and your partner jointly occupy accommodation rented from your educational establishment, and your partner is not a student, the restriction also applies to her/him if s/he is the claimant.[20]

Regardless of any restrictions which may apply during your period of study, you can claim HB if you continue to rent your accommodation from your educational establishment outside that period.[21]

Living in different accommodation during term-time

The rules about claiming HB for two homes are explained on p233.

If you are one of a couple and receive HB for two homes, the assessment of HB for each home is based on your joint income, your couple's applicable amount and, in both cases, the rent deduction (see below) and corresponding income 'disregard' is applied.

4. STUDENTS FROM OVERSEAS

Most overseas students cannot claim housing benefit (HB) because they are persons from abroad (see p236). Even if you are entitled, a successful claim for HB could affect your right to stay in this country and it is best to get immigration advice before making a claim.

Partners of ineligible overseas students

Where you are not eligible, but there are no restrictions on your partner, either as a student or as a person from abroad, s/he may be able to claim instead.[22] However, if s/he receives HB and you are a person from abroad (see p236) this may affect your right to remain in the UK under the immigration rules because a claim by one partner is a claim for both (see p237).

5. CALCULATING STUDENTS' BENEFIT

If you or your partner get income support (IS) or a training allowance, none of the rules below apply to you.

If you do not get IS but you and/or your partner are eligible for housing benefit (HB), your entitlement is calculated in the same way as for other non-IS claimants (see p263), apart from the extra rules below.

Assessing your rent – the student rent deduction

If you are a full-time student, your weekly eligible rent (see p242) is, in most cases, reduced during your period of study by:

- £25.80 if you are attending a course in London; *or*
- £17.85 if you are studying elsewhere.[23]

The level of deduction depends on the area where you study rather than where you live. When it applies, it is made every week during your period of study (see p276), even where a grant is not paid or is paid for term-time only. It does not apply outside your period of study.

In any week in which your eligible rent is reduced, your income is reduced by the same amount. The overall effect of this is that you get less HB.

The rent deduction applies equally where it is the claimant's partner who is a full-time student,[24] but only one rent deduction and income disregard should be made where both partners are full-time students.

When the student rent deduction does not apply

The student deduction is not made if:[25]

- you are on IS or income-based JSA;
- you or your partner receive a training allowance for your own maintenance or for that of your child;
- you are a student on a sandwich course during any period of work experience (industrial, professional or commercial);
- your income for HB purposes is less than the sum of your applicable amount and the amount of the rent deduction, and one of the following also applies:
  - you are a lone parent; *or*
  - the disability premium applies (or would apply if you were not disqualified from incapacity benefit); *or*
  - you have been incapable of work (or treated as incapable) for a continuous 28-week period (including separate periods eight weeks or less apart); *or*
  - you have a partner and only one of you is a full-time student.

If none of these apply to you and the deductions result in hardship, you should ask the authority to make a discretionary addition to your HB, see p272. The authority will not be able to increase your HB above the eligible rent figure calculated under the main rules (see p242) – for students this means your eligible rent before the student rent deduction has been applied.[26]

Assessing your income and capital

The normal rules apply for assessing the income and capital of students, except that there are special rules for assessing the amount of money available from grants, covenants and loans (see pp399-401).

6. PAYMENTS

Students are covered by all the normal rules on the administration and payment of housing benefit (HB). However, there are two provisions which can apply specifically to students.

First, the local authority has the discretion to decide how long your benefit period should last. For most students, there are two benefit periods a year – one during the period of study, and the other during the long summer vacation (see p276).

Secondly, the local authority may decide to pay a rent allowance once each term except that students have the same right as other claimants to insist on fortnightly payments if their entitlement is more than £2 a week (see p291).

CHAPTER FIFTEEN

Claims, payments and reviews

This chapter covers:

1. CLAIMS

Who can make a claim

If you are a single person (this includes a lone parent or a member of a gay or lesbian couple), you make a claim for housing benefit (HB) on your own behalf.

If you are a member of a heterosexual couple, or a partner in a polygamous marriage, you can decide between you who should claim. The choice of claimant will not normally affect the level of HB you receive (but see pp277 and 278 for some important exceptions). In particular, if you are exempt from the local reference rent rules and are considering changing the claim into your partner's name, you should check whether doing so could result in you losing your exemption and becoming subject to the harsher rent restriction rules (see p253). If you cannot agree who should be the claimant, the local authority can decide for you.[1]

If a person is either temporarily or permanently unable to manage her/his own affairs, the local authority must accept a claim made by someone formally appointed to act legally on that person's behalf – eg, someone appointed with power of attorney, a receiver appointed by the Court of

Protection, or, in Scotland, a tutor, curator or other guardian administering the person's estate.[2]

If no-one has been formally appointed to look after the claimant's affairs, the local authority can decide to make someone over 18 an appointee who can act on the claimant's behalf.[3] For the purpose of the claim, an appointee has the responsibility of exercising all rights and duties as though s/he were the claimant.[4] You can write in to ask to be an appointee, and can resign after giving four weeks' notice. The local authority may terminate any appointment at any time,[5] and if someone is given a formal legal appointment, that person automatically takes over from the person appointed by the local authority.[6]

How to make a claim

All claims must be made in writing in a way which is 'sufficient in the circumstances', and accompanied by the information necessary to assess your claim.[7] Claim forms are available from your local authority – but if you are claiming income support (IS) or income-based jobseeker's allowance (JSA) you will find special shortened HB and council tax benefit (CTB) claim forms (NHB1) in your IS/income-based JSA claim form.[8]

DSS guidance suggests that a letter stating that you wish to claim could be regarded as an acceptable alternative to a claim form.[9] Where a claim by letter is not accepted as sufficient, you will be sent an official claim form to fill in. If you return this within four weeks (or longer at the local authority's discretion), it is treated as if it had been received on the date of your original claim.[10] Similarly, if you do not complete the claim form properly but return it properly completed within four weeks (or longer, if the local authority allows more time), it is treated as though it was received on the date of your original claim.[11]

Send your claim form immediately, as other information and evidence can be sent later (see p284).

You cannot claim by telephone. However, if you telephone to ask for a claim form, ask on the form to have your claim backdated to the date of your phone call (or longer, if appropriate) because you have good cause for a late claim (see p285).

You may amend or withdraw your claim in writing at any time before it has been assessed. Amendments must be made in writing and are treated as though they were part of your original claim.[12] A notice to withdraw your claim takes effect from the day it is received.[13]

Usually, you claim HB and CTB together but in Scotland some claimants have to make separate claims for HB and CTB. This is because District Councils are responsible for HB and Regional Councils are responsible for CTB. In most cases, however, District Councils agree to operate the CTB scheme for Regional Councils on an agency basis so that only one claim is necessary.

Where to make your claim

Unless you are claiming IS/income-based JSA as well, you should always return your claim to the address on the form.[14] This will be the address of the authority's 'designated office' for HB/CTB claims. Some local authorities lose a lot of forms. If you can, it is a good idea to keep a copy and to get confirmation that you have delivered it to the designated office.

If you are claiming IS/income-based JSA, you can either send your claim to your Benefits Agency office or to the local authority.[15] If you claim IS/income-based JSA and send your HB/CTB claim to the Benefits Agency, it must forward it to the local authority within two working days of either the date your IS/income-based JSA claim was assessed, or the date your HB/CTB claim was received, whichever is later, or as soon as reasonably practicable after that.[16] If you know there are significant delays at your local Benefits Agency office, it may be wise to send your HB/CTB form directly to the local authority. If you do this, the local authority will want to verify your entitlement to IS/income-based JSA before assessing your HB. This may speed up your HB/CTB claim.

Information to support your claim

Your application for HB should be accompanied by all the information and evidence needed to assess your claim,[17] but you should not delay your claim just because you do not have all the evidence ready to send. You must supply any information requested in connection with your claim within four weeks – or longer if the local authority thinks you need more time.[18] If you fail, without good reason, to provide information which it is reasonable for them to request, the local authority does not have to process your claim.[19] Contact them as soon as possible with the information requested and ask them to extend the four-week period, if you need more time. You do not need to declare receipt of payments, either for yourself or for a non-dependant, from any of the Macfarlane Trusts, the Eileen Trust, the Fund, nor income in kind.[20]

At the time of writing, you cannot be required to produce a national insurance number as a condition of claiming HB or CTB.[21]

Your date of claim

Your date of claim is important because it affects the date from which your HB begins (see p290). Usually, your claim is treated as made on the day it reaches the designated office (see p284).[22] The only exceptions are if:

- you have successfully claimed IS/income-based JSA and your HB claim reached the Benefits Agency within four weeks of your IS/income-based JSA claim – your HB claim is treated as having been made on the first day of entitlement to IS/income-based JSA (including the three waiting days for JSA);[23]
- you have unsuccessfully claimed IS/income-based JSA. Your HB claim is treated as having been made on the day it reached either the Benefits Agency or the authority's designated office, whichever is earlier;[24]
- you have made an advance claim (see below);
- you are on IS/income-based JSA and have just become liable to pay rent. If your HB claim form reaches the authority's designated office or Benefits Agency office within four weeks of you becoming liable, the HB claim is treated as being made on the date that you first became liable.[25]

If you post your claim form, your date of claim will be the date that the local authority receives it, not the date on which you post it (subject to the exceptions above).

Your HB normally starts from the Monday after the date of your claim.[26] This is called your date of entitlement (see p290).

Backdating a claim for 'good cause'

If you failed to claim, you can make a late claim and receive backdated HB, if you can prove you have continuous good cause for your failure throughout the whole time for which you want to claim.[27] Any backdated HB is calculated on both your circumstances and the HB rules which applied over the backdating period.

What amounts to 'good cause' is not spelled out in the HB regulations. Commissioners have decided that it means 'some fact which having regard to all the circumstances (including the claimant's state of health and the information which he received and that which he might have obtained), would probably have caused a reasonable person of his age and experience to act (or fail to act) as the claimant did.'[28] The following are examples of situations where you might have good cause for making a late claim:

- Where you sought advice about your rights but were misled by someone who you were entitled to rely on. You are entitled to rely on officers from the local authority or the Benefits Agency,[29] or independent advisers such as solicitors,[30] Citizens' Advice Bureaux,[31] trade union officials,[32] or accountants.[33] Relying on the advice of work colleagues, friends,[34] or even a doctor,[35] is not enough. The inquiries that you make need not have been specific, provided the situation is such that you ought to have been told about your possible entitlement.

- Where you did not seek advice about your rights either because you mistakenly thought that you understood them, [36] or that you mistakenly thought that you had no entitlement and there was nothing for you to inquire about.[37] Generally, you are expected to find out about your rights but if it was reasonable for you to form one of these views, you can still have good cause.
- Where the delay was due to some factor beyond your control, such as the failure of the post,[38] or the failure of someone you have asked to help you with your claim, provided you have checked whether the claim has arrived in good time.[39]
- Where you are unable to claim due to physical or mental ill-health.[40] However, you might reasonably be expected to seek the assistance of friends or relatives if available.
- If you have difficulty in communicating in English, or understanding documents, or have little knowledge of the benefits system, these matters should be taken into account[41] but are not usually good cause in themselves.[42]

If you think you may be entitled to benefit for an earlier period you should claim as soon as possible. This is because HB cannot be backdated for more than 52 weeks before the date of your request for backdating (which may be after the date of your original claim for HB), so you lose any unclaimed HB in respect of an earlier period.[43] If you would have been entitled to HB for such a period, you could do the following:

- ask for an *ex gratia* payment from the local authority if you were given wrong information or misled by it (see p325);
- complain to the Ombudsman (see p326);
- ask for additional HB on the grounds of exceptional circumstances if, for example, you are in rent arrears through no fault of your own (see p272).

Note: The new Social Security Bill (see Appendix 2) will restrict backdating of HB to one month in most cases, but only in limited circumstances similar to those currently applying to IS (see p134). These changes are likely to be introduced in October 1998. See CPAG's *Welfare Rights Bulletin* for more details.

Advance claims

There are two situations where advance claims can be made.

- If you become liable for rent for the first time but cannot move in until after your liability begins, it is important that you claim HB as soon as you are liable. This is because, once you have moved in, you may be able to receive HB for up to four weeks prior to moving in (providing you satisfy the conditions set out on p233).[44]
- If you are not entitled to HB now, but will become entitled within 13 weeks of claiming, the local authority can treat your claim as having been made in the benefit week immediately before you are first entitled.[45] If this happens, you do not need to make a further claim later on.

Making a further claim when your HB runs out

Your HB is paid to you for a period up to 60 weeks, after which you have to re-apply. The length of this benefit period (see p291) depends on the circumstances of your case[46] and you must be told how long it will last.[47] If you make a repeat claim not more than 13 weeks before, and not less than four weeks after, your current benefit period ends your new benefit period starts immediately your old one finishes.[48] If you have been granted benefit for more than 16 weeks and you have not made a further claim within eight weeks of the end of your existing benefit period, the local authority must send you an application form and remind you to reclaim.[49] It must also invite you to make a further claim if your benefit period expires while your benefit is suspended because you have been required to provide information (see p295). If you claim within four weeks of the expiry of the previous benefit period, your new benefit period starts from the date of expiry.[50]

If you are on IS or income-based JSA or your applicable amount includes the disability, severe disability or higher pensioner premium and you have not made a repeat claim by the last week of your benefit period, the local authority can extend that benefit period by four weeks. DSS guidance says this is to allow them time to issue a reminder or make a home visit if appropriate.[51]

Except where you are moving from IS to income-based JSA or vice versa, if your entitlement to IS/income-based JSA ends you will have to re-apply for HB (see p298).[52] A repeat claim form must be sent to you and, providing you return this within four weeks of the end of your previous benefit period, your new benefit period follows on without a break.[53]

If your partner or former partner was the original claimant but you are now making an HB claim for the same accommodation costs, the DSS guidance suggests that your claim will be treated as a repeat claim.[54]

If your date of claim has been backdated your benefit period begins in the benefit week in which your claim was actually received.[55]

2. DECISIONS

Delays

The local authority must make a decision on your claim, tell you in writing what the decision is, and pay you any housing benefit (HB) you are entitled to within 14 days, or, if that is not reasonably practicable, as soon as possible after that.[56] The local authority is under no duty to deal with your claim if:

- your claim was not accepted because you did not claim on an official form, or your form was not properly filled in and you did not re-submit it within four weeks of being asked to do so (see p283); *or*
- you failed to provide information needed to assess your claim within four weeks of being asked to do so (see p284); *or*
- you have told the local authority you have withdrawn your claim (see p283); *or*
- you have reclaimed benefit more than 13 weeks before the end of your current benefit period (see p287).[57]

In practice, many local authorities take considerably longer than 14 days to deal with claims. If you consider the delay is unreasonable you should write to the HB manager and threaten a formal complaint of 'maladministration' to the Ombudsman (see p326), unless you are paid within 14 days. Send a copy of the letter to your ward councillor and to the councillor who chairs the council committee responsible for HB. If this does not produce results, or if the delay is causing you severe hardship, you should consider court action.

If you are a private tenant and have not received your rent allowance within 14 days of your claim, you can get a payment on account (see p294).

Notification of the decision

Who should be notified

The following should be notified because they are 'persons affected' by the decision:[58]

- the claimant;
- an appointee (see p282);
- your landlord or agent in relation to a decision whether or not to make direct payment to that landlord/agent (see p292);
- the benefit authority;
- any person, including a landlord, from whom the benefit authority decides to recover a recoverable overpayment.

Only a 'person affected' can request reasons for a decision, apply for review or apply for a decision to be set aside, and these must be signed personally by them.[59]

Information a notification should contain

The local authority must include in its notification a minimum amount of information.[60] In addition, it may also include other relevant information.[61]

All notifications must tell you:

- of your right to ask for a further written explanation of the decision, how you can do this, and the time limit for doing so (see p320);[62] *and*
- of your right to ask for the decision to be reviewed, how you can do this, and the time limit for doing so (see p320).[63]

Other information that must be provided varies with the particular circumstances of your case. All the following should be included where relevant:[64]

- the normal weekly amount of HB you are entitled to;
- your weekly eligible rent;
- the amount of any notional fuel deductions, why they have been made, and that they can be varied if you can provide evidence of the actual amount involved;
- the amount and category of any non-dependant deductions;
- if you are a private tenant, the day your HB will be paid and whether payment will be made weekly, monthly etc;
- the date on which your entitlement starts and how long it will last (your benefit period);
- if you are not receiving income support (IS)/income-based jobseeker's allowance (JSA), how your applicable amount is calculated;

- if you are not receiving IS/income-based JSA, how your income has been assessed;
- if your level of HB is less than the minimum amount payable, that this is the reason why you have no entitlement;
- if your claim was successful, your duty to notify the local authority of any changes in circumstances which might affect your entitlement and what kinds of changes should be reported;
- if your claim was unsuccessful, a statement explaining exactly why you are not entitled;
- if it has been decided to pay your rent allowance direct to your landlord, information saying how much is to be paid to your landlord and when payments will start, and also that where recovery of an overpayment is made from a landlord (see p307) and recovery is made from a tenant other than the one who was overpaid, that tenant will be treated as if the full payment of HB had been made;[65]
- if the income and capital of a non-dependant has been used instead of yours to calculate your HB (see p271), additional information saying that this has happened and why.

Local authorities have also been recommended to tell you, in non-IS/JSA cases, if they think you are likely to be entitled to IS or JSA.[66]

3. PAYMENT OF BENEFIT

When your entitlement starts

In most cases your entitlement to housing benefit (HB) starts in the benefit week following your date of claim.[67] A benefit week is a period of seven days running from Monday to Sunday.[68]

However, if you claim in the same week in which you become liable for rent, your HB entitlement starts in that benefit week.[69] This means that:

- if your rent is due weekly or at intervals of a multiple of a week, your HB starts at the beginning of the week in which liability starts – ie, you receive a full week's benefit for that first week, even if your tenancy did not start until part-way through that week;[70]
- if your rent is due at other intervals, your HB starts on the same day your liability actually begins.[71]

When your entitlement ends

Your **benefit period** is the length of time for which your HB is paid before you need to re-apply.[72] Local authorities have discretion as to the length of benefit period they set, up to a maximum of 60 weeks. The benefit period may end early (see **When changes in circumstances take effect,** p298).

If your entitlement to HB ends because you have stopped claiming income support (IS)/income-based jobseeker's allowance (JSA) due to starting work or increasing your hours of or income from work, you may be entitled to an extended payment of HB for four weeks (see p266).

How your benefit is paid

Payment to a claimant

How you are paid

If your landlord is the housing authority responsible for the payment of HB, you receive HB in the form of a reduction in your rent. This is called a rent rebate.[73]

If you are a private tenant, you receive HB in the form of a rent allowance which is usually paid to you[74] although, in some cases, it may be paid direct to your landlord or to someone acting on your behalf (see p292).

Although rent allowances are normally paid in the form of a cheque or giro, the local authority has the discretion to pay you by whatever method it chooses but, in doing so, it must have regard to your 'reasonable needs and convenience'.[75] It should not insist on payment into a bank account if you do not already have a bank or giro account, nor make you collect it if it involves a difficult journey.[76] If it does, you should ask for a review (see p319) and complain to your local councillor (see p325). If that has no effect, ask your MP to take the matter up with the local authority, and also complain to the Ombudsman (see p326).

Time of payment

Housing benefit is normally paid in arrears. Payments are made at intervals of a week, two weeks, four weeks or a month, depending on when your rent is normally due. It can also be paid at longer intervals if you agree.[77]

If your rent allowance is less than £1 a week, the local authority can choose to pay your benefit up to six months in arrears.[78]

You can insist on two-weekly payments if your rent allowance is more than £2 a week unless HB in paid direct to your landlord (see p292).[79] The local authority can pay your rent allowance weekly either to avoid an overpayment or where you are liable to pay rent weekly and it is in your interests for HB to be paid weekly.[80]

The rules for when payments of HB are made changed on 7 October 1996. Before that date, HB was usually paid two weeks before the end of the period in respect of which it was paid (so payments for two weeks were made in advance and payments for four weeks or a month midway through the period).[81] You have transitional protection (ie, the old rules continue to apply to you) if:[82]

- you have been continuously entitled to and in receipt of HB on the same property since 6 October 1996; *or*
- your partner was continuously entitled to and in receipt of HB since 6 October 1996, but has died and you make a new claim within four weeks of the death.

Payment to a claimant's personal representative

Where an appointee, or some other person legally empowered to act for you, has claimed HB on your behalf, that person can also receive the payments (see p282).[83]

If you are able to claim HB for yourself, you can still nominate an agent to receive, or collect it for you. To do this you must make a written request to the local authority. Anyone you nominate must be aged 18 or over.[84] The DSS guidance suggests[85] that this can only be done where you are incapable of receiving or collecting the payment yourself, but the regulations do not make such a restriction.

If a claimant dies, any unpaid HB may be paid to her/his personal representative or, where there is none, to her/his next of kin aged 16 or over. For payment to be made, a written application must be received by the local authority within 12 months of the claimant's death. However, the time limit can be extended at the local authority's discretion.[86] Where HB was being paid to the landlord prior to the claimant's death, the local authority can pay any outstanding HB to clear remaining rent due.

Payment direct to a landlord

When can direct payments be made?

The local authority *must* pay your HB, including payments on account,[87] directly to the landlord (or the person you pay rent to) if:

- you or your partner are on IS/income-based JSA and the Benefits Agency has decided to pay part of your benefit to your landlord for arrears (see p151 and the *Jobseeker's Allowance Handbook 1998/99*);[88] *or*
- you have rent arrears equivalent to eight weeks' rent or more, unless the local authority considers it to be in your overriding interest not to

make direct payments[89] – in which case, your HB is withheld (see p295). Once your arrears have been reduced to less than eight weeks' rent, compulsory direct payments will stop. The local authority can then choose to continue direct payments on a discretionary basis if it considers it to be in your best interests to do so (see below).

The local authority *may* pay your HB directly to the landlord (or person you pay rent to):[90]

- if you have requested or agreed to direct payments; *or*
- without your agreement, if it decides that direct payments are in the best interests of yourself and your family; *or*
- without your agreement, if you have left the address for which you were getting HB and there are rent arrears. In this case, direct payments of any unpaid HB due in respect of that accommodation can be made, up to the total of the outstanding arrears.

The local authority needs to be advised of the above circumstances, and your landlord could contact them about this.[91] Note the impact of the new anti-fraud measures on direct payments (see p294).

If you are granted refugee status and receive a retrospective award of HB, part or all of that award can be paid direct to the landlord (see p241).[92]

If you have just claimed HB, and the local authority thinks you have not already paid your rent and it would be in the interests of the 'efficient administration' of HB, they may make the first cheque payable to the landlord although they will send it to you.[93]

If the local authority implements direct payments, both you and your landlord should be notified accordingly. If it is not in your interests to have HB paid directly to your landlord (eg, because you are deliberately withholding rent to force your landlord to carry out repairs) it is worth trying to persuade the authority to withhold it rather than paying it to your landlord where there are more than eight weeks' arrears. Landlords can sometimes place authorities under pressure to pay them direct and the authority may not use this alternative option as a result.

Time of payment

Payments made direct to your landlord are now made four-weekly or monthly in arrears. If HB is also paid to your landlord for other tenants, the first payment for you can be made at a shorter interval so that your payments are brought into line with the cycle of payments for the other tenants.[94]

If you have transitional protection (see p292), you can continue to have HB paid to your landlord under the pre-October 1996 rules, which allowed payment at other intervals.

When the authority is suspicious about a landlord

Several new provisions have been introduced to try to prevent HB fraud by landlords. If HB is being paid to a landlord, or a request is made for payment to a landlord, and the authority suspects impropriety on the part of the landlord, it may require a landlord or her/his agent to provide information[95] to the authority.[96] The authority may also refuse to make direct payments where it 'is not satisfied that the landlord is a fit and proper person'.[97] Payments cannot then be made in the circumstances where it would normally be mandatory to make direct payments (see p291 above).[98]

However, the authority *may* make direct payments if:[99]

- the requirements for discretionary direct payments (see p293) are met;
- the authority is satisfied that it is in the best interests of you and your family that direct payments be made.

Interim payments on account

Local authorities are required to deal with your claim and pay your HB within 14 days as far as possible.[100] If you are a private tenant and the local authority has not been able to assess your HB within this period, you should receive a payment on account while your claim is being sorted out.[101] The local authority should automatically do this. You do not have to request an interim payment.[102]

Some local authorities treat these interim payments as though they are discretionary. However, the law says the local authority must pay you an amount which it considers reasonable, given what it knows about your circumstances, and DSS guidance reminds it of its duty to pay.[103]

Interim payments can only be refused if it is clear that you will not be entitled or the reason for the delay is that they have asked you for information or evidence in support of your claim and you failed, without good cause, to provide it (see p284).[104] If the delay has been caused by a third party (eg, the rent officer, your bank or employer) this does not affect your right to an interim payment. If your local authority has not made a payment on account, you should complain. You could also argue that it is guilty of maladministration and apply to the Ombudsman (see p326).

If the local authority makes a payment on account, it should notify you of the amount and that it can recover any overpayment which occurs if your actual HB entitlement is different from the interim amount.[105]

If your interim payment is less than your true entitlement, your future HB can be adjusted to take account of the under or overpayment.[106]

Lost and missing cheques and giros

The law says nothing about the replacement of lost or missing giros, as it is seen as an administrative matter. If the local authority refuses to replace a payment which has never arrived, you should threaten to sue them in the county court. The process is the same as for the Benefits Agency (see p147).

Withholding benefit

Your rent allowance *must* be withheld if you have rent arrears equivalent to eight weeks' rent or more but the local authority has decided it is in your overriding interest not to make direct payments to your landlord (see p292).[107]

Housing benefit should not be withheld if either you pay off your arrears or can satisfy the local authority that you will pay off your arrears once you have received your payments.[108]

If the local authority subsequently decides it is no longer in your overriding interest not to pay your landlord, the HB withheld must be paid direct to your landlord unless your arrears have been reduced to less than eight weeks' rent (see p292).

Your rent allowance *may* be withheld in the following circumstances:

- if the authority believes you are not paying your rent regularly to your landlord, payment may be withheld[109] until either you pay off your rent arrears or satisfy the local authority that you will pay off your rent arrears once you have received the amount withheld;[110]
- if the rent officer (see p249) gives seven days notice but you deny her/him entry to your home, the local authority can withhold your HB for as long as you continue to deny entry. If it is your landlord who denies entry, any HB that would have been paid direct to the landlord may be withheld;[111]
- if the authority has evidence which makes it doubt whether your landlord is a 'fit and proper person' to have direct payments of HB.[112] The authority must determine whether this is true within 14 days or as soon as possible thereafter. If it accepts that the landlord is honest, it must then pay her/him direct (see p292).[113] If not, it must pay the arrears to you or someone acting on your behalf;[114]
- if the authority is not sure whether the conditions for direct payment to your landlord are fulfilled.[115] It must decide within 14 days or as soon as possible thereafter and pay the arrears to your landlord[116] or to you or someone acting for you[117] as appropriate;
- if a query has arisen about your entitlement to, or the payment of, your HB, payment is withheld pending a review of your entitlement (see

p319)[118] or while you are required to give information to the authority.[119] In the latter case, you must be notified of the suspension and the information required within seven days or as soon as the authority is able.[120] You must normally provide the information within four weeks or risk having your HB reviewed (see p319-20).[121] On providing the information, further details may be required from you;[122]

- any payment of arrears may be withheld if the local authority thinks you may have been overpaid and that the overpayment is recoverable (see p300);[123]
- if the authority has evidence:
  - which has not been considered by an adjudication officer (AO); *and*
  - which raises a reasonable doubt as to the amount of your income and capital for IS/income-based JSA purposes; *and*
  - which consequently raises a question as to your HB entitlement,
  it can withhold payment until the AO has determined your IS/income-based JSA entitlement and the local authority has renewed your HB.[124]

In the last three situations above, once a decision has been made as to your correct entitlement to HB, the authority *must* immediately pay any benefit withheld to which you were entitled, though it is entitled to deduct any overpayment that is recoverable (see p307).[125]

The local authority must carry out the review within a reasonable time. If it takes an unnecessarily long time to resolve the issue, you should complain to the local authority (see p325). You are not entitled to interest on arrears of HB.[126] If you do not receive an explanation of the delay or are not satisfied, you should complain to the Ombudsman (see p326) or consider applying for judicial review (see p324).

4. CHANGES IN YOUR CIRCUMSTANCES

Duty to report changes of circumstances

From the moment you claim housing benefit (HB), you have a duty to let the local authority know in writing of any changes in your circumstances which you might reasonably know are likely to affect your HB in any way. If you do not, you may be overpaid HB and might have to pay it back, or you may be paid too little HB. If your benefit is paid to someone else on your behalf, the duty to report any relevant changes extends to her/him as well.[127] The local authority must tell you in writing about the changes you have to report.[128] Always keep a copy of this document for reference.

When reporting changes, you should *always* report them in writing and keep a copy of the letter or other document if possible to prevent a dispute later.

You must always report the following changes to the local authority:[129]

- any change to your rent if you are a private tenant;
- when entitlement to income support (IS)/income-based jobseeker's allowance (JSA) ends. You should not assume that the Benefits Agency will do this on your behalf. Make sure that you make a fresh claim for HB if you are still on a low income after coming off IS/income-based JSA;
- if a member of your family is no longer a child for benefit purposes (see p355);
- any change in the number of, or circumstances of, any non-dependants that may affect the level of deductions made to your benefit (see p268).

If you do not receive IS/income-based JSA you must also report:

- any change in family income or capital;
- any change in the number of boarders or sub-tenants or in the payments made by them;
- any change in your status (eg, marriage, cohabitation, separation or divorce).

Other changes

Whether or not you get IS/income-based JSA, there may be other changes which the local authority requires you to report, depending on the particular circumstances of your case. The need to report these additional changes must be drawn to your attention at the time you are notified of your HB entitlement.[130] This is important because you only have a duty to report changes which you 'might reasonably be expected to know' might affect your HB.[131]

You do not have to report:[132]

- any changes in your rent if you are a local authority tenant;
- changes in the ages of members of your family, or of non-dependants, unless the change results in a young person ceasing to be a member of the family.[133]

It is important that you report any changes to the right department. Your duty to notify changes is to the HB department, not to the local authority as a whole.[134]

Remember – if in doubt, always report changes in circumstances. If

you think that the authority might have forgotten to look at your HB entitlement after you report a change, you should check with the authority.

When changes in circumstances take effect

If you have made an application for HB and reported a change of circumstances before the local authority has assessed your claim, your application is assessed on the basis of the revised information you have provided.

If a change of circumstances takes place within your benefit period, the local authority must establish the date on which that change actually occurred.[135] Where you have ceased to be entitled to some other social security benefit, the date the change occurred must always be taken as the day after your last day of entitlement to that benefit.[136]

In most cases, the change takes effect from the start of the benefit week after the one in which the change actually occurred.[137] This means that, on whatever day of the week the change actually occurs, the change is implemented as from the following Monday. This includes cases where IS/income-based JSA stops and HB ends, apart from the exceptions listed below.

- If IS/income-based JSA ends because another benefit becomes payable, the HB benefit period ends at the end of the benefit week in which the payment of IS/income-based JSA ceases.
  (**Note:** The benefit period does not end if you move from IS to income-based JSA or vice versa.[138])
- Where IS/income-based JSA ends in any other case, the HB benefit period ends at the end of the benefit week in which IS/income-based JSA entitlement ceases (ie, the normal rule applies).[139]
- Where a child or young person reaches the age of 11 or 16, the personal allowance in respect of her/him (see p359) increases from the first Monday in September following the 11th or 16th birthday.[140]
- A change in rent is taken into account in the benefit week in which it actually occurs. If you pay your rent weekly, or in a multiple of weeks, the change is taken into account for the whole of the week in which it occurs. This means that the change takes effect on the Monday, though your rent may not have changed until, say, the Thursday of that week. If you pay rent monthly, the change is taken into account on the day it actually occurs.[141]
- A change in your income solely due to a change in tax and national insurance contributions can be disregarded for up to 30 weeks (see p395).[142]

- A change in the HB regulations takes effect from the date the amendment occurs.[143] The annual uprating of other social security benefits, provided it takes place between 1 and 15 April, takes effect from the first Monday in April if you pay rent weekly (or in multiples of weeks). If you pay at other intervals it counts from 1 April.
- A payment of income (or arrears of income) for a past period is taken into account from the date it would have been taken into account had it been paid on time (see p298).[144] Your entitlement for that past period may be reviewed and if you received too much HB, the overpayment may be recoverable (see p300).

If you receive arrears of a social security benefit relating to a period before 6 March 1995, they are taken into account for a forward period from the date the award is actually made.[145] Any lump sum in respect of arrears counts as capital. If arrears of a social security benefit relate to a period after 6 March 1995, DSS guidance says that those arrears should be taken into account from the date they would have been taken into account had they been paid on time.[146] However, you should argue that this is wrong because arrears of benefit are capital not income (see p417) – they would need to be income for the guidance to be right.[147]

If two or more changes occurring in the same benefit week would, according to the above rules, normally take effect in different benefit weeks, they are treated as taking effect in the same benefit week in which they occur. They take effect from the beginning of that benefit week (unless one of the changes relates to monthly rent, in which case all the changes take effect on the same day as the rent changes).[148] If you pay rent weekly (or in multiples of weeks) and the annual uprating occurs at the same time as another change (excluding a change to your rent or the HB Regulations) they all count from the first Monday in April.[149]

Reassessment of your benefit

The local authority may deal with your change of circumstances by ending your benefit period early and inviting you to reclaim so that your entitlement can be completely reassessed.[150] This always happens if you have ceased to be entitled to IS/income-based JSA[151] (unless you have moved from IS to income-based JSA or vice versa).[152] Otherwise, the local authority reviews your existing entitlement and either increases or reduces your existing HB, as appropriate.[153] A review is likely to cause less disruption to your benefit payments than a fresh claim, so you may wish to ask the authority to consider this option, particularly if your circumstances change quite frequently. Local authorities rarely use this option and may need to be persuaded to do so.

5. OVERPAYMENTS

If the information you give the local authority is wrong, or if you do not report a change in your circumstances (see p296), you could end up being paid too much housing benefit (HB). You could also be overpaid as a result of an official error or delay that is not your fault. Not all overpayments are legally recoverable although local authorities sometimes recover them illegally.

What is an overpayment?

An overpayment is an amount of HB which has been paid, and which the local authority subsequently decides that you were not entitled to under the regulations.[154] The reference to HB being 'paid' includes payment to you, your landlord or somebody else and also includes HB credited to your rent account as a rent rebate (see p291).[155]

There are several steps that a local authority must take before an overpayment is recovered. It must:

- decide whether the overpayment is legally recoverable;
- decide whether recovery of the overpayment should be sought, and if so from whom;
- work out the amount of the overpayment and the period over which it occurred;
- decide how the overpayment should be recovered and at what rate;
- notify you of all the above decisions regarding the overpayment and give you an opportunity to request further information or a review.

Is the overpayment recoverable?

Overpayments can have many causes, but the general rule is that an overpayment will be recoverable.[156] There is an exception to that rule (see p301), but an overpayment may be recoverable even if it was caused by an innocent mistake on your part or was somebody else's fault. Remember that, with certain exceptions, just because an overpayment is recoverable does not mean it will necessarily be recovered.

Overpayments fall into two categories: those that are always recoverable, and those that are not recoverable in certain circumstances.

Overpayments that are always recoverable

There are two types of overpayments which are always recoverable:

- An overpayment which is the result of the authority overestimating your HB when making an interim payment (see p294). If you are still receiving HB when the authority makes a final decision as to how much HB you are getting, it is obliged to recover the excess from future HB payments.[157] However, if you are no longer getting HB, this rule does not apply and the overpayment will only be recoverable if the exception does not apply (see below).
- An overpayment of rent rebate that relates to a period after the date that your HB is reviewed and reduced.[158] This does not apply to overpayments of rent rebate relating to a period before the review, which are only recoverable if the exception does not apply (see below).

Overpayments that are not always recoverable

Overpayments that do not fall into the two categories above are not recoverable if you can show that the following three conditions are met:
[159]

- the overpayment was caused by an 'official error' (see below); *and*
- no relevant person caused the official error to be made (see p302); *and*
- no relevant person should have realised that an overpayment was being made (see p303).

Official error

An 'official error' is defined as 'a mistake, whether in the form of an act or omission, by the appropriate authority or by an officer or person acting for that authority or by an officer of the Department of Social Security or the Department of Employment acting as such'.[160] It therefore includes the following:

- a mistake made by the local authority in calculating your entitlement.
- a failure by the local authority to reduce your HB when you inform them of a change of circumstances;
- a failure by an officer of another department of the local authority, such as a social worker, to pass on details of a change of circumstances, where s/he has promised to do so. This is an official error because the definition does not require the mistake to be made by an officer in the department handling HB. A mistake by any local authority officer will be an official error if it results in an overpayment.
- similar mistakes by somebody carrying out functions relating to HB on behalf of the authority;

- a mistake made by the Benefits Agency in calculating your entitlement to IS/income-based JSA which results in a wrong calculation of your entitlement to HB;
- a failure by the Benefits Agency to pass on information to the local authority. DSS guidance says that this is not an official error,[161] but you should argue that there are procedures for the Benefits Agency to pass information to local authorities and if these are not followed it is an omission by the Agency and therefore falls within the definition;
- wrong advice given to you by an officer of the local authority, the Benefits Agency or the Employment Service, provided that s/he is acting as an officer at the time (rather than, say, a friend giving you informal advice).

The list above is not exhaustive. The official error does not have to be the sole cause of the overpayment. An overpayment is 'caused by' an official error if it is one of two or more reasons why the overpayment occurred.[162]

No relevant person caused the official error

The official error will not prevent the overpayment being recoverable if the error was partially or wholly caused by a relevant person, that is:

- a claimant; *or*
- a person acting on your behalf, whether because you are unable to deal with your affairs or because you have asked the authority in writing to deal with her/him on your behalf (see p282); *or*
- a person to whom the payment was made, which would include a different person acting on your behalf or a landlord.

It has been decided that the authority only needs to show that *any* relevant person caused the official error. It can then recover from any person from whom recovery may be sought and does not have to pursue the person who caused the official error.[163] If the authority tries to recover from you and it was another person who caused the official error, you should argue that the court was not obliged to reach a decision on that part of the case. The authority is therefore not bound to follow that decision, and the structure of the regulations means that recovery must be sought from the person causing the official error. You could also argue that the authority should exercise its discretion to recover from that person instead (see p304).

Examples of how a relevant person might cause an official error include:

* making a mistake in information given to the local authority which results in it wrongly calculating your benefit;
* failing to disclose a change of circumstances to the local authority. It is arguable that if you fail to comply with your duty to tell the local authority (see p296), you are contributing to an official error by the Benefits Agency if the Agency fails to pass on the information you have given it to the local authority.

No relevant person should have realised there was an overpayment

Even if the official error was solely the fault of the official, the overpayment will still be recoverable if any relevant person (see p302) knew, or ought reasonably to have known, that an overpayment had been made. The extent to which you can reasonably be expected to realise that an overpayment is being made to you depends on the extent to which the local authority has advised you about the scheme or your duties and obligations, particularly about your duty to notify changes of circumstances. It depends not on what you know, but on what you could have known at the time of the payment or the notification.

Remember, the local authority must show not just that you could have reasonably been expected to know that you might have been overpaid, but that you were overpaid.[164] You should always argue that as a claimant, you cannot be expected to know the intricacies of the HB legislation and that, unless it was glaringly obvious that a change of circumstances would reduce your HB, you should be given the benefit of the doubt.

If you or some other relevant person could only have realised that there was an overpayment at some point during the period of the overpayment, the overpayment will only be recoverable from that date.

Recovery of overpayments

Local authority discretion

Apart from certain interim payments of HB on account (see p294), the local authority has a discretion as to whether an overpayment is recovered.[165] Some recover all recoverable overpayments and others only recover those caused by claimant error.

Nevertheless, local authorities have a legal duty to exercise their judgement on whether or not to make a recovery on the merits of each and every individual case. While they may have general policy guidelines on how to approach the issue in a consistent manner, these must not be so rigid as to effectively decide the outcome of each case in advance. A policy of always recovering recoverable overpayments would, therefore, amount to an unlawful 'fettering' of the local authority's discretion which could be challenged by judicial review.

If you have been overpaid and this was either not your fault or the result of a genuine mistake or oversight on your part, you should ask the local authority not to recover the overpayment, especially if recovery causes you hardship. If the local authority still insists on proceeding with recovery action, you should ask for a review. The rules allow you to ask for a review on the recovery method and the rate of recovery.[166] This is not the same as IS rules where you cannot appeal these decisions. DSS guidance says that a decision to recover a recoverable overpayment is not open to review.[167] You should request a review and argue that this is wrong. A decision to recover is a 'determination' under the HB Regulations and therefore open to review.[168] Furthermore, the review board has the same power to exercise discretion as the local authority.[169]

If the overpayment was caused by someone else, you could suggest that recovery is made from her/him (but where this is the landlord see p310).

You may be asked to repay an irrecoverable overpayment on a voluntary basis. You are under no legal obligation to do so.

Who is the overpayment recoverable from?

An overpayment can be recovered from any of the following:[170]

- you (or your partner where you were members of the same household both at the time the overpayment was made and while it is being recovered);
- the person to whom the payment was made;
- where the overpayment was the result of a misrepresentation or failure to disclose a material fact, from the person who misrepresented or failed to disclose. This means that an overpayment could be recovered from the landlord – eg, even where s/he did not actually receive the payment. For the meaning of 'misrepresentation' and 'failure to disclose', see p159.

In the event of the death of the person from whom recovery is being sought, local authorities may consider recovering any outstanding overpayment from that person's estate.[171]

How much of the overpayment is recoverable?

The authority should distinguish between parts of an overpayment that are recoverable and those which are not. It is a good idea to check the amount of an overpayment to ensure the local authority has calculated it correctly. To calculate an amount, you should do the following:

- determine the dates between which you have been paid too much benefit;
- identify the period or periods over which the authority is entitled to recover;
- work out the total amount of HB you were paid over the period(s) during which the authority can recover;
- work out the correct amount of HB you should have received during the period(s) of recovery. Deduct this from the total benefit.[172]

The authority is not allowed to add any interest to the amount of the overpayment.[173]

Offsets from the overpayment

Besides any amount of HB which you should have been paid, the authority must deduct other amounts from the overpayment:

- if you have been getting a rent rebate over the overpayment period and, for some reason, have paid more into your rent account than you should have paid according to your original (incorrect) benefit assessment, any overpayment arising over that period may be reduced by the amount of the excess payment. The authority will probably not apply this rule where the extra rent is to repay your rent arrears;[174]
- reductions under the diminishing capital rule (see below).[175]

You are not entitled to have other amounts deducted, such as housing costs which ought to have been met under IS or income-based JSA, where you mistakenly claimed HB instead. You could ask the authority to exercise its discretion not to recover the amount of such costs that you would have received in such circumstances.

The diminishing capital rule

The diminishing capital rule only applies in the following circumstances:

- where the overpayment is caused by a misrepresentation of, or a failure to disclose, the amount of your capital (see pp159-61 for the meaning of misrepresentation and failure to disclose); [176]
- where the overpayment is caused by an error as to the claimant's capital, other than an official error (see p301).

It does not have to be your capital that the authority did not know about for the rule to operate. It could be the capital of somebody else, provided that capital is to be taken into account for HB purposes (see p416).

In order to check a diminishing capital calculation made by the local authority, you should do the following:

- work out the period over which the authority can recover. If the period is less than 13 weeks, the rule does not apply; [177]
- work out how much capital you had at the beginning of the period (see Chapter 20);
- work out how much benefit was overpaid for the first 13 benefit weeks of the period;
- deduct the amount of benefit overpaid during that 13-week period from the amount of capital;[178]
- if you spent part of your capital during that period, the regulations do not make it clear whether you can also deduct the amount that you spent. If this applies to you, you should argue that if the deduction is not made, it would not be fair because you do not get the full benefit of the diminishing capital rule and it does not reflect what the reality would have been if the authority had taken your capital into account. However, you should bear in mind the notional capital rule (see p428);
- calculate your entitlement for the next period of 13 weeks taking into account the reduced amount of capital;
- calculate the difference between the amount you were paid during that period of 13 weeks and the amount you should have been paid, to give the amount recoverable for that period;
- this procedure is then repeated for each subsequent block of 13 weeks[179] until: *either*
  - your capital is reduced to below £3,000 (so it has no effect on entitlement), *or*
  - there are less than 14 weeks left before the end of the overpayment period. In that case you should treat your entitlement for that period as being the same as for the last period of 13 weeks;
- add up the overpayment for each period. That is the amount recoverable.

How overpayments can be recovered

If agreement cannot be reached about how an overpayment is to be repaid, there are several different ways in which an authority can seek to recover an overpayment. Except where specifically stated, each method can be adopted for any category of person from whom an overpayment of HB can be recovered (see p304). When an overpayment is recovered from a landlord, you should take careful note of how that affects your liability for rent (see p310).

Recent legislation[180] has significantly expanded the powers of the local authority to recover HB overpayments. It is probable that the new powers can be used to recover overpayments that arose prior to the introduction of the new legislation.[181]

Recovery from payments of HB

An authority is entitled to recover an overpayment by deducting sums from any housing benefit payable to the person from whom recovery is sought.[182] This can be both future payments of HB and any arrears that are owing. There are special rules for recovery from the claimant's partner and from landlords.

Recovery from your partner

The authority may recover from payments of HB made to your partner only if *all* the following conditions are met:[183]

- you are a claimant. This power cannot be used to recover from other categories of people from whom recovery can be made;
- the payment was made to you, rather than to your landlord or someone acting on your behalf;
- you were living in the same household (see p347) *both* at the time of the overpayment *and* when the deduction is made. You must have been living together for the whole period of the overpayment, not just for part of it.

Recovery from a landlord

Before November 1997, the circumstances in which an authority could recover from HB payments to a landlord were restricted. Now the local authority may recover any of the following categories of HB payment:

- HB paid to the landlord personally, as a claimant;[184]
- other benefits paid to the landlord personally (see p308);
- HB paid to the landlord directly in respect of the same claimant who received the overpayment.[185] It is important to distinguish this from cases where the authority recovers from you by reducing the payments that it makes direct to the landlord. The notification of the overpayment (see p312) should make it clear from whom the authority is recovering;
- HB paid to the landlord directly in respect of claimants other than the claimant who received the overpayment.[186]

When HB is recovered from a landlord in this way, there are special rules as to how this affects your liability to pay rent (see p310).

Recovery from other benefits

The local authority can ask the Benefits Agency to recover the overpayment by making deductions from most other social security benefits if:

- a recoverable overpayment has been made as a result of a misrepresentation or failure to disclose a material fact by, or on behalf of, the claimant or some other person to whom HB has been paid; *and*
- the local authority is unable to recover that overpayment from any HB entitlement; *and*
- the person who misrepresented or failed to disclose is receiving at least one of the relevant benefits (see below) at a sufficiently high rate for deductions to be made.[187]

Deductions cannot be made from child benefit or guardian's allowance and, arguably, incapacity benefit because they are not benefits under the Social Security Act 1975. The amount that can be deducted from IS/income-based JSA is unspecified. You should make representations to the Benefits Agency if deductions cause hardship.

Overpayments of HB cannot be recovered by deductions from CTB (and vice versa).[188] If deductions stop because the person ceases to be entitled to that social security benefit, or entitlement drops below the minimum for deductions, the Benefits Agency notifies the local authority which, once again, becomes responsible for any further recovery action.

The authority may use this power to recover from a landlord, if the landlord is receiving benefits.[189]

Adjustment of a rent account

Where the person from whom recovery is sought is a local authority tenant, the authority may recover the overpayment by adding it as a debt on the tenant's rent account.

If a local authority recovers overpaid HB by adjusting its own rent account, the overpayment should be separately identified and you should be informed that the amount being recovered does not represent rent arrears.[190] That means that the local authority cannot usually rely on you owing them that amount to seek possession of your home. This is unaffected by the recent legislation discussed below (see p310) which only applies to private landlords.

Local authorities are reminded in guidance from the DSS that overpayments of HB in respect of their own tenants are not rent arrears and should not be treated as such.[191]

Court action

If the authority cannot use any of the methods of recovery above, and you cannot agree on repayments, the local authority can try to recover the money you owe through the county court (sheriff's court in Scotland) if it thinks you could afford to make repayments. You have six weeks to ask for a review of the decision that the overpayment is recoverable (see p319). This should be borne in mind when local authorities are deciding when to start proceedings.

A local authority is not entitled to use court proceedings for recovery if it has not followed the correct procedure for deciding that there has been a recoverable overpayment. The correct procedure has not been followed if, for example, the local authority has not issued the correct notification (see p312).[192]

An authority may use one of two means of recovering through the courts:

- sue you for the debt created by the overpayment.[193] If the correct procedure has not been followed, you can use this as a defence to the authority's claim.[194] You may also be able to make a counterclaim in certain circumstances (see p325), but you are not allowed to say that you should have received more HB because you must seek a review instead (see p319);[195]
- use the special court procedures to register the overpayment as a debt which can then be recovered using court procedure.[196] This is not the same as suing you and you have to follow a special procedure if you think the authority was not entitled to do this.

If the local authority is successful in using court proceedings against you, you may have to pay legal costs and interest as well as the overpayment. Remember that court procedures often require you to take action within a very short period of time. If the local authority is threatening to use court proceedings, seek advice.

The rate of recovery

A local authority can decide how much of a recoverable overpayment it will actually recover. It can ask for the whole amount at once or recover it by instalments.

If you are not on IS/income-based JSA but your income is below or not much above your IS/income-based JSA level, you should argue for the same weekly maximum (see p162) to apply. You should also ask the local authority to take into account any other debts or financial commitments or health problems you may have.[197] Complain if the rate of recovery is causing you hardship and suggest an amount you think you can afford.

You should check that the methods used by the authority and the rates of recovery are consistent between groups of claimants. For example, council tenants should not be required to repay overpayments in a lump sum (ie, the whole overpayment is debited to their account) where private tenants can repay by instalment – eg, by weekly deductions made to their HB. If this is happening, you should ask for a review.

The effect of recovery from a landlord

When an overpayment is recovered from a landlord, it can mean that you owe the landlord money in certain circumstances. It may also have an effect on the agreement under which you occupy your home, particularly if the agreement allows the landlord to get possession for arrears of rent.

If you received the HB, and then paid your landlord, you will be treated as having paid the amount of HB towards your rent. This is because HB is not the equivalent of rent, it is just money that you can use to pay your rent.[198]

The rules where HB was paid direct to the landlord are different. You should argue that the effect of recovery from a landlord depends on the period during which the overpayments was made, not the time at which recovery of the overpayment was sought, because recent legislation did not affect past transactions between you, your landlord and the local authority. The rules for different periods are set out below.

Whether HB was paid direct to the landlord or not, s/he may still try to claim that even if you owe no rent, you nevertheless owe a debt under the common law, which is probably not correct. If s/he threatens to sue you, seek advice straight away.

Direct payments before 7 April 1997

Where you were overpaid before 7 April 1997, and HB was paid direct to your landlord, you are still treated as having paid that amount towards your rent. This is because the local authority is effectively paying your rent for you, and so your obligation towards your landlord is discharged (subject to you paying any difference between the rent and HB).[199]

What this means is that the landlord cannot say that there are rent arrears of the amount of the overpayment that s/he has had to repay.

Direct payments between 7 April 1997 and 3 November 1997

On 7 April 1997, the Government introduced a new regulation that tried to change the law where HB was paid direct to a landlord.[200] For such payments made after that date, the regulation says that the claimant's liability to pay rent is not discharged when:

- a claimant was not entitled to a payment of HB paid to the landlord or to part of such a payment; *and*

• the HB overpayment was recovered in whole or in part from the landlord.

If your landlord tries to rely on this regulation, you should argue that the Government had no power to make the regulation and the landlord cannot rely on it. This is because at the time the regulation was made, the Government was only allowed to make regulations saying when and how local authorities could make payments to landlords.[201] There was no power to make regulations to say how such payments affected the legal rights of you and your landlord.

Anyone falling within this situation should seek advice *immediately*, since it is not certain whether you would be allowed to use this argument to prevent the landlord claiming that there are rent arrears and that s/he is entitled to possession. You should argue that since you could use the argument if the government was your landlord, you should be allowed to do the same against your landlord.[202]

If it is right that landlords cannot rely on the regulation, you will be in the same position as before 7 April 1997.

Direct payments after 4 November 1997
Where the overpayment relates to HB paid direct after 4 November 1997, the following rules apply:

• where claimant A is overpaid, and the authority recovers the overpayment from the landlord by making deductions from direct payments of claimant B's HB (see p307), claimant B is deemed to have paid the amount of the deduction towards her/his rent;[203]
• where the deductions are made from direct payments of claimant A's HB, claimant A is deemed to have paid the amount of the deduction towards her/his rent where the landlord is convicted of an offence or agrees to pay a penalty (see p317) in relation to that overpayment.[204] In this situation, the authority must notify both the landlord and claimant A that claimant A is to be treated as having paid her/his rent.[205]

In these cases, it is clear that the landlord cannot claim that there are arrears of rent. It is also much easier to argue that the landlord cannot sue under the common law for a debt (see p310).

The legislation does not make clear what happens in other cases where deductions are made from claimant A's HB. If you are in this position, you could argue that the legislation does not say what happens in your case, and so the same rules apply as before the legislation was introduced. As the regulation made in April 1997 is invalid (see above), you are still in the same position as before that date, so you are treated as having paid your rent anyway.

Notification of overpayments

If the local authority decides that a recoverable overpayment has occurred, it must write to the person from whom recovery is being sought (within 14 days, if possible) and notify her/him accordingly.[206] This notification must state:[207]

- the fact that there is an overpayment which is legally recoverable;
- the reason why there is a recoverable overpayment;
- the amount of the recoverable overpayment;
- how the amount of the overpayment was calculated;
- the benefit weeks to which the overpayment relates;
- if recovery is to be made from future benefit, how much the deduction will be;
- if recovery is to be made from a landlord by deduction from direct payments of HB of a claimant other than the claimant who was overpaid, the identity of the claimant overpaid and the claimant whose HB will be deducted;[208]
- that you have a right to ask for a further written explanation of any of the decisions the local authority has made regarding the overpayment, how you can do this and the time limit for doing so;
- that you have a right to ask the local authority to reconsider any of the decisions it has made regarding the overpayment, how you can do this and the time limit for doing so.

It may also include any other relevant matters.

If you write and ask the local authority for a more detailed written explanation of any of the decisions it has made regarding the overpayment, it must send you this within 14 days or, if this is not reasonably practicable, as soon as possible after that.[209] If your local authority does not give proper notification, you should write and point out that the decision to recover the overpayment is not valid until you are given proper notification. No recovery should be sought until after you have been notified and have had a chance to discuss your case or apply for a review.[210]

6. FRAUD AND CRIMINAL OFFENCES

If you deliberately mislead the local authority while claiming housing benefit (HB), you may be at risk of being prosecuted. In their efforts to stop fraud, there is a danger that local authorities will try to prosecute and punish people who have just made mistakes or who do not understand the system.

The best way to avoid misunderstandings is to ensure that the local authority always knows everything about your circumstances and those of people who are part of your family. Tell them everything – even if you are not sure whether they want to know (see p296 above for more details).

Investigation of claims

If a local authority discovers something inconsistent in the information before it, it will often start an investigation into your claim. It does not have to tell you about the inquiries that it is making straight away, but will normally wait until it has gathered all the information it needs and then ask you to attend an interview to explain matters.

Powers of investigation

A local authority has powers to appoint inspectors to look at claims which it thinks may be wrongful.[211] The inspectors are given wide powers to do the following:[212]

- enter premises where a business operates. This does *not* include your home unless the inspector has some reason to think that a business was operating from there and that was the only premises where it was operating;
- make inquiries and examine documents about a person s/he believes to be claiming or receiving HB;
- interview people in premises that are being inspected or who have information or documents about a person s/he believes to be claiming or receiving HB;
- require that information or documents are produced by people who are:
  - in buildings which are inspected; *or*
  - believed by the officer to be claiming or receiving HB; *or*
  - in possession of documents or information about a person claiming or receiving HB.[213]

If you obstruct an inspector or refuse to supply information, you may commit an offence.[214]

While the powers of inspectors are wide, they are not police officers. They cannot come into your home without your permission (except where your home is also where you run a business – see above) and they cannot arrest you. In addition, they cannot make you give information or answer questions in such a way as to confess that you or your spouse (not including your partner if you are not married) are guilty of an offence.[215]

Inspectors are 'persons charged with the duty of investigating offences or charging offenders'[216] and are therefore bound by certain Codes of Practice in investigating a claim. If the Codes are breached, this may restrict the use of evidence that inspectors have obtained.[217] If you think the inspectors have acted unfairly, you should seek advice.

Interviews

Inspectors may carry out formal interviews. These will usually happen at the local authority's offices. You will usually not be told why the interview is happening, so if you get a letter asking you to come for an interview without saying what the interview is about, that may indicate that the authority believes there is something wrong with your claim.

If you think you may be interviewed by inspectors and you think you know why, seek advice before you go. Legal aid may be available if you go to a solicitor. If you are not sure why an interview is happening, try to bring a friend to support you and take notes.

Inspectors sometimes put pressure on claimants to admit to things that are not accurate. It can be very upsetting to be accused of committing an offence, but it is important that you remain calm and listen carefully to the questions you are asked. If you do not understand anything, ask for clarification. Think carefully about the implications of the answers you give.

You may be interviewed under caution. If this happens, you should be advised that you do not have to say anything, but it may harm your defence if you do not mention something you later rely on in court. If you think you can explain the situation that has arisen, you should probably do so, since if you do not mention it at the interview you are more likely to be disbelieved if you are prosecuted.[218] In addition, if you are able to explain matters, your benefit is less likely to be taken away (see p315). Do not confess to something that you did not do, or agree to pay a penalty (see p317) just to finish the interview or to try to prevent your benefit being stopped. If you are interviewed under caution, you may make a written statement if you wish to explain matters.

In a formal interview, someone will write down what you say. You will often be asked to read through the notes of the interview afterwards and sign them to agree that they are accurate. It is important that you check them carefully and challenge anything that you think is wrong, since it may be difficult to do so later. If you do not have anyone with you at the interview, try to write down as much as you can remember about what was said shortly afterwards because it may be difficult to remember later.

The effect on your benefit

The authority is entitled to suspend or withhold your benefit if it has a doubt as to whether you are entitled (see p295). You will often have difficulties in getting your benefit restored during an investigation or after you have been prosecuted. The authority is not entitled to withhold your benefit indefinitely without making a decision as to whether you are in fact entitled or not. If you think the investigation is taking too long, you should complain (see p325).

The decision as to whether you should be prosecuted is separate from a decision to recover an overpayment (see p303). You should not assume that the authority will not recover the overpayment just because you are not prosecuted.

If the authority decides that you should not be getting HB or that you are getting the wrong amount, it will review your entitlement. You are then entitled to seek a further review (see p321).

Whatever the result of an investigation or prosecution, the local authority may take more time assessing future claims because it checks out your circumstances thoroughly. Again, if it takes too long for it to make a decision, you should complain. Remember your entitlement to interim payments on account (see p294).

Prosecution of offences

When have you committed an offence?

There are a number of different offences that you can commit if you mislead an authority. They can broadly be divided into two categories according to the level of penalty and where you are tried. Any fine that you have to pay is in addition to any overpayment that may be found to be recoverable. Remember that the figures given are the maximum penalties – in practice they will usually be much smaller.

Besides the offences set out below, you can also be charged with offences under the Theft Act 1968 – eg, theft, obtaining property by deception and false accounting.[219] These tend to be used only for the most serious offences.

Less serious offences

The maximum penalty for these offences is a £5,000 fine or three months in prison, or both.[220] You commit these offences when you do any of the following:

- make a statement which you know to be false, or give information or documents that you know to be false in some way that is significant.[221] You can commit this offence even if you do not intend to get any HB as a result;[222]
- fail to tell the local authority about a change of circumstances which you know that you have to tell the authority about (see p296), without reasonable excuse.[223] The reasonable excuse could be any reason that might make a reasonable person act as you did, such as wrong advice or personal circumstances such as a bereavement;
- make another person or allow another person to withhold a change of circumstances from the authority when you know s/he has to inform it.[224] You do not 'allow' somebody to do something when you are unable to stop them doing it. You will also have a defence if you have a reasonable excuse – eg, a threat of violence or owing the person in question a duty of confidentiality. Advisers should not come into this category if they give advice in good faith and there is no evidence that they are actively assisting a claimant to defraud the local authority.[225] Any adviser under the threat of prosecution should contact CPAG.

You do not 'know' something if you are merely careless about whether or not something is true, or if you fail to find out.[226] You cannot be convicted of either of the latter two offences due to anything you did or failed to do before 1 July 1997.[227]

More serious offences

You commit these offences if you do any of the above acts, but in addition the following conditions are met:[228]

- you are also acting dishonestly in doing the relevant acts. This means that you are doing something that most people would consider dishonest and that you must have known this; *and*
- you are trying to get benefit paid to yourself or some other person.

If you are convicted in a magistrates' court, you can be fined £5,000 or imprisoned for six months. If you are convicted in the Crown Court, the fine is unlimited and you can be imprisoned for up to seven years.

Will you be prosecuted?

Even if there is evidence which would justify a prosecution you will not necessarily be taken to court. In many cases you may be given the chance to pay a penalty instead (see below). In other cases the authority may decide not to take action against you. The factors that authorities may take into account include such matters as the strength of the evidence, the amount involved, whether an offence was planned, and your personal circumstances.

There are time limits for prosecutions for offences under the two categories set out above. A prosecution must be started by the *later* of the following dates:[229]

- three months from the date the authority thinks that it has enough evidence to prosecute you; *or*
- 12 months from the date you committed the offence.

What to do if you are prosecuted

The most important thing to do is to get advice. You may be entitled to legal aid to have a solicitor or barrister represent you in court. You should check carefully that the authority is able to prove all the parts of the offence you are charged with. Do not plead guilty until you have been able to get advice.

Penalties

Rather than prosecuting you, a local authority may now instead offer you the option of agreeing to pay a financial penalty.

Offering the option

The local authority may *only* offer you the option of paying a penalty when three conditions are fulfilled:[230]

- an overpayment has been found to be recoverable from you. This means that the authority must have gone through the process of reviewing your HB and issuing a determination that the overpayment is recoverable (see p300); *and*
- the overpayment was due to an act or omission on your part. This act or omission must have been after 18 December 1997;[231] *and*
- there are grounds for prosecuting you for any offence.

When the authority decides to offer you the option of paying a penalty, it is required to issue you with a notice which sets out, in broad terms, how the scheme works (see p318)[232] and giving you information as to how you agree to pay a penalty or notify your withdrawal of your agreement.[233] If the authority does not issue a proper notice, it may not be able to enforce the penalty, just as it cannot recover an overpayment (see p312).

The effect of agreeing to pay a penalty

If you decide not to accept the penalty, the authority may proceed to prosecute you if it wishes.

If you do decide to accept the offer, then the effects are as follows:

- The penalty is 30 per cent of the amount of the *recoverable* overpayment (not the total amount including any amounts that are not recoverable from you for some reason). It is added to the overpayment and is recoverable by the same methods (see pp303-09).[234]
- You are immune from prosecution for any offence in relation to the overpayment.[235] Note that this would not stop you being prosecuted in the future if you committed another offence, or in relation to a different overpayment if there was more than one.
- If it is found on review that the overpayment is not recoverable, any penalty that you have paid must be repaid to you.[236] This does not appear to affect the existence of the agreement, so you are still immune from prosecution.
- If the amount of the overpayment is changed on review, the agreement is nullified, so you lose the immunity and the penalty must be repaid, unless you enter into a fresh agreement.[237]

Changing your mind

If you enter into an agreement you are entitled to change your mind within 28 days and tell the authority in the way that is specified on the penalty notice.[238] You then lose your immunity, but you do not have to pay the penalty and if you have paid any part of it, it must be refunded.

The legislation does not allow for the period to be extended. However, if you do not get advice because you are scared of being prosecuted until after the 28-day period expires, and it turns out that the authority had insufficient grounds to prosecute you, it is possible that you may be able to take court proceedings to set aside the penalty agreement on the grounds of the authority's 'undue influence'. [239] If this applies to you, seek advice.

Should you accept the penalty?

The financial incentives on local authorities to get claimants to agree to pay penalties are very substantial and this is likely to lead to authorities offering penalties to claimants when they do not have the evidence to prosecute them. If you are offered a penalty, make sure that you are told what evidence the authority has against you and seek advice as to whether a prosecution is likely to succeed. You may find that if you call the authority's bluff by refusing the penalty, it will not prosecute you.

Remember also that 30 per cent of the overpayment may be a substantial amount of money. For minor offences, it may be that the fine imposed on you is less than the penalty. You may prefer to do community service rather than go further into debt. On the other hand, a penalty does not give you a criminal record. You should seek advice and carefully consider your options.

7. REVIEWS

A review is the process by which a local authority or the housing benefit review board (see p321) looks again at a decision and decides whether it should be altered. Such a review may be in your favour or may reduce the amount of benefit you receive.

If you wish to challenge a decision, you can do so only by asking for a review.

Local authority reviews

The local authority can review any of its own decisions, and those of the review board, at any time if:

- there has been a change of circumstances (see p296); *or*
- it is satisfied the decision was made in ignorance of, or based on a mistake as to, some material fact. In the case of a review board decision, this must be shown by fresh evidence that was not available to the board (and which could not have been put before the board at the time); *or*
- in the case of a local authority decision only, it is satisfied that it was based on a mistake as to the law. However, local authorities cannot decide that a regulation is invalid because the Secretary of State exceeded her/his powers in making it.[240]

If a decision is amended on a review initiated by a local authority, this counts as a fresh decision requiring notification in the normal way, so you can ask for yet another review (see p320) if it is unfavourable to you.[241]

If your HB has been suspended and you have failed to provide information required by the authority within four weeks then the authority *must* review your entitlement.[242] It may extend this period up to 13 weeks. The review is treated as though it was made under the powers set out above, so you have the right to a further review (see p321).

Your right to a review

You can also ask for a review of any decision (including a local authority review decision) simply on the ground that you disagree with it. The right to a review also applies to other people affected by the decision (see p289).[243] Such an application must be received by the local authority within six weeks of the decision being notified to you,[244] although the authority can allow a late application if there are special reasons.[245] The local authority must tell you of your right to apply for a review every time you are notified of a decision.[246] If it fails to do so, that will be a special reason for allowing a late application. An application for an extension must be made in writing, and, if it is refused, the local authority's decision is final[247] (although, in an exceptional case, it might be challenged by judicial review – see p324).

If you want a written explanation from the local authority (see pp289-90) so that you can state your case more effectively, the period between your request reaching the local authority and the explanation being posted to you is ignored when calculating the six-week limit.[248] It is often worth asking the local authority for a written explanation before formally requesting a review, because the law is complicated and you will then know the basis on which the decision was taken. However, if the reasons for the decision are clear or your situation is urgent, you should not delay asking for a review. You can ask for a further written explanation at any time.[249]

There is no time limit laid down within which the authority must carry out the review. Some local authorities have a policy of carrying out the review within 14 days of receiving a request for a review.

You must be notified in writing of the outcome of the review. The information given to you following the review must conform to the normal rules about the notification of decisions (see p289). It must also inform you of your right to ask for a further review by a review board (see p321).[250]

If a decision is altered on review, the revised decision takes effect from the date of the original decision.[251] However, if the review results in an increase in your housing benefit (HB), arrears cannot normally be paid for more than 52 weeks before the date the local authority first received your request for the review. The only exception is where the authority has reversed a decision not to backdate your claim under the 'good cause for a late claim' provisions – in which case any arrears may be paid for up to 52 weeks before the date your request for backdating was made (see p285).[252]

The housing benefit review board

A hearing before a review board is the nearest thing there is to an independent appeal for HB cases. Although review boards are not really independent, they must act as if they are. The review board is made up of local authority councillors.

Applying for a hearing

If you have exercised your right to a review (see p319), and remain dissatisfied with the local authority's decision, you can write and ask for a further review. It is this 'further review' that is carried out by a housing benefit review board.

When you apply, you must give your reasons. These need not be detailed or technical as long as it is clear what it is you disagree with. The request for the further review must reach the local authority within 28 days of the notification of the internal review being posted to you.[253] The review board may extend the deadline if there are special reasons for doing so. An application for an extension must be made to the chair of the review board in writing, and, if it is refused, the review board's decision is final (although, in an exceptional case, it might be challenged by judicial review – see p324).[254]

The hearing

A hearing before a review board should take place within six weeks of your request reaching the local authority or, if that is not reasonably practicable, as soon as possible after that.[255] Some authorities make claimants wait months for a review board hearing. If this has happened in your case, write and threaten to make a complaint of maladministration to the Ombudsman (see p326). However, if you are challenging a decision to restrict your eligible rent (see p248) and the local authority has asked the rent officer to reconsider your case as a result, the review board may decide to defer your hearing pending the outcome.[256]

You must be given at least ten days' notice of the time of the hearing and the place where it will be held, otherwise you have the right to insist on another date being set.[257] If you have been given adequate notice but would like the hearing to be postponed, or if you wish to withdraw your request for a hearing altogether, you must write to the chair of the review board who decides whether the hearing should still proceed.[258]

The review board consists of at least three local authority councillors (or members of the New Town Corporation, Development Board for Rural Wales or Scottish Special Housing Association), one of whom acts as·chair.[259] But if there are only two members of the board present when you attend, the hearing can go ahead provided all parties consent.[260] DSS guidance suggests that the board should not consist of anyone who has had a previous involvement in your case.[261] If the issue to be considered by the review board affects your claim for HB and/or council tax benefit (CTB) and/or community charge benefit (eg, the assessment of your income), the same review board can consider your claim for any combination of all three benefits at the same time, provided everyone concerned in the case agrees.[262]

The chair of the board decides how the hearing should be conducted.[263] You also have the right to attend the hearing and to present your case, call witnesses and question the local authority's witnesses. You can be accompanied to the hearing or be represented. During the hearing your representative has the same rights as you in presenting your case.[264] The local authority should pay your travelling expenses and those of one other person who accompanies or represents you, also any other person affected – eg, called as a witness.[265] The tactics for presenting a case before the review board are similar to those for social security appeal tribunals (see p178).

The review board has the right to ask people to give evidence, but it cannot compel anyone to appear before it who does not wish to.[266] If you fail to attend a hearing, the review board can proceed in your absence.[267] If you were unable to attend through circumstances beyond your control, and the review board has given an unfavourable decision, you may be able to have the decision 'set aside' (see p323).

If the review board decides to adjourn a hearing and the case is subsequently heard by a board composed of any different members, the second board should hear your whole case again.[268]

The decision

After hearing your case, the review board either confirms or alters the decision of the local authority.[269] If the board is not unanimous, a majority decision is taken. If there is an even number of members, the chair has a second or casting vote if necessary.[270] The chair must record the board's decision and its finding on any material question of fact.[271]

In arriving at its decision, the review board is bound only by the law and not by any local authority or DSS policy. It may exercise any discretion open to the local authority under the regulations.[272] It is bound by decisions on HB in the High Court, the Court of Appeal, the House of Lords and the European Court of Justice. Decisions in these courts on other benefits or related issues may be persuasive. It is not bound by any of its own previous decisions, nor by any of the decisions made by social security appeal tribunals or social security commissioners on similar cases and issues in other areas of the social security system, although it can take them into account. In particular, it should be slow to disagree with a commissioner's decision as commissioners are judges with considerable experience of this sort of law.

A copy of the decision must be sent to you within seven days or, if that is not practicable, as soon as possible after that, together with the reasons for the decision and the board's findings of fact.[273] These should give a clear explanation of why you have won or lost.[274] If the review board has altered the local authority's decision in any way, the local authority must implement the board's decision with effect from the date the original decision was made.[275]

If the board has awarded additional HB, arrears may only be paid for up to 52 weeks before the date on which the local authority completed its initial internal review. The only exception is where the review board has overturned a previous local authority decision not to backdate a claim under the 'good cause for a late claim' provisions – in which case any arrears may be paid for up to 52 weeks from the date your claim for backdating is treated as having been made (see p285).[276]

A decision of a review board may be subsequently reviewed by a local authority in certain circumstances (see p319).

There is no right of appeal from a review board's decision but, if the decision was wrong in law, you can apply for judicial review (see p324). This includes a failure to explain its decision properly as required by the regulations.

Correcting a decision

Both local authorities and review boards can correct any accidental errors which have occurred in their decisions.[277] An accidental error is a slip of the pen, a misprint, a mathematical error, or the omission of a word, etc. Corrections may be made at any time and take effect as though they were part of the original decision, or record of a decision, being corrected. Every person affected must be informed of the correction. You cannot seek a review against the correction of a decision, but you can ask for a review of the decision itself.[278]

Setting aside a decision

Both local authorities and review boards also have the power to set aside their own decisions if the interests of justice warrant it.[279] 'Setting aside' means deleting the decision as though it had never been made. A new decision is then made.

The law allows a decision to be set aside if it appears just to do so because:[280]

- you, your representative, or some other person affected by the decision, were not sent, or did not receive, a document relating to the matters concerned in that decision, or the document arrived too late;
- in the case of a hearing before a review board, you, your representative, or some other person affected by the decision were not present;
- for some other reason, the interests of justice require it.

Any person affected by a decision may apply to have that decision set aside.[281] Applications must be in writing and must reach the local authority or review board concerned within 13 weeks of the notification of that decision being posted to the applicant.[282] The 13-week limit cannot be extended but does not include any period before the correction of (or refusal to correct) that decision, or the setting aside of a previous decision.[283] The local authority or review board must send copies of the application to any other persons affected by the decision and give them a reasonable opportunity to comment.[284]

The outcome of an application to have a decision set aside must be notified in writing to every person affected as soon as possible, and this must contain a statement explaining the reasons for meeting or rejecting that request.[285]

If your request to have a decision set aside is rejected, this cannot be challenged by means of a review,[286] but you may still request a review of the original decision itself. In applying the time limits for requesting a review, no account is taken of any period between the date when the notification of the decision, and the notification of the refusal to set it aside, were each posted to you.[287] If you have been denied a fair hearing before the review board and your request to have the board's decision set aside is turned down, you may be able to challenge this by way of a judicial review (see below).

Judicial review

Judicial review is a method of challenging a decision of any form of tribunal, government department or local authority.

Applications are to the High Court (in Scotland, the Court of Session), and should be made within three months.

In practice, it is not a procedure that can be used very much in social security cases except in HB and CTB cases against decisions of review boards. That is because there are two major restrictions on the power of the court to intervene. First, the court very seldom intervenes if there is an alternative right of appeal. Secondly, the court can only intervene to correct an error of law. For these purposes, error of law has the same meaning as for appeals to a social security commissioner in income support (IS) cases (see p181).

Review boards quite often make errors of law (including the failure to make proper findings of fact and give adequate reasons for their decisions). If you consider that one has been made in your case, you should consult a solicitor. Legal aid is available in judicial review cases. CPAG's solicitor may be able to advise if you go through an advice agency.

Claims for damages

If a local authority has failed to carry out its obligations under the HB scheme or has failed to carry them out properly – in other words if it is in 'breach of statutory duty' – you may be able to sue for damages if you can show you have suffered financial loss as a result. An authority would be in breach of statutory duty if, for example, it had not determined a claim where it was under a duty to do so or if it had not paid HB to which you were entitled.

However, the Court of Appeal has held that a landlord cannot sue a local authority for failure to make direct payments (see p292) even if s/he has suffered financial loss as a result.[288] The Court said a landlord would, in these circumstances, simply have to follow the review procedure (see p319). The Court made other comments in this case which appear to indicate that *no one* (whether a claimant, landlord or anyone else) could ever sue for breach of statutory duty. Elsewhere in the judgment it appears to accept that such claims *can* sometimes be brought. You should argue that the case simply related to direct payments and that claims for damages for breach of other statutory duties can be brought. An example is where someone loses their home because the authority failed to make a payment on account of HB (see p294). You should get advice.

8. COMPLAINTS

Complaints

The review procedure enables you to challenge the way that a local authority has applied the law in your case. If you wish to challenge the manner in which your claim was dealt with rather than the actual decision itself, you should make use of the council's complaints procedure. Where there is no formal procedure, you should begin by writing to the supervisor of the person dealing with your claim, making it clear why you are dissatisfied. Include details of everything that has gone wrong, and make it clear what you expect the council to do about it – eg, sort out the claim within seven days, make a formal apology, compensate you for any loss. If you do not receive a satisfactory reply, you should take the matter up with someone more senior in the department and ultimately the principal officer.

Local authority offices are the responsibility of a senior officer (the relevant officer's name or title usually appears on its headed notepaper). In turn, those officers are responsible to councillors and you can write to one of your local councillors or the chair of the relevant council committee. Government departments also monitor local authorities so, if all else fails, you can write to the relevant minister – ie, the Secretary of State for Social Security.

The local government Ombudsman

If you have tried to sort out your complaint with the local authority but you are still not satisfied with the outcome, you can apply to the Commissioner for Local Administration (more commonly known as the local government Ombudsman). The Ombudsman can investigate any cases of maladministration by local authorities. The most common type of maladministration dealt with by the Ombudsman is delays in processing claims or applications for review. Failure to properly apply the procedure for dealing with claims or to give you proper notifications about your entitlement are also covered, though in most cases if there is a right of appeal against a decision the best remedy is to use that right.

You may apply to the Ombudsman by writing to the appropriate local office (see Appendix 3). The Ombudsman has extensive powers to look at documents held by the local authority on your claim. You may be interviewed to check any facts. Straightforward cases can be dealt with in about three months. The Ombudsman can recommend financial compensation if you have been unfairly treated or suffered a loss as a result of the maladministration. A complaint may also make the authority review its procedures, which could be of benefit to other claimants.

CHAPTER SIXTEEN

Council tax benefit

This chapter covers:
1. The basic rules (below)
2. Liability to pay council tax (p329)
3. The amount of benefit (p330)
4. Claims, payments and reviews (p339)
5. Students (p343)
6. People in hospital (p344)

1. THE BASIC RULES

Council tax benefit (CTB) is paid by local authorities and not by the Benefits Agency, although it is a national scheme and the rules are mainly determined by DSS regulations.

The rules for CTB are often the same as for housing benefit (HB). In this chapter, where the rules are the same or similar, reference is made to the preceding three chapters on HB. Footnotes in the three previous chapters contain references to both the HB and CTB legislation where applicable.

You claim CTB for your family (see Chapter 17). To claim you must be liable to pay council tax on a property in which you are resident (see p328).

Basic rules of entitlement

There are two types of benefit: main CTB and alternative maximum CTB, which is usually known as second adult rebate. Most people will only qualify for the former, but if you are eligible for both, you will be paid whichever is the higher.

Main CTB

You can claim main CTB if you fulfil the following basic conditions:

- you are liable for council tax in respect of the home where you are 'resident' (see below); [1] *and*
- your income is low enough.[2] How low it has to be depends on your circumstances (see Chapter 19); *and*
- your savings and other capital are not worth more than £16,000 (see Chapter 20); *and*
- you are not a student.[3] There are certain limited exceptions (see p343); *and*
- you are not a 'person from abroad' (see p329).[4]

Second adult rebate

You can claim a second adult rebate if you fulfil the following basic conditions:

- you are liable for council tax in respect of the home where you are resident (see below);[5] *and*
- with certain exceptions you are the only person liable for the council tax on the home (see p336); *and*
- with certain exceptions no one living in your home pays you rent (see p336);[6] *and*
- there are certain other adults living with you who are on low incomes (see p336);[7] *and*
- you are not a 'person from abroad' (see p329).[8]

For second adult rebate it does not matter if you are a student and/or have capital of more than £16,000.

Where you are resident

For CTB purposes, you are a resident in the home where you have your 'sole or main residence'.[9] This is the same criterion as for liability for council tax (see CPAG's *Council Tax Handbook*), so any decision as to where you have your 'sole or main residence' should be the same for CTB purposes. You can have a property as your 'sole or main residence' even if you spend substantial periods of time away from it, if you consider it to be the main place where you live.[10]

The Government believes that the rules about temporary absence from your home for HB (see p232) also apply to CTB. These rules may sometimes work to your advantage – eg, if you move into a nursing home on a trial basis. However, if you are absent from your home for a period longer than those rules allow, but you think that your home is still your 'sole or main residence', you can argue that you are still entitled to CTB because the regulations set out when you are 'normally occupying' your home.[11] Unlike HB (see p228), it is not a condition of receiving CTB that you are 'normally occupying' the home, as long as it is your 'sole or main residence', which is not the same thing. You should seek advice.

Persons from abroad

The rules for working out whether someone is a person from abroad are the same as for HB (see p236).

The local authority may still make you pay council tax even if you are an asylum-seeker and have no means of paying.[12] However, if you are an asylum-seeker who is not entitled to CTB, you may be retrospectively entitled for that period if you are subsequently granted refugee status.[13] The rules are the same as for HB (see p240).

Other points about CTB

- CTB is non-taxable and is not dependent on you having paid national insurance contributions;
- you must be aged 18 or more to qualify for CTB;
- you may claim CTB regardless of whether or not you or your partner are working or on income support/income-based jobseeker's allowance;
- you can still claim CTB if you have already paid your council tax bill in advance;
- if you are in arrears with your council tax bill this does not affect your right to claim CTB. You may even be able to get your claim backdated for up to one year (see p285).

2. LIABILITY TO PAY COUNCIL TAX

There is not enough space here to describe the rules relating to the council tax itself. For an explanation of the following issues consult CPAG's *Council Tax Handbook* (see Appendix 5):

- which properties are subject to council tax;
- who is liable to pay council tax;
- disability reductions;
- discounts;
- transitional reduction.

3. THE AMOUNT OF BENEFIT

The calculation of council tax benefit (CTB) and second adult rebate is explained below.

Main council tax benefit

The calculation of CTB is based on your net weekly liability for council tax – your bill after any of the following reductions have been applied:[14]

- a disability reduction;
- a discount;
- transitional reduction.

Joint liability

If you are jointly liable for the council tax, the local authority calculate your share of the bill by dividing the total net liability by the number of liable persons. Any liable persons who are students not entitled to CTB (see p343) are ignored.[15] This does not apply where you only share joint liability with your heterosexual partner, as one of you makes a joint claim for both on the total bill.[16] Where a couple are also jointly liable with one or more other residents, the couple can claim on a two-person share of the bill.

Example
Three residents are jointly liable for a net annual council tax bill of £600. They can each make a separate claim on £200 liability (an equal share). If two of the residents were a couple, however, either member of the couple could make a single claim on £400 liability (a two-person share), with the third resident making a separate claim on £200 liability (a one-person share).

If the third resident became a student and was therefore excluded from CTB, the couple could then claim on the full £600 liability.

Under the council tax rules, a person who is jointly and severally liable can be held responsible for the full amount of the tax due on the property while receiving CTB only on her/his 'share'.

Weekly council tax figure

Weekly net liability is assessed by dividing the annual charge by the number of days in the financial year (365 or 366) and then multiplying this by seven.[17]

Example
Net liability £490
Divide this by 365 (or 366, if appropriate) = £1.342466
Multiply this by 7 = £9.397262

DSS guidance recommends that the figures should not be rounded until the final annual amount of CTB is worked out, and that calculations should usually be done to six decimal places.[18] When notifying you of your CTB a rounded figure can be specified.[19]

Reduction for high value homes

From 1 April 1998, if you have a home with a high value, you may not be entitled to the equivalent of your weekly net liability. Whether these new rules affect you or not depends on the 'valuation band' that your home is placed in by the local authority. However, even if your home is high value, there is likely to be some protection if you were claiming before 1 April 1998.

If your home is in valuation band F or above, your weekly net liability is multiplied by a fraction in order to reach your maximum CTB. The fractions are applied *before* any non-dependant deductions (see p332).

The fractions that normally apply are set out in the table below.[20]

Valuation band	Fraction
F	11/13
G	11/15
H	11/18

Example
From the example above, assume that the claimant's home is in valuation band F.
Weekly net liability = £9.397262
Multiplier = 11 divided by 13 = 0.846154
Weekly net liability for CTB purposes = £7.951531

If you are disabled, you are entitled in certain circumstances to a reduction in your council tax.[21] This is achieved by changing the valuation bands. If you have been given a reduction, the fractions are as follows:[22]

Valuation band	Fraction
F	11/13
G	11/15

If you do not think that your home has been placed in the right valuation band, you may be able to appeal against the valuation.[23] See the *Council Tax Handbook* for more details.

Calculation of benefit

The steps below will help to calculate your CTB entitlement. Unlike HB, there is no minimum entitlement.

If you are on income support (IS)/income-based jobseeker's allowance (JSA):

- Work out your maximum CTB. This is your net weekly liability after any reduction (see p330) minus any non-dependant deductions.
- If you are on IS/income based JSA, you are entitled to maximum CTB.

If you are not on IS/income-based JSA:

- Check that your capital is not too high (see Chapter 20).
- Work out your maximum CTB. This is your net weekly liability after any reduction (see p330) minus any non-dependant deductions.
- Work out your applicable amount (see Chapter 18).
- Work out your income (see Chapter 19).
- **If your income is less than or equal to your applicable amount,** you are entitled to maximum CTB.
- **If your income is greater than your applicable amount,** work out the difference. The amount of CTB you are entitled to is maximum CTB **minus 20 per cent** of the difference between your income and applicable amount.

Non-dependant deductions

A non-dependant is a person living with you who, although not liable for council tax, is assumed to be making a contribution to your liability. This assumption takes the form of a reduction in your CTB.

The basic test for whether a person is a non-dependant is the same as for HB (see p268).[24] However, the categories of people who cannot be non-dependants are slightly different.

People who are not non-dependants

The following categories of people cannot be non-dependants:[25]

- a member of your family (see p346);
- if you are in a polygamous marriage, a partner of yours and any child or young person in your household (see p353) for which you or a partner is responsible;
- a child or young person living with you who is not a member of your household (see p346);
- someone who is employed by a charitable or voluntary organisation as a resident carer for you or your partner and you pay for the service. This can also apply if a public body pays on your behalf;
- someone who jointly occupies (see p268) your home and is jointly liable to pay council tax in respect of the home;
- someone who is liable to pay rent on a commercial basis (see p235) to you or your partner.

If the person comes within the last two categories above, s/he can still be treated as a non-dependant if s/he falls within any of the following categories:

- s/he resides with her/his landlord and *either* s/he is a 'close relative' of the landlord *or* the agreement between them is not a commercial one.[26] The meaning of these terms is the same as for HB (see p234);
- her/his liability to the landlord has been created to take advantage of the CTB scheme.[27] For the meaning of 'taking advantage' see p235, but remember that just because someone is taking advantage of the HB scheme does not mean that s/he is taking advantage of the CTB scheme, though the DSS guidance appears to make this assumption.[28] You should argue that the local authority should consider the two schemes separately. As with HB, a person cannot come within this category if s/he had a legitimate liability to the landlord within the eight weeks prior to entering into the agreement that takes advantage of the CTB scheme;
- s/he is jointly liable for council tax on the home and was a non-dependant of one or more residents who were liable for the tax within the last eight weeks. If this is made out, you have to show the local authority that the person is not taking advantage of the CTB scheme by taking on the joint liability.[29]

When deductions are made

Once it is established that you have one or more non-dependants, deductions are usually made for each non-dependant in your household. Only one deduction is made if the non-dependant is part of a couple, whether married or unmarried.[30]

If you share liability for the council tax with others, the amount of the non-dependant deduction is shared equally between you, even if the other person is not claiming CTB. However, if the local authority thinks that the non-dependant only belongs to one resident, the whole deduction is made from that person's benefit.[31] If a couple share liability with a single person, their CTB is reduced by two-thirds of the non-dependant deduction (ie, apportionment is made on the same basis as liability – see p330).

When no deduction is made[32]

The rules as to when a non-dependant deduction is not made are the same as for HB (see p269) except that:

- all non-dependants on IS/income-based JSA are ignored and not just those under 25; *and*
- no deduction is made for the following people with status discounts (for full details see CPAG's *Council Tax Handbook*):
  - people under 19 if child benefit is payable;
  - recent school and college-leavers under 20;
  - student nurses;
  - foreign language assistants;
  - apprentices;
  - people who are severely mentally impaired (see below);
  - certain carers;
  - members of visiting armed forces, members of international headquarters and defence organisations and their dependants; *and*
  - foreign spouses or dependants of students;
- no non-dependant deduction is ever made for a full-time student – even if s/he works during the summer vacation.

A person counts as severely mentally impaired if a doctor has certified that s/he has a severe impairment of intelligence and social functioning which appears to be permanent.[33] S/he must also be entitled to a qualifying benefit.[34]

The amount of the deduction[35]

Circumstances of the non-dependant	*Deduction*
18 or over and in full-time work with a weekly gross income of:	
£250 or more	£6.00
£200-£249.99	£5.00
£116-£199.99	£4.00
up to £115.99	£2.00
Others aged 18 or over (for whom a deduction is made)	£2.00

Only one deduction is made for a couple (or members of a polygamous marriage). Where the individual circumstances of each partner are different, the highest deduction is made.[36] For the purpose of deciding which earnings band applies, their joint income counts even if only one of them is in full-time work.[37]

The definitions of full-time work and earnings and the kinds of income which are ignored are the same as for HB (see p270).

Income and capital of a non-dependant

As with HB, your main CTB can be assessed using the income and capital of a non-dependant, instead of your own, if it is felt you are trying to take advantage of the CTB scheme (see p271).[38]

Increasing the amount of your CTB

You can be awarded more than the normal amount of main CTB if your circumstances are exceptional.[39] The rules are the same as for HB (see p272). Your CTB can be increased up to the total amount of council tax on which you are eligible to claim (see p323). The limit is your apportioned share if you are jointly liable (see p330).

Second adult rebate

Second adult rebate is an alternative type of CTB which can be paid instead of, but not as well as, main CTB. Whenever you claim CTB the local authority must assess you for both types and award whichever is the greater.[40] Second adult rebate is designed to help you if you have certain other residents (referred to as 'second adults') in your home who do not share liability for council tax with you and who do not pay rent to you. In certain cases the presence in your home of a second adult means you have to pay the full council tax without discount, but if their income is low they may not be able to contribute towards the cost. Second adult rebate compensates you for this.

Note that the whole of your income and capital is ignored when you claim second adult rebate. So you can get it even if you have a high income and/or assets worth more than £16,000.[41]

Who counts as a 'second adult'?

A second adult is someone who is resident with you. It does not include anyone who:[42]

- is aged under 18 (they do not count as 'residents'[43] and do not affect any possible discount);
- has a status discount (they are ignored for discount purposes and do not affect any possible discount);[44]
- is your spouse with whom you are jointly liable (they do affect discount entitlement but will be included in any claim for main CTB);[45]
- is residing with you, where you are a member of a couple or polygamous marriage unless both of you (or in the case of a polygamous marriage, at least two of you) have status discounts;[46]
- is jointly liable to pay the council tax on the dwelling with you as a joint owner or tenant, etc (they do affect discount entitlement but can claim main CTB for their own share of the bill – see p330);[47]
- is residing with at least two people jointly liable to pay the tax as joint owners or tenants, etc, and at least two of those people do *not* have status discounts.[48]

In practice, residents classified as second adults will tend to be the same persons as those treated as non-dependants for main CTB purposes (see p332).

Residents liable to pay rent

You are not entitled to second adult rebate if someone is liable to pay rent to you in respect of her/his occupation of the home. This does not apply where any people paying you rent fall into one of the categories of those not treated as second adults (see above).[49]

Some local authorities think you are not entitled to second adult rebate if *any* resident is liable to pay you rent. The DSS guidance refers to second adults who are liable for rent,[50] and so appears to accept that if a person paying you rent does not come within the description of second adult, s/he does not prevent you receiving second adult rebate.

Council tax liability for a second adult rebate

The council tax figure used to work out your second adult rebate is:[51]

- the gross council tax liability for the dwelling as a whole; *less*
- any disability reduction; *and*
- transitional reduction.

Note that this is not the same figure as used for main CTB (see p332). However, the procedure for converting annual to weekly amounts is the same (see p330). Where you have received a discount it must be added back on to the net amount of council tax payable to arrive at the figure used in the second adult rebate calculation. This is only done for the purposes of the CTB calculation – you will still receive your discount in practice.

Reduction for high value homes

From 1 April 1998, if you have a home with a high value, the gross council tax liability calculated as above may be reduced for the purposes of calculating second adult rebate.[52] The circumstances and amount of the deductions are identical to those for main CTB (see p331).

Assessment of second adult income

To obtain a second adult rebate, you must give the local authority details of the gross income of any second adults living with you. Where there is more than one second adult, their combined gross income is used.[53]

Gross income includes the second adult's:

- earnings;
- non-earned income, including social security benefits;
- actual income from capital (as opposed to tariff income). The capital itself is ignored.

Gross income does not include:

- any income of a second adult on IS/income-based JSA;[54]
- any attendance allowance or disability living allowance;[55]
- payments from the MacFarlane Trusts, the Eileen Trust, the Fund and the Independent Living Funds;[56]
- the income of any person with a status discount, except where that person has a partner who is not ignored for discount purposes (in which case the gross income of both partners, less disregarded income, is taken into account).[57]

A basic problem with second adult rebate is that it involves means-testing someone who is not the claimant and who may not always wish to co-operate. If you have difficulty establishing the income of the second adult you may find that the local authority automatically assumes the highest income and that you are not entitled to CTB. If you cannot persuade any second adults to give details of their income to you, they may be prepared to tell the local authority directly. Failing this, you could try finding out the going rate for the type of work they do, or social security benefits they receive, and ask the local authority to make a reasonable estimate based on that.

How much second adult rebate can you get?

The amount of second adult rebate, as a percentage of the gross council tax liability (with any reduction for high value homes), is:[58]

Income of second adult(s)	*Second adult rebate*
2nd adult (or all 2nd adults) on IS/income-based JSA	25%
2nd adult(s) total gross income:	
– up to £116	15%
– £116-£151.99	7.5%
– £152 or more	Nil

Note that the maximum CTB payable is always 25 per cent of liability, even in those cases where you would have received a 50 per cent discount, or would have been exempt altogether, were it not for the presence of two or more second adults in your home – eg, as in the case of a student nurse with two second adults on IS.

Second adult rebates and jointly liable claimants

In contrast to main CTB, where there is more than one resident liable for the council tax in your dwelling, any second adult rebate is always calculated on the (pre-discounted) liability for your dwelling as a whole. Any CTB arising is then split equally between all the jointly liable residents.[59] This does not need to happen where you are jointly liable with your heterosexual partner only, since one of you claims on behalf of both and receives all of the CTB.[60]

Apart from that case, every other jointly liable person must make her/his own separate claim in order to get their share of the CTB. For example, three eligible joint tenants would each be entitled to one-third of the total second adult rebate for the dwelling as a whole. If two of them were a couple, however, then they would be entitled to receive two-thirds, and the other single tenant, one-third, of the total CTB.

Extra benefit in exceptional circumstances

Where you are entitled to a second adult rebate of either 7.5 or 15 per cent, the local authority can increase your CTB up to the 25 per cent figure (or your share of it where you are jointly liable), if it considers your circumstances to be exceptional.[61] As with HB, it is for the local authority to decide what is meant by 'exceptional' in any case (see p272), but you have a right of review (see p343).

Extended payments of CTB

If you were entitled to IS/income-based JSA but your entitlement ceases because you start work or increase your hours of or income from work, you may be entitled to an extended payment of CTB for the four weeks following the end of your entitlement to IS/income-based JSA.[62]

The rules for extended payments are similar to those for HB (see p266). The weekly amount of your extended payment of CTB is the amount of CTB you got in the last week before your entitlement to IS/income-based JSA ceased. If you move, you get the maximum CTB applicable to your new address minus any non-dependant deductions which applied at your old address.[63]

4. CLAIMS, PAYMENTS AND REVIEWS

Claims

The rules for claiming council tax benefit (CTB) are the same as for housing benefit (HB). See p282 for full details, substituting CTB where it says HB. Second adult rebate is a type of CTB so the normal rules apply for claiming.

The rules about advance claims for CTB are slightly different. You can claim up to eight weeks before you become liable for council tax and you are treated as having claimed on the day your liability begins.[64] If you make an unsuccessful claim for CTB but you are likely to become entitled within the next 13 weeks, your claim can be treated as made in the week before your entitlement begins.[65]

There is also a special rule when your local authority has not set its council tax rate by the beginning of the financial year. So long as you claim within four weeks of the council tax being agreed your claim is backdated to 1 April, or the date you first became entitled, if that is later.[66]

Late claims and backdating

The rules about late claims and backdated CTB are the same as for HB (see p285). A special case may arise for CTB where you are jointly liable for the council tax but did not claim because your name was not put on the bill. You could argue that you have good cause for a late claim because you did not realise you were liable as the council had failed (via the bill) to inform you of this.[67]

Decisions and notifications

You will receive separate notifications for HB and CTB. The information which is to be included in a written notification is the same except that those items specifically relating to rent are, of course, excluded in a CTB notification and, instead, it is required that it includes notice of your weekly council tax liability rounded to the nearest penny.[68] The notification should also include the following, where relevant:

- if you have been assessed for, and are entitled to, both main CTB and second adult rebate, the amount of benefit entitlement in each case and the fact that you can only be paid the higher amount;[69]
- if you have been assessed for a second adult rebate, the gross income of any second adult(s) used to determine the rate of CTB, including where any second adult is on IS/income-based jobseeker's allowance (JSA);[70]
- details of how any of the figures supplied on the notification have been rounded (ie, to the nearest penny).[71]

Payment

As with HB, your CTB is paid for a benefit period, which usually runs from the Monday after your date of claim. If you have only just become liable for the council tax and you claim in the same week in which your liability begins, you will be paid from the Monday of that week.[72] The rules about when your benefit period ends are the same as for HB (see p291).

Payment of CTB is normally made by means of a reduction to your annual council tax bill. Your weekly benefit is converted to a daily figure by dividing by seven and then multiplying the answer by the number of days between your first day of entitlement and the following 31 March.

If you are jointly liable for the council tax with one or more other residents, apart from your partner, remember that any CTB they receive will also be credited to the same bill as your own. You will need to take this into account when agreeing with them how any remaining balance of council tax liability should be shared out between you.

Where your CTB cannot be used to reduce your bill, payment can be made direct to you.[73] This is normally only done once you have paid your final instalment of council tax, and usually you must ask for the money. If you do not, your CTB is likely to be credited against your next year's council tax bill.[74]

However, if you are no longer liable for council tax in that authority's area, it should send you any outstanding CTB within 14 days if possible.[75] Payment is normally made to you as the claimant or to your appointee if you have one (see p282).[76]

Withholding of benefit

The local authority can withhold all or part of your CTB in the same circumstances as set out in the *last three* categories of case in which HB may be withheld (see p295).[77]

Payments on death

If a claimant dies, any outstanding CTB can be paid to the personal representative or, if there is none, to the next of kin aged 16 or over. A written application for this must be sent to the local authority within 12 months of the death.[78]

Overpayments

An overpayment of CTB is called 'excess benefit'[79] but the rules about recovery are the same as for HB (see pp300-03), with the following exceptions.

The amount of the overpayment

As with all overpayments, the amount overpaid is the difference between what you were actually paid and what you should have received. However, there are two possible variations of what should have been paid – either a reduced amount of main CTB, or a second adult rebate if you are eligible for this and it would have been higher than the revised amount of main CTB.

When assessing the amount overpaid the local authority should do both calculations, and can only recover the balance between the higher of the two figures and the amount which you in fact received. It is always worth checking that the second adult rebate calculation has been done and that the correct amount is being recovered.

Is the overpayment recoverable?

The criteria for when an overpayment is recoverable are the same as for HB, except that the following categories of overpayments are always recoverable:

- any credit on your council tax account that relates to a period after the date of the review which reduced your CTB entitlement;[80]
- an overpayment which has arisen because you were paid CTB, but then your council tax liability was reduced because of a disability reduction, discount, transitional relief or charge-capping;[81]
- an overpayment that results from the local authority changing the levels of council tax for the financial year.[82]

Recovery of overpaid CTB

Unlike HB, recovery is always from the claimant or the person to whom benefit was paid – eg, an appointee. There can be no recovery from any other person, even if s/he caused the overpayment.[83]

CTB is recoverable by the same methods as HB (see pp303-12) with the following exceptions:

- the overpayment can be recovered by increasing your outstanding council tax liability;[84]
- the local authority cannot use the special court procedures for recovering the overpayment (see p309). If it wishes to recover through the court, it must sue you instead. It may not start proceedings for 21 days after it notifies you of the amount due.[85]

Changes of circumstances

You must always notify the local authority of changes which affect your rights to, or the amount of, CTB.[86] The rules are the same as for HB (see p296) except that you do not need to notify any changes in rent for council tax purposes. Nor do you have to tell the local authority the amount of council tax you pay as they have this information already.[87]

If you are getting second adult rebate, you must write and tell the local authority of any changes in the number of adults living in your home and any changes to their gross income.[88]

The rules about when changes of circumstances take effect are slightly different to those for HB. Normally, a change affects your CTB from the Monday after it occurs.[89] However, the following changes affect your benefit from the date they occur:[90]

- a change in the amount of your council tax;
- changes to the CTB regulations;

- the fact that you have become part of a couple;
- the death of, or separation from, your partner.

If two or more changes occur in the same week and each takes effect from a different date under the above rules, they are all taken into account from the date of the first change.[91]

If you stop getting another social security benefit, the change in circumstances is deemed to occur on the day after your entitlement ends and your CTB is changed from the following Monday.[92]

If your applicable amount includes a personal allowance for a child (see p358), that allowance increases on the first Monday in September following the child's 11th and 16th birthdays. An allowance for childcare costs (see p392) is payable until the first Monday in September after the child's 11th birthday.

The rules for reassessing your CTB following a change of circumstances are the same as for HB (see p299), but remember that the local authority should recalculate both main CTB and second adult rebate and award whichever is currently the higher.

Reviews and complaints

The rules for CTB reviews are the same as those for HB (see pp319-25). The notes to Chapter 15 include CTB legislation. It is always worth applying for a review if you think the decision of the local authority is wrong. If you are applying for a review on both your CTB and your HB, one review board can deal with both claims if everyone agrees[93] (in Scotland, HB is administered by district councils and CTB by regional councils and this situation cannot arise). The local authority can also consider an outstanding review on community charge benefit at the same time as your HB and/or CTB.

If you are dissatisfied with the decision of a review board, judicial review may be possible (see p324). If you wish to complain about the way the local authority has dealt with your claim, see p325.

5. STUDENTS

The definition of full-time student is the same as for HB (see p275).

As with housing benefit (HB), most full-time students cannot get council tax benefit (CTB), but you can claim if:[94]

- you are on income support/income-based jobseeker's allowance;
- you are a pensioner who satisfies the conditions for one of the pensioner premiums;

- you are a lone parent;
- you are a registered lone foster parent and a child has been placed with you by a local authority or voluntary agency;
- you and your partner are both full-time students and have one or more dependent children;
- you are under 19 and not following a course of higher education;
- you qualify for the disability premium or would do if you were not disqualified from incapacity benefit (see p10);
- you have been incapable of work for 28 weeks (see p10). Two or more periods when you are incapable are joined to form a single period if they are separated by less than eight weeks;
- you satisfy the conditions for a grant supplement in the form of a disabled student's allowance awarded because of deafness;
- you are a work trainee on a training allowance.[95]

If you are a student who can claim, you may be entitled to more CTB outside the 'period of study' (see p276) – eg, during the summer vacation.

Overseas students

The rules on overseas students are the same as for HB. To qualify for CTB, overseas students must satisfy both the special rules that allow persons from abroad to claim (see p236) and the special rules for students (see p275). The footnotes covering these matters in Chapter 14 include references to CTB legislation.

Students and second adult rebate

Full-time students are not precluded from getting second adult rebate and should be assessed in the normal way (see p335).

6. PEOPLE IN HOSPITAL

You can continue to get council tax benefit (CTB) while in hospital. The rules are the same as for housing benefit (see p272). If you cease to be treated as residing in your home for council tax purposes because of a prolonged stay in hospital you cannot claim CTB. If this leaves your home unoccupied it will be exempt from council tax altogether. However, if your partner still lives in your former home s/he will now probably be treated as the liable person and can put in her/his own claim for CTB. Your CTB may also be adjusted if the local authority decides you are no longer part of a family and reassesses you as a single person (see p351).

PART FIVE

Common rules

Income support (IS), family credit (FC), disability working allowance (DWA), housing benefit (HB) and council tax benefit (CTB) are all means-tested benefits. The amount you get depends on the size of your family, how much capital you have and how your income compares with your needs (called your 'applicable amount'). The rules for all five benefits are the same or similar. This Part covers those rules which are common to all.

Since 7 October 1996, IS for people who have to register for work has been replaced by income-based jobseeker's allowance (JSA). Income support is now only for people who do not have to register for work – eg, lone parents with dependent children. This Part deals with the common rules which apply to IS. The rules for income-based JSA are set out in CPAG's Jobseeker's Allowance Handbook *(3rd edition published April 1998).*

CHAPTER SEVENTEEN

Who counts as your family

This chapter explains who is included in your benefit claim. It covers:
1. Introduction (below)
2. Claiming as a couple (p347)
3. Claiming for children (p353)

1. INTRODUCTION

What is a 'family'?

You claim income support (IS), family credit (FC), disability working allowance (DWA), housing benefit (HB), council tax benefit (CTB) for yourself, your partner and any dependent children who are members of your household. This is your 'family' for benefit purposes.[1] A partner can include a wife, husband or cohabitee of the opposite sex. When your benefit is worked out, the needs of your partner and any children are usually added to yours and so are your partner's income and capital. There are special rules for the treatment of the income and capital of dependent children (see pp374 and 416).

If one member of your family is claiming IS/FC/DWA/HB/CTB, no other member can claim the same benefit for the same period.[2] However, partners can choose which of them should be the claimant, except for FC which the woman must usually claim,[3] and DWA which the disabled partner must claim.[4] (If both of you are disabled, you can choose which one of you should be the claimant.[5]) For details about how to claim see p128 (IS), p205 (FC), p218 (DWA), p282 (HB) and p339 (CTB).

Membership of the same household

The idea of sharing a household is central to whether you can include a child or a partner in your claim.

However, the term 'household' is not defined. Whether two people should be treated as members of the same household is very much a question of fact. Physical presence together will not in itself be conclusive. There must be a 'particular kind of tie' binding two people together in a domestic establishment (although this could, in appropriate circumstances, include a household within, for example, a hotel or boarding house).[6]

There will be some occasions when you and another person are regarded as members of the same household when you think you should not be. If this arises it will be important to try to show that, although you both live in the same house, you maintain separate **households**.

A separate household might exist if there are:

- independent arrangements for the storage and cooking of food;
- independent financial arrangements;
- separate eating arrangements;
- no evidence of family life;
- separate commitments for housing costs, even if the liability is to another person in the same premises.

You cannot be a member of more than one household at the same time.[7] If two people can be shown to be maintaining separate homes, they cannot be said to be sharing the same household.[8] Even if you have the right to occupy only part of a room, you may have your own household.[9]

Where a child lives for part of the week with each parent, the rules for each benefit allow only one parent to claim that benefit for that child, and s/he is treated as a member of her/his household for the whole week (see p353).

2. CLAIMING AS A COUPLE

You claim as a couple if you and your partner are both 16 or over, and:[10]

- married, and living in the same household (see above for definition); *or*
- not married but 'living together as husband and wife' in the same household.

If you are lesbian or gay partners, you do not count as a couple and must claim as single people.

Special rules apply if one or both partners are under 18 (see pp45, 359 and 374).

Being married to someone does not necessarily mean that you cannot be treated as part of a couple with someone else instead.[11]

You count as polygamously married if you are married to more than one person and your marriages took place in a country which permits polygamy.[12] There are special rules if you are polygamously married.[13]

Living together as husband and wife

If it is decided that you are 'living together as husband and wife' (cohabiting), only one of you will be able to claim benefit. The amount of benefit for a couple is usually less than that for two single people, so it is important to dispute a decision that you are cohabiting if you believe you are not. However, in some cases you may have to *prove* that you are cohabiting – eg, where you want to claim FC, you have children and do not work yourself, but your partner does. You should, of course, be consistent about your circumstances for each benefit. If you are awarded IS, the local authority should not make a separate decision when considering your claim for HB/CTB.[14] However, if you have not been awarded IS, the local authority has a duty to give its own consideration to the cohabitation test, and may reach a different conclusion from that of the Benefits Agency.

The factors considered below are used as 'signposts' in determining whether or not you are cohabiting.[15] No one factor need in itself be conclusive, as it is your 'general relationship' as a whole which is of paramount importance[16] and, just as relationships between couples may often vary considerably, so each case will depend on all its own particular facts and circumstances.

Do you live in the same household?

In all cases you must spend the major part of your time in the same household (see p346 for a discussion of 'household'). If one of you has a separate address where you usually live, the cohabitation rule should not be applied. You cannot be a member of more than one household at the same time (see p347) so, if you are a member of one couple, you cannot also be treated as part of another.

Even if you *do* share a 'household', you may not be cohabiting. It is essential to look at *why* two people are in the same household.[17] For example, where a couple were living in the same household for reasons of 'care, companionship and mutual convenience' they were not 'living together as husband and wife'.[18]

Separated couples living under the same roof should not be treated as couples if they are maintaining separate households.[19] Where a relationship has only recently broken down, continuing financial support and shared responsibilities and liabilities may be particularly inconclusive, especially where there is evidence of active steps being taken to live apart. The way people live and their attitude of mind will be more significant.

Any 'mere hope' of a reconciliation will not be a 'reasonable expectation' where at least one partner has accepted that the relationship is at an end.[20]

Do you have a sexual relationship?

In practice, officers may not ask you about the existence of a sexual relationship, in which case they will only have the information if you volunteer it. If you do not have a sexual relationship, you should tell the officer yourself – and perhaps offer to show her/him the separate sleeping arrangements.

Having a sexual relationship is not sufficient by itself to prove you are cohabiting, and if you have never had a sexual relationship there will be a strong (but not necessarily conclusive) presumption that you are not cohabiting.[21]

A couple who abstain from a sexual relationship before marriage on grounds of principle (eg, religious reasons) should not be counted as cohabiting until they are formally married.[22]

Even if the Benefits Agency or local authority does not go into the question of whether or not there is a sexual relationship, any tribunal or review board has a duty to ask such questions in order to determine whether or not you are cohabiting.[23]

What are your financial arrangements?

If one partner is supported by the other or household expenses are shared, this may be treated as evidence of cohabitation. However, it is important to consider how they are shared. There is a difference between, on the one hand, paying a fixed weekly contribution or rigidly sharing bills 50/50 and, on the other hand, a free common fund attributable to income and expenditure. The former does not imply cohabitation, the latter might.

Is your relationship stable?

Marriage is expected to be stable and lasting. It follows that an occasional or brief association should not be regarded as cohabiting. However, the fact that a relationship is stable does not make it cohabitation – eg, you can have a stable landlord/lodger relationship but not be cohabiting.

Do you have children?

If you have had a child together, and live in the same household as the other parent, there is a strong (but not conclusive) presumption of cohabitation.

How do you appear in public?

Officers may check the electoral roll and claims for national insurance benefits to see if you present yourselves as a couple. Many couples retain their separate identity publicly as unmarried people. They should, however, be aware that they may be regarded as cohabiting.

Challenging a 'living together' decision

Sometimes benefit is stopped or adjusted because someone regularly stays overnight, even though you might have none of the long-term commitments generally associated with marriage. But couples with no sexual relationship who live together (eg, as landlord/lodger, tenant or housekeeper, or as flat-sharers) also sometimes fall foul of the rule. People who provide mutual support and share household expenses are not necessarily cohabiting – this is also the case where people of the same sex or friends of different sexes share a home.[24]

If you are at all unhappy with a decision that you are cohabiting, you should appeal (see p167) or apply for a review (see pp139 and 319), and carefully consider what evidence to put before the tribunal/review board in relation to each of the six questions above and any other matters that you consider relevant. Possibilities include evidence of the other person having another address[25] (eg, a rent book and other household bills), receipts for board and lodging, statements from friends and relatives or, where you have been married, evidence of a formal separation or divorce proceedings.

On an initial application for benefit it is not for you to prove that you are not cohabiting,[26] though you are required to provide the Benefits Agency with any information it reasonably requires to decide your claim.[27] Neither party has the burden of proof in this situation – a decision should simply be made on all the evidence available.[28] By contrast, if your benefit as a single person is stopped because it is alleged that you are cohabiting, the burden of proof is on the Benefits Agency to prove that you are cohabiting.[29]

If your benefit is withdrawn because you are cohabiting, you should re-apply immediately if your circumstances change. You should also apply immediately for any other benefits for which you might qualify – eg, HB/CTB, where the local authority may reach a different decision to that of the Benefits Agency (see p348). You should apply on the basis of low income for other benefits, which you previously qualified for automatically if you were on IS – eg, health benefits (see Chapter 26).

If you are still entitled to benefit, even though it is decided that you are cohabiting, you should be paid as a couple.

If your IS stops and you have diverted a maintenance order to the Benefits Agency (see p108), contact the magistrates' court immediately to get payments sent direct to you. If the Child Support Agency is collecting a child maintenance assessment for you (see p109), ask them to start paying the money to you.

If you have no money at all, you may be able to get a social fund crisis loan (see Part Seven).

Couples living apart

If you separate *permanently* you can claim as a single person immediately. However, you continue to be treated as a couple while you and your partner are *temporarily* apart.[30] Your former household need not have been in this country.[31] The following rules apply in determining whether you still count as a couple.

For FC/DWA

You no longer count as a couple if you or your partner:[32]

- are living apart and do not intend to resume living together (see p348); *or*
- have been in hospital for 52 weeks or more; *or*
- are a compulsory patient detained in hospital under the mental health provisions; *or*
- are detained in custody serving a sentence of 52 weeks or more.

For CTB

You continue to be eligible as a couple as long as you both remain liable for the council tax at your address.[33] Note that the rules for establishing a couple's liability for council tax are not the same as the rules for establishing their entitlement to CTB (see CPAG's *Council Tax Handbook*).

For IS/HB

You will count as a couple, even if you or your partner are living away from your family, if you:[34]

- intend to resume living together (see p348); *or*
- are likely to be separated for less than 52 weeks. However, you can still be treated as a couple if you are likely to be separated for more than 52 weeks provided it is not 'substantially' longer and there are exceptional circumstances such as a stay in hospital, or if there is no control over the length of the absence.

For IS

You will no longer count as a couple if any of the following apply to either of you:[35]

- you are in custody;
- you are on temporary release from prison;
- you are a compulsory patient detained in hospital under the mental health provisions;
- you are staying permanently in local authority residential accommodation, or a residential care or nursing home;
- the *claimant* is abroad and does not qualify for IS. However, where your *partner* is temporarily abroad you continue to be treated as a couple, but after four weeks (eight if s/he has taken a child abroad for medical treatment) the amount of IS you receive is that for a single claimant or lone parent.[36] You can get benefit without signing on if you have children under 16.[37] Your partner's income and capital continue to be treated as yours for as long as the absence is held to be temporary.

If you are no longer treated as a couple for the purposes of calculating your IS, you may still be liable to maintain your partner (see p106).

You are still treated as a couple if you are temporarily living apart and the following applies: one of you is at home or in hospital, or in local authority residential accommodation or in a residential care or nursing home, and the other is:[38]

- resident in a nursing home, but not counted as a patient; *or*
- staying in a residential care home; *or*
- in a home for the rehabilitation of alcoholics or drug addicts; *or*
- in Polish resettlement accommodation; *or*
- on a government training course and has to live away from home (see below for your right to housing costs for more than one home); *or*
- in a probation or bail hostel.

Although your income and capital are calculated in the normal way for a couple, your applicable amount is calculated as if each of you were single claimants if this comes to more than your usual couple rate. If you have children, one of you is treated as a lone parent. If you have housing costs (see p27), your applicable amount includes these as well as any costs of the temporary accommodation of the partner away from home. If you are both away from home, the costs of both sets of temporary accommodation and the family home are met.[39] If both homes are rented, see p233 for when HB can be paid for more than one home at a time. If you own your home and your partner is staying in rented accommodation, you will get your housing costs met by IS and your partner will be able to claim HB.

Additional points

- Where questions of 'intention' are involved (eg, in deciding whether you or your partner intend to resume living with your family), the intention must be unqualified – ie, it must not depend on some factor over which you have no control (eg, where it depends on the right of entry to the UK being granted by the Home Office[40] or on the offer of a suitable job[41]).
- See pp31 and 233 if one of you lives away from home as a student or on a government training course and you have to pay for two homes.
- See p476 if your child is in hospital and you have to stay in lodgings to be nearby.
- See p95 if one or both of you are temporarily in local authority residential accommodation.

3. CLAIMING FOR CHILDREN

You do not have to be a *parent* to receive benefit for a child, but you must be 'responsible' for a child who is living in your household.[42] You claim for any child under 16; or under 19 if they are still in full-time 'relevant' education[43] (see p16 for what this means). Where the same benefit is involved, a child can only be the responsibility of one person in any week.[44] There is no provision allowing benefit to be split between parents where a child divides her/his time equally between the homes of two parents. See p355 for when a child no longer counts as your dependant.

'Responsibility' for a child

You claim IS, FC, DWA, HB or CTB for a child for whom you are 'responsible'. You will be treated as 'responsible' for a child if:

For FC/DWA/HB/CTB

- the child is 'normally living' with you.[45] This means that s/he spends more time with you than with anyone else.[46]

  Where it is unclear whose household the child lives in, or where s/he spends an equal amount of time with two parents in different homes (this may not mean literally 3½ days with each parent[47]), you will be treated as having responsibility if:[48]

- you get child benefit for the child;
- no one gets child benefit, but you have applied for it;
- no one has applied for child benefit, or both of you have applied, but you appear to have the most responsibility;

For IS

- you get child benefit for the child.[49]

Where no one gets child benefit you will be 'responsible' if you are the only one who has applied for it. In all other cases the person 'responsible' will be the person with whom the child *usually lives*.[50]

Where a child for whom you are 'responsible' gets child benefit for another child, you will also be 'responsible' for that child.[51]

Note: For FC/DWA/HB/CTB, it is important to look at who gets child benefit only where it is unclear whose household the child *normally* lives in. For IS it is essential to look first at who gets child benefit, and only where this is not decisive is it relevant to look at where the child *usually* lives. This difference may mean that in some situations one parent may be able to claim IS for a child while the other parent can claim FC/DWA/HB/CTB for the same child at the same time.

Living in the same household[52]

If you are counted as responsible for a child, then that child is usually treated as a member of your household despite any temporary absence. (For the meaning of 'household', see p346.) However, s/he does not count as a member of your household if s/he:

IS/FC/DWA/HB/CTB

- is being fostered by you under a specific statutory provision. However, you can claim benefit for a child you are fostering privately or where social services have made a less formal arrangement for the child to live with you;
- is living with you prior to adoption, and has been placed with you by social services or an adoption agency;

IS/HB/CTB

- is boarded out or has been placed with someone else prior to adoption;
- is in the care of, or being looked after by, the local authority and not living with you. You should receive IS for her/him for the days when s/he comes home – eg, for the weekend or a holiday.[53] Make sure you tell the Benefits Agency in good time so they can pay you the extra money. The local authority can also increase your applicable amount to

include the child for HB/CTB for all of that week whether the child returns for all or only part of it;[54]

IS/FC/DWA

- has been in hospital or a local authority home for more than 12 weeks, and you or other members of your household have not been in regular contact with her/him. For FC/DWA this means 12 weeks prior to the claim.[55] For IS the 12 weeks run from the date s/he went into the hospital or home, or from the date you claimed IS, if later.[56] However, if you were getting income-based JSA immediately before you claimed IS, the 12 weeks run from the date s/he went into the hospital or home;[57]
- has been in hospital or a local authority home for 52 weeks or more because of illness or disability (unless, for IS only, you are still in regular contact);[58]
- is in custody. (For FC/DWA, being in custody on remand does not count.) You should receive IS for any periods your child spends at home;[59]

IS only

- has been abroad for more than four weeks (the four weeks run from the day after s/he went abroad, or from the date you claimed IS, if later), or for more than eight weeks if the absence abroad is to get medical treatment for the child.[60] Note, however, that if you were getting income-based JSA immediately before you claimed IS, the four- or eight-week periods are calculated from the day after the child went abroad;[61]
- is living with you and away from her/his parental or usual home in order to attend school. The child is not treated as a member of your family, but remains a member of her/his parent's household.[62]

When you stop claiming for a child

For IS

You stop claiming for a child as soon as someone else starts receiving child benefit for her/him.

For FC/DWA/HB/CTB

You stop claiming as soon as the child starts 'normally living' elsewhere (see p353).

For IS/HB/CTB

You claim for a child until s/he is 16, or 19 if s/he is in relevant education (see p17). Children count as in relevant education until the 'terminal date' (see p18), or until they get a full-time job if that is earlier. 'Full-time' work for dependent children means at least 24 hours a week.[63]

A 16/17-year-old who has left school or college may continue to be counted as part of your 'family' for a few months after the terminal date. You will get benefit for them during the child benefit extension period (see p18 for details and dates) provided the following apply:[64]

- you were entitled to child benefit for that child immediately before the child benefit extension period started; *and*
- you have made a fresh claim for child benefit in writing for the child benefit extension period; *and*
- s/he has registered for work/Youth Training (YT) at the JobCentre or Careers Office; *and*
- s/he is not in full-time work.

If s/he loses the job or leaves YT before the end of the child benefit extension period, s/he becomes your dependant again and you can claim for her/him as long as the above conditions are satisfied.

Some 16/17-year-olds can get IS in their own right before they are 18 (see p60) and you will not be able to claim for them.[65]

For FC/DWA

A child counts as your dependant for the purposes of your FC/DWA claim where, at the date of the claim, s/he is actually undergoing full-time education. Children do not count as dependants once they have left school, even if you are still getting child benefit for them. They are also not counted as dependants if they become entitled to IS or income-based JSA in their own right[66] (or would be so entitled, had a member of their family not been entitled).

CHAPTER EIGHTEEN

Applicable amounts

This chapter covers:
1. Introduction (below)
2. Personal allowances (p358)
3. Premiums (p360)

I. INTRODUCTION

For income support (IS), housing benefit (HB) and council tax benefit (CTB) the 'applicable amount' is a figure representing your weekly needs for the purpose of calculating your benefit. For IS, your applicable amount is the amount you are expected to live on each week. For HB/CTB, it is the amount used to see how much help you need with your rent or council tax. This chapter explains how you work out your applicable amount for those benefits. For the way benefit payable is calculated, see p26 for IS, p263 for HB and p330 for CTB.

The applicable amount for family credit (FC) is always £79. For disability working allowance (DWA) it is £59.25 for single people (other than lone parents) and £79 for couples/lone parents. For the way FC and DWA are calculated, see pp203 and 217 respectively.

For IS, HB and CTB, your applicable amount is made up of:

- personal allowances: this is the amount the law says you need for living expenses (see p358);
- premiums: this is the amount given for certain extra needs you or your family may have (see p360);
- for IS only, housing costs: (see p27).

For IS, your applicable amount is different if you live in a residential care home, nursing home or local authority residential accommodation (see p87). Your applicable amount is reduced if you are:

- receiving an urgent cases payment (see p86);
- in hospital (see p97);

- a 16/17-year-old, in certain circumstances (see p57);
- a couple, one of whom is a person from abroad (see p69);
- without accommodation (see p102);
- a prisoner (see p101);
- appealing against a decision that you are not incapable of work under the 'all-work' test.[1] (see p55, and CPAG's *Rights Guide to Non-Means-Tested Benefits* for more information on the 'all-work' test).

In addition, there are a number of other reasons why your benefit may be reduced, such as:

- you are subject to a benefit penalty for refusing to co-operate with the Child Support Agency (see p115);
- you are repaying an overpayment of benefit (see p162);
- you are repaying a social fund (SF) loan (see p485);
- the Benefits Agency is making direct payments on your behalf in respect of housing costs, water charges, fuel debts, council tax and community charge arrears, fines or child support maintenance (see pp151-56).

Some IS/HB claimants get an amount of transitional protection on top of their ordinary IS/HB (see pp49 and 273).

2. PERSONAL ALLOWANCES

The amount of your personal allowance for IS, HB and CTB depends on your age and whether you are claiming as a single person or a couple. You also get an allowance for each dependent child (but see pp374 and 416 for the rules on income and capital belonging to children).

If you are polygamously married (see p347) you usually receive an extra amount for each additional partner in your household.[2] For IS, where any additional partner is under the age of 18, you will only receive an extra amount if they are responsible for a child (see p353) or would otherwise meet the special conditions for qualifying for JSA as a 16/17-year-old[3] (see CPAG's *Jobseeker's Allowance Handbook, 3rd edn*, 1998/99). For the treatment of additional partners in polygamous marriages for FC and DWA, see pp203 and 217.

Rates of personal allowances[4]

The rates for people aged 18 or over, and for dependent children, are the same for IS and HB/CTB. No CTB is payable for single people under 18 or for a couple where both are under 18 because they are not liable to pay the tax (see p327). Where one partner is 18 or over, they get the couple rate for over-18s.

Single claimant:

Aged under 18 (some IS cases (see p47) and all HB cases)	£39.85
Aged under 18 (other IS cases only (see p47))	£30.30
Other claimants aged under 25	£39.85
Aged 25 or over	£50.35

Lone parents:

Aged under 18 (some IS cases (see p47) and all HB cases)	£39.85
Aged under 18 (other IS cases only (see p47))	£30.30
Aged 18 or over	£50.35

Couple:

Both aged under 18 (some IS cases (see p48) and all HB cases)		£60.10
Both aged under 18 (other IS cases only (see p48))	*either*	£39.85
	or	£30.30
One aged under 18 (some IS cases (see p48) and all HB and CTB cases)		£79.00
One aged under 18 (other IS cases only (see p48))	*either*	£50.35
	or	£39.85
Both aged 18 or over		£79.00
Polygamous marriages: Each additional qualifying partner living in the same household[5]		£28.65

Children:

Under 11	£17.30*
11-15	£25.35
16-18	£30.30

*This will be increased to £19.80 from November 1998.

For the purpose of calculating the personal allowances above, a child is not treated as being 11 or 16 until the first Monday in September following her/his 11th or 16th birthday.[6]

3. PREMIUMS

Introduction

Premiums are added to your basic personal allowances and are intended to help with extra expenses caused by age, disability or the cost of children. The eight premiums and their rates are:

Family premium	£11.05	
Disabled child premium	£21.45	
(for each qualifying child)		
Severe disability premium		These can be paid
Single (or one partner qualifying)	£38.50	on top of any
Couple (both partners qualifying)	£77.00	other premiums
Carer's premium		
Single (or one partner qualifying)	£13.65	
Couple (both partners qualifying)	£27.30	
Family premium (lone parent increase)		
IS	£ 4.70	
HB/CTB	£11.00	
Disability premium		
Single	£21.45	
Couple	£30.60	Only one of these
Pensioner premium		can be paid; if you
(i) if aged 60-74		qualify for more
Single	£20.10	than one you get
Couple	£30.35	whichever is the
(ii) if aged 75-79		highest.[7]
Single	£22.35	
Couple	£33.55	
Higher pensioner premium		
Single	£27.20	
Couple	£38.90	

Entitlement to some premiums depends on receipt of other benefits. Once you have qualified for a premium, if you or your partner cease to receive a qualifying benefit because of the overlapping benefit rules (ie, because you are receiving another benefit at the same or a higher rate), or because you or your partner are on an employment training course or getting a training allowance, you will continue to receive the relevant premium.[8] In addition, you or your partner (if any) must be getting the benefit for yourself (or for your partner), and not on behalf of someone else – eg, as an appointee.[9]

Sometimes, you may be able to get payment of a premium backdated (see pp134 and 364).

Family premium[10]

You are entitled to this if your family includes a child (see p353). It is paid even if you are not the parent of the child and even if you do not receive a personal allowance for any child because they have capital over £3,000.

Only one family premium is payable regardless of the number of children you have. Where a child who is in the care of or being looked after by a local authority or who is in custody, comes home for part of a week, your IS includes a proportion of the premium, according to the number of days the child is with you;[11] for HB and CTB you may be paid the full premium if your child who is in care or being looked after by a local authority is part of the household for any part of the week: how often and for how long the child visits will be taken into account.[12]

Lone parents[13]

Prior to 6 April 1998, a higher rate of the family premium was payable to lone parents than to couples (unless they were also entitled to the disability premium or one of the pensioner premiums which would be payable instead). The lone parent rate of the family premium is now only payable if:

For IS

- you were both a lone parent and entitled to IS (or income-based JSA) on 5 April 1998, *or*, if you were not, you were on any day within 12 weeks before or after that date and you have not ceased to be both a lone parent and entitled to IS (or income-based JSA) for more than 12 weeks in this time; *and*
- you do not subsequently cease to be both a lone parent and entitled to IS (or income-based JSA), although any periods of less than 12 weeks during which you may cease to be either a lone parent or entitled to IS (or income-based JSA), or both, will be ignored.

For HB/CTB

- you were entitled or treated as entitled to HB/CTB and the lone parent increase on 5 April 1998; *and*
- you do not cease to be a lone parent; *and*
- you do not cease to be entitled or treated as entitled to HB/CTB; *and*

- you do not become or cease to be entitled to IS (or income-based JSA); *and*
- the disability or one of the pensioner premiums does not become payable instead.

You will be treated as entitled to HB/CTB on 5 April 1998 if you were entitled to the other benefit (ie, CTB or HB) as a lone parent from 5 April 1998 to the day before you eventually claim it. You will also be treated as entitled to HB during any rent-free weeks.

Note: Unlike IS, there are no linking periods for HB/CTB, so if you lose the increase even for a short period you will not be able to claim it back (although a change of address does not break your entitlement).[14]

If you lose your entitlement to the lone parent increase for IS/HB/CTB, you may still be entitled to the ordinary rate of the family premium instead.

Disabled child premium[15]

You are entitled to a disabled child premium for each of the children in your family who gets disability living allowance (DLA) or who is blind.

A child is treated as blind if s/he is registered as blind and for the first 28 weeks after s/he has been taken off the register on regaining her/his sight.[16] If DLA stops because the child has gone into hospital, see p99. Where your child is in local authority care or in custody for part of the week, this premium will be affected in the same way as the family premium (see above). For how to qualify for DLA, see CPAG's *Rights Guide to Non-Means-Tested Benefits*.

If the child has over £3,000 capital, you do not get this premium.[17]

Disability premium[18]

The way in which you can get a disability premium differs depending on whether you have a partner or not (see p346). In either case, the person who satisfies the qualifying conditions set out below has to be aged under 60. If you or your partner (if any) are aged 60 or over you may get the higher pensioner premium (see p365). A disability premium will be awarded if:

- you or your partner (if any) are getting a qualifying benefit. For the disability premium, these are attendance allowance (or an equivalent benefit paid to meet attendance needs because of an injury at work or a war injury[19]), disability living allowance, disability working allowance or mobility supplement, and also severe disablement allowance or incapacity benefit paid at the long-term rate. Note that if you are getting the special short-term rate of incapacity benefit because you are terminally ill (see below), this counts as a qualifying benefit.[20] Extra-statutory payments to compensate you or your partner (if any) for not getting these benefits also count.[21] See CPAG's *Rights Guide to Non-Means-Tested Benefits* for who can claim these benefits.

You must be getting the benefit in question for yourself, not on behalf of someone else – eg, as an appointee. The same applies if it is your partner who gets the benefit.[22]

Once you qualify for the premium, you, or your partner (if any), are treated as still getting a qualifying benefit you no longer in fact get, if you would have got it but for the overlapping benefit rules – eg, your severe disablement allowance stops because you start to get a widow's pension;[23]

- you, or your partner (if any), are registered as blind with a local authority. If you, or your partner, regain your sight you still qualify for 28 weeks after being taken off the register;[24]
- you, or your partner (if any), have an NHS invalid trike or private car allowance because of disability;[25]
- you, or your partner (if any), were getting incapacity benefit paid at the long-term rate (or at the short-term rate because of terminal illness) which stopped when retirement pension became payable, since when you have been continuously entitled to IS/HB/CTB.[26] If it is your partner who began receiving a retirement pension, s/he must still be alive (IS),[27] or still be a member of your family (HB/CTB).[28] In the case of IS only, you or your partner (if any), must have previously qualified for a disability premium;[29]
- you, or your partner, were getting attendance allowance or disability living allowance but payment of that benefit was suspended when one of you became a hospital inpatient.[30] In the case of IS only, you or your partner must have previously qualified for a disability premium.
- an adjudication officer has decided that you are 'incapable of work' or you are treated as incapable and you have been so entitled, incapable of work or treated as incapable of work for a continuous period of:[31]
  – 196 days if you have been certified as 'terminally ill' – ie, it can reasonably be expected that you will die within six months in consequence of a progressive disease;[32]
  – 364 days in all other cases;
provided you have claimed incapacity benefit (whether you are entitled to it or not) or (for IS only) you are entitled to statutory sick pay.

Breaks in entitlement/incapacity of up to 56 days are included in these periods. See CPAG's *Rights Guide to Non-Means-Tested Benefits* for more details about statutory sick pay and 'incapacity for work'.

Note: Although the rules for the disability premium include reference to receipt of attendance allowance and retirement pension (see p362), if you or your partner receive either of these benefits you are certain to be entitled to one of the pensioner premiums (see pp365-66) instead of the disability premium.

If you are a couple, you will get the disability premium at the couple rate (£30.60) provided that one of you meets one of the above qualifying conditions, except in the case of the condition concerning statutory sick pay and incapacity for work. In that case, you will not get the premium at all unless the person who qualifies is the claimant.[33] You may, therefore, need to swap who is the claimant (see pp128 and 282).

If you go on a Training for Work (TFW) or Youth Training (YT) course, or for any period you receive a training allowance, you will keep the disability premium even though you may cease to receive one of the 'qualifying benefits', or cease to be entitled to statutory sick pay or be incapable of work during the course, as long as you continue to be entitled to IS/HB/CTB. After the course, the premium continues if you remain entitled to statutory sick pay (for IS only), are still incapable of work, or getting a qualifying benefit.[34]

Note: The Government intends to introduce rules from October 1998 which will allow you to try out work. You will not necessarily lose your disability premium if you give up work and claim IS again.

Backdating

- Your 'qualifying benefit' (see p362) may not be awarded until some time after you claim it. If you are already getting IS/HB/CTB (or you have made a claim but it has been disallowed because you were not yet entitled to the disability premium) you should ask for this to be reviewed and for your disability premium to be backdated either to the same date that your 'qualifying benefit' is awarded from, or to when you first got (or claimed) IS, HB or CTB if that is later. In such circumstances there is no limit to the period for which IS arrears can be paid to you, but any new or increased entitlement to HB/CTB is limited to 12 months.[35]
- If as a result of getting a 'qualifying benefit' backdated you now qualify for but have not previously claimed IS, HB or CTB, you should make a new claim and ask for it to be backdated for up to three months (for IS) or 12 months (for HB/CTB). However, for IS, backdating of up to three months is only possible if you have a specified reason for making a late claim (see p134). For HB/CTB, backdating is possible if you have 'good cause' for not claiming earlier (see pp285 and 339).

Note: From June 1998, backdating of new claims for IS/HB/CTB will be restricted to one month (see Appendix 2).

Similar considerations will apply to backdating the disabled child premium (p362), the higher pensioner premium (see below), the severe disability premium (p367) and the carer's premium (p371).

- If you consider you have been incapable of work for 364/196 days or more, but you have not previously been certified or assessed as incapable of work, you should claim incapacity benefit. You do not have to be awarded incapacity benefit, you only have to show that you have been incapable of work. A medical note is not necessary for any period after 13 April 1995, although one will still be helpful as you will have to persuade an adjudication officer that you have been incapable of work throughout. Even if you have not yet been incapable of work for 364/196 days, it is advisable to claim incapacity benefit as soon as possible so that the disability premium can be awarded to you as soon as you reach the qualifying period.

- For HB/CTB, if you are one of a couple and the person who is incapable of work is not the claimant, you can swap the claimant role and s/he can apply to backdate a new claim if s/he has 'good cause' (see pp285 and 339). In this way you can get the disability premium backdated for up to 12 months.[36]

Note: From June 1998, backdating of new claims will be restricted to one month (see Appendix 2).

Pensioner premium[37]

The pensioner premium is paid at two rates according to age:

- the lower rate if you are aged 60–74 inclusive;
- the enhanced rate if you are 75–79 inclusive.

The couple rate for either is paid even if only one partner fulfils the condition. If you or your partner are sick or disabled check to see if you could get the higher pensioner premium instead (see below).

Higher pensioner premium

You can get this if one of the following applies:[38]

- you or your partner are 80 or over;
- you were getting a disability premium as part of your IS, HB or CTB before you were 60 and you have continued to claim that benefit since reaching that age. You must have been getting a disability premium at some time during the eight weeks before you were 60, and have received

that benefit continuously since you reached 60.[39] But you can have a period off that benefit of up to eight weeks and still qualify. For HB/CTB, if you were entitled to a higher pensioner premium for one benefit in the previous eight weeks you will get a higher pensioner premium with the other if you then qualify or requalify for that benefit.[40]

However, previous entitlement to a premium while on HB/CTB will not help you qualify for the higher pensioner premium when you claim IS, and *vice versa*. In the case of couples, the person who was the claimant for that benefit before s/he was 60 must continue to claim after that, but it is not necessary for the claimant to have been the person who qualified for the disability premium;[41]

• you or your partner are aged 60–79 *and* either of you receive a qualifying benefit (as for the disability premium – see p362), are registered blind, or have an NHS trike or a private car allowance (see p363).
  – If your attendance or disability living allowance stops because you go into hospital – see p97 (IS), pp272 and 344 (HB/CTB).
  – If you, or your partner, stop getting incapacity benefit (or if in the past you stopped getting invalidity benefit) because you get retirement pension instead, you will still get a higher pensioner premium with your IS, HB or CTB, if you remain continuously entitled (apart from breaks of eight weeks or less) to the same benefit.[42] In the case of HB/CTB, if you were entitled to a higher pensioner premium for one of these benefits in the previous eight weeks, you will get a higher pensioner premium with the other if you then qualify or requalify for that benefit.[43] If it is your partner who had changed to a retirement pension, s/he must still be alive (IS), or still be a member of your family (HB/CTB).[44] In the case of IS, the higher pensioner premium or a disability premium must also have been 'applicable' to you or your partner.[45] So, if, up to the time your incapacity (or invalidity benefit) ceased, your applicable amount was calculated by a method that did not include premiums (eg, because you were in a hostel prior to 9 October 1989, or you lived in a residential care or nursing home before 31 March 1993), you will not be able to qualify in this way.[46]
  – If you are getting severe disablement allowance by the time you reach 65, you will be awarded it for life even if you no longer satisfy the incapacity or disability conditions.[47] You will therefore continue to qualify for the higher pensioner premium. This will also apply even if it ceases to be paid because you get retirement pension at a higher rate.[48]

Severe disability premium[49]

You can get the severe disability premium if all of the following apply to you:

- you receive a qualifying benefit. For the severe disability premium this is either attendance allowance (or the equivalent war pension or industrial injury benefit[50]), or the middle or higher rate care component of disability living allowance (or extra-statutory payments to compensate you for not receiving any of these[51]). If you are a couple (or polygamously married), whichever one of you is claiming IS/HB/CTB must be getting a qualifying benefit and your partner(s) must also either be getting a qualifying benefit or else s/he must be registered blind (or treated as blind).[52] However, in either case you are treated as getting the qualifying benefit while still in hospital (see pp97, 272 and 344). The qualifying benefit must be paid in respect of yourself/selves, as receipt of benefit for someone else (eg, a child) does not count;[53]
- no non-dependant aged 18 or over is 'normally residing with you' (see p368) – eg, a grown up son or daughter, or your parents. It does not matter whose house it is, yours or the non-dependant's.[54] For IS/HB, someone is only counted as living with you if you share accommodation apart from a bathroom, lavatory or a communal area such as a hall, passageway or a room in common use in sheltered accommodation. If s/he is separately liable to make payments for the accommodation to the landlord, s/he will not count as living with you.[55] This is not explicitly stated in the rules for CTB, although the same test may in practice be applied for consistency;
- no one gets invalid care allowance for looking after you, or, if you are a couple (or polygamously married), no one gets invalid care allowance for both (or all) of you. Only 'payments' of invalid care allowance count,[56] so no account is taken of any underlying entitlement to invalid care allowance where it is awarded but not paid because of the overlapping benefit rules, or of any extra-statutory payments to compensate for it not being paid. Similarly, no account will be taken of any backdated payments or arrears of invalid care allowance[57] (see **Carers and the severe disability premium**, p372).

Couples will get the couple rate if both (or, in a polygamous marriage, all) of you are getting a qualifying benefit and no one gets invalid care allowance for either one (or any) of you. Note that in this situation a person will be treated as getting attendance allowance (or the higher or middle rate care component of disability living allowance), even though it has stopped because s/he has been in hospital for more than four weeks.

Similarly, a person will be treated as receiving invalid care allowance even if the qualifying benefit of the person for whom s/he is caring has stopped because that person has been in hospital for more than four weeks.[58]

However, if your partner does not get a qualifying benefit but is registered blind (or treated as blind), or if invalid care allowance is paid for one of you, you will still get the single rate.

Non-dependants[59]

The following people who live with you will *not* be counted as non-dependants:

For IS/HB/CTB
- anyone aged under 18;
- any member of your family (see p346 for who counts as part of your family). This may include any child up to the age of 19 (see p353) as well as your partner, although your partner must be getting a qualifying benefit (or would be but for being in hospital, see above) or be registered or treated as blind (see p367) if you are to be paid the severe disability premium (see p367);
- anyone else who receives a qualifying benefit;[60]
- anyone who is registered blind (or treated as blind);[61]
- anyone staying in your home who normally lives elsewhere. In deciding whether someone 'normally' lives with you or elsewhere it may be relevant to consider: why the residence started; the relationship and its history, if any, between those concerned; the motivations involved; the purpose for which residence has been taken up; its duration; and whether there is any other home in which residence is or could be taken up;[62]
- any person (and, for IS only, their partner) employed by a charitable or voluntary body as a resident carer for you or your partner if you pay a charge for that service (even if the charge is only nominal).

For IS only
- any person (or their partner) who jointly occupies (see p370) your home and is either the co-owner with you or your partner, or jointly liable with you or your partner to make payments to a landlord in respect of occupying it. If this person is a close relative, however, s/he *will* count as a non-dependant *unless* the co-ownership or joint liability to make payments to a landlord existed either before 11 April 1988 or

by the time you or your partner first moved in (but see transitional provisions below);

- any person (or any member of their household) who is liable to pay you or your partner on a commercial basis (see p370) in respect of occupying the dwelling (eg, tenants or licensees), unless they are close relatives of you or your partner (but see transitional provisions below);
- any person (or any member of their household) to whom you or your partner are liable to make such payments on a commercial basis, unless they are a close relative (see p370) of you or your partner (but see transitional provisions below);
- transitional provisions. In the three situations above, the presence of close relatives will *not* prevent you from continuing to get the severe disability premium if you fall within the scope of the transitional provisions which applied to claimants entitled to this premium before 21 October 1991. These were set out in the 22nd edition of the *National Welfare Benefits Handbook* (1992/93);
- if someone (other than those listed above) comes to live with you in order to look after you, or your partner, your severe disability premium will remain in payment for the first 12 weeks.[63] After that, you will lose the premium (or get a lower rate premium). The carer should then consider claiming invalid care allowance.

For HB only[64]

- any person who jointly occupies your home and is either the co-owner with you or your partner, or liable with you or your partner to make payments in respect of occupying it. A joint occupier who was a non-dependant at any time within the previous eight weeks will count as a non-dependant if the local authority thinks that the change of arrangements was created to take advantage of the HB scheme;
- any person who is liable to pay you or your partner on a commercial basis in respect of occupying the dwelling unless they are a close relative of you or your partner, or if the local authority thinks that the rent or other agreement has been created to take advantage of the HB scheme (but this cannot apply if the person was otherwise liable to pay rent for the accommodation at any time during the eight weeks before the agreement was made);
- any person, or any member of their household, to whom you or your partner are liable to make payments in respect of your accommodation on a commercial basis unless they are a close relative of you or your partner.

For CTB only[65]
- any person who is jointly and severally liable (see p330) with you to pay ·council tax. If s/he was a non-dependant at any time within the eight weeks before s/he became liable for council tax, s/he will count as a non-dependant if the local authority thinks that the change of arrangements was created to take advantage of the CTB scheme;
- any person who is liable to pay you or your partner on a commercial basis in respect of occupying the dwelling unless they are a close relative of you or your partner, or if the local authority thinks that the liability to make payments in respect of the dwelling has been created to take advantage of the CTB scheme (but this cannot apply if the person was otherwise liable to pay rent for the accommodation at any time during the eight weeks before that liability arose).

Close relative means parent, parent-in-law, son, son-in-law, daughter, daughter-in-law, step-parent, step-son, step-daughter, brother, sister, or partners of any of these.[66]

Jointly occupies has a technical meaning. It is a legal relationship involving occupation by two or more persons (whether as owner-occupiers or as tenants or licensees), with one and the same legal right.[67] It will not exist if people merely have equal access to different parts of the premises (as had previously been decided by a commissioner[68]).

Commercial basis has no technical meaning, and there is no requirement that there need be any intention to make a profit.[69] It may be sufficient if a 'reasonable' charge is made, even if this does not fully cover the cost of the accommodation and meals being provided.[70] The reasonableness of the charge made should be judged solely against the cost of occupying the dwelling, disregarding the additional costs of providing food, clothing and care for the claimant.[71] A useful, but not conclusive, test to apply is to consider whether the same arrangement *might* have been entered into with a lodger rather than with the claimant.[72] It is not relevant to the question of whether the arrangement is on a commercial basis to consider either whether the non-dependant depends financially on the charge being paid or if s/he would take action against the claimant if s/he did not pay.[73] However, these last two matters are relevant to whether there is a *liability* (see below).

Liability means a legal or contractual liability (as distinct from a moral or ethical obligation), although this can always be inferred from the circumstances, there being no requirement that any arrangements need be evidenced in writing.[74] Any liability must arise from the costs of occupying the home. People with no contractual capacity (eg, people with very severe learning disabilities) cannot establish liability under English law. However, there will always be a presumption that capacity exists and the test of capacity may not be very stringent. In any case, a commissioner has urged a consistency of approach for England and Scotland where the law is different in that a liability can exist even where contractual capacity is not established.[75]

Note: The conditions of entitlement to the severe disability premium are considerably more stringent than they used to be. In particular, the rules about living with 'joint occupiers' and those now relating to payments on a 'commercial basis' (see above), have been the subject of considerable legal dispute as a result of which the law has changed several times since it was first introduced in 1988.

If you think you could have qualified for the severe disability premium in an earlier period, you should get advice from a local advice agency and see if it might be possible to put in a late appeal (see p169). For further information see the 24th edition of the *National Welfare Benefits Handbook*, p354.

Carer's premium[76]

You qualify for this if you or your partner are getting, or are treated as getting, invalid care allowance.

- For how to qualify for invalid care allowance, see CPAG's *Rights Guide to Non-Means-Tested Benefits*. Note that if you are entitled to invalid care allowance by the time you reach the age of 65, you will continue to be entitled to it for life even if you stop providing care to a severely disabled person or if you start full-time work.[77]
- You are treated as getting invalid care allowance even if you do not receive it but:
  - you would get it but for the overlapping benefit rules (eg, you get long-term incapacity benefit instead), provided you claimed (or reclaimed) it on, or after, 1 October 1990, and the person you are claiming for continues to get attendance allowance or the care component (middle or higher rate) of disability living allowance.[78] The Benefits Agency may argue that you cannot benefit from this if you originally claimed invalid care allowance before 1 October 1990, but you should argue that that was not the intention of the rule;
  - you are awarded an extra-statutory payment to compensate you for non-payment of invalid care allowance.[79]
- If you stop getting, or being treated as getting, invalid care allowance, your entitlement to a carer's premium continues for a further eight weeks, even if you first claim IS/HB/CTB in this time.
- A double premium is awarded where both you and your partner satisfy the conditions for it.

Carers and the severe disability premium

Before claiming invalid care allowance, carers should consider how their claim may affect the disabled person's entitlement to the severe disability premium (see p367), particularly where the only financial advantage to the carer is the amount of the carer's premium which may be worth considerably less than the severe disability premium (but see p411 for the rules on notional income).

Any backdated award of invalid care allowance will not affect a disabled person's entitlement to the severe disability premium.[80] There may therefore be scope for careful planning to take advantage of this rule so that carers can be paid invalid care allowance or the carer's premium for the same period that the disabled person has already received the severe disability premium.

Note: From June 1998, backdating of new claims for invalid care allowance, like IS/HB/CTB, will be restricted to one month (see Appendix 2).

CHAPTER NINETEEN

Income

This chapter explains the rules for working out your weekly income for income support (IS), family credit (FC), disability working allowance (DWA), housing benefit (HB) and council tax benefit (CTB). It contains:

I. INTRODUCTION

Your entitlement to IS/FC/DWA/HB/CTB and the amount you receive depends on how much income you have. Note that if you get IS you do not need to work out your income again for HB/CTB purposes.[1]

The rules for working out your income are very similar for each benefit. Where there are differences these are indicated. Some of your income may be completely ignored, *or* partially ignored, *or* counted in full. Some income may be treated as capital (see p420), and some capital may be treated as income (see p406). There are some important differences in the rules on income for urgent cases payments under the income support scheme. These are set out at p85.

Note that, if you have to register for work, you will need to claim jobseeker's allowance (JSA) rather than IS (see p53).

Whose income counts

Income of a partner

If you are a member of a couple (see p347), your partner's income is added to yours.[2]

If you receive a reduction of the normal personal allowance for a couple because your partner is under 18 and not eligible for IS (see p48), an amount of her/his income equivalent to the reduction is ignored.[3]

Similar rules apply to additional partners in polygamous marriages.[4]

Example
Kalid is 19. His partner, Kate, is 17 and is not able to claim IS. Kalid's
personal allowance is £39.85 (the rate for a single person aged 18–24.
If Kate was eligible for IS, their personal allowance would be £79.
Up to £39.15 (£79 – £39.85) of any income that Kate has is ignored.

Income of a dependent child

If your child has over £3,000 capital, you do not get benefit for her/him[5]
(although for IS/HB/CTB, the ordinary or lone parent rate of the family
premium may still be payable – see p361) and her/his income is not
counted as yours. However, maintenance paid to, or for, a child does
count as yours.[6]

If your child has capital of £3,000 or less, any of her/his income
(subject to disregards) is usually treated as yours.[7]

With IS/HB/CTB, if that income comes to more than your child's
personal allowance (plus any disabled child premium payable for her/
him), the extra is ignored and not counted as yours.[8] In the case of FC/
DWA, if your child's income (ignoring any maintenance payments)
comes to more than the child credit (plus, for DWA, any disabled child
allowance payable for your child) the whole of your child's income is
ignored, but you do not get any credit/allowance for her/him.[9] However,
in all cases, any maintenance that is not disregarded and which is paid to,
or for, your child counts in full as your income.[10]

Your child's earnings (as opposed to other forms of income) while s/he
is *at school* do not normally count,[11] but if you are on IS/HB/CTB (not
FC/DWA), and your child gets a *full-time* job *after leaving school* but while
you are still claiming for her/him (eg, during the summer holiday), her/his
earnings over £5 count as your income.[12] If the child qualifies for the
disabled child premium (see p362) – or would, but for her/his being in a
residential care or nursing home – and her/his earning capacity is not, as a
result of the disability, less than 75 per cent of what it otherwise would
be, £15 is ignored.[13] In either case, any income that exceeds her/his
personal allowance and any disabled child premium is also ignored.[14]
However, earnings from part-time work (up to 24 hours) are still
completely ignored.

School fees paid by someone other than you or your partner are dealt
with differently for each benefit.

Your entitlement to IS is not affected if someone is paying school
fees directly to the school,[15] except that the payments for the child's

living expenses at the school count as the child's income for the period that the child is there.[16] If your child comes home for part of the week, you receive benefit for the child for the days s/he is at home.[17] If your child spends a night with you s/he does not count as at school on that day.[18]

If your child goes away to school and this is paid for by the local education authority, the child is treated as having income equal to the amount of their IS for the days they are at school.[19] You are entitled to benefit for the child for the days they spend at home.

There are no special rules about school fees for FC/DWA. For HB/CTB, the local authority is advised that boarding school fees met by, for example, a child's grandparents should be ignored unless they are already broken down into separate amounts for education and maintenance. In that case, the education element is disregarded and the living expenses part, if it is taken into account as the child's income under the rules for payments made to someone else on your behalf (see p413), is treated as a charitable or voluntary payment and qualifies for the £20 disregard (see p403).[20] (See p374 for how a child's income is counted.) The education element of school fees paid by a former partner is also ignored, but the living expenses part, if taken into account as income under the rules for payments made to someone else on your behalf (see p413), counts as maintenance (see p398) and qualifies for the £15 disregard (see p398).[21]

Converting income into a weekly amount

IS, FC/DWA, HB and CTB are all calculated on a weekly basis so your income has to be converted into a weekly amount if necessary.

The following rules apply to income from employment[22] (except self-employment – see p390). For other income, see p395.

- If the payment is for less than a week it is treated as the weekly amount.
- If the payment is for a month, multiply by 12 and divide by 52.
- For IS, FC and DWA, multiply a payment for three months by four and divide by 52.
- For IS, FC and DWA, divide a payment for a year by 52.
- For all benefits, multiply payments for other periods by seven and divide by the number of days in the period.

If you work on certain days but are paid monthly, it is necessary to decide whether the payment is for the days worked or for the whole month. This, generally, will depend on the terms of your contract of employment,[23] but may depend on how your employer has arranged to make payments to you.[24]

For IS, where your income fluctuates or your earnings vary because you do not work every week, your weekly income may be averaged over the cycle, if there is an identifiable one; or, if there is not, over five weeks, or over another period if this would be more accurate.[25] If the cycle involves periods when you do no work, those periods are included in the cycle, but not other absences – eg, holidays, sickness.

Example
Ahmed works a cycle of two weeks 'on' and one week 'off'. He works 20 hours a week in the weeks he works for which he is paid £60. In the third week he is paid a retainer of £30. He claims IS in the third week. His average weekly earnings will be £50 a week (£60 + £60 + £30 = £150 ÷ 3 = £50) which will be taken into account in calculating his IS entitlement.

For IS, there are a number of rules about the calculation of income for part-weeks. They are:

- Where income covering a period up to a week is paid before your first benefit week, and part of it is counted for that week; or, if, in any case, you are paid for a period of a week or more, and only part of it is counted in a particular benefit week – multiply the whole payment by the number of days it covers in the benefit week, then divide the result by the total number of days covered by the payment.[26]
- Where any payment of JSA, maternity allowance, incapacity benefit, or severe disablement allowance falls partly into the benefit week, only the amount paid for those days is taken into account. For any payment of IS, that amount is the weekly amount multiplied by the number of days in the part-week and divided by seven.[27]

For IS, where you have regularly received a certain kind of payment of income from one source, and in a particular benefit week you receive that payment and another of the same kind from the same source (eg, where your employer first pays you sick pay in arrears and this then overlaps with a payment in advance), the maximum amount to be taken into account is the one paid first.[28]

This does not apply if the second payment was due to be taken into account in another week, but the overlapping week is the first in which it could practically be counted (see p377).

See p378 for definition of IS benefit week.

The period covered by income for IS

If you are an employed earner, or getting 'other income' and claiming IS, your income counts for a future period. There are special rules for deciding the length of this period and the date from which payments count. This rule does not apply to self-employed earnings (see p388).

- Where a payment of income is made in respect of an identifiable period, it will be taken into account for a period of equal length.[29] For example, a week's part-time earnings will be taken into account for a week.
- If the payment does not relate to a particular period, the amount of the payment will be divided by the amount of the weekly IS to which you would otherwise be entitled. If part of the payment should be disregarded, the amount of IS will be increased by the appropriate disregard. The result of this calculation is the number of weeks that you will not be entitled to IS.[30]

Example
You receive £700 net earnings for work which cannot be attributed to any specific period of time. You are a couple, both aged 28, with one child aged eight, and your rent and your council tax are met by HB/CTB. Your IS is £95.90 (applicable amount of £107.35 less child benefit of £11.45). As a couple you are entitled to a £10 earnings disregard (see p000).
    £700 ÷ (£95.90 + £10 = £105.90) = 6 with £64.60 left over.
This means means that you are not entitled to IS for six weeks and the remaining £64.60 (less a £10 earnings disregard, leaving £54.60) is taken into account in calculating your benefit for the following week.

- Payments made on leaving a job are taken into account for a forward period (see p384).

The date from which a payment is counted

The date from which a payment counts depends on when it was due to be paid. If it was due to be paid before you claimed IS, it counts from the date on which it was due to be paid.[31] Otherwise it is treated as paid on the first day of the benefit week in which it is due, or on the first day of the first benefit week after that in which it is practical to take it into account.[32] Payments of IS, JSA, maternity allowance, incapacity benefit or severe disablement allowance are treated as paid on the day they are officially due.[33]

The benefit week for IS is the seven days running from the day of the week on which benefit is paid. It will often overlap two calendar weeks.[34]

The date that a payment is due may well be different from the date of actual payment. Earnings are due on the employee's normal pay day. If the contract of employment does not reveal the date of due payment, and there is no evidence pointing in another direction, the date the payment was received should be taken as the date it was due.[35] If your contract of employment is terminated without proper notice, outstanding wages, wages in hand, holiday pay and any pay in lieu of notice are due on the last day of employment and are treated as paid on that day, even if this does not happen.[36] If income due to you has not been paid you may be entitled to an urgent cases payment (see p86) or a crisis loan from the social fund (see p479). For the treatment of payments at the end of a job, see p384. If you receive compensation for, say, being dismissed in circumstances constituting sex discrimination, the relevant date is the date when the earnings in question were due to be paid, not when the compensation was awarded.[37]

2. EARNINGS OF EMPLOYED EARNERS

Calculating net earnings from employment

Both your 'gross' earnings and 'net' earnings need to be calculated so that a proper assessment can be made of your income from employment.

'Gross' earnings means the amount of earnings received from your employer less deductions for any expenses wholly, necessarily and exclusively incurred by you in order to carry out the duties of your employment.[38] In appropriate circumstances these could, for example, include tools or work equipment, special clothing or uniform,[39] telephone costs (including rental),[40] postage, fuel costs (including standing charges) and even secretarial expenses,[41] and the costs of running a car (including petrol, tax, insurance, repairs and maintenance and rental on a leased car).[42] It has also been held that an armed forces local overseas allowance (representing the additional cost of essential living expenses incurred from working overseas) also counts,[43] although lodgings allowances to those stationed in the UK cannot be deducted,[44] and there are conflicting decisions on the treatment of rent allowances for police officers.[45] Where any expenditure serves a dual purpose for both business and private use it should be apportioned as appropriate to the circumstances (and any determination by the inland revenue – which commonly allows for 85 per cent business usage – should normally be followed).[46]

'Net' earnings mean your 'gross' earnings less any deductions made for income tax, class 1 national insurance contributions (but not class 3 voluntary contributions[47]) and half of any contribution you make towards a personal or occupational pension scheme.[48] For FC/DWA/ HB/CTB, allowance is also made in certain cases for some childcare costs (see p392).

If your earnings are estimated the authorities estimate the amount of tax and national insurance you would expect to pay on those earnings, and deduct this plus half of any pension contribution you are paying.[49]

For HB/CTB, the local authority has the discretion to ignore changes in tax or national insurance contributions for up to 30 benefit weeks. This can be used, for example, where Budget changes are not reflected in your actual income until several months later. When the changes are eventually taken into account and your benefit entitlement is either increased or reduced accordingly, you are not treated as having been underpaid or overpaid benefit during the period of the delay.[50]

What counts as earnings

Earnings means 'any remuneration or profit derived from...employment'. As well as your wages, this includes:[51]

- any bonus or commission (including tips);
- holiday pay, except if it is not payable until more than four weeks after your job ends or is interrupted, in which case it will be treated as capital.[52]
  Note: For IS, this rule does not apply if you are involved in, or returning to work after, a trade dispute (see p61). For more detail on payments at the end of a job, see p384;
- except for IS, any sick pay.[53] For IS this is treated as other income and counted in full less any tax, class 1 national insurance contributions and half of any pension contributions;[54]
- for HB/CTB, any maternity pay.[55] For FC/DWA, any statutory maternity pay and maternity allowance is ignored altogether,[56] although any additional non-statutory contributions that may be made by an employer should be treated as earnings. For IS, any maternity pay is treated as other income and counted in full less any tax, class 1 national insurance contributions and half of any pension contributions;[57]
- any payments made by your employer for expenses not 'wholly, exclusively and necessarily' incurred in carrying out your job, including any travel expenses to and from work, and any payments made to you for looking after members of your family;

- a retainer fee (eg, you may be paid during the school holidays if you work for the school meals service) or a guarantee payment;[58]
- for DWA, any payment made by your employer towards your council tax;[59]
- for IS/HB/CTB, payments in lieu of wages or in lieu of notice, but only insofar as they represent loss of income;[60]
- an award of compensation for unfair dismissal, or loss of earnings compensation for sex or race discrimination[61] and certain other awards of pay made by an industrial tribunal, and for IS/HB/CTB, certain payments made directly by your employer as compensation for loss of employment (excluding, for IS only, any lump-sum payment made under the Iron and Steel Re-adaptation Benefits Scheme);[62]
- certain other payments from your employer – eg, arrears of wages (but see below for payments from an employer which do not count).

See pp384-86 for definitions of the last three.

The following are examples of payments not counted as earnings:

- payments in kind (eg, petrol)[63] are ignored[64] unless you are on IS and involved in a trade dispute (see p61), but the notional income rules may be applied instead (see p411);[65]
- an advance of earnings or a loan from your employer. This is treated as capital[66] (although it will still be treated as earnings for IS if you or your partner are involved in a trade dispute, or have been back at work after a dispute for no longer than 15 days[67]).
- payments towards expenses that are 'wholly, exclusively and necessarily' incurred, such as travelling expenses during the course of your work.[68] Such disregards from payments by your employer may be in addition to the allowances to be taken into account for expenses incurred by you in the assessment of your 'gross' earnings (see p378);
- if you are a local councillor, travelling expenses and subsistence payments are (and basic allowances may be[69]) ignored as expenses 'wholly, exclusively and necessarily' incurred in your work. However, allowances for attending meetings etc are counted as earnings;[70]
- earnings payable abroad which cannot be brought into Britain – eg, because of exchange control regulations.[71] If your earnings are paid in another currency, any bank charges for converting them into sterling are deducted before taking them into account;[72]
- any occupational pension.[73] This counts as other income and the net amount is taken into account in full.[74]

The value of any accommodation provided as part of your job will be ignored for IS.[75] For FC/DWA, if it is free, the authorities will take account of its value by adding £12 to the calculation of your weekly earnings. If your employer charges you less than £12 rent, the difference between that amount and £12 is added instead. If the accommodation is worth less to you – eg, it is provided but you never use it,[76] no amount will be added.

For CTB, and for HB where job-related accommodation is in addition to the normal home, argue that this is payment in kind[77] and should be disregarded.

How earnings are assessed

For IS, it is necessary to work out the period which payments cover. However, for FC/DWA/HB/CTB a past period is usually used to assess your 'normal weekly earnings'.

For FC

Unless you are employed as a director (see below), the normal rule is to average your weekly earnings over an 'assessment period' of:

- six consecutive weeks immediately preceding the week you claim (or the week before that if this information is not available) if you are paid weekly; *or*
- three consecutive fortnights immediately preceding the week you claim (or, if this information is not available, the three consecutive fortnights leading up to the week before you claim) if you are paid fortnightly; *or*
- three months or three four-week periods if you are paid monthly or four-weekly; *or*
- six consecutive pay periods if you are paid at another interval that is less than a month (eg, daily); *or*
- one year if your pay period is longer than a month.

In the last three cases, the periods in question must immediately precede the week of your claim.[78]

In all cases, it is the earnings which you *received* during the assessment period which count, even though some of these earnings may be for a period falling outside the assessment period – eg, an early payment of holiday pay.[79]

Any weeks/months in the assessment period are ignored and replaced by the next earliest 'normal' pay period if your earnings are reduced because you have been involved in a trade dispute[80] or if you have deliberately chosen to reduce the number of hours you work with the intention of becoming entitled to, or increasing your entitlement to, FC.[81]

Any pay period in which your earnings are 20 per cent or more above or below your average earnings are left out. If this applies to all the weeks/months in your assessment period, only those in which you received no pay or received pay for a longer period than usual (eg, two weeks' holiday pay in one week) are left out. If this still results in all the weeks/months in your assessment period being left out, your employer will be required to provide an estimate of your likely earnings for the period for which you are normally paid.[82]

Where your earnings vary widely you may find that the figure arrived at can be based on just one wage slip which could be up to 20 per cent above or below your real average earnings. Therefore it may sometimes be sensible to delay your claim in order to allow for the lowest possible rate of pay to be taken into account and thus maximise the amount of FC you will receive for the next 26 weeks.

If you are employed as a director of a company, different rules apply.[83] Your normal weekly earnings are worked out by looking at how much you received in the year immediately before the week of your claim. If you have been employed for less than a year, an estimate is made of what you are likely to earn in the first year, taking into account what you have already received. Any week when you do no work and do not get paid is ignored in calculating your weekly earnings.[84]

For DWA

The normal rule is to take your weekly earnings over an 'assessment period' of:

- five consecutive weeks in the last six weeks if you are paid weekly; *or*
- two months if you are paid monthly;

immediately before the week of your claim.[85]

As with FC, it is the earnings which are *received* during the assessment period which count, whether or not they were actually earned in respect of that period.[86]

However, any time in the assessment period during which your earnings were irregular or unusual does not count[87] – eg, any week in which you received, for instance, a one-off bonus or holiday pay, or in which large deductions were made from your wages.

If your earnings fluctuate, or in the five-week or two-month period before your claim do not represent your normal earnings (eg, because you are on unpaid maternity leave[88]), a different period can be used if this gives a more accurate picture of your normal weekly earnings.[89]

If there is a period of short-time working of not more than 13 weeks or a trade dispute at your place of work, your normal weekly earnings will be taken as those prior to the period of short-time working or dispute.

Trade dispute includes a work-to-rule or overtime ban as well as a strike.[90]

For FC/DWA

A bonus or commission paid separately, or for a longer period than other earnings, and which is paid in the year prior to your claim, counts as earnings.[91] The net amount is divided by 52 before it is taken into account.[92]

If you have just started a job or have just returned to work after a break of more than, for FC four weeks, or, for DWA 13 weeks, or your hours have just changed, and the period since the start or resumption of your employment or the change in hours is less than your assessment period, your employer will be required to provide an estimate of your likely earnings for the period for which you are normally paid.[93] If your actual earnings turn out to be lower than the estimate, this will not result in your FC/DWA being reviewed and increased, so it is important that your employer does not overestimate your earnings.

For HB/CTB

Earnings as an employee are usually averaged out over:

- the previous five weeks if you are paid weekly; *or*
- two months if you are paid monthly.[94]

Where your earnings vary, or if there is likely to be or has recently been a change (eg, you usually do overtime but have not done so recently, or you are about to get a pay rise), the local authority may average them over a different period where this is likely to give a more accurate picture of what you are going to earn during the benefit period.[95]

If you are on strike, the local authority should not take into account your pre-strike earnings and average them out over the strike period.[96]

If you have only just started work and your earnings cannot be averaged over the normal period (ie, five weeks/two months), an estimate is made based on any earnings you have been paid so far if these are likely to reflect your future average wage. Where you have not yet been paid or your initial earnings do not represent what you will normally earn over the benefit period, your employer must provide an estimate of your average weekly earnings.[97] Where your earnings change during your benefit period, your new weekly average figure is estimated on the basis of what you are likely to earn over the remainder of the benefit period.[98]

Payments at the end of a job

Redundancy payments are normally treated as capital (see below).

Some redundancy schemes make periodic payments after leaving work; for IS/HB/CTB, these are treated as other income (see p395).[99]

Other payments can cause problems, and are dealt with separately for each benefit.

For IS

In most cases, when you finish a job you will need to claim income-based JSA rather than IS (see the *Jobseeker's Allowance Handbook*, 3rd edn, 1998/99). However, if you do not need to register for work, you may need to claim IS.

If you retire from a full-time job (16 hours or more) and you are aged at least 60 (women) or 65 (men), any payments counted as earnings (eg, final wages, holiday pay, etc) that you receive are disregarded in full.[100] You are not treated as in full-time work for any period covered by those earnings after the end of your job.

In all other cases, only the following final payments that you receive when you leave a *full-time* job affect your right to IS:[101]

- holiday pay which counts as earnings (see p379);
- pay in lieu of notice;
- pay in lieu of wages;
- a compensation payment in respect of employment (ie, where you do not get pay in lieu of notice, or only get part of your pay in lieu of notice, and receive a lump sum instead – ie, *ex gratia*). This is divided by the maximum payable under the statutory redundancy scheme (uprated yearly). The result is the number of weeks the payment will cover up to a maximum of your notice period, whether statutory, contractual or customary.[102] If the amount is less than the statutory maximum for one week or if the calculation creates a fraction, these are treated as capital.[103] If the *ex gratia* payment is not compensation but a gift (eg, a 'golden handshake') it should be treated as capital, not income.

You are treated as in full-time work for the number of weeks covered by these payments after your employment ended.[104] These payments are taken into account consecutively and in the following order:

- any pay in lieu of wages or in lieu of notice; *then*
- payments of compensation for loss of employment; *then*
- holiday pay.[105]

The period for which you are treated as in full-time work starts on the earliest date that any of these payments are due to be paid.[106]

Example

Mary leaves her full-time job with a final week's wages, a week in hand and one week's holiday pay. All three amounts are due to be paid on 30 May. Only the holiday pay will be taken into account, starting from 30 May. Mary will not be entitled to IS for one week.

If you receive an award of compensation for unfair dismissal or certain other awards of pay from an industrial tribunal, these are taken into account as earnings in calculating the amount of your IS from when the award is made.

If your employment is interrupted (eg, you are laid off), any holiday pay that is paid to you affects your right to IS; all other payments are disregarded except that any retainer you are paid is taken into account as earnings in calculating the amount of your IS.[107] If you have been suspended, any payment you receive will be taken into account and affect your right to IS.

If you were working part time (less than 16 hours a week) before you claimed IS, any payments you receive when the job ends or is interrupted, except any retainer, are ignored and do not affect your IS (unless you have been suspended).[108] If, however, you were claiming IS while you were in part-time work, any payments made to you when that job ends are taken into account as earnings in the normal way. Your wages, including any final wages, are counted first, then any pay in lieu of wages or notice, then any compensation paid by your employer for loss of employment (although this will be taken into account for a period of one week only[109]) and then any holiday pay.[110]

Once the period covered by payments at the end of a job has ended, any money remaining will be treated as capital.[111]

For FC/DWA

There are no special FC/DWA rules for payments received at the end of a job. However, if, for example, your partner has just lost her/his job and you apply for FC because you are working full time, any payments that s/he received at the end of the employment (and indeed the amount of previous wages) should not be included as part of your 'normal' weekly income, unless there is evidence that the job will resume while you are getting your current FC award.

For HB/CTB

If you retire from a full-time job (16 hours or more) and have reached the age of 65 (men) or 60 (women), any payments counted as earnings that you receive are disregarded.[112]

In all other cases, only the following final payments that you receive are taken into account as earnings:[113]

- holiday pay which counts as earnings (see p379);
- pay in lieu of notice;
- pay in lieu of wages;
- compensation for loss of employment, but only insofar as it represents loss of income (the detailed rules for IS do not apply);
- an award of compensation for unfair dismissal, or certain other awards of pay from an industrial tribunal;
- any statutory sick pay or statutory maternity pay;
- any retainer fee.

If your work is interrupted, your earnings are disregarded except for holiday pay which counts as earnings (see p379) and any retainer paid to you.

Where you were in part-time work (ie, less than 16 hours a week) before claiming HB/CTB, any earnings paid when your job ended or was interrupted are disregarded, *except* where that payment is a retainer.[114] This disregard does not apply to earnings paid when your job ends if you are already getting HB/CTB.

Disregarded earnings

For FC/DWA, your earnings, worked out in the way described above, are taken into account in full. (Though see provisions on deductions for certain childcare costs, p392.)

For IS and HB/CTB, some of your earnings are disregarded and do not affect your benefit. The amount of the 'disregard' depends on your circumstances. There are three levels.

£25 disregard

Lone parents on HB/CTB but not receiving IS have £25 of their earnings ignored.[115] This does not apply to IS.

£15 disregard

£15 of your earnings (including those of your partner, if any) is disregarded if:

- for IS, you are a lone parent;[116]

- you or your partner (if any) qualifies for a disability premium (see p362).[117] For IS, you are treated as qualifying for the premium if you would do so but for being in hospital, or a local authority home or because you are a person in a residential care or nursing home with preserved rights (see p367);
- for HB/CTB only, you or your partner (if any) qualifies for a severe disability premium (see p365);[118]
- you or your partner (if any) qualifies for the higher pensioner premium (see p365), you or your partner are over 60 and, immediately before reaching that age, you or your partner were in employment (part-time for IS) and you were entitled to a £15 disregard because of qualifying for a disability premium. For HB/CTB this includes where, in the case of a couple, you would have qualified for a disability premium but for the fact that a higher pensioner premium was payable. Since reaching 60, you or your partner must have continued in employment (part-time for IS), although breaks of up to eight* weeks when you were not getting IS (or HB/CTB where you claim either of these benefits) are ignored. For IS, you are treated as qualifying for the higher pensioner premium even if you are in hospital etc;[119]
- you are a member of a couple, your benefit would include a disability premium but for the fact that one of you qualifies for the higher pensioner premium or the enhanced rate of pensioner premium (see p365), one of you is under 60 and either of you are in employment. For IS, you are treated as qualifying for the higher or enhanced pensioner premium if you would do so, but for being in hospital, etc (see above);[120]
- you are a member of a couple, one of you is aged 75-79 and the other over 60, and immediately before that person reached 60 either of you were in part-time employment and you were entitled to a £15 disregard because of qualifying, or being treated as qualifying, for an enhanced pensioner premium (see above). Since then either of you must have continued in part-time employment, although breaks of up to eight* weeks when you were not getting IS (or HB/CTB where you claim either of these benefits), are ignored;[121]
- you or your partner (if any) qualifies for a carer's premium (see p371). The disregard applies to the carer's earnings. For a couple, if the carer's earnings are less than £15, the remainder of the disregard can be used up on her/his partner's earnings as an auxiliary coastguard, etc (see below), or up to £5 (for HB/CTB up to £10) of it can be used up on her/his partner's earnings from another job;[122]
- you or your partner (if any) are an auxiliary coastguard, part-time firefighter or a part-time member of a lifeboat crew, or a member of the Territorial Army.[123] If you earn less than £15 for doing any of

these services you can use up to £5 (for HB/CTB up to £10 if you have a partner) of the disregard on another job[124] or a partner's earnings from another job.[125]

*For IS, this is increased to 12 weeks if you stopped getting IS because you or your partner started full-time work (see p13 for the detailed rules on this). Any period when you were not entitled to IS because you or your partner went on a government training scheme is ignored. But it will count as a period that you were in receipt of IS if you qualify for the £15 disregard as a long-term claimant (see above).[126]

If you qualify under more than one category you still have a maximum of only £15 of your earnings disregarded.

Basic £10 or £5 disregard

If you do not qualify for a £25 or £15 disregard, £5 of your earnings is disregarded if you are single. If you claim as a member of a couple, £10 of your total earnings is disregarded – whether or not you are both working.[127]

3. EARNINGS FROM SELF-EMPLOYMENT

Calculating net earnings

Your 'net profit' over the period before your claim must be worked out. This consists of your self-employed earnings, including any Business Start-Up Allowance,[128] minus:[129]

- reasonable expenses (see below); *and*
- income tax and national insurance contributions; *and*
- half of any premium paid in respect of a personal pension scheme or a retirement annuity contract which is eligible for tax relief.[130] If you and your partner (if any) are aged under 60, you must supply certain information about the scheme or annuity contract to the relevant authority if requested.[131]

For FC/DWA, the Business Start-Up Allowance will not count if it ended before you claimed – so it may be worthwhile delaying your claim.[132] In calculating your earnings any capital grant to set up a business, or a loan of working capital, or the sale of capital assets is excluded,[133] and any capital (eg, a legacy) not generated by the business cannot be treated as earnings.[134]

For IS/HB/CTB, if you receive payments for fostering from a local authority or voluntary organisation, and for IS/FC/DWA/HB/CTB if you receive payments for providing temporary respite care under community care arrangements from a health authority, local authority, voluntary organisation or from the person being looked after, these do not count as earnings[135] but are ignored[136] (although in either case the person you are being paid to look after may not count as a member of your family – see p346). For IS/HB/CTB, if you receive payments for board and lodging charges these do not count as earnings[137] but as other income (less any disregards, see p404). For FC/DWA, these are treated as earnings if, after discounting all the disregards on pp395-40 (other than the boarder's allowance on p404), they form a *major part* of your total income.[138] Otherwise they are treated as other income, as for IS.

Reasonable expenses

Expenses must be reasonable and 'wholly and exclusively' incurred for the purposes of your business.[139] This will involve similar considerations to those that apply in the allowances permitted in the assessment of 'gross' earnings of employed earners (see p378). Where a car or telephone, for example, is used partly for business and partly for private purposes, the costs of it can be apportioned and the amount attributable to business use can be deducted.[140]

Reasonable expenses include:[141]

- repayments of capital on loans for replacing equipment and machinery;
- repayment of capital on loans for, and income spent on, the repair of a business asset except where this is covered by insurance;
- interest on a loan taken out for the purposes of the business;
- excess of VAT paid over VAT received.

Reasonable expenses do not include:[142]

- any capital expenditure;
- depreciation. However, there are conflicting decisions as to whether any decrease (or increase) in the valuation of stock (which can be taken into account for tax purposes) should be taken into account.[143] The most recent case holds that these should be taken into account;[144]
- money for setting up or expanding the business – eg, the cost of adapting the business premises;
- any loss incurred before the beginning of the current assessment period. If the business makes a loss, the net profit is nil. The losses of one business cannot be offset against the profit of any other business in which you are engaged, or against your earnings as an employee,[145] (although where two businesses or employments share expenses these may be apportioned and offset);[146]

- capital repayments on loans taken out for business purposes;
- business entertainment expenses;
- for HB/CTB only, debts (other than proven bad debts), but the expenses of recovering a debt can be deducted.

Working out your average

There are different rules for each benefit.

For IS

The weekly amount is the average of earnings:[147]

- over a period of any one year (normally the last year for which accounts are available);
- over a more appropriate period where you have recently taken up self-employment or there has been a change which will affect your business.[148]

If your earnings are royalties or copyright payments, the amount of earnings is divided by the weekly amount of IS which would be payable if you had not received this income plus the amount which would be disregarded from those earnings.[149] You will not be entitled to IS for the resulting number of weeks.

For FC/DWA

Your normal weekly earnings are worked out by looking at:[150]

- your profit and loss account (and your trading account and/or balance sheet if appropriate), if this covers a period of at least six but not more than 15 months, which ends within 12 months before the date of your claim; *or*
- if you do not provide such a profit and loss account, but do provide a statement of your earnings and expenses for the six calendar months up to and including the month before your claim, your earnings over that period of six months; *or*
- if you do not provide a profit and loss account or statement of earnings and expenses, the six calendar months up to and including the month preceding your claim; *or*
- a different past period, if this represents your normal weekly earnings more accurately.

Your weekly earnings are worked out by averaging the earnings you have received or can expect to receive over the assessment period or, where you have provided a profit and loss account, by averaging the earnings relevant to the period covered by that account.[151]

Any complete week(s) in the assessment period when you are not actually working (eg, because you are sick or on holiday) are ignored.[152]

If you have just started being self-employed (ie, for less than seven calendar months), for FC your normal weekly earnings are worked out over six calendar months, beginning with the month after the one in which you started the business. If you provided a statement of earnings and expenses for those months, up to and including the last month before the month in which you claim, the earnings of those months are taken; if you do not provide such a statement, the earnings up to and including the month before the one preceding your claim are taken. In either case, the amount you can expect to earn for the remainder of the six-month period is added. Any week where you do not work for the business is ignored.[153]

For DWA an estimate will be made of your likely weekly earnings over the next 26 weeks from the date of your claim.[154] If your actual earnings turn out to be lower than the estimate this will not result in your FC/DWA being reviewed and increased.[155] However, if you were not *awarded* FC/DWA because your estimated earnings were too high, but by the time your appeal is heard you would be entitled on the basis of your actual earnings, the tribunal should have regard to your earnings up to the date of the social security appeal tribunal hearing in deciding what your income really was at the date of claim. In this case, the tribunal is deciding whether you are entitled to an award, not dealing with a change of circumstances affecting an existing award.[156]

For HB/CTB

The amount of your weekly earnings is averaged out over an 'appropriate' period (usually based on your last year's trading accounts) which must not be longer than a year.[157]

Childminders

Childminders, in practice, are always treated as self-employed. Your net profit is deemed to be one-third of your earnings less income tax, your national insurance contributions and half of certain pension contributions (see p388).[158] The rest of your earnings are completely ignored.

Disregarded earnings[159]

The rules are the same as for employed earners (see p378).

Childcare costs[160]

More generous allowances for childcare costs will apply to all awards of HB/CTB from 1 June 1998 and all awards of FC/DWA on new or renewal claims starting on or after 2 June 1998 (see p393).

For FC/DWA/HB/CTB an allowance of up to £60* a week may be deducted from your earnings (from employment or self-employment) in respect of childcare costs if you are:

- a lone parent working 16 hours a week or more; *or*
- a couple and both of you work 16 hours a week or more, or else one of you works 16 hours a week or more and the other is 'incapacitated' (see below).

This will only apply if you have any child(ren) in your family under the age of 11* for whom you are paying charges for childcare (not counting charges in respect of compulsory education or charges paid by you to your partner for a child in your family) which is provided:

- by a registered childminder or other registered childcare provider (such as a nursery or after-school club catering for the under-eights); *or*
- by (for children between the ages of eight and 11*) a school on school premises or a local authority – eg, an out-of-hours or holiday play scheme. For FC/DWA it is the age of the child at the start of the claim which counts; *or*
- by a childcare scheme operating on Crown property; *or*
- in schools or establishments exempt from registration.

Note: A child is not treated as having reached the age of 11* until the day before the first Tuesday (for FC/DWA) or first Monday (for HB/CTB) in September *following* her/his 11th* birthday.[161]

You (or your partner) will be treated as 'incapacitated' if:

- you get short-term (higher rate) or long-term incapacity benefit; *or*
- you get severe disablement allowance; *or*
- you get attendance allowance, disability living allowance or constant attendance allowance (or an equivalent award under the war pensions or industrial injuries schemes), or else you would receive one of these benefits but for the fact that you (or your partner) are in hospital; *or*
- you have an invalid carriage or similar vehicle; *or*
- HB/CTB is payable and includes (or would include, but for a disqualification of up to six weeks for misconduct) a disability or higher pensioner premium (see Chapter 18) in respect of the incapacity; *or*

- for HB/CTB, you (but not your partner) have been treated as incapable of work for a continuous period of 196 days or more (disregarding any break of up to 56 days); *or*
- for FC/DWA, you have already been awarded an allowance for childcare costs in HB/CTB.

* From 1 June 1998 (for HB/CTB) or 2 June 1998 (for FC/DWA):

- you can claim for any child(ren) up to the age of 12 instead of 11; *and*
- the maximum allowance will increase from £60 to £100 if you are paying charges for more than one child under the age of 12 (but will still be £60 if you are only paying for one child under 12).

Calculating childcare costs

For FC/DWA[162]

Because childcare costs are likely to vary considerably between term-time and holiday periods, a formula is used to assess the costs that will be taken into account.

Where charges are paid other than monthly, the amount will be: *either*

- 1/52 of the aggregate of:
  - the average weekly charge in the four most recent complete weeks falling in term-time, multiplied by 39; *and*
  - the average weekly charge in the two most recent weeks falling out of term-time, multiplied by 13; *or*
- where your child does not yet attend school, the average weekly charge in the four most recent complete weeks.

Where charges are paid monthly:

- if the charge is for a fixed amount, that amount multiplied by 12 and divided by 52; *or*
- if the charge is variable, 1/52 of the aggregate of charges over the previous 12 months.

However, where there is no, or insufficient, information available in order to assess the childcare costs in any of these ways, an estimate will be made based on information provided by the care provider or, if that is not available, by you.

For HB/CTB[163]

The costs to be taken into account will be estimated over whatever period, not exceeding a year, that will give the best estimate of the average weekly charge over the 'benefit period' (see pp290 and 340), based on information to be provided by the childminder or care provider.

Additional points to note

- These rules do *not* apply to IS.
- Until June 1998, £60 is the maximum amount that can be deducted regardless of the number of children you are paying childcare for. From June 1998, £100 is the maximum even if you have to pay for childcare for more than two children.
- If you are claiming FC or DWA only, the net gain to you of the £60/£100 allowance will be a maximum of £42/£70 (because of the 70 per cent taper used in the calculation of FC/DWA – see pp203 and 217) but you will get no allowance for your childcare costs if your income is less than the appropriate 'applicable amount' (£79 for FC – see p203; £59.25 or £79 for DWA – see p217), because you will be getting the maximum award of FC/DWA anyway. Similar considerations also apply to HB/CTB (see pp264 and 332 for the taper rules).
- The childcare costs calculation will apply both on your claim for FC or DWA and your claims for HB/CTB. If you are claiming more than one of these benefits the effect of their combined tapers is that the maximum gain to you of the allowance may be more than the £42/£70 (70 per cent) if you were claiming FC or DWA only.
- Local authorities may not charge you for nursery services provided under the Children Act if you are on FC/DWA.[164] If your income, but for the childcare allowance, would be too high to qualify for FC/DWA, any charges a local authority makes could be used to enable you to qualify. You should then be able to keep your FC/DWA throughout the 26-week period of the award even though, as soon as you are awarded it, the local authority will have to stop charging you. When your award expires, the local authority will be able to charge you again, and you can then claim again. If, however, you are also claiming HB/CTB, your HB/CTB award may be revised as soon as you no longer have to pay any childcare charges.
- The costs of any childcare provided by a relative or friend (other than your partner) may be allowed so long as s/he is a registered childminder.

4. OTHER INCOME

Most other types of income are taken into account less any tax due on them.[165] For HB/CTB, changes in tax and national insurance rates may be ignored for up to 30 weeks,[166] as for earnings (see p379).

Payments from Training for Work (TFW) and Youth Training (YT) schemes are for the most part taken into account.

All income is converted into a weekly amount (see p375). For IS, this amount is attributed to a forward period (see p377) and affects the benefit payable for that period.

For FC/DWA/HB/CTB, a past period is used where possible to assess normal weekly income, and this figure is used to calculate benefit.

For HB/CTB, an estimate of income is made by looking at an appropriate period (not exceeding one year). The period chosen must give an accurate assessment of your income.[167]

For FC/DWA, your income during the 26 weeks immediately before the week of your claim will be used, unless a different period immediately before your claim would produce a more accurate assessment.[168]

Benefits

Benefits that count in full:

- contribution-based JSA;
- incapacity benefit and severe disablement allowance;
- except for FC/DWA, maternity allowance;
- invalid care allowance;
- widows' benefits (including industrial death benefit);
- retirement pensions;
- industrial injuries benefits (except constant attendance allowance and exceptionally severe disablement allowance);
- except for FC/DWA, child benefit;
- for IS only, guardian's allowance;
- child's special allowance and war orphan's pension;
- for IS, FC/DWA or earnings top-up (ETU). For HB/CTB, any additional FC/DWA/ETU paid because you, or your partner, are working 30 hours or more a week is ignored (see pp203 and 217). Otherwise, FC/DWA/ETU are taken into account;[169]
- for IS only,[170] statutory sick pay and statutory maternity pay – less any class 1 national insurance contributions and half of any pension contributions and any tax. For HB/CTB, statutory sick pay and statutory maternity pay are treated as earnings (see p379) and you may, therefore, benefit from an earnings disregard (see p386). For FC/

DWA, statutory sick pay is counted as earnings but statutory maternity pay is ignored (see p379).

Problems can arise where, for example, the Benefits Agency or local authority try to take into account a benefit you are not receiving, such as child benefit that has been delayed. In such a case, the benefit should not be treated as income possessed by you. For IS, you should get your full benefit and leave the Benefits Agency to deduct the difference from arrears of the delayed benefit when it is eventually awarded.[171]

For IS/FC/DWA/HB/CTB, arrears of all means-tested and some disability benefits should be treated as capital and ignored for 52 weeks (see p426).[172] This rule only applies to arrears of benefit which you actually receive. Therefore, for IS, it will only apply to arrears of benefit which are paid to you *after* the Benefits Agency has made any deductions because the award of the benefit was delayed.

Benefits that are ignored completely:

- attendance allowance (or constant attendance allowance, exceptionally severe disablement allowance or severe disablement occupational allowance paid because of an injury at work or a war injury) or any care component of disability living allowance. For IS only, it is taken into account in full up to a maximum of £51.30 a week if you went to live in a residential care or nursing home before 31 March 1993 and you are a person with preserved rights (see p93), or you are accommodated under The Polish Resettlement Act;[173]
- pensioner's Christmas bonus;[174]
- either of the mobility components of disability living allowance;[175]
- mobility supplement under the War Pensions Scheme;[176]
- any extra-statutory payment made to you to compensate for non-payment of IS, income-based JSA, mobility allowance, mobility supplement, attendance allowance or disability living allowance;[177]
- for FC, disability working allowance.[178] For DWA, family credit;[179]
- social fund payments.[180] For FC/DWA, they are not specifically disregarded, but they should not count as part of your 'normal weekly' income. For IS/FC/DWA/HB/CTB, social fund payments are disregarded as capital indefinitely;[181]
- except for DWA, resettlement benefit paid to certain patients who are discharged from hospital and who had been in hospital for more than a year before 11 April 1988;[182]
- any transitional payment made to compensate you for loss of benefit due to the changes in benefit rules in April 1988;[183]
- HB, CTB, community charge benefit and any community charge or council tax liability;[184]

- IS and income-based JSA are ignored for FC/DWA and HB/CTB.[185] There are special HB/CTB rules for IS/income-based JSA claimants (see pp221 and 332);
- certain special war widows' payments,[186] including any special or supplementary payments (currently £54.70) to pre-1973 war widows;[187]
- for FC/DWA/HB/CTB, guardian's allowance;[188]
- for FC/DWA, child benefit;[189]
- for FC/DWA, maternity allowance and statutory maternity pay;[190]
- for FC/DWA, any payment of ETU (see p210);[191]
- for HB/CTB, any additional payment of FC, DWA or ETU made because you or your partner (if any) are working for 30 hours or more a week;[192]
- any increase for adult or child dependants who are not members of your family (see p346), where you are getting incapacity benefit, maternity allowance, widowed mother's allowance, retirement pension, industrial injuries benefits (including unemployability supplement), invalid care allowance or a service pension.[193]

For the treatment of payments of arrears of benefits, see p426. For the treatment of payments of child maintenance bonuses, see p189, and back to work bonuses, p188.

Benefits that have £10 ignored:

- war disablement pension;
- war widow's pension;
- widow's pension payable to widows of members of the Royal Navy, Army or Royal Air Force;
- an extra-statutory payment made instead of the above pensions;
- similar payments made by another country;
- a pension from Germany or Austria paid to the victims of Nazi persecution.[194]

Only £10 in all can be ignored, even if you have more than one payment which attracts a £10 disregard.[195] However, the £10 disregard allowed on these war pensions is additional to the total disregard of any mobility supplement or attendance allowance (ie, constant attendance allowance, exceptionally severe disablement allowance and severe disablement occupational allowance) paid as part of a war disablement pension (see p396). The £10 disregard may, however, overlap with other disregards on student loans (see p400) and charitable or voluntary payments (see p402) when a combined maximum of £20 is allowed.

Local authorities are given a limited discretion to increase the £10 disregard on war disablement, war widows' pensions and the pension payable to widows of members of the Royal Navy, Army or Royal Air Force, when assessing income for HB/CTB.[196] Check your local authority's policy on this issue.

Maintenance payments

If you are claiming IS and receiving maintenance payments, or child support maintenance payments, from a former partner for yourself or any children, the rules on how this money is treated are considered on p120. Although most maintenance payments count in full as income while you are on IS, you should check to see whether you may be accruing an entitlement to a child maintenance bonus (see p189).

If you claim **FC/DWA** and regular amounts of maintenance payments, or child support maintenance payments, are being made at regular intervals (eg, weekly or monthly) before you claim, the normal weekly amount counts as income.[197] If any child support maintenance payments made are more than the amount due under a maintenance assessment, only the amount due under the assessment is taken into account. If maintenance payments are due to be paid regularly but are not being so, the average of the payments made in the 13 weeks up to the week of your claim counts as income. With child support maintenance payments not paid regularly, you take the average of the payments made over the last 13 weeks, or, if the maintenance assessed was notified to you within the last 13 weeks, over the period since the notification. However, if that average is more than the maintenance assessment, it is the assessment which is taken into account.[198] Payments are taken into account from the date they are received by you, not the date they are received into court or by the DSS (if appropriate).[199] Other payments of maintenance are treated as capital.[200] However, any payments made by the Secretary of State as compensation for a reduction in child support maintenance assessment are disregarded as income and (for 52 weeks) as capital.[201] Maintenance payments to or for a child in your family (see p353) should be treated as yours but only if the payments are actually made.

For **HB** and **CTB**, periodical payments should count as income and lump sums as capital. Maintenance paid to or for your dependent child counts as yours.[202]

If you are a lone parent, or a couple with a child, for FC/DWA, HB and CTB, £15 of any maintenance payment made by your former partner, or your partner's former partner, or the parent of any child in your family is disregarded. If you receive maintenance from more than one person, only £15 of the total is disregarded.[203]

If you *pay* maintenance to a former partner or a child not living with you, your payments are not disregarded for the purpose of calculating your income for IS/FC/DWA/HB/CTB.[204] Even if you are on IS you may still have to pay child support maintenance (see p110).

Grants to students

The term grant includes bursaries, scholarships and exhibitions as well as grants or awards from education authorities.[205] An educational award which is paid by way of a loan does not count as a grant for IS,[206] but is nevertheless taken into account as 'other income' (see p400). You are treated as having the parental or partner's contribution to your grant whether or not it has been paid to you. However, if you are a lone parent, a single foster parent or a disabled student, only the amount of any contribution that you actually receive counts for IS.[207] Grant income is taken into account for the academic year, excluding the summer vacation, unless the grant expressly covers a different period. In each case, it is divided equally over the weeks in the period.[208] In the case of a sandwich course, grant income is averaged out over the period of study excluding the periods of experience – ie, in industry or commerce.[209] Any grant income paid under the Education (Mandatory Awards) Regulations that is intended for the maintenance of a student's dependants or which is an allowance for mature students or lone parents[210] is spread over 52 or 53 weeks.[211] (Benefit weeks and academic years sometimes run to 53 weeks, including part-weeks.) However, for other grants the normal rule (period of study or period for which grant payable) applies. So where a student on a sandwich course received a grant from the Department of Health, the element for his dependants was spread over the period of study only.[212]

The following grant income is ignored:[213]

- a fixed amount of £287 or whatever you get in your grant towards the cost of books and equipment;
- a fixed amount for travelling expenses. Where you are in receipt of a mandatory grant, and living away from your parents' home, this will usually be £161. If you are living at your parents' home it will usually be £249. There is no additional disregard even if your actual travelling expenses are higher;[214]
- any allowance for tuition and examination fees;
- any allowance to meet extra expenses because you are a disabled student;
- any allowance to meet the cost of attending a residential course away from your normal student accommodation during term-time;
- any allowance for the costs of your normal home (away from college) but, for IS, only if your rent is not met by HB;

- any amount for a partner or children abroad is ignored for IS and HB/CTB, but not FC/DWA.

These disregards apply only to the maintenance grant you receive during the academic year, and not to any element for dependants you may receive during the summer vacation.[215]

General points about grant income

- If you receive any payments over and above your grant or top-up loan, to help you with certain expenses (see p399), and these payments are greater than the amounts for those expenses disregarded from your grant income, the excess amount is ignored.[216]
- If you have been required by your education authority to make a contribution to your own grant (eg, because you have other income such as maintenance or part-time earnings), an amount equivalent to that contribution is disregarded as income for IS/FC/DWA/HB/CTB.[217] In the case of a couple, the amount of any contribution that one member has been assessed to pay to her/his partner who is a student does not count as the non-student's income.[218]
- For HB only, if your eligible rent is subject to a flat-rate deduction (see p279), the same amount is disregarded from your income. If your income does not cover the deduction, the balance is ignored from your partner's income.[219]
- For IS only, if you either give up or are dismissed from your course before it finishes, any grant you have received will be taken account of as if you were still a student[220] until you either repay the grant or the academic term or vacation in which you ceased to be a student ends, or until the end of the period covered by the last instalment of your grant, whichever is the earlier.[221]

Student loans[222] under the statutory scheme are treated as income. Weekly income is calculated by dividing the loan over the 52 (or 53) weeks of the academic year. In the final year of the course, or for a one-year course, the loan is divided by the number of weeks from the start of the academic year to the end of the course – ie, the last day of the last term.[223]

There is a £10 disregard on loan income, but it may overlap with other disregards on income from certain war pensions (see p396) and charitable or voluntary payments (see p402). With charitable or voluntary payments, a combined maximum of £20 is allowed.[224]

If you give up your course before it finishes, your loan continues to be counted in the same way, but without any disregard, for each remaining benefit week covered by the loan period following the date you gave it up.[225]

If you fail to take reasonable steps to get a loan to which you are entitled, the maximum amount payable to you is counted as weekly income, calculated as if you actually received it.[226] This does not apply if you have given up your course early (see above), since you are no longer a 'student'.

Career development loans paid under section 2 of the Employment and Training Act 1973 are taken account of as income.[227] For IS, the weekly income is calculated by dividing the loan by the number of weeks of education and training which the loan was paid for.[228] However, for IS/FC/DWA/HB/CTB, this income is ignored – except where it was paid for and is used to meet the cost of food, clothing and footwear, household fuel, rent, mortgage interest charges, certain other accommodation charges, council tax and water charges.[229]

For IS only, any grant income, student loan or career development loan which you have left over at the end of your course is ignored.[230]

Access Fund payments[231] made to students by educational establishments to prevent hardship will be treated as voluntary or charitable payments (see below).

Loans to students from overseas are neither grants nor awards, but should be taken into account as income.[232]

Adoption, fostering and residence order (in Scotland custody) payments

An **adoption allowance** counts in full for IS/FC/DWA/HB/CTB up to the amount of the adopted child's personal allowance or credit and disabled child premium or allowance, if any. Above that level it is ignored completely.[233]

If the child has capital over £3,000, you are not entitled to any benefit for the child (see p416) and the entire adoption allowance is ignored.[234]

The way that a **fostering allowance** is treated depends on whether the arrangement is an official or a private one. If a child is placed or boarded out with you by the local authority or a voluntary organisation under specific legal provisions, any fostering allowances you receive are ignored altogether,[235] but you are not entitled to any benefit for the child (see p354).

If the fostering arrangement is a private one, any money you receive from the child's parent(s) is counted as maintenance (see p398). If the money you receive is not from the child's parent(s), you should probably be treated as a childminder (see p391).

If you are paid a **residence order allowance** (in Scotland, custody allowance) by the local authority, this is treated in the same way as an adoption allowance (see above).[236] Arrears of residence order (in Scotland, custody) allowances are treated as capital for IS.[237] Any payments made by the biological parents count as maintenance (see p398).

If the local authority makes a lump-sum payment to enable you to make adaptations to your home for a disabled child, this is treated as capital and ignored (see p422).[238]

Charitable and voluntary payments

Payments from the Macfarlane and similar trusts

Any payments, including payments in kind, from the Macfarlane Trust, the Macfarlane (Special Payments) Trust, the Macfarlane (Special Payments) (No. 2) Trust, the Fund, the Eileen Trust or either of the Independent Living Funds (see Appendix 1) are disregarded in full.[239]

The Macfarlane Trusts make payments to haemophiliacs. The Fund was set up on 24 April 1992 for people who are not haemophiliacs who have contracted HIV through blood or tissue transfusions.

If you are, or were, a haemophiliac, or have received a payment from the Fund or the Eileen Trust, the following payments from money that originally came from any of the three Macfarlane Trusts, the Fund or the Eileen Trust are also disregarded in full:[240]

- any payment made by you, or on your behalf, to, or for the benefit of:
  - your partner, or former partner from whom you are not estranged or divorced;
  - any child (see p353) who is a member of your family, or who was but is now a member of another family; *or*
- if you have no partner or former partner (other than one from whom you are estranged or divorced), or children, any payment made by you (or from your estate in the event of your death) to:
  - your parent or step-parent; *or*
  - your guardian if you have no parent or step-parent and were a child (see p353) or student at the date of the payment (or at the date of your death).

  In the case of a payment to a parent, step-parent or guardian, this is only disregarded until two years after your death;
- any payment made by your partner, or former partner from whom you are not estranged or divorced, or on her/his behalf, to, or for the benefit of:
  - you;
  - any child who is a member of your family, or who was and is now a member of another family.

Any income or capital that derives from any such payment is also disregarded.

Other payments

Most other charitable or voluntary payments that are made irregularly and are intended to be made irregularly are treated as capital and are unlikely to affect your claim unless they take your capital above the limit.[241] However, if you are on IS it will count as income:

- if you are involved in a trade dispute and for the first 15 days following your return to work after a dispute (see p61);[242] *or*
- where payments made to a child's boarding school are treated as the child's notional income (see p374).[243]

Charitable or voluntary payments made, or due to be made regularly, are completely ignored if:[244]

- for IS/HB/CTB, they are intended, and used, for anything *except* food, ordinary clothing or footwear, household fuel, council tax, water rates and rent (less any non-dependant deductions) for which HB is payable; and, for IS only, housing costs met by IS and residential care or nursing home accommodation charges for people with preserved rights (see p93) met by IS or by a local authority. Where you do not have a preserved right (see p93) and the local authority has placed you in a residential care or nursing home that is more expensive than normal for a person of your needs because you preferred that home, a charitable or voluntary payment towards the *extra* cost will be ignored for IS;[245]
- for FC/DWA, they are intended, and used, for anything *except* food, ordinary clothing or footwear, household fuel, council tax and any housing costs.

School uniform and sportswear are examples of clothing and footwear that is not ordinary.

If not ignored altogether, charitable or voluntary payments have a £20 disregard, although this disregard may overlap with other disregards for certain war pensions (see p396) or student loans (see p400) when a combined maximum of £20 is allowed.[246] Note that this is a weekly disregard so payments spread over different or successive benefit weeks will attract a £20 disregard for each.

For HB/CTB, discretionary grants to Canadian war veterans or their widows settled in the UK should also be treated as voluntary payments and attract a £20 disregard.[247] It is arguable that this disregard should also apply to IS/FC and DWA and to any other discretionary grants paid to any other overseas war veterans (or their widows) who are settled in the UK.

For IS, these rules do not apply where you are involved in a trade dispute, and for the first 15 days following your return to work after a trade dispute. For IS/FC/DWA/HB/CTB, payments from a former partner, or the parent of your child, are dealt with as maintenance (see p398).

See also, payments made to someone else on your behalf, p413, and payments disregarded under miscellaneous income, p408.

Concessionary coal or cash in lieu

Coal that is provided free by British Coal to a former employee or widow is ignored as income in kind (for IS, if you or your partner are involved in a trade dispute, see p61).[248] Cash in lieu of coal is not a voluntary payment[249] but counts in full as income, or as earnings if paid to a current employee.[250]

Income from tenants and lodgers

Lettings without board

If you let out room(s) in your home to tenants/sub-tenants/licensees under a formal contractual arrangement, £4 of your weekly charge for each tenant/sub-tenant/licensee (and her/his family) is ignored, and an extra £9.25 if the charge covers heating costs.[251] The balance counts as income.

If someone shares your home under an informal arrangement, any payment made by them to you for their living and accommodation costs is ignored,[252] but a non-dependant deduction may be made (see p39).

Boarders

If you have a boarder(s) on a commercial basis in your own home, and the boarder or any member of her/his family is not a close relative of yours, the first £20 of the weekly charge is ignored and half of any balance remaining is then taken into account as your income.[253] (With HB/CTB, there is no specific reference to non-commercial arrangements or close relatives, but the rules on contrived tenancies could possibly apply – see p234.) This applies for each boarder you have. The charge must normally include at least some meals.[254]

Note: Whether you let part of your home to a tenant/sub-tenant/licensee or to a boarder, any income left after applying the above disregards may be considered to be intended to be used to meet any housing costs of your own which are not met by IS or HB, and may also therefore be offset accordingly.[255]

Tenants in other properties

If you have a freehold interest in a property other than your home and you let it out, the rent is treated as capital.[256] This rule will also apply if you have a leasehold interest in another property which you are sub-letting. There is disagreement between commissioners as to whether it is the gross rent which should be taken into account, or only the sum left after deducting expenses.[257]

Income from capital

In general, actual income generated from capital (eg, interest on savings) is ignored as income[258] but counts as *capital*[259] from the date you are due to receive it. However, income derived from the following categories of disregarded capital (see p421) is treated as income:[260]

- your home;
- your former home if you are estranged or divorced;
- property which you have acquired for occupation as your home but which you have not yet been able to move into;
- property which you intend to occupy as your home but which needs essential repairs or alterations;
- property occupied wholly or partly by a partner or relative of any member of your family who is 60 or over or incapacitated;
- property occupied by your former partner, but not if you are estranged or divorced (unless – for HB/CTB only – s/he is a lone parent);
- property up for sale;
- property which you are taking legal steps to obtain to occupy as your home;
- your business assets;
- a trust of personal injury compensation.

Income from any of the above categories (other than your current home, business assets or a personal injuries trust) is ignored up to the amount of the total mortgage repayments (ie, capital and interest, and any payments that are a condition of the mortgage such as insurance or an endowment policy),[261] council tax and water rates paid in respect of the property for the same period over which the income is received.[262]

Tariff income from capital over £3,000[263]

If your capital is over £3,000, you are treated as having an assumed income from it, called your tariff income. You are assumed to have an income of £1 for every £250, or part of £250, by which your capital exceeds £3,000 but does not exceed £8,000 (IS/FC) or £16,000 (DWA/

HB/CTB). **Note:** For IS/HB, if you are in residential care or similar accommodation (see p87), tariff income applies between £10,000 and £16,000.

If you are underpaid because of a reduction in your capital affecting your tariff income, you should ask for a review (see p139 for IS, p319 for HB and p322 for CTB). You should report any increase in your capital to the Benefits Agency for IS,[264] and to the local authority for HB/CTB, except where the increase does not stop you getting some IS.[265] If there is a change in your capital which increases the amount of your tariff income and as a result of which you are overpaid, see p156 for IS, p300 for HB and p341 for CTB on recovery of overpayments. For FC/DWA, any increase or reduction in the amount of your capital during the period of your award will not affect your entitlement (see pp209 and 222) and you will not need to notify the Benefits Agency unless or until you renew your claim.

Capital which counts as income

- Instalments of capital outstanding when you claim benefit if they would bring you over whichever capital limit is applicable. For IS, the instalments to be counted are any outstanding either when your benefit claim is decided, or when you are first due to be paid benefit, whichever is earlier, or at the date of any subsequent review.[266] For FC/DWA it is any instalments outstanding at the date of your claim.[267] For HB/CTB it is any instalments outstanding when your claim is made or treated as made, or when your benefit is reviewed.[268] Any balance over the capital limit will be counted as income, by spreading it over the number of weeks between each instalment.[269] Note that for IS, there are two capital limits of £8,000 and £16,000 (see pp415-17).

  If instalments are outstanding in this way on your child's capital, a similar rule applies. If the total of these instalments and your child's existing savings come to more than £3,000, the outstanding instalments should count as your child's income,[270] and be spread over the period between each instalment.[271]
- Any payment from an annuity[272] (see p408 for when this is disregarded).
- Any career development loan paid under section 2 of the Employment and Training Act 1973[273] (see p401 for how such loans are treated).
- For IS only, any educational maintenance grant paid to you as a student if you leave the course before the end of the period for which the grant has been paid (see p400).
- For IS, a tax refund if you or your partner have returned to work after a trade dispute (see p61).[274]

- For IS, a payment from a social services department under sections 17 and 24 of the Children Act 1989 or, in Scotland, a payment from a social work department under sections 12, 24 and 26 of the Social Work (Scotland) Act 1968 (see Appendix 1) – ie, payments from social services to assist children in need or young people who have previously been in care or been looked after by them, if you or your partner are involved in or have returned to work after a trade dispute (see p61).[275]
- For HB/CTB, a local authority will sometimes treat withdrawals from a capital sum as income.[276] This is most likely where a sum was intended to help cover living expenses over a particular period – eg, a bank loan taken out by a mature student. If this is not the intended use of any capital sum, you should dispute the decision. Even where the sum is intended for living expenses, you should argue that unless it is actually paid in instalments it should be treated as capital.[277]

   Any payments of capital, or any irregular withdrawals from a capital sum, which are clearly for one-off items of expenditure and not regular living expenses, should be treated as capital. Further, whatever the intention behind the sum, if no withdrawals are in fact made, it should be treated as capital.[278]
- Some lump sums from liable relatives (see p120).

Capital which is counted as income cannot also be treated as producing a tariff income (see p405).[279]

Income tax refunds

PAYE income tax refunds are not payable to unemployed people receiving jobseeker's allowance (JSA) or IS until the end of the tax year, or until they obtain a job, whichever comes first. Strikers can only get a tax refund on return to work. Other people who are not entitled to JSA or IS can still get tax refunds when they fall due.

- PAYE refunds (employed earners) and tax refunds under schedule D (self-employed) are treated as capital.[280]
- For IS only, if you or your partner have returned to work after a trade dispute (see p61), tax refunds will be treated as income and are taken into account in full.[281]

For treatment of income tax refunds on mortgage interest or loans for repairs and improvements, see below.

Miscellaneous income

The following are counted in full:

- An occupational pension, income from a personal pension or retirement annuity contract (except any discretionary payment from a hardship fund and, for IS, half of a pension or retirement annuity contract in some residential care situations where at least half of it is for your spouse).[282]
- Payments from an annuity. *Except* that in the case of 'home income plans', income from the annuity equal to the interest payable on the loan with which the annuity was bought is ignored if the following conditions are met:
  - you used at least 90 per cent of the loan made to you to buy the annuity; *and*
  - the annuity will end when you and your partner die; *and*
  - you or your partner are responsible for paying the interest on the loan; *and*
  - you, or both your partner and yourself, were at least 65 at the time the loan was made; *and*
  - the loan is secured on a property which you or your partner owns or has an interest in, and the property on which the loan is secured is your home, or that of your partner.

If the interest on the loan is payable after income tax has been deducted, it is an amount equal to the net interest payment that will be disregarded, otherwise it is the gross amount of the interest payment.[283]

The following are ignored:

- For IS only, payments you receive under a mortgage protection policy which you took out, and which you use, to pay the housing costs which are not being met by the Benefits Agency in your IS[284] (for restrictions on housing costs see p41). However, if the amount you receive exceeds the total of:
  - the interest you pay on a qualifying loan which is not met by the Benefits Agency;
  - capital repayments on a qualifying loan; *and*
  - any premiums you pay on the policy in question and any building insurance policy;
  then the excess is counted as your income.

- For IS only, and as long as you have not already used insurance payments for the same purpose, *any* money *you* receive which is given, and which *you* use to make:[285]
  - payments under a secured loan which do not qualify under the housing costs rules;
  - interest payments which are not met under the housing costs rules, even though some interest payments under the loan in question are met;
  - capital repayments on a qualifying loan;
  - payments of premiums on an insurance policy which you took out to insure against the risk of not being able to make the payments in the above three categories, and premiums on a building insurance policy;
  - any rent that is not covered by HB (see Chapter 12);
  - the part of your accommodation charge that is above the maximum payable by IS if you live in a nursing home or residential care home and you are a person with preserved rights (see p93) or above that payable by a local authority.
- For FC/DWA, compensation for a reduced child support maintenance assessment.[286]
- For HB/CTB, payments you receive under a mortgage protection policy are ignored up to the level of your repayments.[287]
- Educational maintenance allowances paid by local authorities or (in Scotland) the Board of Management of Colleges (see Appendix 1).[288]
- Any payment to cover expenses if you are working as a volunteer.[289]
- Payments in kind (unless, for IS, you or your partner are involved in a trade dispute, see p61).[290] These may include food, fuel, cigarettes[291], clothing, holidays, gifts, accommodation, transport[292], or nursery education vouchers[293] (but see p411 for the rules on notional income).
- For FC/DWA, a Jobmatch allowance paid under the Employment and Training Act 1973 if the payments are before your award begins.[294]
- A payment (other than a training allowance) to a disabled person under the Employment and Training Act 1973 or the Disabled Persons (Employment) Act 1944 to assist them to obtain or retain employment.[295]
- If you are participating in arrangements for training under section 2 of the Employment and Training Act 1973 or, in Scotland, section 2 of the Enterprise and New Towns (Scotland) Act 1990 (or an employment rehabilitation course under the 1973 Act), certain travel expenses, living away from home expenses and training premiums[296], as well as, if you are participating in the New Deal (see p58), any childcare expenses[297] and any mandatory top-up payments or discretionary payments for special needs.[298]

- Any payments, other than for loss of earnings or of a benefit, made to jurors or witnesses for attending at court.[299]
- A payment from a social services department under sections 17 or 24 of the Children Act 1989, or, in Scotland, a payment from a social work department under sections 12, 24 or 26 of the Social Work (Scotland) Act 1968 (see Appendix 1) – ie, payments from social services to assist children in need or young people who have been in care or been looked after by them.[300] For IS, such payments are not ignored if you or your partner are involved in or have returned to work after a trade dispute (see p61).
- Any payments made under the Community Care (Direct Payments) Act 1996 or under section 12B of the Social Work (Scotland) Act 1968.[301]
- Any payment you receive for looking after a person temporarily in your care if it is paid under community care arrangements by a health authority, local authority, voluntary organisation or by the person being looked after.[302]
- Victoria Cross or George Cross payments or similar awards.[303]
- Income paid outside the UK which cannot be transferred here.[304]
- If income is paid in another currency, any bank charges for converting the payment into sterling.[305]
- Fares to hospital.[306]
- Payments instead of milk tokens and vitamins.[307]
- Payments to assist prison visits.[308]
- For HB/CTB, if you make a parental contribution to a student's grant, an equal amount of any 'unearned' income you have for the period the grant is paid, is ignored.[309] If your 'unearned' income does not cover the contribution the balance can be disregarded from your earnings.[310] If you are a parent of a student under 25 who does not get a grant (or who only gets a smaller discretionary award) and you contribute to her/his living expenses, the amount of your 'unearned' income that is ignored is the amount equal to your contribution up to a maximum of £38.90 (less the weekly amount of any discretionary award the student has).[311] This is only ignored during the student's term. Again, any balance can be disregarded from your earnings.[312]

5. NOTIONAL INCOME

In certain circumstances you will be treated as having income although you do not possess it, or have used it up.

Deprivation of income in order to claim or increase benefit

If you deliberately get rid of income in order to claim or increase your benefit, you are treated as though you are still in receipt of the income.[313] The basic issues involved are the same as those for the deprivation of capital (see p428). Note that the rule can only apply if the purpose of the deprivation is to gain benefit for *yourself* (or your family); it should not apply if, for example, you stop claiming invalid care allowance solely so that another person (who is not a member of your family) can become entitled to the severe disability premium (see p367).[314] However, a deliberate decision to 'de-retire' and give up your retirement pension (in the expectation of achieving an overall increase in benefit in the future) can come within this rule.[315] For an explanation of de-retirement, see CPAG's *Rights Guide to Non-Means-Tested Benefits*.

Failing to apply for income[316]

If you fail to apply for income to which you are entitled without having to fulfil further conditions, you will be deemed to have received it from the date you could have obtained it.

This does not include income from:

- a discretionary trust; *or*
- a trust set up from money paid as a result of a personal injury; *or*
- funds administered by a court as a result of a personal injury; *or*
- the death of a parent of someone under 18; *or*
- an Employment Service Rehabilitation Allowance; *or*
- where you are under 60, a personal pension scheme or retirement annuity. However, if you are 60 or over, you will be treated as receiving income in certain circumstances if you fail to purchase an annuity.[317]

For IS only, the lone parent element of child benefit, jobseeker's allowance, FC, DWA and ETU are also exempted.

For other income or benefits it must still be certain that it would be paid upon application. It may therefore be difficult to establish that there is 'no doubt' that invalid care allowance, for example, would be paid to a carer who does not wish to claim it because of the effect on another person's severe disability premium (see p367).[318]

Previously, DSS guidance for HB/CTB said that FC (and presumably other benefits as well) should not count as notional income if you might be entitled but had not applied for it, although local authorities should notify the Family Credit Unit where it appeared to them a successful claim could be made. It also said that if you applied for FC/DWA but had not yet been paid, it did not count as income or notional income and should be ignored until you actually received it. Current guidance does not deal with these points, but you should argue that the same still applies.

Any such income must also be available to *you* (or your family) *for your own benefit*. It has been held, for example, that income could not be attributed to the leaseholder of a shop he was forced to sublet to tenants in order to meet his liabilities to the landlord. Although their rents were technically available to him, they were immediately passed on to the landlord so no profit was ever available.[319]

Income due to you that has not been paid

This applies to IS only.[320] You will be treated as possessing any income owing to you. Examples could be wages legally due but not paid, or an occupational pension payment that is due but has not been received. However, this does not apply where an occupational pension has not been paid, or fully paid, because the pension scheme has insufficient funds.[321] The rule also does not apply if any social security benefit has been delayed, or you are waiting for a late payment of a pension under the Job Release Scheme, a government training allowance or a benefit from an EEA country. Nor does it apply in the case of money due to you from a discretionary trust, or a trust set up from money paid as a result of a personal injury.

As above, the income must be due to *you* (or your family) and *for your own benefit*.[322]

If this rule is applied, an urgent cases payment should be considered (see p85).[323]

Unpaid wages

This applies to IS only. If you have wages due to you, but you do not yet know the exact amount or you have no proof of what they will be, you are treated as having a wage similar to that normally paid for that type of work in that area.[324] If your wages cannot be estimated you might qualify for an interim payment[325] (see p145).

Income payments made to someone else on your behalf [326]

If money is paid to someone on your behalf (eg, the landlord for your rent) this can count as notional income. The rules are the same as for notional capital (see p433). For IS, payments of income in kind are ignored, unless you or your partner are involved in a trade dispute, but even then they are ignored if they are from the Macfarlane Trusts, the Fund, the Eileen Trust or either of the Independent Living Funds (see Appendix 1) or in the form of concessionary coal under the Coal Industry Act 1994. [327]

Income payments paid to you for someone else [328]

If you or a member of your family get a payment for somebody not in the 'family' (see p346) (eg, a relative living with you) it will count as your income if you keep any of it yourself or spend it on your family. This does not apply if the payment is from the Macfarlane Trusts, the Fund, the Eileen Trust or either of the Independent Living Funds or in the form of concessionary coal under the Coal Industry Act 1994, or if the payment is a mandatory or discretionary grant for participating in an employment or training programme under the New Deal (see p58). Note that the same exception for payments in kind applies for IS as for income payments made to someone else on your behalf.

Cheap or unpaid labour

If you are helping another person or an organisation by doing work of a kind which would normally command a wage, or a higher wage, you are deemed to receive a wage similar to that normally paid for that kind of job in that area. [329] The burden of proving that the kind of work you do is something for which an employer would pay, and what the comparable wages are, lies with the adjudicating authority. [330]

The rule does not apply if:

either   you can show that the person ('person' in this context includes a limited company [331]) cannot, in fact, afford to pay, or pay more;

or   you work for a charitable or voluntary organisation or as a volunteer, and it is accepted that it is reasonable for you to give your services free of charge, or where your services are provided because you are participating in an employment or training programme under the New Deal (see p58). [332] A 'volunteer' in this context is someone who, without any legal obligation, performs a service for another person without expecting payment. [333]

It has been held that even if you are caring for a sick or disabled relative or another person, it may be reasonable for them to pay you from their benefits, unless you can bring yourself within these exceptions.[334] It may, for example, be more reasonable for a close relative to provide services free of charge out of a sense of family duty,[335] particularly if a charge would otherwise break up a relationship.[336] Whether it is reasonable to provide care free of charge will depend on the basis on which the arrangement is made, the expectations of the family members concerned, the housing arrangements and the reasons (if appropriate) why a carer gave up any paid work. The risk of a carer losing entitlement to invalid care allowance if a charge were made should also be considered[337] as should the likelihood that a relative being looked after would no longer be able to contribute to the household expenses.[338] If there is no realistic alternative to the carer providing services free to a relative who simply will not pay, this may also make it reasonable not to charge.[339] It may also be worth arguing that carers should not charge because they will otherwise lose their statutory right to an assessment of their needs by social services.[340]

Sometimes it may also be reasonable to do a job for free out of a sense of community duty, particularly if the job would otherwise have remained undone, and there would be no financial profit to an employer.[341]

Reducing the number of hours you work

For FC only, if you deliberately choose to reduce the number of hours you work in order to be able to claim or increase your entitlement to FC, any period of reduced hours will be ignored when assessing your normal weekly earnings.[342]

CHAPTER TWENTY

Capital

This chapter covers:
1. Introduction (below)
2. What counts as capital (p417)
3. Disregarded capital (p421)
4. Notional capital (p428)
5. How capital is valued (p435)

1. INTRODUCTION

The capital limit

This chapter explains how capital affects your entitlement to income support (IS), family credit (FC), disability working allowance (DWA), housing benefit (HB) and council tax benefit (CTB). If you get IS, you do not need to work out your capital again for HB/CTB purposes because you receive your maximum HB (see p264) or CTB (see p332),[1] less any deductions for non-dependants.

If you have over £8,000 (IS and FC)[2] or £16,000 (DWA, HB and CTB)[3] you are not entitled to benefit (but for CTB, see p335 for second adult rebate). Some capital is disregarded (see p421), but you may also be treated as having some capital which you do not actually possess (see p428). If you have up to £3,000, it is ignored and does not affect your weekly benefit at all. If you have between £3,000.01 and £8,000 (IS and FC)/£16,000 (DWA, HB and CTB), you may be entitled to benefit but some income will be assumed.[4] This is known as tariff income (see p405).

There are some important differences in the rules on capital for urgent cases payments under the income support scheme (see pp49-52).

Residential care

There are higher capital limits for people in residential or similar accommodation.

For IS[5] the higher limits apply if you live permanently in:

- residential care or a nursing home and in either case you are given board and personal care because of:
  - old age;
  - disablement;
  - past or present dependence on alcohol or drugs; *or*
  - past or present mental disorder;
- residential accommodation. For what is meant by residential accommodation see p95, but note that for the higher capital rules the exceptions for people under 18 or for people not receiving board do not apply;
- Abbeyfield Society homes; *or*
- a home provided under the Polish Resettlement Act in which you are receiving personal care because of:
  - old age;
  - disablement;
  - past or present dependence on alcohol or drugs;
  - past or present mental disorder; *or*
  - a terminal illness.

Note that you are treated as living permanently in one of these homes for periods of absence of up to 13 weeks. However, if you are over pensionable age or (in some cases) were getting supplementary benefit as a residential care home boarder before 27 July 1987, it can be up to 52 weeks.

For HB[6] the higher limits apply, broadly speaking, if you live permanently in one of the limited categories of accommodation referred to on p247. Some temporary absences (see p92) are again ignored.

For both IS and HB, tariff income starts at £10,000 (instead of £3,000) and the upper limit is £16,000 (for HB that is the limit for other claimants too).

Whose capital counts

Your partner's capital is added to yours.[7] Your child's capital does not count as belonging to you,[8] but if it is over £3,000 you will not get benefit for that child[9] (although, for IS/HB/CTB, the ordinary or lone parent rate of the family premium is still payable – see p361), in which case any income of the child will not be counted as yours either.[10]

However, maintenance paid to, or for, a child does count as yours.[11] The rules used to work out your child's capital also apply to you.[12]

2. WHAT COUNTS AS CAPITAL

The term 'capital' is not defined. In general, it means lump-sum or one-off payments rather than a series of payments.[13] It includes, for example, savings, property and redundancy payments. It also includes any payments of child maintenance bonus[14] (see p189) or back to work bonus[15] (see p188).

Capital payments can normally be distinguished from income because they are not payable in respect of any specified period or periods, and they do not form nor are intended to form part of a regular series of payments[16] (although capital can be paid by instalments).

However, some capital is treated as income (see p406), and some income is treated as capital (see p420).

Savings

Your savings generally count as capital – eg, cash you have at home, premium bonds, stocks and shares, unit trusts, and money in a bank account or building society.

Your savings from past earnings can only be treated as capital when all relevant debts, including tax liabilities, have been deducted.[17] Savings from other past income (including social security benefits) will be treated as capital (see p426). There is no provision for disregarding money put aside to pay bills.[18] If you have savings just below the capital limit, it may be best to pay bills for gas, electricity, telephone etc by monthly standing order, or by use of a budget account, to prevent your capital going above the limit.

Fixed-term investments

Capital held in fixed-term investments counts. However, if in reality it is presently unobtainable, it may have little or no value (but see p436 for jointly held capital). If you can convert the investment into a realisable form, sell your interest, or raise a loan through a reputable bank using the asset as security, its value counts. If it takes time to produce evidence about the nature and value of the investment, you may be able to get an interim payment for IS, FC or DWA (see p145) or HB[19] (see p294) or a crisis loan from the social fund (see p479).

Property and land

Any property or land which you own counts as capital. Many types of property are disregarded (see p421). See also proprietary estoppel – p419.

Loans

A loan usually counts as money you possess. However, a loan granted on condition that you only use the interest but do not touch the capital should not be counted as part of your capital because the capital element has never been at your disposal.[20] Where you have been paid money to be used for a particular purpose on condition that the money must be returned if not used in that way, it should not be treated as part of your capital.[21] Where you have bought a property on behalf of someone else who is paying the mortgage,[22] or where you are holding money in your bank account on behalf of another person which is to be returned to them at a future date,[23] the capital should not count as yours.

For HB/CTB some loans might be treated as income even though paid as a lump sum (see p407).

Trusts

A trust is a way of owning an asset. In theory, the asset is split into two notional parts: the legal title owned by the trustee, and the beneficial interest owned by the beneficiary. A trustee can never have use of the asset, only the responsibility of looking after it. An adult beneficiary, on the other hand, can ask for the asset at any time. Anything can be held on trust – eg, money, houses, shares etc.

If you are the adult beneficiary of:

- a non-discretionary trust, you can obtain the asset from the trustee at any time. You effectively own the asset, and so its market value will count as your capital;
- a discretionary trust, you cannot insist on receiving payments from the trust. Payments are at the discretion of the trustee within the terms of the trust. Any payments made will be treated in full as income or capital depending on the nature of the payment. The trust asset itself would not normally count as your capital because you cannot demand payment (of either capital or income);
- a trust which gives you the right to receive payments in the future (eg, on reaching 25), this is a right that has a present capital value, unless disregarded (see p425).

If you have a life interest only in an asset, the value of your right to receive income is disregarded[24] (see p425), but not the income itself if you get any.

If the beneficiary is under 18, even with a non-discretionary trust, s/he has no right to payment until s/he is 18 (or later if that is what the trust stipulates). Her/his interest may nevertheless have a present value.[25]

If you hold an asset as a trustee, it is not part of your capital. You are only a trustee either if someone gives you an asset on the express condition that you hold it for someone else (or use it for their benefit), or if you have expressed the clearest intention that your own asset is for someone else's benefit, and renounced its use for yourself[26] (assets other than money may need to be transferred in a particular way to the trust).

It is not enough to only *intend* to give someone an asset. However, in the case of property and land, proprietary estoppel may apply. This means that if you lead someone to believe that you are transferring your interest in some property to them, but fail to do so (eg, it is never properly conveyed), and they act on the belief that they have ownership (eg, they improve or repair it, or take on a mortgage), it would then be unfair on them were they to lose out if you insisted that you were still the owner.[27] In this case, you can argue the capital asset has been transferred to them, and you are like a trustee. Thus you can insist that it is not your capital asset, but theirs, when claiming benefit.

If money (or another asset) is given to you to be used for a special purpose, it may be possible to argue that it should not count as your capital. This is called a purpose trust[28] (see also p418).

Trust funds from personal injury compensation

Where a trust fund has been set up out of money paid because of a personal injury, the value of the trust fund is ignored.[29] Although the regulations refer to 'personal injury to the claimant' only, in practice the capital value of the trust fund is ignored regardless of whether the money was paid in respect of you, your partner (if any), or your children.

It is not necessary for the trust to be set up by a formal deed. For these purposes, personal injuries compensation held by the Court of Protection (because the injured person is incapable of managing her/his own affairs) and administered by that Court and/or the Public Trustee will be treated in the same way as a trust.[30] The important point is that the person who is awarded the compensation should not be able to have any direct access to it.

In this context, 'personal injury' includes not only accidental and criminal injuries, but also any disease and injury suffered as a result of a disease. Thus, a trust fund for a child who had both legs amputated following meningitis and septicaemia could be disregarded for the purposes of the parent's claim.[31]

Any payments actually made to you from these trusts may count in full as income or capital depending on the nature of the payment.[32] However, trustees may have a discretion to use such funds to purchase items that would normally be disregarded as capital such as personal possessions (see p424) – eg, a wheelchair, car, new furniture – or to arrange payments that would normally be disregarded as income – eg, for IS/HB/CTB, ineligible housing costs. Similarly, they may have discretion to clear debts or pay for a holiday, leisure items or educational or medical needs. See p402 for the treatment of voluntary payments and pp413 and 433-34 for the treatment of payments made to third parties. Note that the notional income and capital rules (see pp411 and 428) cannot apply to trusts or funds administered by the court which, in either case, have been set up as a result of a personal injury.

If there is no trust, or until one can be set up, the whole of the compensation payment counts as capital, even if the money is held by your solicitor.[33]

Infant funds in court[34]

Where damages are awarded to minors (ie, under the age of 18) in respect of personal injury or compensation for the death of one or both parents, the money may be paid into a special fund to be administered by, and at the discretion of, the court. The same rules on capital disregards, notional income, and treatment of payments apply to these funds as to other funds from personal injuries administered by the court (see p419).

Income treated as capital

Certain payments which appear to be income are nevertheless treated as capital. These are:[35]

- an advance of earnings or loan from your employer;*
- holiday pay which is not payable until more than four weeks after your employment ends or is interrupted;*
- income tax refunds;*
- income from capital (eg, interest on a building society account) and income from rents on properties let to tenants (see pp404 and 425). However, income from disregarded property listed on p421 (eg, a home you are trying to move into or sell, or which is occupied by elderly relatives) and income from business assets or personal injury trusts counts as income not capital;

- for IS/HB/CTB, a lump sum or 'bounty' paid to you not more than once a year as a part-time firefighter or part-time member of a lifeboat crew, or as an auxiliary coastguard or member of the Territorial Army – for FC/DWA this will normally count as earnings;[36]
- irregular (one-off) charitable payments;*
- for IS only, the part, or the whole, of a compensation payment for loss of employment that is treated as capital under the IS rules (see p385);
- for IS only, a discharge grant paid on release from prison;
- for IS only, arrears of residence order (in Scotland, custody) payments from a local authority (see p401);
- for FC/DWA only, irregular maintenance payments (see p398).[37]

*Except, for IS, in the case of people involved in, or returning to work after, a trade dispute (see p61).

Any income treated as capital is disregarded as income.[38]

3. DISREGARDED CAPITAL

Your home

If you own the home you normally live in, its value is ignored.[39] Your home includes any garage, garden, outbuildings and land, together with any premises that you do not occupy as your home but which it is impractical or unreasonable to sell separately – eg, croft land.[40] If you own more than one property, only the value of the one normally occupied is disregarded under this rule.[41]

The value of property can be disregarded even if you do not live in it, in the following circumstances.

- **If you have left your former home following a marriage or relationship breakdown,** the value of the property is ignored for six months from the date you left. It may also be disregarded for longer if any of the steps below are taken. For HB/CTB, if it is occupied by your former partner who is a lone parent its value is ignored as long as s/he lives there.[42]
- **If you have sought legal advice or have started legal proceedings in order to occupy property** as your home, its value is ignored for six months from the date you first took either of these steps.[43] The six months can be extended, if it is reasonable to do so, where you need longer to move into the property.
- **If you are taking reasonable steps to dispose of any property,** its value is ignored for six months from the date you *first* took such steps.[44] This may include a period before you claimed benefit.[45] The

definition of 'property' here includes land on its own, without any buildings on it.[46] Putting the property in the hands of an estate agent or getting in touch with a prospective purchaser should constitute 'reasonable steps'.[47] The test for what constitutes 'reasonable steps' is an objective one. Any period when the house is advertised at an unrealistic sale price would not count.[48] But if you need longer to dispose of the property, the disregard can continue for years if it is reasonable – eg, where a husband or wife attempts to realise their share in a former matrimonial home but the court orders that it should not be sold until the youngest child reaches a certain age.

- **If you are carrying out essential repairs or alterations** which are needed so that you can occupy a property as your home, for IS/FC/ DWA/HB/CTB the value of the property is ignored for six months from the date you first began to carry them out.[49] If you cannot move into the property within that period because the work is not finished, its value can be disregarded for as long as is reasonable.

- **If you sell your home** and intend to use the money from the sale to buy another home, the capital is ignored for six months from the date of the sale.[50] This also applies even if you do not actually own the home but, for a price, you surrender your tenancy rights to a landlord.[51] If you need longer to complete a purchase, the authorities can continue to ignore the capital if it is reasonable to do so. You do not have to have decided within the six months to buy a *particular* property. It is sufficient if you intend to use the proceeds to buy *some* other home although your 'intention' must involve more than a mere 'hope' or 'aspiration'.[52] There must be an element of 'certainty' which may be shown by evidence of a practical commitment to another purchase, although this need not involve any binding obligation.[53] If you intend to use only part of the proceeds of sale to buy another home, only that part is disregarded even if, for example, you have put the rest of the money aside to renovate your new home.[54]

- **If you have acquired a house or flat for occupation** as your home but have not yet moved in, its value is ignored if you intend to live there within six months.[55] If you cannot move in by then the value of the property can be ignored for as long as seems reasonable.

- **If your home is damaged or you lose it altogether**, any payment, including compensation, which you intend to use for its repair, or for acquiring another home, is ignored for a period of six months, or longer if it is reasonable to do so.[56]

- **If you have taken out a loan or been given money for the express purpose of essential repairs and improvements** to your home, it is ignored for six months, or longer if it is reasonable to do so.[57] If it is a condition of the loan that the loan must be returned if the improvements are not carried out, you should argue that it should be ignored altogether.[58]

- **If you have deposited money with a housing association as a condition of occupying your home,** this is ignored indefinitely.[59] If money which was deposited for this purpose is now to be used to buy another home, this is ignored for six months, or longer if reasonable, in order to allow you to complete the purchase.[60]
- **Grants made to local authority tenants to buy a home or do repairs/ alterations** to it can be ignored for up to 26 weeks, or longer if reasonable, to allow completion of the purchase or the repairs/ alterations.[61]

When considering whether to increase the period of any disregard, all the circumstances should be considered – particularly your and your family's personal circumstances, any efforts made by you to use or dispose of the home (if relevant) and the general state of the market (if relevant). In practice, periods of around 18 months are not considered unusual.

It is possible for property to be ignored under more than one of the above paragraphs in succession.[62]

Some income generated from property which is disregarded is ignored (see p405).

The home of a partner or relative

The value of a house will also be ignored if it is occupied wholly or partly as their home by:[63]

- *either* your partner[64] – ie, your husband/wife, provided you are both still treated as living in the same household (see p346) or your cohabitee, provided you are still treated as living together as husband and wife (see p348);
  or a relative of yours, or any member of your family;
  who in either case, is aged 60 or over or is incapacitated (see below);
- your former partner from whom you are not estranged or divorced. This means your husband/wife where you are not still treated as living in the same household or your former cohabitee where you are not still treated as living together as husband and wife;
- for HB/CTB only, your former partner from whom you are estranged or divorced if s/he is a lone parent.[65]

'Incapacitated' is not defined, but guidance for IS/FC/DWA/HB/CTB suggests it refers to someone who is getting an incapacity or disability benefit, or who is sufficiently incapacitated to qualify for one of those benefits.[66] However, you should argue for a broader interpretation, if necessary. For FC/DWA, the relative must have been incapacitated throughout the 13 weeks before you claim.[67]

Relative includes: a parent, son, daughter, step-parent/son/daughter, or parent/son/daughter-in-law; brother or sister; or a partner of any of these people; or a grandparent or grandchild, uncle, aunt, nephew or niece.[68] It also includes half-brothers and sisters and adopted children.[69]

Personal possessions

All personal possessions, including items such as jewellery, furniture or a car, are ignored unless you have bought them in order to be able to claim or get more benefit[70] (in which case the sale value, rather than the purchase price, is counted as actual capital, and the difference is treated as notional capital[71] - see p428).

Compensation for damage to, or the loss of, any personal possessions, which is to be used for their repair or replacement is ignored for six months, or longer if reasonable.[72]

Business assets

If you are self-employed, your business assets are ignored for as long as you continue to work in that business. For IS/FC/DWA, as little as half an hour's work a week may be sufficient.[73] If you cannot work because of physical or mental illness, but intend to work in the business when you are able, the disregard operates for 26 weeks, or for longer if reasonable in the circumstances.[74] If you stop working in the business, you are allowed a reasonable time to sell these assets without their value affecting your benefit. For FC/DWA, if you have sold a business asset but intend to reinvest the proceeds in that business within 13 weeks (or longer if reasonable) the money is ignored.[75] It will sometimes be difficult to distinguish between personal and business assets. The test is whether the assets are 'part of the fund employed and risked in the business'.[76] Note that letting out a single house does not constitute a business.[77]

Tax rebates

Tax rebates for the tax relief on interest on a mortgage or loan obtained for buying your home or carrying out repairs or improvements are ignored.[78]

Personal pension schemes and retirement annuity contracts

The value of a fund held under a personal pension scheme or retirement annuity is ignored.[79]

Insurance policy and annuity surrender values

The surrender value of any life assurance or endowment policy is ignored. Note that the life assurance aspect need not be the sole or even the main aspect of the policy (although the other features of any policy may still be considered under the actual or notional income and capital rules).[80] The surrender value of any annuity is also ignored.[81] Any payment under the annuity counts as income[82] (but see p408 for when this is ignored).

Personal injuries trust funds

The value of a trust fund or fund administered by the court and set up out of money paid because of personal injury is ignored (see p419).

Future interests in property

A future interest in most kinds of property is ignored. A future interest is one which will only revert to you, or become yours for the first time, when some future event occurs.[83]

However, this does not include a freehold or leasehold interest in property which has been let *by you* to tenants. If you did not let the property to the tenant (eg, because the tenancy was entered into before you bought the property), then your interest in the property should be ignored as a future interest in the normal way. In addition, a commissioner has recently suggested that if you grant someone an '*irrevocable* licence' to occupy property, your interest in that property is a future one and should be ignored.[84]

An example of a future interest is where someone else has a life interest in a fund and you are only entitled after that person has died.

The right to receive a payment in the future

If you know you will receive a payment in the future, you could sell your right to that payment at any time so it has a market value and therefore constitutes an actual capital resource. The value of this will be ignored where it is a right to receive:

- income under a life interest or, in Scotland, a liferent.[85] When the income is actually paid, it will count in full (see p405);
- any earnings or income which are ignored because they are frozen abroad (see pp380 and 410);[86]
- any outstanding instalments where capital is being paid by instalments (see p406);[87]
- an occupational or a personal pension;[88]
- any rent if you are not the freeholder or leaseholder;[89]
- any payment under an annuity (see p408);[90]
- any payment under a trust fund that is disregarded (see p418).[91]

Benefits and other payments

Arrears of certain benefits are ignored for 52 weeks after they are paid.[92] These are mobility allowance, attendance allowance (or, for FC/DWA only, an equivalent benefit paid because of a war or work injury), mobility supplement, disability living allowance, DWA, income-based jobseeker's allowance, IS, supplementary benefit, FC, earnings top-up, family income supplement, HB/CTB, or concessionary payments made instead of any of these, certain war widows' payments,[93] and refunds on community charge and council tax liability.[94]

For IS, any backdated payments of IS/HB/CTB made once the Home Office has accepted you are a refugee (see p78) are ignored for 52 weeks from the date of receipt.[95] The same rule also applies in relation to backdated payments of IS and HB (for HB)[96] and IS and CTB (for CTB)[97]. For special capital rules and urgent cases, see pp51-52.

For FC, DWA, HB and CTB only, any child maintenance bonus (see p189) or back to work bonus (see p188) is ignored for 52 weeks from the date you receive it.[98]

The following payments are ignored for 52 weeks from receipt:

- fares to hospital;[99]
- payments in place of milk tokens or vitamins;[100]
- payments to assist prison visits;[101]
- for FC/DWA only, payments made by the Secretary of State as compensation for a reduction in your child support maintenance assessment;[102]
- any mandatory top-up payments or discretionary payments for special needs for participating in the New Deal (see p58).[103]

Social fund payments are ignored indefinitely.[104]

A payment to a disabled person under the Disabled Persons (Employment) Act 1944 or the Employment and Training Act 1973 (other than a training allowance or training bonus) to assist with employment, or a local authority payment to assist blind homeworkers is ignored.[105]

Any payments made to holders of the Victoria or George Cross are ignored.[106]

Payments by social services

A payment under section 17 of the Children Act 1989 from a social services department or, in Scotland, a payment from a social work department under section 12 of the Social Work (Scotland) Act 1968 (see Appendix 1), is ignored. 'Section 24' (or, in Scotland, 'section 24 or 26') payments made by local authorities to young people who have previously been in care or been looked after by social services are also ignored. But if you or your partner are involved in a trade dispute or it is paid during the first 15 days following your return to work after the dispute, it counts as income for IS.[107]

Charitable payments

Any payment in kind by a charity is ignored.[108] All payments from the Macfarlane Trusts, the Fund, the Eileen Trust and either of the Independent Living Funds (see Appendix 1) are ignored.[109] Payments from the Macfarlane Trusts, the Fund or the Eileen Trust do not have to be declared for HB/CTB at all, or to the Benefits Agency, if they are kept separately from the claimant's other capital and income.[110] Certain payments from money that originally came from any of the three Macfarlane Trusts, the Fund or the Eileen Trust are also ignored – the rules are the same as for income (see p402).

Payments to jurors and witnesses

Any payments made to jurors or witnesses for attending at court are ignored, except for payments for loss of earnings or of benefit.[111]

Training bonus

A training bonus of up to £200 is ignored,[112] but only for a year for HB/CTB, FC and DWA. For IS only, this disregard does not apply to trainees in Scotland.

Payments in other currencies

Any payment in a currency other than sterling is taken into account after disregarding banking charges or commission payable on conversion to sterling.[113]

Capital treated as income

Some payments which appear to be capital are treated as income. See p405 for the detailed rules.

Any capital treated as income is ignored as capital.[114]

4. NOTIONAL CAPITAL

In certain circumstances, you are treated as having capital which you do not, in fact, possess. This is called 'notional capital' and it counts in the same way as capital you actually do possess.[115] There is a similar rule for notional income (see p411).

Deprivation of capital in order to claim or increase benefit

If you deliberately get rid of capital in order to claim or increase your benefit, you are treated as still possessing it.[116] You are likely to be affected by this rule if, at the time of using up your money, you know that you may qualify for benefit (or more benefit) as a result, or qualify more quickly. It should not be used if you know nothing about the effect of using up your capital (eg, you do not know about the capital limit for claiming benefit),[117] or if you have been using up your capital at a rate which is reasonable in the circumstances. Knowledge of capital limits can be inferred from a reasonable familiarity with the benefit system as a claimant,[118] but if you fail to make enquiries about the capital limit, this does not constitute an intention to secure benefit. This is because you cannot form the required intention if you do not know about the capital rules.[119]

Even if you do know about the capital limits, it still has to be shown that you intended to obtain, retain or increase your benefit.[120] For example, where a claimant, facing repossession of his home, transferred ownership to his daughter (who, he feared, would otherwise be made homeless), in spite of having been warned by Benefits Agency staff that he would be disqualified from benefit if he did so, it was held that, under the circumstances, he could not be said to have disposed of the property with the intention of gaining benefit.[121] The longer the period that has elapsed since the disposal of the capital, the less likely it will be that it was for the purpose of obtaining benefit.[122] However, no matter how long it has been since you may have disposed of an asset, there is no set 'safe' period after which it may be said that benefit can be claimed without the need for further enquiry.[123]

A person who uses up her/his resources may have more than one motive for doing so. Even where qualifying for benefit as a result is only a subsidiary motive for your actions, and the predominant motive is something quite different (eg, ensuring your home is in good condition by spending capital to do necessary repairs and improvements) you may still be counted as having deprived yourself of a resource in order to gain benefit.[124] Local authorities tend to apply this test less stringently in the case of HB and CTB. Examples of the kinds of expenditure that could be caught by the rule are an expensive holiday and putting money in trust. (For IS/FC/DWA, putting money in trust for yourself does not constitute deprivation if the capital being put in trust came from compensation paid for any personal injury.[125]) But the essential test is not the kind of item that the money has been spent on but the *intention* behind the expenditure.

If you pay off a debt which you are required by law to repay immediately, you will not be counted as having deprived yourself of money in order to gain benefit.[126] However, even if you pay off a debt which you are not required by law to repay immediately, it is still for the Benefits Agency (for IS/FC/DWA) or the local authority (for HB/CTB) to prove that you did so in order to get benefit.[127]

In practice, arguing successfully that you have not deprived yourself of capital to get or increase benefit may boil down to whether you can show that you would have spent the money in the way you did (eg, to pay off debts or reduce your mortgage), regardless of the effect on your benefit entitlement. Where this is unclear, the burden of proving that you did it in order to get benefit lies with the Benefits Agency (IS/FC/DWA) or local authority (HB/CTB). In one case a man lost over £60,000 speculating on the stock market. Due to his wife's serious illness which affected his own health and judgement, he did not act to avoid losses when the stock market crashed. It was held that the adjudication officer had not discharged the burden of proving that this had been done for the purpose of obtaining IS.[128]

For IS, FC and DWA, you can only be treated as having notional capital under this rule if the capital of which you have deprived yourself is *actual* capital.[129] So if you are counted as owning half a joint bank account under the rule about jointly held capital (see p436), but your real share is only a quarter, you should not be caught by the deprivation rule in relation to the other quarter. It is also arguable that the deprivation rule should not apply even to the quarter you actually hold.[130] There is no express rule spelt out in HB/CTB law that for the notional capital rule to apply you must have deprived yourself of actual capital, but you should argue that the same principle applies.

Note that where a disposal of capital is not effective (eg, where there is a disposal between the serving of a bankruptcy notice and the appointment of a trustee in bankruptcy) the notional capital rules will not apply (but the actual capital rules will apply if you still own the asset in question).[131] If, on the other hand, a person acting on your behalf as your attorney has misspent your money for her/his own benefit, the amount spent cannot be notional capital (because the disposal was unlawful) or actual capital (because you no longer have it), but your right to recover the money may still have an actual capital value.[132]

If you are treated as possessing notional capital, it is calculated in the same way as if it were actual capital[133] and the same disregards usually apply. The only possible exception is that you may not be able to rely on the disregard for the 26 weeks (or longer) you would otherwise be allowed to take steps to dispose of a property, even if the new owner is trying to sell it. However, there is conflicting commissioner case law on this.[134]

Other points on deprivation of capital

Any deprivation must be found to have been for the purposes of claiming or increasing your entitlement to that benefit.

Deprivation for the purposes of obtaining supplementary benefit cannot be said to have been deprivation for the purposes of obtaining IS,[135] because IS did not exist at that time. It should also, therefore, be argued that there could have been no deprivation for the purposes of obtaining FC prior to April 1988, DWA prior to April 1992, and CTB prior to April 1993, as those benefits did not come into existence until those dates.

Where an intentional deprivation has been found for the purposes of obtaining IS, for example, it does not necessarily follow that there has also been any intention to gain HB/CTB. Where your circumstances change (eg, you start work and claim FC) any finding of intentional deprivation for IS will not necessarily be relevant to your claim for FC.

Each adjudicating authority must reach its own decision on each benefit. Even decisions on deprivation for HB must be made independently of decisions for CTB.[136] This may result in different conclusions being drawn on any disposal for each benefit. And even where intent is found in two different benefits, there may be different views about the amount of capital that has been intentionally disposed of.[137]

However, where you are held to have deprived yourself of capital for the purposes of claiming HB/CTB, and you then submit a successful claim for IS, the notional capital rules for HB/CTB should be put in abeyance for as long as IS remains in payment.[138]

The diminishing notional capital rule

This rule provides a calculation for working out how your notional capital may be treated as *spent*.[139] Prior to 1 October 1990 there was a different rule (see p433). The rule starts to operate from the first week (or, for IS/CTB only, part-week) after the week in which it is first decided that the notional capital will be taken into account. The rule provides that:

- **where your benefit has been refused altogether** because of your notional capital, the amount of your notional capital will be reduced by the weekly total of any of the following benefits (or the additional amounts of the benefits, unless it is IS) that you would have been entitled to but for the notional capital rule:

for IS	–	IS/HB/CTB (or, formerly community charge benefit (CCB))
for FC	–	FC/HB/CTB (or CCB)
for DWA	–	DWA/HB/CTB (or CCB)
for HB	–	IS/FC/DWA/HB/CTB (or CCB)
for CTB	–	IS/FC/DWA/HB/CTB

  In order to ensure that account is taken of as many other benefits as possible, it is important (where you are not already doing so) to make a claim for any of the other benefits (where appropriate) as soon as the notional capital rule has been applied. Any notice you are then given of any amounts of benefits you have 'lost' can then be supplied as evidence of the total weekly aggregate that should be taken into account;

- **where your IS/FC/DWA/HB/CTB is reduced because of tariff income from your notional capital,** that capital is diminished by the amount of that reduction each week (or part-week). For example, if your notional capital is £3,750, giving a tariff income of £3 a week, the reduction is £3 a week until it reaches £3,500, when it will be £2 and so on. Account should be taken of any anticipated reduction in your tariff income band during any assessment period.[140]

  For FC/DWA/HB/CTB, the amount of your notional capital will also be reduced by the weekly aggregate of the following benefits (or any additional amounts of these benefits, unless it is IS) which you would have been entitled to but for the notional capital rule:

for FC   –   HB/CTB (or CCB)
for DWA –   HB/CTB (or CCB)
for HB   –   IS/FC/DWA/CTB (or CCB)
for CTB   –   IS/FC/DWA/HB;

• **the reduction in your notional capital is calculated on a weekly basis**. However, where your benefit has been stopped altogether because of the notional capital rule, the amount is fixed for a period of 26 weeks. Even if the amount you would have been entitled to increases during this period, there will be no change in the amount by which the capital is reduced (except for HB/CTB where guidance[141] states that in circumstances not related to capital – eg, you have married or a baby has been born – a new assessment can be made). The aggregate of your benefit entitlement can, however, be recalculated from the end of this 26-week period when you reclaim benefit, and will be increased if it is more than it was before, but it will stay the same as in the earlier assessment if it is unchanged or less. You do not have to reclaim at the end of every 26-week period but there can be no recalculation unless and until you do. However, you cannot renew a claim until at least 26 weeks (IS/HB/CTB), 22 weeks (FC) or 20 weeks (DWA) have passed since the last assessment. Once the amount of reduction has been recalculated in this way, it is again fixed for the same period.

For IS, you should ask the Benefits Agency for a forecast of when your notional capital will reduce to a point where a further claim might succeed, but the onus will be on you to reclaim when it is to your advantage to do so[142] – ie, when you may qualify for an increased assessment, or because you have requalified for benefit. Timing will be important. If you delay you may lose out as new assessments cannot take effect before you reclaim. However, if you reclaim too soon you will have to wait until the fixed periods have lapsed before you can apply for a fresh determination;

• **where you have both actual and notional capital**, you may have to draw on your actual capital to meet your living expenses, which may include (and will probably exceed) amounts equivalent to benefits you have 'lost'. There is no reason why this should affect the amount by which your notional capital is diminished, even if this effectively results in double-counting. Any reduction in your actual capital should be taken into account in calculating any tariff income arising from your combined actual and notional capital, unless, of course, you have spent it at such a rate and in such a way that it raises questions of intent, when you may find that the notional capital rules are applied all over again.

Note: It has been decided that these rules on how your capital was *spent* only apply from 1 October 1990. Prior to that date, any reasonable living and other expenditure was counted, which was far more generous.[143] Any notional capital you have been held to possess until 30 September 1990 will be reduced under the earlier rules, and any notional capital carried forward to 1 October 1990 and onwards will be reduced under the current rules.[144] Note that the current rules apply to deprivation of capital only; the earlier rules still apply to other forms of notional capital (see below).

For IS or FC, where the current more restrictive rules have been applied to you for any period before 1 October 1990, you should consider submitting a late appeal (see p169) to take advantage of the more generous treatment. For HB, the position on how the rules should have applied in earlier periods is less clear, although you should argue that as the law was essentially the same, the more generous rules should apply.

Failing to apply for capital[145]

Under this rule you are treated as having capital you could get if you applied for it. Examples of failure to apply could be where money is held in court which would be released on application, or even an unclaimed premium bond win! For IS, HB and CTB, you are only treated as having such capital from the date you could obtain it. Although the FC/DWA rules do not make the same point, you should argue that the same applies.

This rule does not apply if you fail to apply for:

- capital from a discretionary trust; *or*
- capital from a trust (or fund administered by the court[146]) set up from money paid as a result of a personal injury; *or*
- capital from a personal pension scheme or retirement annuity contract; *or*
- a loan which you could only get if you gave your home or other disregarded capital (see p421) as security.

Capital payments made to a 'third party' on your behalf

If someone else pays an amount to a 'third party' (eg, the electricity board or a building society) for you or a member of your family (if any), this may count as your capital.[147] It counts if the payment is to cover you or your family's food, household fuel, council tax or ordinary clothing or footwear. (School uniforms and sportswear are not ordinary clothing;[148] nor are, for example, special shoes because of a disability.[149])

It also counts if it is to cover:

- **for IS, HB and CTB**, rent for which HB is payable (less any non-dependant deductions) or water charges;
- **for IS alone**, housing costs met by IS or a residential care or nursing home accommodation charge for a person with preserved rights (see p88) met by IS;
- **for FC/DWA**, any housing costs (or any outstanding community charge, but not any standard community charge).

If the payment is for other kinds of expenses – eg, children's school fees (see pp374-75), a TV licence, accommodation charges above the IS limit, or (except for FC/DWA) mortgage capital repayments – it does not count. Also remember that payments from the Macfarlane Trusts, the Fund, the Eileen Trust or either of the Independent Living Funds, or any payments made for participating in the New Deal (see p58), do not count, whatever they are for.

Payments made for the food etc, of any member of the family, count as the capital of the member of the family in respect of whom they are paid. Since a child's capital is not counted as belonging to the claimant, a payment to, for example, a clothes shop for your child, should count as the child's notional capital and not yours.

For IS only, payments *derived* from certain social security benefits (including war disablement pensions and war widows' pensions) and paid to a third party count:

- as yours, if you are entitled to the benefit; *and*
- as a member of your family's, if it is the family member who is entitled to the benefit.[150]

For IS, there are different rules if you could be liable to pay maintenance as a liable relative (see p121).

Capital payments paid to you for a 'third party'[151]

If you or a member of your family get a payment for someone not in your family (eg, a relative who does not have a bank account) it only counts as yours if it is kept or used by you. Payments from the Macfarlane Trusts, the Fund, the Eileen Trust or either of the Independent Living Funds, or any payments made for participating in the New Deal (see p58), do not count at all.

Companies run by sole traders or a few partners

This applies if, as a sole trader or a small partnership, you have registered your business as a limited company. For IS/FC/DWA the value of your shareholding is ignored but you will be treated as possessing a proportionate share of the capital of the company.[152] This does not apply while you are working for the company.[153] Even if you work for the company for, say, only half an hour a week, this will suffice.[154] DSS guidance for FC/DWA indicates that it is not necessary for the work to be paid.[155] It has, however, been held that a 'sleeping partner' in a business managed and worked exclusively by others may not benefit from this disregard. As well as having a financial commitment to the business you must also be involved or engaged in it in some practical sense as an earner.[156]

For HB/CTB, the local authority has a discretion whether to apply the same rules as for IS/FC/DWA, but if it decides to it must apply them all.[157]

5. HOW CAPITAL IS VALUED

Market value

Apart from national savings certificates (see below), your capital is valued at its current market or surrender value.[158] This means the amount of money you could raise by selling it or raising a loan against it, etc. The test is the price that would be paid by a willing buyer to a willing seller on a particular date.[159] So if an asset is difficult, or impossible, to realise, its market value should be very heavily discounted or even nil.[160]

In the case of a house, an estate agent's figure for a quick sale is a more appropriate valuation than the District Valuer's figure for a sale within three months.[161]

Appeal if you disagree with the valuation of your capital (see p167).

Expenses of sale

If there would be expenses involved in selling your capital, 10 per cent is deducted from its value for the cost of sale.[162]

Debts

Deductions are made from the 'gross' value of your capital for any debt or mortgage secured on it.[163] If a creditor (eg, a bank), holds the land certificate to your property as security for a loan and has registered notice of deposit of the land certificate at the Land Registry, this counts as a debt secured on your property.[164] Where a single mortgage is secured on a house and land and the value of the house is disregarded for benefit purposes, the whole of the mortgage can be deducted when calculating the value of the land.[165]

If you have debts which are not secured against your capital (eg, tax liabilities), these cannot be offset against the value of your capital.[166] However, once you have paid off your debts, your capital may well be reduced. You can be penalised if you deliberately get rid of capital in order to get benefit (see p428).

National savings

For IS, a certificate bought from an issue which ceased before the 1 July before your claim is decided, or your benefit is first payable (whichever is earlier), or the date of any subsequent review, has the value it would have had on that 1 July if purchased on the last day of the issue. For FC/ DWA, it is the 1 July before the date of your claim; for HB/CTB, it is the 1 July before your claim is made or treated as made or when your benefit is reviewed. In any other case, the value is the purchase price.[167] DSS guidance contains a convenient valuation table for each issue.[168]

Capital that is jointly owned with someone other than your partner

If you jointly own a capital asset with one or more other people (other than your partner), the way your capital is valued depends on whether you have 'joint beneficial ownership' of it or whether you own 'undivided beneficial shares'.

Joint beneficial ownership exists where:

- no one co-owner has any greater or lesser right than another or any separate right of ownership at all; *and*
- if the co-owners were to sever their joint ownership they would be left with equal beneficial shares, *or*
- if one died the whole asset would be left in the beneficial ownership of the surviving beneficial owner(s).

In such circumstances, the capital is treated as being shared equally between you and the other joint beneficial owner(s).[169] The value of your deemed share is then calculated by taking the net value of the whole asset and dividing it by the number of joint beneficial owners.

If you are caught by this rule, and treated as owning capital of greater value than it is actually worth to you, you should consider selling your share if this is possible, because as soon as it is sold only the actual proceeds of your actual share should be treated as your capital. Unless you have sold it at less than it is actually worth, the notional capital rules (see p428) should not apply here. In the meantime, you may be able to apply for a crisis loan from the social fund (see p479).

Undivided beneficial shares exist where each co-owner has their own share which does not extend to the whole asset but represents only a portion of it (equal or unequal) but which is held with the other undivided shares on a collective basis. In relation to ownership of land (eg, a house) this is referred to as a *'tenancy in common'*.

In such circumstances it is only your actual share that is to be valued.[170] If the shared asset is, for example, a house, the market value of your share may even be nil, particularly where it is occupied and the other owner(s) are unwilling to sell their share(s) and there is a possibility that the sale of the property cannot be forced.[171]

Sometimes it will not be clear which type of joint ownership exists. If, for example, you have held savings in a joint bank account with your separated spouse there is a presumption that you have 'joint beneficial ownership' of the whole account. But if there is clear evidence that part of the sum in the account is in your sole ownership, and the joint account has merely been used for convenience, that amount will be your own 'undivided beneficial share'.[172]

Although a social security commissioner has decided that capital held by two or more people in 'undivided beneficial shares' should be treated differently (and usually more favourably to you), it is understood that the DSS considers this case to have a limited application and may nevertheless treat all jointly owned capital as if it is in 'joint beneficial ownership'.[173] If this happens to you, you may need to seek specialist advice from one of the agencies listed in Appendix 4.

Treatment of assets following the breakdown of a relationship

When partners separate, assets such as their former home or a building society account may be in joint or sole names. For example, if a building society account is in joint names, under the rule about jointly owned capital, you and your former partner are treated as having a 50 per cent share each (see above). But if your former partner is claiming sole ownership of the account, DSS guidance for FC/DWA says that your interest in the account should count as having a nil value until the question of ownership is settled.[174] Arguably, the same should apply to IS/HB/CTB. The guidance deals only with a marriage breakdown, but there is no reason why the same should not apply if you were not married. If your former partner puts a stop on the account, in effect freezing it, the account should be disregarded until its ownership is resolved.

On the other hand, a former partner may have a right to some or all of an asset that is in your sole name – eg, s/he may have deposited most of the money in a building society account in your name. If this is established, then the partner in whose name the account is held may well, depending on the circumstances, be treated as not entitled to the whole of the account but as holding part of it as trustee for her/his former partner.[175] In that event, the rule about jointly owned capital may have the effect of treating you as owning half of the amount in the account. However, the point made in the DSS guidance referred to above (p437) should logically apply equally here, so you should not be treated as owning half the capital (or indeed any of it) unless or until it is established that you do own at least some share of it, and the value of your interest can be assessed.

Shares

Shares are valued at their current market value less 10 per cent for the cost of sale[176] and after deducting any lien held by brokers for sums owed for the cost of acquisition and commission. Market value should be calculated in accordance with Inland Revenue guidance which is based on the bid price plus a quarter of the difference between this and the offer price (rather than *Financial Times* figures which rely on the mean between the bid and offer prices).[177] Fluctuations in price between routine reviews of your case are normally ignored. Where a claimant has a minority holding of shares in a company, the value of the shares should be based on what the claimant could realise on them, and not by valuing the entire share capital of the company and attributing to the claimant an amount calculated according to the proportion of shares held.[178] Although there may be some practical difficulties in selling shares held by children, there are no obstacles to sale that cannot be overcome by courts, if necessary. They would, therefore, still have a value, even though allowance would have to be made for some inducement to overcome the reluctance of stockbrokers, registrars and potential purchasers in contracting with minors for an immediate sale.[179]

Unit trusts

These are valued on the basis of the 'bid' price quoted in newspapers. No deduction is allowed for the cost of sale because this is already included in the 'bid' price.[180]

The right to receive a payment in the future

The value of any such right that is not ignored (see p425) is its market value – what a willing buyer will pay to a willing seller.[181] For something which is not yet realisable this may be very small.

Overseas assets

If you have assets abroad, and there are no exchange controls or other prohibitions that would prevent you transferring your capital to this country, your assets are valued at their current market or surrender value in that country.[182] If there are problems getting benefit because it is difficult to get the assets valued, you may be able to get an interim payment of IS, FC or DWA (see p145), or a 'payment on account' of HB (see p294).

If you are not allowed to transfer the full value of your capital to this country, you are treated as having capital equal to the amount that a willing buyer in this country would give for those assets.[183] It seems likely that the price such a person (if there is one) would be willing to pay may bear little relation to the actual value of the assets.

The same deductions of 10 per cent if there are expenses of sale, and for any debts or mortgage secured on the assets abroad, are made. If the capital is realised in a currency other than sterling, charges payable for converting the payment into sterling are also deducted.[184]

PART SIX

The regulated social fund

CHAPTER TWENTY-ONE

The regulated social fund

This chapter covers:
1. Maternity expenses payments (below)
2. Funeral expenses payments (p444)
3. Cold weather and winter fuel payments (p451)
4. Reviews and appeals (p453)

The social fund (SF) is a government fund which makes payments to people in need. Eligibility normally depends on receipt of certain means-tested benefits. There are two types of payments available from the social fund:

- **grants available by right for maternity expenses, funeral expenses, periods of cold weather and winter fuel.** Unlike the discretionary payments, you are *legally entitled* to these grants if you satisfy the eligibility conditions, which are laid down in regulations.
- **discretionary grants and loans to meet a variety of needs.** These are covered in Part Seven – see p456.

I. MATERNITY EXPENSES PAYMENTS

The basic rules

You are entitled to a maternity expenses payment if you satisfy all of the following rules:

- You or your partner (see note on p443) have been awarded a qualifying benefit when you claim a maternity expenses payment. The following are qualifying benefits: income support (IS), income-based jobseeker's allowance (JSA) – including hardship payments, family credit (FC) and disability working allowance (DWA).[1] See p443 for issues relating to the award of qualifying benefits.
- One of the following applies:[2]
  - you or a member of your family (see note p443) are pregnant or have given birth (including stillbirth after 24 weeks of pregnancy[3]);

- you or your partner have adopted a child who is less than 12 months old when you claim a maternity expenses payment;
- you and your spouse have been granted a parental order allowing you to have a child by a surrogate mother.

In the last two cases, you are entitled to a payment even if one has already been made to the natural mother or a member of her family.[4]

- You do not have too much capital. Any capital you and your partner have in excess of £500 (£1,000 if either of you is aged 60 or over) is deducted from the maternity expenses payment.[5] As the payment is a flat-rate £100 (see p444 – Amount), this means if you have capital of more than £600 (or £1,100) you will not get a payment. Capital is calculated as for IS or income-based JSA, except that lump-sum widow's payment (£1,000) is ignored for 12 months after your husband's death.[6]

- You or your partner are not involved in a trade dispute (see p61) unless:
  - either of you is getting IS or income-based JSA and the trade dispute has been going on for six weeks or more when you claim a maternity expenses payment; *or*
  - either of you is getting FC or DWA, which you claimed before the trade dispute started.[7]

- You claim within the time limits (see p444).

Note: The terms 'partner' and 'family' in the above rules have virtually the same meaning as for IS (see p346).[8]

Award of qualifying benefits

- A backdated award of a qualifying benefit which covers the date you claim a maternity expenses payment should render you eligible for a payment.
- If you are refused a payment because although you have claimed a qualifying benefit, it has not yet been awarded and:
  - you are subsequently awarded the qualifying benefit; *and*
  - you reclaim a maternity expenses payment within three months of the decision awarding you the qualifying benefit;
  your claim is backdated to the date of your original claim or to the date from which the qualifying benefit has been awarded, whichever is later.[9]
- If you are under 19 and cannot claim a qualifying benefit in your own right, a member of your 'family' (see note above) can claim a payment for you, if s/he is getting a qualifying benefit.

Amount

The maternity expenses payment is £100 for each child.[10] If this is insufficient to meet your needs, you could try making an application to the discretionary social fund, but see p464.

Time limits[11]

You can claim a maternity expenses payment at any time from eleven weeks before the first day of your expected week of confinement until three months after your actual date of confinement. If you adopt a child or have a child by a surrogate mother, you can claim up to three months following the date of the adoption or parental order.

There is no provision for claiming outside the above time limits. If your claim is refused because you are not getting a qualifying benefit – see Award of qualifying benefits, p443.

Claiming and getting paid

You should claim on form SF100 which you can get from your local Benefits Agency. The date of claim is normally the date the form is received by the Benefits Agency.[12] If you make a written claim in some other way, you should be sent the appropriate form to complete. If you return it within one month or such longer period as the Secretary of State considers reasonable, the date of claim will be the date the Benefits Agency received your initial application.[13] See p443 for when your claim can be backdated if you are subsequently awarded a qualifying benefit.

If you claim before confinement, you will need to submit a maternity certificate (form MAT B1), a note from your doctor or midwife or an ante-natal clinic appointment card showing your expected date of confinement. If you claim after the child is born, you will usually be asked for a maternity, birth or adoption certificate.[14]

The rules for getting paid and the recovery of overpayments are the same as for IS (see pp144 and 156).

2. FUNERAL EXPENSES PAYMENTS

The basic rules

You are entitled to a funeral expenses payment if all of the following rules are satisfied:

- You or your partner (see p447 – Meaning of terms) have been awarded a qualifying benefit when you claim a funeral payment (see p451 for date of claim).[15] The following are qualifying benefits: IS, income-based JSA, FC, DWA, housing benefit (HB) and council tax benefit (CTB – including second adult rebate, see p335). See p448 for issues relating to the award of qualifying benefits.

- You or your partner are in one of the categories of eligible persons, listed below, who can be treated as responsible for the funeral expenses.
- You or your partner 'accept responsibility' for funeral expenses.[16] If you are claiming as a close relative or close friend (see p447), it must also be 'reasonable' for you to accept responsibility. See p448 (Accepting responsibility for funeral costs) for more details.
- The funeral (ie, burial or cremation[17]) takes place in the UK, unless you or your partner are covered by specified EC legislation, in which case the funeral can take place in any EEA state[18] (see p448 – EEA nationals, for details).
- The deceased was 'ordinarily resident' in the UK when s/he died.[19] See p198 for the meaning of ordinarily resident.
- You do not have too much capital (see p450 – Deductions from awards).
- You claim at any time from the date of death up to three months after the date of the funeral.[20] There is no provision for late claims (but if your claim is refused because you are not getting a qualifying benefit, see p448 – Award of qualifying benefits). See p451 for details of the date your claim is treated as made.

Notes:

- Involvement in a trade dispute has no effect on entitlement to a funeral payment.
- You cannot get a funeral payment if one has already been awarded for the same funeral. You can, however, get an increase in the amount awarded on review, up to the maximum allowed under the rules (see p449 – Amount).[21]

Eligible persons

You are only eligible for a funeral payment if you or your partner fall into one of the following categories of people who can be treated as responsible for the funeral costs:

- You were the partner of the deceased when s/he died.[22]
- The deceased was a child for whom you were 'responsible' when s/he died and there is no 'absent parent', or there is an absent parent but s/he (or her/his partner) was getting a qualifying benefit (see p445)

when the child died (see p447 for meaning of terms). If the deceased was a 'stillborn child' (see p447 for meaning), you must have been the parent or parent's partner and it does not matter whether there is an 'absent parent'.[23]
- You were a 'close relative' (see p447) or 'close friend' of the deceased and it is reasonable for you to accept responsibility for the funeral expenses.[24] Whether it is reasonable is determined by the nature and extent of your contact with the deceased (see p448 – Accepting responsibility for funeral costs).[25] You cannot get a payment, however, if you are excluded under the rules below.

Exclusion of close relatives/friends

If you claim as a 'close relative' or 'close friend' of the deceased, you cannot get a payment if any of the following circumstances apply:

- The deceased had a partner (unless that partner died before the funeral without making a claim for a funeral payment).[26]
- There is a parent, son or daughter of the deceased, apart from the following:[27]
  - anyone who was a 'child' (see p447 for meaning) when the deceased died;
  - anyone who (or whose partner) has been awarded a qualifying benefit (see p445);
  - anyone estranged from the deceased when s/he died ('estranged' is not defined but has connotations of emotional disharmony);[28]
  - students under 19 doing a full-time course of advanced education, or aged 19 to pension age doing any full-time course;
  - members of a religious order which fully maintains them;
  - prisoners (including those in youth custody or a remand centre) who or whose partner were getting a qualifying benefit immediately before being detained;
  - in-patients receiving free treatment in a hospital or similar institution, who or whose partner were getting a qualifying benefit immediately before becoming a patient.
- There is a 'close relative' (see p447 for meaning) of the deceased who was in *closer contact* with the deceased than you were, taking into account the nature and extent of such contact.[29]
- There is a 'close relative' of the deceased who was in *equally close contact* with the deceased as you were and either:
  - s/he (or her/his partner) is not getting a qualifying benefit; *or*
  - s/he (and her/his partner) has more capital than you have and that capital exceeds £500 (or £1,000 if s/he and her/his partner are both aged 60 or over).[30]

Note: The last two bullet points do not apply where:

- the close relative was a child when the deceased died;[31] *or*
- the deceased was a child or stillborn child and the circumstances set out on p445 (last bullet point) apply.[32]

Example 1
Jane is not entitled to a funeral payment because although she looked after her brother for many years before he died, he has a son who is not getting a qualifying benefit. Although the son rarely saw his father, they were not estranged.

Example 2
Yuri is entitled to a funeral payment when his close friend Robert dies because although Robert has two surviving close relatives, a son and a sister-in-law, the son is getting HB and Yuri was in closer contact with Robert than either of them were.

Meaning of terms

- 'Child' is defined as for IS purposes (see p353).[33] You are 'responsible' for a child if you get or could get child benefit for her/him (see CPAG's *Rights Guide to Non-Means-Tested Benefits*).[34]
- 'Stillborn child' means a child born dead after 24 weeks of pregnancy.[35]
- 'Absent parent' means a parent of a deceased child, where the child:
  - was not living in that parent's household at the date of death; *and*
  - was living with another person who was responsible for her/him.[36]
- 'Close relative' means parent, parent-in-law, son, son-in-law, daughter, daughter-in-law, step-parent, stepson, stepson-in-law, stepdaughter, stepdaughter-in-law, brother, brother-in-law, sister, sister-in-law.[37]
- 'Partner' is defined in virtually the same way as for IS (see p346).[38] You also count as a partner, however, if you were living in residential or nursing care (as defined on p94) when the deceased died, and:
  - you and your spouse were living in the same home; *or*
  - you were a member of a couple before one or both of you moved into such a home.[39]
  This rule is designed to enable a surviving partner to claim a funeral payment where one or both partners were in a home at the date of death.

Accepting responsibility for funeral costs

To qualify for a funeral payment, you or your partner must 'accept responsibility' for funeral expenses.[40] The key factor is whether you are liable to pay for the costs of a funeral, rather than whether you have made the arrangements for the funeral.[41]

If the funeral director's account or contract is in your name, you should normally be treated as having accepted responsibility. If the account or contract is in someone else's name (or, in the first case below, another person has paid the bill), you can still be 'responsible' if:

- s/he is acting as your 'agent' – eg, because you are too distressed to act on your own behalf;[42] *or*
- s/he transfers liability to you, prior to full payment, with the consent of the funeral director ('novation' of the contract).[43]

If you are a 'close relative' or 'close friend' of the deceased, it must also be 'reasonable' for you to accept responsibility for the funeral expenses, determined by the nature and extent of your contact with the deceased.[44] In one case, it was held reasonable for a person to accept responsibility for his father's funeral even though he had not seen him for 24 years. This did not erase the contact they had had in the previous 30 years.[45]

Award of qualifying benefits

- A backdated award of a qualifying benefit which covers the date you claim a funeral payment should render you eligible for a payment.
- If you are refused a payment because although you have claimed a qualifying benefit, it has not yet been awarded, and,
  - you are subsequently awarded the qualifying benefit; *and*
  - you reclaim a funeral payment within three months of the decision awarding you the qualifying benefit;
  your claim is backdated to the date of your original claim, or to the date from which qualifying benefit has been awarded, whichever is the later.[46]

EEA nationals

You can get a funeral payment for a funeral which takes place in any state of the European Economic Area (EEA) (see p75) if you fall into one of the following categories:[47]

- You are a 'worker' for the purposes of EC Regulations 1612/68 or 1251/70 (see p76).

- You are a member of the family of a worker for the purposes of EC Regulation 1612/68, or a member of the family of a worker who has died and who was covered by EC Regulation 1251/70. The following count as family members:[48]
  - the worker's spouse;
  - the worker's or spouse's children, grandchildren and other descendants who are either under 21 or dependent;
  - dependent relatives of the worker or spouse in the ascending line – eg, parents, grandparents.
- You have the right to reside in the UK under EC Directive 68/360 or 73/148 (see p77).

If you have ever been refused a payment for a funeral which took place in an EEA state and you satisfied the above rules, you should ask for a review. You could try asking for lost interest or compensation for past non-payment.

Amount

You are entitled to a payment sufficient to cover the following expenses:[49]

- The necessary costs of purchasing a new burial plot (with the exclusive right of burial in it) and of the actual burial.[50]
- The necessary costs of cremation, including medical references and certificates and the fee for removing a pacemaker (restricted to £20 if not carried out by a doctor).[51]
- The costs of documentation necessary for the release of the deceased's assets.[52]
- The reasonable cost of transport for the portion of journeys in excess of 50 miles, undertaken for the following purposes:
  - transporting the body within the UK to a funeral director's premises or to a place of rest;[53]
  - transporting the coffin and bearers in a hearse and the mourners in another vehicle from the funeral director's premises or place of rest to the funeral.[54] The cost of this transport plus burial in an existing plot cannot exceed the cost of such transport plus the purchase and burial costs of a new plot.[55]
- The necessary expenses of one return journey within the UK for you or your partner to arrange *or* attend the funeral. The maximum allowed is the cost of a return journey from your home to the place where the burial or cremation costs are incurred.[56]
- Up to £600 for any other funeral expenses – eg, funeral director's fees, religious costs, flowers, other transport costs.[57]

Note:

- . The cost of any items or services provided under a pre-paid funeral plan or equivalent arrangement cannot be met. Expenses not covered by the plan can be met if they fall into the above categories but the maximum allowed under the last category is restricted to £100.[58]
- Costs relating to religious requirements cannot be included in the amount allowed for burial and transport.[59]
- If the amount awarded does not cover your funeral expenses, you could try making an application to the discretionary SF (eg, for the cost of a headstone or funeral clothes), but see p464.

Deductions from awards

The following amounts are deducted from an award of a funeral payment:

- Any capital you or your partner have in excess of £500 (£1,000 if either of you is aged 60 or over).[60] Capital is calculated as for IS (see p415) except that lump-sum widow's payment (£1,000) is ignored for 12 months after your husband's death.[61] Any money you have been given or loaned for the express purpose of meeting the funeral expenses is disregarded.[62] If, however, you have used any of your capital (apart from disregarded capital) to pay for funeral expenses, you are treated as though you still possessed it.[63]
- Any of the deceased's assets available to you or a member of your family (defined as for IS purposes) without probate or letters of administration.[64] Assets at the date of death count, even if you have spent or distributed them prior to your claim for a funeral payment.[65] Arrears of the deceased's attendance allowance (and probably other benefits) paid to you as next of kin also count.[66]
- Any lump sum legally due to you or a member of your family from an insurance policy, occupational pension scheme, burial club or equivalent source on the death of the deceased.[67]
- Any contribution towards funeral expenses made to you or a member of your family by a charity or a relative of your's or of the deceased.[68]
- Any funeral grant paid by the government for a war disablement pensioner.[69]
- Any amount paid or payable under a pre-paid funeral plan or equivalent arrangement (whether or not the plan was fully paid for).[70]

Note: Any payments from the Macfarlane Trust, the Macfarlane (Special Payments) Trusts, the Fund or the Eileen Trust (see Appendix 1) are disregarded from the above deductions.[71]

Recovery from the deceased's estate

The Secretary of State is entitled to recover funeral expenses payments from the deceased's estate and will normally seek to do so.[72] Funeral expenses are a first charge on the estate, in priority to anything else (although there may be insufficient assets for full repayment).[73] Personal possessions left to relatives and the value of a house occupied by a surviving partner should be disregarded.

Claiming and getting paid

You should claim on form SF200, which you can get from your local Benefits Agency office. When completing the form, bear in mind the rules about 'accepting responsibility' for the funeral expenses and your contact with the deceased.

The date of claim is normally the date the form is received by the Benefits Agency.[74] If you do not complete the SF200 properly or apply in writing but not on the form, you should be sent the form to complete or correct. If you submit it within one month, or such longer period as the Secretary of State considers reasonable, the claim is treated as made on the date you originally applied.[75] See p448 for when your claim can be backdated if you are subsequently awarded a qualifying benefit.

The Benefits Agency will usually pay by giro, made payable to the funeral director, unless you have already paid the bill.[76]

The rules for getting paid and the recovery of overpayments are as for IS (see p128) but see above for recovery from the deceased's estate.

3. COLD WEATHER AND WINTER FUEL PAYMENTS

The basic rules for cold weather payments

You are entitled to a cold weather payment if:

- a 'period of cold weather' has been forecast or recorded for the area in which your normal home is situated (see below);[77] *and*
- you have been awarded income support (IS) or income-based jobseeker's allowance (JSA) for at least one day during the period of cold weather; *and*
- *either* your income support (IS) or income-based jobseeker's allowance (JSA) includes one or more of the following premiums:

pensioner; disability; higher pensioner; severe disability; disabled child (see p360);

or you have a child under five.[78] The exclusion of claimants with children over five may be challengeable.

Notes:

- The amount of capital you have does not affect the payment.
- You are not entitled to a payment if you live in residential or nursing care and do not have preserved rights (see p87).[79]

A 'period of cold weather'

This is a period of seven consecutive days during which the average of the mean daily temperature forecast or recorded for that period is equal to or below 0° Celsius. The 'mean daily temperature' is the average of the maximum and minimum temperatures recorded for that day.[80] The regulations divide the country into 72 areas, each covered by a weather station at which temperatures are forecast or recorded.[81] The area your home is in is normally determined by your postcode.

The amount of the payment

The sum of £9.50 is paid for each week of cold weather.[82]

Claiming and getting paid

You do *not* need to make a claim for a cold weather payment. The Benefits Agency should automatically send you a giro if you qualify.[83] Your district Benefits Agency should publicise when there are periods of cold weather in your area by placing advertisements in local newspapers, by radio broadcasts, and by distributing posters and leaflets – eg, to doctors' surgeries and local advice centres.[84] If you do not receive a giro and you think you are entitled, contact your local Benefits Agency. If you do not receive a payment or are told you are not entitled, submit a written claim and ask for a written decision. You can then appeal against an unfavourable decision.[85]

The rules for getting paid and the recovery of overpayments are the same as for IS.

Winter fuel payments

You are entitled to a one-off winter fuel payment of £50 if you were receiving IS, including the pensioner or higher pensioner premium, in the week beginning 5 January 1998.[86]

You are entitled to a payment of £20 if you are over pension age and were ordinarily resident in GB and receiving one of the following benefits in the week beginning 5 January 1998: attendance allowance, disability living allowance, incapacity benefit, invalid care allowance, severe disablement allowance, retirement pension, war pension, widow's pension, widowed mother's allowance, and IS or JSA if you have no accommodation (see p102). If another person in your household is also entitled to a payment, you only get £10.[87]

You are not entitled to a payment if you are in residential care and receiving a residential allowance (see p93) unless you are temporarily in care and your partner is living at home or is in hospital.[88] You are not entitled to a £20 payment if you have been in hospital for more than 52 weeks or are in residential care with 'preserved rights' (see p88) or in a local authority home (unless you are only temporarily there and your partner is at home).[89]

You do not need to claim winter fuel payments. They should be paid automatically. If you do not receive a payment to which you think you are entitled, contact your local Benefits Agency office.

4. REVIEWS AND APPEALS

The rules relating to reviews and appeals are almost the same as for IS (see pp140 and 167). Most decisions are made by adjudication officers and are subject to review and appeal. If an application for review is made more than one month outside the time limits for claiming a payment, a revised payment can only be made if the circumstances set out on p142 are satisfied (payment of more than one month's arrears of IS on review).[90]

PART SEVEN

The discretionary social fund

General principles

This chapter covers:

I. INTRODUCTION

In addition to the grants available by right for maternity expenses, funeral expenses and cold weather and winter fuel described in Part Six, the social fund (SF) also provides discretionary grants and loans to meet a variety of other needs. This part of the SF is very different in character to all other social security provision:

- It is strictly **budget-limited**. Each district office of the Benefits Agency is given an annual budget which it must not exceed.
- Payments are **discretionary**. There is no legal entitlement to a payment. The rules are only concerned with eligibility and how discretion is to be exercised.
- Many payments are in the form of **loans**. These have to be repaid to the Benefits Agency, usually by deductions from weekly benefit.
- Decisions are made by **social fund officers**.
- There is **no right of appeal** to an independent tribunal. Instead there is a system of internal review with a right to a further review by quasi-independent **social fund inspectors**.

Despite the unpopularity and inherent problems of the discretionary SF, its wide scope makes it an important and valuable (though unpredictable) source of help and you should *always apply* if you have a need which can be met by the fund.

Decisions are governed by law, guidance and district budgets.

2. THE LAW

Primary legislation

The social fund (SF) exists by Act of Parliament.[1] The Act empowers social fund officers (SFOs) to make discretionary payments from the fund. In deciding whether to make a payment, the Act requires SFOs to take into account all the circumstances of each case and, in particular:[2]

- the nature, extent and urgency of the need;
- the existence of resources which could meet the need;
- whether any other person or body could meet the need;
- whether a loan is likely to be repaid;
- the amount of the Benefits Agency district office budget (see p459);
- SF directions and guidance (see below).

The Act also empowers the Secretary of State to issue directions to SFOs which are legally binding.[3]

The directions

The directions establish three types of discretionary payment available from the SF:

- community care grants (CCGs) (see p468);
- budgeting loans (see p477);
- crisis loans (see p479).

The directions set out the eligibility conditions for each type of payment. They also exclude payments for certain expenses (see p462) and cover reviews (see pp492 and 496) and control of budgets (see p459).

The regulations[4]

These deal with procedures. They cover:

- applications for grants and loans;
- applications for reviews;
- the acceptance and recovery of loans.

The Act, directions and regulations are included in CPAG's *Income Related Benefits: The Legislation* (see Appendix 5).

Case law

Decisions of the higher courts (eg, judicial reviews in the High Court) create binding precedent although they are often only relevant to the particular case in question. Social fund inspector decisions do not create binding case law but can be useful guidance (see p459).

3. GUIDANCE

National guidance

The Secretary of State issues national guidance on how to interpret the directions and administer the social fund (SF). The guidance and directions are published in an *SF Guide* (see Appendix 5). The guidance suggests the circumstances in which a payment should be made and for what items and services. It also sets out which types of need should normally be given high, medium or low priority.

Social fund officers (SFOs) must take account of the guidance,[5] but it is *not* legally binding. The guidance repeatedly reminds SFOs that they must exercise discretion according to the individual circumstances of each case.[6] The absence of guidance on a particular situation does not mean that help should be refused.[7] The guidance on priorities is not exhaustive[8] and stresses that '... the overriding concern in determining priority is the assessment of *individual* need'.[9] Despite this, SFOs tend to use the *SF Guide* as a rule book.

Local guidance

Local guidance is issued by SF managers in Benefits Agency district offices.[10] Copies should be available from your local office and is public information.

The main purpose of local guidance is to specify which levels of priority need (ie, high, medium or low), determined in accordance with the national guidance, can be met from the district budget.[11] It must be reviewed at least every month.[12] The guidance may also include details of the district budget and a monthly expenditure profile – ie, planned expenditure (see p459).

SFOs must take account of the local guidance but it is not legally binding and must not conflict with the directions or national guidance by, for example, excluding groups of claimants from payments.[13] In practice, however, SFOs tend to only award payments to meet rigidly defined high priority needs which may not be explicitly set out in the local guidance.

Social fund inspectors' decisions

Social fund inspector (SFI) decisions can be useful guidance because they indicate how discretion can be exercised by SFOs. However, they apply only to the case under review and do not create precedents. The SF Independent Review Service (see Appendix 3) issues a thrice-yearly *Journal* which includes a digest of SFI decisions.

Advice and practice notes

'Advice Notes' were issued to SFIs by the legal adviser to the Social Fund Commissioner from 1993 to 1995. They are not binding but can be useful on difficult problems of interpretation. They are included in *The Social Fund: Law & Practice* (see Appendix 5).

'Best Practice Notes' on the law and practice are issued by the Independent Review Service and are included in their *Journal* (see above).

4. THE BUDGET

The government sets the total budget for the discretionary social fund (SF) each year. Each Benefits Agency district office is then allocated a fixed sum for grants and another for loans.[14]

The district SF manager is responsible for planning and monitoring expenditure on a monthly basis.[15] Any under- or overspend in a particular month should lead to a revision of planned monthly expenditure for the rest of the year. However, there is no monthly limit on expenditure and it would be unlawful to refuse a payment solely because planned expenditure for a particular month had been exceeded.[16]

The only limit on district expenditure is the total budget allocated for the year. The directions prohibit social fund officers (SFOs) from spending more than their annual district budget.[17] It is possible, however, for the Secretary of State to allocate additional funds to a district in the course of the year,[18] and there is nothing to stop district managers asking for more funds if their budget is likely to be overspent. However, many appear to be unaware that this action is open to them and are usually reluctant to do anything which could be interpreted as an inability to manage the budget (see p462 – Tactics).

SFOs must have regard to the budget when deciding whether to make a payment and how much to award.[19] However, the budget is only one factor they must take into account when making decisions. The High Court has ruled that need should be assessed before budgetary considerations are taken into account (see How decisions are made, below). Refusal of an application on budgetary grounds alone is unlawful, unless the budget is exhausted. You should consider asking for a review if your application is refused because of the budget (see p492).

The directions require SFOs to manage the budget so as to give priority to 'high-priority needs' throughout the year.[20] There is no legal definition of what constitutes a high-priority need but SFOs are advised to take account of guidance (see p458) and try to treat applications consistently throughout the year.[21] If you are refused a payment on the grounds of insufficient priority, you can request a review (see p492).

5. HOW DECISIONS ARE MADE

The theory

The legal demands placed on social fund officers (SFOs) when making decisions are onerous and in some respects, contradictory. They must:

- carefully consider all the circumstances of each case including the nature, extent and urgency of the need and the other matters set out on p457, and use their discretion to decide whether to award a payment;
- follow the directions (see p457);
- take account of national and local guidance (see p458), without being rigidly bound by either;
- have regard to the budget (see p459);
- decide on the priority of the application and give priority to high-priority needs (see above).

The High Court has ruled that the assessment of need is separate from and precedes budgetary considerations. If a need is assessed to have the level of priority which the local guidance says the district budget can meet, an award should normally be made.[22] SFOs are also expected to:

- exercise discretion flexibly but consistently;[23]
- ensure their decisions are not in any way affected by bias or prejudice on such grounds as race, colour, religion, gender or sexual orientation;[24]

- liaise with local social services departments, the probation service and other local organisations about the operation of the fund and priorities as well as individual applications, subject to normal confidentiality rules.[25]

The practice

Not surprisingly, the practice rarely matches the theory. Many people would argue that there is a basic conflict between meeting need and having regard to the budget; or between exercising discretion on an individual basis and taking account of the guidance. Also, most SFOs have neither the training nor the time to achieve the standard of decision-making imposed by all the above requirements.

In practice, SFOs tend to use the *SF Guide* as a rule book and only make payments to meet rigidly defined 'high priority needs' in order to stay within budget. Other applications are routinely rejected, regardless of the circumstances of the applicants.

The SF has been likened to a lottery by many critics because your chances of success can depend on when you apply (ie, the state of the budget at that time) and where you live (there is little national consistency in decision-making).

6. TACTICS

- Do not be put off from applying for any payment you need. The SF can pay for anything other than excluded items (see p462) as long as you satisfy the basic eligibility rules (see pp467, 477 and 479).
- Refer to the national guidance on priorities, if it helps your case. The high priority category for community care grants (CCGs), for example, is wide in scope and can be used to frame your application (see p469).
- Get a copy of your district office's local guidance and refer to it in your application if it helps your case.
- Always ask for a grant, rather than a loan, if you satisfy the conditions on p467. However, any application is to the SF as a whole and the SFO should always consider whether you are eligible for a grant even if you ask for a loan.
- Tips on completing the application forms are on p489.
- If you are unhappy about a decision, *you should consider asking for a review and, if necessary, a further review by the* social fund inspectors (SFIs) (see p492). This could apply if you have been refused a payment, been given less than you asked for, or been offered a loan rather than a grant. SFO decisions are often overturned by SFIs – in particular a

loan award may be replaced by a CCG. *A decision may, however, not be made in your favour,* see p492.

- A local campaign could be persuasive in highlighting the need for an increase in the district budget. Such a campaign could involve local MPs and highlight the hardship resulting from refusals of applications to the SF.

7. EXCLUDED ITEMS

The directions exclude payments from the SF for the items listed below.[26]

The general list of exclusions

- A need which occurs outside the UK. This rule may constitute unlawful discrimination in the case of EEA nationals (see p75). For details, see CPAG's *Migration and Social Security Handbook* (Appendix 5).
- An educational or training need, including clothing and tools.
- 'Distinctive' school uniform, or any equipment or sports clothes for school use (see Appendix 1 for grants available from the local authority).
- Travel expenses to and from school (but see Appendix 1).
- School meals and meals taken during the holidays by children entitled to free school meals (but see Appendix 1).
- Expenses in connection with court proceedings (including a community service order) – eg, legal fees, court fees, fines, costs, damages and travel expenses. You can get a crisis loan, however, for emergency travel expenses (see p484).
- Removal charges where you are permanently rehoused following a compulsory purchase order, a redevelopment or closing order, or where there is a compulsory exchange of tenancies or you are permanently rehoused as homeless under the Housing Acts. In all these circumstances your local authority may help you.
- The cost of domestic assistance or respite care. This would include the cost of home care or short breaks in residential care.[27]
- Repairs to property owned by public sector housing bodies including Councils, most housing associations, housing co-operatives and housing trusts.[28]
- Medical, surgical, optical, aural or dental items or services. A medical item does not include an ordinary everyday item needed because of a medical condition – eg, cotton sheets and non-allergic bedding when a

person is allergic to synthetics, built-up shoes, special beds, incontinence pads.[29] If an item is not in ordinary, everyday use, it should only be treated as a medical item if it cures, alleviates, treats, diagnoses or prevents a medical condition. Wheelchairs (or parts for them) should not be an excluded item under this test.[30] Social fund officers, however, are told to find out whether help is available from the NHS or other relevant agencies.[31]

- Work-related expenses. The guidance says this includes fares when seeking work and the cost of work clothes.[32] You may be able to get help with fares to interviews from the Employment Service.
- Debts to government departments. These could include national insurance arrears, income tax liabilities and customs charges.[33] Debts to other organisations or people, however, are not excluded, even if they are incurred in respect of an excluded item.[34]
- Investments.
- Council tax, council water charges, arrears of community charge, collective community charge contributions and community water charges.
- Most housing costs, including:[35]
  - repairs and improvements to your home, including garage, garden and outbuildings. (**Note:** repairs and improvements are no longer defined with reference to the income support (IS) regulations);
  - deposits to secure accommodation;
  - mortgage payments, rent, service charges, water and sewerage rates and any other accommodation charges.

Housing costs which are not excluded

You can get a payment for the following housing costs:

- a community care grant (CCG) or loan for minor repairs and improvements (the type of work, rather than the cost should determine whether a repair is major or minor[36]);
- a CCG for overnight accommodation as part of a travel expenses payment (see p476);
- a loan for rent in advance for fresh accommodation where the landlord is not a local authority;
- a loan for housing costs not met by housing benefit (HB), IS or income-based jobseeker's allowance (JSA) (see pp246 and 38) or not eligible for direct deductions from IS or income-based JSA (see p151)
  - eg, emptying cesspits or septic tanks;
- a crisis loan for board and lodging or hostel charges *or* a budgeting loan for such charges in advance (excluding meals, services, deposits);

• a CCG or loan for repayment of a debt incurred to pay for a housing expense – eg, money borrowed to pay for a deposit or repair.[37]

Additional items excluded from community care grants[38]

• The cost of purchasing, renting or installing a telephone and of any call charges (help may be available from your local authority if you are chronically sick or disabled – see Appendix 1).
• Any expenses which the local authority has a *statutory duty* to meet (discretionary powers do not trigger the exclusion, nor should statutory duties not accepted by the local authority).
• The cost of any fuel and standing charges.
• Any daily living expenses such as food and groceries except where incurred in caring for a prisoner on temporary release or where the maximum amount for a crisis loan has already been awarded (see p483).
• Any item worth less than £30, or several items which together are worth less than £30 (unless the award is for daily living expenses or travel expenses).[39]

Additional items excluded from budgeting loans[40]

• The cost of 'mains' fuel and standing charges. This exclusion does not apply to help with liquid gas, paraffin and coal.
• Any item worth less than £30, or several items which together are worth less than £30.[41]

Additional items excluded from crisis loans[42]

• Telephone purchase, installation, call and rental charges (see Appendix 1 if you are chronically sick or disabled and need a telephone).
• Mobility needs (this does not include travel expenses).
• Holidays.
• Television or radio, TV licence, aerial, TV rental.
• Garaging, parking, purchase and running costs of any motor vehicle – except where payment is being considered for emergency travel expenses.

Help with maternity and funeral expenses

The regulated SF covers maternity and funeral expenses (see p442). The discretionary SF covers 'other needs'.[43] According to the *SF Guide*, this means that any maternity or funeral expense not covered by a regulated grant, cannot be met by the discretionary SF.[44] It was argued unsuccessfully in a legal challenge that items not paid for by a regulated grant could be met by the discretionary SF.[45] The *SF Guide* concedes, however, that there is no definition of 'maternity' and 'funeral' expenses[46] and that items such as clothing for a pregnant mother or a growing (as opposed to newborn) baby may not be maternity expenses,[47] while items such as a headstone or clothing to attend a funeral may not be funeral (ie, burial or cremation) expenses.[48]

8. PEOPLE INVOLVED IN A TRADE DISPUTE

There are special rules affecting people involved in a trade dispute. See p61 for the meaning of 'involvement in a trade dispute'.

Community care grants

If you or your partner are involved in a trade dispute, you are not eligible for a community care grant (CCG) other than for travel expenses to visit somebody who is ill and then only in the following circumstances:[49]

- **You are involved in a trade dispute and are visiting:**
  - your partner in hospital or a similar institution;
  - a dependant in hospital or similar institution, but only if you have no partner living with you who could get a grant, or your partner is also in hospital or a similar institution;
  - a close relative or member of your household who is critically ill (whether or not in hospital or a similar institution).
- **You are not involved in a trade dispute but you are the partner or dependant of somebody who is, and you are visiting:**
  - a close relative or member of your household who is a patient in a hospital or similar institution or who is critically ill (whether or not in hospital or a similar institution).

To get a CCG you must be receiving IS or income-based JSA or would be but for the trade dispute. For how your travel expenses will be calculated, see p476.

Budgeting loans

You are not eligible for a budgeting loan if you or your partner are involved in a trade dispute.[50]

Crisis loans

If you or your partner are involved in a trade dispute, you are only entitled to a crisis loan for:[51]

- expenses arising from a disaster (see p482);
- the cost of items needed for cooking or space heating (including fireguards). This could include cooking utensils as well as a cooker.

CHAPTER TWENTY-THREE

Community care grants

This chapter covers:
1. Introduction (below)
2. Moving out of institutional or residential accommodation (p470)
3. Staying out of institutional or residential accommodation (p472)
4. Planned resettlement (p473)
5. Easing exceptional pressures on families (p474)
6. Travel expenses (p476)

I. INTRODUCTION

Community care grants (CCGs) are intended to promote community care by helping people live independently in the community.

There is no legal entitlement to a CCG. Payments are discretionary. However, you can ask for a review if you are not paid what you ask for (see p492). Unlike loans, CCGs are not repayable.[1]

The basic rules

You must satisfy all the following rules to be eligible for a CCG. The rules are laid down in legally binding directions. None of the words used are defined. 'Partner' and 'family' are not, therefore, restricted to their meanings for the purposes of income support (IS) or income-based jobseeker's allowance (JSA).

- **You must be in receipt of IS or income-based JSA when your application for a CCG is treated as made** (see p488).[2] The only exception to this rule is if you are due to leave institutional or residential accommodation (see p471) within six weeks of your application for a CCG and you are likely to get IS or income-based JSA when you leave.[3] You will not be treated as receiving income-based JSA if you make your application for a CCG on one of the three 'waiting days' for JSA (see p53), unless you are applying for a grant in order to move out of institutional or residential care.[4] You are treated as receiving income-based JSA if you get a hardship payment of JSA[5] (see CPAG's *Jobseeker's Allowance Handbook*). You should be treated as 'in receipt of' IS or income-based JSA if you receive a backdated award covering the date of your CCG application.[6] According to advice to the social fund inspectors (SFIs), you are not 'in receipt' of benefit if your partner is the claimant.[7] Arguably, this is a very restrictive way to interpret the directions of a discretionary safety net scheme and could be challenged.

- **You must not have too much capital.** Any CCG awarded is reduced by the amount of capital you have in excess of £500 (£1,000 if you or your partner are 60 or over).[8] Capital is calculated as for IS or income-based JSA, depending on which benefit you are getting[9] (see p415 and CPAG's *Jobseeker's Allowance Handbook*). Payments made from the family fund to you, your partner or child are ignored.[10] Any back to work bonus counts as capital.[11] Capital held by your children should be disregarded.[12] **Note:** When deciding whether or not to make an award, *all* your income and capital resources can be taken into account, apart from the mobility component of disability living allowance.[13] The £500/£1,000 rule only affects the *amount* of an award.
- **You or your partner must not be involved in a trade dispute** unless your claim is for travel expenses to visit a sick person (see p476). For what counts as being involved in a trade dispute, see p61.
- **You cannot get a CCG for an excluded item** (see p462).
- **You must be awarded a CCG of at least £30**, unless your award is for daily living expenses or travel expenses,[14] but see p464 (excluded items).
- **You must need a CCG for one or more of the following purposes:**[15]
  - to help you, or a member of your family, or other person for whom you or a member of your family will be providing care, to establish yourself in the community following a stay in institutional or residential accommodation in which you received care (see p470);
  - to help you, or a member of your family, or other person for whom you or a member of your family will be providing care, to remain in the community rather than enter institutional or residential accommodation in which you will receive care (see p472);
  - to help you to set up home in the community as part of a planned resettlement programme following a period during which you have been without a settled way of life;
  - to ease exceptional pressures on you and your family (see p474);
  - to allow you, or your partner, to care for a prisoner or young offender on temporary release (see p470);

– to help you, or one or more members of your family, with travel expenses within the UK in certain circumstances (see p476).

The guidance and priorities

The Secretary of State and district office managers issue guidance to social fund officers (SFOs) to help them decide which applicants should get a CCG (see p458).

The guidance is *not legally binding* and SFOs must exercise discretion in each individual case, taking into account the nature, extent and urgency of the need (see p457). They are told to use their discretion sensitively and with imagination to promote the objectives of community care; to avoid a rigid interpretation of the guidance; and to consider circumstances not covered by the guidance.[16] In practice, however, SFOs tend to use the *SF Guide* as a rule book and only award CCGs to meet rigidly defined high priority needs.

The *SF Guide* suggests needs are prioritised as follows:[17]

• High priority should normally be given if a CCG will have a significant and substantial impact in resolving or improving the circumstances of the applicant and be very important in fulfilling the purpose of CCGs (see p468).
• Medium priority should normally be given if a CCG will have a substantial impact in resolving or improving the circumstances of the applicant but is less important in fulfilling the purpose of CCGs.
• Low priority should normally be given if the need in question is indirectly limited to the circumstances of the applicant or will be of minor importance in fulfilling the purpose of CCGs.

Examples given of circumstances which may affect priority include:[18]

• mental or physical disability and illness and general frailty;
• physical or social abuse or neglect;
• a long period of sleeping rough;
• unstable family circumstances and broken homes;
• behavioural problems – eg, due to drug or alcohol misuse.

Social fund officers are reminded that the above guidance is not exhaustive.[19] They might, for example, identify circumstances which would give an application higher priority than normally given to the need in question.

The *SF Guide* suggests higher priority is given to a new type of expense (particularly if unforeseeable) than to items which need replacing in the normal course of events – eg, a broken cooker.[20] Nothing in the law justifies this distinction, however, and it has been criticised by the legal adviser to the Social Fund Commissioner.[21] The guidance also implies that you should meet the cost of replacing items from weekly IS/income-based JSA.[22] This suggests that benefit rates cover these needs but there is, in fact, no legal definition of the needs IS or income-based JSA should meet.[23]

Local guidance will state which level of priority (usually high only) can be met by the budget. Unfortunately, the vagueness of the above definition of high priority needs gives district offices considerable leeway to interpret 'high priority' as they want.

The High Court has ruled that if a need is assessed to have the level of priority which the local guidance says the district budget can meet, a CCG should normally be paid (see p460).

The important thing to remember is that the only legal requirement for eligibility for a CCG is that you satisfy the basic rules set out on pp467-68. Always give *your* reasons why your needs are high priority and how a CCG will help your circumstances and promote community care.

Items and amounts

You can ask for a payment for any item or service which is not excluded by law (see p462).

The *SF Guide* states that the amount you request should normally be allowed unless it is unreasonable.[24]

Local offices often refer to well known catalogue shop prices as a guide as to what is reasonable. There is no legal maximum award. The minimum that can be awarded in most cases is £30 (see p468).[25]

If you have borrowed money to obtain an item or service, even if help for that item is excluded by the directions, you can apply for a CCG to repay the debt.[26]

If you are caring for a prisoner or young offender on temporary release, the *SF Guide* suggests it is normally reasonable to award one-seventh of your IS or income-based JSA for each day. If the prisoner is your partner, the *SF Guide* suggests one-seventh of the difference between the couple rate and your personal allowance.[27]

2. MOVING OUT OF INSTITUTIONAL OR RESIDENTIAL ACCOMMODATION

A CCG can be paid to help you, or a member of your family, or other person for whom you or a member of your family will be providing care, to establish yourself in the community, following a stay in institutional or residential accommodation in which you received care.[28]

Interpretation

- None of the above terms are defined in the SF Directions. They are, therefore, open to interpretation to fit your circumstances.
- The *SF Guide* says institutional or residential accommodation means accommodation where residents receive '... a significant and substantial amount of care, supervision or protection because they are unable to live independently in the community or might be a danger to others in the community ...'[29] Examples of accommodation given are hospitals, residential care and nursing homes, prisons and youth centres, foster care, group homes, supported lodgings, sheltered housing and various types of hostel.[30]
- You should be covered where you are establishing yourself in the community for the first time because, for example, you have always lived in care or you have recently arrived in the UK and have been in a refugee camp overseas or a refugee hostel in the UK (the High Court has ruled that 'the community' is restricted to the UK[31]). The High Court has said that you must be actually or imminently in the community to qualify.[32]
- The *SF Guide* suggests that a 'stay in' institutional or residential accommodation normally means at least three months, or a pattern of frequent or regular admission.[33] The High Court has ruled, however, that undue importance should not be attached to the reference to three months.[34]
- See p475 for the meaning of 'family'.
- If you cannot establish that you lived in 'institutional or residential accommodation', you may still qualify for a grant. See 'Staying out of institutional or residential accommodation' (p472) and 'Planned resettlement' (p473).

What to claim for

You can claim for help with any expenses which are necessary to help establishment in the community. Examples include:

- furniture, cookers, beds, bedding, kitchen, cleaning and household equipment, floor-covering, curtains and connection charges, when setting up home;
- moving expenses including fares, connection charges and storage charges.
- clothing and footwear;
- items needed because of a disability (including wheelchairs,[35] or extra clothing etc).

3. STAYING OUT OF INSTITUTIONAL OR RESIDENTIAL ACCOMMODATION

A CCG can be paid to help you, or a member of your family, or other person for whom you or a member of your family will be providing care, to remain in the community, rather than enter institutional or residential accommodation in which you will receive care.[36]

Interpretation

- None of the above terms are defined in the SF directions. They are, therefore, open to interpretation to fit your circumstances.
- See p471 for the guidance on the meaning of 'institutional or residential accommodation'. See p475 for the meaning of 'family'.
- There is no requirement that a CCG must be able to 'prevent' you going into institutional or residential accommodation. The legal test is whether a CCG will 'help' you remain in the community. SFOs are told to consider whether a CCG 'would improve the applicant's independent life in the community and therefore lessen the risk of admission into care' or 'delay such an admission'.[37] Going into hospital, even for a short admission, counts as entering care in this context.[38] The risk of care does not have to be immediate, but should be more than a remote possibility (if it is immediate, the application should be given higher priority).[39] If your condition makes you liable to stays in care, you could still get a CCG if it could reduce the frequency or length of such stays.
- Actual or potential risk to physical or mental health because of a lack of items such as basic furniture, cooking facilities, clothes, bedding and heaters can be used to argue that a CCG for such items will lessen the risk of entry into hospital or other types of institutional or residential accommodation.

What to claim for

You can claim for help with any expenses which will help you remain in the community by lessening the risk of you ending up in care – eg, hospital. Examples include:

- Minor repairs, redecoration and refurbishment, a survey fee which cannot be included in a mortgage/loan met by IS/income-based JSA, heaters, fuel reconnection charges, installation of a pre-payment meter, bedding, a washing machine to improve your living conditions.[40]

- Moving expenses, furniture and household equipment if a move to more suitable accommodation will help you to remain in the community, or if you are moving to help look after a vulnerable person.
- Items needed because of a disability (including wheelchairs,[41] special clothing, an orthopaedic mattress or an upright armchair).
- Expenses of setting up home where, for example, you have been living rough or in temporary accommodation.

4. PLANNED RESETTLEMENT

A CCG can be paid to help you set up home in the community as part of a planned resettlement programme following a period during which you have been without a settled way of life.[42]

Interpretation

- None of the above terms are defined in the SF Directions. They are, therefore, open to interpretation to fit your circumstances.
- The *SF Guide* says people without a settled way of life may have been in a night shelter, hostel, emergency shelter, temporary supported lodging scheme or sleeping rough but that this is not an exhaustive list.[43]
- The *SF Guide* also says planned resettlement programmes may be run by local authorities, voluntary organisations, housing associations and registered charities.[44] Again, this is not an exhaustive list and you can argue you are part of a programme planned by any other organisation or person. SFOs are told they may need to check that a resettlement programme exists at the accommodation you are moving from and that you are on such a programme.[45]
- SFOs are told to 'give priority to those who have for a substantial amount of time led an unsettled way of life'.[46]
- If you cannot qualify for a CCG under this section, you may qualify under 'Staying out of institutional or residential accommodation' (p472).

What to claim for

You can claim for help with any expenses which will help you set up home. Examples include:

- furniture and household equipment;
- removal expenses, storage charges and fares on moving home;
- connection charges.

5. EASING EXCEPTIONAL PRESSURES ON FAMILIES

You can get a CCG to ease exceptional pressures on you and your family.[47] The scope for applications is very wide.

When making your application, always fully explain all the pressures your family is experiencing and how a CCG will ease those pressures and help you to continue living independently in the community.

If your application is refused on the grounds of insufficient priority, consider asking for a review (see p492).

'Exceptional pressures'

The term 'exceptional pressures' is not defined in the SF directions and should be given its normal, everyday meaning. The following points may be of relevance:

- Comparisons with 'normal' families by SFOs are usually based on generalised assumptions. The level of pressure should be considered in terms of its effect on the individual family in question.[48] Clearly though, 'exceptional' means something greater than the normal range of pressures experienced by all families.
- The overall effect of the different pressures on a family should be assessed, including their cumulative impact. You should always, therefore, list all the pressures affecting your family and explain their overall effect.
- Whether the pressures were foreseeable or are common is irrelevant.
- The breakdown of a relationship, particularly involving domestic violence, is a common source of exceptional stress.
- Low income, lone parenthood and poor or overcrowded living conditions can be the source of exceptional pressures.
- Pressures that arise from a sudden event (eg, a disaster) can be exceptional and traumatic. Pressures which have existed for a long time do not necessarily become easier to handle.
- There does not have to be any risk of a person going into care for exceptional pressures to exist.
- Mental stress, anxiety, depression, disability and illness are all sources and symptoms of exceptional pressures. The fact that an applicant does not appear stressed at an interview does not mean that exceptional pressures do not exist. A recent 'Best Practice Note' (see p459) states, 'where there are physical and/or mental health problems affecting daily life, and/or disability premiums are in

payment, it is probable that the family will be under exceptional pressure'.[49]

- Exceptional pressures experienced by children are entirely valid – eg, shame, discomfort, health risks from lack of clothes or facilities in the home.
- The *SF Guide* suggests higher priority should be given to a new type of expense[50] but this approach should be challenged (see p469).

'Family'

The law refers to 'easing exceptional pressures on a person and his family'. This implies that people not living in a family are excluded. This interpretation was endorsed in a High Court case.[51]

The word 'family' is not defined. The *SF Guide* says it should be given a flexible interpretation.[52] It could encompass:

- a couple (married or not) with or without children;
- a lesbian or gay couple;
- a household with grown-up children;
- adult brothers and sisters or relatives living together;
- a parent living with children for part of the week only;
- a pregnant woman – most likely to be accepted if she is at least 24 weeks pregnant.[53]

What to claim for

You can claim for any non-excluded items which will help ease the exceptional pressures your family is facing. Examples include:

- items which will improve your family's living conditions or physical or mental health;
- maternity and funeral expenses that are arguably not covered by the Regulated SF (see p464);
- moving and setting-up home expenses if you move to more suitable accommodation or following the breakdown of a relationship;
- minor structural repairs;
- repairs or replacement of items damaged by behavioural problems;
- items needed because of a disability (including wheelchairs,[54] extra clothing, bedding, etc).

6. TRAVEL EXPENSES

A CCG can be paid to assist you and/or a member of your family with travel expenses in the UK (including overnight accommodation charges) to:[55]

- visit someone who is ill (in hospital or elsewhere); *or*
- attend a relative's funeral; *or*
- ease a domestic crisis (not defined); *or*
- visit a child who is with the other parent pending a court decision on which parent the child is to live with; *or*
- move to suitable accommodation.

The amount of the payment

The *SF Guide* suggests that grants for travel expenses should be calculated as follows:[56]

- the cost of 'standard' rate public transport (excluding air fares); *or*
- the cost of petrol, either up to the cost of public transport if available or in full if public transport is not available or you are unable to use it; *or*
- taxi fares, if public transport is unavailable or you or your partner cannot use public transport and have no access to private transport; *plus*
- the cost of an escort's fare if you cannot travel alone; *plus*
- the reasonable cost of necessary overnight accommodation.

According to the *SF Guide* a CCG for hospital fares may be reduced by the amount of any IS or income-based JSA personal allowance you are receiving for a hospital patient which exceeds the hospital personal allowance (see p97).[57] CCGs for travel expenses can be paid in advance or by instalment if you are making regular visits.[58]

The £30 minimum rules (see p468) do not apply to CCGs for travel expenses.[59]

CHAPTER TWENTY-FOUR

Loans

This chapter covers:

1. Budgeting loans (see below)
2. Crisis loans (p479)
3. Repayments (p485)

Budgeting loans are intended to help people who have been receiving income support (IS) or income-based jobseeker's allowance (JSA) for at least 26 weeks to meet one-off expenses. Crisis loans are not restricted to those on benefit, but are only available to deal with special problems.

There is no legal entitlement to a loan. Payments are discretionary. You can, however, ask for a review if you are refused a loan or awarded less than you asked for (see p492).

Loans are obviously far less attractive than grants because they must be repaid although they are, at least, interest-free.[1] Another problem with loans is that they cannot exceed what the Benefits Agency thinks you can afford to repay.

It is always better, therefore, to ask for a grant if you are elibible to do so (see Chapter 23). There is nothing to stop you asking for a grant and a loan for the same item at the same time. Legally, your application is to the social fund (SF) as a whole and should be automatically considered for a grant and a loan.[2] If you are awarded a loan, you can accept it and request a review to get it changed to a grant (see p492).

I. BUDGETING LOANS

The basic rules

You must satisfy all the following rules in order to be eligible for a budgeting loan. The rules are laid down in directions which are legally binding. None of the words used are defined in the directions:

- **You must be in receipt of IS or income-based JSA when your budgeting loan application is determined by the Benefits Agency.**[3]

According to advice to the social fund inspectors (SFIs), you are not in 'receipt' of benefit if your partner is the claimant.[4] Arguably, this is a very restrictive way to interpret the directions of a discretionary safety net scheme and could be challenged.

- **You, or your partner, between you must have been receiving IS or income-based JSA throughout the 26 weeks before the date on which your application is determined.**[5] One break of 14 days or less when IS/JSA was not being paid can be included in the 26 weeks.[6] A period covered by benefit paid in arrears counts towards the 26 weeks.[7] If you received benefit while in Northern Ireland, that also counts.[8] The *SF Guide* says that you can have had more than one partner during the 26 weeks.[9] *Note:* The three 'waiting days' at the start of a jobseeking period (see CPAG's *Jobseeker's Allowance Handbook*) do not count towards the 26-week qualifying period.[10]
- **You must not have too much capital.** The rules are the same as for community care grants (CCGs) (see p468 for details).
- **You, or your partner, must not be involved in a trade dispute** (see p465).
- **The loan must be to assist you to meet important intermittent expenses** for which it may be difficult to budget.[11]
- **The loan must not be for an excluded item** (see p462).
- **The loan must be at least £30** (if you need a loan of less than £30, you are not entitled to anything). The maximum you can get is £1,000 less any outstanding SF loan(s) you have.[12]
- **The loan must not exceed an amount which you are likely to be able to repay** (see p486).[13]

The guidance and priorities

The Secretary of State and district office managers issue guidance to social fund officers (SFOs) to help them decide who should get a budgeting loan (see p458).

The guidance is not legally binding and SFOs must exercise discretion in each individual case, taking into account the nature, extent and urgency of the need (see p460). They are told to avoid a rigid interpretation of the guidance and consider circumstances not covered by it.[14] In practice, however, SFOs tend to use the *SF Guide* as a rule book and only award loans to meet rigidly defined 'high priority' needs.

The *SF Guide* gives the following examples of high, medium and low priority needs:[15]

- **High priority**: Essential furniture and household equipment; bedclothes; essential removal charges; fuel meter installation and reconnection charges; non-mains fuel costs; essential minor repairs

and maintenance for owner-occupiers, which could not be met by a local authority grant.
- **Medium priority**: Non-essential furniture and household equipment; clothing; debts; redecoration.
- **Low priority**: Leisure items; removal charges and rent in advance if a move is not essential.

Social fund officers are reminded that the examples are not exhaustive and that they should identify circumstances which might give an application higher priority than normally given to the need in question.[16] Local guidance will state which level of priority (usually only high) can be met by the budget.

If you are applying for a high priority need as defined above, point this out in your application. Otherwise, do not be put off from applying by the guidance. Always give *your* reasons why your needs are high priority and consider requesting a review if your application is refused. You should also make sure the items you need the loan for are worth £30 or more (see p478).

The amount of the loan

The amount awarded must be between £30 and £1,000.[17]

There is no guidance on how much should be paid for specific items or services. SFOs are told to accept your estimate of the cost if it is 'within the broad range of prices considered appropriate for an item of serviceable quality'.[18] Local offices often refer to well known catalogue shop prices as a guide as to what is reasonable. Ask for a review if you are unhappy about the amount awarded to you (but see p492).

You cannot be awarded more than you can afford to repay.[19] The amount you can afford to repay is usually calculated by multiplying your weekly repayment rate by 78 (see p486). If you already have one or more loans, you may find you are offered less than you ask for.

2. CRISIS LOANS

The basic rules

You must satisfy all the following rules in order to be eligible for a crisis loan. The rules are laid down in directions which are legally binding. None of the words used are defined in the directions:

- You must be 16 or over.[20]
- You must not be an 'excluded person' (see p480). [21]

- The loan must not be for an excluded item (see p462).
- The loan must not exceed an amount which you are likely to be able to repay.[22] There are maximum awards (see p485), but no minimum amount is laid down in law.[23] See p485 for how a loan for living expenses is calculated.
- You must be without sufficient resources to meet the immediate short-term needs of yourself and/or your family (see p482).[24]
- The loan must be for expenses in an emergency, or as a consequence of a disaster, and be the only means by which serious damage or serious risk to the health or safety of yourself or a member of your family may be prevented (see p482);[25] *or* the loan must be for rent in advance payable to a non-local authority landlord and a CCG is being awarded following a stay in institutional or residential care (see p470).[26]

Making an application

It is common for Benefits Agency counter staff to advise potential applicants (eg, homeless or young people without money) that they will not be given a crisis loan. Do not be put off. Always insist on completing an application form and being given a written decision. See p490 for more details.

Excluded persons

Those excluded in all circumstances

The following people are excluded by the directions from getting a crisis loan in all circumstances.[27]

- People in hospital, nursing homes or residential care homes (private or local authority), *unless* their discharge is planned to take place within the next two weeks.
- Prisoners and people lawfully detained, including those on temporary release (but not those released on parole or on bail pending a court hearing[28]).
- Members of religious orders who are fully maintained by the order.
- People in 'relevant education' who are not entitled to IS or income-based JSA.

Those excluded in some circumstances

The following people are excluded by the directions from getting a crisis loan except in very limited circumstances:

- Full-time students not on IS or income-based JSA can only claim a crisis loan for expenses arising out of a disaster.[29]

- 'Persons from abroad' for the purposes of IS and income-based JSA who are not entitled to these benefits either at the ordinary or the urgent cases rate (see p67) can only claim a crisis loan for expenses arising out of a disaster.[30] Many asylum-seekers are now in this position as most are no longer entitled to benefit (see p80). To get a crisis loan, they would have to show that their situation constitutes a disaster and that they are likely to be able to repay the loan. Social fund officers (SFOs) are told to give particular attention to the clothing needs of asylum-seekers and refugees.[31] **Note:** If you are an overstayer, subject to a deportation order, or an illegal entrant, you should not apply for a crisis loan before getting advice about regularising your status here.
- People involved in a trade dispute (see p465 for details).
- People subject to certain JSA disallowances or sanctions (see below for details).

Those subject to JSA disallowances or sanctions

Excluded persons

If you are subject to a JSA disallowance or sanction in any of the following circumstances, you can only get a crisis loan for expenses arising from a disaster (see p482), or for items needed for cooking or space heating (including fireguards), for the periods specified. The restriction does not apply, however, if you are receiving hardship payments of JSA.[32]

- Your claim for JSA has been disallowed because you do not satisfy the labour market conditions (eg, you are not available for or actively seeking work). A crisis loan can only be paid for the above expenses for 14 days, from the first day of the benefit week following the disallowance decision, or the day of the decision if it is made on the first day of a benefit week.[33]
- You are not getting JSA because you have been sanctioned for failing to take up or complete a 'New Deal' employment or training option for 18/26-year-olds. A crisis loan can only be paid for the above expenses during your sanction period, which will either be two or four weeks.[34] If, for example, you receive a two-week sanction from 9–22 April 1998 (your JSA due on 24 April will not be paid), your crisis loan restriction applies during that period.[35]
- You are not getting JSA because you have been sanctioned for another reason (eg, for leaving a job without just cause). A crisis loan can only be paid for the above expenses for 14 days, from the first day of the benefit week following the sanction period.[36] If, for example, you

receive a two-week sanction, the crisis loan restriction applies during the following two weeks, coinciding with the period you are without JSA (which is paid in arrears).

Notes:

- For details of JSA disallowances, sanctions and hardship payments and the 'New Deal' employment and training options, see CPAG's *Jobseeker's Allowance Handbook*.
- After the periods specified have expired and during any period you are receiving JSA hardship payments, you are eligible for a crisis loan without any restrictions.
- See p485 for details of how much crisis loan is payable for living expenses when you are subject to JSA disallowance or sanction.

Emergencies and disasters

Most crisis loans can only be awarded in an emergency or following a disaster. Neither of these terms is defined in the directions. You should always explain why a particular situation constitutes an emergency or disaster for you or your family. The consequences, rather than the causes, of the crisis should be the key issue. Self-inflicted crises are not excluded and SFOs should not deny you a crisis loan based on their judgements about your behaviour. Loss of money in the past should not prejudice the payment of a crisis loan needed because of a further loss.

Serious damage/risk to health or safety

A crisis loan has to be the only means of preventing serious damage or risk to health or safety. You will have to show there are no other resources or ways of meeting your need. This is often interpreted very strictly by SFOs. If an SFO suggests other means which are impractical or unavailable to you, ask for a review.

The potential serious risk to your health or safety might be obvious – eg, you have no money for food or other essentials. Any supporting evidence you can get from your doctor, social worker, etc will help your case.

Survival for a period without money or a crisis loan does not mean that a crisis loan is not the only means of preventing serious damage or risk to your health or safety.

Resources

You must be without sufficient resources to meet the immediate short-term needs of yourself and/or your family. 'Resources' are not defined in the SF directions. The *SF Guide* says all resources which '... are actually available to the applicant or could be obtained in time to meet the need' should be taken into account.[37] Resources available on credit should only be taken into account if the applicant is not on IS or income-based JSA and can afford the required repayments.[38]

The *SF Guide* says the following resources should be disregarded:[39]

- other SF payments, housing benefit, disability living allowance (mobility component);
- the value of your home, premises acquired for occupation within the next six months, and premises occupied by a relative or your ex-partner;
- the value of any reversionary interest – ie, an interest in property or capital which you will only be able to enjoy in the future, when a specified event occurs;
- your business assets;
- any sum paid to you because of damage to, or loss of, your home or personal possessions and intended for their repair or replacement;
- any sum acquired on the express condition that it is used for essential repairs or improvements to your home;
- any personal possessions, except those acquired for the purpose of qualifying for a crisis loan;
- any payments from the Independent Living Funds, and the Macfarlane Trusts (see Appendix 1).

Social fund officers are told not to routinely refer applicants to employers, relatives or close friends 'unless there is reason to believe their help will be forthcoming'.[40] They are reminded that social services do not normally meet financial needs.[41] Emergency payments for children should be disregarded unless they meet the need for which the crisis loan is requested.[42]

The *SF Guide* suggests it may be reasonable to disregard other resources at least for a temporary period.[43] You could argue that money set aside to meet forthcoming bills (eg, council tax, fuel bills) is not available and should be disregarded.

Guidance on crisis loan situations

The Secretary of State and district office managers issue guidance to SFOs to help them decide who should get a crisis loan (see p458).

The guidance is *not legally binding*. SFOs must consider each application on its merits, taking into account the nature, extent and urgency of the need in each case (see p460). The guidance says that it would be rare for the budget to be insufficient to pay a crisis loan to avoid serious damage or risk to health and safety.[44] If you are refused a crisis loan, ask for a review (see p492).

The *SF Guide* gives a few examples of situations where a crisis loan may be appropriate. Remember, however, you are eligible for a loan in *any* situation as long as you satisfy the basic rules set out on p479.

Living expenses for a short period

The *SF Guide* suggests a crisis loan could be awarded to meet day-to-day living expenses in the following situations:

- you are waiting for your first benefit payment or wages and your employer will not give you an advance;[45]
- you are suffering hardship because your employer has imposed a compulsory unpaid holiday;[46]
- you have lost money or you have lost a giro and replacement is delayed (see p147 on lost giros);[47]
- you cannot get IS or income-based JSA because your capital is over £8,000 but you cannot realise your assets immediately;[48]
- you are homeless and need living expenses. The *SF Guide* stresses the risk to physical and mental health brought about by sleeping rough and prolonged homelessness.[49]

The guidance suggests a crisis loan should only cover living expenses for more than 14 days in exceptional circumstances – eg, a continuing crisis, loss of money which would normally cover you until your next income is due, or no money because of misfortune or mismanagement.[50]

Other situations

- Emergency travel expenses if you are stranded away from home or emergency fares to hospital.[51]
- Fuel reconnection charges[52] and fuel debts[53]. The *SF Guide* says that if you need a crisis loan to pay for a powercard or token, an amount to meet fuel arrears should be awarded separately from amounts for current consumption, which would come under living expenses (see above), and which are subject to the minimum on p485.[54]
- Rent in advance payable to a non-local authority landlord if you are also awarded a CCG on leaving care – the rules about serious risk to health and safety do not apply in this situation.[55]
- Disasters – eg, fire or flood[56] (see p482).

The amount of the loan

There is no legal minimum. There is a general legal maximum of £1,000 less any outstanding SF loan(s) you have.[57] You also cannot be awarded more than you can afford to repay,[58] usually calculated by multiplying your weekly repayment rate by 78 (see p486). If you already have one or more loans you may find you are offered less than you asked for.

There are also more specific legal maximums for items, services and living expenses.

Items and services:[59] the maximum you can get is the reasonable cost of purchase (including delivery and installation) or the cost of repair, if cheaper.

Living expenses:[60]

- the normal maximum you can get is 75 per cent of the appropriate IS/income-based JSA personal allowance for you *and* any partner plus £17.30 for each child;
- if you have been disallowed JSA because you have been sanctioned, or have failed to satisfy the labour market conditions (see p481), the maximum crisis loan payable to your partner for living expenses is restricted to 75 per cent of her/his JSA personal allowance;
- if you are getting a 'hardship payment' of JSA, the maximum crisis loan you can get for living expenses is the lesser of:
  - 75 per cent of the normal income-based JSA personal allowance for you and any partner plus £17.30 for each child;
  - the hardship rate of income-based JSA payable for you and any family.

See CPAG's *Jobseeker's Allowance Handbook* for details of hardship payments.

3. REPAYMENTS

All loans must be repaid to the Benefits Agency. The rate of repayment, the repayment period and the method of recovery are technically decided by the Secretary of State and not by SFOs.[61] In practice, decisions are made on her/his behalf by SFOs. Guidance, which is *not legally binding*, is issued in a *Social Fund Decision and Review Guide* (see Appendix 5).

Unlike SFO decisions (eg, the amount of loan awarded), which can be challenged by review, Secretary of State decisions are not subject to review. You can request that a Secretary of State's decision is reconsidered, however, by 'making a complaint' (see p487 – 'Challenging repayment terms').

The rate and period of repayment

There is no law specifying repayment rates or periods. The guidance says loans should normally be recovered over a period of 78 weeks,[62] or exceptionally 104 weeks,[63] at the weekly rate of:

- 15 per cent of your IS/income-based JSA applicable amount, excluding housing costs (see p27) if you have no 'continuing commitments';[64]
- 10 per cent if you have 'continuing commitments' of up to £7.55 a week;[65]
- 5 per cent if you have higher 'continuing commitments'.[66]

Recovery of a loan should be deferred until any existing loans are repaid.[67]

You should argue that if you are getting the hardship rate of JSA, you should not be required to repay until income-based JSA is restored to its normal rate, or that recovery should be at the 5 per cent rate.

Recovery of loans

Methods of recovery

Loans are nearly always recovered by direct deductions from benefit, although you can make a direct payment at any time to partially or wholly pay off the debt. Deductions can only be made from the following benefits:[68]

- IS;
- family credit;
- JSA (contributory or income-based);
- incapacity benefit;
- severe disablement allowance;
- invalid care allowance;
- disability working allowance;
- disablement benefit, reduced earnings allowance and industrial death benefit;
- widows' benefits (excluding the lump-sum widow's payment);
- retirement pensions (all types);
- maternity allowance.

No recovery can be made from the back to work bonus paid with either IS or income-based JSA.[69]

Increases of benefit for age and dependants, and additional benefit under SERPS are also subject to deduction.

Deductions from benefit can be made even where an order for bankruptcy or sequestration has been made.[70]

Who they can be recovered from

A loan can be legally recovered from:

- you (the applicant) or the person who the loan was for;[71]
- your partner, if you are living together as a married or unmarried couple as defined for IS purposes (see p346);[72]
- a 'liable relative' (see p106) or a 'person who has given a sponsorship undertaking' (see p85).[73] If you claim IS or income-based JSA, a crisis loan will be recovered from you. If you cannot claim IS/JSA, a crisis loan can be recovered from your liable relative or sponsor.[74]

There is no right of review or appeal against a decision about the rate of repayment of a loan.

Challenging repayment terms

If you are unhappy about the repayment terms when a loan is offered, you should write to the Benefits Agency and explain why. This is technically known as 'making a complaint'.[75] You should do this before accepting the offer of a loan. If loan repayments are causing you hardship, you can write to the Benefits Agency at any time, outlining your commitments, and ask for rescheduling – ie, lower repayments over a longer period.[76]

CHAPTER TWENTY-FIVE

Applications, payments and reviews

This chapter covers:
1. Applications (below)
2. Decisions and payments (p491)
3. Internal reviews (p492)
4. Social fund inspector reviews (p496)

1. APPLICATIONS

Making an application

Applications for a social fund (SF) payment must be made in writing, either on a standard application form obtainable from the Benefits Agency or in some other way which is acceptable to the Secretary of State – eg, a letter with all the necessary details.[1] If your application is incomplete, the Benefits Agency can ask you to provide additional information either in writing, or by calling in at your local office.[2]

An application can be made on your behalf by somebody else, as long as you give your written consent (this is not necessary if an appointee is acting for you – see p129).[3] If you are a member of a couple and claim a community care grant (CCG) or budgeting loan, you will only be treated as 'in receipt of' income support (IS) or income-based jobseeker's allowance (JSA) if you are the benefit claimant (see pp468 and 478).

Your application is treated as having been made on the day it is received at a Benefits Agency office.[4] If your application was incomplete and you comply with a request for additional information, your application will be treated as made on the day it was originally received.[5]

Each application is made to the fund as a whole and should be considered for a CCG, budgeting loan or crisis loan as appropriate.[6]

Where to apply

You should normally apply to the Benefits Agency office which covers the area in which you live.[7] If you are applying for a crisis loan, however, you can apply to the office where your need arises.[8] In an emergency, social services or other agencies can contact the Benefits Agency 'out of hours' service on your behalf (see p148).

If you are moving out of care and claiming a CCG, you should apply to the office which covers the area you are moving to, unless you are only claiming removal expenses and/or fares.[9]

Evidence and information

Your application should normally be decided on the information you give on your application form, unless this is incomplete.[10] Exceptionally, you may be asked for corroborating evidence such as an estimate or a medical note.[11] You should not be asked to get evidence for which you have to pay.[12] Evidence from a third party should be made known to you on request, although its source may remain confidential.[13] Third party evidence can be used *without* that person's consent.[14]

Community care grants and budgeting loans

You should apply on form SF300, which you can obtain from the Benefits Agency and advice centres. The form is for both CCGs and budgeting loans.

Tips on completing the application form

- In part 3 of the form, you are asked whether you want a grant or loan. Always ask for a grant if you satisfy the eligibility rules (see p467). You can ask for a grant and a loan. *Legally, your application is to the fund as a whole* and each application should automatically be considered for a grant *and* a loan.[15]
- You should complete part 6 of the form with full details of what you need. Be as specific as possible (do not write just 'furniture' or 'clothes', list each item needed). Write down the actual cost or a reasonable estimate for each item. It is not usually necessary to supply written estimates from a supplier (unless you are asking for removal expenses, when two written estimates are usually required).
- Part 6 also asks why the items are needed. Part 7 asks more specific questions about why you need help. It is important to establish that you satisfy the rules of eligibility for a CCG or budgeting loan (see Chapters 23 and 24), including the purposes for which a CCG can be

awarded. It is also important to show why your application should be given high priority. Refer to the local or national guidance if it helps your case (you can obtain a copy of the local guidance from your local Benefits Agency office). Use the space in Part 10 of the form and continue in a letter, if necessary.

- Submit any supporting evidence with your application – eg, a letter from your doctor or social worker.

Crisis loans

You can apply for a crisis loan on form SF400 at the Benefits Agency which will normally be completed while you are being interviewed. Alternatively, you can submit a self-completion form SF401 available from the Benefits Agency or advice centres. It is common for Benefits Agency counter staff to 'advise' potential applicants that they will not be given a loan. Do not be put off. Always insist on completing an application form and receiving a written decision. Make sure the form fully records your needs and circumstances. You will usually be interviewed in connection with your application. Crisis loan decisions should be based on your circumstances at the date of decision and social fund officers (SFOs) should never deliberately delay a decision until the need has passed.

Repeat applications

If you have been awarded or refused a payment for an item or service, you cannot get a payment for the same item or service within 26 weeks of a previous application unless:[16]

- there has been a relevant change of circumstances; *or*
- you are applying for a budgeting loan for which you were ineligible when you made your first application because neither you nor your partner had been on IS or income-based JSA, or a combination of both benefits, for 26 weeks.

You should note the following points:

- Applications by different partners are not caught by the above rule. The second application must be made by the same person who made the first application for the rule to apply.[17]
- The rule does not apply if your first application was incomplete; *or* you withdrew it before a decision was made; *or* you declined or did not respond to a loan offer.[18]
- Only payments for the 'same item or service' are excluded. An application for bedding may be different from an application for

sheets, pillow cases and eiderdown. Applications for different items of clothing should not be caught by the rule. An application for a bed for one child is different to an application for a bed for another child.[19]

• Where there are a number of repeat applications for the same item or service, the 26 weeks should run from the date of the first.[20]

• The Act refers to 'any relevant change of circumstances'[21] (which could include changes in the budget) whereas the SF direction refers to 'a relevant change in the applicant's circumstances'.[22] It can be argued that the direction wrongly restricts the powers laid down in the primary legislation.

If you think the rule about repeat applications has been wrongly applied, you are entitled to request a review (see p492).[23]

2. DECISIONS AND PAYMENTS

Decisions

You should receive a written decision on your application. If a payment is wholly or partly refused, the decision should explain why and state that you have the right to request a review. The reasons given are usually very general and sketchy – eg, your application is not high enough priority or is not for one of the purposes for which a payment can be made. If you are not satisfied you should consider asking for a review, see p492.

There are no legal time limits within which the Benefits Agency must make decisions. The *SF Guide*, however, says that 'all decisions should normally be made within 28 days of the date of the application'.[24] Decisions on urgent applications (eg, crisis loans) should be made within one working day.[25]

If there are unreasonable delays in getting a decision, you should complain to the social fund manager in your district office. If this does not help, you should ask your MP to take up your case with the manager, the Secretary of State or the Ombudsman. The Benefits Agency has published a *Customer Charter* for claimants. This gives target times for processing crisis loans (the day the need arises or the application is made) and community care grants (an average of seven days). There are no targets for dealing with budgeting loans.

Payments

You should normally be paid by giro made out to you.[26] The Benefits Agency can, however, choose to pay a supplier directly.[27] Payment can also be made in the form of travel warrants, food vouchers or cash, and in instalments. You can ask for a review of any decision to pay a supplier rather than you, or to pay in instalments.[28]

Note: Under the new Social Security Bill, overpayments will be recoverable where you have misrepresented or failed to disclose a material fact (see Appendix 2).

3. INTERNAL REVIEWS

Introduction

There is no right of appeal against decisions regarding the discretionary social fund (SF). There is instead a review system, which is divided into two distinct stages.

First, you ask for a review of a decision and your case is reconsidered by the office which made the decision. Internal reviews are carried out by reviewing officers (ROs) who are social fund officers (SFOs) or specially appointed social fund review officers.[29]

Second, if you are dissatisfied with the outcome, you can ask for a further review by a social fund inspector (SFI) based in an office in Birmingham, who reconsiders the case independently.[30]

You should always consider asking for a review if you are unhappy about a decision. If the decision is not changed following an internal review, you should always consider requesting a further review by an SFI who will reconsider your application more thoroughly and independently.

You should note, however, that a review decision may be unfavourable to you and result in the award of a loan rather than a CCG, or a smaller loan than the one originally awarded. The Benefits Agency can always recover a loan.

Note: At the time of writing, there is no power to recover a CCG which has been paid to you. Under the new Social Security Bill (see Appendix 2), however, overpayments will be recoverable where you have misrepresented or failed to disclose a material fact.

If you want to get a CCG award reviewed, wait until it has been paid and then request the review. But check the time limits for requesting a review (see p492). You should get advice if you are not sure whether to ask for a review. In general, but not always, decisions by SFIs appear to give greater weight to the urgency of the need.

The law regarding reviews is set out in legislation and the SF directions.

Decisions subject to review

All SFO decisions are subject to review, including:[31]

- the refusal of a grant or loan;
- the amount awarded;
- payment to a third party or by instalments;
- refusal to determine a repeat application.

Decisions about the repayment of loans are made by the Secretary of State and not subject to review, but can still be challenged (see p487).

Applying for a review

The basic rules

You must apply for a review of a decision by writing to the Benefits Agency **within 28 days** of the date the decision was issued to you.[32] Your application must include your grounds for requesting a review (see below – Tactics).[33] If somebody is making an application on your behalf, it must be accompanied by your written authority (unless the person is your appointee).[34]

Late applications can be accepted for 'special reasons'.[35] 'Special reasons' are not defined. They could include reasons why the application is late (eg, ill-health, domestic crises, wrong advice) or any other reasons – eg, you will suffer hardship without a review. The restrictive definition given to the phrase 'special reasons' for late appeals (see p170) does not apply to the SF. If the Benefits Agency does not accept there are special reasons, get advice. You may have to threaten judicial review if its refusal is unreasonable.

If your application is out of time, you can also ask the RO to use her/his powers to conduct an 'any time' review (see p494).

The Benefits Agency can ask you to submit further information in connection with your application if reasonably required.[36]

You can withdraw your application in writing at any time.[37]

Tactics

- Your application must be in writing. Keep a copy if possible. Quote your national insurance number if possible. If you do not have a national insurance number your application can be dealt with clerically. Begin by stating that you are requesting a review and clearly identify the decision you are unhappy about.
- If your application is late, give your 'special reasons' why it should be considered out of time (see above). Alternatively, you could ask the RO to conduct an 'anytime' review (see p494).

- Explain, as fully as possible, why you disagree with the SFO's decision.
- CCGs are often refused on the grounds that your application was not for one of the purposes for which a grant can be given. You can challenge such decisions by explaining how your application *is* for one of the purposes for which a CCG can be given (see p468).
- CCGs and loans are often refused on the grounds of 'insufficient priority' (see Chapter 22). You can challenge such decisions by stating you are not satisfied your particular needs and circumstances have been properly looked at. You should then explain why your application should be high priority.
- If you are unhappy about the amount you have been awarded, you should state that you are not satisfied that the SFO has assessed your needs properly. Explain why you need the amount you asked for, giving any further evidence or information which was not in your original application.
- If you are awarded a loan rather than a CCG, you can refuse or accept the loan and also ask for a review explaining why you think you should be awarded a CCG.
- Bear in mind that however good your case, a decision on review may be unfavourable (see p492).

'Any time' reviews

An RO *must* review a decision at any time, with or without an application from you, which appears:[38]

- to have been based on a mistake about the law or directions; *or*
- to have been made in ignorance of a material fact or based on a mistake about a material fact; *or*
- where there has been a relevant change of circumstances since the decision was given.

A relevant change in circumstances is not restricted to changes in *your* circumstances or those of your family. It could include, for example, any additional allocations to a district office budget during the year (see p459).

An RO *may* also review a decision at any time, with or without an application from you, '... in such other circumstances as he thinks fit'.[39] This is a wide discretionary power, not subject to any time limits or particular grounds for review.[40]

You can ask an RO to initiate a review under the above powers at any time – eg, if you are out of time to apply for a review.

Deciding reviews

The theory

When carrying out a review, ROs must take into account all the factors listed on p457 (eg, the nature, extent and urgency of the need, the SF directions and guidance and the budget).[41] Note also, the High Court ruling referred to on p460 about the assessment of need preceding budgetary considerations. In addition, they must consider:

- *first*, whether the original decision was legally correct (in particular, sustainable on the evidence and based on all relevant considerations and a correct interpretation of the law), reasonable, procedurally correct and unbiased and that the applicant had sufficient opportunity to put her/his case;[42]
- *second*, all the circumstances which existed at the time of the original decision and any new evidence and relevant changes in circumstances since the decision was made.[43]

The practice

Not surprisingly, reviews are rarely conducted with the thoroughness demanded by the legal requirements. In practice, budget considerations and the guidance on priorities tend to be the major determinants of review decisions. Also there is a tendency for ROs only to change original decisions in the light of new evidence.

Review procedure

Interview

If a decision is not wholly revised in your favour, you must be given the opportunity to attend an interview.[44] You have the legal right to be accompanied by a friend or representative.[45] At the interview, you must be given an explanation of the reasons for the review decision and an opportunity to put your case, including any additional evidence you have.[46]

The interview should take place in a private room and can be held in your home if, for example, you are severely disabled or ill.[47] The RO must make an accurate written record of your representations, to be agreed and signed by you.[48]

Tactics

- Always ask to be interviewed in a private room and complain if one is not offered.
- Do not sign the written record unless you agree with it and everything you want to say has been recorded. It is particularly important to include any new evidence or information you have.
- If you do not wish to attend an interview, tell the Benefits Agency, making it clear you still want the review to go ahead. Unless you withdraw your review application in writing, the Benefits Agency must proceed with the review and issue you with a review decision.
- Always insist on an interpreter if you are not familiar with English.

Decisions

Review decisions must be notified to you in writing and inform you of your right to request a further review by an SFI if you do not agree with the decision.[49]

4. SOCIAL FUND INSPECTOR REVIEWS

Introduction

If you are dissatisfied with a review decision, you have a right to request a further review by a social fund inspector (SFI).[50] You should always consider asking for a further review as your chances of success are generally higher than with the internal review, but see p492.

Social fund inspectors are based in the office of the Independent Review Service for the SF in Birmingham (see Appendix 3) and conduct their reviews independently of the Benefits Agency. They tend to produce a much higher standard of decision-making than review officers, and are generally better trained and have more time. They also tend to be less influenced by guidance and district budgets.

The law regarding SFI reviews is set out in legislation and SFI directions.

Applying for a further review

The basic rules

You must apply for a further review in writing within 28 days of the date the review decision was issued to you.[51] Your application must include your grounds for requesting a further review (see p497 – Tactics).[52] If somebody is applying on your behalf, you must send your written authority[53] (unless the person is your appointee). You should specifically authorise the person to make an application for further review by an SFI on your behalf. You will need to do this even if you supplied written authority when you first applied for an internal review.

Late applications can be accepted for 'special reasons' (see p493).[54] You must send your application to the local Benefits Agency office and not directly to the SFI office in Birmingham. The local office will send your application together with all relevant papers to Birmingham. Decisions about late or incomplete applications must be made by the SFI and not the local office. The SFI will write to you direct for further information or evidence.

Tactics

- Your application must be in writing to your local Benefits Agency office. Begin by stating you are requesting a further review by an SFI, identify clearly the decision you are unhappy about and quote your national insurance number, if possible. If your application is late, explain in full why this is the case.
- Your grounds for review are likely to be similar to the grounds for the initial review (see p494). Explain as fully as possible why you are unhappy with the review decision.
- It is a good idea to contact the SFI office a few days after submitting your application to make sure they have received it. Local Benefits Agency offices are told to send applications on to Birmingham by courier on the day they are received whenever possible.[55] Complain to the SF manager and, if necessary, your MP, if there are delays.
- If your case is urgent, state this and explain why. There is a special express procedure if you are seeking a review of a crisis loan decision; you can ask the local office to fax the decision and papers to the SFI office rather than rely on a courier.[56] You could also ask the local office to consider reviewing a decision where it is urgent but the request is for a CCG or budgeting loan.

Deciding SFI reviews

The law

When conducting a review, SFIs are legally bound to take into account the same matters as apply to internal reviews (see p495), including any new evidence and relevant changes of circumstances since the review decision – eg, the current state of the district office budget or any change in your circumstances.[57] Note the High Court ruling referred to on p460 about assessment of need preceding budgetary considerations. The High

Court has also ruled that it must be clear from the SFI's decision that s/he has taken the Secretary of State's guidance into account.[58] In another case, the Court ruled that the SFI must apply the law at the time of the SFI decision, not the law at the time of the original SFO decision.[59]

The procedure

Reviews are almost always conducted on the basis of written information. You have no right to an oral hearing although an SFI can interview you, if necessary, 'at a mutually convenient location'.[60]

You will be sent copies of all the papers which the SFI has about your case before the review takes place. You should look through the papers and send any written comments you have to the SFI on the form provided. It will help your case if you can identify any inconsistencies, judgemental assumptions or incorrect interpretations of the directions in the RO's decision, which should be set out in full in the papers you receive.

Social fund inspector decisions

SFIs can:[61]

- confirm the decision of the local office; *or*
- substitute their own decision; *or*
- refer the case back to a social fund review officer for redetermination.

You will receive a detailed written decision from the SFI. There are long delays (often several weeks) with SFI reviews and you could complain to your MP about these. Crisis loan reviews should be done urgently (see above). If you are unhappy about an SFI decision, get advice. There is no right of appeal, but you can ask an SFI to reconsider her/his decision – eg, because it is unreasonable or wrong in law.[62] You can also apply for a judicial review of the decision in the High Court.

If a case is referred back for another internal review, the SFI should identify the factors which need further consideration. The social fund review officer must redetermine the case and send you a new decision, with a full explanation of how this was reached, taking into account the SFI's comments.[63] If you are dissatisfied with the new decision, you have the right to request a further review by an SFI.

Further SFI reviews

The rules and procedure are identical to initial SFI reviews (see above).

PART EIGHT

Health service benefits

Health service benefits

This chapter covers:

I. INTRODUCTION

Although the National Health Service (NHS) generally provides free health care, there are charges for some goods and services. Some people are **exempt from charges**, including anyone getting income support (IS), income-based jobseeker's allowance (JSA), family credit (FC) or disability working allowance (DWA).

You can also get a **full or partial reduction of charges** on the grounds of 'low income' if you have less than £8,000 capital. The low-income calculation is explained below. It is only relevant if you cannot gain exemption from charges on other grounds.

You can claim a **refund of charges** if you have already paid them, but think you would have qualified for an exemption or reduction.

2. HOW LOW INCOME IS WORKED OUT

The Benefits Agency decides if your income is 'low' by comparing your 'requirements' with your 'resources'. If your 'resources' are less than or the same as your 'requirements', you do not have to pay NHS charges. If your resources are more than your 'requirements' you may still qualify for partial help with dental costs, sight tests, glasses, wigs and fabric supports and fares to hospital. You cannot get partial help with prescriptions (you may be better off using a pre-payment certificate – see p505).

'Requirements' and 'resources' are calculated as at the date on which you claim help with charges, or the date you paid them if you are claiming a refund.[1]

Requirements[2]

Your 'requirements' are based on your IS/income-based JSA applicable amount (see p357) but there are important differences.

To calculate your requirements, add up the following items:

- Your IS personal allowance(s) (see p358). The reductions which apply to IS (eg, because of involvement in a trade dispute) do not apply. Nor do the special rules for people from abroad or members of religious orders. 16/17-year-olds are assumed to have the requirements of 18-year-olds if they are in full-time work or training, or are eligible for the disability premium. Couples under 18 who have children, are eligible for a disability premium or have housing costs, or where one is on youth training or in full-time work, are assumed to have the requirements of a couple over 18. Child allowances are based on their actual age at the date of claim.
- Your IS premiums (see p360). The disability premium can be added to your requirements if you, or your partner, have been getting incapacity benefit, statutory sick pay or have been incapable of work for 28 weeks, (not 52 as for IS). If you jointly own your own home or share liability for rent with a close relative such that you would *not* get the severe disability premium included in IS, you nevertheless include this premium in your requirements. The higher pensioner premium (HPP) is added to the requirements of anyone aged 60 or over.
- Your rent *less* any housing benefit.
- Your council tax *less* any council tax benefit.
- Your housing costs, as for IS (see p27), but with the following differences:
  - you can include *all* interest and capital payments on house purchase loans and other loans secured on your home (with no waiting periods) and all payments on loans (whether secured or not) where these are made for adapting the home to take account of the special needs of a disabled person;
  - you can also include endowment policy payments if they are in connection with the purchase of your home;
  - the rules for non-dependant deductions (see p39) and housing costs payable when you are temporarily away from your home (including in a residential care home/nursing home) are modified.

Resources

Your resources are based on IS (see p373), but with some differences.[3]

Maintenance payments

Maintenance payments (including child support payments) are treated as follows:

- If you are due to receive regular payments, your normal weekly income will be:
  - the weekly amount of those payments if they are made regularly; *or*
  - the average weekly amount you have actually received in the 13 weeks immediately before you claimed, if the payments were not made regularly.
- Payments which are not part of a regular series (ie, lump sums), are treated as capital.

Earnings

In the case of employees the rules for deciding the *period* for which income is paid (see p377) and *when* income is treated as paid (see p378) do not apply. If you receive a payment of income it is likely that it will be counted as income in the week in which it is paid.

If you are affected by a trade dispute, your earnings are taken to be those you would have received had there been no dispute.[4] None of the modifications to treatment of income under IS which apply to people affected by a trade dispute apply.

The calculation of the earnings of self-employed people is usually based on the net profit over a longer period, with reference to accounts if available.

Disregards

- If you are one of a couple not entitled to a £15 disregard (see p386) you will have £10 of your earnings disregarded. If one partner's earnings are less than £10, the remainder of the disregard can be used on any earnings of the other partner.
- There is a £15 earnings disregard if you are entitled to the HPP (see p365).
- Payments you receive from an insurance policy to pay for housing costs not met under the IS regulations are normally taken into account as income. Most of the housing costs not eligible for IS are added into the calculation on the requirements side. However, payments from an insurance policy on your home which you use to repay unsecured

loans to do repairs and improvements or to pay any premiums on those loans do not count.

- There is no provision for dealing with the situation in which you receive two payments of earnings or income of the same kind from the same source in the same week. Your actual income or earnings for one week should be counted when calculating your resources.
- The £10 disregard from student loans only applies to student claimants who are eligible for a disability premium or who are deaf (in certain circumstances), and to non-student claimants with a student partner.

Applications for low-income certificates

To apply for a reduction of the charges on the grounds of low income, you need to complete form HC1, obtainable from doctors' surgeries, dentists, opticians, hospitals, advice agencies or the Benefits Agency. If your income is low enough to qualify for free services you get certificate HC2. If your income is higher, you may still qualify for partial reduction of the charges, in which case you get certificate HC3. If you are applying because you are entitled to IS or income-based JSA of less than 10p, you should send in your DSS award letter which will then entitle you to free help. A person awarded benefit of less than 10p is not paid IS/income-based JSA. If you do not have the letter apply on form HC1.

Another person can apply on your behalf if you are unable to act.[5] If you live in a residential care or nursing home and your place is being partly or wholly funded by the local authority, you can complete a special short application form HC1(RC).

Certificates are normally valid for six months but for some applicants the certificates will last for up to 12 or 13 months from the date of the claim.[6] If your circumstances change, you can ask for a fresh assessment. You should make a repeat claim on form HC1 shortly before the expiry date. There is no right of appeal against a decision, but if you feel a mistake has been made, you can ask for your case to be reconsidered.

3. PRESCRIPTIONS

Free prescriptions

You qualify for free prescriptions if:[7]

- you receive IS, income-based JSA, FC or DWA, or you are a member of the family of someone who does (see p346); *or*

- you are entitled to IS or income-based JSA of less than 10p (see p503); *or*
- your income is low enough (see p500); *or*
- you are under 16, or under 19 and in full-time education; *or*
- you are aged 60 or over;[8] *or*
- you are a permanent resident in a residential care or nursing home and your place is being partly or wholly funded by the local authority (see p96); *or*
- you are pregnant; *or*
- you have given birth within the last 12 months (even if the child was stillborn or has since died); *or*
- you are a war disablement pensioner and you need the prescription for your war disability (in which case you claim from your War Pensions Office); *or*
- you suffer from one or more of the following conditions:
  - a continuing physical disability which prevents you leaving your home except with the help of another person;
  - epilepsy requiring continuous anti-convulsive therapy;
  - a permanent fistula, including a caecostomy, ileostomy, laryngostomy or colostomy, needing continuous surgical dressing or an appliance;
  - diabetes mellitus, except where treatment is by diet alone;
  - myxoedema;
  - hypoparathyroidism;
  - diabetes insipidus and other forms of hypopituitarism;
  - forms of hypoadrenalism (including Addison's disease) for which specific substitution therapy is essential;
  - myasthenia gravis.

Claims

You claim by ticking a box on the back of the prescription.

If you are pregnant, you should obtain a form from your doctor, midwife or health visitor (or, in Scotland, the Primary Care Division of the Health Board) and send it to the Family Health Services Authority (in Scotland, the Health Board). You will be sent an exemption certificate which lasts until a year after it is expected you will give birth.

If you are claiming on the ground that you have given birth within the last year (and do not already have an exemption certificate) or you are suffering from one of the conditions listed above, you should complete the form in DSS leaflet P11 which you can obtain from your doctor's surgery, a chemist or a Benefits Agency office.

If you are claiming on the grounds of low income or because you are in residential care, see p503.

Refunds[9]

If you think you may be entitled to free prescriptions but do not have an exemption or low-income certificate, ask the chemist for a special receipt – form FP57 (in Scotland, EC57) – when you pay the charge. The form explains how to claim a refund. You must apply within three months. This period can be extended for as long as you can show good cause.[10]

Pre-payment certificates[11]

If you need a lot of prescriptions, but are not entitled to them free, you can reduce the cost by buying a pre-payment certificate for four months or a year. It saves money if you need more than five prescription items in four months or 14 items in a year. You apply for a certificate on form FP95 (EC95 in Scotland) which you can get at the Benefits Agency, post office or chemist. A refund can be given if you buy a pre-payment certificate and then, within a month, qualify for free prescriptions. If you die within a month, your survivor can also claim a refund.

4. DENTAL TREATMENT AND DENTURES

Free NHS dental treatment and dentures

You qualify for free treatment (including check-ups) and appliances (including dentures and bridges) if:[12]

- you receive IS, income-based JSA, FC or DWA, or you are a member of the family of someone who does (see p346); *or*
- you are entitled to IS or income-based JSA of less than 10p (see p503); *or*
- your income is low enough (see p500); *or*
- you are under:
  - 16 (for treatment, dentures or bridges),
  - 18 (for treatment),
  - 19 (for treatment, dentures or bridges if you are still in full-time education); *or*
- you are pregnant and were pregnant when the dentist accepted you for treatment or you have given birth within the last 12 months (even if the child was stillborn or has since died); *or*
- you are a war disablement pensioner and need the treatment or appliances because of your war disability (in which case you claim a refund from the War Pensions Directorate); *or*
- you are a permanent resident in a residential care or nursing home and your place is being partly or wholly funded by the local authority.

Claims

You claim by ticking a box on a form provided by the dentist, so tell the receptionist that you think you qualify for free treatment *before* you have it.

A woman who is pregnant or has a child under the age of one may be asked to show her Family Health Services Authority Exemption Certificate, so it is best to get one before you go for the treatment (see p503).

If you are claiming on the grounds of low income or because you are in residential care, see p503.

Reduced charges

If you do not qualify for *free* treatment, you may qualify for *partial* help with charges for dental treatment and appliances **on low-income grounds**. Your resources must not exceed your requirements (see pp501-02)' by more than one-third of the charge, and you must have less than £8,000 capital. You will be entitled to the difference between the charge for one course of treatment, including any appliances, and three times the amount by which your resources exceed your requirements.[13] To qualify you need certificate HC3 (see p503). If you paid the full charge when you need not have done, you can obtain a refund (see below).

Refunds[14]

If you paid a charge when you could have had appliances or treatment free or at reduced cost you can obtain a refund. You should get a receipt for the items or treatment you have paid for. You must apply, within three months of paying the charge, using form HC5 (and HC1 if you do not have a current HC2 or HC3 certificate). This period will be extended for as long as you can show good cause.

5. SIGHT TESTS AND GLASSES

Free sight tests and vouchers for glasses

There is no set charge for sight tests so it may be worth shopping around for them. Some opticians do not charge at all.

You qualify for a free NHS test if:[15]

- you receive IS, income-based JSA, FC or DWA, or you are a member of the family of someone who does (see p346); *or*

- your income is low enough (see p500); *or*
- you are under 16 or under 19 and in full-time education; *or*
- you are registered blind or partially sighted; *or*
- you have been prescribed complex lenses; *or*
- you have been diagnosed as suffering from diabetes or glaucoma; *or*
- you are aged 40 or over and are the parent, brother, sister or child of someone suffering from glaucoma; *or*
- you are a war disablement pensioner and require the sight test because of your war disability (in which case you claim from your War Pensions Office); *or*
- you are a patient of the Hospital Eye Service.

Claims

To claim, tell the optician before you have the test. You will need certificate HC2 if you need help because of low income (see p503). You must sign a voucher, which can then be redeemed by the optician.

Reduced-cost sight tests

If you do not qualify for a *free* eye test, you may be entitled to *partial* help with the cost of a private sight test on **low-income grounds**.[16] You pay the smaller of the actual sight test charge or what your certificate says you can pay. To qualify, you need certificate HC3 (see p503). If you do not have an HC3 before the test, you must apply for one within two weeks of the test and then apply for a refund (see p508).

'Full-value' vouchers for glasses and contact lenses

If your sight test shows you need glasses, you are given a prescription by the optician which is valid for two years.

You will qualify for a 'full-value' voucher to meet the cost of glasses or contact lenses if:[17]

- you receive IS, income-based JSA, FC or DWA; *or*
- you are a member of the family of someone who does (see p346); *or*
- you are entitled to IS or income-based JSA of less than 10p (see p503); *or*
- your income is low enough (see p500); *or*
- you are under 16 or under 19 and in full-time education; *or*
- you are a Hospital Eye Service patient needing frequent changes of glasses or contact lenses; *or*
- you have been prescribed complex lenses.

Certain war pensioners can obtain refunds of charges for glasses or contact lenses, even though they do not qualify for vouchers (see below). If you qualify for a voucher, the optician will give you one if:[18]

- you require glasses or contact lenses for the first time; *or*
- your new prescription differs from your old one; *or*
- your old glasses have worn out through fair wear and tear; *or*
- you are under 16 and have lost or damaged your old glasses or contact lenses and the cost of repair or replacement is not covered by insurance or warranty; *or*
- you are ill and, as a result of your illness, have lost or damaged your glasses or contact lenses and the cost of repair or replacement is not covered by insurance or warranty *and*:
  - you receive IS, income-based JSA, FC or DWA, or you are a member of the family of someone who does (see p346); *or*
  - your income is low enough (see p500); *or*
  - you have been prescribed complex lenses.

A hospital can issue you a voucher if it has prescribed complex lenses or you need to change your lenses frequently. The voucher is valid for six months.[19] Its value depends on the type of lenses or repair you need.[20] (A Benefits Agency booklet called *NHS sight tests and vouchers for glasses* (G11) lists the different value vouchers available.) You can use the voucher to buy (or repair) the glasses or lenses prescribed for you from any supplier. Prices vary, however, and you may have to shop around to find glasses or lenses for the value of your voucher.

Reduced-value vouchers

If you do not qualify for a full-value voucher, you may qualify for a lesser-value voucher on low-income grounds. It will be worth a full-value one less twice the amount by which your resources exceed your requirements (see p501).[21] To qualify, you need certificate HC3 (see p503) before you pay for the glasses or contact lenses.

Refunds

If you pay for a sight test or glasses without a voucher, you can apply for a refund on a special form, from the Family Health Services Authority. You will need to send a receipt of your charges and evidence that you are entitled to full or reduced help with those charges. You must apply for a refund within three months. The time limit can be extended, however, if there is 'good cause'.[22]

War pensioners

If you can only qualify for a free sight test, free glasses or contact lenses because you are a war pensioner, you must pay the charges and then claim a refund from Treatment Group, War Pensions Directorate, DSS, Norcross, Blackpool FY5 3TA.

6. WIGS AND FABRIC SUPPORTS[23]

Free wigs and fabric supports

You qualify for free NHS wigs and fabric supports if:

- you receive IS, income-based JSA, FC or DWA, or you are a member of the family of someone who does (see p346); *or*
- you are entitled to IS or income-based JSA of less than 10p (see p503); *or*
- your income is low enough (see p500); *or*
- you are under 16 or under 19 and in full-time education; *or*
- you are a hospital in-patient when the wig or fabric support is supplied; *or*
- you are a war disablement pensioner and need the wig or fabric support for your war injury; *or*
- you are a permanent resident in a residential care or nursing home and your place is being partly or wholly funded by the local authority (see p96).

Claims

You claim when you go to the hospital to have the wig or fabric support fitted. You may have to show some proof that you are entitled to free provision. You need certificate HC2 (see p503).

Refunds

The rules are the same as for dental treatment (see p506).

Reduced charges

The rules are the same as for dental treatment (see p506). To qualify, you need certificate HC3 (see p503).

7. FARES TO HOSPITAL[24]

Who can get full help

You qualify if you are attending an NHS hospital for treatment, or a disablement services centre *and*:

- you receive IS, income-based JSA, FC or DWA, or you are a member of the family of someone who does (see p346); *or*
- you are entitled to IS or income-based JSA of less than 10p (see p503); *or*
- your income is low enough (see p500); *or*
- you are a patient at a sexually transmitted disease clinic more than 15 miles from your home; *or*
- you are a war disablement pensioner and the treatment is for your war injury; *or*
- you are a permanent resident in a residential care or nursing home and your place is being partly or wholly funded by the local authority (see p503).

You also get help travelling to a mainland hospital if you live in the Highlands and Islands of Scotland or the Isles of Scilly.

Claims

Payment is made at the hospital each time you visit.

You usually have to get yourself to hospital, but once you are there you are paid the cost of the return trip. If you receive a qualifying benefit, you will need to show proof of this. However, you can ask the hospital to send you the money in advance. If you cannot get this in time you may be able to get a crisis loan from your local Benefits Agency office (see p479). You will need certificate HC2 (see p503).

What costs can be paid

You are expected to use the cheapest form of transport available. You can claim for:

- normal public transport fares;
- estimated petrol costs;
- a reasonable contribution to a local voluntary car scheme;
- taxi fares, but only if there is no alternative for all or part of the journey, or you cannot use public transport because of a disability.

The travelling costs of a companion will also be paid if it is necessary for you to be accompanied on medical grounds.

Refunds

The rules are the same as for dental treatment (see p506).

Partial help

If your resources exceed your requirements and you have savings of less than £8,000, you will get the difference between your excess income and your weekly fares. To qualify, you need certificate HC3 (see p503).

Visiting patients

If you are receiving IS or income-based JSA and are visiting a close relative or partner, you may be entitled to help from the social fund (see p476).

If you are visiting a war pensioner who is being treated for her/his war injury, you may also be entitled to help.

8. FREE MILK AND VITAMINS[25]

Free milk tokens

The following people qualify for free milk tokens:

- Disabled children aged five to 16 who cannot go to school because of their disability (claim on form FW20 available from your Benefits Agency office).
- Expectant mothers who are receiving IS or income-based JSA (or who are a member of the family of someone who is – see p346). You do not have to wait for the Certificate of Expected Date of Confinement. A note from your doctor or midwife will entitle you to free milk tokens at once.
- Children under five whose family receives IS or income-based JSA.

The milk tokens for each person entitled can be exchanged for 7 x 568 millilitres/8 half litres of liquid cow's milk a week. If they are for a child under one they can be exchanged for 900 grammes of dried milk or to buy milk for the mother if she is breastfeeding. You can use milk tokens at a clinic to get dried milk or they can be exchanged for fresh milk from suppliers who are then reimbursed by the Secretary of State. Tokens cannot be used to purchase soya milk. Suppliers can accept milk tokens as part-payment if the milk you buy is more expensive than the basic-cost milk.[26] If you cannot find a supplier who will accept your tokens you can apply to the Benefits Agency to cash them.[27]

If you lose your milk tokens or they are stolen or accidentally destroyed, the Benefits Agency will replace them.[28]

If you do not receive milk tokens to which you are entitled, they should be replaced by the Benefits Agency if this was due to '... some act or omission on [its] part'.[29]

If you are absent from home, with the result that you miss some of the milk covered by your token, your supplier can give you a refund for the pints you have missed. You have to ask the supplier to do this during the period within which the token is valid.[30]

Free milk for children in day-care

Children under five with a registered childminder, a registered day nursery, or a local authority or day nursery which is not required to register, can get 189 millilitres of milk or dried milk free each day they are looked after for two hours or more.[31] This entitlement is in addition to any entitlement outlined above. The childminder or organiser of the nursery applies to the Benefits Agency. Children under one are allowed the equivalent amount of dried milk instead.

Reduced-cost milk

Anyone attending a maternity or childcare clinic can buy dried milk at a reduced price.

Families on family credit (FC) with children under one can get dried milk at an even lower price from maternity and child health clinics.[32] You are allowed to buy up to 900 grammes of dried milk a week for each child under one. You need evidence that you get FC and of your child's age. If you do not have this evidence through 'some act or omission' on the part of the Secretary of State, you can get a refund.[33]

Free vitamins

The following qualify for free vitamins:[34]

* Expectant mothers or those breastfeeding a child under one who are receiving IS or income-based JSA (or who are a member of the family of someone who is – see p346).
* Children under five whose family receives IS or income-based JSA.

Entitlement gives 20 millilitres of vitamin drops every 13 weeks for children and expectant mothers. Breastfeeding mothers can have the same or 90 tablets instead. Vitamins are available from child health and maternity clinics.

If you are not entitled to free vitamins, you can buy them cheaply if you are attending a maternity or childcare clinic.

Other benefits and sources of help

This appendix covers briefly other means-tested benefits and sources of help for people on low incomes. It does not cover non-means-tested social security or other benefits. For details of these, see CPAG's *Rights Guide to Non-Means-Tested Benefits* and the *Disability Rights Handbook* (see Appendix 5).

1. Education benefits

Free school meals

Children of families receiving income support (IS) or income-based jobseeker's allowance (JSA) are entitled to free school meals as are 16/18-year-olds receiving these benefits in their own right.

Clothing grants

Education authorities can give grants for school uniforms and other school clothes. Each authority can determine its own eligibility rules.

School transport

Education authorities must provide free transport to school for pupils living more than three miles away (two miles if aged under eight or under 11 in Northern Ireland).

Education grants

Some grants are mandatory, others discretionary. Contact your education authority for details.

2. Housing grants

Local authority grants

Various types of grant are available to help with the cost of improving your home. These include housing renovation grants, disabled facilities grants and minor works grants. Some grants are mandatory, most are discretionary and all are subject to a means test. Contact your local authority for details.

Home insulation grants

These are available under the Government's Home Energy Efficiency Scheme for loft insulation and draught-proofing. For details, contact the EAGA Ltd, Freepost, PO Box 130, Newcastle-upon-Tyne NE99 2RP (tel: 0800 181 667; minicom: 0191 233 1054).

3. Social Services

Local authority social services departments have statutory duties to provide a range of practical and financial help to families, children, young people, older people and people with disabilities. These include:

- help and support for children in need, including financial assistance under sections 17 and 24 of the Children Act 1989 or section 12 of the Social Work (Scotland) Act 1968;
- home care, meals, telephones, aids, adaptations, travel concessions for people with disabilities (reasonable charges can be made for these services);
- provision and funding of residential or nursing care (see p96) for older people and people with disabilities;
- accommodation, food and other services for people who are destitute or at risk, including asylum-seekers (see p84), under the National Assistance Act 1948.

Contact your local authority social services department for details.

4. The Independent Living (1993) Fund

The fund gives grants to help severely disabled people aged 16-65 inclusive pay for care services in their own home. To qualify, you must be receiving the highest rate care component of disability living allowance and have less than £8,000 capital. You must be receiving at least £200 worth of services a week from social services and need additional care up to a total value of £500 a week. For more details, contact your local authority social services department, or the Independent Living Fund, PO Box 183, Nottingham NG8 3RD (tel: 0115 9428191/2).

5. The Family Fund

The Family Fund gives grants and other help to families with children who have severe disabilities. It commonly helps with things like holidays, furniture, equipment and transport needs. For details, contact the Family Fund, PO Box 50, York YO1 1UY.

6. The Macfarlane and Eileen Trusts and the Fund

The Macfarlane Trust gives grants to people who have haemophilia and have been infected with HIV through treatment for their haemophilia. It also administers the Eileen Trust which helps people infected with HIV through NHS blood transfusions, or transplants etc.

For further information, contact the Macfarlane Trust, PO Box 627, London SW1H 0QG (tel: 0171 233 0342).

7. Charities

There are hundreds of charities which provide a variety of help to people on low incomes. Your local authority social services department may know about appropriate charities or you can consult the *Charities Digest*, in your local library.

The Social Security Bill

The Government says it intends to develop a modern, integrated benefit system that is simpler, streamlined and more efficient. To this end, as this book goes to press, a new Social Security Bill is making its way through Parliament. It is likely that the bill will become law in June 1998 although many of its provisions will not take effect until, at the earliest, April 1999. See below for the provisions that come in sooner.

The Bill's main provisions are outlined on pp517-20. CPAG's *Welfare Rights Bulletin* (see Appendix 5) will provide further information as it becomes available.

When do the provisions take effect?

The Government says that most of the provisions in the Social Security Bill will not begin to come in until April 1999 at the earliest. The following will take effect sooner:

- When the Bill becomes law, where someone has applied to a commissioner for leave to appeal against a tribunal decision and the parties agree there has been an error of law, an appeal *must* be referred back to another tribunal. Note, however, that when the other provisions relating to appeals come in (from April 1999), this will be discretionary (see p518).
- From summer 1998, if it is correctly decided following a claim that someone is not entitled to benefit, s/he cannot be entitled to benefit on the basis of any change in circumstances after the date of the decision without making a fresh claim.
- Tribunals will no longer be allowed to consider an appellant's circumstances beyond the date of the decision in dispute (ie, 'down to the date of the hearing') from summer 1998 (see p518).
- Where a 'test case' is pending, suspension of payment of benefit in 'look-alike cases' will be allowed when the bill becomes law (see p518).
- When the Bill becomes law, the current anti-test case rule will apply whether a request for a review is made before or after the date of the

test case (see p144 for information about the current rule and p519 for information about the Bill).

- The higher (lone parent) rate of child benefit is likely to be abolished in June 1998 (see p519).
- Backdating of benefit is likely to be restricted to one month from June 1998 (October 1998 for housing benefit and council tax benefit) (see p520).
- Social fund overpayments are likely to be recoverable from June 1998 (see p520).

A summary of the main provisions

The system for decision making, reviews and appeals will be radically altered. Adjudication officers, child support officers and social fund officers will be abolished and all decision-making powers transferred to the Secretary of State. Benefits Agency chief executives (rather than the Chief Adjudication Officer) will draw up guidance on advice from DSS solicitors.

Reviews

The present system for reviewing decisions (see p140) will be replaced with powers to 'revise' or 'supersede' decisions. Under the new system:

- Claimants can ask for a decision to be revised if this is done within one month of the decision being made – the 'dispute period'. The Secretary of State can also initiate a revision. No grounds will be needed. It is not mandatory for claimants to seek revisions. Instead, they can choose to appeal straight away. If an appeal is pending and a decision is revised even if only in part, except in certain circumstances, the appeal will lapse and a claimant will have to appeal again within a time-limit.
- Claimants can ask for a decision to be superseded at any time, so long as there are grounds. The Secretary of State can also initiate a supersession. The grounds for superseding decisions are likely to be those that are currently grounds for review (see p141).

Appeals

Appeals tribunals are to be unified and the appeal system administered by the Secretary of State. There will no longer be a range of different types of tribunals (ie, SSATs, MATs, DATS, and CSATs) to hear different sorts of appeals. Tribunals will be made up of one, two or three members. The chair will not always be legally qualified. Regulations will set out the type of tribunal appropriate to hear a particular type of case. For example, the Government intends that tribunals dealing with questions about incapacity for work will be two person tribunals – a doctor and a solicitor. The Government says that appellants will be able to make representations if they consider their appeal is to be heard by an inappropriately constituted tribunal.

- The time-limit for appealing (see p168 for the current rules) is to be reduced from three months to one month.
- The types of decision which can be appealed to a tribunal will be those that are currently made by adjudication officers (see p137).
- So-called 'hopeless cases' are likely to be heard by one person tribunals or to be struck out (see p173 for the current rules).
- Tribunals will no longer be required to consider issues that come up in the course of an appeal – this will be discretionary.
- Tribunals will only be allowed to look at a claimant's circumstances as they were at the time of the decision being appealed. They will no longer be allowed to take any changes of circumstance into account that have happened between the date of the decision being appealed and the date the appeal is heard (what is known as 'looking down to the date of hearing'). This will particularly affect appeals about incapacity, disability and the habitual residence test. Appellants will therefore have to make fresh claims when their circumstances change.
- Where someone seeks leave to appeal to the commissioner, the tribunal chair (or one person tribunal) will have to set aside a decision and refer the appeal back to be heard by another tribunal if s/he thinks, or the parties to the appeal agree, that the tribunal made an 'error of law' (see p181). Commissioners will have the discretion to do this in similar circumstances when applications for leave to appeal are made direct to them.

Suspension of payment of benefit

As currently, there will be powers to suspend benefit in certain circumstances (see p146 for the current rules that are similar).

- The power to suspend benefit in so called 'look-alike' cases will be reinstated. Where an appeal to a commissioner or court is pending in a different case (a 'test case') the Secretary of State will be allowed to suspend benefit in a 'look-alike' case if it appears that, were the 'test case' decided in a particular way, it would mean that the award of benefit in the 'look-alike' case should be revised or superseded (see p517).
- The power to suspend benefit will be extended to housing benefit and council tax benefit for the first time.

• The Secretary of State will also be able to suspend and terminate payment of benefit where someone fails to provide information or submit to a medical examination.

Postponing of decisions

New powers will be introduced to allow for postponing of decisions where a 'test-case' is pending. Where the Secretary of State postpones making a decision, the anti-test case rule (see below) will apply if s/he makes a decision in the 'look-alike' case after the decision in the 'test-case'.

• The Secretary of State will be allowed to postpone making a decision in a case (a 'look-alike' case) if an appeal is pending against the decision of a commissioner or a court in another case – a 'test case'. This will be allowed where the Secretary of State thinks it possible that the result of the 'test case' may mean there is no entitlement to benefit for the claimant in the 'look-alike' case.
• Where a decision is pending in a 'test case' against a commissioner or court decision and someone has appealed to a tribunal or commissioner in a 'look-alike' case, the Secretary of State will be able to require the tribunal or commissioner in the 'look-alike' case:
  – not to decide the appeal and refer the case back to her (s/he could then postpone making a decision (see above); *or*
  – postpone making a decision until the 'test case' is decided; *or*
  – decide the appeal in the 'look-alike' case as if the 'test case' had been decided in the way that is the most unfavourable to the appellant.

Anti-test case rule

The current anti-test case rule limits the effect of a 'test case' for certain decisions made after the date of the 'test case' (see p144). This is to be extended.

• The rule will apply when someone makes a claim or seeks a revision or a supersession of a decision (see p517).
• The rule will apply to Secretary of State decisions made after the decision in the 'test case' even where someone has sought a review before that date.
• The rule will apply where regulations are found to be *ultra vires*.

Lone parent benefit

The Government intends to abolish the higher (lone parent) rate of child benefit for new claims from June 1998. The Government says that:

• lone parents already getting the higher (lone parent) rate of child benefit will continue to do so;

- those who were already lone parents and who were getting income support or income-based jobseeker's allowance on 5 April 1998 will be able to claim the higher (lone parent) rate of child benefit if they leave benefit to move into work.

The Government says it intends to restore the value of the lost benefit by increasing child benefit for all parents by £2.50 a week from April 1999 and via Working Families Tax Credits from October 1999. See CPAG's *Welfare Rights Bulletin* for further details.

Backdating of benefit

Backdating of benefit is to be reduced from three months to one month where someone makes a late claim. Some benefits will automatically be backdated one month. Means-tested benefits (including housing benefit and council tax benefit) will only be backdated for up to one month if certain conditions apply. The Government says that the conditions are likely to be similar to those that currently allow up to one or three months backdating (see p135).

As is now the case, further backdating will be allowed in certain circumstances. The Government says this include cases where a claim for one benefit is dependent on the claimant's or another person's entitlement to another benefit *or* for income support, housing benefit and council tax benefit, where an asylum-seeker is granted refugee status *or* where claims for certain incapacity or maternity benefits are delayed because an employer is late in informing an employee s/he was not entitled to statutory sick pay or statutory maternity pay.

The social fund

The application process for budgeting loans will be separated from that for crisis loans and community care grants. It will therefore no longer be possible for people to ask for a review of a decision to award a budgeting loan on the grounds that a community care grant should have been paid instead.

- The Government is proposing a fact-based decision-making process for budgeting loans. Discretion will remain for a limited number of cases.
- Social fund overpayments will be recoverable in cases where the applicant has misrepresented or failed to disclose material facts.

Useful addresses

The President of the Independent Tribunal Service and regional chairs

The President
HH Judge Michael Harris
The President's Office
4th Floor, Whittington House
19-30 Alfred Place
London WC1E 7LW
Tel: 0171 814 6500

The President (Northern Ireland)
Mr CG MacLynn
6th Floor, Cleaver House
3 Donegal Square North
Belfast BT1 5GA
Tel: 01232 539900

Social Security Appeal Tribunals

Acting National Chair
Mr D Turrell
The President's Office
4th Floor, Whittington House
19-30 Alfred Place
London WC1E 7LW
Tel: 0171 814 6500

Regional Chairs

North East
Mr JW Tinnion
3rd Floor, York House
York Place
Leeds LS1 2ED
Tel: 0113 245 1246

Midlands
Mr R Martin
3rd Floor, Auchinleck House
Broad Street
Birmingham B15 1DL
Tel: 0121 643 6464

South East
Mr RG Smithson
ITS, Copthal House
9 The Pavement
Grove Road
Sutton
Surrey SM1 1DA
Tel: 0181 710 2908

North West
Mr RS Sim
36 Dale Street
Liverpool L2 5UZ
Tel: 0151 236 4334

Wales and South West
Mr CB Stephens
Oxford House
Hills Street, The Hayes
Cardiff CF1 2DR
Tel: 01222 378071

Scotland
Mrs LT Parker
Wellington House
134-36 Wellington Street
Glasgow G2 2XL
Tel: 0141 353 1441

Child Support Appeal Tribunals and Disability Appeal Tribunals

An Operations Manager is located in each regional tribunal office (see above for addresses). In addition there is an Operations Manager at:

8th Floor
Anchorage 2
Anchorage Quay
Salford Quays M5 2YN
Tel: 0161 848 9999

Manorview House
Kings Manor
Newcastle upon Tyne
NE1 6PA
Tel: 0191 201 2300

Pearson Building
57 Upper Parliament Street
Nottingham NG1 6AZ
Tel: 0115 909 3600

Offices of the Social Security Commissioners

England and Wales
Harp House
83 Farringdon Street
London EC4A 4DH

Address for administration:
5th Floor, Newspapers House
8-16 Great New Street
London EC4A 3BN
Tel: 0171 353 5145

Scotland
23 Melville Street
Edinburgh EH3 7PW
Tel: 0131 225 2201

Northern Ireland
Lancashire House
5 Linenhall Street
Belfast BT2 8AA
Tel: 01232 332344

Benefits Agency Chief Executive

Mr P Mathison
Quarry House
Quarry Hill
Leeds LS2 7UA
Tel: 0113 232 4000

Severe Hardship Claims Unit (16/17-year-olds)

174 Pitt Street
Glasgow G2 4DZ
Tel: 0141 225 4259
(From late summer 1998, the unit is moving to Sheffield.)

DSS Solicitor
New Court
48 Carey Street
London WC2A 2LS
Tel: 0171 962 8000

Disability Working Allowance Unit
Diadem House
2 The Pavilion
Preston PR2 2GN
Tel 01772 883300

Earnings Top-up Customer Services
Room 306
Norcross
Blackpool FY5 3TA
Tel: 0345 114422

Family Credit Unit
Government Buildings
Cop Lane
Preston PR1 0SA
Tel: 01253 500050

Independent Review Service for the Social Fund
4th Floor, Centre City Podium
5 Hill Street
Birmingham B5 4UB
Tel: 0121 606 2100

Central Adjudication Services
Quarry House, Quarry Hill
Leeds LS2 7UA
Tel: 0113 2324000

The Pricing Prescription Authority
(previously Health Benefits Division)
Sandyford House
Osborne Road
Jesmond
Newcastle upon Tyne NE2 1DB
Tel: 0191 213 5000

Health Service Ombudsman
Millbank Tower
London SW1P 4QP
Tel: 0171 217 4051

Local Government Ombudsman

England
21 Queen Anne's Gate
London SW1H 9BU
Tel: 0171 915 3210

Scotland
23 Walker Street
Edinburgh EH3 7HX
Tel: 0131 225 5300

Wales
Derwen House
Court Road
Bridgend CF31 1BN
Tel: 01656 661325

Northern Ireland
Progressive House
33 Wellington Place
Belfast BT1 6HN
Tel: 01232 233821

The Parliamentary Ombudsman
Office of the Parliamentary
Commissioner
Church House
Great Smith Street
London SW1P 3BW
Tel: 0171 276 2130

Getting information and advice

Independent advice and representation

It is sometimes difficult for unsupported individuals to get a positive response from the Benefits Agency. You may be taken more seriously if it is clear you have taken advice about your entitlement or have an adviser assisting you.

If you want advice or help with a benefit problem the following agencies may be able to assist.

- Citizens Advice Bureaux (CABx) and other local advice centres provide information and advice about benefits and may be able to represent you.
- Law Centres can often help in a similar way to CABx/advice centres.
- Local authority welfare rights workers provide a service in many areas and some arrange advice sessions and take-up campaigns locally.
- Local organisations for particular groups of claimants may offer help. For instance, there are Unemployed Centres, pensioners groups, centres for people with disabilities, etc.
- Claimants Unions give advice in some areas. For details of your nearest group contact your local Council for Voluntary Services (CVS).
- Some social workers and probation officers (but not all) help with benefit problems, especially if they are already working with you on another problem.
- Solicitors can give free legal advice under the green form scheme (pink form in Scotland). This does not cover the cost of representation at an appeal hearing but can cover the cost of preparing written submissions and obtaining evidence such as medical reports. However, solicitors do not always have a good working knowledge of the benefit rules and you may need to shop around until you find one who does.
- Refugee Council, 3 Bondway, London SW8 1SJ.
- Joint Council for the Welfare of Immigrants (JCWI), 115 Old Street, London EC1V 9JR.

If you cannot find any of these agencies in the telephone book your local library should have details.

Unfortunately, CPAG is unable to deal with enquiries directly from members of the public but if you are an adviser you can phone the advice line, which is usually open from 2.00 to 4.00 pm on Monday to Thursday – 0171 253 6569. This is a special phone line; do not ring the main CPAG number. Alternatively, you can write to us at Citizens' Rights Office, CPAG, 4th Floor, 1-5 Bath Street, London EC1V 9PY. We can take up a limited number of test cases including appeals to the Social Security Commissioners or courts.

Advice from the Benefits Agency

You can obtain free telephone advice on benefits on the following numbers. These are for general advice and not specific queries on individual claims.

Enquiry line for people with disabilities 0800 882 200
(in Northern Ireland 0800 220 674)
(minicom: 0800 243 355)
Disability Working Allowance Helpline 01772 883 300
(this is not a freephone line)
Family Credit Helpline 01253 500 050 (this is not a freephone line)
Some information about benefits and a selection of leaflets is available on the Benefits Agency Website at: http://www.dss.gov.uk

If English is not your first language, ask your local Benefits Agency office to arrange for advice in your own language.

Books, leaflets and periodicals

Many of the books listed here will be in your main public library. Stationery Office books are available from Stationery Office bookshops and also from many others. They may be ordered by post, telephone or fax from: The Publications Centre, PO Box 276, London SW8 5DT (tel: 0171 873 9090; fax: 0171 873 8200. General enquiries tel: 0171 873 0011; fax: 0171 873 8247).

1. Textbooks

Claim in Time by M Partington (Legal Action Group, 3rd edn, 1994). Detailed study of the rules on the time limits for claiming benefits. Available from Legal Action Group, 242 Pentonville Road, London N1 9UN.

Overpayments and Recovery of Social Security Benefits by P Stagg, Legal Action Group, 1996. Detailed information on the rules on overpayments. Available from Legal Action Group, see address above.

2. Case law and legislation

Social Security Case Law – Digest of Commissioners' Decisions by D Neligan (Stationery Office, looseleaf in two volumes). Summaries of commissioners' decisions grouped together by subject.

The Law Relating to Child Support (Stationery Office, looseleaf in one volume).

The Law Relating to Social Security (Stationery Office, looseleaf in 11 volumes). All the legislation but without any comment. Known as the 'Blue Book'. Volumes 6, 7, 8 and 11 deal with means-tested benefits.

Child Support: The Legislation by E Jacobs and G Douglas (Sweet & Maxwell), 3rd edn, £36 incl p&p from CPAG Ltd, 1-5 Bath Street, London EC1V 9PY – if you are a CPAG member. Contains the primary legislation with a detailed commentary. A Supplement is available from summer 1998, £11.50 (prov), which is reduced to £10.50 if ordered from CPAG before 31 July 1998.

CPAG's Income Related Benefits: The Legislation (Mesher) updated by P Wood (Sweet & Maxwell), 1998/99 edn available from September, £52 (prov) with December supplement, incl p&p from CPAG Ltd, 1-5 Bath Street, London EC1V 9PY – if you are a CPAG member. Contains the most useful legislation with a detailed commentary. If ordered from CPAG before 31 July 1998, the price is reduced to £48.

CPAG's Housing Benefit and Council Tax Benefit Legislation by L Findlay, R Poynter, P Stagg and M Ward (CPAG Ltd), 1998/99 edn available late 1998, £48 (incl Supplement) incl p&p from CPAG Ltd, 1-5 Bath Street, London EC1V 9PY. Contains the main legislation with a detailed commentary. If ordered from CPAG before 31 July 1998, the price is reduced to £44. The 1997/98 Findlay (10th edn) is also available at £43.95 per set.

Medical and Disability Appeal Tribunals: The Legislation by M Rowland (Sweet & Maxwell), 3rd edn, 1998, £36 incl p&p from CPAG Ltd, 1-5 Bath Street, London EC1V 9PY – if you are a CPAG member. A Supplement is available from late 1998, £15 (prov), but reduced to £13.50 if ordered from CPAG before 31 July 1998.

3. Official guidance

*Since the HMSO became the Stationery Office, certain Departmental guides have not been updated and appear to be no longer available to the public.

Adjudication Officers' Guide (Stationery Office, looseleaf in 13 volumes). Volumes 4-8 deal with means-tested benefits. Supplementary guidance notes are issued internally – eg, Memo AOG Vol 3/77.

Benefits Agency Guide, *IS for 16/17-year-olds*, Stationery Office, amended February 1996.

Charging for Residential Accommodation Guide (Department of Health, in one volume).

Child Support Adjudication Guide (Stationery Office, looseleaf in one volume).

Child Support Guide (Child Support Agency, looseleaf in eight volumes). Replaced the *Child Support Manual* during 1996.

Field Officers' Guide (Child Support Agency, looseleaf in one volume).

Housing Benefit and Council Tax Benefit Guidance Manual (Stationery Office, looseleaf in one volume).

Income Support Guide (Stationery Office, looseleaf in eight volumes). Procedural guide issued to Benefits Agency staff.

The Social Fund Guide (Stationery Office, looseleaf in two volumes).

The Social Fund Cold Weather Payments Handbook (Stationery Office, looseleaf in one volume).

**The Social Fund Customer and Application Details Guide*, (Stationery Office, looseleaf in one volume).

**The Social Fund Decision and Review Guide*, (Stationery Office, looseleaf in one volume).

The Social Fund Maternity and Funeral Payments Guide (Stationery Office, looseleaf in one volume).

4. Tribunal handbooks

Social Security Appeal Tribunals: A Guide to Procedure (Stationery Office).

5. Leaflets

The Benefits Agency publishes many leaflets which cover particular benefits or particular groups of claimants or contributors. They have been greatly improved in recent years and the bigger ones extend to 48-page booklets. They are free from your local Benefits Agency office or on Freephone 0800 666 555. If you want to order larger numbers of leaflets, or receive information about new leaflets, you can join the Benefits Agency Publicity Register by writing to the Benefits Agency, 3rd Floor South, 1 Trevelyan Square, Leeds LS1 6EB or by phoning 0645 540 000 (local rate). Free leaflets on HB/CTB are available from the relevant department of your local council.

A selection of leaflets is available on the Benefits Agency Website at:
http://www.dss.gov.uk

6. Periodicals

The *Welfare Rights Bulletin* is published every two months by CPAG. It covers developments in social security law and updates this *Handbook* between editions. The annual subscription is £21 but it is sent automatically to CPAG Rights and Comprehensive Members. For subscription and membership details, contact CPAG, 4th Floor, 1-5 Bath Street, London EC1V 9PY.

7. Other publications – general

Rights Guide to Non-Means-Tested Benefits, £8.95 (£3 for claimants)
Jobseeker's Allowance Handbook, £8.95 (£3 for claimants)
Child Support Handbook, £11.95 (£3.50 for claimants)
Council Tax Handbook, £9.95
Debt Advice Handbook, £10.95
A Guide to Money Advice in Scotland, £14.95
Migration and Social Security Handbook, £10.95
Fuel Rights Handbook, £10.95 (autumn 1998)
Guide to Housing Benefit and Council Tax Benefit, £15.95
Rights Guide for Home Owners, £9.95 (autumn 1998)
Disability Rights Handbook, £11
Benefits: CHAR's Guide (for single homeless), £9.95
Youthaid's Guide to Training and Benefits for Young People, 1997 edn, £6.95
Unemployment and Training Rights Handbook (Unemployment Unit), 1997 edn, £9.95
Immigration and Nationality Law Handbook (JCWI), £16.95

Most of these are available from CPAG Ltd, 4th Floor, 1-5 Bath Street, London EC1V 9PY. Prices include p&p.

Abbreviations used in the notes

AC	Appeal Cases
All ER	All England Reports
Art(s)	Article(s)
CA	Court of Appeal
CAO	Chief Adjudication Officer
CSBO	Chief Supplementary Benefit Officer
DC	Divisional Court
ECJ	European Court of Justice
ECR	European Court Reports
FLR	Family Law Reports
HBRB	Housing Benefit Review Board
HC	High Court
HL	House of Lords
HLR	Housing Law Reports
JPR	Justice of the Peace Reports
IRS	Independent Review Service for the Social Fund
para(s)	paragraph(s)
QBD	Queen's Bench Division
r	rule
reg(s)	regulation(s)
RSC	Rules of the Supreme Court
s(s)	Section(s)
SBAT	Supplementary Benefit Appeal Tribunal
SBC	Supplementary Benefits Commission
Sch(s)	Schedule(s)
WLR	Weekly Law Reports

Acts of Parliament

AIA 1996	Asylum and Immigration Act 1996
CA 1989	Children Act 1989
CSA 1991	Child Support Act 1991
HSS&SSA Act 1983	Health and Social Services and Social Security Adjudication Act 1983
JSA 1995	Jobseekers Act 1995
LAA 1988	Legal Aid Act 1988
LGFA 1992	Local Government Finance Act 1992
NAA 1948	National Assistance Act 1948

NHSA 1977 National Health
      Service Act 1977
NHSCCA National Health
  1990   Service and
      Community Care
      Act 1990
NHS(S)A National Health
  1978   Service (Scotland)
      Act 1978
RHA 1984 Registered Homes
      Act 1984

SSAA 1992 Social Security
      Administration
      Act 1992
SSA(F)A Social Security
  1997   Administration
      (Fraud) Act 1997
SSCBA 1992 Social Security
      Contributions
      and Benefits Act
      1992

European law

Secondary legislation is made under the Treaty of Rome 1957, the Single European Act and the Maastricht Treaty in the form of Regulations (EEC Reg) and Directives (EC Dir).

Regulations

Each set of regulations has a statutory instrument (SI) number and a date. You ask for them by giving their date and number.

CB Regs   The Child Benefit (General) Regulations 1976 No.965

CC(DIS) Regs   The Community Charge (Deductions from Income Support) Regulations 1990 No.107

CS(AIAMA) Regs The Child Support (Arrears, Interest and Adjustment of Maintenance Assessments) Regulations 1992 No.1816

CS(C&E) Regs   The Child Support (Collection and Enforcement) Regulations 1992 No.1989

CS(CEOFM) Regs The Child Support (Collection and Enforcement of Other Forms of Maintenance) Regulations 1992 No.2643

CS(IED) Regs   The Child Support (Information, Evidence and Disclosure) Regulations 1992 No.1812

CS(MA) Regs   The Child Support (Miscellaneous Amendments) Regulations 1996 No.1945

CS(MAP) Regs   The Child Support (Maintenance Assessment Procedure) Regulations 1992 No.1813

CS(MASC) Regs   The Child Support (Maintenance Assessments and
                     Special Cases) Regulations 1992 No.1815
CSAT(P) Regs   The Child Support Appeal Tribunals (Procedure)
                     Regulations 1992 No.2641
CT(DIS) Regs   The Council Tax (Deductions from Income Support)
                     Regulations 1993 No.494
CTB Regs   The Council Tax Benefit (General) Regulations 1992
                     No.1814
DWA Regs   The Disability Working Allowance (General)
                     Regulations 1991 No.2887
DWA&IS Regs   The Disability Working Allowance and Income
                     Support (General) Amendment Regulations 1995
                     No.482
F(DIS) Regs   The Fines (Deductions from Income Support)
                     Regulations 1992 No.2182
FC Regs   The Family Credit (General) Regulations 1987
                     No.1973
HB Regs   The Housing Benefit (General) Regulations 1987
                     No.1971
HB(Amdt) Regs   The Housing Benefit (General) Amendment
                     Regulations 1995 No.1644
HB(Amdt) Regs   The Housing Benefit (General) Amendment
1996   Regulations 1996 No.965
HB(Amdt 2) Regs   The Housing Benefit (General) Amendment (No.2)
                     Regulations 1997 No.1974
HB(ILA) Regs   The Housing Benefit (Information from Landlords
                     and Agents) Regulations 1997 No.2436
HB(RO) Regs   The Housing Benefit (Recovery of Overpayments)
                     Regulations 1997 No.2435
HB&CTB(Amdt)   The Housing Benefit and Council Tax Benefit
Regs   (General) Amendment Regulations 1997 No.852
I(EEA)O   Immigration (European Economic Area) Order 1994
                     No.1895
IRB&JSA(PA)   The Income-related Benefits & Jobseeker's
  Amdt Regs   Allowance (Personal Allowances for Children and
                     Young Persons) (Amendment) Regulations 1996
                     No.2545
IRBS(Amdt 2)   The Income-related Benefits Schemes (Miscellaneous
  Regs   Amendments) (No.2) Regulations 1995 No.1339
IRBS(MA) Regs   The Income-related Benefits Schemes (Miscellaneous
                     Amendments) (No.3) Regulations 1994 No.1807

IRBS&SF(MA) Regs	The Income-related Benefits Schemes and Social Fund (Miscellaneous Amendments) Regulations 1996 No.1944
IS Regs	The Income Support (General) Regulations 1987 No.1967
IS(AT) Regs	The Income Support (General) Amendment and Transitional Regulations 1995 No.2287
IS(JSACA) Regs	The Income Support (General) (Jobseeker's Allowance Consequential Amendments) Regulations 1996 No.206
IS(LR) Regs	The Income Support (Liable Relatives) Regulations 1990 No.1777
JSA Regs	The Jobseeker's Allowance Regulations 1996 No.207
NA(AR) Regs	The National Assistance (Assessment and Resources) Regulations 1992 No.2977
NHS(CDA) Regs	The National Health Service (Charges for Drugs and Appliances) Regulations 1980 No.1503
NHS(GOS) Regs	The National Health Service (General Ophthalmic Services) Regulations 1986 No.975
NHS(OCP) Regs	The National Health Service (Optical Charges and Payments) Regulations 1997 No.818
NHS(TERC) Regs	The National Health Service (Travelling Expenses and Remission of Charges) Regulations 1988 No.551
RA(RPORE) Regs	The Residential Accommodation (Relevant Premises, Ordinary Residence and Exemptions) Regulations 1993 No.477
RCH Regs	The Residential Care Homes Regulations 1984 No.1345
RO(AF)O	The Rent Officers (Additional Functions) Order 1995 No.1642
RO(HBF)O	The Rent Officers (Housing Benefit Functions) Order 1997 No.1984
SF(App) Regs	The Social Fund (Applications) Regulations 1988 No.524
SF(AR) Regs	The Social Fund (Application for Review) Regulations 1988 No.34
SF(Misc) Regs	The Social Fund (Miscellaneous Provisions) Regulations 1990 No.1788
SF(RDB) Regs	The Social Fund (Recovery by Deductions from Benefits) Regulations 1988 No.35
SFCWP Regs	The Social Fund Cold Weather Payments (General) Regulations 1988 No.1724

SFM&FE Regs	The Social Fund Maternity and Funeral Expenses (General) Regulations 1987 No.481
SFWFP	The Social Fund Winter Fuel Payment Regulations 1998 No.19
SS(AA) Regs	The Social Security (Attendance Allowance) Regulations 1991 No.2740
SS(Adj) Regs	The Social Security (Adjudication) Regulations 1995 No.1801
SS(BWB) Regs	The Social Security (Back to Work Bonus) Regulations 1996 No.193
SS(BWB) (No.2) Regs	The Social Security (Back to Work Bonus) (No.2) Regulations 1996 No.2570
SS(CMB) Regs	The Social Security (Child Maintenance Bonus) Regulations 1996 No.3195
SS(C&P) Regs	The Social Security (Claims and Payments) Regulations 1987 No.1968
SS(Cr) Regs	The Social Security (Credits) Regulations 1975 No.556
SS(DLA) Regs	The Social Security (Disability Living Allowance) Regulations 1991 No.2890
SS(ICA) Regs	The Social Security (Invalid Care Allowance) Regulations 1976 No.409
SS(ICB) Trans Regs	The Social Security (Incapacity Benefit) (Transitional) Regulations 1995 No.310
SS(HIP) Regs	The Social Security (Hospital In-Patients) Regulations 1975 No.555
SS(MA) Regs	The Social Security (Miscellaneous Amendments) Regulations 1998 No.563
SS(PAOR) Regs	The Social Security (Payments on account, Overpayments and Recovery) Regulations 1988 No.664
SS(PFA)MA Regs	The Social Security (Persons from Abroad) Miscellaneous Amendments Regulations 1996 No.30
SS(PN) Regs	The Social Security (Penalty Notices) Regulations 1997 No.2813
SS(SDA) Regs	The Social Security (Severe Disablement Allowance) Regulations 1984 No.1303
SSCP Regs	The Social Security Commissioners Procedure Regulations 1987 No.214
WF Regs	The Welfare Foods Regulations 1996 No.1434

Other information

See Appendix 5 for fuller details of the following publications.

Advice Notes	Social Fund Inspectors' Advice Notes.
AOG	The *Adjudication Officers' Guide.*
CSAG	The *Child Support Adjudication Guide.*
CSRCG	The *Child Support Requirement to Co-operate Guide.*
CWPH	The *Social Fund Cold Weather Payments Handbook.*
GM	The *Housing Benefit and Council Tax Benefit Guidance Manual.*
HC Handbook	IS for Homeless Customers, Hostels, Residential Care and Nursing Homes.
IS Guide	This is a largely procedural guide to the implementation of income support, which is issued to adjudication officers/DSS staff.
SF Dir/SFI Dir	Direction(s) on the discretionary social fund. They are printed in the *Social Fund Guide* and Mesher Wood.
SFCADG	The *Social Fund Customer and Application Details Guide.*
SFDRG	The *Social Fund Decision and Review Guide.*
SFG	The *Social Fund Guide.*
SFROG	The *Social Fund Review Officers' Guide.*

References like CIS/142/1990 and R(SB) 3/89 are references to commissioners' decisions (see p180).

Notes

References are to the statutes and regulations as amended up to 24 March 1998. All regulations are (General) Regulations unless otherwise stated. There is a full list of abbreviations in Appendix 5.

PART TWO: INCOME SUPPORT

Chapter 2: The basic rules of entitlement
(pp8-24)

1 s124 SSCBA 1992
2 Reg 4ZA and Sch 1B IS Regs
3 Sch 1B paras 16 and 17 IS Regs
4 Sch 1B paras 7-9, 13, and 24-27 IS Regs
5 Reg 22A IS Regs; reg 19(5) DWA&IS Regs
6 para 18339 AOG
7 Sch 1B paras 1-6 and 14 IS Regs
8 Sch 1B paras 10-12, 15 and 28 IS Regs
9 Sch 2 para 12(5) IS Regs
10 Sch 1B para 18-22 IS Regs
11 Reg 5 IS Regs
12 Reg 5(3A) IS Regs
13 R(IS) 5/95
14 R(IS) 1/93
15 CIS/434/1994
16 Reg 5(7) IS Regs
17 Reg 5(2)(b)(i) and (3B) IS Regs
18 Reg 5(2)(b)(ii) IS Regs
19 Reg 5(2)(a) IS Regs; R(IS) 8/95
20 Reg 5(3) IS Regs
21 CIS/14661/1996
22 R(U) 2/87
23 Reg 5(5) IS Regs
24 Reg 5(4) IS Regs
25 Reg 6 IS Regs
26 para 25216 AOG
27 CIS/649/1992
28 CIS/514/1990; *Smith v CAO*, (CA) (unreported)
29 s124(1)(d) SSCBA 1992
30 Reg 12 IS Regs; s142 SSCBA 1992 and reg 5(2) CB Regs
31 Regs 4ZA and 13(2)(a)-(e) IS Regs
32 R(IS) 9/94
33 CIS/11766/1996
34 R(IS) 9/94
35 R(SB) 2/87
36 CIS/11441/1995
37 R(IS) 9/94
38 Reg 7(4), (5) and (6) CB Regs
39 Reg 12 IS Regs; reg 7 CB Regs
40 Regs 4ZA and 61 IS Regs, definition of 'student
41 Reg 61, definitions of 'student' and 'course of advanced education
42 Reg 61 IS Regs definitions of 'full-time course of advanced education'
43 para 35045 AOG
44 R(SB) 40/83; R(SB) 41/83
45 CIS/152/1994
46 See note 42
47 Regs 4ZA and 61 and Sch 1B IS Regs
48 Sch 1B paras 10, 11 and 12 IS Regs
49 CIS/368/1992
50 CIS/13276/1996
51 CIS/13986/1996 (CIS/15594/1996 decided that this was incorrect, but the claimant has appealed to the Court of Appeal); *CAO v Webber* (CA), *Times Law Report*, 10 July 1997
52 *Driver v CAO*, CA, 6 December 1996 (unreported)
53 *CAO v Webber* (CA), *Times Law Report*, 10 July 1997; CIS/152/1994
54 Reg 4(1) and (2)(a) and (b) IS Regs
55 Reg 4(2)(c) IS Regs
56 Sch 7 paras 11 and 11A IS Regs

Chapter 3: How your benefit is calculated
(pp 25-52)

2. Housing costs
(pp 27-47)

1 s124(4) SSCBA 1992
2 Sch 3 para 4(1) IS Regs
3 Sch 3 para 1 IS Regs
4 Sch 3 paras 15-17 IS Regs
5 Sch 3 para 2 IS Regs
6 CSB/213/1987
7 Sch 3 para 5(5) IS Regs; CIS/743/1993
8 Reg 2(1) IS Regs; reg 2(1) HB Regs; R(SB) 22/87
9 CIS/636/1992 (confirmed by the Court of Appeal in *Brain v CAO*, 2 December 1993)
10 Sch 3 para 2(2) IS Regs
11 Sch 3 para 3(1) IS Regs
12 CIS/297/1994
13 s137(1) SSCBA 1992, definition of 'dwelling'; reg 2(1) IS Regs, definition of 'dwelling occupied as the home'
14 Sch 3 para 3(7) IS Regs
15 Sch 3 para 3(10) IS Regs
16 Sch 3 para 3(11) IS Regs
17 Sch 3 para 3(8) and (9) IS Regs
18 *R v Penwith District Council ex parte Burt*
19 Sch 3 para 3(5) IS Regs
20 CIS/719/1994
21 Sch 3 para 3(6) IS Regs
22 CIS/543/1993
23 CIS/339/1993
24 Sch 3 para 3(6)(b) IS Regs
25 Sch 3 para 3(3) IS Regs

26 Sch 3 para 3(11)(c)(viii) IS Regs
27 Sch 3 para 3(4) and regs 2 and 61 IS Regs
28 Sch 3 para 15 IS Regs
29 R(IS) 11/94
30 R(IS) 4/95
31 R(IS) 7/93
32 R(IS) 6/94
33 CIS/465/1994
34 Sch 3 para 5 IS Regs
35 Sch 3 para 4 IS Regs
36 Sch 3 para 4(4) IS Regs
37 Sch 3 para 4(4A) IS Regs
38 Sch 3 para 4(2) and (4) and paras 28481 and 28486-87AOG, definition of 'relevant period'
39 Sch 3 paras 1(3) and (4) and 4(9) IS Regs
40 CIS/7273/1995
41 Sch 3 para 4(10) IS Regs
42 CIS/14657/1996
43 Sch 3 para 4(6)(a) IS Regs
44 Sch 3 para 4(6)(b) IS Regs; CIS/7273/1995
45 CIS/11293/1995
46 Sch 3 para 4(8) IS Regs
47 R(IS) 8/94
48 Sch 3 para 4(11) IS Regs
49 Sch 3 para 10 IS Regs; R(SB) 46/83
50 Sch 3 para 10 IS Regs
51 Sch 3 para 12 IS Regs
52 Sch 3 para 16 IS Regs
53 CIS/6010/1995
54 R(IS) 5/96
55 CIS/14657/1996
56 CIS/14468/1996
57 CIS/14657/1996
58 Sch 3 para 17 IS Regs
59 Sch 3 para 17(4) IS Regs

60 R(IS) 3/91; R(IS) 4/91; CIS/1460/1995
61 R(IS) 4/92; R(IS) 19/93
62 CIS/4/1988
63 Sch 3 para 17(2) IS Regs
64 Sch 3 para 18 IS Regs
65 CSIS/185/1995
66 Reg 3(4) and (5) IS Regs
67 Reg 3 IS Regs
68 CSB/1163/1988
69 Sch 3 para 18(6) and (7) IS Regs
70 Sch 3 para 18(8) IS Regs
71 Sch 10 para 26 IS Regs
72 Sch 9 para 22 IS Regs
73 Sch 3 para 11(4) and (5) IS Regs
74 Sch 3 para 11(6) IS Regs
75 Sch 3 para 13 IS Regs
76 R(IS) 12/91
77 Sch 3 para 13(2) IS Regs
78 Sch 3 para 13(4) and (5) IS Regs
79 R(SB) 7/89
80 R(SB) 6/89; R(SB) 7/89
81 R(IS) 10/93
82 CIS/347/1992
83 CSB/617/1988. This case has been reported as R(SB) 4/89, but the reported version omits the relevant paragraphs
84 R(SB) 7/89
85 Sch 3 para 13(6) and (7) IS Regs; *Secretary of State for Social Security v Julien*, reported as appendix to R(IS) 13/92
86 R(SB) 7/89
87 R(IS) 9/91
88 Sch 3 paras 6 and 8 IS Regs
89 Sch 3 para 9 IS Regs

90 Sch 3 paras 1(2) and 6
IS Regs
91 Sch 3 paras 1(2) and 8
IS Regs
92 Sch 3 para 8(2) and (3)
IS Regs
93 Sch 3 para 11(2) IS
Regs
94 Sch 3 para 14 IS Regs
95 Reg 32 IS(JSACA) Regs
96 Sch 3 paras 14(4), (5),
(5A) and (5B) IS Regs
97 Reg 3 IS(AT) Regs
98 Sch 3 para 7 IS Regs
99 s16 Interpretation Act
1978;

3.   Rates of benefit paid to 16/17-year-olds
(pp47-49)
100 Sch 2 para 1(1)(a), (b)
and (c) and (2)(a), (b)
and (c) IS Regs
101 Sch 2 paras 1(1)(b) and
(c), (2)(b) and (c), and
1A IS Regs
102 Sch 2 para 1(3) IS Regs

5.   Urgent cases payments
(pp49-52)
103 Reg 70(2) IS Regs
104 Reg 70(4) IS Regs
105 Reg 71(1)(a) IS Regs
106 Reg 71(1)(b) and (c) IS
Regs
107 Reg 71(1)(a) and (b) IS
Regs
108 Reg 72(1) IS Regs
109 Reg 72(1)(c) IS Regs
110 Reg 72(2) IS Regs

Chapter 4: Jobseeker's allowance
(pp53-59)
1 Reg 47(1) and (2) JSA
Regs
2 Sch 1 para 4 JSA 1995;
reg 46 JSA Regs

3 ss1-3 JSA 1995
4 s6 JSA 1995; reg 5 JSA
Regs
5 Reg 8 JSA Regs
6 Reg 10 JSA Regs
7 s6(5) and (7) JSA 1995;
reg 16 JSA Regs
8 Reg 14 JSA Regs
9 Reg 15 JSA Regs
10 Reg 18 JSA Regs
11 Reg 18(3) JSA Regs
12 Reg 19 JSA Regs
13 s9 JSA 1995
14 s9(1) JSA 1995; reg 31
JSA Regs
15 s19 JSA 1995
16 Reg 140 JSA Regs
17 Reg 145(1) JSA Regs
18 s124(1)(f) SSCBA 1992;
ss2(1)(d) and 3(1)(b)
JSA 1995

Chapter 5: Special rules for special groups
(pp60-103)

1.   16/17-year-olds
(pp60-61)
1 s124(1)(a) SSCBA 1992
and Sch 1B IS Regs
2 s124(1)(e) SSCBA 1992
and Sch 1B IS Regs
3 s124(1)(d) SSCBA 1992
and reg 13 IS Regs
4 Reg 61(1)(c) JSA Regs
5 s124(1)(f) SSCBA 1992;
s3(1)(b) JSA 1995

2.   People involved in a trade dispute
(pp61-66)
6 s14 JSA 1995
7 ss126 and 127 SSCBA
1992 and Sch 1B para
20 IS Regs
8 ss126 and 127 SSCBA
1992; s15 JSA 1995
9 s35(1) JSA 1995
10 s14(1) and (2) JSA 1995

11 s14(4) and (5) JSA 1995
12 R(U) 4/62; R(U) 1/70
13 s126(1)(b) and (2)
SSCBA 1992
14 s14(1) JSA 1995; *Presho
v Insurance* Officer
[1984] (see R(U) 1/84);
paras 37210 and 37245
AOG
15 s14(3) JSA 1995
16 Regs 55 and 56(1)(b)
and (3)(a) SS(Adj) Regs
17 Reg 5(4) IS Regs
18 s124(1)(c) SSCBA 1992
19 paras 37677-78 AOG
20 Reg 5(4) JSA Regs;
para 37676 AOG
21 s126(3) SSCBA 1992
22 Sch 3 para 2(2) IS Regs
23 Sch 9 para 34 IS Regs
24 s126(5)(b) SSCBA 1992
and Sch 9 para 34 IS
Regs
25 s126(5)(a)(ii) SSCBA
1992; reg 41(4) IS Regs
26 Sch 9 para 28 and Sch
10 para 17 IS Regs
27 Reg 48(9) and (10)(a)
and (c), Sch 9 paras 15
and 39 and Sch 10 para
22 IS Regs
28 Sch 9 para 21 and reg
42(4) IS Regs
29 Reg 35(1)(d) IS Regs
30 Reg 48(6) IS Regs
31 s126(5)(a)(i) SSCBA
1992
32 s127 SSCBA 1992
33 Reg 6(e) IS Regs
34 s127(b) SSCBA 1992
35 para 37790 AOG
36 Reg 26(4) SS(C&P)
Regs
37 s127(c) SSCBA 1992;
reg 20 SS(PAOR) Regs
38 Reg 26 SS(PAOR) Regs
39 Reg 19(3), (4) and (5)
SS(PAOR) Regs

40 Reg 18(2) SS(PAOR) Regs
41 Reg 22(2) SS(PAOR) Regs
42 Reg 22(3) SS(PAOR) Regs
43 Reg 22(4) SS(PAOR) Regs
44 Reg 20(1) and (2) SS(PAOR) Regs
45 Reg 22(5)(a) SS(PAOR) Regs
46 Reg 22(6) SS(PAOR) Regs
47 Reg 21(1) SS(PAOR) Regs
48 Reg 25 SS(PAOR) Regs
49 Reg 28 SS(PAOR) Regs
50 Reg 29 SS(PAOR) Regs
51 Regs 27 and 29 SS(PAOR) Regs
52 Reg 27(5) SS(PAOR) Regs
53 SF Dir 26
54 SF Dir 17
55 SF Dir 8(c)

3. People from abroad
(pp66-87)

56 Regs 70 and 71 and Sch 7 para 17 IS Regs
57 Reg 21(3) IS Regs
58 s7(1) Immigration Act 1988; reg 23(3)(a) IS Regs
59 Reg 21(3)(a) IS Regs
60 s124 SSCBA 1992; reg 21(3) IS Regs
61 Reg 21(3) and Sch 7 para 17 IS Regs
62 Sch 7 para 17(c)(i) IS Regs
63 Sch 7 para 17(c)(i) IS Regs
64 Sch 7 para 17 IS Regs; para 28831 AOG
65 Sch 7 para 17(b) and (c)(ii) and (iii) IS Regs
66 Reg 21(3)(a) IS Regs

67 Reg 16(3)(d) and Sch 7 para 11 IS Regs
68 Reg 16 IS Regs
69 CIS/13805/1996
70 CIS/508/1992; CIS/13805/1996
71 Reg 21(3) IS Regs; reg 85 JSA Regs; reg 7A(4)(e) HB Regs; reg 7A(4)(e) CTB Regs
72 Reg 21(3) and (3F) IS Regs; Reg 85(4) and (4A) JSA Regs
73 Reg 4(2) IRBS(MA) Regs
74 EEC Reg 1408/71; *Di Paolo v Office National de l'Emploi*, Case 76/76 [1977] ECR 315; R(U) 8/88
75 CIS/2326/1995; paras 20747-48 AOG
76 CIS/1067/1995; CIS/2326/1995; paras 20747-48 AOG
77 CIS/1067/1995, para 28
78 CIS/2326/1995, para 24
79 *Re F (child abduction)* [1992] 1 FLR 548
80 CIS/1067/1995, para 29
81 CIS/2326/1995, para 28
82 CIS/2326/1995; *Nessa v CAO*
83 CIS/1067/1995, para 15
84 CIS/2326/1995; CIS/11481/1995 (CA, 5 Feb 1998)
85 *R v Secretary of State ex parte Sarwar, Getachew and Urbanek* (CA), October 1996
86 CIS/7201/1995: *Swaddling* - reference to ECJ
87 Arts 48, 52 and 59 Treaty of Rome; I(EEA)O
88 s124 SSCBA 1992; reg 21(3)(a) IS Regs;

s1(2)(i) JSA 1995 and reg 85 JSA Regs
89 Reg 21(3) IS Regs
90 *R v Immigration Appeal Tribunal and Surinder Singh ex parte Secretary of State for the Home Department* (ECJ) Case 370/90 [1992] 3 All ER 798
91 *Levin* Case 53/81 [1982] ECR 1035; EEC Reg 1251/70
92 *Levin; Kempf* Case 139/85 [1986] ECR 1741; *Raulin* Case 357/89 [1992] ECR 1027
93 *Scrivner* Case 122/84 [1985] ECR 1027; Art 7 I(EEA)O; CIS/12909/1996
94 *Lair* Case 39/86 [1988] ECR 3161; *Raulin*; Art 7(2) EEC Reg 1612/68
95 *Raulin*; Art 7(2) EEC Reg 1612/68
96 para 22680 AOG
97 CIS/4521/1995, para 13; Art 7(1) EEC Reg 1612/68
98 *Lair*, Art 7(1) EEC Reg 1612/68
99 *Lebon* Case 316/85 [1989] ECR 2811; CIS/4521/1995
100 *Lair, Raulin*; CIS/4521/1995, para 14
101 Art 2(b) EEC Reg 1251/70
102 Art 2(a) EEC Reg 1251/70
103 Arts 2(c) and 4 EEC Reg 1251/70
104 Arts 1 and 4 EEC Dir 68/360
105 *Antonissen*, Case 292/88 [1991] ECR 1-745; CIS/4521/1995

106 Arts 1 and 4 EC Dir 73/148
107 para 22680 AOG; C10/95 (IS)
108 Arts 4(1), 5(1) and 6(2)(b) I(EEA)O
109 Art 1(b) EC Dir 73/148
110 *Cowan* Case 186/87 [1989] ECR 195; *Humbel* Case 263/86 [1988] ECR 5365; *Luisi* Case 286/82 [1988] ECR 5365
111 Art 1 EC Dir 68/360; Art 10 EEC Reg 1612/68; Art 1 EC Dir 73/148
112 *Royer* [1976] ECR 497; *Echternach* [1989] ECR 723; *Raulin*
113 Art 15(2) I(EEA)O
114 *Antonissen* Case 292/88 [1991] ECR 1-745
115 EC Dirs 90/364, 90/365 and 93/96
116 Reg 21(3)(h) IS Regs; reg 85(4)(h) JSA Regs; reg 7A(4)(d) HB Regs; reg 4A(4)(d) CTB Regs
117 *Wolke and Remilien v Secretary of State for Social Security and CAO*, (27 November 1997)
118 Reg 21ZA(1) IS Regs; reg 85(4) JSA Regs
119 Reg 21(3) IS Regs; reg 85(4) JSA Regs
120 Reg 21ZA(2) and (4) IS Regs; reg 4(3C) and 19(1A) SS(C&P) Regs
121 s124(1)(f) SSCBA 1992
122 Sch 10 para 49 IS Regs; Sch 8 para 12(b) JSA Regs
123 Arts 2 and 3 EEC Reg 1408/71; CIS/564/1994
124 Reg 21(3) IS Regs; reg 85(4) JSA Regs
125 SS(PFA)MA Regs

126 *R v Secretary of State for Social Security ex parte Re B and JCWI*
127 s11 and Sch 1 AIA 1996
128 Regs 21(3)(j) and 70(3)(b) IS Regs
129 Reg 70(3)(b) and (3A)(a) IS Regs
130 CIS/143/1997
131 para 36144 AOG
132 Reg 70(3A)(b)(i) IS Regs
133 Reg 70(3A)(aa) IS Regs
134 Reg 70(3A)(b)(i) IS Regs
135 Reg 12(1) SS(PFA)MA Regs; Sch 1 para 6(2)(a) AIA 1996
136 Reg 70(3A)(b)(ii) IS Regs
137 *R v Secretary of State for Social Security ex parte Okito, Zaheer, Vijeikis* (10 July 1997); CIS/16992/1996
138 *R v Secretary of State for Social Security ex parte 'T'* (18 March 1997)
139 Sch 1 para 5 AIA 1996
140 Reg 21(3)(j) IS Regs
141 Reg 147(3)(b) JSA Regs
142 s124(1)(f) SSCBA 1992
143 Reg 70(3A)(b)(i) IS Regs
144 *R v Secretary of State ex parte Karaoui and Abbad* (HC, 11 March 1997)
145 *Ibid.*
146 Reg 70(3A)(b)(ii) IS Regs
147 s17(6) CA 1989
148 *R v Hammersmith and Fulham London Borough and others*, CA, *The Times*, 19 February 1997
149 *R v Newham ex parte Gorenkin*, HC, 14 May 1997

150 para 5205 SFG
151 Reg 21(3)(i) IS Regs
152 Reg 21(3)(i) IS Regs
153 Reg 70(3)(c) IS Regs
154 Reg 12(2) SS(PFA)MA Regs
155 ss105 and 106 SSAA 1992
156 ss78(6)(c), 105 and 106 SSAA 1992
157 Reg 70(3)(a) IS Regs
158 Reg 70(3)(b) IS Regs
159 Reg 70(3)(c) IS Regs
160 Reg 72 IS Regs

4. Residential and nursing care
(pp87-97)

161 NHSCCA 1990
162 Reg 19(1ZB)-(1ZR) IS Regs
163 Reg 19 IS Regs
164 Reg 19(1ZF) IS Regs
165 Reg 40 and Sch 9 para 9 IS Regs
166 Sch 4 para 13 IS Regs
167 Sch 4 para 1(1)(a) IS Regs
168 Sch 4 para 2(2) IS Regs
169 Sch 4 para 2(1) IS Regs
170 Sch 4 para 3 IS Regs
171 Sch 4 para 5 IS Regs
172 Sch 4 paras 6 and 7 IS Regs
173 Sch 4 para 9 IS Regs
174 Sch 4 para 10 IS Regs
175 Sch 4 paras 9(b) and 10(4) IS Regs
176 CIS/263/1991
177 s55 RHA 1984
178 Reg 1(2) RCH Regs
179 CSB/1171/1986
180 s20(1) RHA 1984
181 Sch 4 para 6(2) IS Regs
182 Sch 4 para 12(1) and (2) IS Regs
183 Sch 4 para 12(1) and (2) IS Regs

184 Sch 4 para 12(3) and
(4) IS Regs
185 Sch 9 para 30(1)(e) IS
Regs
186 s26A NAA 1948;
RA(RPORE) Regs
187 Sch 4 paras 14 and 15
IS Regs
188 Sch 7 para 16 IS Regs
189 CIS/5415/1995; CSIS/
833/1995
190 Sch 3 para 4(1)(b) IS
Regs; reg 7(1)(e) HB
Regs
191 Sch 2 para 2A IS Regs
192 Sch 3C IS Regs
193 Sch 2 para 2A(4A) IS
Regs
194 Reg 17(1)(bb) and Sch
2 para 2A(3) IS Regs
195 Reg 19(3) and Sch 2
para 2A(3) IS Regs
196 Sch 2 para 2A(4) IS
Regs
197 Regs 7 and 8 SS(AA)
Regs; regs 9 and 10
SS(DLA) Regs
198 Sch 9 para 15A IS Regs
199 Sch 9 para 30A IS Regs
200 Reg 21(3)-(4) IS Regs
201 Reg 21(3A) IS Regs
202 Sch 7 paras 10A-C and
13 IS Regs
203 Part III NAA 1948
204 s22(1) NAA 1948
205 NA(AR) Regs
206 s22 HSS&SSA Act
1983
207 s22(5A) NAA 1948

5. People in hospital
(pp97-101)
208 Reg 21(3) IS Regs; reg
2(2) SS(HIP) Regs;
NHSA 1977; NHS(S)A
1978; NHSCCA 1990
209 Reg 2(2) SS(HIP) Regs;
s65 NHSA 1977 (s58

NHS(S)A 1978); Sch 2
para 14 NHSCCA 1990
210 *Botchett v CAO* (CA),
The Times, 8 May 1996;
paras 29332-33 and
29341-54 AOG
211 Sch 3 paras 1(1) and
3(11) IS Regs
212 Sch 2 para 13(3A) IS
Regs
213 s70(1) and (2) SSCBA
1992; Sch 2 para 14ZA
IS Regs
214 Sch 7 para 1(a) IS Regs
215 Sch 7 para 2(b) IS Regs
216 Sch 7 para 2(a) IS Regs
217 Sch 2 para 13(3A) IS
Regs
218 s70(2) SSCBA 1992;
Sch 2 para 14ZA IS
Regs
219 Sch 7 para 1(b) IS Regs
220 Reg 16(2)(b) IS Regs
221 Sch 2 para 15(5) IS
Regs
222 s70 SSCBA 1992; Sch 2
para 14ZA IS Regs
223 Sch 7 para 1(c) and Sch
2 para 12(1)(c)(ii) IS
Regs
224 Reg 16(2)(b) IS Regs
225 Sch 7 para 2 IS Regs
226 Reg 16(2) and Sch 7
para 1(b) IS Regs
227 Reg 16(2) and Sch 7
para 1(a) IS Regs
228 Sch 7 para 3(a) IS Regs
229 Sch 2 para 14(b) IS
Regs
230 Sch 7 para 3(b) IS Regs
231 Sch 7 para 18(a)(i) and
(ii) IS Regs
232 Sch 7 para 18(a)(iii) and
(iv) IS Regs
233 Sch 2 para 2A(4A) IS
Regs
234 Sch 7 para 13 IS Regs
235 Sch 7 para 18(b) and
(c) IS Regs

236 Sch 7 para 13 IS Regs
237 Sch 7 para 2A IS Regs
238 Sch 7 para 7(1)
SS(C&P) Regs; paras
29386-87 AOG
239 Reg 21(2) IS Regs
240 Sch 7 para 7(3)(d)
SS(C&P) Regs
241 R(S) 4/84, CS/249/1989,
CIS/571/1994, CIS/192/
1991 and CDLA/11099/
1995
242 para 29372 AOG; CIS/
571/1994
243 CDLA/11099/1995
244 CDLA/11099/1995;
CIS/571/1994; para
29373 AOG

6. Prisoners
(pp101-102)
245 Sch 7 para 8 IS Regs
246 Reg 16(3)(b) IS Regs
247 Reg 16(5)(f) IS Regs
248 Reg 21(3) IS Regs
249 para 29526 AOG; R(IS)
17/93
250 Reg 16(1) and (2) and
Sch 7 para 9 IS Regs
251 Reg 48(7) IS Regs

**7. People without
accommodation**
(pp102-103)
252 Sch 7 para 6 IS Regs
253 para 29503 AOG
254 para 42 HC Handbook
255 para 15 HC Handbook
256 *R v Hammersmith and
Fulham* London
Borough and others,
CA, *The Times*, 19
February 1997

Chapter 6: Maintenance payments
(pp104-127)

2. Who is 'liable to maintain'?
(pp106-108)

1 s105(3) SSAA 1992
2 ss78(6)-(9) and 105(3) SSAA 1992
3 ss78(6)-(9) and 105 SSAA 1992
4 s1 CSA 1991
5 s106 SSAA 1992
6 ss8(3) and 9 CSA 1991
7 *NAB v Parkes* [1955] 2 QBD 506; *Hulley v Thompson* [1981] 1 WLR 159
8 s106(2) SSAA 1992
9 *NAB v Parkes* [1955] 2 QBD 506
10 s105(1) SSAA 1992

3. Getting maintenance
(pp108-110)

11 s108 SSAA 1992
12 s108(5) SSAA 1992; reg 3 IS(LR) Regs
13 s106(4)(a) SSAA 1992
14 s30(1) CSA 1991; CS(CEOFM) Regs
15 s29(3) CSA 1991; reg 2 CS(C&E) Regs
16 *Residual Liable Relative and Proceedings Guide*, paras 1630-42

4. The child support scheme
(pp110-119)

17 s6(1) CSA 1991; reg 34 CS(MAP) Regs
18 s2 CSA 1991
19 s6(8) CSA 1991
20 s6(1) and (11) CSA 1991
21 s6(9) CSA 1991; regs 2 and 3 CS(IED) Regs

22 App 1 CSRCG
23 para 2553 CSAG
24 s46(5) CSA 1991
25 Reg 35 (1) and (2) CS(MAP) Regs
26 Reg 35(3) CS(MAP) Regs
27 s46(10) CSA 1991
28 R(SB) 33/85
29 s46(3) and (4) CSA 1991
30 Reg 25(2) CS(MA) Regs
31 s46(5) CSA 1991
32 s2 CSA 1991; para 2556 CSAG; CCS/1037/1995
33 Reg 35A CS(MAP) Regs
34 s46(7) CSA 1991
35 Reg 3 CSAT(P) Regs
36 s6(8) CSA 1991
37 Reg 40 CS(MAP) Regs
38 Reg 39 CS(MAP) Regs
39 Reg 36(8) CS(MAP) Regs
40 Reg 47(1) CS(MAP) Regs
41 Reg 36(2) CS(MAP) Regs
42 Reg 37 CS(MAP) Regs
43 Reg 36(7) CS(MAP) Regs
44 Reg 36(4) CS(MAP) Regs
45 Reg 25(3) and (4) CS(MA) Regs
46 Reg 47(2) CS(MAP) Regs
47 Reg 47(4) and (5) CS(MAP) Regs
48 Reg 25(4) CS(MA) Regs
49 Reg 46 CS(MAP) Regs
50 Reg 41 CS(MAP) Regs
51 Reg 38 CS(MAP) Regs
52 Reg 48 CS(MAP) Regs
53 Reg 48 CS(MAP) Regs
54 Reg 40 CS(MAP) Regs

55 Regs 43 and 44 CS(MAP) Regs
56 Reg 49 CS(MAP) Regs
57 Reg 25(4) CS(MA) Regs
58 Reg 42 CS(MAP) Regs
59 s43 CSA 1991; regs 13 and 28 CS(MASC) Regs
60 Reg 28(1) and Sch 4 CS(MASC) Regs
61 s43 and Sch 1 para 5(4) CSA 1991; reg 28(3) CS(MASC) Regs; Sch 9 para 7A SS(C&P) Regs
62 Reg 28(5) and Sch 5 CS(MASC) Regs

5. How maintenance affects your income support
(pp120-127)

63 Reg 60B IS Regs
64 Reg 60C IS Regs
65 s74(1) SSAA 1992; reg 7 SS(PAOR) Regs
66 s41(2) CSA 1991; reg 8 CS(AIAMA) Regs
67 Reg 60D(aa) IS Regs
68 Regs 54-60 IS Regs
69 Reg 54 IS Regs
70 Reg 54 IS Regs, definition of 'periodical payment'; *Bolstridge v CAO*
71 Reg 58 IS Regs
72 Reg 58(4) IS Regs
73 Reg 59(1) IS Regs
74 s74(1) SSAA 1992; reg 7(1) SS(PAOR) Regs
75 Reg 54 IS Regs, definition of 'periodical payment'
76 *Regina v West London SBAT ex parte Taylor* [1975] 1 WLR 1048 (DC); *McCorquodale v CAO* (CA) reported as an appendix to R(SB) 1/88

77 Reg 60 IS Regs
78 Reg 60(2) IS Regs
79 Reg 54 IS Regs,
definition of 'payment'
and reg 55 IS Regs
80 Regs 57(4) and 59(2) IS
Regs
81 Reg 57(1) IS Regs
82 Reg 57(2) IS Regs
83 Reg 57(3) IS Regs
84 Reg 54 IS Regs,
definition of 'payment'
85 Regs 54, definition of
'payment', 55 and 60(1)
IS Regs
86 CSB/1160/1986;
R(SB) 1/89
87 R(SB) 1/89

**Chapter 7: Claims,
reviews and getting paid**
(pp128-166)

I. Claims
(pp128-136)
1 s1 SSAA 1992
2 Reg 4(3C) SS(C&P)
Regs
3 Reg 4(3) SS(C&P) Regs
4 Reg 4(4) SS(C&P) Regs
5 Reg 33 SS(C&P) Regs
6 R(SB) 5/90
7 CIS/642/1994
8 CIS/379/1992
9 Reg 4(1A) SS(C&P)
Regs
10 Reg 4(5) SS(C&P) Regs
11 Reg 5(2) SS(C&P) Regs
12 s1(1A) SSAA 1992; reg
2A IS Regs
13 Reg 2A IS Regs
14 Reg 4(1A) SS(C&P)
Regs
15 Reg 4(1B) SS(C&P)
Regs
16 Reg 7 SS(C&P) Regs
17 Reg 7(4) and (5)
SS(C&P) Regs
18 Reg 56 SS(Adj) Regs

19 Reg 19(1) and Sch 4
para 6 SS(C&P) Regs
20 Reg 6(1A) SS(C&P)
Regs
21 R(SB) 8/89
22 CIS/759/1992
23 Reg 13(1) SS(C&P)
Regs
24 Reg 6(1A) SS(C&P)
Regs
25 Reg 6(28) SS(C&P)
Regs
26 R(SB) 9/84
27 Reg 19(8) SS(C&P)
Regs
28 Reg 19(6) and (7)
SS(C&P) Regs
29 Reg 19(4) and (5)
SS(C&P) Regs
30 s68 SSAA 1992
31 R(SB) 17/83; R(IS)
5/91; CIS/812/1992
32 R(P) 2/85
33 Reg 32(1) SS(C&P)
Regs

**2. Decisions and
reviews**
(pp137-144)
34 ss20 and 21 SSAA
1992
35 Reg 56 SS(Adj) Regs
36 Reg 9(1) and Sch 1
SS(C&P) Regs
37 Reg 55(1), (3) and (4)
SS(Adj) Regs
38 Reg 55(7) SS(Adj) Regs
39 Reg 55(5) SS(Adj) Regs
40 s21(1) SSAA 1992
41 s25 SSAA 1992
42 CSB/376/1983; R(I) 1/
71; CI/11/1977
43 R(I) 50/56
44 *CAO v Eggleton &
Others* (CA) March 1993
45 Reg 17(4) SS(C&P)
Regs; CSIS/137/1994(T)
46 s25(1) SSAA 1992
47 CIS/767/1994

48 *CAO v McKiernon*
(CA) 8 July 1993
49 R(S) 4/86
50 CSIS/137/1994(T); CIS/
856/1994
51 Regs 63(5) and 64
SS(Adj) Regs
52 Sch 7 para 7 SS(C&P)
Regs
53 CIS/714/1991
54 s36 SSAA 1992; R(IS)
15/93
55 Reg 63(1) SS(Adj) Regs
56 Reg 57(3) SS(Adj) Regs
57 Reg 57(2) SS(Adj) Regs
58 *Saker v Secretary of State
for Social Services*, R(I)
2/88
59 Reg 63(1A) SS(Adj)
Regs
60 CSIS/80/1995;
AM(AOG)66, 17
February 1998
61 Reg 63(1B) SS(Adj)
Regs
62 R(IS) 11/92
63 s69 SSAA 1992; reg 58
SS(Adj) Regs; *CAO and
Another v Bate* (HL)
[1996] 2 All ER 790
64 *CAO and Another v
Woods* (CA),
unreported, 12
December 1997 (the
CAO is seeking leave
to appeal to HL)
65 CIS/566/1991;
CIS/788/1991

3. Payments of benefit
(pp144-156)
66 Reg 20 SS(C&P) Regs
67 Reg 21 SS(C&P) Regs
68 para 5039 IS Guide
(payments volume)
69 Reg 38(1) SS(C&P)
Regs
70 Reg 38(2A) SS(C&P)
Regs

71 Sch 7 para 5 SS(C&P) Regs

72 Reg 28 SS(C&P) Regs

73 Reg 26(1) and Sch 7 SS(C&P) Regs

74 Sch 7 para 1 SS(C&P) Regs

75 Sch 7 para 6(1) SS(C&P) Regs

76 Sch 7 para 3(2) SS(C&P) Regs

77 Sch 7 para 3(1) SS(C&P) Regs

78 Reg 2 SS(PAOR) Regs

79 *Factortame Ltd and others v Secretary of State for Transport (No.2)* [1991] 1 AC 603 [1991] 1 All ER 70

80 Regs 3 and 4 SS(PAOR) Regs

81 Reg 37(1)(a) SS(C&P) Regs

82 Reg 37(1)(b) SS(C&P) Regs

83 Reg 37(1)(c) SS(C&P) Regs

84 Reg 37B SS(C&P) Regs

85 In *R v Secretary of State ex parte Sutherland* (QBD) 7 November 1996, the court found reg 37A SS(C&P) Regs to be *ultra vires*

86 *R v Secretary of State for Social Security ex parte Mulgrew* (unreported case)

87 Reg 37AA SS(C&P) Regs

88 Reg 37AB SS(C&P) Regs

89 *Walsh v DSS*, Bromley County Court, 12 February 1990. Not reported – see *Welfare Rights Bulletin 96*

90 R(IS) 7/91

91 *Hansard*, 4 May 1993;

paras 137-140 'Financial Redress for Maladministration'

92 Reg 33 SS(C&P) Regs

93 Reg 34 SS(C&P) Regs

94 Reg 34A and Sch 9A para 2 SS(C&P) Regs

95 Sch 9A paras 8 and 9 SS(C&P) Regs

96 Sch 9A para 3 SS(C&P) Regs

97 Sch 9A paras 3 and 5 SS(C&P) Regs

98 Sch 9A para 6 SS(C&P) Regs

99 *Pazio v Secretary of State for Social Security* (Birmingham County Court, 1996) – see report in *Welfare Rights Bulletins 133*, p14 and *138*, p14

100 Sch 9A para 3 SS(C&P) Regs

101 Reg 35 and Sch 9 SS(C&P) Regs

102 Sch 9 para 2 SS(C&P) Regs

103 Sch 9 para 5 SS(C&P) Regs

104 Sch 9 para 5(1)(c)(i) SS(C&P) Regs

105 Sch 9 para 5(1)(c)(ii) SS(C&P) Regs

106 Sch 9 para 5(6) SS(C&P) Regs; R(IS) 14/95

107 Sch 9 para 5(7) SS(C&P) Regs

108 Sch 9 para 3 SS(C&P) Regs

109 Sch 9 para 3(5) SS(C&P) Regs

110 Sch 9 para 1 SS(C&P) Regs

111 Sch 9 para 3(4) SS(C&P) Regs

112 CIS/15146/1996

113 Sch 9 para 4 SS(C&P) Regs

114 Sch 9 paras 1 and 7 SS(C&P) Regs

115 Sch 9 para 7(1) SS(C&P) Regs

116 Sch 9 para 7(2) SS(C&P) Regs

117 Sch 9 para 7(7) SS(C&P) Regs

118 Sch 9 para 6 SS(C&P) Regs

119 Sch 9 para 6(1) SS(C&P) Regs

120 Sch 9 para 6(4) SS(C&P) Regs

121 CC(DIS) Regs; CT(DIS) Regs; CIS/ 11861/1996

122 Sch 9 para 4A SS(C&P) Regs

123 Regs 1-7 F(DIS) Regs

124 s43 CSA 1991

125 Sch 9 SS(C&P) Regs

126 Sch 9 paras 1 and 2(2) SS(C&P) Regs

127 Reg 2 CC(DIS) Regs; regs 2-3 CT(DIS) Regs

128 Sch 9 para 3(2A) SS(C&P) Regs

129 Sch 9 para 8(1) SS(C&P) Regs

130 Sch 9 paras 5(5), 6(6), 7(8) and 8(2) and (3) SS(C&P) Regs

131 Sch 9 para 9 SS(C&P) Regs

132 Regs 15 and 16 SS(PAOR) Regs; reg 3 SF(RDB) Regs

133 Reg 4 CC(DIS) Regs; reg 8 CT(DIS) Regs

4. Overpayments and fraud

(pp156-165)

134 s74 SSAA 1992

135 R(SB) 3/91

136 Sch 9A para 11
SS(C&P) Regs
137 *R v Secretary of State for Social Security ex parte Golding* (CA), *The Times,* 15 March 1996
138 CIS/5206/1995
139 CIS/5206/1995
140 s71 SSAA 1992
141 CSB/688/1982
142 s71(5A) SSAA 1992; CSSB/621/1988 and CSB/316/1989; R(SB) 7/91
143 CIS/451/1995, following this case s71 SSAA 1992 was amended
144 CSB/1006/1985
145 R(SB) 21/82; R(SB) 28/83; R(SB) 54/83; R(A) 1/95
146 Reg 32(1) SS(C&P) Regs
147 CSB/688/1982; R(SB) 12/84; R(SB) 20/84; R(SB) 40/84
148 R(SB) 18/85
149 CWSB/2/1985
150 CSB/347/1983; R(SB) 10/85
151 R(SB) 33/85; CSB/1195/1984
152 R(SB) 54/83
153 CSB/393/1985
154 *Page v CAO* (CA), *The Times,* 4 July 1991
155 *Jones/Sharples v CAO* [1994] 1 All ER 225; R(SB) 9/85
156 R(SB) 3/90
157 CIS/222/1991
158 *Sheriff v CAO, The Times,* 10 May 1995
159 *Jones/Sharples v CAO* [1994] 1 All ER 225; *Franklin v CAO, The Times,* 29 December 1995; CIS/674/1994; CIS/583/1994

160 CIS/674/1994
161 *Franklin v CAO, The Times,* 29 December 1995
162 CIS/53/1994
163 CIS/159/1990; CS/11700/1996
164 R(SB) 20/84; R(SB) 24/87
165 Reg 13 SS(PAOR) Regs
166 R(IS) 5/92
167 *Commock v CAO* reported as appendix to R(SB) 6/90; CSIS/8/1995
168 Regs 15 and 16(3) SS(PAOR) Regs
169 Reg 14 SS(PAOR) Regs
170 Reg 15 SS(PAOR) Regs
171 s74(2)(b) SSAA 1992
172 Reg 16(3) SS(PAOR) Regs
173 Reg 16(4), (5) and (6) SS(PAOR) Regs
174 Reg 16(6) SS(PAOR) Regs
175 Reg 17 SS(PAOR) Regs
176 CIS/332/1993; CIS/12022/1996 decided the opposite
177 *Secretary of State for Social Services v Solly* [1974] 3 All ER 922; R(SB) 21/82

Chapter 8: Appeals
(pp167-185)

1. Appealing to social security appeal tribunals
(pp167-177)

1 R(SB) 29/83; R(SB) 12/89; CIS/807/1992
2 Reg 3(5A) SS(Adj) Regs
3 para 1003, Code of Appeals Procedure
4 Reg 55(7) SS(Adj) Regs
5 Reg 3 and Sch 2

SS(Adj) Regs; CIS/550/1993
6 Reg 3(6C) SS(Adj) Regs
7 Reg 3(6) and (6B) SS(Adj) Regs
8 Reg 3(6A) SS(Adj) Regs
9 Reg 3(5) SS(Adj) Regs
10 Reg 3(3) and (3A) SS(Adj) Regs
11 Reg 3(3E) SS(Adj) Regs
12 Reg 3(3B) and (3C) SS(Adj) Regs
13 Reg 3(5) SS(Adj) Regs
14 Reg 3(3D) SS(Adj) Regs
15 Reg 3(8) and (9) SS(Adj) Regs
16 R(SB) 24/82
17 s29 SSAA 1992
18 Reg 22(1A) SS(Adj) Regs
19 Reg 22(1) SS(Adj) Regs
20 Reg 22(1c) SS(Adj) Regs
21 Reg 2(1)(b) SS(Adj) Regs
22 para 38(1) *Social Security Appeal Tribunals: A guide to procedure,* HMSO
23 Reg 4(2B) SS(Adj) Regs
24 Reg 2(1)(aa) and (ab) SS(Adj) Regs
25 Regs 4(2A) and 7 SS(Adj) Regs
26 Reg 7 SS(Adj) Regs
27 Reg 7(3) SS(Adj) Regs
28 Reg 6(2) and (2A) SS(Adj) Regs
29 R(IS) 5/94)
30 Reg 4(2) SS(Adj) Regs
31 Reg 4(3A) SS(Adj) Regs
32 Reg 5(1) SS(Adj) Regs
33 Reg 4(3) SS(Adj) Regs
34 CIS/566/1991; CS/99/1993
35 Reg 4(4) SS(Adj) Regs
36 s41 SSAA 1992

37 Regs 22(2) and 23(1)
SS(Adj) Regs
38 Sch 2 para 7 SSAA
· 1992
39 para 05328 AOG
40 CS/12054/1996, CIB/
14430/1996 and CIS/
12015/1996(T)
41 CIS/643A/1992
42 President's Circulars
No.1 and No.9, June
1997
43 Reg 22(3) SS(Adj) Regs
44 CSIS/118/1990;
CSIS/110/1991
45 Reg 23(3) SS(Adj) Regs
46 Reg 23(3A) SS(Adj)
Regs
47 CDLA/16902/1996
48 Reg 23(3D) SS(Adj)
Regs
49 Reg 37 SS(C&P) Regs
50 Reg 10 SS(Adj) Regs
51 R(SB) 4/90
52 CSB/172/1990
53 CI/79/1990;
CIS/373/1994
54 Reg 9 SS(Adj) Regs

2. How to prepare an appeal
(pp178-180)
55 s36 SSAA 1992; R(SB)
1/82; R(FIS) 1/82
56 R(SB) 6/82
57 R(SB) 33/85;
R(SB) 12/89
58 R(SB) 10/86
59 R(IS) 6/91
60 R(SB) 1/81
61 s123(2) SSCBA 1992
62 s39(2) SSAA 1992
63 s23 SSAA 1992
64 R(I) 12/75

3. Appealing to the social security commissioner
(pp181-184)
65 s23 SSAA 1992
66 R(A) 1/72;
R(SB) 11/83
67 CS/1939/1995
68 R(IS) 4/93
69 s23(9) SSAA 1992
70 Reg 24(1) SS(Adj) Regs;
reg 3(1) SSCP Regs
71 Regs 3(3) and 24 and
Sch 2, para 7 SS(Adj)
Regs
72 Reg 3(1) and (3) SSCP
Regs; CIS/550/1993
73 Reg 3(2) and (5) SSCP
Regs; CIS/500/1993
74 Reg 7(1) SSCP Regs
75 Reg 5(2) SSCP Regs
76 Regs 10, 11 and 12
SSCP Regs
77 Reg 27(3) and (4) SSCP
Regs
78 Reg 15 SSCP Regs
79 s57 SSAA 1992
80 Reg 17(4) SSCP Regs
81 Reg 22(2) SSCP Regs
82 s23(7)(b) SSAA 1992
83 s23(7)(a) SSAA 1992
84 *Innes v CAO* (CA)
(unreported), 19
November 1986
85 Regs 24 and 25 SSCP
Regs

4. Appealing to the courts
(pp184-185)
86 s24 SSAA 1992
87 Regs 27(2) and 31(1)
SSCP Regs
88 *White v CAO* [1986] 2
All ER 905 (CA), also
reported as an
Appendix to
R(S) 8/85
89 s24(2)(b) SSAA 1992

90 RSC 0.59 r.21(2)
91 RSC 0.3 r.5 and 0.59
r.14(2)
92 RSC 0.59 r.14(2), (2A),
(2B)
93 RSC 0.59 r.4(3) and
r.21(2)
94 *Bland v CSBO* [1983]
1 WLR 262 (CA), also
reported as
R(SB) 12/83
95 ss2(4)(a) and 15(1)
LAA 1988

PART THREE: BACK TO WORK BENEFITS, FAMILY CREDIT AND DISABILITY WORKING ALLOWANCE

Chapter 9: Back to work benefits
(pp188-196)
1 SS(BWB) (No.2) Regs
2 Reg 1(2) SS(CMB)
Regs
3 Reg 3 SS(CMB) Regs
4 Reg 3(2) and (3)
SS(CMB) Regs
5 Reg 14 SS(CMB) Regs
6 Reg 4 SS(CMB) Regs
7 Reg 4(2)-(5) SS(CMB)
Regs
8 Reg 5 SS(CMB) Regs
9 Reg 1(5) SS(CMB)
Regs
10 Reg 5(5) SS(CMB) Regs
11 Regs 2(2) and 6
SS(CMB) Regs
12 Reg 10(1) SS(CMB)
Regs
13 Reg 9 SS(CMB) Regs
14 Reg 9(4) and (5)
SS(CMB) Regs
15 Reg 10 SS(CMB) Regs
16 Reg 11(3) SS(CMB)
Regs

17 Reg 11(4) SS(CMB)
Regs
18 Reg 10(3)-(5) SS(CMB)
Regs
19 Reg 11(1) and (2)
SS(CMB) Regs
20 Reg 8(1) and (2)
SS(CMB) Regs
21 Reg 8(4) and (5)
SS(CMB) Regs
22 Reg 8(3) SS(CMB) Regs
23 Reg 13 SS(CMB) Regs
24 Reg 7 SS(CMB) Regs

Chapter 10: Family credit
(pp197-211)

2. The basic rules
(pp198-203)
1 s128(1) SSCBA 1992
2 Reg 3(1) FC Regs
3 R(P) 1/78; R(M) 1/85
4 *Shah v Barnet LBC*
[1983] All ER 226
5 Reg 9(1) FC Regs; CIS/
508/1992
6 R(FC) 2/93
7 Reg 3(2) FC Regs
8 para 50100 AOG
9 Reg 3(1)(aa) FC Regs
10 Reg 3(1A) FC Regs; reg
12 SS(PFA)MA Regs
11 CIS/16992/1996;
CIS/2809/1997;
CFC/1580/1997
12 ss128(1)(b) and
129(1)(a) SSCBA 1992
13 R(FIS) 6/83; R(FIS) 1/
84; R(FIS) 1/86
14 *Kevin Smith v CAO*, 11
October 1994
(unreported)
15 CFC/33/1993
16 R(FIS) 1/83
17 Reg 4(3)(c) FC Regs;
reg 6(3)(c) DWA Regs
18 R(FIS) 1/86; CDWA/1/
1992

19 Reg 4(3)(a) FC Regs;
reg 6(3)(a) DWA Regs
20 Reg 4(3)(b) FC Regs;
reg 6(3)(b) DWA Regs
21 Reg 4 FC Regs; reg 6
DWA Regs
22 R(IS) 1/93
23 Reg 4(5) FC Regs; reg
6(5) DWA Regs
24 Reg 4(6)(b) FC Regs;
reg 6(6)(b) DWA Regs
25 Reg 4(6) FC Regs; reg
6(6) DWA Regs
26 R(FIS) 2/83
27 R(FIS) 6/83; R(FIS) 1/
84
28 R(FIS) 6/83
29 R(FIS) 1/85; *R v Ebbw
Vale & Merthyr Tydfil
SBAT ex parte Lewis*
[1982] 1 WLR 420
30 R(FIS) 2/81; R(FIS) 2/
82
31 R(FC) 1/92
32 Reg 4(4)(a) FC Regs;
reg 6(4)(a) DWA Regs
33 paras 50381-82 AOG
34 R(FIS) 6/85; para 50372
AOG
35 Reg 4(4)(b) FC Regs;
reg 6(4)(b) DWA Regs
36 Reg 4(4)(c)(ii)(bb) FC
Regs
37 Reg 4(4)(c)(i) FC Regs;
reg 6(4)(c)(i) DWA
Regs; CIS/261/1990
38 Reg 4(4)(c)(ii)(aa) FC
Regs; reg 6(4)(c)(ii)
DWA Regs
39 Reg 4(4A) FC Regs
40 Reg 5(1A) IS Regs; reg
4(1) FC Regs
41 s128(1)(d) SSCBA 1992
42 Reg 52 FC Regs

3. The amount of benefit
(pp203-204)
43 s128(1)(a) SSCBA 1992;
reg 47(1) FC Regs
44 s128(2)(b) SSCBA
1992; reg 48 FC Regs
45 Reg 46(1) FC Regs
46 Sch 4 FC Regs
47 Reg 46(4)-(6) FC Regs
48 Regs 5 and 6
IRB&JSA(PA) Amdt
Regs amending reg 46
of, and Sch 4 to, the
FC Regs
49 Reg 46(1)(aa) and Sch 4
para 1A FC Regs
50 Reg 4A FC Regs
51 Reg 28 SS(C&P) Regs
52 Reg 27(2) SS(C&P)
Regs

4. Special rules for special groups
(p205)
53 Reg 14(3) FC Regs
54 s128(3) SSCBA 1992

5. Claims and getting paid
(pp205-210)
55 Reg 4(2) SS(C&P) Regs
56 Reg 6(1) SS(C&P) Regs
57 Reg 6(1)(aa) SS(C&P)
Regs
58 Reg 4(7) SS(C&P) Regs
59 Reg 6(27) SS(C&P)
Regs
60 Reg 19(7)(e) SS(C&P)
Regs
61 Reg 19(7)(f) SS(C&P)
Regs
62 Reg 5 SS(C&P) Regs
63 Reg 19 and Sch 4 para
7 SS(C&P) Regs
64 Reg 16(1) and (3)
SS(C&P) Regs
65 Reg 16(1B) SS(C&P)
Regs

66 Reg 13(6) SS(C&P)
   Regs
67 Reg 9 and Sch 1 Part 1
   SS(C&P) Regs
68 CFC/25/1993; see also
   '4th Report of the
   Parliamentary
   Commissioner for
   Administration 1993/
   94', Case C-761/93
69 Reg 7(3) SS(C&P) Regs
70 s21(1) SSAA 1992
71 DSS Press Release 95/
   176, December 1995
72 Reg 20 SS(Adj) Regs
73 Reg 27(1A) SS(C&P)
   Regs
74 Reg 27(2) SS(C&P)
   Regs
75 Reg 27(1) SS(C&P)
   Regs
76 Reg 21 SS(C&P) Regs
77 s128(3) SSCBA 1992
78 s128(4) SSCBA 1992;
   reg 50 FC Regs
79 Reg 49A FC Regs
80 Reg 49 FC Regs
81 Reg 51 FC Regs
82 CFC/18/1989
83 Regs 15 and 16
   SS(PAOR) Regs

6. Challenging a family credit decision
(p210)
84 Reg 65 SS(Adj) Regs

Chapter 11: Disability working allowance
(pp212-225)
1 Reg 4 NHS(TERC)
   Regs
2 Reg 7B SS(Cr) Regs
3 s129(1) SSCBA 1992
4 Reg 5 DWA Regs
5 s129(1)(b) SSCBA 1992
6 s11(2) SSAA 1992; reg
   4 DWA Regs

7 Reg 3 and Sch 1 DWA
   Regs
8 Sch 1 para 24 DWA
   Regs
9 s129(1), (2) and (4)
   SSCBA 1992; reg 7
   DWA Regs
10 Reg 17 SS(ICB) Trans
   Regs; regs 7A and 7B
   DWA Regs
11 s129(2A) and (2B)
   SSCBA 1992
12 s11(3) SSAA 1992
13 s129(1)(d) SSCBA 1992
14 Reg 57 DWA Regs
15 Reg 51(1A) DWA Regs
16 s129(5) SSCBA 1992;
   reg 53 DWA Regs
17 Reg 51 and Sch 5
   DWA Regs
18 Regs 8 and 9
   IRB&JSA(PA) Amdt
   Regs
19 Reg 51(1)(bb) and Sch
   5 para 2A DWA Regs
20 Reg 6A DWA Regs
21 Reg 28 SS(C&P) Regs
22 Reg 27(2) SS(C&P)
   Regs
23 Reg 16(3) and (4)
   DWA Regs
24 Reg 4(1) SS(C&P) Regs
25 Reg 4(3A) SS(C&P)
   Regs
26 Reg 4(7) SS(C&P) Regs
27 Reg 5 SS(C&P) Regs
28 Reg 9 and Sch 1 Part 1
   SS(C&P) Regs
29 Reg 6(1) SS(C&P) Regs
30 Reg 6(1)(aa) SS(C&P)
   Regs
31 Reg 6(10) SS(C&P)
   Regs
32 Reg 6(27) SS(C&P)
   Regs
33 Reg 6(13) SS(C&P)
   Regs
34 Reg 6(12) SS(C&P)
   Regs

35 Reg 6(15) SS(C&P)
   Regs
36 Reg 6(14) SS(C&P)
   Regs
37 s30(13) SSAA 1992
38 Reg 6(11) SS(C&P)
   Regs
39 Reg 19(7)(h) SS(C&P)
   Regs
40 Reg 19(7)(f) SS(C&P)
   Regs
41 Reg 19(1) and Sch 4
   para 11 SS(C&P) Regs
42 Reg 7(1) SS(C&P) Regs
43 Reg 7(3) SS(C&P) Regs
44 ss20 and 21 SSAA
   1992
45 s11(2) SSAA 1992; reg
   4 DWA Regs
46 s54 SSAA 1992
47 s54(2) SSAA 1992
48 Reg 20 SS(Adj) Regs
49 Reg 16(1) and (3)
   SS(C&P) Regs
50 Reg 16(1C) SS(C&P)
   Regs
51 Reg 16(1B) SS(C&P)
   Regs
52 s129(6) SSCBA 1992
53 Reg 21 SS(C&P) Regs
54 Reg 27(1A) and (2)
   SS(C&P) Regs
55 Reg 36 SS(C&P) Regs
56 s129(6) SSCBA 1992
57 Reg 55 DWA Regs
58 Reg 54 DWA Regs
59 Reg 56 DWA Regs
60 s71 SSAA 1992
61 s30(5) SSAA 1992
62 Reg 66(1) SS(Adj) Regs
63 Reg 66(2) SS(Adj) Regs
64 ss42 and 68(10) SSCBA
   1992
65 s93 SSCBA 1992
66 Regs 12 and 19
   SS(ICB) Trans Regs

PART FOUR: HOUSING BENEFIT AND COUNCIL TAX BENEFIT

Chapter 12: The basic rules
(pp228-262)

1. Introduction
(pp228-242)

1 s130 SSCBA 1992
2 Reg 6(1)(a) HB Regs
3 Reg 6(1)(b) HB Regs
4 Reg 6(1)(c)(i) HB Regs
5 Reg 6(1)(c)(ii) HB Regs
6 Reg 6(1)(d) HB Regs
7 Reg 6(1)(e) HB Regs
8 s134(2) SSCBA 1992; reg 71(1) HB Regs
9 Reg 10(5) HB Regs
10 Reg 10(3) HB Regs
11 *R v Rugby BC HBRB ex parte Harrison* [1994] 28 HLR 36, QBD
12 *R v Poole BC ex parte Ross* [1995] 28 HLR 351, QBD; *R v Warrington BC ex parte Williams*, 28 January 1997, QBD
13 *R v Cambridge CC ex parte Thomas*, 10 February 1995, QBD
14 Reg 6(2) HB Regs
15 s130(1) SSCBA 1992; reg 5(1) and (2) HB Regs
16 Reg 5(3) HB Regs
17 Reg 5(4) HB Regs
18 R(SB) 10/81
19 Reg 5(7A) HB Regs
20 Reg 5(7B) and (7C) HB Regs
21 Reg 5(8) HB Regs
22 Reg 5(8B) HB Regs
23 *R v Penwith DC ex parte Burt* [1988] 22 HLR

292, QBD; para A3.25 GM
24 Reg 5(8A) HB Regs
25 para A3.20 GM
26 Reg 5(6) HB Regs
27 Reg 5(5)(a) HB Regs
28 Reg 5(5)(b) HB Regs
29 Reg 5(5)(c) HB Regs
30 Reg 5(5)(d) HB Regs
31 Circular HB/CTB A41/97
32 Reg 5(5)(e) HB Regs
33 Reg 48A(1) HB Regs
34 Reg 7A HB Regs
35 Reg 7(1)(d) HB Regs
36 Reg 7(1)(e) HB Regs
37 Reg 7(1)(a)(i) HB Regs
38 Reg 3(4) HB Regs
39 *Thamesdown BC v Goonery*, 13 February 1995, CA
40 Reg 2(1) HB Regs
41 R(SB) 27/87; Circular HB/CTB A27/97
42 paras A3.70-74 GM
43 *R v Rugby BC HBRB ex parte Harrison* [1994] 28 HLR 36, QBD
44 para A3.66(iii) GM
45 *R v Poole BC ex parte Ross* [1995] 28 HLR 351, QBD
46 *R v Sutton LBC ex parte Partridge* [1994] 28 HLR 315, QBD
47 Para A3.66(iv) GM
48 Reg 7(1)(b) HB Regs
49 Reg 7(1)(c) HB Regs
50 *R v Solihull MBC ex parte Simpson* [1995] 1 FLR 140, CA
51 *R v Sutton LBC HBRB ex parte Keegan* [1992] 27 HLR 92, QBD
52 Para A3.76 GM
53 *R v Manchester CC ex parte Baragrove Properties Ltd* [1991] 23 HLR 337, QBD

54 *R v Gloucestershire CC ex parte Dadds* [1997] 29 HLR 700, QBD
55 *R v Poole BC ex parte Ross* (1995) 28 HLR 351, QBD
56 Reg 8(2)(b) HB Regs
57 Reg 8(2ZA) HB Regs
58 Reg 10(2)(a) and (c) HB Regs
59 Reg 2(1) HB Regs
60 Reg 8(2) HB Regs
61 Reg 8(3) HB Regs
62 Reg 10(2)(e) HB Regs; Part A8 GM
63 Reg 10(2)(b) HB Regs
64 Reg 10(2)(d) HB Regs
65 Circular HB/CTB A7/94
66 Reg 7A(5) HB Regs
67 Reg 7A(2) HB Regs
68 Reg 7A(3) HB Regs
69 Reg 7A(4)(a) HB Regs
70 Reg 7A(4)(b) HB Regs
71 Reg 7A(4)(c) HB Regs
72 Reg 7A(4)(d) HB Regs
73 Reg 7A(4)(e) HB Regs
74 Circular HB/CTB A7/94
75 Command Paper Cm 2609, para 31
76 Reg 7A(4)(e) and (5) HB Regs
77 Reg 18 SS(MA) Regs
78 Reg 7A(4)(f) and (5) HB Regs
79 Reg 12(2) SS(PFA)MA Regs
80 Reg 7A(5) HB Regs
81 Reg 12(1) SS(PFA)MA Regs
82 *R v Secretary of State for Social Security ex parte Vijeikis*, 10 July 1997, QBD; CIS/16992/1996
83 CIS/16992/1996
84 Reg 7A(5A) HB Regs
85 Sch A1 para 2(4) HB

Regs; Sch A1 para 2(4) CTB Regs

86 Sch A1 para 2(5) HB Regs; Sch A1 para 2(5) CTB Regs

87 Sch A1 para 2(1) HB Regs; Sch A1 para 2(1) CTB Regs

88 Sch A1 para 1(2) HB Regs; Sch A1 para 1(2) CTB Regs

89 Sch A1 paras 1(3) and 2(3) HB Regs; Sch A1 paras 1(3) and 6 CTB Regs

90 Sch A1 para 9 HB Regs; Sch A1 para 8 CTB Regs

91 Sch A1 para 5(1) HB Regs; Sch A1 para 4(1) CTB Regs

92 Sch A1 paras 4 and 5(2) HB Regs; Sch A1 para 4(2) and (4) CTB Regs

93 Sch A1 para 6 HB Regs; Sch A1 para 5 CTB Regs

94 Sch A1 para 5(3) HB Regs; Sch A1 para 4(3) CTB Regs

95 Reg 7B(1)(b) HB Regs; Reg 10(5A) HB(Amdt) Regs as amended

96 Sch A1 para 8(1) HB Regs; Sch A1 para 7(1) CTB Regs

97 Sch A1 para 8(5) HB Regs

98 Sch A1 para 8(4) HB Regs

99 Reg 7(1)(e) HB Regs

100 Reg 7(2) HB Regs

101 Reg 7(4)-(12) HB Regs

2. 'Eligible rent'
(pp 242-247)

102 Reg 10(1) HB Regs

103 Reg 2(4)(a) HB Regs

104 Reg 10(3)(a) and (6) HB Regs

105 Reg 10(4) HB Regs

106 Reg 8(2A) HB Regs

107 Reg 10(6A) HB Regs

108 Sch 1 para 5(1) HB Regs

109 Sch 1 para 5(1)(a) HB Regs

110 Sch 1 para 5(2) and (2A) HB Regs

111 Reg 10(3)(b) HB Regs

112 Sch 1 para 5(3) and Sch 6 para 9(c) HB Regs

113 para A4.90(iii) GM

114 Sch 1 paras 4 and 5(1)(b) HB Regs; para A4.95 GM

115 Sch 1 para 7 HB Regs

116 Sch 1 para 7 HB Regs

117 Reg 10(1)(e) HB Regs

118 Sch 1 para 1(a)(iii) HB Regs

119 Sch 1 para 1(a)(ii) HB Regs

120 Sch 1 para 1(b) HB Regs

121 Sch 1 para 1(a)(iv) HB Regs

122 Sch 1 para 1(a)(iv) HB Regs

123 Sch 1 para 1(c) HB Regs; para A4.75 GM

124 Sch 1 para 1(f)(i) HB Regs

125 *R v Sutton LBC HBRB ex parte Harrison*, 23 July 1997, QBD. The claimants in this and other cases heard with it are appealing to the Court of Appeal.

126 Sch 1 para 1(f)(ii) HB Regs; paras A4.77-79 GM

127 Sch 1 para 1(f)(iii) HB Regs

128 Sch 1 para 7 HB Regs

129 Reg 3 HB(Amdt 2) Regs

130 Sch 1 para 3 HB Regs

131 Sch 1 para 1 HB Regs

132 Reg 10(3)(c) and Sch 1 para 2(1A) HB Regs

133 Sch 1 para 2 HB Regs

134 Sch 1 para 1(a)(i) HB Regs

135 Sch 1 para 1A(1) HB Regs

136 Sch 1 para 1A(5) and (6) HB Regs

3. Rent restrictions
(pp 247-262)

137 Reg 12A HB Regs

138 Reg 12A(2)(b) and Sch 1A HB Regs

139 Reg 12A HB Regs

140 Sch 1A para 2 HB Regs

141 Sch 1 para 1 RO(HBF)O

142 Sch 1 para 2 RO(HBF)O

143 Sch 2 RO(AF)O

144 Art 2(1) RO(HBF)O

145 Sch 1 para 3 RO(HBF)O

146 Sch 1 para 5 RO(HBF)O

147 Reg 2(1)(a) HB Regs definition of 'young individual'

148 Reg 2(1)(b)-(e) HB Regs definition of 'young individual'

149 Reg 11(3B)(b) HB Regs

150 Reg 11(3B)(c) HB Regs

151 Sch 1 para 4 RO(HBF)O

152 Sch 1 para 6 RO(HBF)O

153 Sch 1 paras 4(5) and 6(2) RO(HBF)O

154 Sch 1 para 6(1) RO(HBF)O

155 Sch 1 para 4(3)(b) and (5) RO(HBF)O

156 Sch 1 para 5(2)(c)
RO(HBF)O
157 Sch 1 para 9
RO(HBF)O
158 Reg 10 HB(Amdt) Regs
159 Reg 10(2) HB(Amdt)
Regs
160 Reg 10(6) HB(Amdt)
Regs
161 Reg 10(6) HB(Amdt)
Regs
162 Reg 11(13) HB Regs
163 Reg 11(3) and (4) HB
Regs
164 Reg 11(8A) HB Regs
165 Reg 4(2)
HB&CTB(Amdt) Regs
166 Reg 4(2A
HB&CTB(Amdt) Regs
167 Reg 11(6) HB Regs
168 Reg 11(6A) and (6B)
HB Regs
169 Reg 11(7) HB Regs
170 Reg 11(9) and (10) HB
Regs
171 Reg 61(3) HB Regs
172 para A12.03 GM
173 Reg 61(4) HB Regs
174 Reg 10(6B) HB Regs
175 Reg 12A(1)(c) HB Regs
176 Reg 12A(3) HB Regs
177 Sch 1 para 9
RO(HBF)O
178 Reg 79(5B) HB Regs
179 Reg 11(2) HB Regs
(pre-January 1996)
180 *R v Kensington and
Chelsea RBC HBRB ex
parte Pirie,* 26 March
1997, QBD
181 *R v Beverley DC HBRB
ex parte Hare* [1995] 27
HLR 637, QBD
182 *R v Kensington and
Chelsea RBC HBRB ex
parte Sheikh,* 14 January
1997, QBD
183 *R v Kensington and
Chelsea RBC ex parte*

Abou-Jaoude, 10 May
1996, QBD
184 *Macleod v Banff and
Buchan District HBRB*
[1988] SLT 753, CS;
*Malcolm v Tweedale
District HBRB* [1994]
SLT 1212, CS
185 *R v Kensington and
Chelsea RBC ex parte
Abou-Jaoude,* 10 May
1996, QBD
186 *R v Coventry CC ex parte
Waite,* 7 July 1995,
QBD
187 *R v East Devon DC
HBRB ex parte Gibson*
[1993] 25 HLR 487,
QBD
188 para A4.110 GM; *R v
Waltham Forest LBC ex
parte Holder* [1996] 29
HLR 71, QBD
189 *R v Kensington and
Chelsea RBC HBRB ex
parte Sheikh,* 14 January
1997, QBD
190 Reg 11(6)(a) HB Regs
(pre-January 1996)
191 Reg 11(7) HB Regs
(pre-January 1996)
192 Reg 11(8) HB Regs
(pre-January 1996)
193 *R v Lambeth LBC
HBRB ex parte
Harrington,* 22
November 1996, QBD
194 Reg 11(6)(a) HB Regs
(pre-January 1996)
195 *R v Kensington and
Chelsea RBC ex parte
Pirie,* 26 March 1997,
QBD
196 *R v Coventry CC ex parte
Waite,* 7 July 1995,
QBD
197 *R v Sefton BC HBRB ex
parte Brennan* [1996] 29
HLR 735, QBD

198 *R v Waltham Forest LBC
ex parte Holder* [1996] 29
HLR 71, QBD; *R v
Slough BC ex parte Green,*
15 November 1996,
QBD
199 Reg 11(3) HB Regs
(pre-January 1996)
200 Reg 11(3) HB Regs
(pre-January 1996)
201 *R v East Devon DC
HBRB ex parte Gibson*
[1993] 25 HLR 487,
QBD
202 *R v Waltham Forest LBC
ex parte Holder* [1996] 29
HLR 71, QBD
203 *R v Oadby and Wigston
DC ex parte Dickman*
[1995] 28 HLR 806,
QBD
204 Reg 11(6)(b) HB Regs
(pre-January 1996)
205 *R v Kensington and
Chelsea RBC HBRB ex
parte Sheikh,* 14 January
1997
206 *R v Kensington and
Chelsea RBC HBRB ex
parte Carney* [1997]
Crown Office Digest
124, QBD
207 Reg 11(3) HB Regs
(pre- January 1996)
208 *R v Brent LBC HBRB
ex parte Connery* [1989]
22 HLR 40, QBD
209 Reg 11(3A) HB Regs
210 Reg 11(4) and (5) HB
Regs (pre-January 1996)
211 Reg 12(b) HB Regs;
para A4.125 GM
212 Reg 12 HB Regs

Chapter 13: The amount of benefit
(pp 263-273)

1. The basic calculation
(pp 263-266)

1 Reg 61 HB Regs
2 Sch 4 para 4 HB Regs; Sch 5 para 5 CTB Regs; *R v Penwith DC ex parte Menear* [1991] 24 HLR 120, QBD
3 Reg 64(2) HB Regs
4 Reg 2 HB Regs
5 Reg 69 HB Regs
6 Reg 69(2)(b) HB Regs
7 Reg 70(3) and Sch 1 para 6(2) HB Regs; paras A5.49-53 GM
8 Reg 70(3)(a) and Sch 1 para 6(2)(a) HB Regs
9 Reg 70(3)(b) and Sch 1 para 6(2)(b) HB Regs

2. Extended payments of HB/CTB
(pp 266-267)

10 Sch 5A para 1 and reg 62A(2) and (3) HB Regs; Sch 5A para 1 and reg 53A(2) and (3) CTB Regs
11 Reg 62A(1)(b) and Sch 5A para 3(3)(b) HB Regs; reg 53A(1)(b) and Sch 5A para 3(3)(b) CTB Regs
12 Reg 76(4) HB Regs; reg 66(4) CTB Regs
13 Sch 5A para 4 HB Regs
14 Sch 5A para 6 HB Regs
15 Sch 5A para 10 HB Regs
16 Reg 62A(5) HB Regs; reg 53A(5) CTB Regs
17 Sch 5A para 11 HB Regs; Sch 5A para 7 CTB Regs

3. Deductions for non-dependants
(pp 268-271)

18 Reg 3(1) HB Regs; reg 3(1) CTB Regs
19 CIS/14850/1996
20 para A5.11 GM
21 Reg 3(4) HB Regs
22 Reg 3(4) and Sch 1 para 7 HB Regs
23 para C1.34 GM
24 *Thamesdown BC v Goonery*, 13 February 1995, CA
25 Reg 3(2) HB Regs; reg 3(2) CTB Regs
26 *R v Chesterfield BC ex parte Fullwood* [1993] 26 HLR 126, CA
27 Reg 3(3) HB Regs
28 Reg 63(6) HB Regs; reg 52(6) CTB Regs
29 Reg 63(7) HB Regs; reg 52(7) CTB Regs
30 Reg 63(1) HB Regs; reg 52(1) CTB Regs
31 Reg 63(8) HB Regs
32 Reg 63(1) and (2) HB Regs
33 Reg 4(1) HB Regs; reg 4(1) CTB Regs
34 Reg 4(4) HB Regs; reg 4(4) CTB Regs
35 Reg 4(1) and (2) HB Regs; reg 4(1) and (2) CTB Regs
36 Reg 4(5) HB Regs; reg 4(5) CTB Regs
37 paras A5.30-32 GM
38 Reg 4(6) HB Regs; reg 4(6) CTB Regs; para A5.16 GM
39 Reg 63(9) HB Regs; reg 52(9) CTB Regs
40 para A5.23 GM
41 Reg 63(3) HB Regs; reg 52(3) CTB Regs
42 Reg 63(4) HB Regs; reg 52(4) CTB Regs
43 Reg 63(5) HB Regs
44 Reg 20(1) HB Regs; reg 12(1) CTB Regs
45 Reg 20 HB Regs; reg 12 CTB Regs

4. Extra benefit in exceptional circumstances
(p 272)

46 Reg 61(2) HB Regs
47 *R v Maidstone BC ex parte Bunce* [1994] 27 HLR 375, QBD
48 Reg 61(2) HB Regs
49 Reg 61(2) HB Regs
50 ss134(8) and 139(6) SSAA 1992

5. People in hospital
(pp 272-273)

51 Reg 18(1)(a) HB Regs; reg 10(1)(a) CTB Regs
52 Reg 18(1)(b) HB Regs; reg 10(1)(b) CTB Regs
53 Reg 18(1)(c)(i) HB Regs; reg 10(1)(c)(i) CTB Regs
54 Reg 18(1)(c)(ii) HB Regs; reg 10(1)(c)(ii) CTB Regs
55 Reg 18(1)(d)(i) HB Regs; reg 10(1)(d)(i) CTB Regs
56 Reg 18(1)(d)(ii) HB Regs; reg 10(1)(d)(ii) CTB Regs
57 Reg 18(3) HB Regs; reg 10(3) CTB Regs

Chapter 14: Special rules for students
(pp274-281)

1 Reg 46 HB Regs; reg 38 CTB Regs
2 Reg 46 HB Regs; reg 38 CTB Regs
3 Reg 46 HB Regs; reg 38 CTB Regs
4 para C5.03 GM
5 Lord Justice Hobhouse in *Chief Adjudication Officer v Webber* [1997] 4 All ER 274. The case was about IS, but the HB and CTB legislation is almost identical.
6 *Chief Adjudication Officer v Webber* [1997] 4 All ER 274; CIS 152/1994
7 Circular HB/CTB A26/96
8 Reg 7 IRBS&SF(MA) Regs
9 Reg 46 HB Regs; reg 38 CTB Regs
10 Reg 46 HB Regs; reg 38 CTB Regs
11 Reg 48A(2) HB Regs; reg 40(3) CTB Regs
12 s131 SSCBA 1992; reg 6(1)(e) HB Regs
13 Reg 52 HB Regs
14 Reg 48(1) HB Regs
15 Reg 48(2) HB Regs
16 para C5.26 GM
17 Reg 50(1) HB Regs
18 Reg 50(2) HB Regs
19 Reg 50(3) HB Regs
20 Reg 52 HB Regs
21 Reg 50(1) HB Regs; para C5.33 GM
22 s131 SSCBA 1992; regs 6(1)(b) and 52 HB Regs
23 Reg 51(1) HB Regs
24 Reg 52 HB Regs
25 Reg 51(2) HB Regs
26 Reg 61(2) HB Regs

Chapter 15: Claims, payments and reviews
(pp282-326)

1. Claims
(pp282-288)

1 Reg 71(1) HB Regs; reg 61(1) CTB Regs
2 Reg 71(2) HB Regs; reg 61(2) CTB Regs
3 Reg 71(3) and (5) HB Regs; reg 61(3) and (5) CTB Regs
4 Reg 71(6) HB Regs; reg 61(6) CTB Regs
5 Reg 71(4) HB Regs; reg 61(4) CTB Regs
6 Reg 71(4)(c) HB Regs; reg 61(4)(c) CTB Regs
7 Reg 72(1) HB Regs; reg 62(1) CTB Regs
8 Reg 72(2) HB Regs; reg 62(2) CTB Regs
9 para A2.09 GM
10 Reg 72(7)(b) and (8) HB Regs; reg 62(7)(b) and (8) CTB Regs
11 Reg 72(7)(a) and (8) HB Regs; para A2.24 GM; reg 62(7)(a) and (8) CTB Regs
12 Reg 74(1) HB Regs; reg 64(1) CTB Regs
13 Reg 74(2) HB Regs; reg 64(2) CTB Regs
14 Reg 72(4)(a) and (b) HB Regs; reg 62(4)(a) and (b) CTB Regs
15 Reg 72(4)(a) and (b) HB Regs; reg 62(4)(a) and (b) CTB Regs
16 Reg 72(4)(c) HB Regs; reg 62(4)(c) CTB Regs
17 Reg 72(1) HB Regs; reg 62(1) CTB Regs
18 Reg 73(1) HB Regs; reg 63(1) CTB Regs
19 Reg 76(2)(b) HB Regs; reg 66(2)(b) CTB Regs

20 Reg 73(1) and (3) HB Regs; reg 63(1) and (3) CTB Regs
21 s1(1C) SSAA 1992; reg 2A HB Regs; reg 2A CTB Regs
22 Reg 72(5)(c) HB Regs; reg 62(5)(d) CTB Regs
23 Reg 72(5)(a) HB Regs; reg 62(5)(a) CTB Regs
24 Reg 72(5)(b) HB Regs; reg 62(5)(b) CTB Regs
25 Reg 72(5)(bb) HB Regs; reg 62(5)(c) CTB Regs
26 Reg 65(1) HB Regs; reg 56(1) CTB Regs
27 Reg 72(15) HB Regs; paras A2.14-16 and B2.29 GM; reg 62(16) CTB Regs
28 CS/371/1949; para A2.23 and Part A2 Annex A GM
29 R(SB) 6/83
30 CS/50/1950
31 R(U) 35/36
32 CI/146/1991; CI/142/1993
33 *R v Canterbury CC ex parte Goodman*, 11 July 1995, QBD; CFC/39/1993
34 R(U) 5/56
35 R(S) 5/56
36 R(SB) 6/83
37 CI/37/1995
38 R(S) 25/52
39 R(P) 2/85
40 R(S) 10/59; R(SB) 17/83
41 CSB/813/1987
42 R(G) 1/75
43 Reg 72(15) HB Regs; reg 62(16) CTB Regs
44 Reg 5(6) HB Regs
45 Reg 72(11) HB Regs; reg 62(12) CTB Regs
46 Reg 66 HB Regs; paras

A6.07 and B4.7 GM; reg 57 CTB Regs
47 Sch 6 paras 9(g)-(h) and 10(a) HB Regs; Sch 6 paras 9(d)-(e) and 10(a) CTB Regs
48 Reg 72(12) and (13) HB Regs; reg 62(13) and (14) CTB Regs
49 Reg 72(14) HB Regs; para A6.12 GM; reg 62(15) CTB Regs
50 Reg 96A(10) HB Regs; reg 81A(10) CTB Regs
51 Reg 66(4) HB Regs; paraA6.10 GM; reg 57(4) CTB Regs
52 Reg 67(1)(a) and (2) HB Regs; reg 58(1)(a) and (2) CTB Regs
53 Reg 72(13) HB Regs; para A6.12 GM; reg 62(14) CTB Regs
54 Reg 72(12) and (13) HB Regs; para A6.13 GM
55 Reg 66(1)(b) HB Regs; reg 57(1)(b) CTB Regs

2.   Decisions
(pp288-290)
56 Regs 76(3), 77(1)(a) and 88(3) HB Regs; regs 66(3), 67(1)(a) and 77(3)(b) and (c) CTB Regs
57 Reg 76(2) HB Regs; reg 66(2) CTB Regs
58 Reg 2(1) HB Regs; reg 2(1) CTB Regs
59 Regs 77(4), 79(2) and 86(1) and (2) HB Regs; regs 67(2), 69(2) and 75(1) CTB Regs
60 Reg 77 and Sch 6 HB Regs; reg 67 and Sch 6 CTB Regs
61 Sch 6 para 6 HB Regs; Sch 6 para 6 CTB Regs

62 Sch 6 para 2 HB Regs; Sch 6 para 2 CTB Regs
63 Sch 6 para 3 HB Regs; Sch 6 para 3 CTB Regs
64 Sch 6 paras 9-13 HB Regs; Sch 6 paras 9-13 CTB Regs
65 Reg 4(1) HB(RO) Regs
66 para C12.10 GM

3.   Payment of benefit
(pp290-296)
67 Reg 65(1) HB Regs; reg 56(1) CTB Regs
68 Reg 2(1) HB Regs; reg 2(1) CTB Regs
69 Reg 65(2) HB Regs
70 Reg 69(4)(a) HB Regs
71 Reg 69(2)(b), (5)(a) and (6) HB Regs
72 Reg 66 HB Regs; reg 57 CTB Regs
73 s134(1)(b) SSAA 1992
74 s134(1)(c) SSAA 1992; reg 92(1) HB Regs
75 Reg 88(1)(b) HB Regs; reg 77(1) and (3) CTB Regs
76 para A6.24 GM
77 Reg 90(1) and (4) HB Regs
78 Reg 88(2) HB Regs
79 Reg 90(3) HB Regs
80 Reg 90(4) HB Regs; para A6.30 GM
81 Reg 90(2) HB Regs (pre-October 1996)
82 Reg 11 HB(Amdt) Regs 1996
83 Reg 92(2) HB Regs; reg 78(2) CTB Regs
84 Reg 92(3) HB Regs
85 para A6.44 GM
86 Reg 96 HB Regs; reg 81 CTB Regs
87 *R v Haringey LBC ex parte Azad Ayub* [1992] 25 HLR 566
88 Reg 93(a) HB Regs;

Sch 9 para 1(2) SS(C&P) Regs
89 Regs 93(b) and 95(1) HB Regs
90 Reg 94(1) HB Regs
91 *R v Haringey LBC ex parte Azad Ayub* (1992) 25 HLR 566, QBD
92 Sch A1 para 8(4) HB Regs; Sch A1 para 7(4) CTB Regs
93 Reg 94(1A) HB Regs
94 Reg 90(2A) and (2B) HB Regs
95 Reg 4 HB(ILA) Regs sets out the information that may be required.
96 s126A SSAA 1992; reg 3 HB(ILA) Regs
97 Regs 93(3) and 94(1B) HB Regs
98 Reg 93(3) HB Regs
99 Reg 94(1B) HB Regs
100 Reg 88(3) HB Regs
101 Reg 91(1) HB Regs
102 *R v Haringey LBC ex parte Azad Ayub* [1992] 25 HLR 566, QBD
103 para A6.36 GM
104 Reg 91(1) HB Regs; *R v Haringey LBC ex parte Azad Ayub* [1992] 25 HLR 566, QBD
105 Reg 91(2) HB Regs
106 Reg 91(3) HB Regs
107 Reg 95(1) HB Regs
108 Reg 95(3)(a) and (b) HB Regs
109 Reg 95(2) HB Regs
110 Reg 95(3) HB Regs
111 Reg 95(7) and (8) HB Regs
112 Reg 95(1A) HB Regs
113 Reg 95(6A)(a) HB Regs
114 Reg 95(6A)(b) HB Regs
115 Reg 95(1B) HB Regs
116 Reg 95(6B)(a) HB Regs
117 Reg 95(6B)(b) HB Regs

118 Reg 95(4) HB Regs; reg
80(1) CTB Regs
119 Reg 96A HB Regs; reg
81A CTB Regs
120 Reg 96A(4) HB Regs;
reg 81A(4) CTB Regs
121 Reg 96A(8) HB Regs;
reg 81A(8) CTB Regs
122 Reg 96A(5) HB Regs;
reg 81A(5) CTB Regs
123 Reg 95(5) HB Regs; reg
80(2) CTB Regs
124 Reg 95(4A) HB Regs;
reg 80(2A) CTB Regs
125 Reg 95(6) HB Regs
126 *R v Kensington and
Chelsea RBC ex parte
Brandt* [1995] 28 HLR
528, QBD

4. Changes in your circumstances
(pp296-299)

127 Reg 75(1) HB Regs; reg
65(1) CTB Regs
128 Sch 6 paras 9(i) and
10(a) HB Regs; Sch 6
paras 9(f) and 10(a)
CTB Regs
129 Reg 75(1), (2)(e) and
(3) HB Regs; paras
A6.52 and B4.10 GM;
reg 65(1), (2)(d), (3)
and (4) CTB Regs
130 Regs 73(2) and 75 HB
Regs; regs 63(2) and 65
CTB Regs
131 Reg 75(1) HB Regs; reg
65(1) CTB Regs
132 Reg 75(2) HB Regs; reg
65(2) CTB Regs
133 Reg 75(3) HB Regs; reg
65(3) CTB Regs
134 Regs 2(1), 73(2) and
75(1) HB Regs; regs 2,
63(2) and 65(1) CTB
Regs
135 Reg 68 HB Regs; reg
59 CTB Regs

136 Reg 68(1) HB Regs; reg
59(1) CTB Regs
137 Reg 68(1) HB Regs; reg
59(1) CTB Regs
138 Reg 67(1)(b) and (2)
HB Regs
139 Reg 67(1)(a) and (b)
HB Regs; reg 58(1)(a)
and (b) CTB Regs
140 Sch 2 para 2 HB Regs;
Sch 1 para 2 CTB Regs
141 Reg 68(2) HB Regs
142 Regs 26 and 68(1) HB
Regs; regs 18 and 59(1)
CTB Regs
143 Reg 68(3) HB Regs; reg
59(4) CTB Regs
144 Reg 68(6) and (7) HB
Regs
145 *R v Middlesbrough BC ex
parte Holmes*, 15
February 1995, QBD
146 Circular HB/CTB A9/95
147 *Welfare Rights Bulletin
135*, p9; Sch 5 para 8
HB Regs; Sch 5 para 8
CTB Regs
148 Reg 68(4) HB Regs; reg
59(7) CTB Regs
149 Reg 68(5) HB Regs
150 Reg 67(c) HB Regs; reg
58(c) CTB Regs
151 Reg 67(1)(a) and (b)
HB Regs; reg 58(1)(a)
and (b) CTB Regs
152 Reg 67(2) HB Regs
153 Reg 79(1)(a) and (3)(a)
HB Regs; reg 69(1)(a)
and (3)(a) CTB Regs

5. Overpayments
(pp300-312)

154 Reg 98 HB Regs; reg
83 CTB Regs
155 Reg 98 HB Regs; reg
83 CTB Regs
156 Reg 99(1) HB Regs; reg
84(1) CTB Regs
157 Reg 91(3) HB Regs

158 Reg 99(4) HB Regs
159 Reg 99(2) HB Regs; reg
84(2) CTB Regs
160 Reg 99(3) HB Regs; reg
84(3) CTB Regs
161 para A7.14 GM
162 *Duggan v Chief
Adjudication Officer, The
Times*, 13 March 1988,
CA
163 *Warwick DC v Freeman*
[1994] 27 HLR 616
164 *R v Liverpool City Council
ex parte Griffiths* [1990]
22 HLR 312
165 Reg 100 HB Regs; reg
85 CTB Regs
166 Regs 79(2) and 101-102
HB Regs; regs 69(2)
and 86 CTB Regs
167 para A7.51 GM
168 Reg 79(2) HB Regs; reg
69(2) CTB Regs; *Welfare
Rights Bulletin 120*, p9
169 Reg 83(2) HB Regs; reg
72(2) CTB Regs; *R v
Ellesmere Port and Neston
HBRB ex parte Williams*,
15 November 1996, CA
170 Reg 101 HB Regs; reg
86 CTB Regs
171 paras A7.54-56 GM
172 Reg 104(a) HB Regs;
reg 90(a) CTB Regs
173 *R v Kensington and
Chelsea RBC ex parte
Brandt* [1995] 28 HLR
528 at 537, QBD
174 Reg 104(b) HB Regs;
para A7.27 GM; reg
90(b) CTB Regs
175 Reg 103(1) HB Regs;
reg 89(1) CTB Regs
176 Reg 103(1) HB Regs;
reg 89(1) CTB Regs
177 Reg 103(2) HB Regs;
reg 89(2) CTB Regs
178 Reg 103(1)(a) HB Regs;
reg 89(1)(a) CTB Regs

179 Reg 103(1)(b) HB Regs;
reg 89(1)(b) CTB Regs

180 ie, the SSA(F)A 1997
and regulations made
under it

181 *R v Secretary of State for
Social Security ex parte
Britnell* [1989] Crown
Office Digest 487, DC

182 Reg 102 HB Regs; reg
87(2)(a) CTB Regs

183 Reg 101(2) HB Regs;
reg 86(2) CTB Regs

184 s75(5)(a) SSAA 1992;
reg 2(2)(a) HB(RO)
Regs

185 s75(5)(b) SSAA 1992;
reg 2(3) HB(RO) Regs

186 s75(5)(c) SSAA 1992;
reg 2(3) HB(RO) Regs

187 Regs 102 and 105 HB
Regs; regs 87(3) and 91
CTB Regs

188 Reg 105 HB Regs; reg
91 CTB Regs

189 Reg 2(4) HB(RO) Regs

190 *R v Haringey LBC ex
parte Azad Ayub* [1992]
25 HLR 566, QBD

191 paras A7.40-43 GM

192 *Warwick DC v Freeman*
[1994] 27 HLR 616,
CA

193 Reg 88 CTB Regs; para
A7.38 GM

194 *Warwick DC v Freeman*
[1994] 27 HLR 616,
CA

195 *Plymouth CC v Gigg*, 16
May 1997, CA

196 s75(7) SSAA 1992

197 para A7.44 GM

198 *DPP v Huskinson* [1988]
20 HLR 562, QBD

199 *R v Haringey LBC ex
parte Azad Ayub* [1992]
25 HLR 566, QBD

200 Reg 93(2) HB Regs

201 s5(1)(p) SSAA 1992

202 *Wandsworth BC v Winder*
[1985] AC 461, HL

203 s75(6) SSAA 1992

204 s75(6) SSAA 1992; reg
3(1) and (2) HB(RO)
Regs

205 Reg 3(3) HB(RO) Regs

206 Reg 77(1)(b) HB Regs;
reg 67(1)(b) CTB Regs

207 Sch 6 paras 2, 3, 6 and
14 HB Regs; para
A7.42 GM; Sch 6 paras
2, 3, 6 and 16 CTB
Regs

208 Reg 4(4) HB(RO) Regs

209 Reg 77(4) and (5) HB
Regs; reg 67(2) and (3)
CTB Regs

210 para A7.51 GM

6. Fraud and criminal offences
(pp313-319)

211 s110A SSAA 1992

212 s110B(1) SSAA 1992

213 s110B(2) and (7) SSAA
1992

214 s111(1) SSAA 1992

215 s110B(5) SSAA 1992

216 s67(9) Police and
Criminal Evidence Act
1984

217 s78(1) Police and
Criminal Evidence Act
1984

218 s34 Criminal Justice and
Public Order Act 1994

219 *Osinunga v DPP, The
Times*, 26 November
1997, DC

220 s112(3) SSAA 1992

221 s112(1) SSAA 1992

222 *Clear v Smith* [1981] 1
WLR 399, DC

223 s112(1A)(a) SSAA 1992

224 s112(1A)(b) SSAA 1992

225 *Hansard*, House of
Commons Standing
Committee E, 21

January 1997, cols 316-
7

226 *Taylor's Central Garages v
Roper* [1951] 115 JPR
445

227 s25(5) SSA(F)A 1997

228 s111A(1) SSAA 1992

229 s116(2)(b) SSAA 1992

230 s115A(1) SSAA 1992

231 s25(7) SSA(F)A 1997;
Art 2(1)(b) SSA(F)A
1997 (Commencement
No 5) Order 1997 SI
No 2766 art 2(1)(b)

232 s115A(2)(a) SSAA 1992;
reg 2(1) SS(PN) Regs

233 s115A(2)(b) SSAA
1992; reg 2(2) SS(PN)
Regs

234 s115A(3) and (4)(a)
SSAA 1992

235 s115A(4)(b) SSAA 1992

236 s115A(6) SSAA 1992

237 s115A(7) SSAA 1992

238 s115A(5) SSAA 1992

239 *Williams v Bayley* [1866]
1 House of Lords 200
(HL)

7. Reviews
(pp319-325)

240 Reg 79(1) and (1A) HB
Regs; reg 69(1) and
(1A) CTB Regs

241 Reg 79(6) HB Regs; reg
69(7) CTB Regs

242 Reg 91A(8) HB Regs;
reg 81A(8) CTB Regs

243 Reg 79(2) HB Regs; reg
69(2) CTB Regs

244 Reg 79(2) HB Regs; reg
69(2) CTB Regs

245 Reg 78(3) and (4) HB
Regs; reg 68(3) and (4)
CTB Regs

246 Sch 6 para 3 HB Regs;
Sch 6 para 3 CTB Regs

247 Reg 78(3), (4) and (5)

HB Regs; reg 68(3), (4) and (5) CTB Regs

248 Reg 79(4) HB Regs; reg 69(4) CTB Regs

249 Reg 77(4) and (5) HB Regs; reg 67(2) and (3) CTB Regs

250 Reg 79(2) and Sch 6 paras 4 and 5 HB Regs; reg 69(2) and Sch 6 paras 4 and 5 CTB Regs

251 Reg 79(3)(b) HB Regs; reg 69(3)(b) CTB Regs

252 Reg 79(3)(c) and (5)(a) HB Regs; reg 69(3)(c) and (5)(a) CTB Regs

253 Reg 81(1) and (2) HB Regs; reg 70(1) and (2) CTB Regs

254 Reg 78(3)-(5) HB Regs; reg 68(3)-(5) CTB Regs

255 Reg 82(1) HB Regs; reg 71(1) CTB Regs

256 Reg 82(2) and (1A) HB Regs

257 Reg 82(3) HB Regs; regs 70(5) and 71(3) CTB Regs

258 Reg 82(5) HB Regs; reg 71(5) CTB Regs

259 Sch 7 HB Regs; Sch 7 CTB Regs

260 Reg 82(7) HB Regs; reg 71(7) CTB Regs

261 paras A6.66 and B6.18 GM

262 Reg 81(4) HB Regs; reg 70(4) CTB Regs

263 Reg 82(2)(a) HB Regs; reg 71(2)(a) CTB Regs

264 Reg 82(2)(c) HB Regs; reg 71(2)(c) CTB Regs

265 Reg 82(9) HB Regs; paras A6.68 and B6.22 GM; reg 71(9) CTB Regs

266 Reg 82(2)(c)(ii) HB Regs; reg 71(2)(c)(ii) CTB Regs

267 Reg 82(4) HB Regs; reg 71(4) CTB Regs

268 Reg 82(5) and (6) HB Regs; reg 71(5) and (6) CTB Regs

269 Reg 83(1) HB Regs; paras A6.70 and B6.24 GM; reg 72(1) CTB Regs

270 Reg 82(8) HB Regs; reg 71(8) CTB Regs

271 Reg 83(4) HB Regs; reg 72(4) CTB Regs

272 Reg 83(2) HB Regs; reg 72(2) CTB Regs

273 Reg 83(5) HB Regs; reg 72(5) CTB Regs

274 *R v HBRB of Sefton MBC ex parte Cunningham* [1991] 23 HLR 534, QBD

275 Reg 84 HB Regs; reg 73 CTB Regs

276 Regs 79(3)(c), (5) and 83(3) HB Regs; regs 69(3)(c) and (5) and 72(3) CTB Regs

277 Regs 85(1) and 87(1) HB Regs; regs 74(1) and 76(1) CTB Regs

278 Reg 87(3) HB Regs; reg 76(3) CTB Regs

279 Reg 86(1) HB Regs; paras A6.79-82 and B6.33-6 GM; reg 75(1) CTB Regs

280 Reg 86(1) HB Regs; reg 75(1) CTB Regs

281 Reg 86(1) HB Regs; reg 75(1) CTB Regs

282 Regs 78(2) and 86(2) HB Regs; regs 68(2) and 75(2) CTB Regs

283 Reg 87(2) HB Regs; reg 76(2) CTB Regs

284 Reg 86(3) HB Regs; reg 75(3) CTB Regs

285 Reg 86(4) HB Regs; reg 75(4) CTB Regs

286 Reg 87(3) HB Regs; reg 76(3) CTB Regs

287 Regs 78(2) and 87(2) and (3) HB Regs; regs 68(2) and 76(2) and (3) CTB Regs

288 *Haringey LBC v Cotter* [1996] 29 HLR 682

Chapter 16: Council tax benefit
(pp 327-344)

1. The basic rules
(pp 327-329)

1 s131(3) SSCBA 1992

2 s131(5) SSCBA 1992

3 s131(3)(b) SSCBA 1992; reg 40 CTB Regs

4 s131(3)(b) SSCBA 1992; reg 4A CTB Regs

5 s131(3) SSCBA 1992

6 s131(6)(a) SSCBA 1992

7 s131(6)(b) SSCBA 1992

8 s131(3)(b) SSCBA 1992; reg 4A CTB Regs

9 s6(5) LGFA 1992

10 *Ward v Kingston-upon-Hull MBC* [1993] Rating Appeals 71, QBD

11 Regs 4B and 4C CTB Regs

12 *R v Hackney LBC ex parte Adebari, The Times,* 5 November 1997, QBD

13 Reg 4D and Sch A1 CTB Regs

3. The amount of benefit
(pp 330-339)

14 Reg 51(1)(a) and (2)(a) CTB Regs

15 Reg 51(3) CTB Regs
16 Reg 51(4) CTB Regs
17 Reg 51(1) CTB Regs
18 para B3.27 GM
19 Sch 6 paras 9-10 CTB
   Regs
20 Reg 51(2A) CTB Regs
21 Council Tax
   (Reductions for
   Disabilities) Regulations
   1992 SI No.554;
   Council Tax
   (Reductions for
   Disabilities) (Scotland)
   Regulations 1992 SI
   No.1335
22 Reg 51(2B) CTB Regs
23 s16 LGFA 1992
24 Regs 2(2) and 3(1)
   CTB Regs
25 Reg 3(2) CTB Regs
26 Reg 3(3)(a) CTB Regs
27 Reg 3(3)(b) CTB Regs
28 paras B3.17 and C1.30-
   34 GM
29 Reg 3(3)(c) HB Regs
30 Reg 52(3) CTB Regs
31 Reg 52(5) CTB Regs
32 Reg 52(6)-(8) CTB
   Regs
33 Sch 1(2) LGFA 1992
34 Reg 3 Council Tax
   (Discount Disregards)
   Order 1992 SI No.548
35 Reg 52(1), (2) and (9)
   CTB Regs
36 Reg 52(3) CTB Regs
37 Reg 52(4) CTB Regs
38 Reg 12 CTB Regs
39 Reg 51(5) CTB Regs
40 s131(9) SSCBA 1992
41 Reg 54, Schs 2 and 5
   para 45(1) CTB Regs
42 s131(7) SSCBA 1992
43 s6(5) LGFA 1992
44 s131(7)(a) SSCBA 1992;
   Sch 1 LGFA 1992
45 s131(7)(b) SSCBA

1992; reg 55(a) CTB
Regs
46 s131(7)(b) SSCBA
   1992; reg 55(b) CTB
   Regs
47 s131(7)(b) SSCBA
   1992; reg 55(c) CTB
   Regs
48 s131(7)(b) SSCBA
   1992; reg 55(d) CTB
   Regs
49 ss131(6)(a) and (7)
   SSCBA 1992
50 Para B3.30ii GM
51 Reg 54 and Sch 2 para
   1(2) CTB Regs
52 Sch 2 para 1(3) and (4)
   CTB Regs
53 Reg 54 and Sch 2 para
   1 Table CTB Regs
54 Sch 2 para 2(a) CTB
   Regs
55 Sch 2 para 2(b) CTB
   Regs
56 Sch 2 para 2(c) CTB
   Regs
57 Reg 54 and Sch 2 para
   3 CTB Regs
58 Reg 54 and Sch 2 para
   1 Table CTB Regs
59 Reg 54(2) CTB Regs
60 Reg 54(3) CTB Regs
61 Reg 54(4) CTB Regs
62 Reg 53A CTB Regs
63 Sch 5A paras 4 and 5
   CTB Regs

4. Claims, payments and reviews
(pp339-343)

64 Reg 62(10) CTB Regs
65 Reg 62(12) CTB Regs
66 Reg 62(11) CTB Regs
67 Reg 62(16) CTB Regs
68 Sch 6 paras 9(a) and
   10(a) CTB Regs
69 Sch 6 paras 12(b), 14(b)
   and 15 CTB Regs

70 Sch 6 para 13(c) and (f)
   CTB Regs
71 Sch 6 paras 9, 10, 13
   and 15 CTB Regs
72 Reg 56(2) CTB Regs
73 Reg 77(1)(b) and (3)
   CTB Regs
74 Reg 77(3)(a)(ii) CTB
   Regs
75 Reg 77(3)(b) CTB Regs
76 Reg 78 CTB Regs
77 Regs 80 and 81A CTB
   Regs
78 Reg 81 CTB Regs
79 Reg 83(1) CTB Regs
80 Reg 84(5) CTB Regs
81 Regs 83(a) and 84(4)
   CTB Regs
82 Regs 83(b) and 84(4)
   CTB Regs
83 Reg 86(1) CTB Regs
84 Reg 87(2)(b) CTB Regs
85 Reg 88 CTB Regs
86 Reg 65(1) CTB Regs
87 Reg 65(2) CTB Regs
88 Reg 65(4) CTB Regs
89 Reg 59(1) CTB Regs
90 Reg 59(2)-(6) CTB
   Regs
91 Reg 59(7) CTB Regs
92 Reg 59(1) CTB Regs
93 Reg 70(4) CTB Regs

5. Students
(pp343-344)

94 Reg 40(3) CTB Regs
95 Reg 38 CTB Regs

PART FIVE: COMMON RULES

Chapter 17: Who counts as your family
(pp346-356)

1 s137 SSCBA 1992
2 s134(2) SSCBA 1992
3 Reg 4(2) SS(C&P) Regs
4 s129(1) SSCBA 1992

5 Reg 4(3A) SS(C&P) Regs

6 *Santos v Santos* [1972] 2 All ER 246; CIS/671/1992; CIS/81/1993

7 R(SB) 8/85

8 R(SB) 4/83

9 CSB/463/1986

10 s137 SSCBA 1992

11 R(SB) 8/85

12 **IS** Reg 2(1) IS Regs **HB** Reg 2(1) HB Regs **CTB** Reg 2(1) CTB Regs

13 **IS** Regs 18 and 23 IS Regs **FC** Reg 10 FC Regs **DWA** Reg 12 DWA Regs **HB** Regs 17 and 19 HB Regs **CTB** Regs 9 and 11 CTB Regs

14 *R v HBRB of Penwith District Council ex parte Menear*, 24 HLR 120 (11 October 1991)

15 *Crake and Butterworth v SBC* [1982] 1 All ER 498

16 R(SB) 17/81; R(G) 3/71; CIS/87/1993

17 *Crake and Butterworth v SBC* quoted in R(SB) 35/85

18 R(SB) 35/85

19 para 15027 AOG

20 CIS/72/1994

21 CIS/87/1993

22 CSB/150/1985

23 CIS/87/1993

24 CSSB/145/1983

25 R(SB) 13/82

26 CIS/317/1994

27 Reg 7(1) SS(C&P) Regs

28 CIS/317/1994

29 R(I) 1/71

30 **IS** Reg 16(1) IS Regs **FC** Reg 9 FC Regs

DWA Reg 11 DWA Regs **HB** Reg 15(1) HB Regs **CTB** Reg 7(1) CTB Regs

31 CIS/508/1992

32 **FC** Reg 9 FC Regs **DWA** Reg 11 DWA Regs

33 Reg 7(1) CTB Regs

34 **IS** Reg 16(1) and (2) IS Regs **HB** Reg 15(1) and (2) HB Regs

35 Reg 16(3) IS Regs

36 Sch 7 paras 11 and 11A IS Regs

37 Sch 1 para 22 IS Regs

38 Sch 7 para 9 IS Regs

39 Sch 7 para 9 col (2) IS Regs

40 CIS/508/1992; CIS/13805/1996

41 CIS/484/1993

42 s137 SSCBA 1992

43 **IS** Reg 14 IS Regs **FC** Reg 6 FC Regs **DWA** Reg 8 DWA Regs **HB** Reg 13 HB Regs **CTB** Reg 5 CTB Regs

44 **All** s134(2) SSCBA 1992 **IS** Reg 15(4) IS Regs **FC** Reg 7(3) FC Regs **DWA** Reg 9(3) DWA Regs **HB** Reg 14(3) HB Regs **CTB** Reg 6(3) CTB Regs

45 **FC** Reg 7(1) FC Regs **DWA** Reg 9(1) DWA Regs **HB** Reg 14(1) HB Regs **CTB** Reg 6(1) CTB Regs

46 CFC/1537/1995

47 CFC/1537/1995

48 **FC** Reg 7(2) FC Regs **DWA** Reg 9(2) DWA Regs **HB** Reg 14(2) HB Regs **CTB** Reg 6(2) CTB Regs

49 Reg 15(1) IS Regs

50 Reg 15(2) IS Regs

51 Reg 15(1A) IS Regs

52 **IS** Reg 16 IS Regs **FC** Reg 8 FC Regs **DWA** Reg 10 DWA Regs **HB** Reg 15 HB Regs **CTB** Reg 7 CTB Regs

53 Regs 15(3) and 16(6) IS Regs

54 **HB** Reg 15(5) HB Regs **CTB** Reg 7(4) CTB Regs

55 **FC** Reg 8(2)(a) FC Regs **DWA** Reg 10(2)(a) DWA Regs

56 Reg 16(5)(b) IS Regs

57 Reg 16(5A) IS Regs

58 **IS** Reg 16(5)(b)(ii) IS Regs **FC** Reg 46(6) FC Regs **DWA** Reg 51(6) DWA Regs

59 Regs 15(3) and 16(6) IS Regs

60 Reg 16(5a) and (aa) IS Regs

61 Reg 16(5A) IS Regs

62 Reg 16(5)(a) IS Regs

63 Regs 1(2) (definition of 'remunerative work') and 7 CB Regs

64 **All** Reg 7D(1) CB Regs **IS** Reg 15(1) IS Regs **HB** Reg 13 HB Regs **CTB** Reg 5 CTB Regs

65 s134(2) SSCBA 1992

66 **FC** Reg 6(2) FC Regs
DWA Reg 8(2) DWA
Regs

**Chapter 18: Applicable
amounts**
(pp357-372)

1 Reg 22A IS Regs
2 **IS** Reg 18 IS Regs
HB Reg 17 HB Regs
CTB Reg 9 CTB Regs
3 Reg 18(2) IS Regs
4 **IS** Part I Sch 2 IS Regs
HB Part I Sch 2 HB
Regs
CTB Part I Sch 1 CTB
Regs
5 **IS** Reg 18(1)(b) IS Regs
HB Reg 17(b) HB
Regs
CTB Reg 9(b) CTB
Regs
HB/CTB paras C4.05-
06 GM
6 **IS** Sch 2 para 2 IS
Regs
HB Sch 2 para 2 HB
Regs
CTB Sch 1 para 2 CTB
Regs
7 **IS** Sch 2 para 5 IS
Regs
HB Sch 2 para 5 IS
Regs
CTB Sch 1 para 5 HB
Regs
8 **IS** Sch 2 para 7 IS
Regs
HB Sch 2 para 7 HB
Regs
CTB Sch 1 para 7 CTB
Regs
9 **IS** Sch 2 para 14B IS
Regs
HB Sch 2 para 14B
HB Regs
CTB Sch 1 para 18
CTB Regs
10 **IS** Sch 2 para 3 IS Regs

HB Sch 2 para 3 HB
Regs
CTB Sch 1 para 3 CTB
Regs
11 Regs 15(3) and 16(6) IS
Regs
12 **HB** Reg 15(4)-(5) HB
Regs
CTB Reg 7(3)-(4) CTB
Regs
13 **IS** Sch 2 para 3 IS Regs
HB Sch 2 para 3 HB
Regs
CTB Sch 1 para 3 CTB
Regs
14 **HB/CTB** A45/97 and
A10/98
15 **IS** Sch 2 paras 14 and
15(6) IS Regs
HB Sch 2 paras 14 and
15(6) HB Regs
CTB Sch 1 paras 15
and 19(7) CTB Regs
16 **IS** Sch 2 paras
12(1)(a)(iii) and (2) and
14(c) IS Regs
HB Sch 2 paras
12(1)(a)(v) and (2) and
14(c) HB Regs
CTB Sch 1 paras
13(1)(a)(v) and (2) and
15(c) CTB Regs
17 **IS** Sch 2 para 14(a) IS
Regs
HB Sch 2 para 14(a)
HB Regs
CTB Sch 1 para 15(a)
CTB Regs
18 **IS** Sch 2 para 11 IS
Regs
HB Sch 2 para 11 HB
Regs
CTB Sch 1 para 12
CTB Regs
19 **IS** Reg 2(1) IS Regs
HB Reg 2(1) HB Regs
CTB Reg 2(1) CTB
Regs

All Definition of
'attendance allowance'
20 **IS** Sch 2 para 12(6) IS
Regs
HB Sch 2 para 12(7)
HB Regs
CTB Sch 1 para 13(6A)
CTB Regs
21 **IS** Sch 2 para 14A IS
Regs
HB Sch 2 para 14A
HB Regs
CTB Sch 1 para 17
CTB Regs
22 **IS** Sch 2 para 14B IS
Regs
HB Sch 2 para 14B
HB Regs
CTB Sch 1 para 18
CTB Regs
See also R(IS) 10/94
23 **IS** Sch 2 para 7(1)(a) IS
Regs
HB Sch 2 para 7(1)(a)
HB Regs
CTB Sch 1 para 7(1)(a)
CTB Regs
24 **IS** Sch 2 para
12(1)(a)(iii) and (2) IS
Regs
HB Sch 2 para
12(1)(a)(v) and (2) HB
Regs
CTB Sch 1 para
13(1)(a)(v) and (2) CTB
Regs
25 **IS** Sch 2 para
12(1)(a)(ii) IS Regs
HB Sch 2 para
12(1)(a)(iv) HB Regs
CTB Sch 1 para
13(1)(a)(iv) CTB Regs
26 **IS** Sch 2 para 12(1)(c)(i)
IS Regs
HB Sch 2 para
12(1)(a)(ii) HB Regs
CTB Sch 1 para
13(1)(a)(ii) CTB Regs

27 Sch 2 para 12(1)(c)(i) IS Regs
28 **HB** Sch 2 para 12(1)(a)(ii) HB Regs **CTB** Sch 1 para 13(1)(a)(ii) CTB Regs
29 Sch 2 para 12(1)(c) IS Regs
30 **IS** Sch 2 para 12(1)(c)(ii) IS Regs **HB** Sch 2 para 12(1)(a)(iii) HB Regs **CTB** Sch 1 para 13(1)(a)(iii) CTB Regs
31 **IS** Sch 2 para 12(1)(b) IS Regs **HB** Sch 2 para 12(1)(b) HB Regs **CTB** Sch 1 para 13(1)(b) CTB Regs
32 s30B(4) SSCBA 1992
33 **IS** Sch 2 paras 11(b) and 12 IS Regs **HB** Sch 2 paras 11(b) and 12 HB Regs **CTB** Sch 1 paras 12(b) and 13 CTB Regs
34 **IS** Sch 2 paras 7(1)(b) and 12(5) IS Regs **HB** Sch 2 paras 7(1)(b) and 12(5) HB Regs **CTB** Sch 1 paras 7(1)(b) and 13(5) CTB Regs
35 **IS** Reg 63(1A) SS(Adj) Regs **HB** Reg 79 HB Regs **CTB** Reg 69 CTB Regs
36 CSIS/66/1992; CIS/706/1992
37 **IS** Sch 2 paras 9 and 9A IS Regs **HB** Sch 2 paras 9 and 9A HB Regs **CTB** Sch 1 paras 9 and 10 CTB Regs
38 **IS** Sch 2 para 10 IS Regs **HB** Sch 2 para 10 HB

Regs **CTB** Sch 1 para 11 CTB Regs
39 **IS** Sch 2 para 10(1)(b)(ii) and (3) IS Regs **HB** Sch 2 para 10(1)(b)(ii) and (3) HB Regs **CTB** Sch 1 para 11(1)(b)(ii) and (3) CTB Regs
40 **HB** Sch 2 para 10(3)(c) HB Regs **CTB** Sch 1 para 11(3)(c) CTB Regs
41 **IS** Sch 2 para 10(2)(b)(ii) IS Regs **HB** Sch 2 para 10(2)(b)(ii) HB Regs **CTB** Sch 1 para 11(2)(b)(ii) CTB Regs
42 **IS** Sch 2 para 12(1)(c)(i) IS Regs **HB** Sch 2 para 12(1)(a)(ii) HB Regs **CTB** Sch 1 para 13(1)(a)(ii) CTB Regs
43 **HB** Sch 2 para 10(3)(c) HB Regs **CTB** Sch 1 para 11(3)(c) CTB Regs
44 **IS** Sch 2 para 12(1)(c)(i) IS Regs **HB** Sch 2 para 12(1)(a)(ii) HB Regs **CTB** Sch 1 para 13(1)(a)(ii) CTB Regs
45 Sch 2 para 12(1)(c) IS Regs
46 CIS/458/1992
47 CIS/458/1992
48 **IS** Sch 2 para 7(1)(a) IS Regs **HB** Sch 2 para 7(1)(a) HB Regs **CTB** Sch 1 para 7(1)(a) CTB Regs
49 **IS** Sch 2 para 13 IS

Regs **HB** Sch 2 para 13 HB Regs **CTB** Sch 1 para 14 CTB Regs
50 **IS** Reg 2(1) IS Regs **HB** Reg 2(1) HB Regs **CTB** Reg 2(1) CTB Regs
51 **IS** Sch 2 para 14A IS Regs **HB** Sch 2 para 14A HB Regs **CTB** Sch 1 para 17 CTB Regs
52 **IS** Sch 2 para 13(2A) IS Regs **HB** Sch 2 para 13(2A) HB Regs **CTB** Sch 1 para 14(2A) CTB Regs
53 **IS** Sch 2 para 14B IS Regs **HB** Sch 2 para 14B HB Regs **CTB** Sch 1 para 18 CTB Regs *See also* R(IS) 10/94, upheld in *Rider v CAO* (CA), *The Times*, 30 January 1996
54 *Bate v CAO* [1996] 2 All ER 790 (HL)
55 **IS** Reg 3(4) and (5) IS Regs **HB** Reg 3(4) HB Regs
56 **IS** Sch 2 para 13(2)(a)(iii) and (b) IS Regs **HB** Sch 2 para 13(2)(a)(iii) and (b) HB Regs . **CTB** Sch 1 para 14(2)(a)(iii) and (b) CTB Regs
57 **IS** Sch 2 para 13(3ZA) IS Regs **HB** Sch 2 para 13(4) HB Regs

CTB Sch 1 para 14(4)
CTB Regs

58 IS Sch 2 para 13(3A) IS
Regs
HB Sch 2 para 13(3A)
HB Regs
CTB Sch 1 para 14(3A)
CTB Regs

59 IS Reg 3 IS Regs
HB Reg 3 HB Regs
CTB Reg 3 CTB Regs

60 IS Sch 2 para 13(3)(a)
IS Regs
HB Sch 2 para 13(3)(a)
HB Regs
CTB Sch 1 para
14(3)(a) CTB Regs

61 IS Sch 2 para 13(3)(d)
IS Regs
HB Sch 2 para 13(3)(c)
HB Regs
CTB Sch 1 para
14(3)(c) CTB Regs

62 CIS/14850/1996 para 10

63 Sch 2 para 13(3)(c) and
(4) IS Regs

64 Regs 3 and 7(1) HB
Regs

65 Reg 3 CTB Regs

66 IS Reg 2(1) IS Regs
HB Reg 2(1) HB Regs
CTB Reg 2(1) CTB
Regs
All Definition of 'close
relative'

67 *Bate v CAO* [1996] 2
All ER 790 (HL)

68 CIS/180/1989

69 CIS/529/1994 (Tribunal
of Commissioners)

70 CSIS/43/1989

71 CIS/754/1991 and CIS/
529/1994 para 12

72 CIS/529/1994 para 8

73 CIS/529/1994 paras 10
and 11

74 CIS/754/1991

75 CIS/754/1991 referring

to CSIS/28/1992 and
CSIS/40/1992

76 IS Sch 2 para 14ZA IS
Regs
HB Sch 2 para 14ZA
HB Regs
CTB Sch 1 para 16
CTB Regs

77 s70(6) SSCBA 1992;
reg 11 SS(ICA) Regs

78 IS Sch 2 paras 7 and
14ZA(2) IS Regs
HB Sch 2 paras 7 and
14ZA(2) HB Regs
CTB Sch 1 paras 7 and
16(2) CTB Regs

79 IS Sch 2 para 14A IS
Regs
HB Sch 2 para 14A
HB Regs
CTB Sch 1 para 17
CTB Regs

80 IS Sch 2 para 13(3ZA)
IS Regs
HB Sch 2 para 13(4)
HB Regs
CTB Sch 1 para 14(4)
CTB Regs

Chapter 19: Income
(pp 373-414)

1. Introduction
(pp 373-378)

1 HB Sch 3 para 10 and
Sch 4 para 4 HB Regs
CTB Sch 3 para 10 and
Sch 4 para 4 CTB Regs

2 s136(1) SSCBA 1992

3 Reg 23(4) IS Regs

4 Reg 23(5) IS Regs

5 IS Reg 17(b) IS Regs
FC Reg 46(4) FC Regs
DWA Reg 51(4) DWA
Regs
HB Reg 16(b) HB
Regs
CTB Reg 8(b) CTB
Regs

6 IS Regs 25 and 44(5)
IS Regs
FC Reg 27(3) FC Regs
DWA Reg 30(3) DWA
Regs
HB Reg 36(2) HB
Regs
CTB Reg 27(2) CTB
Regs

7 s136(1) SSCBA 1992

8 IS Reg 44(4) IS Regs
HB Reg 36(1) HB
Regs
CTB Reg 27(1) CTB
Regs

9 FC Regs 27(2) and
46(5) FC Regs
DWA Regs 30(2) and
51(5) DWA Regs

10 IS Reg 25 IS Regs
FC Reg 27(2) FC Regs
DWA Reg 30(2) DWA
Regs
HB Reg 36(1) HB
Regs
CTB Reg 27(1) CTB
Regs

11 IS Sch 8 para 14 IS
Regs
FC Sch 1 para 2 FC
Regs
DWA Sch 2 para 2
DWA Regs
HB Sch 3 para 13 HB
Regs
CTB Sch 3 para 13
CTB Regs

12 IS Sch 8 para 15(b) IS
Regs
HB Sch 3 para 14(b)
HB Regs
CTB Sch 2 para 14(b)
CTB Regs

13 IS Sch 8 para 15(a) IS
Regs
HB Sch 3 para 14(a)
HB Regs
CTB Sch 3 para 14(a)
CTB Regs

14 **IS** Reg 44(4) IS Regs
HB Reg 36(1) HB
Regs
CTB Reg 27(1) CTB
Regs
15 Reg 42(4)(a)(ii) IS Regs
16 Reg 44(2)(a) IS Regs
17 Reg 44(2)(b) IS Regs
18 Reg 44(9) IS Regs
19 Reg 44(3) IS Regs; CIS/
164/1994
20 **HB** Reg 35(3)(a) and
Sch 4 para 13(1), (2)
and (5) HB Regs
CTB Reg 26(3)(a) and
Sch 4 para 13(1), (2)
and (5) CTB Regs
Both paras C3.107 and
C3.112 GM
21 **HB** Reg 35(3)(a) and
Sch 4 paras 13(3) and
47 HB Regs
CTB Reg 26(3)(a) and
Sch 4 paras 13(3) and
46 CTB Regs
Both paras C3.89,
C3.110 and C3.112 GM
22 **IS** Reg 32(1) IS Regs
FC Reg 18(1) FC Regs
DWA Reg 20(1) DWA
Regs
HB Reg 25 HB Regs
CTB Reg 17 CTB Regs
23 R(IS) 3/93
24 CIS/242/1989 (to be
reported as R(IS) 10/
95)
25 Reg 32(6) IS Regs
26 Reg 32(2) and (3) IS
Regs
27 Reg 32(4) IS Regs
28 Reg 32(5) and Sch 8
para 10 IS Regs
29 Reg 29(2)(a) IS Regs
30 Reg 29(2)(b) IS Regs
31 Reg 31(1)(a) IS Regs
32 Reg 31(1)(b) IS Regs
33 Reg 31(2) IS Regs
34 Reg 2(1) IS Regs

35 R(SB) 33/83
36 R(SB) 22/84; R(SB) 11/
85
37 CIS/590/1993

2. Earnings of employed earners

(pp378-388)

38 *Parsons v Hogg* [1985] 2
All ER 897, CA,
appendix to R(FIS) 4/
85
39 R(FC) 1/90
40 CFC/26/1989
41 R(FIS) 4/85
42 R(IS) 13/91; R(IS) 16/
93; CFC/26/1989
43 CCS/318/1995 (applying
the identical provisions
in child support law)
44 CCS/5352/1995
45 CCS/12769/1996 held
that the rent allowances
were deductible; CCS/
10/1994 and CCS/
12598/1996 held that
the rent allowances
were not.
46 R(U) 2/72; R(FIS) 4/85;
R(FC) 1/91; R(IS) 13/91
47 CIS/521/1990
48 **IS** Reg 36(3) IS Regs
FC Reg 20(3) FC Regs
DWA Reg 22(3) DWA
Regs
HB Reg 29(3) HB
Regs
CTB Reg 20(3) CTB
Regs
49 **FC** Regs 14(2) and
20(4) FC Regs
DWA Regs 16(7) and
22(4) DWA Regs
HB Regs 22(2) and
29(4) HB Regs
CTB Regs 14(2) and
20(4) CTB Regs
HB/CTB para C3.22
GM

50 **HB** Reg 26 HB Regs
CTB Reg 18 CTB Regs
HB/CTB paras C3.03-
04 GM
51 R(SB) 21/86
IS Reg 35(1) IS Regs
FC Reg 19(1) FC Regs
DWA Reg 21(1) DWA
Regs
HB Reg 28(1) HB
Regs
CTB Reg 19(1) CTB
Regs
52 **IS** Reg 48(3) IS Regs
FC Reg 31(2) FC Regs
DWA Reg 34(2) DWA
Regs
HB Reg 40(3) HB
Regs
CTB Reg 31(3) CTB
Regs
53 **FC** Reg 19(1)(g)-(h) FC
Regs
DWA Reg 21(1)(g)-(h)
DWA Regs
HB Reg 28(1)(i)-(j) HB
Regs
CTB Reg 19(1)(i)-(j)
CTB Regs
54 Regs 35(2)(b) and 40(4)
and Sch 9 paras 1, 4
and 4A IS Regs
55 **HB** Reg 28(1)(i)-(j) HB
Regs
CTB Reg 19(1)(i)-(j)
CTB Regs
56 **FC** Sch 2 paras 27 and
31 FC Regs
DWA Sch 3 paras 27
and 31 DWA Regs
57 Regs 35(2)(b) and 40(4)
and Sch 9 paras 1, 4
and 4A IS Regs
58 R(IS) 9/95
59 Reg 21(1)(i) DWA Regs
60 **All** R v NIC ex parte
Stratton [1979] QBD
361
IS Reg 35(1)(c) IS Regs

HB Reg 28(1)(c) HB
Regs
CTB Reg 19(1)(c) CTB
Regs
61 CIS/590/1993
62 Reg 35(2)(e) IS Regs
63 **IS** Reg 35(2)(a) IS Regs
FC Reg 19(2)(a) FC
Regs
DWA Reg 21(2)(a)
DWA Regs
HB Reg 28(2)(a) HB
Regs
CTB Reg 19(2)(a) CTB
Regs
64 **IS** Sch 9 para 21 IS
Regs
FC Sch 2 para 20 FC
Regs
DWA Sch 3 para 20
DWA Regs
HB Sch 4 para 21 HB
Regs
CTB Sch 4 para 22
CTB Regs
65 CIS/11482/1995
66 **IS** Reg 48(5) IS Regs
FC Reg 31(5) FC Regs
DWA Reg 34(5) DWA
Regs
HB Reg 40(5) HB
Regs
CTB Reg 31(5) CTB
Regs
67 Reg 48(6) IS Regs
68 **IS** Reg 35(2)(c) IS Regs
FC Reg 19(2)(b) FC
Regs
DWA Reg 21(2)(b)
DWA Regs
HB Reg 28(2)(b) HB
Regs
CTB Reg 19(2)(b) CTB
Regs
69 CIS/77/1993; CIS/89/
1989
70 R(IS) 6/92
IS paras 29155-166
AOG

HB/CTB para C3.10
GM
71 **IS** Sch 8 para 11 IS
Regs
FC Sch 1 para 1 FC
Regs
DWA Sch 2 para 1
DWA Regs
HB Sch 3 para 11 HB
Regs
CTB Sch 3 para 11
CTB Regs
72 **IS** Sch 8 para 12 IS
Regs
FC Sch 1 para 3 FC
Regs
DWA Sch 2 para 3
DWA Regs
HB Sch 3 para 12 HB
Regs
CTB Sch 3 para 12
CTB Regs
73 **IS** Reg 35(2)(d) IS Regs
FC Reg 19(2)(c) FC
Regs
DWA Reg 21(2)(c)
DWA Regs
HB Reg 28(2)(c) HB
Regs
CTB Reg 19(2)(c) CTB
Regs
74 **IS** Reg 40(4) and Sch 9
para 1 IS Regs
FC Reg 24(5) and Sch
2 para 1 FC Regs
DWA Reg 27(4) and
Sch 3 para 1 DWA
Regs
HB Reg 33(4) and Sch
4 para 1 HB Regs
CTB Reg 24(5) and
Sch 4 para 1 CTB Regs
75 Reg 35(2)(a) IS Regs;
para 29126 AOG
76 **FC** Reg 19(3) FC Regs
DWA Reg 21(3) DWA
Regs
77 **HB** Reg 28(2)(a) HB
Regs

CTB Reg 19(2)(a) CTB
Regs
78 Reg 14(1) and (2) FC
Regs
79 Reg 14(1) FC Regs
80 Reg 14(3) FC Regs
81 Reg 14(2A) FC Regs
82 Reg 20(5) FC Regs
83 Reg 14A FC Regs
84 Regs 14(1), 14A, 17(b)
and 18(3) FC Regs
85 Reg 16(2)-(4) DWA
Regs
86 Reg 16(1) DWA Regs
87 Reg 19(a) DWA Regs
88 R(FIS) 1/87; R(FIS) 2/
87
89 Reg 16(5) DWA Regs
90 s27(3)(b) SSCBA 1992;
reg 16(3), (4)(b) and
(9)(b) DWA Regs; R(U)
5/87
91 **FC** Regs 14(4) and 20A
FC Regs
DWA Regs 16(6) and
23 DWA Regs
92 **FC** Reg 20A FC Regs
DWA Reg 23 DWA
Regs
93 **FC** Reg 14(5) and (6)
FC Regs
DWA Reg 16(7) and (8)
DWA Regs
94 **HB** Reg 22(1)(a) HB
Regs
CTB Reg 14(1)(a) CTB
Regs
HB/CTB para C3.16
GM
95 **HB** Reg 22(1)(b) HB
Regs
CTB Reg 14(1)(b) CTB
Regs
HB/CTB para C3.17
GM
96 R v HBRB of the
London Borough of
Ealing ex parte Saville
[1986] 18 HLR 349

97 **HB** Reg 22(2)(a)-(b)
HB Regs
CTB Reg 14(2)(a)-(b)
CTB Regs
HB/CTB para C3.19
GM
98 **HB** Reg 22(3) HB
Regs
CTB Reg 14(3) CTB
Regs
99 **IS** Regs 35(1)(b) and
40(1) IS Regs
HB Regs 28(1)(b) and
33(1) HB Regs
CTB Regs 19(1)(b) and
24(1) CTB Regs
100 Sch 8 para 1(a)(i) IS
Regs
101 Sch 8 para 1(a)(ii) IS
Regs
102 Reg 29(4B) and (4D)(b)
IS Regs
103 Reg 48(11) IS Regs
104 Regs 5(5) and 29(3)(a)
IS Regs
105 Reg 29(4) IS Regs
106 Reg 29(3)(b) IS Regs
107 Reg 5(5) and Sch 8
para 1(b) IS Regs
108 Sch 8 para 2 IS Regs
109 Regs 29(4C) and 32(7)
IS Regs
110 Reg 29(4) and (4C) IS
Regs
111 R(IS) 3/93; CIS/104/
1989
112 **HB** Sch 3 para 1(a)(i)
HB Regs
CTB Sch 3 para 1(a)(i)
CTB Regs
113 **HB** Sch 3 para 1(a)(ii)
HB Regs
CTB Sch 3 para 1(a)(ii)
CTB Regs
114 **HB** Sch 3 para 2 HB
Regs
CTB Sch 3 para 2 CTB
Regs
115 **HB** Sch 3 para 4 HB

Regs
CTB Sch 3 para 4 CTB
Regs
116 Sch 8 para 5 IS Regs
117 **IS** Sch 8 para 4(2) IS
Regs
HB Sch 3 para 3(2) HB
Regs
CTB Sch 3 para 3(2)
CTB Regs
118 **HB** Sch 3 para 3(2) HB
Regs
CTB Sch 3 para 3(2)
CTB Regs
119 **IS** Sch 8 para 4(4) IS
Regs
HB Sch 3 para 3(4) HB
Regs
CTB Sch 3 para 3(4)
CTB Regs
120 **IS** Sch 8 para 4(3) and
(5) IS Regs
HB Sch 3 para 3(3) and
(5) HB Regs
CTB Sch 3 para 3(3)
and (5) CTB Regs
121 **IS** Sch 8 para 4(6) IS
Regs
HB Sch 3 para 3(6) HB
Regs
CTB Sch 3 para 3(6)
CTB Regs
122 **IS** Sch 8 paras 6A and
6B IS Regs
HB Sch 3 paras 4A and
4B HB Regs
CTB Sch 3 paras 4A
and 4B CTB Regs
123 **IS** Sch 8 para 7(1) IS
Regs
HB Sch 3 para 6(1) HB
Regs
CTB Sch 3 para 6(1)
CTB Regs
124 **IS** Sch 8 para 8 IS Regs
HB Sch 3 para 7 HB
Regs
CTB Sch 3 para 7 CTB
Regs

125 **IS** Sch 8 para 7(2) IS
Regs
HB Sch 3 para 6(2)(b)
HB Regs
CTB Sch 3 para 6(2)(b)
CTB Regs
126 Reg 3A and Sch 8 para
4(7) IS Regs
127 **IS** Sch 8 paras 6 and 9
IS Regs
HB Sch 3 paras 5 and
8 HB Regs
CTB Sch 4 paras 5 and
8 CTB Regs

3. Earnings from self-employment
(pp388-394)

128 **IS** Reg 37(1) IS Regs
FC Reg 21(1) FC Regs
DWA Reg 24(1) DWA
Regs
HB Reg 30 HB Regs
CTB Reg 21 CTB Regs
129 **IS** Reg 38(3) IS Regs
FC Reg 22(3) FC Regs
DWA Reg 25(3) DWA
Regs
HB Reg 31(3) HB Regs
CTB Reg 22(3) CTB
Regs
130 **IS** Reg 2(1) IS Regs
FC Regs 2(1) and
22(12)-(13) FC Regs
DWA Regs 2(1) and
25(14)-(15) DWA Regs
HB Regs 2(1) and
31(11)-(12) HB Regs
CTB Regs 2(1) and
22(11)-(12) CTB Regs
131 **IS**/FC/DWA Reg 32(3)
SS(C&P) Regs
HB Reg 73(4) HB Regs
CTB Reg 63(4) CTB
Regs
132 **FC** Reg 21(1) FC Regs
DWA Reg 24(1) DWA
Regs

133 CFC/24/1989; CFC/3/
1992

134 CFC/4/1991
(Kostanczwk v CAO);
CFC/23/1991

135 **IS** Reg 37(2) IS Regs
FC Reg 21(3) FC Regs
DWA Reg 24(3) DWA
Regs
HB Reg 30(2) HB Regs
CTB Reg 21(2) CTB
Regs

136 **IS** Sch 9 paras 26-27 IS
Regs
FC Sch 2 para 24 FC
Regs
DWA Sch 3 para 24
DWA Regs
HB Sch 4 paras 24-25
HB Regs
CTB Sch 4 paras 25-26
CTB Regs

137 **IS** Reg 37(2)(a) IS Regs
HB Sch 4 para 42 HB
Regs
CTB Sch 4 para 21
CTB Regs

138 **FC** Reg 21(2) FC Regs
DWA Reg 24(2) DWA
Regs

139 **IS** Reg 38(3)(a), (4), (7)
and (8)(a) IS Regs
FC Reg 22(3)(a), (4),
(7) and (8)(a) FC Regs
DWA Reg 25(3)(a),
(4)(a), (5), (6), (9) and
(10)(a) DWA Regs
HB Reg 31(3)(a), (4),
(7) and (8)(a) HB Regs
CTB Reg 22(3)(a), (4),
(7) and (8)(a) CTB
Regs

140 R(IS) 13/91; R(FC) 1/
91; CFC/26/1989

141 **IS** Reg 38(6) and (8)(b)
IS Regs
FC Reg 22(6) and
(8)(b) FC Regs
DWA Reg 25(8) and

(10)(b) DWA Regs
HB Reg 31(6) and
(8)(b) HB Regs
CTB Reg 22(6) and
(8)(b) CTB Regs

142 **IS** Reg 38(5) IS Regs
FC Reg 22(5) FC Regs
DWA Reg 25(7) DWA
Regs
HB Reg 31(5) HB Regs
CTB Reg 22(5) CTB
Regs

143 Compare CFC/19/1993
and CFC/41/1993 with
CFC/22/1989, CFC/19/
1992 and CFC/10/1993

144 CFC/41/1993 (to be
reported as R(FC) 1/96)

145 **IS** Reg 38(11) IS Regs
FC Reg 22(11) FC
Regs
DWA Reg 25(13) DWA
Regs
HB Reg 31(10) HB
Regs
CTB Reg 22(10) CTB
Regs; R(FC) 1/93

146 CFC/836/1995

147 Reg 30 IS Regs

148 Regs 30(1)(b) and
38(10) IS Regs; CIS/
166/1994; CIS/14409/
1996

149 Reg 30(2) IS Regs

150 **FC** Reg 15(1) FC Regs
DWA Reg 17(1) DWA
Regs

151 **FC** Reg 18(2) FC Regs
DWA Reg 20(2) DWA
Regs

152 **FC** Reg 17 FC Regs
DWA Reg 19(b) DWA
Regs

153 Regs 15(2) and (4) and
17(a) FC Regs

154 Reg 17(3) DWA Regs

155 **FC** s128(3) SSCBA
1992

DWA s129(6) SSCBA
1992

156 CFC/24/1989; CFC/14/
1991

157 **HB** Regs 23(1) and
25(2) HB Regs
CTB Regs 15(1) and
17(2) CTB Regs

158 **IS** Reg 38(9) IS Regs
FC Reg 22(9) FC Regs
DWA Reg 25(11) DWA
Regs
HB Reg 31(9) HB Regs
CTB Reg 22(9) CTB
Regs

159 **IS** Reg 38(2) IS Regs
FC Reg 22(2) FC Regs
DWA Reg 25(2) DWA
Regs
HB Reg 31(2) HB Regs
CTB Reg 22(2) CTB
Regs

160 **FC** Regs 13(1)(c) and
13A FC Regs
DWA Regs 15(1)(c) and
15A DWA Regs
HB Regs 21(1)(c) and
21A HB Regs
CTB Regs 13(1)(c) and
13A CTB Regs

161 **FC** Reg 13A(2) FC
Regs
DWA Reg 15A(2)
DWA Regs
HB Reg 21A(2) HB
Regs
CTB Reg 13A(2) CTB
Regs
FC/DWA Reg 10(3)
IRB&JSA(PA) Amdt
Regs

162 **FC** Reg 13A FC Regs
DWA Reg 15A DWA
Regs

163 **HB** Reg 21A HB Regs
CTB Reg 13A CTB
Regs

164 s29 CA 1989

4. Other income

(pp395-410)

165 **IS** Reg 40 and Sch 9 para 1 IS Regs
FC Reg 24 and Sch 2 para 1 FC Regs
DWA Reg 27 and Sch 3 para 1 DWA Regs
HB Reg 33 and Sch 4 para 1 HB Regs
CTB Reg 24 and Sch 4 para 1 CTB Regs

166 **HB** Reg 26 HB Regs
CTB Reg 18 CTB Regs

167 **HB** Reg 24 HB Regs
CTB Reg 16 CTB Regs

168 **FC** Reg 16(1) FC Regs
DWA Reg 18(1) DWA Regs

169 **HB** Sch 4 paras 57, 58 and 60 HB Regs
CTB Sch 4 paras 56, 57 and 59 CTB Regs

170 Reg 35(2) and Sch 9 para 4 IS Regs

171 s74(2) SSAA 1992

172 **IS** Sch 10 para 7 IS Regs
FC Sch 3 para 8 FC Regs
DWA Sch 4 para 8 DWA Regs
HB Sch 5 para 8 HB Regs
CTB Sch 5 para 8 CTB Regs

173 **IS** Sch 9 para 9 IS Regs
FC Sch 2 paras 4 and 7 FC Regs
DWA Sch 3 paras 4 and 7 DWA Regs
HB Sch 4 paras 5 and 8 HB Regs
CTB Sch 4 paras 5 and 8 CTB Regs

174 **IS** Sch 9 para 33 IS Regs
FC Sch 2 para 28 FC Regs

DWA Sch 3 para 28 DWA Regs
HB Sch 4 para 31 HB Regs
CTB Sch 4 para 32 CTB Regs

175 **IS** Sch 9 para 6 IS Regs
FC Sch 2 para 4 FC Regs
DWA Sch 3 para 4 DWA Regs
HB Sch 4 para 5 HB Regs
CTB Sch 4 para 5 CTB Regs

176 **IS** Sch 9 para 8 IS Regs
FC Sch 2 para 6 FC Regs
DWA Sch 3 para 6 DWA Regs
HB Sch 4 para 7 HB Regs
CTB Sch 4 para 7 CTB Regs

177 **IS** Sch 9 paras 7-8 IS Regs
FC Sch 2 paras 5-6 FC Regs
DWA Sch 3 paras 5-6 DWA Regs
HB Sch 4 paras 6-7 HB Regs
CTB Sch 4 paras 6-7 CTB Regs

178 Sch 2 para 4 FC Regs

179 Sch 3 para 46 DWA Regs

180 **IS** Sch 9 para 31 IS Regs
HB Sch 4 para 30 HB Regs
CTB Sch 4 para 31 CTB Regs

181 **IS** Sch 10 para 18 IS Regs
FC Sch 3 para 19 FC Regs
DWA Sch 4 para 19 DWA Regs

HB Sch 5 para 19 HB Regs
CTB Sch 5 para 19 CTB Regs

182 **IS** Sch 9 para 38 IS Regs
FC Sch 2 para 33 FC Regs
HB Sch 4 para 37 HB Regs
CTB Sch 4 para 39 CTB Regs

183 **IS** Sch 9 paras 40-42 IS Regs
FC Sch 2 paras 35-37 FC Regs
DWA Sch 2 paras 34-36 DWA Regs
HB Sch 4 paras 35-36 and 48 HB Regs
CTB Sch 4 paras 37-38 and 47 CTB Regs

184 **IS** Sch 9 paras 5, 45-46 and 52 IS Regs
FC Sch 2 paras 3, 41-42 and 49 FC Regs
DWA Sch 3 paras 3, 39, 40 and 47 DWA Regs
HB Sch 4 paras 40-41 and 51 HB Regs
CTB Sch 4 paras 36, 41 and 50 CTB Regs

185 **FC** Sch 2 para 3 FC Regs
DWA Sch 3 para 3 DWA Regs
HB Sch 4 para 4 HB Regs
CTB Sch 4 para 4 CTB Regs

186 **IS** Sch 9 para 47 IS Regs
FC Sch 2 para 43 FC Regs
DWA Sch 3 para 41 DWA Regs
HB Sch 4 para 43 HB Regs

CTB Sch 4 para 42
CTB Regs
187 **IS** Sch 9 paras 54-56 IS
Regs
FC Sch 2 paras 52-54
FC Regs
DWA Sch 3 paras 50-
52 DWA Regs
HB Sch 4 paras 53-55
HB Regs
CTB Sch 4 paras 52-54
CTB Regs
188 **FC** Sch 2 para 50 FC
Regs
DWA Sch 3 para 48
DWA Regs
HB Sch 4 para 50 HB
Regs
CTB Sch 4 para 49
CTB Regs
189 **FC** Sch 2 para 15 FC
Regs
DWA Sch 3 para 15
DWA Regs
190 **FC** Sch 2 paras 27 and
31 FC Regs
DWA Sch 3 paras 27
and 31 DWA Regs
191 **FC** Sch 2 para 56 FC
Regs
DWA Sch 3 para 54
DWA Regs
192 **HB** Sch 4 paras 57, 58
and 60 HB Regs
CTB Sch 4 paras 56,
57 and 59 CTB Regs
193 **IS** Sch 9 para 53 IS
Regs
FC Sch 2 para 51 FC
Regs
DWA Sch 3 para 49
DWA Regs
HB Sch 4 para 52 HB
Regs
CTB Sch 4 para 51
CTB Regs
194 **IS** Sch 9 para 16 IS
Regs
FC Sch 2 para 14 FC

Regs
DWA Sch 3 para 14
DWA Regs
HB Sch 4 para 14 HB
Regs
CTB Sch 4 para 14
CTB Regs
195 **IS** Sch 9 para 36 IS
Regs
FC Sch 2 para 29 FC
Regs
DWA Sch 3 para 29
DWA Regs
HB Sch 4 para 33 HB
Regs
CTB Sch 4 para 34
CTB Regs
196 ss134(8) and 139(6)
SSAA 1992; regs 7 and
8 IRBS(Amdt 2) Regs
197 **FC** Reg 16(2)(a) and
(2A)(a) FC Regs
DWA Reg 18(2)(a) and
(2A)(a) DWA Regs
198 **FC** Reg 16(2)(b) and
(2A)(b) FC Regs
DWA Reg 18(2)(b) and
(2A)(b) DWA Regs
199 CFC/48/1993
200 **FC** Reg 31(6) FC Regs
DWA Reg 34(6) DWA
Regs
201 **FC** Sch 2 para 55 and
Sch 3 para 48 FC Regs
DWA Sch 3 para 53
and Sch 4 para 47
DWA Regs
202 s136(1) SSCBA 1992
203 **FC** Sch 2 paras 13(3)
and 47 FC Regs
DWA Sch 3 paras 12(3)
and 13 DWA Regs
HB Sch 4 paras 13(3)
and 47 HB Regs
CTB Sch 4 paras 13(3)
and 46 CTB Regs
204 CIS/683/1993
205 **IS** Reg 61 IS Regs
FC Reg 37 FC Regs

DWA Reg 41 DWA
Regs
HB Reg 46 HB Regs
CTB Reg 38 CTB Regs
All Definition of 'grant'
206 R(IS) 16/95
207 **IS** Reg 61 IS Regs
FC Reg 37 FC Regs
DWA Reg 41 DWA
Regs
HB Reg 46 HB Regs
CTB Reg 38 CTB Regs
All Definition of 'grant
income'
208 **IS** Reg 62(3) IS Regs
FC Reg 38(3) FC Regs
DWA Reg 42(3) DWA
Regs
HB Reg 53(3) HB Regs
CTB Reg 42(4) CTB
Regs
209 **IS** Reg 62(4) IS Regs
FC Reg 38(4) FC Regs
DWA Reg 42(5) DWA
Regs
HB Reg 53(4) HB Regs
CTB Reg 42(5) CTB
Regs
210 R(IS) 15/95
211 **IS** Reg 62(3A) IS Regs
FC Reg 38(3A) FC
Regs
DWA Reg 42(4) DWA
Regs
HB Reg 53(3)(b) HB
Regs
CTB Reg 42(4)(b) CTB
Regs
HB/CTB para C5.47
and Annex A GM
212 CIS/109/1991
213 **IS** Reg 62(2) IS Regs
FC Reg 38(2) FC Regs
DWA Reg 42(2) DWA
Regs
HB Reg 53(2) HB Regs
CTB Reg 42(2) CTB
Regs
214 R(IS) 7/95

215 CIS/91/1994
216 **IS** Reg 66(1) IS Regs
FC Reg 42 FC Regs
DWA Reg 46 DWA
Regs
HB Reg 57 HB Regs
CTB Reg 46 CTB Regs
217 **IS** Reg 67A IS Regs
FC Reg 43A FC Regs
DWA Reg 48A DWA
Regs
HB Reg 58A HB Regs
CTB Reg 48A CTB
Regs
218 **IS** Reg 67 IS Regs
FC Reg 43 FC Regs
DWA Reg 48 DWA
Regs
HB Reg 58(1) HB Regs
CTB Reg 48 CTB Regs
219 Reg 58(2) HB Regs
220 Reg 32(6A) IS Regs
221 Reg 29(2B) IS Regs
222 **IS** Reg 66A IS Regs
FC Reg 42A FC Regs
DWA Reg 47 DWA
Regs
HB Reg 57A HB Regs
CTB Reg 47 CTB Regs
223 **IS** Reg 61 IS Regs
FC Reg 37 FC Regs
DWA Reg 41 DWA
Regs
HB Reg 46 HB Regs
CTB Reg 38 CTB Regs
All Definition of 'last
day of the course'
224 **IS** Sch 9 para 36 IS
Regs
FC Sch 2 para 29 FC
Regs
DWA Sch 3 para 29
DWA Regs
HB Sch 4 para 33 HB
Regs
CTB Sch 4 para 34
CTB Regs
225 **IS** Reg 40(3A) IS Regs
FC Reg 24(4A) FC

Regs
DWA Reg 27(5) DWA
Regs
HB Reg 33(3A) HB
Regs
CTB Reg 24(4) CTB
Regs
226 **IS** Reg 66A(3) IS Regs
FC Reg 42A(3) FC
Regs
DWA Reg 47(3) DWA
Regs
HB Reg 57A(3) HB
Regs
CTB Reg 47(3) CTB
Regs
227 **IS** Reg 41(6) IS Regs
FC Reg 25(3) FC Regs
DWA Reg 28(3) DWA
Regs
HB Reg 34(4) HB Regs
CTB Reg 25(4) CTB
Regs
228 Reg 29(2A) IS Regs
229 **IS** Sch 9 para 59 IS
Regs
FC Sch 2 para 58 FC
Regs
DWA Sch 3 para 56
DWA Regs
HB Sch 4 para 63 HB
Regs
CTB Sch 4 para 63
CTB Regs
230 Sch 9 paras 60-61 IS
Regs
231 Excluded from
definition of 'grant' in:
IS Reg 61 IS Regs
FC Reg 37 FC Regs
DWA Reg 41 DWA
Regs
HB Reg 46 HB Regs
CTB Reg 38 CTB Regs
232 R(IS) 16/95
233 **IS** Sch 9 para 25(1)(a)
and (2)(b) IS Regs
FC Sch 2 para 22(1)(a)
and (2)(b) FC Regs

DWA Sch 3 para
22(1)(a) and (2)(b)
DWA Regs
HB Sch 4 para 23(1)(a)
and (2)(b) HB Regs
CTB Sch 4 para
24(1)(a) and (2)(b) CTB
Regs
234 **IS** Sch 9 para 25(2)(a)
IS Regs
FC Sch 2 para 22(2)(a)
FC Regs
DWA Sch 3 para
22(2)(a) DWA Regs
HB Sch 4 para 23(2)(a)
HB Regs
CTB Sch 4 para
24(2)(a) CTB Regs
235 **IS** Sch 9 para 26 IS
Regs
FC Sch 2 para 23 FC
Regs
DWA Sch 3 para 23
DWA Regs
HB Sch 4 para 24 HB
Regs
CTB Sch 4 para 25
CTB Regs
236 **IS** Sch 9 para 25(1)(b)
and (2) IS Regs
FC Sch 2 para 22(1)(b)
and (2) FC Regs
DWA Sch 3 para
22(1)(b) and (2) DWA
Regs
HB Sch 4 para 23(1)(b)
and (2) HB Regs
CTB Sch 4 para
24(1)(b) and (2) CTB
Regs
237 Reg 48(8) IS Regs
238 **IS** Sch 10 para 8(b) IS
Regs
FC Sch 3 para 9(b) FC
Regs
DWA Sch 4 para 9(b)
DWA Regs
HB Sch 5 para 9(b) HB
Regs

CTB Sch 5 para 9(b)
CTB Regs

239 **IS** Reg 48(10)(c) and
Sch 10 para 22 IS Regs
FC Sch 2 para 34 FC
Regs
DWA Sch 3 para 33
DWA Regs
HB Sch 4 para 34 HB
Regs
CTB Sch 4 para 35
CTB Regs

240 **IS** Sch 9 para 39 IS
Regs
FC Sch 2 para 34 FC
Regs
DWA Sch 3 para 33
DWA Regs
HB Sch 4 para 34 HB
Regs
CTB Sch 4 para 35
CTB Regs

241 **IS** Reg 48(9) IS Regs
FC Reg 31(3) FC Regs
DWA Reg 34(3) DWA
Regs
HB/CTB There are no
specific provisions for
HB/CTB but such
payments are obviously
capital

242 Reg 48(10)(a) IS Regs

243 Reg 48(10)(b) IS Regs

244 **IS** Sch 9 para 15 IS
Regs
FC Sch 2 para 13 FC
Regs
DWA Sch 3 para 12
DWA Regs
HB Sch 4 para 13 HB
Regs
CTB Sch 4 para 13
CTB Regs

245 Sch 9 para 15A IS Regs

246 **IS** Sch 9 paras 15(4)
and 36 IS Regs
FC Sch 2 paras 13(4)
and 29 FC Regs
DWA Sch 3 paras 12(4)

and 29 DWA Regs
HB Sch 4 paras 13(4)
and 33 HB Regs
CTB Sch 4 paras 13(4)
and 34 CTB Regs

247 **HB/CTB** Circular A17/
97

248 **IS** Sch 9 para 21 IS
Regs
FC Sch 2 para 20 FC
Regs
DWA Sch 3 para 20
DWA Regs
HB Sch 4 para 21 HB
Regs
CTB Sch 4 para 22
CTB Regs

249 *R v Doncaster MBC ex
parte Boulton* [1992] 25
HLR 195; R(IS) 4/94

250 **IS** para 31047 AOG
FC/DWA para 51166
AOG
HB/CTB para C3.90
GM

251 **IS** Sch 9 para 19 IS
Regs
FC Sch 2 para 19 FC
Regs
DWA Sch 3 para 19
DWA Regs
HB Sch 4 para 20 HB
Regs
CTB Sch 4 para 20
CTB Regs

252 **IS** Sch 9 para 18 IS
Regs
FC Sch 2 para 18 FC
Regs
DWA Sch 3 para 18
DWA Regs
HB Sch 4 para 19 HB
Regs
CTB Sch 4 para 19
CTB Regs

253 **IS** Sch 9 para 20 IS
Regs
FC Sch 2 para 40 FC
Regs

DWA Sch 3 para 38
DWA Regs
HB Sch 4 para 42 HB
Regs
CTB Sch 4 para 21
CTB Regs

254 **All** Definition of 'board
and lodging
accommodation'
IS Reg 2(1) IS Regs
HB Sch 4 para 42(2)
HB Regs
CTB Sch 4 para 21(2)
CTB Regs

255 CIS/13059/1996

256 **All** *CAO v Palfrey and
Others, The Times,* 17
February 1995
IS Reg 48(4) IS Regs
FC Reg 31(4) FC Regs
DWA Reg 34(4) DWA
Regs
HB Reg 40(4) HB Regs
CTB Reg 31(4) CTB
Regs

257 *See* CIS/25/1989; CIS/
563/1991; CIS/85/1992
(Palfrey)

258 **IS** Sch 9 para 22(1) IS
Regs
FC Sch 2 para 16(1)
FC Regs
DWA Sch 3 para 16(1)
DWA Regs
HB Sch 4 para 15(1)
HB Regs
CTB Sch 4 para 15(1)
CTB Regs

259 **IS** Reg 48(4) IS Regs
FC Reg 31(4) FC Regs
DWA Reg 34(4) DWA
Regs
HB Reg 40(4) HB Regs
CTB Reg 31(4) CTB
Regs

260 **IS** Sch 9 para 22(1) IS
Regs
FC Sch 2 para 16(1)
FC Regs

DWA Sch 3 para 16(1)
DWA Regs
HB Sch 4 para 15(1)
HB Regs
CTB Sch 4 para 15(1)
CTB Regs
261 CFC/13/1993
262 **IS** Sch 9 para 22(2) IS
Regs
FC Sch 2 para 16(2)
FC Regs
DWA Sch 3 para 16(2)
DWA Regs
HB Sch 4 para 15(2)
HB Regs
CTB Sch 4 para 15(2)
CTB Regs
263 **IS** Reg 53 IS Regs
FC Reg 36 FC Regs
DWA Reg 40 DWA
Regs
HB Reg 45 HB Regs
CTB Reg 37 CTB Regs
264 Reg 32(1) SS(C&P)
Regs
265 **HB** Reg 75 HB Regs
CTB Reg 65 CTB Regs
266 Reg 41(1) IS Regs
267 **FC** Reg 25(1) FC Regs
DWA Reg 28(1) DWA
Regs
268 **HB** Reg 34(1) HB Regs
CTB Reg 25(1) CTB
Regs
269 **IS** Reg 29(2)(a) IS Regs
FC Reg 18 FC Regs
DWA Reg 20 DWA
Regs
HB Reg 25 HB Regs
CTB Reg 17 CTB Regs
270 **IS** Reg 44(1) and (5) IS
Regs
FC Reg 27(1) and (3)
FC Regs
DWA Reg 30(1) and (3)
DWA Regs
HB Reg 36(2) and (5)
HB Regs

CTB Reg 27(2) and (5)
CTB Regs
271 **IS** Reg 32(1) IS Regs
FC Reg 18(1) FC Regs
DWA Reg 20(1) DWA
Regs
HB Reg 25(1) HB Regs
CTB Reg 17(1) CTB
Regs
272 **IS** Reg 41(2) IS Regs
FC Reg 25(2) FC Regs
DWA Reg 28(2) DWA
Regs
HB Reg 34(2) HB Regs
CTB Reg 25(2) CTB
Regs
273 **IS** Reg 41(6) IS Regs
FC Reg 25(3) FC Regs
DWA Reg 28(3) DWA
Regs
HB Reg 34(4) HB Regs
CTB Reg 25(4) CTB
Regs
274 Regs 41(4) and 48(2) IS
Regs
275 Reg 41(3) IS Regs
276 *R v SBC ex parte Singer*
[1973] 1 All ER 931; *R
v Oxford County Council
ex parte Jack* [1984] 17
HLR 419; *R v West
Dorset DC ex parte
Poupard* [1988] 20 HLR
295; para C3.118 GM
277 paras C2.09(xix) and
3.118 GM
278 *R v West Dorset DC ex
parte Poupard* [1988] 20
HLR 295
279 **IS** Sch 10 para 20 IS
Regs
FC Sch 3 para 21 FC
Regs
DWA Sch 4 para 21
DWA Regs
HB Sch 5 para 21 HB
Regs
CTB Sch 5 para 21
CTB Regs

280 **IS** Reg 48(2) IS Regs
FC Reg 31(1) FC Regs
DWA Reg 34(1) DWA
Regs
HB Reg 40(2) HB Regs
CTB Reg 31(2) CTB
Regs
281 Regs 41(4) and 48(2) IS
Regs
282 **IS** Reg 40(4) and Sch 9
para 15B IS Regs
FC Reg 24(5) FC Regs
DWA Reg 27(4) DWA
Regs
HB Reg 33(4) HB Regs
CTB Reg 24(5) CTB
Regs
All Definition of
'occupational pension'
in reg 2(1) of each of
those regs
283 **IS** Reg 41(2) and Sch 9
para 17 IS Regs
FC Reg 25(2) and Sch
2 para 17 FC Regs
DWA Reg 28(2) and
Sch 3 para 17 DWA
Regs
HB Reg 34(2) and Sch
4 para 16 HB Regs
CTB Reg 25(2) and
Sch 4 para 16 CTB
Regs
284 Sch 9 para 29 IS Regs;
para 33240 AOG
285 Sch 9 para 30(a)-(d) IS
Regs
286 **FC** Sch 2 para 55 FC
Regs
DWA Sch 3 para 53
DWA Regs
287 **HB** Sch 4 para 28 HB
Regs
CTB Sch 4 para 29
CTB Regs
288 **IS** Sch 9 para 11 IS
Regs
FC Sch 2 para 9 FC
Regs

DWA Sch 3 para 9
DWA Regs
HB Sch 4 para 10 HB
Regs
CTB Sch 4 para 10
CTB Regs

289 **IS** Sch 9 para 2 IS Regs
FC Sch 2 para 2 FC
Regs
DWA Sch 3 para 2
DWA Regs
HB Sch 4 para 2 HB
Regs
CTB Sch 4 para 2 CTB
Regs

290 **IS** Sch 9 para 21 IS
Regs
FC Sch 2 para 20 FC
Regs
DWA Sch 3 para 20
DWA Regs
HB Sch 4 para 21 HB
Regs
CTB Sch 4 para 22
CTB Regs

291 para C3.73(xiii) GM

292 *See* para 63596 AOG on
related provisions for
child benefits

293 HB/CTB Circular A17/
97

294 **FC** Sch 2 para 12 FC
Regs
DWA Sch 3 para 11A
DWA Regs

295 **IS** Sch 9 paras 14 and
51 IS Regs
FC Sch 2 paras 12 and
48 FC Regs
DWA Sch 3 para 45
DWA Regs
HB Sch 4 paras 12 and
49 HB Regs
CTB Sch 4 paras 12
and 48 CTB Regs

296 **IS** Sch 9 para 13 IS
Regs
FC Sch 2 para 11 FC
Regs

DWA Sch 3 para 11
DWA Regs
HB Sch 4 para 11 HB
Regs
CTB Sch 4 para 11
CTB Regs

297 **IS** Sch 9 para 13(d) IS
Regs
FC Sch 2 para 11(d)
FC Regs
DWA Sch 3 para 11(d)
DWA Regs
HB Sch 4 para 11(d)
HB Regs
CTB Sch 4 para 11(d)
CTB Regs

298 **IS** Sch 9 paras 62 and
63 IS Regs
FC Sch 2 paras 59 and
60 FC Regs
DWA Sch 3 paras 57
and 58 DWA Regs
HB Sch 4 paras 64 and
65 HB Regs
CTB Sch 4 paras 64
and 65 CTB Regs

299 **IS** Sch 9 para 43 IS
Regs
FC Sch 2 para 38 FC
Regs
DWA Sch 3 para 37
DWA Regs
HB Sch 4 para 38 HB
Regs
CTB Sch 4 para 40
CTB Regs

300 **IS** Sch 9 para 28 IS
Regs
FC Sch 2 para 25 FC
Regs
DWA Sch 3 para 25
DWA Regs
HB Sch 4 para 26 HB
Regs
CTB Sch 4 para 27
CTB Regs

301 **IS** Sch 9 para 58 IS
Regs
FC Sch 2 para 57 FC

Regs
DWA Sch 3 para 55
DWA Regs
HB Sch 4 para 66 HB
Regs
CTB Sch 4 para 62
CTB Regs

302 **IS** Sch 9 para 27 IS
Regs
FC Sch 2 para 24 FC
Regs
DWA Sch 3 para 24
DWA Regs
HB Sch 4 para 25 HB
Regs
CTB Sch 4 para 26
CTB Regs

303 **IS** Sch 9 para 10 IS
Regs
FC Sch 2 para 8 FC
Regs
DWA Sch 3 para 8
DWA Regs
HB Sch 4 para 9 HB
Regs
CTB Sch 4 para 9 CTB
Regs

304 **IS** Sch 9 para 23 IS
Regs
FC Sch 2 para 21 FC
Regs
DWA Sch 3 para 21
DWA Regs
HB Sch 4 para 22 HB
Regs
CTB Sch 4 para 23
CTB Regs

305 **IS** Sch 9 para 24 IS
Regs
FC Sch 2 para 30 FC
Regs
DWA Sch 3 para 30
DWA Regs
HB Sch 4 para 32 HB
Regs
CTB Sch 4 para 33
CTB Regs

306 **IS** Sch 9 para 48 IS
Regs

FC Sch 2 para 44 FC Regs
DWA Sch 3 para 42 DWA Regs
HB Sch 4 para 44 HB Regs
CTB Sch 4 para 43 CTB Regs

307 **IS** Sch 9 para 49 IS Regs
FC Sch 2 para 45 FC Regs
DWA Sch 3 para 43 DWA Regs
HB Sch 4 para 45 HB Regs
CTB Sch 4 para 44 CTB Regs

308 **IS** Sch 9 para 50 IS Regs
FC Sch 2 para 46 FC Regs
DWA Sch 3 para 44 DWA Regs
HB Sch 4 para 46 HB Regs
CTB Sch 4 para 45 CTB Regs

309 **HB** Sch 4 para 17 HB Regs
CTB Sch 4 para 17 CTB Regs

310 **HB** Sch 3 para 9 HB Regs
CTB Sch 3 para 9 CTB Regs

311 **HB** Sch 4 para 18 HB Regs
CTB Sch 4 para 18 CTB Regs

312 **HB** Sch 3 para 9 HB Regs
CTB Sch 3 para 9 CTB Regs

313 **IS** Reg 42(1) IS Regs
FC Reg 26(1) FC Regs
DWA Reg 29(1) DWA Regs
HB Reg 35(1) HB Regs

CTB Reg 26(1) CTB Regs

5. Notional income
(pp411-414)

314 paras 33608-16 AOG; *see also* CIS/15052/1996
315 CSIS/57/1992
316 **IS** Reg 42(2) IS Regs
FC Reg 26(2) FC Regs
DWA Reg 29(2) DWA Regs
HB Reg 35(2) HB Regs
CTB Reg 26(2) CTB Regs
317 **IS** Reg 42(2A) IS Regs
FC Reg 26(2A) FC Regs
DWA Reg 29(2A) DWA Regs
HB Reg 35(2A) HB Regs
CTB Reg 26(2A) CTB Regs
318 paras 33608-16 AOG
319 CIS/15052/1996, para 11
320 Reg 42(3) IS Regs
321 Reg 42(3A) and (3B) IS Regs
322 CIS/15052/1996, para 10
323 Reg 70(2)(b) IS Regs
324 Reg 42(5) IS Regs
325 Reg 2 SS(PAOR) Regs
326 **IS** Reg 42(4)(a)(ii), (4A) and (9) IS Regs
FC Reg 26(3)(a) FC Regs
DWA Reg 29(3)(a) DWA Regs
HB Reg 35(3)(a) and (8) HB Regs
CTB Reg 26(3)(a) and (8) CTB Regs
327 Reg 42(4) IS Regs
328 **IS** Reg 42(4)(b) IS Regs
FC Reg 26(3)(b) FC Regs

DWA Reg 29(3)(b) DWA Regs
HB Reg 35(3)(b) HB Regs
CTB Reg 26(3)(b) CTB Regs
329 **IS** Reg 42(6) IS Regs; CIS/191/1991
FC Reg 26(4) FC Regs
DWA Reg 29(4) DWA Regs
HB Reg 35(5) HB Regs
CTB Reg 26(5) CTB Regs
330 R(SB) 13/86
331 R(SB) 13/86
332 **IS** Reg 42(6) IS Regs
FC Reg 26(4) FC Regs
DWA Reg 29(4) DWA Regs
HB Reg 35(5) HB Regs
CTB Reg 26(5) CTB Regs
333 R(IS) 12/92
334 *Sharrock v CAO* (CA) 26 March 1991; CIS/93/1991
335 CIS/93/1991
336 CIS/422/1992
337 CIS/701/1994
338 CIS/422/1992
339 CIS/701/1994
340 s1(3)(a) Carers (Recognition and Services) Act 1995 excludes those who care 'by virtue of a contract of employment or other contract' which according to policy guidance issued by the Department of Health means, 'anyone who is providing personal assistance for payment either in cash or in kind'.
341 CIS/147/1993
342 Reg 14(2A) FC Regs

Chapter 20: Capital
(pp415-439)

1. Introduction
(pp415-417)

1 HB Sch 5 para 5 HB
Regs
CTB Sch 5 para 5 CTB
Regs

2 IS Reg 45 IS Regs
FC Reg 28 FC Regs

3 DWA Reg 31 DWA
Regs
HB Reg 37 HB Regs
CTB Reg 28 CTB Regs

4 IS Reg 53 IS Regs
FC Reg 36 FC Regs
DWA Reg 40 DWA
Regs
HB Reg 45 HB Regs
CTB Reg 37 CTB Regs

5 Regs 45 and 53(1A),
(1B), (1C) and (4) IS
Regs

6 Regs 7(9) and 45(1A),
(1B), (1C), (4) and (5)
HB Regs

7 s136(1) SSCBA 1992

8 IS Reg 47 IS Regs
FC Reg 30 FC Regs
DWA Reg 33 DWA
Regs
HB Reg 39 HB Regs
CTB Reg 30 CTB Regs

9 IS Reg 17(1)(b) IS Regs
FC Reg 46(4) FC Regs
DWA Reg 51(4) DWA
Regs
HB Reg 16(b) HB
Regs
CTB Reg 8(b) CTB
Regs

10 IS Reg 44(5) IS Regs
FC Reg 27(3) FC Regs
DWA Reg 30(3) DWA
Regs
HB Reg 36(2) HB
Regs

CTB Reg 27(2) CTB
Regs

11 IS Regs 25 and 44(5)
IS Regs
FC Reg 27(3) FC Regs
DWA Reg 30(3) DWA
Regs
HB Reg 36(2) HB
Regs
CTB Reg 27(2) CTB
Regs

12 IS Reg 17(1)(b) IS Regs
FC Reg 46(4) FC Regs
DWA Reg 51(4) DWA
Regs
HB Reg 16(b) HB
Regs
CTB Reg 8(b) CTB
Regs

**2. What counts as
capital**
(pp417-421)

13 para C2.09 GM; para
34020 AOG

14 Reg 14 SS(CMB) Regs

15 Reg 22 SS(BWB) Regs

16 *R v SBC ex parte Singer*
[1973] 1 WLR 713

17 R(SB) 35/83

18 CIS/654/1991

19 IS/FC/DWA Reg 2
SS(PAOR) Regs
HB Reg 91(1) HB
Regs

20 R(SB) 12/86

21 R(SB) 53/83; R(SB) 1/
85

22 R(SB) 49/83

23 R(SB) 23/85

24 IS Sch 10 para 13 IS
Regs
FC Sch 3 para 14 FC
Regs
DWA Sch 4 para 14
DWA Regs
HB Sch 5 para 14 HB
Regs

CTB Sch 5 para 14
CTB Regs

25 *Peters v CAO* reported
as an appendix to
R(SB) 3/89

26 R(IS) 1/90

27 R(SB) 23/85

28 *Barclays Bank v Quistclose
Investments Ltd* [1970]
AC 567; R(SB) 49/83;
CFC/21/1989

29 IS Sch 10 para 12 IS
Regs
FC Sch 3 para 13 FC
Regs
DWA Sch 4 para 13
DWA Regs
HB Sch 5 para 13 HB
Regs
CTB Sch 5 para 13
CTB Regs

30 IS Sch 10 paras 44 and
45 IS Regs
FC Sch 3 paras 46 and
47 FC Regs
DWA Sch 4 paras 45
and 46 DWA Regs
HB Sch 5 paras 46 and
47 HB Regs
CTB Sch 5 paras 46
and 47 CTB Regs

31 R(SB) 2/89

32 IS Regs 40 and 46 IS
Regs
FC Regs 24 and 29 FC
Regs
DWA Regs 27 and 32
DWA Regs
HB Regs 33 and 38
HB Regs
CTB Regs 24 and 29
CTB Regs
All CIS/559/1991

33 *Thomas v CAO*
(appendix to R(SB) 17/
87)

34 IS Sch 10 paras 44-45
IS Regs
FC Sch 3 paras 46-47

FC Regs
DWA Sch 4 paras 45-46 DWA Regs
HB Sch 5 paras 46-47 HB Regs
CTB Sch 5 paras 46-47 CTB Regs

35 **IS** Reg 48 IS Regs
FC Reg 31 FC Regs
DWA Reg 34 DWA Regs
HB Reg 40 HB Regs
CTB Reg 31 CTB Regs

36 paras 51162 and 51172 AOG

37 **FC** Reg 31(6) FC Regs
DWA Reg 34(6) DWA Regs

38 **IS** Sch 9 para 32 IS Regs
FC Sch 2 para 26 FC Regs
DWA Sch 3 para 26 DWA Regs
HB Sch 4 para 29 HB Regs
CTB Sch 4 para 30 CTB Regs

3. Disregarded capital
(pp421-428)

39 **IS** Sch 10 para 1 IS Regs
FC Sch 3 para 1 FC Regs
DWA Sch 4 para 1 DWA Regs
HB Sch 5 para 1 HB Regs
CTB Sch 5 para 1 CTB Regs

40 **IS** Reg 2(1) IS Regs meaning of 'dwelling occupied as the home'; R(SB) 3/84; CIS/427/1991
FC Sch 3 para 1 FC Regs
DWA Sch 4 para 1

DWA Regs
HB Sch 5 para 1 HB Regs
CTB Sch 5 para 1 CTB Regs

41 **IS** Sch 10 para 1 IS Regs
FC Sch 3 para 1 FC Regs
DWA Sch 4 para 1 DWA Regs
HB Sch 5 para 1 HB Regs
CTB Sch 5 para 1 CTB Regs

42 **IS** Sch 10 para 25 IS Regs
FC Sch 3 para 26 FC Regs
DWA Sch 4 para 26 DWA Regs
HB Sch 5 para 24 HB Regs
CTB Sch 5 para 24 CTB Regs

43 **IS** Sch 10 para 27 IS Regs
FC Sch 3 para 28 FC Regs
DWA Sch 4 para 28 DWA Regs
HB Sch 5 para 26 HB Regs
CTB Sch 5 para 26 CTB Regs

44 **IS** Sch 10 para 26 IS Regs
FC Sch 3 para 27 FC Regs
DWA Sch 4 para 27 DWA Regs
HB Sch 5 para 25 HB Regs
CTB Sch 5 para 25 CTB Regs
All CIS/6908/1995; CIS/7319/1995

45 CIS/562/1992

46 CIS/7319/1995

47 R(SB) 32/83

48 CIS/7319/1995, para 22

49 **IS** Sch 10 para 28 IS Regs
FC Sch 3 para 29 FC Regs
DWA Sch 4 para 29 DWA Regs
HB Sch 5 para 27 HB Regs
CTB Sch 5 para 27 CTB Regs

50 **IS** Sch 10 para 3 IS Regs
FC Sch 3 para 3 FC Regs
DWA Sch 4 para 3 DWA Regs
HB Sch 5 para 3 HB Regs
CTB Sch 5 para 3 CTB Regs

51 R(IS) 6/95

52 CIS/685/1992

53 CIS/8475/1995; CIS/15984/1996

54 R(SB) 14/85

55 **IS** Sch 10 para 2 IS Regs
FC Sch 3 para 2 FC Regs
DWA Sch 4 para 2 DWA Regs
HB Sch 5 para 2 HB Regs
CTB Sch 5 para 2 CTB Regs

56 **IS** Sch 10 para 8(a) IS Regs
FC Sch 3 para 9(a) FC Regs
DWA Sch 4 para 9(a) DWA Regs
HB Sch 5 para 9(a) HB Regs
CTB Sch 5 para 9(a) CTB Regs

57 **IS** Sch 10 para 8(b) IS Regs

FC Sch 3 para 9(b) FC
Regs
DWA Sch 4 para 9(b)
DWA Regs
HB Sch 5 para 9(b)
HB Regs
CTB Sch 5 para 9(b)
CTB Regs

58 *Barclays Bank v Quistclose
Investments Ltd* [1970]
AC 567; CSB/975/1985

59 IS Sch 10 para 9(a) IS
Regs
FC Sch 3 para 10(a) FC
Regs
DWA Sch 4 para 10(a)
DWA Regs
HB Sch 5 para 10(a)
HB Regs
CTB Sch 5 para 10(a)
CTB Regs

60 IS Sch 10 para 9(b) IS
Regs
FC Sch 3 para 10(b)
FC Regs
DWA Sch 4 para 10(b)
DWA Regs
HB Sch 5 para 10(b)
HB Regs
CTB Sch 5 para 10(b)
CTB Regs

61 IS Sch 10 para 37 IS
Regs
FC Sch 3 para 39 FC
Regs
DWA Sch 4 para 38
DWA Regs
HB Sch 5 para 37 HB
Regs
CTB Sch 5 para 36
CTB Regs

62 CIS/6908/1995

63 IS Sch 10 para 4 IS
Regs
FC Sch 3 paras 4 and
30 FC Regs
DWA Sch 4 paras 4
and 30 DWA Regs
HB Sch 5 para 4 HB

Regs
CTB Sch 5 para 4 CTB
Regs

64 IS Reg 2(1) IS Regs
definition of 'partner'
FC Reg 2(1) FC Regs
definition of 'partner'
DWA Reg 2(1) DWA
Regs definition of
'partner'
HB Reg 2(1) HB Regs
definition of 'partner'
CTB Reg 2(1) CTB
Regs definition of
'partner'
All s137(1) SSCBA
1992 definition of
'married couple' and
'unmarried couple'

65 HB Sch 5 para 24 HB
Regs
CTB Sch 5 para 24
CTB Regs

66 para 34429 AOG
HB/CTB para C2.12.ii.a
and b GM

67 FC Sch 3 para 4 FC
Regs
DWA Sch 4 para 4
DWA Regs

68 IS Reg 2(1) IS Regs
definition of 'relative'
FC Reg 2(1) definition
of 'close relative' and
Sch 3 para 4 FC Regs
DWA Reg 2(1)
definition of 'close
relative' and Sch 4 para
4 DWA Regs
HB Reg 2(1) HB Regs
definition of 'relative'
CTB This is not
defined for CTB but
presumably the same
definition will apply

69 CSB/209/1986; CSB/
1149/1986; R(SB) 22/87

70 IS Sch 10 para 10 IS
Regs

FC Sch 3 para 11 FC
Regs
DWA Sch 4 para 11
DWA Regs
HB Sch 5 para 11 HB
Regs
CTB Sch 5 para 11
CTB Regs

71 CIS/494/1990

72 IS Sch 10 para 8(a) IS
Regs
FC Sch 3 para 9(a) FC
Regs
DWA Sch 4 para 9(a)
DWA Regs
HB Sch 5 para 9(a) HB
Regs
CTB Sch 5 para 9(a)
CTB Regs

73 IS para 34375 AOG
FC para 53271 AOG

74 IS Sch 10 para 6 IS
Regs
FC Sch 3 para 6 FC
Regs
DWA Sch 4 para 6
DWA Regs
HB Sch 5 para 7 HB
Regs
CTB Sch 5 para 7 CTB
Regs

75 FC Sch 3 para 7 FC
Regs
DWA Sch 4 para 7
DWA Regs

76 R(SB) 4/85

77 CFC/15/1990

78 IS Sch 10 para 19 IS
Regs
FC Sch 3 para 20 FC
Regs
DWA Sch 4 para 20
DWA Regs
HB Sch 5 para 20 HB
Regs
CTB Sch 5 para 20
CTB Regs

79 IS Sch 10 para 23A IS
Regs

FC Sch 3 para 24A FC
Regs
DWA Sch 4 para 24A
DWA Regs
HB Sch 3 para 39A
HB Regs
CTB Sch 5 para 30A
CTB Regs
80 **IS** Sch 10 para 15 IS
Regs
FC Sch 3 para 16 FC
Regs
DWA Sch 4 para 16
DWA Regs
HB Sch 5 para 16 HB
Regs
CTB Sch 5 para 16
CTB Regs
All CIS/7330/1995
81 **IS** Sch 10 para 11 IS
Regs
FC Sch 3 para 12 FC
Regs
DWA Sch 4 para 12
DWA Regs
HB Sch 5 para 12 HB
Regs
CTB Sch 5 para 12
CTB Regs
82 **IS** Reg 41(2) IS Regs
FC Reg 25(2) FC Regs
DWA Reg 28(2) DWA
Regs
HB Reg 34(2) HB
Regs
CTB Reg 25(2) CTB
Regs
83 **IS** Sch 10 para 5 IS
Regs
FC Sch 3 para 5 FC
Regs
DWA Sch 4 para 5
DWA Regs
HB Sch 5 para 6 HB
Regs
CTB Sch 5 para 6 CTB
Regs
84 CIS/635/1994
85 **IS** Sch 10 para 13 IS

Regs
FC Sch 3 para 14 FC
Regs
DWA Sch 4 para 14
DWA Regs
HB Sch 5 para 14 HB
Regs
CTB Sch 5 para 14
CTB Regs
86 **IS** Sch 10 para 14 IS
Regs
FC Sch 3 para 15 FC
Regs
DWA Sch 4 para 15
DWA Regs
HB Sch 5 para 15 HB
Regs
CTB Sch 5 para 15
CTB Regs
87 **IS** Sch 10 para 16 IS
Regs
FC Sch 3 para 17 FC
Regs
DWA Sch 4 para 17
DWA Regs
HB Sch 5 para 17 HB
Regs
CTB Sch 5 para 17
CTB Regs
88 **IS** Sch 10 para 23 IS
Regs
FC Sch 3 para 24 FC
Regs
DWA Sch 4 para 24
DWA Regs
HB Sch 5 para 30 HB
Regs
CTB Sch 5 para 30
CTB Regs
89 **IS** Sch 10 para 24 IS
Regs
FC Sch 3 para 25 FC
Regs
DWA Sch 4 para 25
DWA Regs
HB Sch 5 para 31 HB
Regs
CTB Sch 5 para 31
CTB Regs

90 **IS** Sch 10 para 11 IS
Regs
FC Sch 3 para 12 FC
Regs
DWA Sch 4 para 12
DWA Regs
HB Sch 5 para 12 HB
Regs
CTB Sch 5 para 12
CTB Regs
91 **IS** Sch 10 para 12 IS
Regs
FC Sch 3 para 13 FC
Regs
DWA Sch 4 para 13
DWA Regs
HB Sch 5 para 13 HB
Regs
CTB Sch 5 para 13
CTB Regs
92 **IS** Sch 10 para 7 IS
Regs
FC Sch 3 para 8 FC
Regs
DWA Sch 4 para 8
DWA Regs
HB Sch 5 para 8 HB
Regs
CTB Sch 5 para 8 CTB
Regs
93 **IS** Sch 10 para 41 IS
Regs
FC Sch 3 para 43 FC
Regs
DWA Sch 4 para 42
DWA Regs
HB Sch 5 para 38 HB
Regs
CTB Sch 5 para 37
CTB Regs
94 **IS** Sch 10 para 36 IS
Regs
FC Sch 3 para 38 FC
Regs
DWA Sch 4 para 37
DWA Regs
HB Sch 5 para 36 HB
Regs

CTB Sch 5 para 35
CTB Regs

95 Sch 10 paras 47-49 IS
Regs

96 Sch 5 paras 50-51 HB
Regs

97 Sch 5 paras 50-51 CTB
Regs

98 FC Sch 3 paras 49 and
50 FC Regs
DWA Sch 4 paras 48
and 49 DWA Regs
HB Sch 5 paras 50 and
51 HB Regs
CTB Sch 5 paras 50
and 51 CTB Regs

99 IS Sch 10 para 38 IS
Regs
FC Sch 3 para 40 FC
Regs
DWA Sch 4 para 39
DWA Regs
HB Sch 5 para 39 HB
Regs
CTB Sch 5 para 38
CTB Regs

100 IS Sch 10 para 39 IS
Regs
FC Sch 3 para 41 FC
Regs
DWA Sch 4 para 40
DWA Regs
HB Sch 5 para 40 HB
Regs
CTB Sch 5 para 39
CTB Regs

101 IS Sch 10 para 40 IS
Regs
FC Sch 3 para 42 FC
Regs
DWA Sch 4 para 41
DWA Regs
HB Sch 5 para 41 HB
Regs
CTB Sch 5 para 40
CTB Regs

102 FC Sch 3 para 48 FC
Regs

DWA Sch 4 para 47
DWA Regs

103 IS Sch 10 paras 50 and
51 IS Regs
FC Sch 3 paras 52 and
53 FC Regs
DWA Sch 4 paras 51
and 52 DWA Regs
HB Sch 5 paras 53 and
54 HB Regs
CTB Sch 5 paras 53
and 54 CTB Regs

104 IS Sch 10 para 18 IS
Regs
FC Sch 3 para 19 FC
Regs
DWA Sch 4 para 19
DWA Regs
HB Sch 5 para 19 HB
Regs
CTB Sch 5 para 19
CTB Regs

105 IS Sch 10 paras 42-43
IS Regs
FC Sch 3 paras 44-45
FC Regs
DWA Sch 4 paras 43-
44 DWA Regs
HB Sch 5 paras 43-44
HB Regs
CTB Sch 5 paras 42-43
CTB Regs

106 IS Sch 10 para 46 IS
Regs
FC Sch 3 para 49 FC
Regs
DWA Sch 4 para 48
DWA Regs
HB Sch 5 para 48 HB
Regs
CTB Sch 5 para 48
CTB Regs

107 IS Sch 10 para 17 IS
Regs
FC Sch 3 para 18 FC
Regs
DWA Sch 4 para 18
DWA Regs
HB Sch 5 para 18 HB

Regs
CTB Sch 5 para 18
CTB Regs

108 IS Sch 10 para 29 IS
Regs
FC Sch 3 para 31 FC
Regs
DWA Sch 4 para 31
DWA Regs
HB Sch 5 para 32 HB
Regs
CTB Sch 5 para 32
CTB Regs

109 IS Sch 10 para 22 IS
Regs
FC Sch 3 para 23 FC
Regs
DWA Sch 4 para 23
DWA Regs
HB Sch 5 para 23 HB
Regs
CTB Sch 5 para 23
CTB Regs

110 IS para 34454 AOG
FC/DWA para 53471
AOG
HB Reg 73(1) and (3)
HB Regs
CTB Reg 63(1) and (3)
CTB Regs

111 IS Sch 10 para 34 IS
Regs
FC Sch 3 para 36 FC
Regs
DWA Sch 4 para 36
DWA Regs
HB Sch 4 para 38 HB
regs
CTB Sch 4 para 40
CTB Regs

112 IS Sch 10 para 30 IS
Regs
FC Sch 3 para 32 FC
Regs
DWA Sch 4 para 32
DWA Regs
HB Sch 5 para 33 HB
Regs

CTB Sch 5 para 33
CTB Regs

113 **IS** Sch 10 para 21 IS
Regs
FC Sch 3 para 22 FC
Regs
DWA Sch 4 para 22
DWA Regs
HB Sch 5 para 22 HB
Regs
CTB Sch 5 para 22
CTB Regs

114 **IS** Sch 10 para 20 IS
Regs
FC Sch 3 para 21 FC
Regs
DWA Sch 4 para 21
DWA Regs
HB Sch 5 para 21 HB
Regs
CTB Sch 5 para 21
CTB Regs

4. Notional capital
(pp428-435)

115 **IS** Reg 51(6) IS Regs
FC Reg 34(6) FC Regs
DWA Reg 37(6) DWA
Regs
HB Reg 43(6) HB Regs
CTB Reg 34(6) CTB
Regs

116 **IS** Reg 51(1) IS Regs
FC Reg 34(1) FC Regs
DWA Reg 37(1) DWA
Regs
HB Reg 43(1) HB Regs
CTB Reg 34(1) CTB
Regs

117 CIS/124/1990; CSB/
1198/1989

118 R(SB) 9/91

119 CIS/124/1990

120 CIS/40/1989

121 CIS/621/1991

122 CIS/264/1989

123 CIS/7330/1995, para
12(3)

124 R(SB) 38/85

125 **IS** Reg 51(1) IS Regs
FC Reg 34(1) FC Regs
DWA Reg 37(1) DWA
Regs

126 R(SB) 12/91

127 CIS/2627/1995

128 CIS/236/1991

129 **IS** Reg 51(7) IS Regs
FC Reg 34(7) FC Regs
DWA Reg 37(7) DWA
Regs

130 CIS/240/1992

131 CIS/634/1992

132 CIS/12403/1996

133 **IS** Reg 51(6) IS Regs
FC Reg 34(6) FC Regs
DWA Reg 37(6) DWA
Regs
HB Reg 43(6) HB Regs
CTB Reg 34(6) CTB
Regs

134 CIS/30/1993, but other
commissioners have
taken a different view
(*see*, eg, CIS/25/1990
and CIS/81/1991)

135 R(IS) 14/93

136 para C2.69 GM

137 para C2.97 GM

138 para C2.92 GM

139 **IS** Reg 51A IS Regs
FC Reg 34A FC Regs
DWA Reg 38 DWA
Regs
HB Reg 43A HB Regs
CTB Reg 35 CTB Regs

140 s25(1)(c) SSAA 1992
HB Reg 66(2) HB Regs
CTB Reg 57(2) CTB
Regs

141 para C2.84 GM

142 R(IS) 9/92

143 R(IS) 1/91; R(IS) 9/92

144 R(IS) 9/92

145 **IS** Reg 51(2) IS Regs
FC Reg 34(2) FC Regs
DWA Reg 37(2) DWA
Regs
HB Reg 43(2) HB Regs

CTB Reg 34(2) CTB
Regs

146 CIS/368/1994

147 **IS** Reg 51(3)(a)(ii) and
(8) IS Regs
FC Reg 34(3)(a) FC
Regs
DWA Reg 37(3)(a)
DWA Regs
HB Reg 43(3)(a) and
(7) HB Regs
CTB Reg 34(3)(a) and
(7) CTB Regs

148 **IS** Reg 51(8) IS Regs
FC Reg 34(3)(a) FC
Regs
DWA Reg 37(3)(a)
DWA Regs
HB Reg 43(7)(b) HB
Regs
CTB Reg 34(7) CTB
Regs

149 **IS** para 34866 AOG

150 Reg 51(3)(a)(i) IS Regs

151 **IS** Reg 51(3)(b) IS Regs
FC Reg 34(3)(b) FC
Regs
DWA Reg 37(3)(b)
DWA Regs
HB Reg 43(3)(b) HB
Regs
CTB Reg 34(3)(b) CTB
Regs

152 **IS** Reg 51(4) IS Regs
FC Reg 34(4) FC Regs
DWA Reg 37(4) DWA
Regs

153 **IS** Reg 51(5) IS Regs
FC Reg 34(5) FC Regs
DWA Reg 37(5) DWA
Regs
HB Reg 43(5) HB Regs
CTB Reg 34(5) CTB
Regs

154 **IS** para 34375 AOG; *see
also* R(IS) 13/93
FC/DWA para 53372
AOG

155 para 53373 AOG

156 *CAO v Knight* (CA) 9
     April 1997
157 **HB** Reg 43(4) HB Regs
     CTB Reg 34(4) CTB
     Regs

**5. How capital is
valued**
(pp435-439)
158 **IS** Reg 49(a) IS Regs
     FC Reg 32(a) FC Regs
     DWA Reg 35(a) DWA
     Regs
     HB Reg 41(a) HB Regs
     CTB Reg 32(a) CTB
     Regs
159 R(SB) 57/83; R(SB) 6/
     84
160 R(SB) 18/83
161 R(SB) 6/84
162 **IS** Reg 49(a)(i) IS Regs
     FC Reg 32(a)(i) FC
     Regs
     DWA Reg 35(a)(i)
     DWA Regs
     HB Reg 41(a)(i) HB
     Regs
     CTB Reg 32(a)(i) CTB
     Regs
163 **IS** Reg 49(a)(ii) IS Regs
     FC Reg 32(a)(ii) FC
     Regs
     DWA Reg 35(a)(ii)
     DWA Regs
     HB Reg 41(a)(ii) HB
     Regs
     CTB Reg 32(a)(ii) CTB
     Regs
164 CIS/255/1989
165 R(SB) 27/84
166 R(SB) 2/83; R(SB) 31/
     83
167 **IS** Reg 49(b) IS Regs
     FC Reg 32(b) FC Regs
     DWA Reg 35(b) DWA
     Regs
     HB Reg 41(b) HB
     Regs
     CTB Reg 32(b) CTB
     Regs

168 **IS** Part 34 Appendix 3
     AOG
     FC/DWA Part 53
     Appendix 2 AOG
     HB/CTB C2: Annex B
     GM; Circular A24/97
     (July 1997)
169 **IS** Reg 52 IS Regs
     FC Reg 35 FC Regs
     DWA Reg 39 DWA
     Regs
     HB Reg 44 HB Regs
     CTB Reg 36 CTB Regs
170 CIS/7097/1995
171 CIS/391/1992, para 53
172 CIS/7097/1995
173 These arguments are to
     be dealt with by a
     Tribunal of
     Commissioners in CIS/
     15936/1996, CIS/267/
     1997 and CIS/3283/
     1997
174 **FC/DWA** para 53056
     AOG
     HB/CTB para 2.42 GM
175 R(IS) 2/93
176 **IS** Reg 49(a) IS Regs
     FC Reg 32(a) FC Regs
     DWA Reg 35(a) DWA
     Regs
     HB Reg 41(a) HB Regs
     CTB Reg 32(a) CTB
     Regs
177 R(IS) 18/95
178 R(SB) 18/83; R(IS)
     2/90
179 CIS/654/1993
180 **IS** para 34681 AOG
     FC/DWA para 53132
     AOG
     HB/CTB para C2.34
     GM
181 *Peters v CAO* (appendix
     to R(SB) 3/89)
182 **IS** Reg 50(a) IS Regs
     FC Reg 33(a) FC Regs
     DWA Reg 36(a) DWA
     Regs
     HB Reg 42(a) HB Regs

     CTB Reg 33(a) CTB
     Regs
183 **IS** Reg 50(b) IS Regs
     FC Reg 33(b) FC Regs
     DWA Reg 36(b) DWA
     Regs
     HB Reg 42(b) HB
     Regs
     CTB Reg 33(b) CTB
     Regs
184 **IS** Sch 10 para 21 IS
     Regs
     FC Sch 3 para 22 FC
     Regs
     DWA Sch 4 para 22
     DWA Regs
     HB Sch 5 para 22 HB
     Regs
     CTB Sch 5 para 22
     CTB Regs

PART SIX: THE
REGULATED
SOCIAL FUND

Chapter 21: The
regulated social fund
(pp442-453)
 1 Reg 5(1)(a) SFM&FE
    Regs
 2 Reg 5(1)(b) SFM&FE
    Regs
 3 Reg 3(1) SFM&FE
    Regs
 4 Reg 4(2) SFM&FE
    Regs
 5 Reg 9(1) SFM&FE
    Regs
 6 Reg 9(2) SFM&FE
    Regs
 7 Reg 6 SFM&FE Regs
 8 Reg 3(1) and (2)
    SFM&FE Regs
 9 Reg 6(24) and (25)
    SS(C&P) Regs
10 Reg 5(2) SFM&FE
    Regs
11 Reg 19 and Sch 4 para
    8 SS(C&P) Regs

12 Reg 6(1)(a) SS(C&P)
   Regs
13 Regs 6(1) and 4(7)
   SS(C&P) Regs
14 para 44012 AOG
15 Reg 7(1)(a) SFM&FE
   Regs
16 Reg 7(1)(e) SFM&FE
   Regs
17 Reg 3(1) SFM&FE
   Regs
18 Reg 7(1)(b) SFM&FE
   Regs
19 Reg 7(1)(c) SFM&FE
   Regs
20 Sch 4 para 9 SS(C&P)
   Regs
21 Reg 4(3) and (4)
   SFM&FE Regs
22 Reg 7(1)(e)(i) SFM&FE
   Regs
23 Reg 7(1)(e)(ii)
   SFM&FE Regs
24 Reg 7(1)(e)(iii) and (iv)
   SFM&FE Regs
25 Reg 7(5) SFM&FE
   Regs
26 Reg 7(1)(e)(iii) and (iv)
   and (2) SFM&FE Regs
27 Reg 7(3) and (4)
   SFM&FE Regs
28 R(SB) 2/87
29 Reg 7(6)(a) SFM&FE
   Regs
30 Reg 7(6)(b) and (c)
   SFM&FE Regs
31 Reg 7(7) SFM&FE
   Regs
32 Reg 7(6) SFM&FE
   Regs
33 Reg 3(1) SFM&FE
   Regs
34 Reg 7(1)(e)(ii)(aa)
   SFM&FE Regs
35 Reg 3(1) SFM&FE
   Regs
36 Reg 3(1) SFM&FE
   Regs

37 Reg 3(1) SFM&FE
   Regs
38 Reg 3(1) SFM&FE
   Regs
39 Reg 3(1A) SFM&FE
   Regs
40 Reg 7(1)(e) SFM&FE
   Regs
41 CSB/488/1982
42 CIS/12344/1996 and
   CIS/975/1997
43 CIS/85/1991
44 Reg 7(1)(e)(iii) and (iv)
   and (5) SFM&FE Regs
45 CIS/12783/1996
46 Reg 6(24) and (25)
   SS(C&P) Regs
47 Reg 7(1A) SFM&FE
   Regs
48 Art 10 EEC Reg 1612/
   68; Art 2 EEC Reg
   1251/70
49 Reg 7A(1) SFM&FE
   Regs
50 Reg 7A(2)(a) SFM&FE
   Regs
51 Reg 7A(2)(b) SFM&FE
   Regs
52 Reg 7A(2)(c) SFM&FE
   Regs
53 Reg 7A(2)(d) SFM&FE
   Regs
54 Reg 7A(2)(e) SFM&FE
   Regs
55 Reg 7A(4A) SFM&FE
   Regs
56 Reg 7A(4B) SFM&FE
   Regs
57 Reg 7A(2)(g) SFM&FE
   Regs
58 Reg 7A(5) SFM&FE
   Regs
59 Reg 7A(4) SFM&FE
   Regs
60 Reg 9(1) SFM&FE
   Regs
61 Reg 9(2) and (3)(b)
   SFM&FE Regs

62 Reg 9(3)(a) SFM&FE
   Regs
63 Reg 9(3)(c) SFM&FE
   Regs
64 Reg 8(1)(a) SFM&FE
   Regs
65 R(IS) 14/91
66 R(IS) 12/93
67 Reg 8(1)(b) SFM&FE
   Regs
68 Reg 8(1)(c) SFM&FE
   Regs
69 Reg 8(1)(d) SFM&FE
   Regs
70 Reg 8(1)(e) SFM&FE
   Regs
71 Reg 8(2) SFM&FE
   Regs
72 s78(4) SSAA 1992; CIS/
   616/1990
73 R(SB) 18/84
74 Reg 6(1) SS(C&P) Regs
75 Regs 4(7) and 6(1)(b)
   SS(C&P) Regs
76 Reg 35(2) SS(C&P)
   Regs
77 Reg 2(1) and (2)
   SFCWP Regs
78 Reg 1A SFCWP Regs
79 Reg 1A(i) SFCWP Regs
80 Reg 1(2) SFCWP Regs
81 Schs 1 and 2 SFCWP
   Regs
82 Reg 3 SFCWP Regs
83 para 104 CWPH
84 paras 500-511 CWPH
85 paras 603 and 701-04
   CWPH
86 Regs 2(2) and 3(1)(a)
   SFWFP Regs
87 Regs 2(5) and (6) and
   3(1)(b) SFWFP Regs
88 Reg 2(3), (4) and (5)
   SFWFP Regs
89 Reg 2(7) and (8)
   SFWFP Regs
90 Regs 57 and 67 SS(Adj)
   Regs

PART SEVEN: THE DISCRETIONARY SOCIAL FUND

Chapter 22: General principles
(pp456-466)

1 s167 SSAA 1992
2 s140(1) and (2) SSCBA 1992
3 s140(2)-(4) SSCBA 1992
4 SF(App) Regs; SF(AR) Regs; SF(RDB) Regs; SF(Misc) Regs
5 s140(2) SSCBA 1992
6 paras 1043, 3011, 3705, 4055 and 5011 SFG
7 paras 1045, 3702, 4351 and 5011 SFG
8 paras 3704 and 4355 SFG
9 para 2147 SFG
10 s64(3) SSAA 1992; SF Dir 41
11 SF Dir 41(b)
12 SF Dir 41(c)
13 s140(5) SSCBA 1992
14 s168 SSAA 1992
15 SF Dir 41
16 para 2144 SFG
17 SF Dir 42
18 s168(3)(c) and (d) SSAA 1992
19 s140(1)(e) SSCBA 1992
20 SF Dir 40
21 paras 2122 and 2124 SFG
22 *R v SFI ex parte Taylor*
23 paras 2124-25 SFG
24 para 1027 SFG
25 paras 1080-1103 SFG
26 SF Dirs 12, 23 and 29
27 paras 4222-23 SFG
28 para 4224 SFG
29 CSB/1482/1985; para 4233 SFG; Advice Note 7; *R v SFI ex parte*

Connick, 8 June 1993 (unreported)
30 Advice Note 13
31 para 4234 SFG
32 para 4236 SFG
33 para 4237 SFG
34 Advice Note 1
35 SF Dirs 12(o), 23(2)(f) and 29(d)
36 paras 3142 and 4226 SFG
37 Advice Note 1
38 SF Dir 29
39 SF Dir 28(a)
40 SF Dir 12(n)
41 SF Dir 10
42 SF Dir 23
43 s138(1)(b) SSCBA 1992
44 paras 3124 and 4201 SFG
45 *R v SFI ex parte Harper*
46 paras 3125 and 4202 SFG
47 paras 3129-30 and 4206-07 SFG
48 paras 3136 and 4213 SFG
49 SF Dir 26
50 SF Dir 8(1)(b)
51 SF Dir 17(a) and (f

Chapter 23: Community care grants
(pp467-476)

1 SF Dir 6
2 SF Dir 25(1) and (2)(a)
3 SF Dir 25(2)(b)
4 SF Dir 25(3)
5 para 7002 SFG
6 Advice Note 5
7 Advice Note 11
8 SF Dir 27
9 SF Dir 27(2)
10 SF Dir 27(2)
11 SF Dir 27(3)
12 para 3752 SFG
13 s140(1)(b) SSCBA 1992; Advice Note 10
14 SF Dir 28(b)

15 SF Dir 4
16 para 3011 SFG
17 para 3709 SFG
18 para 3710 SFG
19 paras 3704, 3710 and 3713 SFG
20 paras 3707-08 SFG
21 Advice Note 16
22 para 3706 SFG
23 Advice Note 16
24 para 3800 SFG
25 SF Dir 28
26 Advice Note 1
27 para 3622 SFG
28 SF Dir 4(a)(i)
29 para 3201 SFG
30 para 3208 SFG
31 *R v The SFI ex parte Mohammed, The Times,* 25 November 1992
32 *R v Secretary of State for Social Security ex parte Healey, The Times,* 22 April 1991
33 para 3203 SFG
34 *R v The SFI ex parte Sherwin, The Times,* 23 February 1990
35 Advice Note 13
36 SF Dir 4(a)(ii)
37 paras 3353-54 SFG
38 BPN, IRS *Journal,* Summer 1997
39 BPN, IRS *Journal,* Summer 1997
40 paras 3359-3467 SFG
41 Advice Note 13
42 SF Dir 4(a)(v)
43 paras 3634-35 SFG
44 para 3637 SFG
45 para 3639 SFG
46 para 3641 SFG
47 SF Dir 4(a)(iii)
48 para 3500 SFG
49 BPN, IRS *Journal,* Winter 1997
50 para 3502 SFG
51 *R v Secretary of State for Social Security ex parte*

Healey, *The Times*, 22
April 1991
52 para 3503 SFG
53 Advice Note 12; para
3503 SFG
54 Advice Note 13
55 SF Dir 4(b)
56 paras 3666-69 SFG
57 para 3652 SFG
58 paras 3670-72 SFG
59 SF Dir 28(b))

Chapter 24: Loans
(pp477-487)
1 SF Dir 5
2 paras 3000 and 4000
SFG
3 SF Dir 8(1)(a)
4 Advice Note 11
5 SF Dir 8(1)(c)
6 SF Dir 8(2)
7 para 4101 SFG
8 para 4102 SFG
9 para 4105 SFG
10 SF Dir 8(3)
11 SF Dir 2
12 SF Dir 10
13 SF Dir 11
14 para 4351 SFG
15 paras 4356-58 SFG
16 paras 4355 and 4363
SFG
17 SF Dir 10
18 para 4603 SFG
19 SF Dir 11
20 SF Dir 14(a)
21 SF Dirs 15-17
22 SF Dir 22
23 SF Dir 21
24 SF Dir 14(b)
25 SF Dir 3(a)
26 SF Dir 3(b)
27 SF Dir 15
28 para 5155 SFG
29 SF Dir 16(a)
30 SF Dir 16(b)
31 para 5205 SFG
32 SF Dir 17(b)-(f)
33 SF Dir 17(b)

34 SF Dir 17(d)
35 para 7069 SFG
36 SF Dir 17(c)
37 para 5051 SFG
38 para 5052 SFG
39 paras 5053-105 SFG
40 para 5107 SFG
41 para 5108 SFG
42 para 5053 SFG
43 para 5104 SFG
44 para 5504 SFG
45 paras 5420-22 SFG
46 para 5423 SFG
47 para 5416 SFG
48 paras 5424-25 SFG
49 paras 5429-33 SFG
50 paras 5417-19 SFG
51 paras 5413 and 5427
SFG
52 para 5428 SFG
53 para 5559 SFG
54 para 5559 SFG
55 SF Dir 3(b)
56 paras 5409-12 SFG
57 SF Dirs 18, 20 and 21
58 SF Dir 22
59 SF Dir 21
60 SF Dirs 18 and 20
61 s78(1) and (2) SSAA
1992
62 para 4003 SFDRG
63 para 4004 SFDRG
64 para 4013 SFDRG
65 para 4014 SFDRG
66 para 4015 SFDRG
67 para 4019 SFDRG
68 Reg 3 SF(RDB) Regs
69 Reg 3(a) and (c)
SF(RDB) Regs
70 *Mulvey v Secretary of State*,
13 March 1977;
*R v Secretary of State ex
parte Taylor and
Chapman, The Times*, 5
February 1996; s78(3A)
and (3B) SSAA 1992
71 s78(3)(a) SSAA 1992
72 s78(3)(b) SSAA 1992
73 s78(3)(c) SSAA 1992

74 para 4054 SFDRG
75 para 11001 SFDRG
76 paras 4040 and 11029
SFDRG

**Chapter 25:
Applications, payments
and reviews**
(pp488-498)
1 Reg 2(1) and (2)
SF(App) Regs
2 Reg 2(5) SF(App) Regs
3 Reg 2(4) SF(App) Regs
4 Reg 3(a) SF(App) Regs
5 Reg 3(b) SF(App) Regs
6 paras 1046, 3000 and
4000 SFG
7 para 2100 SFG
8 para 2100 SFG
9 paras 2106-07 SFG
10 paras 3013, 4056 and
5012 SFG
11 paras 3017, 4060 and
5016 SFG
12 paras 3018, 4061 and
5017 SFG
13 paras 3020-26, 4066-69
and 5019-25 SFG
14 paras 3024, 4067 and
5023 SFG
15 paras 1046, 3000 and
4000 SFG
16 s140(4)(a) SSCBA 1992;
SF Dir 7
17 s140(4)(a) SSCBA 1992;
Advice Note 8
18 paras 3100, 4150 and
5300 SFG
19 Advice Note 17
20 Advice Note 17
21 s140(4)(a) SSCBA 1992
22 SF Dir 7(b)
23 Advice Note 17
24 para 2062 SFG
25 para 2061 SFG
26 para 4003 SFCADG
27 s138(3) SSCBA 1992
28 para 8052 SFG

29 s66 SSAA 1992; SF Dir 31

30 s66 SSAA 1992; SFI Directions

31 s66(1)(a) SSAA 1992; para 8052 SFG

32 Reg 2(1) and (2)(a) SF(AR) Regs

33 Reg 2(4) SF(AR) Regs

34 Reg 2(6) SF(AR) Regs

35 Reg 2(3) SF(AR) Regs

36 Reg 2(5) SF(AR) Regs

37 SF Dir 37

38 SF Dir 31

39 s66(1)(b) SSAA 1992

40 *R v SFO ex parte Hewson* (HC), 22 June 1995

41 s66(6) SSAA 1992

42 SF Dir 39

43 SF Dir 32

44 SF Dir 33

45 SF Dir 33

46 SF Dir 34

47 para 8500 SFG

48 SF Dir 35

49 SF Dir 36; para 8600 SFG

50 s66(3) SSAA 1992

51 Reg 2(1) and (2)(b) SF(AR) Regs

52 Reg 2(4) SF(AR) Regs

53 Reg 2(6) SF(AR) Regs

54 Reg 2(3) SF(AR) Regs

55 para 5004 SFROG

56 paras 5006-07 SFROG

57 s66(6) and (7) SSAA 1992; SFI Dirs 1 and 2

58 *R v IRS ex parte Connell* (QBD) 3 November 1994

59 *R v SFI ex parte Ledicott* (QBD) reported 24 May 1995

60 para 9013 SFG

61 s66(4) SSAA 1992

62 s66(5) SSAA 1992

63 SF Dir 38; paras 8753-55 SFG

PART EIGHT: HEALTH SERVICE BENEFITS

Chapter 26: Health service benefits
(pp 500-512)

1 Reg 6(2) NHS(TERC) Regs

2 Reg 6 and Sch 1 Part II NHS(TERC) Regs

3 Sch 1 para 1 and Table A NHS(TERC) Regs

4 Reg 6(5) NHS(TERC) Regs

5 Reg 7(1A) NHS(TERC) Regs

6 Reg 7(6) and Sch 1A NHS(TERC) Regs

7 Reg 4 NHS(TERC) Regs; regs 3-7 NHS(CDA) Regs

8 Reg 7 NHS(CDA) Regs; *R v Secretary of State for Health ex parte Cyril Richardson,* Case C-137/94

9 Reg 9 NHS(CDA) Regs

10 Reg 8(2) NHS(TERC) Regs

11 Reg 8 NHS(CDA) Regs

12 Regs 3 and 4 NHS(TERC) Regs

13 Reg 5(1), (2) and (3) NHS(TERC) Regs

14 Reg 8 NHS(TERC) Regs

15 Reg 13 NHS(GOS) Regs

16 Reg 3 NHS(OCP) Regs

17 Regs 8 and 15 NHS(OCP) Regs

18 Regs 9 and 15 NHS(OCP) Regs

19 Reg 12(1) NHS(OCP) Regs

20 Sch 1 NHS(OCP) Regs

21 Regs 1(2), 14(3) and 19(4) NHS(OCP) Regs

22 Regs 6 and 20 NHS(OCP) Regs

23 Regs 3, 4, 5 and 5A NHS(TERC) Regs

24 Regs 3, 4, 5 and 5A NHS(TERC) Regs

25 Regs 3-5 WF Regs

26 Reg 14(3) WF Regs

27 Reg 14(3) WF Regs

28 Reg 13(4) WF Regs

29 Reg 12 WF Regs

30 Reg 14(2) WF Regs

31 Reg 18 WF Regs

32 Reg 7 WF Regs

33 Reg 8 WF Regs

34 Reg 5 WF Regs

Index

How to use this index

Because the *Handbook* is divided into separate sections covering the different benefits, many entries in the index have several references, each to a different section. Where this occurs, we use the following abbreviations to show which benefit each reference relates to:

(IS)	Income support	(CTB)	Council tax benefit
(FC)	Family credit	(RSF)	Regulated social fund
(DWA)	Disability working allowance	(SF)	Social fund
(HB)	Housing benefit		

References to common provisions appear first in the sequence. We list individual references in the order above, which reflects the order of the sections of the *Handbook*.

Entries against the bold headings direct you to the general information on the subject, or where the subject is covered most fully. Sub-entries are listed alphabetically and direct you to specific aspects of the subject.

unit trusts 417, 439
unreasonably high rent (old scheme)
(HB) 258
rent increases
(HB) 262
suitable alternative accommodation
(HB) 259
unreasonably large accommodation
(HB) 259
urgent cases payments 49–52
asylum-seekers 81
backdated payments for refugees
(IS) 79
benefit reduction while appealing a BA
decision 50
overseas students 21
person from abroad 85, 86

V

vacations 399
(HB) 274, 281
valuation of capital 435
Victoria Cross payments 410, 427
violence
applying for maintenance 113
benefit paid for two homes
(HB) 231
housing costs for two homes
(IS) 31
visits
hospital in patient
(SF) 476
hospital inpatient
(IS) 511
prisoner **102**
vitamins 410, 426, 512
voluntary/charitable payments 402
voluntary unemployment reduction
urgent cases payments
(IS) 50
voluntary work 413
(FC/DWA) 200
expenses 409
hours of work
(IS) 15
vouchers
glasses and contact lenses 506–9
SF payments 492

W

wages
arrears 380

crisis loans while waiting for first payment
484
due but not paid 412
payments in lieu 380
(IS) 384
war disability
free prescriptions 504
war disablement pension
income disregards
(HB) 272
treatment as income 397
war pension
qualifying for DWA 215
war widow's pension
income disregards
(HB) 272
treatment as income 397
water charges
(HB) 243
(IS) 38
debts paid by deductions from benefit
(IS) 152
widows' benefits
treated as income 395
wigs 509
winter fuel payments 452
withdrawal of benefit
cohabitation rule applied 350
withdrawing a claim
(DWA) 219
(FC) 206
(HB) 283
(IS) 130
withholding benefit
(CTB) 341
(HB) 295, 315
(IS) 146
withholding rent for repairs
(HB) 293
witnesses
allowances 410, 427
entitlement to IS 12
work
absence from work
(FC/DWA) 201
(IS) 9, 15
expenses
(IS) 15
full-time work
(FC/DWA) **199–201**
(IS) 9, 13
giving up work through ill health
(DWA) 224
incapable of work, disability premium
(IS/HB/CTB) 362

RIGHTS GUIDE TO NON-MEANS-TESTED BENEFITS

21st edition: 1998/99

Revised and updated to give authoritative, practical guidance to most non-means-tested benefits and how to claim them. There is full coverage of incapacity benefit, disability benefits, maternity pay and benefits, statutory sick pay, pensions, how contributions are worked out, calculating earnings, widows' benefits, equal treatment rules for women and men, and industrial injuries and diseases. Also how benefits are administered and how to appeal.

New features of this edition include: improved and updated coverage of disability benefits, with information on reviews (eg, under the Benefits Integrity Project); the latest incapacity benefit developments, particularly challenging decisions and appeals; abolition of the higher rate of child benefit, with some information on transitional arrangements.

There is some information on benefit for unemployed claimants, but you will need to use the *Jobseeker's Allowance Handbook* for full details of contribution-based jobseeker's allowance.

Fully indexed and cross-referenced to law, regulations, official guidance, court and commissioners' decisions.

'So easy to follow ... a godsend. Many of us would be lost without (them)' – A CLAIMANT

'The most complete guides to social security benefits' – SUNDAY TIMES

'The best value in publishing ... Anyone who advises those in receipt of benefit will struggle without them' – SOLICITORS JOURNAL

April 1998   0 901698 05 X   **£8.95**
Individual benefit claimants (direct from CPAG) £3.00

One copy sent automatically to CPAG Rights and Comprehensive members

Send a cheque/PO for £8.95 (incl.p&p) to CPAG Ltd, 1-5 Bath Street, London EC1V 9PY

JOBSEEKER'S ALLOWANCE HANDBOOK

3rd edition: 1998/99

The new edition is revised, updated and expanded to give full coverage of the New Deal for 18–24-year-olds, together with details of other schemes from the Government's 'welfare to work' strategy, as well as all other changes relevant to jobseeker's allowance. There is practical guidance to benefit entitlement as it applies from April 1998.

There are full details of: contribution- and income-based JSA; signing on and interviews; availability and actively seeking work tests; negotiating with and getting help from the Employment Service; when benefit can be withheld; the back to work bonus; which other benefits can be claimed; special groups – students and people with disabilities; fraud and overpayments; challenging decisions, including appeals.

Along with New Deal coverage, other new features of this edition include: the latest on JSA sanctions and hardship payments; expanded coverage of the rules for 16/17-year-olds; new rules on backdating and claiming JSA.

Fully indexed and cross-referenced to law, regulations, official guidance, relevant decisions – and to its companion volumes.

'So easy to follow ... a godsend. Many of us would be lost without (them)' – A CLAIMANT

'The most complete guides to social security benefits' – SUNDAY TIMES

'The best value in publishing ... Anyone who advises those in receipt of benefit will struggle without them' – SOLICITORS JOURNAL

April 1998   0 901698 06 8   **£8.95**
Individual benefit claimants (direct from CPAG) £3.00

Send a cheque/PO for £8.95 (incl.p&p) to CPAG Ltd, 1-5 Bath Street, London EC1V 9PY

CPAG COURSES

CPAG courses provide comprehensive rights training for advisers, and detailed coverage of up-to-the minute legislative changes. Our tutors are expert in their area of work and draw on the extensive training experience of the Citizens' Rights Office.

CPAG courses range from introductory to more technical and legal courses for advisers with more knowledge or experience. We also run courses with a skills base, or where the emphasis is on campaigning or challenging decisions. Our current programme includes a broad range of popular courses for both new and experienced advisers. We have introduced a number of new courses in response to demand and to reflect current issues and developments. The new courses for this programme are: Employment Rights for Beginners, Fraud and the 'Fraud Act', Fraud and Housing Benefit, The New Social Security Act – Changes in Decision Making, Reviews and Appeals, 'Welfare to Work' and the New Deal. **CPAG's Welfare Rights for Franchising Lawyers course has been chosen by the Law Society as the approved course for all lawyers needing to qualify for legal aid work.**

Our courses can also be tailored to meet the needs of specific groups, including those not normally concerned with welfare rights. To assess your training needs, we are happy to discuss your requirements for 'in-house' training to meet the internal needs of your organisation. For further information, contact Judy Allen at the address given below.

Fees:	Lawyers	Statutory Organisations	Voluntary Organisations
One-day	£170	£120	£80
Two-day	£230	£180	£150
Three-day	£270	£230	£200
Week-long	£390	£310	£230
Half-day	£90	£65	£55

Most of CPAG's courses are Law Society accredited and carry continuing education points.

For a full programme please contact Judy Allen, Training Administrator, Child Poverty Action Group, 1-5 Bath Street, London ECIV 9PY. Tel: 0171 253 3406; Fax: 0171 490 0561.

CHILD SUPPORT HANDBOOK

6th edition: 1998/99

The new *Child Support Handbook* is fully revised and updated to give clear, practical guidance to the child support scheme as it applies in 1998/99. New features of this edition include procedural changes to the requirement to co-operate, new January and April 1998 regulation changes and the incorporation of significant new case law.

The *Child Support Handbook* covers:
- what the key terms mean and who is affected
- how to apply for maintenance and how to withdraw an application
- the powers of the CSA to pursue maintenance and seek information
- the requirement to co-operate for parents with care on benefit
- the right to refuse to co-operate and the benefit penalty
- how the formula for calculating maintenance payment works and the system of departure from the formula
- collection and enforcement, and negotiating payment in arrears
- reviews, appeals and making complaints

There are practical examples, and tactical hints and arguments for use when seeking exemption, withdrawal of applications, review or appeal. Fully indexed and cross-referenced to legislation, case law and to its companion volumes, the CPAG benefit guides. The *Child Support Handbook* is the standard guide for claimants and other parents affected, solicitors, welfare rights advisers, CABx, social workers, women's' groups and children's charities.

'Struggling parents baffled by the changing rules of the troubled Child Support Agency can find practical guidance in the latest Child Support Handbook' – NEWS OF THE WORLD

'Gives a thorough explanation of the system' – WOMAN'S OWN

'It is difficult to recommend this book too highly' – FAMILY LAW

June 1998   1 901698 07 6   **£11.95**
Individual benefit claimants (direct from CPAG) £3.50

Send a cheque/PO for £8.95 (incl.p&p) to CPAG Ltd, 1-5 Bath Street, London EC1V 9PY